THIRD EDITION

Family Systems
in
America

IRA L. REISS *Department of Sociology and the Family Studies Center, University of Minnesota*

HOLT, RINEHART AND WINSTON

NEW YORK   CHICAGO   SAN FRANCISCO   DALLAS
MONTREAL   TORONTO   LONDON   SYDNEY

To my mother's brother
Dr. Murray Jacobs, 1888–1979
A man who tended to other people's crises.

The author gratefully acknowledges the following authors and publishers for permission to reprint their works:

pp. 116–117—Quotations from Ovid, reprinted by permission of the publisher, Indiana University Press.

pp. 118–121—Quotations from Andreas Capellanus, *The Art of Courtly Love*, trans. by John Jay Parry, edited and abridged by Frederick Locke. Copyright © 1957 Frederick Ungar Publishing Co., Inc.

Tables 6.1 and 6.2—Copyright © 1978 by Alan P. Bell and Martin S. Weinberg. Reprinted by permission of Simon & Schuster, a division of Gulf & Western Corporation.

Table 7.2—Reprinted from Lewis M. Terman, *Psychological Factors in Marital Happiness*, 1938. Used with permission of McGraw-Hill Book Co.

Figures 7.2, 8.1, 8.4, and Tables 7.3, 8.1, 8.2, 8.3, 8.4, and 8.5 reprinted with permission of *Family Planning Perspectives*.

Table 9.4, 9.5, and 9.6 © 1975 by Sage Publications, Inc., Beverly Hills, CA.

Figure 9.4—Copyright © 1979 by The Free Press, a division of Macmillan Publishing Company.

Tables 11.1, 11.9, and 11.11 reprinted by permission of the Institute for Sex Research, Inc.

Tables 11.3, 11.4, 11.5, and 11.8 reprinted with permission of Playboy Press from *Sexual Behavior in the 1970s*, by Morton Hunt. © 1974 by Morton Hunt.

Tables 11.5 and 11.6 courtesy of *Redbook*.

Figure 12.4—From *Courtship, Marriage, and the Family*, 3d ed. by R. K. Kelley, © 1979 by Harcourt Brace Jovanovich and reprinted with their permission.

Table 17.2—Reprinted with permission from *International Journal of Sociology of the Family* 5 (Autumn 1975): 168–177.

Library of Congress Cataloging in Publication Data
Reiss, Ira L
Family systems in America.

Bibliography: p. 507
Includes indexes.
1. Family—United States. 2. Marriage—United States. 3. Courtship. I. Title.
HQ536.R44 1980 306.8'0973 80–10168
ISBN 0-03-047246-6

Printed in the United States of America
0 1 2 3 4 038 9 8 7 6 5 4 3 2 1

Preface

Every once in a while you write something you feel good about—something that captures the essence of your thinking and clearly expresses the state of the art at this point in history. That is how I feel about this third edition of *Family Systems in America*. From the very beginning of the revision, I felt the excitement of a project that was fitting together and gathering momentum. My goal was to better integrate the entire family field and to more clearly explicate each major aspect of that field. One reason I was able to accomplish the task so much better now is that there has been an immense improvement in the state of knowledge in this field during the last five years.

The family field was building up to a quantum leap forward for many years but the actual takeoff occurred only in the last few years. Government reports have vastly improved both in the variety of research projects with which they deal and in the skill and clarity of their presentation. This is a significant development. The government, with its census files and its annual surveys of tens of thousands of households, is in one of the best positions to improve the overall understanding of our society. Individual social science research has also made notable advances in terms of both the quality of the research and the attempt to integrate theoretical explanations with the research undertaking. There may well have been a critical mass of researchers needed for a breakthrough to occur. Whatever the reason, I felt the stimulation of the increased availability of strategic data and ideas. This made the development of integrative explanations much more feasible. I sensed this opportunity the moment I began to examine the recent literature in the family field. The elation I felt due to the increased ability to integrate and explain took hold of me to such an extent that I completely rewrote two-thirds of the second edition and the remaining third has been noticeably altered. I spent as much time and energy on this revision as I did on the first edition.

One way that I sought to integrate the total material was to reduce the number of chapters from twenty-four to eighteen, while keeping the size of the book the same. I dispersed some material throughout the text, integrated some in particular places, discarded a good deal, and brought in much new relevant information. I consolidated those areas that were able to clarify and relate to each other. In this way the overall unity has been greatly enhanced.

Let me cover some of the highlights and new elements of this third edition. The first chapter is entirely new and basically affords the reader a background of the study of the family over the past century. This sort of background knowledge helps in seeing the relationship of some recent work to the older accomplishments in this area of study. One can gain some insight from this chapter into the flavor of the family field and obtain an initial orientation to the approach of the book.

I have stressed even more strongly than before the importance of gender roles for the understanding of the family. The ways in which our culture defines the role of males and females is fundamental to understanding how we act toward each other in regard to love, marriage, sexuality, and occupation, to name but a few

iii

important areas. Chapter 3 lays the foundation for the important place of gender roles and other chapters further develop this theme.

I have taken the issue of sexual partner preferences and written an entire chapter on it. Instead of a separate discussion of homosexuality and heterosexuality, I have put forth the beginnings of a theory of sexuality that integrates both the development of heterosexual and homosexual preferences. I have also completely reorganized the treatment of premarital sexuality so as to integrate the discussion of trends and causes. This is followed by a discussion of outcomes such as contraceptive behavior, pregnancy, and abortion. In this way there is a more holistic quality about the discussion of premarital sexuality.

The treatment of marital power relationships has been expanded and I have added some discussion of the new research on violence in the family. The entire section on marriage is related to the study of patterns of communication and commitment in marriage as brought out in the latest research. Another integrative mechanism was the combination of marital and extramarital sexuality into one chapter. After all, extramarital sexuality does have crucial connections to the entire marital relationship and it seems obvious that marital sexuality must be explored if one is to have complete understanding of extramarital sexuality. Thus it made sense to treat these two types of sexuality together.

In a culture with the highest divorce rate in the Western world, it seemed sensible to pay increased attention to the entire area of remarriage. Over a quarter of all the marriages made each year are remarriages. Until very recently there was virtually no research on remarriage, despite its commonness. I have incorporated the recent thinking and research on this topic in Chapter 12.

Probably the central role change for women in the last generation was in the occupational area. Forty-two out of every one hundred mothers of preschool children are now employed. Just thirty years ago only twelve out of every one hundred were employed. The acceptance and pursuit of employment by mothers of small children is a vital aspect of the changing female role. The stresses and strains of the dual-earner family is another important aspect that is discussed in depth. The change in the female occupational role helps spell out the gender-role alterations that are occurring now in the Family Systems in America. The occupations we work at have major effects on the values we hold and so it is worth examining just what type of work married men and women are now engaged in. I deal with this and other gender-role changes in terms of all age groups and for both black and white racial groups, so that the diversity that exists can be clearly portrayed. Such breakdowns, particularly by race and social class, are present throughout the book.

The last section of this edition is almost all new. I have added a chapter on Sweden. One reason for this was that I spent my 1975–1976 Sabbatical at Uppsala University. But even without that experience I would have felt that Sweden, as the leader in the Western world's equalitarian gender-role changes, is well worth studying. Not that we are in the same exact situation as the Swedes, but rather because they have faced many of the same problems as we are now facing and it is instructive to study their experience. Furthermore, we can better develop an understanding of social change by such comparisons.

In the last chapter I seek to develop a new synthesis of explanations of the Family Systems in America based upon what has been covered in the earlier chapters. I use the term "Family Systems" to include three institutions: (1) family institution; (2) marital institution, and (3) courtship institution. I allow myself the luxury of predictions regarding future trends in all three institutions. The book ends with an examination of the People's Republic of China and how the Chinese have tried to equalize gender roles in their new country. China too is not a model for America but its experience—both successes and failures—help test some of the ideas put forth regarding trends and changes in Western society.

Each chapter has its own list of references. These can serve as the basis for further inquiry for those who are so inclined. I have not attempted to include all research. Instead I have tried to pick out those that were among the best in the field and which more clearly incorporate explanatory value and are therefore helpful in affording understanding of an area. Of necessity, only a few works could be explored in any depth and inevitably some fine research could only be mentioned. In order to facilitate easy location of references, there is at the end of the book a master bibliography containing the total set of references used in this edition.

There are four appendixes which are optional for student and instructor use. For the person who wishes to go further into the research and theory dimensions these appendixes should be of value. They are written as introductory pieces and are not very technical.

I am a sociologist by training and thus my emphasis is upon sociological research. Nevertheless, I have also utilized a good deal of anthropological, historical, and psychological work. My goal is to explain the way courtship, marital, and family relationships operate in our society. These other disciplines are often quite useful in achieving this goal and thus they are brought into focus on occasion. The emphasis throughout is upon the Family Systems in America today. But societies are not born full-grown anymore than are we humans and therefore it is important to gain some historical perspective so as to better appreciate the nature of our current system. Recent anthropological and historical work is invaluable for affording such perspective. The overall approach is one that would be appropriate for more than just sociology courses on the family. Courses in family relations and child development units often cover much of the same material as do sociological courses. I believe that any course with a fundamental interest in an overall scientific understanding of the family would find this book relevant.

Finally, I am pleased to report that G. C. Sponaugle, a doctoral student at the University of Minnesota, has prepared an *Instructor's Manual* for this text. Sponaugle has been extremely thorough and innovative in the development of this manual. He has included the usual test questions and discussion topics but he also has developed ideas that he found useful in his own teaching in this area and from which many of you no doubt will also benefit.

The entire process of writing this third edition has been a most exciting experience. Now that the work is at an end, I have a deep feeling of satisfaction. I hope I have been able to transmit some of this excitement and that you will gain much satisfaction, as I have, from the study of Family Systems in America.

In a sense my first debt is to Burton Taylor, emeritus professor from Bowdoin College in Maine. It was he who after hiring me for my first position asked me to teach a course on the family. Although I had interests in various aspects of that field, I had never taken a course in the family as a graduate student. I immediately found the idea attractive and of considerable interest but I did feel that in many respects the family field was in need of improved research and theorizing. My interest was aroused sufficiently so that I wrote my first book in 1960 on the topic of premarital sexuality. I have since found an increasing degree of satisfaction in the study of the family and thus am indebted to Professor Taylor for inviting me to teach that course.

All of us who teach are in debt to our students. Students impose a challenge upon the professor to organize ideas, to encourage critical thinking, to motivate, and to make explanations exciting. Colleagues are a source of support that must be acknowledged. At all the colleges I have taught and, specifically in the last ten years here at the University of Minnesota, I have found much stimulation from my colleagues and am grateful for their willingness to help in any project I undertook.

Three of my fellow sociologists have been kind enough to read a full draft of this book and let me benefit from their responses; Reuben Hill, Hyman Rodman, and Carlfred Broderick have been readers for all three editions. This is indeed a series of acts beyond the normal call of duty and I am most grateful for their careful and concerned assistance. In addition, three new readers—Thomas Ramsbey, Ralph Locke, and Marilyn Aronoff—have given me useful comments.

My research assistant has been G. C. Sponaugle, a doctoral student at the University of Minnesota. He too worked with me on the second edition of this book. On this third edition he labored long and hard searching for new data sources which I needed, drawing some of the graphs, suggesting key articles to read that I might have otherwise missed, and in many other ways being most valuable. Sponaugle is also the author of the *Instructors Manual* that accompanies this text. He always was there when I needed him for all kinds of help.

My wife, Harriet, has aided me in all my books and was in charge of an important part of the composition of this one. Understanding my need for photographs to improve the esthetic appeal and add greater clarity to some of the ideas being discussed, Harriet located historical sources for many interesting sketches and found relevant photographs of sculptures, as well as more traditional photographic sources. In addition to that massive task she edited the entire manuscript. She also discussed many of the topics in the book and gave me the benefit of her insight. Her efforts were essential to the project and I am deeply grateful.

The Family Study Center at the University of Minnesota has always been very generous with its assistance and I am particularly appreciative to Mary Ann Beneke and Fae Bjurquist. Linda Day and others attached to the Sociology Department also aided in many ways. I thank them all.

Minneapolis, Minn.   Ira L. Reiss
February, 1980

Contents

7

Premarital Sexual Permissiveness: Trends and Causes

166

8

The Management of Premarital Pregnancy

193

Part III **THE MARITAL INSTITUTION**   **219**

9

The Marital Relationship: Roles, Power, and Communication

221

Part IV THE FAMILY INSTITUTION

13

The Parental Choice

353

14

The Interweave of Children and Parents

374

15

Occupation and Parenthood

390

16

Kinship Ties: From the Cradle to the Grave

413

Part V **MODELS OF THE FUTURE**   433

17

Sweden: The Western Model
435

18

The Future of the Family Systems in America
457

Appendixes

Appendix 1

Value Judgments and Science
474

Appendix 2

An Elementary Approach to Probability Statistics

483

Appendix 3

Causal Analysis: The Fascinating Search for Answers

490

Appendix 4

Theory Construction: The Building of Explanations

500

Ira L. Reiss is professor of Sociology and also on the staff of the Family Study Center at the University of Minnesota. His primary interests are in the sociology of the family area, with emphasis on sexual relationships and gender roles, and his secondary interests are in theory construction and the study of deviant behavior. He has served as associate editor on journals such as *The American Sociological Review*; *Social Problems*; *Journal of Marriage and the Family*; and *Archives of Sexual Behavior*. He was Director of the University of Minnesota Family Study Center from 1969 to 1974. In 1971 he was elected President of the Midwest Sociological Society; in 1975 Chairperson of the family section of the American Sociological Association, and in 1979 President of the National Council on Family Relations. He has published eight books and monographs, including: *Premarital Sexual Standards in America* (The Free Press of Macmillan, 1960); *The Social Context of Premarital Sexual Permissiveness* (Holt, Rinehart and Winston, Inc., 1967); and *Contemporary Theories About the Family*, 2 vols. (with W. Burr, R. Hill, and I. Nye; The Free Press of Macmillan Co., 1979). He has also published approximately 90 articles and commentaries in professional journals and has received federal and university research grants. Professor Reiss lectures to numerous universities, professional, and other groups around the country and abroad. His current writing centers on the development of a theory of extramarital sexual permissiveness.

Photo by Ivan Kalman

Part One BY WAY OF BACKGROUND

Our Approach
to the Family System

ONE

Introduction

The 1980s are starting out as a quite different decade than the 1970s. The year 1970 was a year of violent protest concerning the war in Vietnam. Campuses across the nation were in upheaval. It was in that year that Cambodia was invaded and four students were slain at Kent State University. Rioting had occurred in the ghettoes of many United States cities. Experimentation with new family forms was widespread among novices. X-rated movies and some "unrated" pornographic films were appearing all over the country in public theaters. Divorce rates were sky-rocketing at a pace rarely seen in this century. Birth rates were dropping sharply and the age at marriage was rising.

The indicators of the 1980s are quite distinct from those of a decade ago. As you will see during the course of reading this book, the vital signs of the Family Systems in America seem to be stabilizing.[1] Divorce rates are moving up only very slowly; marriage rates are rising and birth rates seem to have stabilized. To be sure, there are changes occurring. Cohabitation is increasing rapidly, as it is in the rest of the Western World. There appears to be increasing popularity in the legitimacy of certain choices like whether to have premarital intercourse, when to marry, how many children to have, whether to pursue a career and a marriage, and what rights and privileges are accorded to husbands and wives. There appears to be in all these areas a consolidation of the changes that occurred in the late 1960s and the 1970s. This does not mean that all the new life-styles that were introduced in the last fifteen years have become accepted or that all those that were accepted were rated

[1]The term Family Systems will be capitalized throughout the book. This is done to distinguish it more clearly from the term "family institutions." Both these concepts will be discussed at length in Chapter Two.

as being of identical value. It does mean that instead of continued explanation of alternatives, there is now occurring a ranking and filtering of judgments about what has changed. Although I will not try to morally evaluate these changes, I do believe this book will help the reader in arriving at his or her own judgment on the new Family Systems in America. My major objective is to afford the reader a way of viewing, a way of understanding and making sense of the operation of the courtship, marital, and family institutions which comprise the Family Systems in American society in the 1980s.

The basic perspective that I offer is a sociological one. Specifically, this means that we will focus upon the various *shared* ways of feeling, thinking, and believing that exist in our culture today and look at the *shared* patterns of behaving that are occurring today in our society. The psychic life of the individual must, of necessity, be viewed but essentially it will be examined in terms of how the individual's thoughts, feelings, and actions relate to the social and cultural setting in which that person exists. Perspectives of other disciplines will be presented. In particular, this is true for social psychology, anthropology, and history and to a lesser extent we will draw upon the discipline of psychology and biology. But all of these other disciplines will be utilized to help organize and improve our sociological under-standing of the multitude of life-styles that go to make up the diverse Family Systems in America. In short, where other disciplines can help throw light on how sociological factors operate or where their limits are, we shall discuss that body of knowledge. My hope is that instead of ending up with a hodgepodge of discrete facts and unrelated perspectives, the student will develop an integrated and coherent understanding of Family Systems from a sociological perspective. Such a coherent, organized view is only possible if we create a clear focus. The focus in this book is adjusted to the vision of the sociologist. No claim is made that only sociological vision is 20/20. Rather, it is asserted that this is one very popular and valuable way to understand the family and once one achieves knowledge of the sociological perspective, other orientations can more easily be added.

The sociological orientation is a scientific one and thus research evidence is of crucial concern. We will deal with value controversies in many sections of this book but not with the aim of recommending a moral solution but rather with the aim of clarifying our understanding of the causes and consequences operating therein (see Appendix 1 for a full discussion of value judgments). It should be clear that the aim is *not* to cover all the research studies that have been carried out or to memorize all the statistical facts that have been published, but rather to build up your ability to *explain* and *understand* the various phenomena operative in the Family Systems in America. Thus, when we cover research studies and their findings we will be looking for the insights and clues they afford toward an explanation of the family customs we are examining. In some areas there will be competing scientific explanations as is the case in explaining the development of love rela-tionships. In other areas, as extramarital sexual relationships, explanations are just beginning to be developed and only a few parts of the puzzle are available. But in all cases, we will strive as much as we can toward developing such explanations for that is the basic goal of all science. The development of such scientific explanations cannot but help those who wish to apply themselves to the solution of social or personal problems. But our major goal here is to clarify the operation of the human Family Systems in America in the 1980s. It is left to others to apply this knowledge as they wish.

Brief Overview of the Sociology of the Family Field

A. EVOLUTIONARY APPROACHES (1850 TO DATE):

The term "sociology" was coined in the 1830s by a French social philosopher named August Comte. Comte thought of sociology as the "queen of the sciences." To Comte sociology was the most general of the social sciences in that it dealt with all of human society. Other social sciences would deal with specific institutions such as the economic or political institutions, but sociology tried to arrive at an integrative view of the total society. Comte was a positivist and as such strongly believed that science could supply the answers to the social problems that had been produced by the industrial revolution. Needless to note, this expectation has not been fulfilled!

During the last half of the nineteenth century the Darwinian evolutionary mood of all sciences showed itself in the sociological writings about the family. Since there were no Ph.D. degrees given in sociology until the last decade of the nineteenth century, the writers who were called sociologists were often trained as historians, anthropologists, and philosophers. One such person was Lewis Henry Morgan, a lawyer who was also an anthropologist. In 1877 Morgan wrote a book entitled *Ancient Society*, in which he described the evolution of the family from the very beginning of time up to date. A most ambitious undertaking, to be sure.

Morgan had spent a great many years studying and living with the Iroquois Indians and was made a member of the Seneca Indian tribe. In line with the evolutionary notions of his time, Morgan pictured the different forms of the family evolving through the stages of savagery, barbarism and finally into civilization. The earliest male-female interaction was assumed to be a stage of "primitive promiscuity." From this stage of unrestricted sexual matings evolved five types of families:

1. *The consanguine family*: Group marriage between all those of one generation. All such people would call each other brothers and sisters.
2. *Punaluan family*: Derives from the consanguine family by excluding biological brothers and sisters from being part of the same group marriage. (The name of this form comes from the study of the Hawaiian kinship system.)
3. *Pairing family*: Consists of single males and females who are married by parental arrangement based on considerations of convenience. The marriage is easily dissolved and continues only at the pleasure of the two people. This form is thought to be an evolution from the larger Punaluan family.
4. *Patriarchal family*: A strongly male dominant form, usually with multiple wives.

Lewis Henry Morgan (1818–1881).
Source: Brown Brothers.

5. *Monogamian family:* Involves a single male and female but the male is less dominant in this form of marriage. (After reading Chapter 2, the reader will appreciate that Morgan did not make a clear distinction between marital and family institutions.)

There were other evolutionary views of the family. The Swiss classicist Bachofen's book, *The Mother-Right* (1861), was perhaps one of the earliest to catch the attention of the European intelligentsia and was perhaps influential on Morgan's thinking. Bachofen also posited an original state of promiscuity which developed into a system based upon "mother-rights" wherein females raised the children and were the stable element in the society while males were geographically mobile due to their hunting activity. The males would return to bring food and mate with the females who were raising the resulting children collectively. These views are compatible with the later views of Lewis Henry Morgan, particularly the early consanguine family stage.

Morgan's ideas are of greater historical interest to us predominantly because Friedrich Engels came upon his work and adopted much of it as part of the official position of the Communist Party. Engels did not accept Morgan's total analysis. In fact, he rejected Morgan's views on the importance of private property as well as his most recent evolutionary form of the family (the monogamian family). Engels instead preferred the pairing family and made it the ideal family form of the Communist philosophy. He transposed some of the meaning of the pairing family for he removed parental arrangement and made the basis of it love and affection rather than convenience and efficiency. In short, Engels made the pairing family into the "free love" type of union that was so popular in the late nineteenth century with European intellectuals. The essence of the "free love" notion was that you live with someone if you love them and if you stop loving them, you leave. No marriage ceremony or legal conditions were stipulated. Some of the forms of cohabitation today, particularly in Sweden, are similar to these "free love" notions and will be discussed in detail later on. Suffice to say here that Engels found the pairing family of Morgan's schema to be compatible with his own free love notions. He also was provided by Morgan with a historical explanation of how this form evolved and this pleased him, for historical explanations were a typical part of the Communist philosophy. It is ironic that the Communist Party should get its ideal family form from an American lawyer who found it to be the prevailing form among the American Iroquois Indians. The pairing family was seen by Morgan as developing during the hunting and gathering phase and as being replaced by the more male dominant patriarchal family when agriculture appeared on the scene. Engels saw the patriarchal family as evolving in direct relationship to the increased concern by males to control female sexual behavior so as to ensure that their own biological offspring would inherit their farmland. It was precisely this patriarchal family that Engels saw as a type of oppression of females by males and which he therefore fully rejected. He also rejected the monogamian family which is the modern-day family because it still had too much male dominance and its legal basis was also seen as a means of passing down property through the male line. The Communist view of history incorporated the idea that there once existed a more equalitarian type of society and that we will eventually return to such a society. The pairing family of Morgan seemed to Engels to fit that more equalitarian past and thus he embraced it.

The above description of Morgan's work and its relation to other late-nineteenth-century conceptions about the family should afford the reader some of the flavor of the evolutionary stage theories that prevailed at that period in our history. However, it is important to realize that those specific evolutionary ideas are rejected today by the social science community. Morgan made the mistake of assuming that the fact that all people of one generation called each other brother and sister was evidence that in the past there must have been a group marriage of all such brother-sister kinship types. We now know that in societies wherein all people of one generation call each other brother and sister there still is clear awareness of a biological mother and father and there is differential treatment given to biological brothers and sisters. Thus the use of the same kinship term does not necessarily mean that no distinctions are being made among all with that label or that they participated in a group marriage.

Even in the nineteenth century there were many opponents to the idea of "primitive promiscuity" as well as the related notion of an original mother-centered society in which all women reared the children collectively and all men roamed the land and occasionally came home to casually mate. Henry Maine, Herbert Spencer, Charles Darwin, and Edward Westermarck were a few of the opponents. Westermarck, a Finnish anthropologist, wrote a massive work on the history of

Edward Westermarck (1862–1939).
Source: Elina Haavio-Mannila,
University of Helsinki.

marriage and published it before he was thirty years of age (1891). The primitive promiscuity notion was premised on the idea that males did not know their role in paternity and thus did not participate in raising children. Westermarck presents a great deal of evidence indicating that males did know their role in paternity and thus would have been involved in a Family System that reared children. Others have noted societies in which males lived in small families even though they did not know their paternity role. The role of jealousy was also argued. It was felt that jealousy would make promiscuity among all brothers and sisters in a large group unlikely because males would protect their sexual rights over particular women. It was also argued that mothers would feel closer to their biological children than to other children and thus distinct family units would be present.

Westermarck also questioned some of the evidence presented in favor of the primitive promiscuity notion. The quotation below from Westermarck (1891:110) catches some of the flavor of this debate:

> In the very chapter where Pliny states that among the Garamantians men and women lived in promiscuous intercourse he tells us of another African tribe, the Blemmyans, that they were said to have no head and to have the mouth and eyes in the breast. I have never seen this statement quoted in any book on human anatomy, and can see no reason to assume that our author was so much better acquainted with the sexual habits of the Garamantians than he was with the personal appearance of the Blemmyans.

The twentieth century has seen the almost total rejection of the type of evolutionary theory put forth by Morgan, Bachofen, and Engels. The work of George Peter Murdock (1949) clearly summarized the position of anthropologists in the 1940s. Murdock cites Australian tribes who are ignorant of physical paternity but view their children as their descendants. Descent and kin ties depend on group membership and not necessarily on recognition of biological connections. Murdock also pointed out that several modes of tracing descent occur within the same "level

TABLE 1.1
Forms of Descent*

	PATRILINEAL	MATRILINEAL	BILATERAL	DOUBLE DESCENT
From which grandparent is descent traced	Father's father	Mother's mother	All four	One from the mother's parents and one from the father's parents
Percent distribution in Murdock's 1,138 societies (1967)	50%	14%	33%	3%

*Our society is bilateral today but it has traces of patrilineal descent from our past, e.g., we are patronymic and take the male name. But this too is changing today.

of culture," i.e. hunting, agriculture or modern societies, and thus evolutionary notions of new family forms for each cultural level seem in error (Murdock, 1949: Chap. 8). There is also little support for the nineteenth-century evolutionary notion that we first traced our descent only through the female line (matrilineal descent) and then shifted when agriculture arose to tracing descent only through the male line (patrilineal descent) and then recently shifted to tracing descent through both male and female lines (bilateral descent). It seems that all systems of tracing descent have wide distributions in many different types of societies (Schusky, 1965). Table 1.1 presents the distribution of various types of descent. Once again, the evolutionary notions of fixed stages and fixed lines of development seem not to fit the data we possess. This is not to deny that there may be more complex designs that will be found in the historical development of family forms, but it is rather to assert that we have made little progress in discovering such forms and that the simplistic nineteenth-century notions seem not to fit the world as we now know it.

There is one aspect of the nineteenth-century evolutionary theory that is somewhat supported by examination of present-day societies around the world. The evolutionary view asserted that there was a marked increase in male dominance in agricultural societies as compared to the older hunting societies. The evidence (Middleton, 1962; Gough, 1971) from several studies indicates that hunting societies have milder degrees of male dominance than do agricultural societies. So there is some evidence that the advent of agriculture with its ownership of land and more settled life may have increased the power of males at the expense of females. Of course, one can argue that this difference in male dominance may be true of hunting and agricultural societies today but that 12,000 years ago, when agriculture was just beginning, the situation was different and hunting and agricultural societies were not then as they are today. Nevertheless, if one examines sources such as the Code of Hammurabi and the Old Testament, written three or four thousand years ago, one does find evidence of male dominance codified into law. Wives were legally treated as property, and rights to divorce were much more available to males.

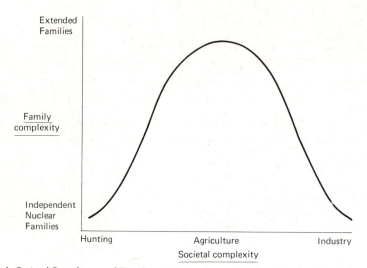

Figure 1.1. Societal Complexity and Family Complexity. (Composed from Winch and Blumberg, 1972.)

Sexual restrictions were much more heavily placed on females and political power was wielded by males. So there is suggestive evidence supporting agriculture as a time of great male dominance.

More recent evidence concerning the evolution of family types comes from the work of Winch and Blumberg (1972, 1977). These researchers used the cross-cultural evidence that is available in our libraries today and sought to relate societal complexity (degree of simple hunting to the greater complexity of agricultural and industrial activity) to family complexity (degree to which households are made up of several families living together, i.e. extended family systems). Figure 1.1 shows the result of their research.

It appears that agriculture was a time of large family groups wherein several generations and relatives of the same generation lived together within the same household. The complexity of the family forms in agricultural societies may also have promoted male dominance as a way of ordering the numerous relationships involved. In contrast, in both hunting at one extreme and industrial societies at the other, the husband-wife-and-child unit (nuclear family) operated separately from their elderly parents and other relatives to a much greater degree. Such independence may have promoted greater male-female equality.

Perhaps of equal importance is the fact that it now seems that our modern-day type of small family group is not the last stage of an evolutionary process but is very similar to the earliest forms of the family found in primitive hunting societies. Thus, compulsory simple straight-line theories of evolutionary stages which proceed from simple to complex forms have to be rejected. We need to be open to a wide variety of possible trends throughout history.

Many formidable difficulties faced the nineteenth-century evolutionary writers and those writers today who attempt to deal with long-term trends in the human family. Humans have been on this planet for over two million years and for all but the last 12,000 of those years we have been hunters and gatherers. For only the last 200 years have we had industrial societies. Thus, the world we are most familiar with is a brand-new world. Writing goes back only 5,000 years. Even cave drawings go back only 30,000 years. So we have pitifully little to base any theory of origins of the family upon. Even historical accounts are often biased and picture but a narrow segment of the population. Some people still find the search worthwhile and try to find suggestive evidence; others seek to limit their comparisons to societies in existence today. There has arisen in the last fifteen years a new type of social history of the family. The historians in this scientific branch strive to use the best available data in ingenius ways to examine the last few centuries of our history (see, for example, Modell, et al., 1976; Demos, 1977; Laslett, 1977). These are all legitimate pursuits. Indeed, there still are those who search for our origins in the distant past and new theories are appearing (Winch, 1977). We are today much more scientific and sophisticated than a hundred years ago when the early social science writings on the family began to appear.

B. SOCIAL PSYCHOLOGICAL-SOCIAL REFORM APPROACHES (1900 TO DATE):

Many of the early sociologists wrote about the family. For example, the term "primary group" as coined by Charles Horton Cooley (1909) was most clearly illustrated by the family. A primary group was defined as a small, face-to-face, durable group of great importance to the individual. Cooley called it primary in part because he had in mind the family as the group that *first* contacted the individual and was primary in that sense. George Herbert Mead's work (1934) in the first three decades of this century also gave importance to family socialization because of his emphasis on interpersonal relationships with people who are significant in one's life. Thus, in the early decades of this century there developed an emphasis upon studying the family as a particularly important type of small group. In 1926, Ernest Burgess, a sociologist at the University of Chicago, defined the family as a "unity of interacting personalities, each with its own history." This definition further showed the emphasis on the internal processes of the family group. The larger society was not lost sight of in this approach for it was the pressures of other social institutions like the occupational, religious, political, and educational that were seen as impacting on the ways in which parents would interact with each other and with their children. But the focus was on the internal operations of the family members. This basic orientation is what I am calling the social psychological approach. It was born and bred in the midwest and reflects the dominance of the University of Chicago.

The nineteenth-century interest in sociology as a possible source of solutions to social problems remained powerful in the early twentieth century. Much of the interest in the social psychological study of the family was based upon the feeling that to study the family would enable us to gain insight into how marital happiness might be produced or how divorce might be avoided or how marital crises might be handled (Terman, 1938; Burgess and Cottrell, 1939; Hill, 1949; Burgess and Wallin, 1953).

Courses in marriage and the family, the forerunners of the one you are now enrolled in, began in the 1920s with this same problem-centered emphasis. They began in an attempt to help students prepare for getting engaged and eventually getting married. To be sure there was a scientific and research component which was supposed to help clarify the problem areas but the stress was clearly on finding the "correct" answer to the problem of marital happiness, premarital sexuality, or divorce.

C. THE SCIENTIFIC APPROACH VIA RESEARCH AND THEORY BUILDING (1950 TO DATE):

Despite the heavy reform and problem-centered approach of the early twentieth century, there also was a scientific approach being emphasized by sociologists even as far back as the late nineteenth century (Durkheim, 1893, 1897). In fact, there was a constant battle between the more scientific minded sociologists and the more social problem oriented sociologists. This struggle was clearly visible throughout the entire first half of this century. In particular, the decades up until the 1950s were dotted by the battles of people like George Lundberg and Samuel Stouffer arguing with people like Robert MacIver and Howard Becker (Lundberg, 1939; Stouffer, 1949; MacIver, 1942; Becker and Barnes, 1938).

Those who stressed scientific interests as primary gained increasing power during World War II. The Information and Education branch of the U. S. Army was heavily staffed with social scientists and the government utilized these people to help with several practical concerns. One of these concerns centered on the integration of black and white troops in combat. A later concern was in devising a fair system of discharging the millions of service personnel when World War II ended. The social scientists undertook objective studies of attitudes, developed scales and other measuring instruments and helped in many ways to answer the questions posed to them (Stouffer, et al. 1949, 4 vols.). The favorable reaction of the government and business groups led to the establishment of federal research organizations and to the funding of social science research by these agencies in the years after World War II. Social scientists had shown that they could be useful and the public prestige of social science rose. All this encouraged a scientific research emphasis in sociological studies of the family.

The sociological research on the family from 1950 on showed this increased scientific rigor. Relatedly, there was an emphasis on doing more than just gathering descriptive data on how many people said yes and how many people said no to a particular question. The emphasis increasingly came on developing explanations or what more technically we call "theory." In short, rather than just stating that divorce rates are lower for college educated people, the demand was for a hypothesis or proposition that would assert why divorce rates were lower. One explanation that has been proposed is simply that a college degree is a good predictor of a higher than average income and that income is a good predictor of being able to keep economic strains from producing marital difficulties or divorce. This, on a simple level, is part of an explanation or the beginning of a theory. A theory would be an integrated set of such explanations. Once you formulate and test such explanations you can deduce other hypotheses from them, e.g., one could deduce that if the college degree becomes more common, it will be less of a good predictor of a high-paying job, and then the divorce rate for the college educated would become closer to the average. Such predictions can be checked when those conditions are met by a particular society. The reader will find many examples of such explanations in this book and their usefulness will become clear. For now, it is only necessary to note that the emphasis upon building and testing explanations (theories) is the most recent trend and is most visible in the work done in the last fifteen years. (See Appendix 4 for further elaboration on theory building.)

The Orientation of This Book to the Family

In light of what has been written in this chapter it is best to clarify just which of the three major directions of sociological research will be followed. We will not focus on evolutionary or social problem concerns. The basic orientation of this book is a scientific one. This does not mean that we will not deal with areas relevant to evolutionary interests and to social problems—we certainly will. But when we deal with issues relevant to a social problem, we will not attempt to solve these problems, nor to give the reader moral advice about the problems, nor even to deal with all the pros and cons that have been thought up about those problems. For example, we will deal with areas of human courtship relationships, marital relationships, and family relationships that are controversial but our interest will be to understand what social factors are causally at work, what are the trends, how do people's attitudes divide on the area, and how does this area relate to other parts of our social life.

Thus, our interest is in increasing your ability to understand what is going on in the Family Systems in America. You may judge for yourself what is worthwhile and what you personally would like to see happen. Surely, what we cover here will make it easier to arrive at personal value judgments. One might say that this approach is more likely to lead to informed and carefully reasoned judgments than if we focused on the problem itself and concentrated predominantly on personal arguments of each side. My goal is to enable you to be better able to evaluate research which you read about in the popular press or in scientific journals and to enable you to have an overall understanding of what is happening to the family, marital and courtship institutions in America. In this way you become more independent from reliance on what those in authority say. Your intellectual curiosity will be developed as will your ability to objectively understand societal trends and relationships. I cannot guarantee that this will make you a happier or a better person, but you will possess a deeper and more objective understanding of the world in which you live. If that is your goal, read on; if not, you may be reading the wrong book.

References

Bachofen, J. J. 1948. *Das Mutterrecht*. Basel, Switzerland: Benno Schwabe. (Originally published in 1861.)

Becker, Howard, and H. E. Barnes. 1938. *Social Thought From Lore to Science*. 2 vols. Washington, DC: Harren Press.

Burgess, Ernest W., and Leonard S. Cottrell, Jr. 1939. *Predicting Success or Failure in Marriage*. New York: Prentice-Hall.

———, and Paul Wallin. 1953. *Engagement and Marriage*. Philadelphia: Lippincott.

Cooley, Charles Horton. 1909. *Social Organization*. New York: Schocken.

Demos, John. 1977. "The American Family in Past Time." Pp. 59–77 in A. S. Skolnick and J. H. Skolnick (eds.), *Family in Transition*. Boston: Little, Brown.

Engels, Friedrich. 1902. *The Origin of the Family, Private Property, and the State*. Chicago: Charles H. Kerr. (Originally published in 1884.)

Gough, Kathleen E. 1971. "The Origin of the Family," *Journal of Marriage and the Family* 33 (November):760–771.

Hill, Reuben. 1949. *Families Under Stress*. New York: Harper & Row.

Laslett, Peter. 1977. *Family Life and Illicit Love in Earlier Generations*. Cambridge, England: Cambridge University Press.

Lévi-Strauss, Claude. 1969. *The Elementary Structures of Kinship*. Boston: Beacon.

Linton, Ralph. 1936. *The Study of Man*. New York: Appleton.

Lundberg, George A. 1939. *Foundations of Sociology*. New York: Macmillan.

MacIver, Robert M. 1942. *Social Causation*. Boston: Ginn.

Mead, George Herbert. 1934. *Mind, Self and Society*. Chicago: University of Chicago Press.

Middleton, Russell. 1962. "Brother-Sister and Father-Daughter Marriage in Ancient Egypt," *American Sociological Review* 27 (October):603–611.

Modell, John, Frank Furstenberg, and Theodore Hershberg. 1976. "Social Change and Transitions to Adulthood in Historical Perspective," *Journal of Family History* 1 (Autumn):7–33.

Morgan, Lewis Henry. 1877. *Ancient Society*. Chicago: Charles H. Kerr.

Murdock, George Peter. 1949. *Social Structure*. New York: Macmillan.

———. 1967. "Ethnographic Atlas: A Summary,' *Ethnology* 6 (April): 109–236.

Nimkoff, Meyer F., and Russell Middleton. 1960. "Types of Family and Types of Economy," *American Journal of Sociology* 66 (November): 215–225.

Radcliffe-Brown, A. R., and Daryll Forde (eds.). 1950. *African Systems of Kinship and Marriage*. New York: Oxford University Press.

Schusky, Ernest L. 1965. *Manual for Kinship Analysis*. New York: Holt, Rinehart and Winston.

Shorter, Edward. 1975. *The Making of the Modern Family*. New York: Basic Books.

Stouffer, Samuel A., et al. 1949. *The American Soldier*. 4 vols. Princeton, NJ: Princeton University Press.

Terman, Lewis M. 1939. *Psychological Factors in Marital Happiness*. New York: McGraw-Hill.

Westermarck, Edward. 1922. *The History of Human Marriage*. 3 vols. 5th ed. New York: Allerton Book Co. (Originally published in 1891.)

Winch, Robert F. 1977. *Familial Organization*. New York: Free Press.

Winch, Robert F., and Rae Blumberg. 1972. "Societal Complexity and Familial Complexity: Evidence for the Curvilinear Hypotheses." *American Journal of Sociology* 77 (March: 898–920.

The Wheat from the Chaff—

Universality and Family Systems

TWO

Introduction

The first step in clear and open communication is to make sure that the basic concepts one is talking about are defined in precise and agreed upon fashions. In this book we shall be talking about three basic institutions: courtship, marriage, and the family. Therefore, it is well to spend this chapter clarifying the meaning we will give to these institutions.

The census bureau defines a family as "two or more people related by blood, marriage or adoption, living together." That obviously is an arbitrary definition, that is, it is not aimed at defining the essence of the family but rather at just getting a convenient way to count and measure what is called a family by this definition. Such definitions cannot be true or false and they are commonly used. Burgess's famous definition of the family stated in 1926 is: "The family is a unity of interacting personalities each with its own history." Here too we have a "convenient" definition, and *not* one that aims at putting forth the essential qualities of the institution in a way that is testable. Both these definitions merely point to what is of interest to a particular person or group about the family. They are what the philosopher would call a "nominal" definition, that is, they are arbitrary and for convenience and they have no "truth value" and thus are not empirically testable (Bierstedt, 1959). There is nothing wrong with using such definitions and they are useful if others are also interested in a phenomenon so defined.

Although I too use nominal definitions, I prefer not to use them for the Family System and instead will seek a "real" definition of these three institutions which will incorporate what is universally essential in that institution. We will learn more about the Family System by seeking to find out what qualities it possesses that are essential for the continuation of human society rather than if we simply pick an arbitrary definition that fits some particular narrow interest of ours. Also, by trying to define what is universally required about the family, marital, and courtship institutions, we will arrive at a conception that can be scientifically tested. Thus, we have a way to discern if our view is in line with the evidence available. This type of definition is what philosophers call a "real" definition or one that asserts the essence of something in a way that is testable. Nominal definitions, discussed above, simply state an agreed way to use a concept and are not testable. (Bierstedt, 1959; Lee, 1975 and 1977). Finally, if our goal is to learn something about these institutions that is true not only for America in 1980 but which has some more general truth value, then we must conceptualize these institutions in a universal way that allows for comparisons within our own society and with other societies.

Before we begin discussing the universal aspects of these institutions, we should arrive at some preliminary understanding of each of the three. Each has a logical and empirical relationship to each other. It is through courtship that one gets married and it is through being married that one is legitimized as a potential parent in a family. It would thus seem useful to have one term that referred to all three of these institutions. Accordingly, I propose that we call the integrated set the "Family System." Since there is often more than one acceptable way of courting, mating, or starting a family, we may properly speak of Family Systems. Together, these three institutions comprise the means of replacing the present generation with a new generation. The family institution is seen as the most central of the three institutions and thus the overall term "Family System" seems appropriate.

How does one establish what is universally required about Family Systems? The search for universals in any form is a difficult one and always falls short of certainty. Some of the nineteenth-century evolutionary writers sought for universals but the lack of scientifically sound cross-cultural data hindered them greatly. So one requirement in the search for what is universally required is to have good information on a variety of cultures around the world. If a particular characteristic is universally *required* for society to exist, then that characteristic should be present in all known cultures. To be sure, just being universally *present* is not final proof that the characteristic is universally *required*—it may be a characteristic that is difficult to do without, but not essential to societal survival, or it may be present in all societies just by chance. Nevertheless, to entertain the idea that a particular characteristic is universally required, it must be universally present.

The difficulties involved in finding characteristics that are universally required can be illustrated by the case of incest. Incest taboos of some sort seem present in all societies today, and it was thought that such a custom was necessary for societal survival. However, in 1962 Russell Middleton published findings indicating that during the Roman occupation of Egypt (30 B.C. to 324 A.D.), brother–sister and father–daughter marriages constituted about a quarter of all marriages that took place. It was widely known that such brother–sister marriage was common in royal lines in Egypt (the same was true in Hawaii and among the Incas in Peru). But it was believed that the masses in a society had never participated in such incestuous unions. Despite that belief, Middleton's historical data makes it apparent that such marriages were quite common and usually for the same reasons that they occurred among the royalty—namely, as a means of keeping wealth within one's own family.

Biological consequences do not rule out incest. Marriage to a close relative simply increases the chances that recessive traits that are present in that family line will show up in the offspring. Those recessive traits are often socially disvalued, but on occasion they may also be positively valued such as traits related to height, coordination, or intelligence. The negatively evaluated outcomes are only rarely destructive to life and often are not present. Further, in some small isolated cultures, all the people are very closely biologically related and yet there are still incest taboos that do not always restrict those most closely biologically related. Thus, biological consequences do not seem to be at the heart of an explanation of incest taboos.

Sociological reasons asserting how difficult it would be to allow incest have been advanced. Claude Lévi-Strauss (1969) and Davis (1950) have submitted sociological reasons favoring the incest taboo. Lévi-Strauss stressed the advantage of linking two different nuclear families by marriage so they might help each other in times of need. Perhaps among the wealthier families in a society, the need for outside help is reduced and thus the possibility of incestuous unions is increased. Davis posed an alternative explanation which stressed that there was inherent difficulty in combining the role of father and lover in one's relationship to a daughter and relatedly the potential conflict with the wife-mother that such incest might involve.

Thus, there are some reasons that make acceptance of incest difficult and quite rare but at least for brother-sister incest and to a lessor extent father–daughter incest, there is evidence of some societies that have not had such restrictions. One might still argue that it is very difficult to overcome the social pressures stated above against such incestuous marriage. I will not pursue the question of incest taboos here. I use this example simply to enlighten the reader on some of the difficulties present in establishing that a custom is universally required. One reward of such a difficult search is that one has to think through the nature of human relationships and what they might contribute to societal continuity, as we see in the thoughts put forth by Lévi-Strauss and Davis. Such analysis affords insight into the operation of human society. So, although the search for universals is not the easiest quest, nor the one with the most abundant available evidence, it is still a worthwhile investigation.

If we are to look for the essential aspects of family systems, it is well to begin with some overall view of what types of marital and family forms are found in cultures throughout the world today. Table 2.1 shows the several forms of marriage and the family as delineated by George Peter Murdock, a renowned anthropologist who studied hundreds of societies to arrive at this classification.

Marriage has two basic types: monogamy and polygamy. Polygamy is divisible into three types. By far the most widespread type is polygyny, where one male has several wives. The rarity of polyandry and the extreme lack of group marriage around the world are not just idle facts. As we discuss emerging family forms in America, the question of group marriage will come up, and we shall then give some attention to the reasons for its rarity around the world.

TABLE 2.1

Basic Forms of Marriage and the Family*

MARITAL FORMS

---

1. Monogamy: one male and one female
2. Polygamy: many males and/or many females
   a. Polygyny: one male and several females
   b. Polyandry: one female and several males
   c. Group marriage: many males and many females

FAMILY FORMS (WHICH DEVELOP FROM THE ABOVE MARITAL FORMS)

---

1. Nuclear family: one husband and wife and their children
2. Polygamous family: many husbands and/or wives and their children (see three main types of polygamous marital unions under marital forms)
3. Extended family: either a nuclear or polygamous family extended to include the parental generations and also sometimes to include relatives such as aunts and uncles

---

The classification schema used is basically that of George P. Murdock and is widely utilized by anthropologists.

A few words about polygyny: Americans have some rather inaccurate notions of how and why polygynous marriages occur. Perhaps, because of our sexually restrictive past, Americans tend to view the taking of multiple wives as mainly sexually motivated behavior. In short, Americans view polygyny as motivated by the desire for sexual variety. This is generally an erroneous view, for in most all societies in the world those males who wish sexual variety obtain it by having extramarital relationships, by taking mistresses or concubines or via prostitution, and not by taking extra wives. The major motivation for extra wives is economic. Predominantly it is wealthy men who take extra wives and then mainly to help manage their property and take care of their possessions and to produce heirs. Perhaps a brief description of a common form of polygyny will be helpful.

The Madagascar polygynous family, which Ralph Linton (1936) described, starts out with a first marriage that usually is a love match. Other wives are added at the suggestion of the first wife, but the first wife clearly outranks the secondary wives. It is she who suggests the addition of other wives as the simplest means of obtaining help in her task of taking care of her husband's land. Madagascar society has a marital custom that is mentioned in the Bible, namely, the levirate. This custom requires that when a man dies, his brother should marry his widow. A similar custom that is frequently found is called the sororate, and this involves a woman marrying the husband of her deceased sister.

In the Madagascar case, each wife has a separate house in which to live. The husband is supposed to spend each night with a different wife. If he violates this rotation custom by spending an extra night with one wife, he then has committed "adultery" and such an act would be viewed with the same emotional intensity as adultery in our society. Later on in this book we shall discuss the strikingly similar arrangements made by present-day people in America who are involved in group marriages (Chapter 11). In Madagascar each wife is also given a separate piece of land to work. It can be seen that this system is organized to minimize jealousy and conflict among the wives by clearly structuring their relationships to each other and to the husband. It is hardly a system designed to achieve sexual satisfaction for the male. In fact, the male who wants sexual pleasure often utilizes other women such as concubines. Polygyny seems to be basically a system dependent on economic wealth and a custom that is a sign of prestige. Almost everywhere that polygyny is allowed as an optional form of marriage one finds that it is preferred over monogamy because of its high-status associations. Often the wealthy are the only ones who can afford multiple wives. Table 2.2 shows that of the various forms of marriage, Murdock (1957) found that 75 percent of the societies in his sample preferred polygyny, 1 percent preferred polyandry and 24 percent preferred monogamy. Group marriage was nowhere preferred. This overview affords some cross-cultural perspective on the dominant place of exclusive monogamy in the West.

The family forms that are present in Figure 2.1 should be familiar to all readers. The nuclear family is our type of family with its emphasis on husband, wife, and their children, and it derives from monogamous marriages. The polygamous family simply derives from polygamous marriages, and very often, as noted above, the wives have separate residences with their own children. The extended family is familiar to us and simply involves adding grandparents and perhaps their relatives to the same household. As we shall soon see, the extended family was never as common as many Americans think, and William Goode (1963) has therefore called it the "family of Western nostalgia."

A Universal View of the Family Institution

Let us start our search for a universal definition with the family institution and then proceed to examine the marital and courtship institutions.

Anthropologists in particular have offered their conception of what is universally true regarding the family institution. George Peter Murdock's conception is perhaps the best known of all (1949). Murdock's ideas are especially provocative in that they were so boldly stated. Murdock asserted that the nuclear family is a universally required feature of human society. In the polygamous and extended forms of the

TABLE 2.2
Distribution of Preferred Types of Marriage

75%	24%	1%
Polygyny	Monogamy	Polyandry

Source: Table data composed from Murdock, 1957:686.

family, the nuclear subunit still operates; that is, in the polygynous family the husband, each wife, and their children make up separate nuclear family units. In the extended family, the parental generation operates as a separate nuclear family from its married children. In short, the nuclear family is viewed as the essential building block of all family institutions, even those that use it to construct more elaborate family structures.

Murdock goes one step further and posits that this universal nuclear family structure of husband–wife–child will have four universal functions: (1) reproduction, (2) sexual relations, (3) economic cooperation, and (4) socialization of offspring. Thus, Murdock is asserting that every culture will not only have the nuclear family but in every culture that nuclear family unit will have the above four functions. The explicitness and boldness of Murdock's views make it relatively easy to test. If one can find a society that lacks the structure of the nuclear family or where that structure does not perform each of the four functions, then Murdock's conception of what are the universally required features of the family will have to be altered.

One way to test such a conception is to examine the more exotic types of Family Systems and see if they fit. There is no need to check Murdock's ideas on typical Western societies because they do clearly seem to fit there. America does have the nuclear family, and within it one can find the functions relating to socialization of children, economic cooperation of mates, sexual relations, and reproduction. One may quibble on particular points as to just how closely America fits Murdock's conception, but clearly it does generally fit. Thus, let us turn to look at some more "unusual" family institutions and see how Murdock fares there.

THE NAYARS OF INDIA

The Nayars are an excellent society to study for our purposes because their family form presents an extreme that helps pinpoint which aspects of the family are essential and which are not. The Nayars are located on the south-western coast (Malabar Coast) of India. The ties between females dominate among the Nayars (Linton, 1936; Gough, 1960; Mencher, 1965); that is, descent is traced through the female line and inheritance passes through the female line. This type of system is called matrilineal. People view themselves as descended from their mother's line only and *not* also from their father's line, as we do in America. (See Table 1.1 for further information.)

The traditional household consists of kin all descended from a common female ancestor. Typically this would be a woman, her children, her daughters' and granddaughters' children, her brothers, descendants through her sisters, and her relations through her dead female ancestors. Men do not live with their wives; they live with their mothers and visit their wives after the evening meal for a few hours. Males in Nayar society are basically engaged in warfare and often are away fighting.

In classic times (and that is the time period we are discussing) there were two types of marriage among the Nayars. The first was based upon a "tali-tying" ceremony and involved young, premenstrual females marrying, en masse, males who were chosen for them by the village astrologer. At this group ceremony each girl was married to a particular boy. The tali was a gold-leaf-shaped pendant on a chain, which the man would place around the girl's neck. The couple would then spend four days together, after which the groom left and might never see the girl again. However, the wife wore the tali around her neck the rest of her life, and when her tali-husband died, she mourned him. Thus not all ties were broken after the four days of cohabitation. The significance of the ceremony seems to be as a societal sanction for childbearing. In short, it was a legitimation of parenthood ceremony.

After this ceremony the woman was free to take on a second type of husband called *sambandham*. Usually her uncle or father would arrange the first such relationship. After that she could add additional husbands, and it was not unusual for a Nayar woman to have six or seven husbands at one time. A system allowing multiple wives and multiple husbands is one which allows both polyandry and polygyny. It is not group marriage in the sense that lasting relationships among all those involved did not usually occur. Many unions were sequential and temporary. (See Table 2.1 for brief descriptions of various forms of marriage and the family.) As long as the man chosen was from the same or a higher caste and the relation not incestuous, all offspring were recognized as socially legitimate. Even with several husbands allowed, the woman might enter into additional brief affairs. When pregnant the woman had to name a man of an appropriate caste as the father of her child. If he was willing to step forward and acknowledge paternity by giving small gifts and paying incidental expenses connected with the delivery of the child, then the child was considered legitimate. Males were not particularly concerned with the question of biological parenthood (as we are in America), and they were willing to step forward without knowing if they were the biological father.

The male's key time, when he was not fighting, was taken up with responsibilities within his own matrilineage, that is, with his sister and her children and other relatives from his mother's line. His ties to his wife and her children were minimal. His wife would have her brothers and her mother to help her rear her children, and in any case the children belonged to the female line and thus were not considered part of their father's descent group. Males in the Nayar system are not treated as inferiors. In fact, the final authority was almost always exercised by a male relative in the matrilineage, and this is still the case today. This system has gradually weakened under British rule, but even today there are many matrilineal remnants left (Fuller, 1976). The reader should keep in mind, in this and all cultures described, that I am speaking of the classic time of the culture and that in most cases recent contact with other societies has broken down the full pattern of the classical way of life.

The importance of this culture for our purposes is that it seems to lack much of what Murdock called the nuclear family structure and even some of the functions of which he spoke. The nuclear family is defined as a set of social relations between husband, wife, and child. In the Nayar case the husband–wife relations are often tenuous. The tali-tying husband may never be seen again; the sambandham husbands may be very tentative relationships also. In any case, even if there should happen to be stable husband–wife relations, the husband has virtually nothing to

A recent Nayar wedding. Photo courtesy of K. R. Vijayan Nair.

do with the rearing of his wife's children. Further, he makes practically no contribution toward the economic support of his wife. Thus, in terms of two of the four nuclear-family functions (socialization of children and economic cooperation of mates), the Nayars do not seem to fit Murdock's definition. Even when we measure the other two functions of sexuality and reproduction, there is some lack of fit because there are numerous nonmarital affairs, and socially legitimate children at times result from these. Some observers of the Nayars have postulated that only the tali-tying husband is "really" a husband, for the girl's marriage to him is necessary if she is to bear legitimate children, but none of the sambandham husbands are required for the legitimation of offspring. The main requirement after the tali-tying ceremony is that the father of the child be from the proper caste. In this view the majority of all sexual and reproduction activity would be with lovers rather than with the tali-tying husband, and Murdock's approach would have even less relevance.

Thus, the Nayars would seem to be a society that is not congruent with Murdock's conception of what is universally required in a family system. The very structure of the nuclear family seems to be lacking because of the relative absence of requirements for husbands in relation to their wives and children. Structure, as we define it, is an interrelated set of social roles or relationships. The social role of husband seems to involve very little required interaction in his family in relation to his wife and children, and thus one can question whether the nuclear family exists at all (Gough, 1960; Mencher, 1965). Even if we assume that the nuclear family roles are clear and strong enough structurally, it has been shown above that there are serious questions about the socialization and economic cooperation functions. The husband typically performs these functions for his sister's family instead of for his wife's family. This is so, of course, because he belongs to his sister's descent group, and in this society the line of descent takes precedence over the marital relationship. This type of integration of males is a common occurrence in societies that trace descent in the female line.

It is interesting to note here that Murdock, in correspondence with the author, contended that the Nayars are not really an exception to his theory, for they are but the old warrior caste of the Kerala society and not really an entire society in and of themselves. There is reason to take issue with this defense. For one thing, few societies are entirely independent of other neighboring groups. Are some of the American Indian groups societies? Equally important is the fact that Murdock had no doubts about the Nayars being a society when he included them as one of his 250 cultures in his 1949 book. Only many years later, after the anthropological evidence indicated that the Nayars did not meet his universal conception, did he come to the conclusion that they were not a society. One can never be disproved if the rules of proof can be changed to eliminate every negative case. We shall soon also see that there are other societies that do not fit with Murdock's views concerning the universal features of the family.

It is well at this point to give credit where credit is due. Murdock's work has led to a tremendous amount of valuable thinking and research, and his efforts have rarely been equaled by others. Even if his universality notions can be shown to be in part ill-founded, it must be acknowledged that he has demonstrated a remarkable amount of cross-cultural conformity to his universal notions. No other human institution shows as much similarity in various cultural settings as does the family. Political, religious, and other institutions vary considerably more around the world. Murdock has shown us the high degree of similarity in family forms and has given us many valid generalizations as to the operation of human societies. Let us not reject him in toto because we find exception to some of his many ideas.

JAMAICAN SOCIETY

The entire Caribbean area has been a center of social scientific investigation for many decades now. One major reason for this is the very high rate of illegitimacy in this area of the world. Judith Blake, when she was a Ph.D. candidate working under Kingsley Davis, studied one culture in the Carribbean area—Jamaica (Blake, 1961). She studied the large lower-class black population on the island and reported that about two-thirds of all births were illegitimate. By contrast, the percentage of births in 1977 that were illegitimate in the United States was 15.5 percent. (U.S. Department of Health, Education, and Welfare 27:11, 1979).

The marriage and family system in Jamaica is "mother centered" or what is more technically called a *matrifocal* system. This is seen in the small role that is played by the father in child rearing. In this sense one can see a similarity to the Nayar system described earlier, but there is one important difference in that ideally the Jamaicans want the father to participate more in the marital institution. Further, the Jamaicans lack the socially organized help of the mother's brother which the Nayars have. In short, the Jamaican system seems one that evolved out of social pressures that were not in line with the culture's ideals, whereas the Nayar system is in line with their cultural ideals. The economic strain in Jamaica is one key causal factor in their family situation. The unemployment rate for males is quite high—about 25 percent, and thus many men shun marriage until they are much older and better off economically. As a comparison, the 1978 male unemployment rate in the United States was under 6 percent. Many of the Jamaican men feel inadequate in fulfilling the role of a husband in terms of housing, income, and job permanency, and thus they avoid this role. Females are brought up quite ignorant of contraception (for reasons we shall discuss in Part II of this book) and quite often get pregnant while still unmarried. This premarital pregnancy adds a further economic burden to any legal marriage.

The lower-class black Jamaicans have accommodated themselves to this economic and social stituation by practicing a type of "consensual" union; that is, they tend to live with each other for a period of several years and bear children under these conditions. We shall later distinguish these consensual unions from the cohabitation of college students which most commonly lacks children. A good proportion of these consensual unions are later legalized by marriage, but many end up with the male leaving. Although the Jamaicans do *prefer* legal marriage to these consensual unions, Rodman's analysis (1966) suggests that they view these consensual unions as an *accepted* means of obtaining legitimate children. The baby born out of a casual encounter is not viewed in the same way as the baby born from a consensual union. The child of a consensual union is the typical child. The child of a legal marriage is less typical, but by no means rare. There appears then to be a legitimacy hierarchy with casual union at the bottom, consensual next, and legal at the top.

Now if we ask whether the Jamaican society fits Murdock's conception concerning the universal aspects of the nuclear family, we again would have to answer, at least in part, no. For example, the very presence of the structure of the nuclear family is in question in the many cases where the male lives only briefly, or not at all, with the female. The presence of stable father roles is in doubt for large segments of the population, since the average consensual union lasts somewhat less than four years. The woman is often helped by her mother in rearing the resultant children, and property is often in her name (Otterbein, 1965).

The four functions that Murdock postulated are not all occurring. Most obviously missing is the one of economic cooperation, for in many consensual unions the male lives with or visits the female in her house and doesn't contribute a significant amount of food, clothing, or shelter. The frequent absence of a male also means that socialization of the children is largely a female task. Jamaica then is an exception, in part at least, to Murdock's thesis regarding what is universal about the family.

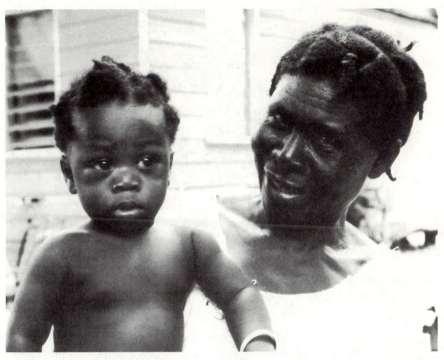

Jamaican mother and child. Photo by Luther P. Gerlach.

I hope that in covering the Nayar and the Jamaican cultures the reader has begun to gain a broader conception of the human family. Let us look now at another culture and introduce another dimension of the human family that is not found in our own society and thereby test Murdock's views further.

THE ISRAELI KIBBUTZIM

Unlike the Nayar and the Jamaican systems, the Israeli kibbutz family is not a "mother-centered" family system. Instead, it is a classic example of a highly collectivized family. The family in the kibbutz conforms to the family that Marx and Engels described as the Communist ideal (Engels, 1902). (Remember Morgan's "pairing family" in Chapter 1.) It is *not* the common form of the Israeli family, but is typical for about 4 percent of the Israeli population who live in the collective settlements called kibbutzim.

The kibbutz husband and wife live together in a communal agricultural society. There is virtually no private property. Norms regarding equalitarian male–female roles are strong, and females work full time. However, according to Spiro's study (1956), the females do not usually work at so prestigious a set of tasks as do males. More females work at running the laundry, the schools, and the community dining halls. Agricultural work has much higher prestige. Children are brought up communally, but see their parents at the evening meal each day and all day Saturday.

Ein Harrod Kibbutz with Mount Gilboa in the background. Courtesy American Zionist Youth Foundation.

The children still identify with their parents and seem to have their strongest love feelings for them, although they often call the nurses by a name meaning mother (Spiro, 1958).

Until recently legal marriage was lacking, and a man and woman who wanted to live permanently together would simply request that they be assigned to the same room. It is well to keep this custom in mind, for we find here, as in the Jamaican society, a lack of legal marriage. However, in the kibbutz situation, legal marriage was not preferred. The main point here is that it is the social sanction that establishes whether a couple is "married." The crucial question is whether the people of a society recognize it as a legitimate union and recognize therefore that the resultant children will be legitimate; that is, they will be given full birth status. The settlers of the kibbutzim came from eastern Europe starting about 1910. While there is a wide range of political and religious ideology among the over 90,000 members of the kibbutzim, the above description of the family structure is fairly typical.

Now, if we apply Murdock's conception of what is universal to the Israeli kibbutz, we note that once again we have found a family form that does not quite fit. One can agree that even though the family of husband, wife, and child do not live together, a psychological identity exists among them. Strong love feelings predominate; the child does call his parents' room his home; and the ties among members of such nuclear families are stronger than the ties to other adults or children. Thus, one can argue that the structure of the nuclear family is present.

Nevertheless, the four functions are not found fully intact. Most conspicuously absent is the function of economic cooperation of husband and wife. Since there is no private wealth to speak of and since each individual is provided for whether married or single, there is no economic cooperation within the nuclear family.

One may argue that such economic cooperation occurs within the entire kibbutz and that it can be conceived of as a large family. But such an argument is hardly relevant to Murdock, for he speaks of a nuclear family which by definition is just one husband and wife and their children. A kibbutz of several hundred people could hardly be thought of as this type of family. The other function *somewhat* qualified is socialization of offspring. The collective upbringing means that three types of child socialization—caretaking, disciplining, and value inculcation—occur largely outside of the family. However, a fourth type of socialization—nurturant socialization (giving of emotional support and response)—does occur within the family. So it is mainly economic cooperation of mates that is missing and parts of child socialization.

THE TROBRIANDERS

Trobriand culture was made famous by Bronislaw Malinowski (1929), who spent several years living there during World War I. Malinowski was an alien in England when war broke out and asked to be left in the Trobriand Island on the east coast of New Guinea in Melanesia for the duration of the war. His request was granted. The result was a series of books that made Malinowski one of the world's most renowned anthropologists.

Trobriand society has a matrilineal descent system wherein the female line is emphasized.[1] Residence after marriage consists of the man and woman residing with the husband's mother's brother. This is called "avunculocal residence." Note that such residence stresses the female line, but uses male relatives in that line. It is the mother's line that is stressed, but through her brother. This is further evidence that where matrilineal descent is present, males are still of considerable importance. Women typically turn over their power to a male relative, such as a brother. In the Trobriand case residence in the groom's village with his male relatives further strengthens male power. Cross-culturally, male–female power distribution runs from strong male control to equalitarian systems, and practically never do we find societies with strong female control. We shall look into this matter in depth in the next chapter.

Socialization of children follows descent lines and thus, in a matrilineal system like the Trobrianders, it is the child's mother's line that must take care of the socialization for only they know the customs of that lineage. The child's biological father is heavily involved in the socialization of his sister's child and not his own biological child. Unlike the Nayar case, wherein the husband sleeps within his mother's household and gives little economic support to his wife, the Trobriand husband sleeps with his wife and gives her half her food supply—the other half comes from her brother. The father of the child does give a great deal of nurturance to his children. He is the disciplinarian to his sister's children, but to his own children he is one of the key nurturers for he is not responsible for disciplining

[1]A more recent account of the Trobrianders by Weiner (1976) calls into question some of Malinowski's interpretations. The interested reader should consult this source.

Trobriand Islanders, 1978. Courtesy of Oir Niugini.

them nor for teaching them basic values. The father's role in this sense is analogous to the grandfather's role in our culture.

In terms of Murdock's thesis, the Trobrianders fit better than the other three cultures examined. However, there still are serious deficiencies in the fit with Murdock's ideas. Economic cooperation is severely limited since the brother supplies so much of his sister's needs. Also, most of the socialization, other than nurturance, is performed by the mother's brother, and not the father. Clearly, the Trobrianders resemble the Nayar matrilineal system although they are a more moderate case.

In passing one should note that the societies discussed such as the Nayar, kibbutz, Jamaican, and Trobriand are not that unique among human cultures. Driver (1961), in his discussion of American Indians, illustrates many cases where Family Systems similar to those we have analyzed exist in our own American Indian heritage. There may be a difference of degree of emphasis on communal organization, or on matrilineal descent, or on consensual unions, but the general characteristics are not that rare. So we conclude that societies which do not fit Murdock's notions occur particularly in matrilineal societies with matrilocal residence (descent through the female line and residence among female relatives). Thus, although perhaps most cultures do fit Murdock's ideas rather well, there are many that do not. Since our search is for a universal definition, that is, one that will hold up for any society and that points to the essential nature of the family, we must somehow modify Murdock's position.

A PROPOSED DEFINITION OF THE FAMILY INSTITUTION

If Murdock's attempt at defining the universal qualities of the family has serious flaws, then do we simply admit that there are no universal aspects of the family or is there an alternate definition that better fits the existing cross-cultural evidence? The best way to answer this is to look over the evidence on family types we have just examined and see if that can help us arrive at a new conception.

Looking at Murdock's four nuclear family functions, it becomes clear that economic cooperation must be dropped because of the occurrence of communal societies such as the kibbutz and matrilineal cultures such as the Nayar. Also, sex and reproduction seem rather secondary in importance since among the Nayars the key factor seemed to be more that sex and reproduction occur with a person of the proper caste rather than that they occur between a man and woman who would stay together and rear the child. Also, a good deal of the socialization function was often very largely performed by individuals outside the nuclear family: the mother's brother in the Nayar and the Trobriand cases, the mother's mother in the Jamaican case, and the communal school in the kibbutz case.

What is left then? The four functions of Murdock seem to have the real possibility of being carried out in good measure by other segments of the society. Let us be clear: These four functions that Murdock attributes to the nuclear family are universal in the societal sense; for example, no society could survive if somehow it did not achieve socialization, economic cooperation, sex, and reproduction. But the weight of Murdock's argument was that these four functions would largely be achieved *within the nuclear family*. It is here that we have found exceptions.

Nevertheless, there is one strand of Murdock's thesis that still seems to hold universally for the family. Even in the kibbutz one notes that the nurturant socialization, that is, the giving of emotional support and response to the newborn infant, was done predominantly by the mother and the father, particularly during the early years of life. The same nurturance of the newborn was found in Jamaica and among the Trobrianders and Nayars. It is the one type of socialization that seems to have been present in all of the families we have examined. Have we here then a base for another attempt at a universal definition of the family?

Murdock's definition was applicable to one type of family structure (nuclear) and spelled out specifically four types of family functions. I shall attempt a much less ambitious universal definition. First, my definition will apply to *any type of family structure* whether it is a nuclear family or some other form; for we have seen that the nuclear family, although widespread, is not universal. Second, instead of delineating four universal functions, I shall select but one universal function, for that is all that the evidence has indicated exists. This one function shall be the nurturance of the newborn. The structure shall simply be defined as that of a small kinship-structured group. Thus, my definition of the universal essence of the family would be: *The family institution is a small kinship-structured group with the key function of nurturant socialization of the newborn* (Reiss, 1965). Let me now explain this further. (See Lee, 1975 and 1977, for recent elaboration.)

Kinship ties are often defined socially, not biologically. Photo by G. C. Sponaugle.

The phrase "kinship-structured group" is perhaps most in need of explanation. What is kinship? We all have some idea of the meaning of this term for we all know we are kin to our parents and to our children. The heart of the meaning of kinship to a social scientist refers to the tie among people who are descended from each other (parents–children) or have common descent relations (brothers and sisters). Kinship can involve a sort of biological reckoning concerning relation among individuals. However, *it is the social definition and not the biological ties that determines who is kin*. Scientific understanding of biology is limited to only some cultures. One interesting case showing the importance of the social definition of kinship is that of the Trobrianders (Malinowski, 1929). The Trobrianders do not understand the father's role in the production of children, and yet the father is viewed as kin to the child. In other societies where there are widespread adoption and exchange of children, kinship notions are still central, but in those cases the offspring are viewed as kin of the persons with whom they live, rather than as kin of their biological mother and father (Landy, 1959; Whiting, 1963). Thus, although the biological tie is most often present, it is the social definition of who is "descended" from whom or who "belongs" to whom that carries the most weight. If that definition includes people who are not biologically related, these people are still socially viewed as kin. (For a valuable discussion of this, see Coale et al., 1965, pp. 83–101 and Radcliffe-Brown, 1959, pp. 1–85.)

The tie of kinship is a special tie in every society of which we have any record. It invariably defines a bond that is generally closer than that of any other in a society. It is closer than friendship. It involves special rights of possession. Marriage ties may, in some societies, be equally (or more) intense than parent–child ties, but one must note that husband and wife are kin to each other, for they stand in the same kinship relation to their children. Husband–wife ties are usually called *affinal kinship ties* as distinguished from parent–child or brother–sister ties which are called *consanguineal kinship ties.* In societies where the new family created by marriage lives far away from the parental families, we are more likely to find stress on the affinal kinship ties of husband–wife and reduced emphasis on the parent–child ties. However, even in our own society with its stress on husband–wife ties, living in one's own home, and being economically independent of one's parents, one finds that parent–child ties are still quite powerful. (See Part IV for a full discussion of parent–child ties.)

The basic type of kin of whom we speak is called primary kin, and it consists of those whose descent relation is closest, such as father, mother, brother, and sister. Other, more distant kin are those related to us through these individuals such as father's brother, sister's husband, and so on. The heart of the kinship tie is descent, and other individuals become involved only because of their tie to one's descent relationship with primary kin. Thus your father's brother is a type of kin for he is a kin to your father and therefore indirectly to you.

Parsons and Bales (1955) have argued that only in kinship groups can the child learn the marital and parental roles to be played later and that only in such groups is there sufficient stability for adequate socialization. Now one can argue that children could be brought up in formal organizations by technically trained nurses and thus the family is not needed. However, no society has achieved this, and in the case of the kibbutz where something like the formal organizational setup is present, we find that the nurturant socialization ties are still predominantly with the parents (the kin) and that the family still exists as a separate group.

It would not seem possible to give nurturance to someone in a large, impersonal group. Some form of small group seems essential even if this were part of a larger formal organization. We would still have a kinship tie even if babies were artificially produced by the state in mechanical wombs, with people donating the egg and the sperm, and were then given over to nurses in small groups to raise. This I believe to be so because kinship, as we have defined it, is not dependent on biological connections, but rather it is dependent on socially defined connections. In a society that assigned nurses to rear newborn infants, the ties between the nurse and the infants given to her/him would be defined as distinctive and special. Such ties of nurse and children, because they begin from infancy and last a period of years, would possess special emotional significance and would invest both the nurse and the children with special rights and duties relative to each other. What would such a small group of nurse and children be but a kinship group or a family? The notion of special rights of possession in one another because of a feeling of belonging to or "descending" from one another is at the heart of the kinship notion, and thus a type of small kinship-structured group would exist whenever this developed. The earliest memories of a child are of those who nurtured that child, and these memories are what comprise the feelings of descent.

In my thinking, the structure of a kinship group, like the family, can vary tremendously. The biological mother can be alone with her child or, in rare societies, she may not be present at all, as in the nurse–child illustration above. Other adults can be involved or it may even be older siblings who perform the nurturant function. Now, it is true that in almost all societies the biological mother is at least one of those who is involved in the nurturant function. But the point here is that whoever performs the major share of the nurturant function for the newborn comprises the heart of the family unit. Other individuals may attach to this core element in the family by marriage or kinship ties. In the kibbutz case the husband often does almost as much nurturance as the wife and is himself a part of the core of the family. In the Nayar case a strict application of our definition of the family would leave the husband, at least as family member, of quite secondary importance—if we include him at all. In fact, the mother's brother would have more claim to be involved in the nurturance of his sister's children.

A particular society may have more than one family structure, that is, more than one way of carrying out the nurturant function. For example, in our own society, because of divorce and widowhood and desertion, there are several million households with young children where only one parent is present; there are a good number of other households wherein grandparents participate heavily in the nurturance of the newborn. The involvement of grandparents is an even more common phenomenon in the Soviet Union, since the great loss of husbands and fathers during World War II increased the necessity of grandparents helping out (Geiger, 1968). Working wives in both societies also increase this pressure for grandparent support. One could certainly say that *if these family forms are socially viewed as acceptable* ways to nurture the newborn in the communities involved, then they are alternate ways of structuring a family for that society.

However, there are other ways of nurturing children that we would not give the tab of "family institution" for they are not acceptable as family forms in our society, e.g. being raised in orphanages or by nurses in a formal organizational setting. Now you may wonder why having said earlier that a society that raised its children by nurses in an organizational setup would develop the nurse–child relation into a family institution, I now seem to be saying that today we would not call such a relationship "family." The answer is simple. I am speaking of a family *institution*. Any institution whether it be political, economic, or family is an integrated set of relations among people that has become *internalized or accepted* by the people in any given society as a proper structure for carrying out those relationships. In a society wherein all children would be raised by nurses *and this was the accepted way*, we would meet the requirements of what constitutes a family *institution* as an acceptable, internalized way of carrying out family relations. The nurses in such a society would be an accepted functional equivalent of parents in our society. However, in a society such as ours today where being raised in an orphanage is tolerated in emergency situations but is not an *accepted* way to carry out family relations and where one tries actively to get children out of such organizations and into private families, then it is not a family in the sense of being an accepted kinship institution of society. Also, where it is not an accepted way, the nurse–child relation will not develop into a kin type of relation, for it stands in contrast to the accepted kin type of relation and the children will therefore feel deprived of socially acceptable kin ties. To make the point more sharply, let me note that in a society wherein the nurse–child relation was the accepted way to raise infants, the biological parent–child relation might not be an acceptable relation for nurturing. In such a case, the parent–child relation would be viewed as an exception and would not be accepted as a kin-type relation.

By virtue of the importance of social acceptance or institutionalization, we make our definition of the family more specific and thereby stress both the structural and functional aspects of the family institution. So while in our society, a nurse with several children in her care may well be performing the family *function* of nurturance, if she is not involved in what the society accepts as a kinship-structured group, then she is not in a family structure. We can see the importance of this distinction of structure and function in looking at other institutions. In the Soviet Union, many have contended that communism is performing a religious function in that it maintains the motivation and feeling of meaningful existence of the Soviet people. Now if we define a religious structure in terms of the church or similar forms, then the Soviet system achieves this religious *function*, but lacks a religious *structure* and thus lacks an institution of religion which is so defined. It is similar with the family. If our definition is truly applicable to all cultures, then each culture must have an accepted definition of a small kinship group (in whatever way the people agree to define it) and that group must perform the bulk of nurturant socialization of the newborn.

Nurturance here is defined as the giving of emotional support or response or both. The amount of time such nurturance is required after birth is open to question. One could argue that it is essential throughout life, but the question here is how long it is needed within a kinship group of parent and child. I would give a rough answer of at least two or three years and perhaps as many as seven or eight. I base this answer on the actual practice of various societies, and it is, of course, put forth tentatively.

If nurturant socialization occurs outside a small kinship-structured group and if such outside nurturance becomes typical and accepted, then our definition is not universally valid, for then the family, as we have defined it, is not doing the bulk of the nurturance of the newborn in that society. My own feeling, as noted above, is that if an alternate form of giving nurturance develops and eliminates our current family institutions, then the new form would soon become defined by the community as a kinship group in terms similar to those used to define kinship groups today. But if this did not occur and no special descent or kinship relation was given, then the family, as we have defined it, would cease to exist, and our definition would have been proved inadequate as a statement of the universal aspects of the family. Further, if a society was found where nurturance was not present in the relations with small children, then my definition would also be shown to be in error. The definition posits a universal relation of small kin groups and nurturant socialization and is a testable proposition. Now let us look at the evidence available for evaluating this new definition.

RELEVANT EVIDENCE FOR THE PROPOSED UNIVERSAL VIEW OF THE FAMILY

One basic reason why I believe an internalized set of norms defining the obligations of kin to their newborn child is essential is that the failure of any one generation to provide nurturance would severely limit the ability of its children to grow up into adults who could function in that society. Such a situation, therefore, would severely threaten the survival of that society. If I am right about the essential quality of nurturance, then it seems that societies would have to achieve clarity and certainty in the nuturant function; that means that nurturance cannot be treated casually but must be carefully structured and assigned to the individuals most intimately involved with one another, that is, assigned to kin to perform. Now, all this assumes that the nurturant function is essential if the society is to survive. I am assuming that infants brought up without nurturance would not grow up into fully functioning adults, for they would not have educated their emotions to the point where they could relate adequately to other individuals. But what evidence is there of this? Also, even if one agrees that nurturance is essential to the survival of human society, what evidence is there that it must be done in kinship groups?

There are three basic types of evidence that one can present for my proposed definition of the universal aspects of the family. The first source of data consists of evidence from other societies. All the societies we examined and all that I have been able to find accounts of in the human relations area files and elsewhere exhibit a small kinship-structured group that is performing the bulk of the nurturant socialization of the newborn. (For good cross-cultural accounts see Stephens, 1963; Blitsten, 1963; Goode, 1963; Lee, 1977; Whyte, 1978. See also Murdock's 1975 Ethnographic Atlas of over 600 cultures.) Thus, we have one body of evidence supporting the universality of the kind of family we have spoken of. However, such evidence really indicates only that we *may* be correct in our understanding of what is universally required about the family. It does not indicate that we are correct, for it is possible that an institution found in every society is not essential to the survival of those societies. This could occur because (as mentioned in our discussion of incest) such a set of customs might be *important* although not *essential*, or it might just be *convenient* but not essential, for survival. Thus we need other evidence that will show that not only is it universally *found* today but, in addition, that it is universally *required*.

Work done by Colin Turnbull (1972) on the Ik culture is important to touch upon here. Turnbull reports a society wherein newborns are often left to die and are neglected in many ways. One could take this as evidence against our definition. However, the Ik culture is under severe economic strain and is going out of existence. In this sense it supports our view for it is an interesting case in point showing the consequences of low nurturance.

A second source of evidence consists of the work done on our "cousins," the nonhuman primates. If we can find supportive evidence here, it will strengthen our case concerning the human family. The work of Harry Harlow (1958, 1962a, 1962b) on rhesus monkeys is most relevant here. Harlow separated monkeys from their natural mothers and raised them with surrogate "cloth" and "wire" mother dolls. In some experiments the wire mother surrogate was equipped with milk, while the cloth mother was not. Even under these conditions the monkeys preferred the cloth mother to the wire mother. The monkeys showed this preference by running more to the cloth mother when threatened and by exerting themselves more to press a lever to see the cloth mother. This preference was supposedly due to the softer contact and resultant comfort afforded by the cloth mother. Harlow's work indicates that infant–mother love is not simply a result of the mother supplying the food needs of the infant but is strongly related to affording comfort, particularly comfort resulting from physical contact. This contact "need" of the monkeys can be argued to be a rudimentary need for nurturance, that is, for emotional comfort.

Further investigation of these monkeys revealed some additional important findings. The monkeys raised by surrogate mothers, either cloth or wire, became emotionally disturbed and were unable to relate to other monkeys or to perform sexually. This result was irreversibly produced in about six months. Although the comfort of contact with the cloth mother seemed important, it also was necessary to have other live monkeys to give the infants some sort of emotional response. Some of the surrogate-raised females were forcibly impregnated. They became very poor mothers, and their infants had to be taken away from them to ensure their survival, for the mothers would not nurse the infants and would often injure them.

Harlow found that it was not the mother per se that was essential, for when an infant monkey was raised just with other siblings, emotional stability and sexual competence were much improved. Nevertheless, the presence of a mother helped to increase the likelihood of a successful outcome even when siblings were present. These results seem to support the assertion concerning a need for emotional support and responses or what we have called nurturance. Surely this evidence is not conclusive. Although monkeys and humans are both primates, what holds for one may not hold for the other. Also, the evidence on monkeys is only suggestive of support. Human infants are far more helpless at birth than monkey infants. Thus it is highly doubtful that a group of human siblings could survive and nurture one another to anywhere near the extent found among monkeys. The human infant requires someone older and more aware of the environment.

In a very real sense, it seems that the existence of human society is testimony to the concern of humans for one another. Unless older humans care for the newborn, the society will cease to exist. Every adult member of society is alive only because some other member of society took the time and effort to raise him or her. One may argue that this care need be only of a physical nature, but our assertion is that the emotional care involved in nurturance is equally essential.

A third and final type of evidence concerns the effects on human infants of maternal separation or formal organizational upbringing away from parents. The kibbutz family has formal organizational rearing of children, but there is a strong emotional exchange between parents and children and thus nurturance is not absent. We need to find cases wherein nurturance was low and then see if the result is such that adult role performance of low nurtured infants is hindered in a way analogous to the effects on Harlow's rhesus monkeys.

Leon J. Yarrow published an excellent summary of over 100 studies involving mother separation (1964). Since before World War I there have been reports supporting the view that maternal separation has deleterious effects on children. The first such reports came from pediatricians pointing out physical and psychological deterioration in hospitalized infants. In 1951 Bowlby reviewed the literature in this area for the World Health Organization and arrived at similar conclusions (1951). More recent and careful studies have made us aware of the importance of distinguishing the effects of maternal separation from the effects of formal organizations. Certainly the type of organizational care afforded the child is quite important. Further, the previous relation of the child with the mother before entering the formal organization and the age of the child are important variables. In addition, one must look at the length of time separation endured and whether there were reunions with the mother at a later date. Yarrow's view is that while there is a tendency toward disturbance in mother separation, this can best be understood when we learn more about the precise conditions under which it occurs and cease to think of disturbance as inevitable under any conditions. Bowlby's more recent work (1969, 1973) is relevant to further specification of the consequences of mother separation.

Evidence indicates that children separated from mothers with whom they had poor relationships display less disturbance than other separated children. Further, infants who were provided with mother substitutes of a personal sort showed much less severe reactions. Children who were in an all-day nursery (in line with the findings on the kibbutz) gave no evidence of serious disturbance. Many studies in the area of child rearing in formal organizations show the importance of the structural characteristics of the organizational environment. When care is impersonal and inadequate, there is evidence of language retardation, impairment of motor functions, and limited emotional responses toward other people and objects. Interestingly, the same types of characteristics are found among children living in "deprived" family environments. One of the key factors in avoiding such "negative" results in an organizational setup is the presence of a stable parental figure for the child. Individualized care and attention seem to be capable of reversing or preventing the impairments mentioned. Without such care, there is evidence that ability to form close interpersonal relations later in life is greatly weakened.

The evidence in this area thus indicates that some sort of emotionally nurturant relationship in the first few years of life between the child and some other individual is vital in the child's development. Disease and death rates have been reported to rise dramatically in children deprived of such nurturance. In addition, there is support for the position that some sort of kin-type group relationship is the structural prerequisite of this nurturant function. Indeed, it seemed that the closer the institution's child-nurse relation approximated a stable, personal kinship type of relationship, the more successful was the institution in achieving emotional nurturance and avoiding later impairments.

SUMMARY AND CONCLUSIONS ON THE FAMILY INSTITUTION

In this book the family will be conceived as a small kinship-structured group with the key function being nurturant socialization. With this definition one ought to be able to find the core of the family in America as well as in any other society. One will always find other characteristics of the family added to this universal core. For example, there very often are the four functions of which Murdock spoke. But none of these other characteristics is found in *every* family institution. Although we shall speak of a wide variety of characteristics of the American family, it is well to keep in mind the core of the family. In this way we can avoid joining those who, every time one of its characteristics changes, cry that the family is disintegrating. If we know what is essential to the family institution, we can then make more accurate judgments as to what changes affect the future of the family most deeply (Bane, 1976).

One of the goals of this text is to inculcate in the reader a spirit of scientific tentativeness, that is, a willingness to examine the evidence and an unwillingness to take things on authority alone. In this vein I should note that there are those who would question the universality of the family. Barrington Moore, Jr. (1958) feels that it is largely a middle-class sentimentality that makes social scientists believe that the family is universal. More recently many writers have pictured the family as on its way out in our society. I shall deal with such views later on in this book. Also, some whose view of the family is very similar to my own position, like Marion Levy (Levy and Fallers, 1959; Coale et al., 1965, pp. 1–100), would add specifications that I would not. Levy feels that biological mothers and infants naturally incline toward each other and that only the biological mother can be counted on to be sufficiently motivated to nurture the newborn infant. Thus, Levy feels that we can specify that at least one of the major nurturers of the child will be the biological mother. While I would agree that most of the anthropological literature gives little indication of any family form where biological mothers do not have a major role in nurturance, I hesitate to include it in my definition of what is universally necessary until more supportive evidence is available.

I shall, in the next sections, briefly define the courtship and marital institutions in terms of what is universally required. These institutions are, of course, intimately related to the family institution, and with our definition clear for the family, it will be a much simpler and quicker matter to show the relation of courtship and marriage. I have dealt with the family *institution* first because the courtship and marital institutions are more transitory in the lives of individuals. Typically, one spends only a limited number of years courting and even fewer years in marriage without forming a family by having children. If one parent dies, the marriage may end but parenthood continues. Thus, the longest lasting of these three institutions is the family. Further, it will soon become clear that the courtship and marital functions are instrumental to the family function of nurturance of the newborn. Thus, the family institution is the central one and I have, therefore, dealt with it first and called all three institutions the Family System.

A Proposed Universal Definition of the Courtship Institution

The family institution rears children in ways that prepare them for courtship so I will consider that institution next. Every society has some type of courtship institution that functions as the means by which selection of mates occurs. It is valuable to understand the selective process by which individuals choose their marital partners and the mutual parent of their future children. The best way to gain perspective on our particular method of mate selection is to examine briefly how courtship has occurred at other times and places. I use the term "courtship" here to cover all mate-selection institutions, but the reader should be aware that the term derived from the medieval romantic love affairs in the royal courts of Europe.

Individual courtship institutions can vary infinitely in specific details, but the myriad approaches can all be classified by one common function and by two basic types of structure. The universal function of courtship institutions is the selection of future mates. The two structured ways in which this is accomplished are by parental arrangement or by the arrangement of the young people themselves. Of course, most courtship systems have elements of both parental choice and autonomous choice of mates. Even in our own society where the individual's ability to choose his mate is an accepted right, one can find much evidence of parental influence in various direct and indirect ways. Still, societies can be classified according to the degree to which the young people or their parents are socially sanctioned to arrange marriages.

Are courtship institutions a universally required aspect of human society? We have already asserted that family institutions are universally required—but what about courtship institutions? The answer here is rather easy to arrive at, for if we are agreed that the family institution is essential, then each society must somehow arrange for the selection of the individuals who will do much of the nurturing of the newborn. The courtship system is one major part of such a societal selection system. Thus, we can safely predict that every society will have some kind of courtship institution to select some of the key people who will later on nurture the infants who will become the citizens of the next generation.

What can we say about the structure, the integrated set of roles, that constitutes the way in which the function of mate selection is achieved? To keep our approach consistent we must specify that courtship will be a chief concern of the kinship groups in the society; that is, the parents of the people who will marry will be deeply concerned and, directly or indirectly, influence the outcome of the process. Parents in our society influence the process in the first place by the schools to which they send their children. Sending a child to a parochial school, for example, helps load the outcome toward a homogamous religious match. Sending a child to a state or a private school, or to college, also determines the likely type of mate the offspring will find. Parents also influence the outcome by the neighborhood in which they live. White Protestant parents who live in all-white, Protestant suburbs increase the chances of homogamous matings. Most of all, of course, parents influence by inculcating attitudes that affect the likelihood of one's getting along with certain types of people. If parents consistently display antiblack, anti-Jewish, or anti-Catholic attitudes and such attitudes are socially supported by other significant adults, their children will likely internalize such attitudes and tend to minimize contact and intimacy with such racial and religious groups. In other chapters we shall deal with specific studies that support these contentions, but all we need do now is generally establish the basic role of parental power in mate-selection decisions.

Using the same approach as in our definition of the family, we shall seek here for a clear definition that will state what is essential about courtship and do so briefly. I would define the courtship institution thus: *The courtship institution consists of interactive patterns among young unmarried people and/or their parental kin with the key function of mate selection.* In our system the young people and parents interact in ways that allow a direct influence to the desires of the young people and allow an indirect influence to those of the parents. Other systems reverse this priority. All courtship institutions fall somewhere on this continuum with societies like ours at one end and more traditional societies such as India at the other end (Nimkoff, 1965). Before we look at our own system, let us briefly look at the courtship systems of those same societies we just examined in terms of their family institutions.

NAYAR COURTSHIP

The Nayars offer considerable contrast to our courtship system, for they marry their daughters off at about ages ten to twelve (Mencher, 1965). The marriage is approved by the girl's maternal kin, but, as noted before, the particular choice of mate is usually made by the village astrologer. In this system, then, the young person's role in courtship is minimal, and the adults conduct most of the courtship for this first marriage (the tali-tying union). However, all subsequent unions are increasingly arranged by the young girl and her lover. We noted earlier that such additional unions are usually considered marriages, but of a different sort than the tali marriage. These additional marital unions are at first aided by choices of the girl's uncle or father, but as the girl gets older, she arranges such matters herself. As in all courtship systems, there are certain people one cannot mate with because of incest taboos, age differentials, religious or racial differentials, and so forth. In the Nayar case the female cannot mate with a man from a lower caste or with a man who is not a Hindu or who is living in the same matrilineal household. It is interesting to note that the Nayar system incorporates in the first marital union a type of strong parentally run courtship, but in the latter unions it more closely resembles our own system of participant-run courtship. However, there is one basic difference: The Nayars lack the strong norm we have regarding the association of marriage with a deep love relationship, and thus many of their unions do not start out with as much emotional commitment as do ours. The reader should be aware that we are talking about the classic period, and what was true in the classical period of Nayar culture may not be true today (Fuller, 1976).

KIBBUTZ COURTSHIP

The kibbutz courtship system is closer to our own (Spiro, 1956, 1958). Free choice of mate by young people is the norm, although indirect parental influence is present just as it is in our own system. Affectionate ties are important in choosing a mate, although the Hollywood version of love (inability to concentrate, walking into walls, not eating, and so on) is not popular. Premarital coitus is permitted to those who have finished high school (usually accomplished at about age eighteen). Sexual intimacy before that time is frowned upon by the adults (Spiro, 1958, p. 328), but evidently not so much by the young people themselves. Spiro (1958, p. 333) describes some young teenage females who strip to the waist when males come into their work area in the fields. This would seem to be an open attempt to sexually interest males. This difference in the normative orientation of young people and their parents regarding courtship will be a major point to be developed as we proceed. Here, however, it is sufficient to say merely that one fundamental proposition of sociology is that one's role position affects one's beliefs and behaviors. In simplistic terms this can be seen in the fact that when we cross the street on foot, we are annoyed at the carelessness of the automobile drivers, whereas when we are driving, we are annoyed at the carelessness of the pedestrians. Similar differences in belief and behavior in line with social role positions can be clearly seen in labor and management relations, business and government, student and administrator contacts, and many other areas.

In an overall sense the dating patterns in the kibbutz are similar to our own, although obviously the type of "dates" are different. Discos and supper clubs are urban phenomena, and agricultural kibbutzim have little contact with such dating activities. Nevertheless, they do find less commercial things to do together. There is one fundamental difference, however, between the general dating patterns of the kibbutz youngsters and our own, and that is their lack of *casual dating*. This is the same difference that distinguishes our dating patterns from even some European countries'. Steady dating, engagement dating, and other relatively exclusive and seriously committed forms of dating are quite common in the kibbutz, but the idea of dating just for fun—perhaps even going out with someone you have never seen and will likely never see again—that idea is more alien to the kibbutz as it is to some European cultures even today. With increased transportation and communication advances, this, too, is changing, but casual dating is still the most distinctive feature of our dating system compared with that of the kibbutz.

Casual dating is more than just an accidental custom that arose here more quickly than in European societies. The widespread nature of this custom testifies to the greater participant control given to American young people. When youngsters date in a focused and committed fashion, it is easier for parental control to be exercised, for fewer dating partners are involved and parents can direct their children

TABLE 2.3

Marriage Patterns in 125 Kibbutz Sabra* Marriages

TYPE OF MARRIAGE PARTNER	PERCENT
From same peer group	0
From other similarly aged peer group	3
From other part of the kibbutz	31
From another kibbutz	23
From within the youth movement	27
From outside the youth movement	16
	100 (N = 125)

*A Sabra is a person born in Israel.
Source: Yonina Talmon, 1964:495.

toward certain partners. When casual dating is common, then parents cannot possibly know all the potential partners, and since steady dating arises from such casual dating, the parental control of marriage is further weakened. The kibbutz member has some tendency toward casual dating because of the high proportion of people who meet their future mate during the compulsory military service required of all males and females. Also, many youngsters meet their future mates in the high schools that join children from several kibbutzim. Yonina Talmon (1964) examined a sample of 125 marriages among young people born and bred in a kibbutz; the results can be seen in Table 2.3. Only 16 percent marry outside of the generally common ideology shared by the kibbutzim and the various youth movements. About twice that percent marry within their own kibbutz, and about half marry outside their own kibbutz, but to someone who is in another kibbutz or who is a member of a youth movement with a common ideology.

The Talmon data make it clear that most young people marry someone outside their own kibbutz, and thus parental control of a direct sort is limited and the chance for casual dating patterns to develop is much higher. I believe casual dating is a *functional equivalent* to parental arrangement of mate selection. Casual dating occurs where the complexities of one's social world are such that it is difficult for the young person to abide by formal parental introductions and still contact most of the other young people in his or her social world. In the kibbutz the public high school and army service create the setting for meeting new people. In America, our public school system, university system, and work situations also operate as a way of meeting the eligible population that, in a simpler society, one's parents might have known. The low rate of peer-group endogamous marriage in the kibbutz has at times been thought of as an incest taboo (Shepher, 1971; Spiro, 1958). However, Talmon (1964) argues convincingly that it more likely results from introducing the kibbutz youngsters to outsiders during the crucial dating years in high school and in the army. Finally, one notes that there is no "horror" of endogamous peer-group marriage and no strong prohibition. It just does not often happen. This, too, makes it different from the usual incest taboo.

JAMAICAN COURTSHIP

Jamaican courtship practices offer some interesting patterns. It will be recalled that in one particular segment of the population about two-thirds of the births that occur are out of legal wedlock (Blake, 1961). However, it should be kept in mind that the percentage of children born outside of the consensual unions is much less; that is, the percentage of births resulting from casual unions is nowhere near as large. Consensual unions are called "living" by the natives in the Caribbean. Less permanent unions are called "friending," and below that is the very casual union. The Jamaican case is particularly instructive, for the high proportion of births out of legal wedlock does not result from mothers rearing their daughters to prefer this system. Rather, it results from a set of unintended consequences that I shall briefly comment upon.

The mother of an "illegitimate"child still feels that it would have been preferable to have been legally married. There is a debate, which we shall explore later on, regarding the extent of this preference. My position is that although a consensual union is not usually viewed as preferable to legal marriage, it is still felt to be within the limits of social acceptability. However, the mother would prefer that her daughter be legally married and avoid casual sexual relationships. In order to help ensure the outcome she desires, the mother tends to restrict the daughter's freedom as much as possible. In addition, the mother gives practically no information regarding sexuality to her daughter. The result of this is that males learn quite a bit more about sexuality because of their greater freedom, and by the time a female is sixteen or seventeen she has found ways to meet males and is in the process of being persuaded by the boys to have coitus. Blake (1961: 46, 52) reports that at age seventeen two-thirds of the females are ignorant of the possibility of pregnancy—despite the fact that seventeen is the average age for a female to have her first coitus. Blake estimates that half of the females become pregnant during their first affair, substantially because of their ignorance of pregnancy fundamentals. Thus, the very effort of Jamaican mothers to protect their daughters backfires and leads to exactly the kind of consequences which the effort was aimed at avoiding. If the Jamaican example is a valid basis for arriving at a conclusion, it would seem that the promotion of ignorance does not prevent premarital intimacy and illegitimate children. However, I would hasten to add that it does not follow that the removal of ignorance would thereby eliminate premarital pregnancy. Many factors besides ignorance lead to premarital pregnancy, and these will be discussed in Chapter 8.

Another factor that supports the high rate of premarital sexuality is the economic position of the male. The high unemployment rate means that many males are unable to afford setting up a home for a legal wife, supporting a wife and children on their own, or even having a "proper"wedding. These reasons discourage males from marrying until they are well into their thirties, but do not discourage them from entering into casual and consensual unions. Since I conceive of consensual unions as a functional equivalent to marriage, it is only the casual unions that would technically contain *premarital sexuality* in Jamaica. Such casual unions often occur in the younger years of life, and more permanent consensual and especially legal marital unions occur during the third and fourth decades of life.

Courtship in Jamaica differs, then, from that in either the kibbutz or the Nayar society by its lack of fully accepted social forms. As a result of sexual ignorance and economic pressures, casual unions occur which are not fully desired by the community, and the desired legal marriage is also further postponed in favor of consensual unions. One should note that strong emotional attachment between the mates is valued and sought for in Jamaica, even though it is not often achieved. Compatibility between the husband and wife is considered a good thing in almost all cultures; cultures differ mostly in that some stress the value of such compatibility as the prime goal (our own society), whereas others (like the Nayar) minimize such compatibility although they, too, value it.

TROBRIAND COURTSHIP

The Trobriand courtship system is particularly interesting in that they are a highly permissive society: Girls at seven or eight and boys at ten or eleven start having sexual intercourse. The emotional commitment to sexual intercourse increases with age among Trobriand youth. By the time the boy reaches puberty, he moves out of his parental home into a large bachelors' house which he shares with other boys his age. It is understood that the girls he brings into this bachelors' house will not be just casual friends. He is supposed to entertain only serious "dates" there. He may carry on less committed relationships, but they will have to occur elsewhere. The increasing commitment over the years leads to eventual marriage. The basis for marriage among Trobrianders is not so different from our own in that the emotional attachment of the couple plays a large part. The choice of marriage partner is free for all but royalty, although there are incest taboos and restrictions on marrying people from the same village. In all cultures, rules that stress choosing a partner from outside a particular group are called "exogamous rules." Rules that do the reverse are called "endogamous." In America we are exogamous in terms of encouraging a girl to marry into a higher class, and endogamous regarding the race of one's mate.

Despite their openness regarding premarital coitus, the Trobrianders condemn some courtship practices that American youth freely accept. Close dancing on a frequent basis with strangers is not promoted there. Also eating together in the boy's home is not allowed, for that is in effect the marriage ceremony in their society. Another anomalous custom is the strong double standard that prevails after, but not before, marriage. Despite the fact that before marriage girls and boys are given relatively equal rights sexually, after marriage adultery on the part of the female is much more severely punished. This is not because of any fear of illegitimate offspring, because the Trobrianders do not believe there is any causal relation between coitus and pregnancy. We shall return to this interesting point and discuss explanations in Chapter 11.

A CROSS-CULTURAL VIEW OF COURTSHIP

The four cultures we have covered illustrate some of the cross-cultural range that exists in courtship. Jamaica serves as an example of a somewhat disorganized form of courtship because of economic and other pressures. The Nayar courtship system offers us an instance wherein the participants have very little control over the first marriage (tali-tying union). Instead, the parents, in cooperation with other adult members of the community, arrange the mate choice. However, the additional marriages (sambandham unions) are left up to the individuals involved. The kibbutz courtship system shows signs of external control in their homogamous mating patterns. Although young people typically do not marry someone they were reared with, they do typically marry someone from a kibbutz or at least from a like-minded group, such as one of the youth movements. However, the precise choice of a mate is left up to the individual. Here in the kibbutz then is evidence of the influence of parents and other adults on the choice of mate even in a society that allows the young person the final say regarding mate choice.

The Trobriand case does help to elaborate the way communal forces shape mate choice. There are rules regarding village exogamy, rules against marrying somebody from one's own descent grouping, and so forth. Now, here, too, the young person within these limits is given considerable free choice. But the point here is that even though we have examined societies where free mate choice is in most cases accepted, it is obvious that there are still many restraints on such mate choice. We can perhaps see this more clearly in other societies rather than in our own. That is why I have made this point here before going on in other chapters to show similar restrictions within our own "free" mate-choice system.

The cultures we examined fit our universal definition of courtship as an institution consisting of interactive patterns among young unmarried people and their parental kin with the key function of mate selection. We shall discuss this institution further in the concluding pages of this chapter and elaborate upon its place in the Family System.

A Universal Definition of the Marital Institution

The courtship institution is the means by which a society puts in contact those individuals who will eventually be sanctioned as potential parents. Now let us turn to the marriage institution and see how it fits with the courtship institution and with the family institution.

In a society like our own, with its history of a "forbidden" orientation to sex, it would be expected that the sexual motivation for marriage would be overemphasized. One frequently hears people comment on recent increases in permissiveness before marriage as a threat to the motivation to marry. Such people believe that men marry in order to have coitus, and thus they will cease to marry if coitus is available outside of marriage. If availability of premarital coitus deterred one from marriage, then the marriage rates of the majority of the world's societies would be considerably lower than they are. Most societies allow premarital coitus and still have almost universal marriage.

Two most powerful groups that are involved in courtship embody the two basic universal reasons that motivate people to marry. These powerful groups are parents and young people. The parental motivation in many cultures involves a sense of duty and a desire to maintain one's social standing. The youth group embodies a basic emphasis on the satisfactions of an intense, emotionally close relationship. In societies like ours, where young people have the key balance of power in courtship, the major motivations for marriage are the satisfactions that arise from a stable, emotionally close relationship. In cultures all over the world this is increasingly becoming a motivation to marry as those cultures adopt a participant-run, autonomous type of courtship system. Sexual satisfaction may well be one of the rewards derived from a stable, emotionally close relationship, but it would hardly be sufficient in itself to motivate marriage in any but a tiny fraction of cases. One may enjoy premarital coitus with a number of partners even more than with the person he or she marries. Only a few can marry the most sensuous-looking person, and thus most, by numerical necessity, must marry someone less than their sexual ideal. Initial desire for coitus may well support much of the dating that goes on in our society, and it may be the initial attraction in relationships that will lead to love. However, that is quite a different thing from saying it is the basic reason for legal marriage in our society.

Sexual interests may be pursued, but the marital partner will most likely be chosen for nonsexual qualities that contribute to close emotional rapport. One becomes interested in some people for nonsexual reasons in addition to the initial sexual reasons. Sexuality is, of course, integrated with these other qualities, but it is hardly the key element, although it might well be the initial reason for interest in a particular person. How well that interest is sustained depends on much more than sexual attraction. Further, it is well to add that the greater open interest of females in sexuality and the greater interest of males in close emotional relations deny the validity of the view that sexuality is important only for males and that it is the key element in marital choice. This will be discussed further in later chapters.

In societies where parents have the dominant power, young people are taught that they should cooperate with their parents in the choice of a mate and should marry from a sense of duty to their family and the community. Here too the sexual motive is not the dominant one in the choice of a mate. In many of these societies, as in the youth-dominated societies, premarital coitus is allowed, particularly between potential mates. Thus marriage is *not* the legitimation of sex, but rather marriage is the legitimation of parenthood. Marriage, as Malinowski long ago stated (1930), legitimizes the people involved as potential future parents. Many other writers during the twentieth century have supported this conception of marriage (Davis, 1939; Gough, 1960; Radcliffe-Brown, 1959). An examination of a few cultures will help document this position.

NAYAR, TROBRIAND, AND KIBBUTZ MARRIAGE FORMS

One of the most interesting marriage and family systems exists among the Nayars—a group we have already spoken of. The tali-tying ceremony that every prepubertal girl is supposed to go through is the marriage ceremony of the Nayars. It is important to note that if a female has not gone through this ceremony and has a baby, the child is considered socially unacceptable, that is, illegitimate. If the same female has the exact same child but has gone through the tali-tying ceremony, then her child is considered legitimate. It seems clear then that the ceremony operates as a societal device to approve of certain people as potential parents. The parental aspects of the ceremony are further visible in the requirement that the tali-tying ceremony occur before the onset of first menses. Clearly the ceremony is tied with potential parenthood in the people's minds.

The Trobriand marriage ceremony is rather simple. The boy invites the girl to supper in his parental home. The meal together signifies their marriage. It bears repeating that even though the Trobrianders start coitus in their prepubertal years, they are shocked by the European practice of taking women out casually to eat. Sharing a meal means marriage, and the implications that go with this are that the young people can now become legitimate parents. Prior to this time, despite their great sexual freedom, the Trobrianders do not want children. The ceremonial meal is the start of accepting the possibility of parenthood.

In the kibbutz studied by Spiro (1956), the request for a room to share, instead of two private rooms, signified the beginning of a marriage. The members of the kibbutz claim that they do not make distinctions between babies born before and those born after the parents had requested a shared room. However, Spiro's own account of the nurses' handling of children (1958) affords clear evidence of the nurses making such a distinction and using the illegitimate status of certain children as an explanation for their disapproved behavior. Moreover, he even found the nurses using such status as an insult directly to the child (Spiro, 1958, p. 349).

THE QUESTION OF LEGITIMACY—THE JAMAICAN CASE

The Jamaican case is somewhat more puzzling. Two out of three babies are born out of legal wedlock. Then, is it true that marriage is missing, that legitimization of parenthood does not occur? Blake (1961), Goode (1960, 1961), Otterbein (1965), and Rodman (1966) have been some of the many contestants in a heated debate on this question. My own views are that marriage is present in a functional sense among the Jamaicans, although absent in a legal sense. Clearly, legal marriage cannot be the criterion for the presence or absence of marriage because most cultures lack a formal legal system. A more impartial approach would be to search for evidence that the society was legitimizing parenthood—in short, to examine the society to see if the function of marriage was present in any fashion whatsoever.

I believe that those who contend that marriage, or legitimization of parenthood, is absent in Jamaica are viewing legitimization as an all-or-none quality. Goode, for example, takes this position—as do Blake and Davis—partly on the basis that

TABLE 2.4

Percentage Distribution of Responses to Marriage versus Living Question by Gender and Class in Trinidad

	MALES		FEMALES		
Responses to Marriage Versus Living Question	*Upper-Lower Class*	*Lower-Lower Class*	*Upper-Lower Class*	*Lower-Lower Class*	*Total*
Marriage is good and living is wrong	37	17	59	42	34
Marriage is better, but living is also good	49	48	41	53	49
Living is good, and marriage is wrong	0	0	0	0	0
Living is better, but marriage is also good	3	12	0	5	7
No difference	11	23	0	0	10
Total	100	100	100	100	100
Number of cases	(35)	(58)	(17)	(55)	(165)

Source: Hyman Rodman (1966:680).

80 percent of the Jamaican natives will assert that they prefer the legal-type marriage to their consensual (living together) type of marriage (Blake, 1961:118). Such an assertion indicates a preference, but I do not think it indicates that consensual unions are not acceptable. After all, one may state that he would "really rather have a Buick," but that hardly means that such a person thinks his old Ford is not "really" an acceptable car. Preference does not imply that all else is unacceptable, but rather implies that all else is *less* acceptable. It is easy to understand why black Jamaicans might prefer the upper-class white form of marriage with all the prestige she or he feels it confers. Table 2.4 shows the results of Rodman's (1966) check in Trinidad (a similar Caribbean culture) and reveals that only 34 percent of these respondents thought that consensual unions were *not* acceptable. Rodman uses the Trinidadians' term for consensual union, which is "living." Besides the fact that only 34 percent thought that living was wrong, it is worth noting in Table 2.4 that this answer varied by class and gender. More females than males were likely to think that living was wrong, and upper-lower-class respondents were more likely to condemn living than were lower-lower-class respondents. In fact, among lower-lower-class males, 12 percent thought living was better than marriage, and another 23 percent thought there was no difference. These findings further support the notion that what is accepted as a legitimate way to bear a child varies by social class, and that this is true even though the legitimization fashions of the upper classes may well have an appeal that all these groups find hard to resist.

In short, I am proposing that legitimacy is not an all-or-none matter in human society. Rather, it is a matter of more or less. Societies seem to rank-order various ways of becoming parents. For example, in our own society it may be that in some circles a church wedding is much preferred over a simple justice of the peace ceremony, but both are acceptable. However, every group has a limit to what it will sanction as acceptable.

If in our society there exists a group of people living in a community that sanctions young couples becoming parents provided they have asked for a common room, and thereby made their intention public, then this would become their marriage system. (This, of course, is one marriage system in the kibbutzim.) However, all groups seem to have limits beyond which they will not go. The Jamaicans feel a child born out of a casual encounter should be afforded considerably lower status than a child born out of a consensual living arrangement or from other less casual arrangements (Rodman, 1969). They may go further and state that children born out of a legal marriage and from a consensual union are considered "acceptable," whereas the children born out of the casual encounter are not. In short, the legitimacy norms have socially defined limits in Jamaica as well as everywhere else.

In this same vein one may note how even within a single culture the "cutoff" point on the legitimacy–illegitimacy continuum varies. An excellent case in point is the Soviet Union. During World War II about 15 million Russian men were killed (Geiger, 1968, 120). This meant that a similar number of Russian women would never have a husband. If those 15 million Russian women had abided by the strictest legitimacy norms, they would have had to forgo becoming mothers permanently. Millions of these women instead chose to have babies out of legal wedlock, and Geiger (1968) reports that the social norms of legitimacy altered accordingly. There was a general liberalization of socially acceptable limits concerning parenthood. The state gave support to women bearing children out of wedlock [in 1949, 3,312,000 unmarried mothers received child support from the Soviet government (Geiger, 1968: 259)], and the social condemnation was considerably reduced despite the 1944 law that allowed the fact of illegitimacy to be stamped on the child's birth certificate. During the 1960s when this group of Russian women, whose potential husbands had been killed, was nearing the end of their reproductive period, the laws and the customs began to revert back to a stricter interpretation of legitimacy and more stress on legal marriage. Here is a modern-day example of the flexibility in the social norms concerning legitimacy, and it illustrates well the danger of taking an all-or-none view of legitimacy. (See also Mandel, 1975).

STRUCTURAL VARIATIONS OF MARRIAGE

If legitimation of parenthood is the universal function of the marital institution, what is the structure of that institution, that is, what established roles go with this institution? The answer basically is that it includes at the minimum a husband role and a wife role filled by individuals almost always from different primary-kin groups (families). The historical presence of occasional incest (as in ancient Egypt) forces us to qualify and say "*almost* always" from different families.

The reader should be careful to understand that the roles of husband and wife need not be filled by any particular gender. A marriage can occur between two men or between two women. Also, one role may be defined as having a great deal more stability or importance than the other in a particular society. Let me illustrate these points.

The Nuer, an African tribe, were studied by E. E. Evans-Pritchard (1951). Evans-Pritchard reports (151: 108–109) that one form of marriage which existed was between two women. When one woman believed herself to be sterile, she would contract with a younger woman to arrange a marriage. The two would marry in the same ceremony in which male–female couples married. The older woman would be the husband and the younger the wife in such a union. The woman would then arrange for a male friend to have intercourse with her bride and thereby impregnate her. The children born in this way would call the older woman "Father" and the younger woman "Mother." They would be viewed as legitimate children by the community.

On our own Northwest Pacific coast, the Kwakiutl have a man-man form of marriage described by Driver (1961: 270) as follows:

> A custom known as fictive marriage was occasionally practiced by the Kwakiutl of the Northwest Coast. Among these Indians, chieftainship and other statuses tended to pass from a man to his son-in-law and then to his daughter's son. When a chief had no daughter, he acquired a legal son-in-law by means of a sham marriage between his son and the man who was to be the son-in-law. The fictive son-in-law produced children through a real wife of another family, normally one of lower rank, and carried on in the role of the chief.

The Nuer and Kwakiutl customs illustrate unusual forms of marriage, but exactly for that reason they throw a penetrating light on the universal structure of the marital institution. They demonstrate that the husband and wife role positions can be occupied by individuals of any gender because these roles are adequately performed as long as they accomplish the function of legitimation of parenthood. When the usual male–female occupancy of those roles will not accomplish that function, a society will allow for alternative role occupants (for other examples, see Brain, 1976).

The husband and wife roles in the Nayar culture illustrate another extreme example in that both roles are in many ways very lightly spelled out in the Nayar society. Wives and husbands are both free to switch to another mate at any time, or to add another mate. Residence is matrilocal and does not change after marriage. Wives and husbands both live with their respective mothers and not with their mates. The father role is also not very demanding, for a male will be obligated more to the raising of his sister's children than to his wife's children. The mother role is more the typical role that we are familiar with in America. The husband–wife roles are sufficient to establish legitimacy of the parents, and they are not embellished with other demands from society among the Nayars. The Nayars meet the structural minimums of the marital institution. The important structural prerequisite is that there be a socially defined fashion for instructing those who are to be legitimized as parents as to how to proceed. The role incumbents can vary considerably, and one person may be by far the key individual. But the social selection, in one way or the other, sets the stage for the occurrence of legitimate children.

In those cases where the couple decides not to have children, they are electing not to take the option bestowed on them when they go through the marriage ceremony. This is similar to people who court and never select a mate or parents who do not give nurturance to their offspring. In all three cases the structure or roles of the institution are present, but the function does not occur. As long as these are not the majority of cases the institutions are still fulfilling the requirements of the social system.

The definition of the marital institution which we arrive at then would be that it is *a socially accepted union of individuals in husband and wife roles with the key function of legitimation of parenthood.* I am here speaking of a universal definition of marriage. In all cultures there are specific structural and functional qualities added to what I have stated above. For certain groups the married pair may have more than just a parenthood role to prepare for; many rights and duties other than parenthood preparation may be involved. But the above is the only structure and function that is universally present and universally required. Note that I have said "husband and wife roles." By this I mean first to imply that there can be more than one husband and wife. More specifically, by husband and wife roles I mean that behavior pursuant to pregnancy and childbirth will not only be allowed but will moreover be expected. Now, I have not said "heterosexual intercourse" because we have seen that in the Nuer and the Kwakiutl cases of same gender mates, this would not be possible. But in those cases the mates would still be expected to pursue the goal of pregnancy by bringing in persons of the opposite gender. Regardless of the gender of the people involved in a marriage, they are expected to pursue the goal of bearing children, and that activity is the universal script written into husband and wife roles.

What is there about the marital institution that makes it universally required for a society? I think there are two basic arguments to support the universal nature of marriage. First, what sort of group would it be that would lack a principle of legitimacy? What sort of group would it be that would not set up criteria that stated under what conditions certain people could get together and prepare to produce children? I would suggest that any group that lacked such a principle of legitimation would be at a survival disadvantage. A group would at least have to state that certain age attainment, certain stability, certain mental competence, and the like were required for individuals to be legitimized as parents. Otherwise people who would be unable to rear children would be allowed to bear children. I do not believe that we are sure of all the factors that go into producing parents who could best produce stable adults capable of fulfilling adult roles. However, that is not the point. It is not such knowledge that is fully required, for clearly no society has a monopoly on that. It is, rather, *having a concern* for the situation into which the next generation will be born. Such concern would evidence a survival advantage over a society that lacked this concern and had no principle of legitimization. Assuming a similar level of knowledge of how to produce the best adults for the society, that society which tries to utilize such knowledge is at an advantage. Also, the very effort shows a degree of concern, which increases the likelihood of "successful" selection of parents. The Caribbean people show this concern in their preference for legal marriage and consensual unions over casual affairs. The Nayars show it in their required tali-tying ceremony. We in America show it in our own customs. All such marital customs lay out a clear path of responsibility for bearing children on certain people and give a clear social place for the child to be born into. It is this that I am assuming is universally required for societal survival.

A second line of reasoning, which one can present for the marital institution being universally required, concerns its tie to the family institution. If one accepts the family institution as universally required and if one can show that the marital institution is essential to the family, then one has shown marriage to be universally required also. Nurturance of the newborn was the key function of the family institution as we discussed it. For this function to be successfully performed, some degree of care in selecting who will do the nurturance is necessary. The marital institution embodies that concern with the selection of some of those who will eventually do the nurturance, for it legitimizes certain individuals to become parents. Thus, one can argue that the marital institution is essential as a means of selecting adequate nurturers for the family institution. In this same vein, courtship becomes essential as the institution that focuses upon the processes by which the marital pair come to be selected.

The definition of marriage which we propose can be disproved by finding a society that lacks the legitimation-of-parenthood function or by finding a society wherein this is done through a different set of roles than husband and wife. These exceptions could occur if there were a society that allowed, without censure, almost anyone to become a parent and thus would lack a legitimization *function*. In addition, the *structure* of husband–wife roles could be done away with in a society that produced babies in test tubes from banks of sperm and eggs. In such a case the state might still exercise caution regarding whom to allow to nurture the newborn, but the state would have taken the place of the marriage ceremony that sanctions a couple to try to be parents. Instead, the state and its scientists would be sanctioned to produce babies. Such a situation would break the structural connection between husband–wife and father–mother roles which now universally exists. At present, at least one of the people who strive to produce children is involved in the nurturance of those children produced. I believe the impersonal aspect of the state-produced baby system will prevent it from ever becoming accepted. Also, it seems that even in such a system, before a couple would apply for a child, they still would require some assurance of permanency in their relationship. Thus, it is likely that some agreed upon type of living together of couples will occur before parenthood. If that does occur and social approval of these unions as a prerequisite to parenthood develops, then the husband and wife roles are present in the culture. To do away with such roles, even in the test-tube society, would seem to require that there be no courtship or mating structure that is a prerequisite to parenthood. But without some criterion of a type of preexisting socially approved relationship, and without people feeling that rearing children is part of their "roles," would the motivation to parenthood for females and males maintain itself? I am betting that it would not and, therefore, I assume that the structure of socially accepted individuals in husband and wife roles is a universal requirement.

I have accepted the minimum of two people in the marital roles because this is universally the case and because I believe one can argue for the almost universal conception that marriage is a union of individuals from two families. Such a union

TABLE 2.5

Composition of Family Systems

INSTITUTIONS	STRUCTURE*	FUNCTION†
1. Family	Small kinship-structured group (kin roles)	Nurturance of the newborn
2. Marital	Husband and wife roles	Legitimation of parenthood
3. Courtship	Parent and youth roles	Mate selection

Structure is defined as a pattern or design composed typically of social roles.
†*Function is defined as a consequence of a custom or behavior pattern which tends to maintain a part or all of society. (See Merton, 1957, Chap. 1 for a discussion of the concept of function).*

of two families of orientation helps build social solidarity and lays a foundation for the placement of any children that result. In short, it ensures support for the marital dyad and for their future venture into parenthood. This is not to deny that a single parent can raise a child but rather it asserts that such a procedure will not be viewed as a cultural ideal unless, as in the Nayar and Trobriand cases, other kin are assigned to aid in child rearing.

Summary and Conclusions on the Family System

Let me briefly list the definitions and discuss the interrelations among the three institutions that comprise the Family System.

> 1. The family institution is a small, kinship-structured group with the key function of nurturant socialization.
> 2. The marital institution is a socially accepted union of individuals in husband and wife roles with the key function of legitimization of parenthood.
> 3. The courtship institution consists of interactive patterns among young unmarried individuals and/or their parental kin with the key function of mate selection.

Table 2.5 illustrates the definitions of these key institutions in structure and function terms.

The courtship and marital institutions are functionally integrated with the family institution. The functions of mate selection (courtship) and legitimization of parenthood (marital) are essential for the function of nurturance of the newborn (family) to occur. In short, one must somehow have a system whereby people select one another, have that selection socially sanctioned, and thereby supply individuals for the nurturance function. The close interrelation of these institutions has caused me to think of them as one system, and since the nurturance of the newborn appears to be the most crucial and central function, I have chosen to call these three institutions the *Family System*, while reserving the term "institution" for each of the three interrelated parts of the Family System.

Of course, the closeness of fit of these three institutions with one another, the efficiency and cost with which they achieve their major functions, and the extent to which other structures and functions are added to the basic ones vary considerably around the world. What I have tried to extract and isolate was the essential, universal characteristics of the structure and function of these three institutions. The overall Family System is, in effect, a society's way of replacing the older generation with a younger generation. In that sense it is surely of crucial importance toward the understanding of any human society.

References

Aberle, David F., et al. 1950. "The Functional Prerequisites of a Society," *Ethics* 60 (January): 100–111.

Bane, Mary Jo. 1976. *Here to Stay: American Families in the Twentieth Century.* New York: Basic Books.

Bierstedt, Robert. 1959. "Nominal and Real Definitions in Sociological Theory," Chap. 4 in Llewellyn Gross (ed.), *Symposium on Sociological Theory.* Evanston, Il: Row, Peterson.

Blake, Judith. 1961. *Family Structure in Jamaica: The Social Context of Reproduction.* New York: Free Press.

Blitsten, Dorothy R. 1963. *The World of the Family.* New York: Random House.

Bowlby, John. 1951. *Maternal Care and Mental Health.* Geneva: World Health Organization.

_____. 1969. *Attachment.* New York: Basic Books.

_____. 1973. *Separation.* New York: Basic Books.

Brain, Robert. 1976. *Friends and Lovers.* New York: Basic Books.

Carpenter, Clarence R. 1953. "Life in the Trees: The Behavior and Social Relations of Man's Closest Kin," in Carleton S. Coon (ed.), *A Reader in General Anthropology.* New York: Holt, Rinehart and Winston, pp. 2–45.

Coale, Ansley J., et al. 1965. *Aspects of the Analysis of Family Structure.* Princeton, NJ: Princeton University Press.

Davis, Kingsley. 1939. "Illegitimacy and the Social Structure," *American Journal of Sociology* 45 (September): 215–233.

_____, 1950. *Human Society.* New York: Macmillan.

Driver, Harold H. 1961. *The Indians of North America.* Chicago: University of Chicago Press.

Engels, Friedrich. 1902. *The Origin of the Family,*

Private Property, and the State. Chicago: Charles H. Kerr. (Originally published in 1884.)

Evans-Pritchard, E. E. 1951. *Kinship and Marriage Among the Nuer.* London: Oxford University Press.

Fuller, C. J. 1976. *The Nayars Today.* Cambridge, England: Cambridge University Press.

Geiger, Kent. 1968. *The Family in Soviet Russia.* Cambridge, MA: Harvard University Press.

Goode, William J. 1960. "Illegitimacy in the Caribbean," *American Sociological Review* 25 (January): 21–30.

_____. 1961. "Illegitimacy, Anomie, and Cultural Penetration," *American Sociological Review* 26 (December): 910–925.

_____. 1963. *World Revolution and Family Patterns.* New York: Free Press.

Gough, Kathleen E. 1960. "Is the Family Universal: the Nayar Case," in Norman Bell and Ezra Vogel (eds.), *A Modern Introduction to the Family.* New York: Free Press, pp. 76–92.

_____. 1971. "The Origin of the Family," *Journal of Marriage and the Family* 33 (November): 760–770.

Harlow, Harry F. 1958. "The Nature of Love," *American Psychologist* 13 (December): 673–685.

_____. 1962a. "The Heterosexual Affection System in Monkeys," *American Psychologist* 17 (January): 1–9.

_____, and Margaret K. Harlow. 1962b. "Social Deprivation in Monkeys," *Scientific American* 206 (November): 1–10.

Landy, David. 1959. *Tropical Childhood.* Chapel Hill: University of North Carolina Press.

Lee, Gary. 1975. "The Problem of Universals in Comparative Research: An Attempt at Clarification," *Journal of Comparative Family Studies* 6 (Spring):89–100.

———. 1977. *Family Structure and Interaction: A Comparative Analysis.* Philadelphia: Lippincott.

Lévi-Strauss, Claude. 1969. *The Elementary Structures of Kinship.* Boston: Beacon Press.

Levy, Marion J., Jr., and Lloyd A. Fallers. 1959. "The Family: Some Comparative Considerations," *American Anthropologist* 61 (August): 647–651.

Linton, Ralph. 1936. *The Study of Man.* New York: Appleton.

———. 1955. *The Tree of Culture.* New York: Knopf.

Malinowski, Bronislaw. 1929. *The Sexual Life of Savages in North-Western Melanesia.* New York: Harvest Books. (Published by Harcourt Brace Jovanovich.)

———. 1930. "Parenthood, the Basis of Social Structure," in V. F. Calverton and Samuel Schmalhausen (eds.), *The New Generation.* New York: Citadel, pp. 137–138.

Mandel, William M. 1975. *Soviet Women.* New York: Anchor Books.

Mencher, Joan P. 1965. "The Nayars of South Malabar," in Meyer F. Nimkoff (ed.), *Comparative Family Systems.* Boston: Houghton Mifflin, pp. 163–191.

Merton, Robert K. 1957. *Social Theory and Social Structure.* New York: Free Press.

Middleton, Russell. 1962. "Brother–Sister and Father–Daughter Marriage in Ancient Egypt," *American Sociological Review* 27 (October):603–611.

Moore, Barrington, Jr. 1958. *Political Power and Social Theory.* Cambridge, MA: Harvard University Press.

Murdock, George P. 1949. *Social Structure.* New York: Macmillan.

———. 1957. "World Ethnographic Sample," *American Anthropologist* 59 (August):664–687.

———. 1967. "Ethnographic Atlas: A Summary," *Ethnology* 6 (April):109–236.

———. 1975. *Outline of World Cultures.* New Haven, CT: Human Relation Area Files.

Nimkoff, Meyer F. (ed.). 1965. *Comparative Family Systems.* Boston: Houghton Mifflin.

Otterbein, Keith F. 1965. "Caribbean Family Organization: A Comparative Analysis," *American Anthropologist* 67 (February):66–79.

Parsons, Talcott, and Robert F. Bales. 1955. *Family: Socialization and Interaction Process.* New York: Free Press.

Radcliffe-Brown, A. R. 1959. *African Systems of Kinship and Marriage.* New York: Oxford University Press.

Reiss, Ira L. 1965. "The Universality of the Family: A Conceptual Analysis," *Journal of Marriage and the Family* 27 (November):443–453.

Rodman, Hyman, 1966. "Illegitimacy in the Caribbean Social Structure: A Reconsideration," *American Sociological Review* 30 (October):673–683.

———. 1969. "Fidelity and Forms of Marriage: The Consensual Union in the Caribbean," in Gerhard Neubeck (ed.), *Extramarital Relations.* Englewood Cliffs, NJ: Prentice-Hall, pp. 108–127.

Shepher, Joseph. 1971. "Mate Selection Among Second Generation Kibbutz Adolescents and Adults: Incest Avoidance and Negative Imprinting," *Archives of Sexual Behavior* 1, No. 4:291–307.

Spiro, Melford E. 1956. *Kibbutz: Venture in Utopia.* Cambridge, MA: Harvard University Press.

———. 1958. *Children of the Kibbutz.* Cambridge, MA: Harvard University Press.

Stephens, William N. 1963. *The Family in Cross-Cultural Perspective.* New York: Holt, Rinehart and Winston.

Talmon, Yonina. 1964. "Mate Selection in Collective Settlements," *American Sociological Review* 29 (August):491–508.

Turnbull, Colin. 1972. *The Mountain People.* New York: Simon & Schuster.

U. S. Department of Health, Education, and Welfare. 1979. *Monthly Vital Statistics Report: Final Natality Statistics, 1977,* 27 (11), February 5.

Voydanoff, Patricia, and Hyman Rodman. 1978. "Marital Careers in Trinidad," *Journal of Marriage and the Family* 40 (February): 157–163.

Weiner, Annette. 1976. *Women of Value; Men of Renown.* Austin: University of Texas Press.

Whiting, Beatrice B. (ed.). 1963. *Six Cultures: Studies in Child Rearing.* New York: Wiley.

Whyte, Martin King. 1978. *The Status of Women in Preindustrial Societies.* Princeton, NJ: Princeton University Press.

Yarrow, Leon J. 1964. "Separation from Parents during Early Childhood," in Martin L. Hoffman and Lois W. Hoffman (eds.), *Review of Child Development Research,* vol. 1. New York: Russell Sage, pp. 89–136.

Gender Roles:

Men and Women in Society

THREE

Introduction

It is important that you possess some basic overview of the specific social roles of women and men in Western society before we start discussing and analyzing various parts of the Family System. A society's shared conception of what males and females are supposed to be like permeates all aspects of courtship, marital, and family relationships and thus it is of first importance in understanding these areas of human behavior. Gender roles comprise the entire set of rights and duties that are expected to be characteristics of females and males in a particular group. All roles entail rights and duties, and gender roles simply imply the specific set of rights and duties that go with each gender.

Gender role, unlike most other social roles (e.g., student, congregant) contains cultural prescriptions that apply to virtually all major institutional settings (Davidson and Gordon, 1979; Schlegel, 1977; Weitz, 1977). For example, our culture promulgates views regarding the place of males and females in religion—with few exceptions males are to be the priests, rabbis, and ministers and females the lower-ranked members of the religious organization. Females in politics are not equally endorsed for the top power positions as can be seen in Table 3.1. Only if we included volunteer services would females be in the majority in any political type of activity. In educational and economic activity, women are clearly the less influential group. The more prestigious the degree, the more likely males will dominate (See Table 3.2.). In the area of sexuality, male privileges are still greater than are those granted females. Thus, in all areas of social life, women and men are defined in distinct ways and these definitions are what we call gender roles. We shall spell this out in greater detail later on in this chapter.

The reader should be aware that the terms "gender role" and "sex role" are often

TABLE 3.1

Political Power of Men and Women in America: 1978

	PERCENT MEN	PERCENT WOMEN
U.S. Population	48.7	51.3
U.S. Senate	99	1
U.S. House	96	4
U.S. Supreme Court	100	0
Federal Judges	99	1
Governors	96	4
State Representatives	90	10
State Senators	95	5
Statewide Elective/Appointive Offices	89	11
County Governing Boards	97	3
Mayors and Councilors	92	8
School Board Members	75	25

Source: Center for the American Woman in Politics, 1521 New Hampshire Ave., NW, Washington, DC 20036, 1979. P. 1.

used interchangeably in the research literature. I prefer the term gender role because the term sex has several different meanings. Sex is used to mean sexual contact of various sorts as in "to have sex with someone." Secondly, it sometimes is used to mean biological or genetic sex—that is chromosomal sex (XX or XY). On the other hand, gender role refers to a cultural role that is obviously highly correlated with genetic sex but it is still clearly a cultural role. No society does a chromosomal check to be sure that someone is a genetic male before letting them perform a male gender role (there are rare exceptions as in some professional athletic events). Even though most all the occupants of each gender role are of one genetic sex, when we talk of the role of males and females we are talking of rights and duties that, for the most part, can be learned by either genetic sex. Thus, to use the word sex might

TABLE 3.2

Earned Academic Degrees in 1976

TYPE OF DEGREE	PERCENT EARNED BY MALES	PERCENT EARNED BY FEMALES
Bachelor's	56	44
Master's	54	46
Ph.D.	77	23
Medicine	84	16
Law	81	19
Dentistry	96	4

Source: U.S. Bureau of the Census, Statistical Abstracts of the United States: 1978: 168, Tables 277 and 278.

confuse gender role with one's genetic sex. For these reasons I find gender role a much clearer concept to utilize. Nevertheless, the reader should be aware that there is a split in common usage in this new area of research and theorizing.

Gender Roles: A Limit of Two Per Culture?

If one thinks of gender roles as part of culture and not totally tied to genetic sex, then it becomes possible that some cultures may have recognized more than two genders. Such a possibility is documented in the recent anthropological literature (Martin and Voorhies, 1975, Chap. 4). Just as some cultures recognize various shades of color and other cultures recognize only broad categories of color, so it is with gender roles. One biological reason for a third gender category revolves about the fact that a small percent of all births involve individuals with genitalia that are "ambiguous." Ambiguous genitalia refers to genitalia which contain either an exceptionally small penis that could be confused with a clitoris and/or a partially open vulva that could be confused with a scrotum. When such infants were born in the traditional Navajo groups, they were given the name "nadle" (Hill, 1935). The gender role of nadle has two subtypes: (a) those who have ambiguous genitalia, and (b) those who have normal genitalia but do not wish to identify as either the male or female gender. Nadle have different dress codes—allowing for either male or female clothing (or both) to be worn. Nadles can perform the duties of either the male or female gender if they wish. Only hunting and warfare are ruled out for this third gender. In practice nadles seem to prefer female clothing and female activities. They may live in a marriage-like status with another individual of either genetic sex or with someone with ambiguous genitalia. Navajo mythology has a figure called "May-des tzihi" who is described as having been both man and woman. This belief further supports the recognition of a third gender. There are a few other societies that also display acceptance of more than two genders but we will not take the time to go into them here. It is sufficient for the reader to be aware that the very common practice of recognizing only two genders is not universal. The relationship between the biological sex and gender categories is thus obviously not perfect, and the cultural aspect of gender roles should now be more obvious. Some societies which recognize only two biological sexes still permit some individuals of either biological sex to choose whether they wish to be members of the female or male gender. The Mohave and Churkchee cultures allow this (Martin and Voorhies, 1975, Chap. 4). This creates four gender role possibilities. The cultural demand that all biological creatures fit into two genders is itself important insight into the flexibility of the gender role ideology of a particular society.

Heredity and Gender Roles

One vital question that needs to be addressed in order to understand gender roles is: Are there any inherited characteristics of genetic males and females that form the basis for the particular division of gender roles we have in America? In short, are gender roles purely arbitrary and fully alterable and exchangeable or are there some parts of gender roles that are based on inherited biological characteristics of each particular genetic sex? To attempt to answer this complex question involves some basic understanding of the biological basis of sex differentiation in utero and I will briefly turn to that now.

One major point about genetic male-female differentiation is that the human embryo will normally develop a female genital appearance unless something is added in the way of male hormones. Without male hormones (and in fact without female hormones either), the newborn will have the appearance of a female. To produce a male there must first be added a substance that suppresses the development of the Mullerian ducts which would develop into the womb, tubes, and vagina. A genetic male (XY) who lacks this suppressant can (despite the fact that he is a genetic male) be born with female genitalia. To produce a male, androgen (male sex hormone) must be present. This hormone promotes the development of the Wolffian ducts which form the male reproductive structures. The XY (male) fetus is programmed so that during the third month of pregnancy, an "androgen bath" will occur and the absorption of this androgen by the fetus will promote the development of the Wolffian ducts. Without these events occurring, a genetic male fetus will not develop the genital appearance of a male. In the female case, a genetic female fetus will appear like a female if the male hormone bath is absent and will develop the full ability to reproduce if the female hormone is present and promotes the Mullerian ducts.

The above description briefly indicates how the genetic male and female fetus develops into a fully functioning male or female. Incomplete differentiation of the reproductive system can occur and produce ambiguous genitalia or what Money and Ehrhardt (1972) call hermaphroditism, that is, an infant with genitalia of both sexes. It should be clear that all fetuses have both sets of ducts. It is the development of the Mullerian ducts that produce the female genitalia and internal reproductive organs and it is the development of the Wolffian ducts that produce the male genitalia and reproductive organs. Some hormonal event in utero can encourage the development of one of these ducts regardless of the genetic sex of the fetus. One of the best-known examples is the andrenogenital syndrome, occurring in a genetic female fetus. In such a case there is an excess of male hormones (androgen) and this leads to the suppression of the Mullerian ducts and the development of the Wolffian ducts and a resultant male genitalia that is more or less developed despite the fact that the fetus is a genetic female. Also, in a genetic male fetus (XY) who is androgen insensitive, that is, whose body does not respond normally to the androgen bath, there will be a failure to inhibit the Mullerian ducts and activate the Wolffian ducts, and female genitalia will develop. In many cases the genitalia of both sexes are partially present, but in some instances the genetic sex is completely hidden by developed genitalia of the opposite sex. The power of hormones in these instances is striking. The third gender category in some societies, referred to in our earlier discussion, is often occupied by such people with ambiguous genitalia.

This should afford the reader some insight into a few of the processes involved in producing male or female genitalia in humans and some of the ways in which "errors" can creep in. These errors are relatively rare, but they do afford us insight into gender identity. Money and Ehrhardt (1972) report on research they did on infants born with ambiguous genitalia. They found that the child would accept whichever gender was assigned regardless of the genetic sex. This does not establish learning as the only factor in gender identity, but it does show the crucial role of such learning. Money does report evidence that androgenized genetic females tend to behave more as tomboys when they grow up. One can take this as evidence that male hormones (androgen) produce more aggression. Nevertheless, this situation may also be the result of parents, aware of the androgenized conditions of their daughters, treating their offspring in ways that promote tomboyism (Quadagno et al. 1977). In any case the hormonal factors do not produce situations that lead to the inability of such children to adopt the female gender role of our society.

So the basic androgen difference in genetic males and females is a key factor to search out for possible connections to a society's gender role differences. Maccoby and Jacklin (1974) report that they found most of the research studies they examined indicated that males were more aggressive than females. They also found this to be the case in our close cousins, the great apes. They believe that aggression is likely based on the higher androgen levels in male animals. Androgen is five to ten times more plentiful in the male than in the female. Androgen has been found to produce aggressive actions when injected into animals. Surely there is a learned component to aggression but Maccoby and Jacklin conclude that they feel there is a genetic sex difference based on androgen. If one accepted this position, this hormonal difference could be supposed to be the basis for gender role differences in aggression that are expected in male and female roles. This same hormone, androgen, is also able to increase sexual desire in some men and, more generally, in women. Here too one may raise the question whether gender role differences in sexual assertiveness is partially based on hormonal differences.

It may be well to enter a caveat to the reader at this point. Those readers who are equalitarian may well resist accepting any biological differences between the sexes whereas those who are traditional may well look for as many differences as possible to help support their conception of more differentiated roles. Such self-inflicted pressures are unnecessary. No matter how many differences are found, one can still argue that with extensive enough training those differences could be overcome. Also, even if no differences are found, one could argue that there are religious, ethical, pragmatic, or other reasons for differentiating gender roles. In short, although it is important to know what biological differences exist, that knowledge does not establish what the "proper" set of gender roles are, and it also does not describe unalterable differences. It simply states the parameters of the biological situation that must be dealt with through cultural training of genetic females and males.

It is important to also keep in mind the interrelatedness of heredity and environment. The influence of Darwinian evolution in the late nineteenth century led to a strong bias which asserted that everything was inherited. Instinct theories grew which assumed that every personality trait had an instinctual base. In sum, we inherited our "natural" characteristics. By the 1920s the psychological profession had rejected the instinct approach and was increasingly accepting a behavioristic approach such as that put forth by Watson and others (Rossi, 1977). This new approach rejected biological factors as fully as the earlier approach had rejected learning factors. The new conception held that human relationships were fully determined by learning. Around the time of World War II and shortly after, a synthesis of biological and learning theory approaches emerged. It was becoming clear that biology might make certain types of behavior more likely but not determine them fully, and, relatedly, it was increasingly apparent that the way a person thought could affect that person's biological responses. One could make oneself ill through mental stress as in various forms of psychosomatic illness (ulcers, rashes, and so on).

This new biosocial perspective can be seen directly in the area of genetic sex differences. For example, it is known that the physiology of the male and female is affected by hormones which led to the female being more "cyclical." By cyclical we mean that female hormones produce cyclical patterns of hormonal secretions, and the hormonal synthesis related to the menstrual cycle. The older perspective was that the pituitary gland regulated these hormonal secretions and they, in turn, produced other hormonal secretions which eventually signaled the pituitary to start the cycle over again. This view is one that posits a closed system of hormonal forces. The newer view that came in vogue in the 1960s gave the brain a role in this entire process. Thus, it was assumed that the brain (the hypothalamus, to be specific) signaled the pituitary to start this process of hormonal secretion and synthesis. This was an important alteration because if the brain had a direct role in these hormonal processes, then learning and thinking could affect such hormonal processes. This new perspective posited a basic difference, not only in brain structure of the male and female but, more importantly, it introduced a joining together of biological and social influences. Experiments were performed on rats that transformed the pituitary gland from a male animal to a female animal and noted that the male pituitary once transplanted in a female became cyclical and regulated the menstrual cycle. Thus, the female brain must have been programmed differently and must have been able to promote a different functioning of the transplanted pituitary. For our purposes, this very interesting finding has an additional meaning—since learning can affect the brain and the brain can affect the hormonal processes, then the hormonal system was no longer simply a closed physiological system that had no point of entry. One's emotional and mental state could interact with one's hormonal system and dramatically affect the hormonal outflow.

The new biosocial perspective is important for our focus because it leads us to conclude that no matter what biological differences we may find between males and females, they are alterable in various ways by training. Thus the reader, regardless of personal values, may relax and try to find out what males and females are like biologically and not feel that his or her personal values on gender roles are being threatened by any particular findings.

Some of this biosocial research revealed the role of another hormone called oxytocin. Females have much greater quantities of oxytocin than do males. Oxytocin is released after childbirth and helps the uterus to contract and heal. It is also released during coitus, particularly if the female has an orgasm. The contractions induced in the vaginal track by oxytocin help transport the sperm into the uterus (Nalbandov, 1964; Newton, 1967; Rossi, 1977). The older views of the speed of sperm traveling in the vaginal passageway have been rejected in favor of the catalytic role of oxytocin. This finding also implies that pregnancy may indeed be more likely if the female is orgasmic. Of course, orgasm is not at all a prerequisite for pregnancy, but the orgasm and the related oxytocin do help in promoting pregnancy. Oxytocin is released in the mother upon the crying of her infant. Oxytocin causes the nipples to become erect and in that sense prepares the female for nursing. Now one could conclude that this finding supports a gender role that ties the mother, rather than the father, closer to the infant. However, taken a step further, women could be taught to avoid breast feeding and thus the oxytocin pressure toward mother-infant ties would be reduced. In fact, this is exactly what has happened in American society today where most women bottle-feed rather than nurse their newborn infants. This illustrates the plasticity of genetic sex differences and supports the perspective that such knowledge does not force us to accept any one type of gender role system.

There are several summary statements that can be made concerning the biological differences between females and males that are relevant to gender roles today. First, we must assert that our knowledge in this area is in its infancy. Much of what we know dates from the beginnings of the field of neuroendocrinology in the 1960s. Nevertheless, we can say that there are differences in androgen and oxytocin hormones that seem relevant to understanding some basic gender role differences. Oxytocin may have been one factor that helped link females more with infant care and androgen may have tied males more to aggression and eroticism. *But,* as we have discussed here, there are so many other learned factors that can link one to infant care or that can motivate one to be aggressive or erotic, that we can certainly not conclude that these biological factors are the necessary and sufficient causes of present-day gender roles. There is an ample range of interest in child care, aggression, and eroticism *within each genetic sex* to make it clear that the interaction of biology with learning is a major context to be explored. The educated woman's orgasmic behavior differs from that of the uneducated woman; California females seem more sexually permissive than New York females; American males seem more aggressive than Swedish males (Kinsey, 1953; Reiss, 1967; 1979). All these facts argue for the power of learning to modify and supplement whatever biological base is present. This is not to say that the biological tendencies are unimportant but rather that they interact with learning and are constantly being modified. The evidence would indicate that we can create any type of gender role society that we want—the most that biology can do is make some changes more difficult to accomplish, but there is no evidence of the inevitability of any aspect of gender role. The key question is better put as what type of gender role system do we desire and are we willing to receive the rewards and pay the cost of achieving that system?

The very facts of pregnancy, lactation, and menstruation do not force a particular type of gender role outcome. However, these factors do produce outcomes that tie the mother to the newborn child, and that basic tie is at the heart of virtually every gender role system in the world. The close ties to motherhood make work outside the home more problematic. Not that women in most cultures do only minor work outside the home—on the contrary, women in most cultures do a large share of the work outside the home. It has been estimated that cross-culturally, women contribute about 44 percent of the subsistence production (Aronoff and Crano, 1975).

Nevertheless, despite this large share of work outside the home, the female's primary responsibility has been child care, and thus the likelihood of gaining power and dominance in a society is greatly reduced. Males have been assigned as their number one priority to full-time work outside the home, and they accordingly control the power structures in economic and political areas. As has been noted earlier, although some societies are closer to equalitarianism, there are no societies where females have the dominant share of power and only the Amazonian and other myths even talk of such cultures occurring in the past (Hammond and Jablow, 1975; Schlegel, 1977). *Two features of gender roles in all cultures then are: (1) female ties to child rearing and (2) male ties to economic and political power.* While it is true that in many cultures males do a large share of the child rearing and, conversely, women do a large share of the economic work, this does not alter the basic gender role priorities for the two genders. The basic root cause of this crucial division of labor in gender roles is the tie of the female to the child which historically gave males the reins of power. I hasten to add here that such a division of labor is not necessitated by the biological differences between the sexes. One could design a culture in which child care was more evenly shared and was in part taken care of by the state. In fact, that goal is precisely incorporated in the Swedish government's official policy on child care (see Chapter 17). All Western cultures have been slowly moving in that direction during this century. It is also possible that economic and political power could be more evenly divided between the genders and there are minor trends in this direction in the Western world also.

One difficulty in changing gender roles is in creating the motivation for males to want to participate in child care. Some men have moved in this direction but basically child care is still very heavily a female activity (Petras, 1975; Komarovsky, 1976). How do you get males to move from their powerful economic and political positions to the child-care positions? Clearly, this is not an easy area in which to effect change. Few groups have voluntarily given up their power. One could redefine child care to make it as high on rewards of prestige and power as are other activities and thereby lure males to participate more. But this situation has not come about.

Surprising as it may seem, there are large numbers of women who prefer the child-care role and do not want to participate in the economic and political power areas to a greater extent. The debate in recent years on the Equal Rights Amendment (ERA) has made us all aware of this. In part, this should not surprise us. If we train women to assume the child-care role, we should expect resistance if we then try to resocialize women to accept the choice of other activities outside the home. Marjori Galenson (1973:6) reports in her book on working women in various Western nations that women are more easily satisfied than men are with low paid and low status work. Surely, this is changing today as the rights of women and equalitarian gender relations become more widespread. Further, more recent research presents strong evidence that the behaviors and policies of employers are much more important causes of gender differences in the workplace than the attitudes and behavior of women employees (Wolf and Fligstein, 1979; Duncan and Morgan, 1978; U.S. Department of Labor, 1978).

As we shall see in later chapters, many women are quite ambivalent about child care and employment—they feel guilty about the possible neglect of their children if they work outside the home and yet they feel less worthwhile if they do not have outside employment. Many women then are caught on the horns of a dilemma, namely, our changing gender role notions. We have still not achieved a full measure of choice in the female and male roles. These issues will become clearer as we discuss the case of Sweden and other relevant data in future chapters. For now it is sufficient to say that although the tie-up of gender roles to biology is alterable and although the entire Western world seems to be striving toward greater gender equality, change has been slow.

Socialization into Gender Roles

How do we learn our gender roles? People learn gender roles the same way they learn the common aspects of student roles, child roles and peer-group roles. In short, they learn roles by role-taking. George Herbert Mead (1934) put forth what has come to be the most widely accepted description of role-taking and the process by which we learn social roles and develop a social self. I will briefly describe Mead's thought here as a background explanation for our discussion of gender roles.

GEORGE HERBERT MEAD AND THE SOCIAL SELF

Mead has the distinction of having never written a book during his life (1879–1931) and yet having several books today with his name as author. To have graduate students who have thought enough of your lectures to keep their class notes is a rarity. To have, in addition, students who were willing to help create a book posthumously for a professor is almost unheard of. For such students to actually contribute their time and energy to the production of three books is something of a miracle. The books have been extensively read, especially *Mind, Self and Society* (1934) and have been influential in the thinking of most all sociologists on the topic of role socialization.

Mead starts out by positing that society is prior to the individual. This basic assumption should not be taken to be historical fact. Of course, a human society cannot occur unless human individuals are present, and thus society cannot be temporally prior. However, what Mead meant was that in a logical sense, one cannot produce a human individual unless that individual is raised in the company of other humans. We do have evidence from studies of children brought up in isolation which support this assumption. Years ago, Davis (1940, 1947) reported on studies of "attic children," that is, children, often illegitimate, who are kept in almost full isolation by their mothers; because of guilt feelings and other attitudes, contact is made only to feed and clean the child. Such children when found are often thought to be deaf and feebleminded. They cannot speak intelligibly, and they do not respond when spoken to. They have the human biological equipment, but they lack the societal setting; therefore a human social self fails to develop. With special educational efforts such children can be taught normal social behavior. However, the degree of success depends upon their age when they are found, and there are definite limits.

Now, Mead did not mean to imply that the societal setting is all that is required. Clearly there are biological requirements of human heredity. His point is that the societal setting is a necessary condition of producing a social self. It is by contact with other humans that attitudes are learned. This occurs via "role-taking." Role-taking is an innate process that involves putting oneself in the place of the other person and arriving at an impression of what the other person is thinking or feeling. Such role-taking can be seen in its elementary forms in the baby understanding the moods of parents, or making the most of the type of responses the parents give to crying (Flavell, 1975). Role-taking is a prerequisite of all communication. If someone is talking to you and you are not "listening," not role-taking, then no meaning can be transferred and no communication is possible. We all have experienced such a situation wherein someone says to us, "Well, what do you think?" and our response is "What?—I guess I wasn't paying attention." The words created sound waves that hit our eardrums, but without role-taking there is no transference of meaning. The same sort of thing often happens to some people when they are reading a book. Their minds wander, and they do not role-take with the author of the words they are reading. After several minutes they may realize that they do not remember a thing that their eyes passed over. I hope that is not happening now!

By role-taking we tend to learn the feelings of others because we constantly (consciously or not) put ourselves in their shoes. In this way we pick up and internalize the attitudes of others. We may do this inaccurately or be better at it with some people than with others. Thus, the result is a selective process, and we do not become simply a rubber-stamp version of all those we contact. Also, some infants are more sensitive to areas such as music, smell, or sight. This further indicates selectivity in role-taking and in accuracy and response. Once we develop, through role-taking, certain attitudes in an area, future role-taking in that area is affected. People differ as to the degree they keep their minds open to change, but clearly there is a tendency to close out certain areas to outside influence as one gets older. Here too, then, is a selective factor.

One easy way to see the effects of role-taking in children is to observe them playing house. The young female who plays the mother will usually indicate strong elements of her mother's role in her own play behavior. This indicates that she has learned her mother's role and, thus, has role-taken with her mother. The entire area of anticipatory socialization is involved here. We socialize our children ahead of time by our own behavior in the roles they will later perform. One can see this in everyday areas such as driving and drinking and smoking, but even more broadly in parental roles. The kind of parental-role conceptions children develop will be heavily influenced by their own parents' role behavior. Of course, parents are not the sole influence on role conceptions. As the child ages, peers increasingly become important influences.

The relatively integrated set of attitudes which one develops as one grows up is what George Herbert Mead defines as the "social self." The self, in addition to these attitudes, has a reflexive quality. That is, it can take itself as object. This means that the self has an awareness of itself. The attitudes that compose the self are attitudes that are shared with others, for that is their source. Idiosyncratic views are not part of the social self. Nevertheless, Mead makes it clear that one's attitudes are a selective assortment of the many attitudes one has contacted over the years. One way to note which attitudes are selected is to give a special name to those *others* who are most influential. Mead calls such others "significant others." Significant others are usually parents, close friends, lovers, and relatives. We internalize the attitudes of these people who are significant to us much more easily than others. Clearly, then, the social self develops through a selective process. I stress this point because many people believe that sociologists view people as merely rubber stamps of the groups they contact. Mead's conceptions do not support such a mechanical reproduction of attitudes.

The reflexive quality of the self makes pride and guilt possible. We evaluate ourselves by looking at ourselves in the mirror of those attitudes of others *that we accept.* I stress the last three words, for it is not just the general community's attitudes by which we judge ourselves. The more influential criterion we use is the attitudes that we have accepted and internalized. Just being exposed to a set of attitudes in a community does not by any means guarantee acceptance of such attitudes. The great diversity of attitudes and the number of contradictory attitudes in most American communities necessitates choice and selectivity. This also means that one can internalize contradictory attitudes in several areas. For example, one can learn from one's parents that premarital coitus is wrong and learn from one's peer group that it is right. If one group's definition of the situation is more influential than the other, the potential conflict is reduced. But when both groups have equal influence on a person, the internal conflict can become quite intense. Under such conditions, when one looks into the mirror of the internalized attitudes of others, what one sees is a blurred image, and self-evaluation becomes uncertain. Just as a clear mirror is necessary to view oneself physically, so a clear mirror composed of accepted attitudes is necessary to clearly view oneself socially.

Mead asserted that people develop their ability to role-take. At first a person is able to role-take only with one other person; later on one learns to role-take with small groups of people. This group role-taking is particularly important in team sports, for one cannot be a good team player unless one can anticipate the moves of all teammates. Finally, Mead feels that people develop the ability to role-take with what he calls the "generalized other," or the entire community or, in large cities, with what an entire segment of the community feels and thinks. Here one can envisage how a community would react to a certain behavior that is contemplated. By virtue of this ability, the individual has shown great interdependence with others. We are dependent upon the community's judgment of us—particularly if it is a community whose attitudes we share.

On the other hand, the other members of that community are affected by what our feelings and thoughts are. Mead was very much concerned with the ethical basis of modern society. He felt that his theoretical conception of how the social self developed, with its stress on the interdependence of human beings, would provide an integrative basis for modern urban–industrial society. Mead felt that if a human being is a social creature, shaped by his or her contact with fellow humans and constantly subject to influencing them and being influenced by them, then the ethical basis of society was obvious: A human being must consider the consequences of his or her actions on fellow creatures, and even in modern society such consequences are ever present. Whether one agrees with this philosophical argument or not, it is true that almost fifty years later, Mead's conception of how the social self developed is still widely accepted by sociologists. Sociologists and social psychologists are trying now to specify more precisely the general process that Mead outlined. (For relevance to the family, see two articles by Stryker, 1964, 1968, and see Flavell et al., 1975.)

What about the broader social and cultural factors that influence the social self's development? The basic institutional structure of the family and the political, economic, and religious institutions in a community will shape the prevailing attitudes. Mead talks about the ways in which one acquires attitudes in terms of a social–psychological process of developing a self in society. But Mead does not talk about the different ways the very processes of socialization are organized. In one community there may be stress on openness in parent–child relations and on creative public schools; in another community the stress may be on respect for parents by children and on a conventional public school education. Such social and cultural differences are not part of Mead's focus. His focus is the classic social–psychological focus of how the individual's interaction with group members shapes attitudes and behaviors. This is not said to criticize Mead, but rather to sharpen the reader's appreciation for differences in perspective and orientation. In this book we shall utilize the social–psychological, as well as the more purely sociological, perspectives.

It should be clear that when we talk of *role-taking*, we are speaking of a *psychological process* wherein an individual puts himself in the place of another and estimates the other's feelings and thoughts. When we speak of *role-playing*, we are speaking of *a sociological process* wherein the individual carries out the rights and duties of a particular position in society. For example, when a student comes to class, participates in discussions, takes exams, and so forth, he is playing the role of a student. In the course of that role-playing he will role-take with the teacher, for that is his only way of understanding what the teacher is saying. Role-*taking* with people who are in roles that we shall someday be in is one key way to learn how to play that role when we get older. The reverse is also true: By role-*playing* as a student we learn more skills at role-taking with the teacher. Thus, there is a clear interrelation of these concepts, but yet they are distinct in meaning.

Finally, I hope the reader is aware that the term role-playing does not imply that the person is putting on an act and does not really mean what he or she is doing. Rather, this is simply a way of noting that the role is socially defined as to how one should act, and in this sense there is a script written for each role, and one learns the script and usually acts accordingly. The possibility of acting differently is always present, but most people choose to conform. This can be seen in the courtship system we have. It is a participant-run courtship system, and thus young people have a great deal of freedom to do what they want. Yet most young people do not greatly exceed the approved limits or act fully impulsively. Through role-taking they have learned both parental and peer expectations in courtship. Most youngsters abide by the dominant expectations of their significant others and do not strike off on their own and make up their own sets of rules.

Learning Gender Roles

Let us go from this general description of how the social self emerges to a more specific analysis of the way in which gender roles are learned (Hartley, 1960; Maccoby, 1966; Kagan, 1964; Maccoby and Jacklin, 1974; Yorburg, 1974). The first eighteen months are crucial in learning gender roles. The extensive research of John Money (Money and Ehrhardt, 1972) has led to the conclusion that you can bring up either genetic sex to accept either gender role providing you start early enough. After about eighteen months, it becomes increasingly difficult to accomplish any change in gender identity. If clarity is not present in the way a child is treated, that may be hard to correct after eighteen months.

Young children from ages three to seven years old already realize a good deal of the cultural definitions of what goes with being a genetic male or female. Despite considerable change in what adult females do today, children this age will often indicate that they believe a girl should be pretty and small and a boy should be large and strong (Kagan, 1964, p. 139; Yorburg, 1974). Girls are likely to be viewed as less aggressive verbally and physically than boys are. Both genders generally view their fathers as more aggressive than their mothers and believe that girls, more than boys, can express dependency, passivity, and conformity. Both genders commonly view their mothers as more nurturant than their fathers. Now, these differences are sharper in the lower social classes than in the middle social classes. We shall see later on that such social-class differences fit with studies by Kohn (1959, 1969) and others which also show sharper gender-role differentiation in the lower classes. The middle and upper middle classes seem to have endorsed more fully the feminist changes we discussed in part earlier. Particularly, one might say that the middle classes accept the increased freedom in courtship and the freedom for the female to work for satisfaction outside the home. It is generally agreed that parents are the original prototypes of masculinity and femininity for the young child; thus, if the classes differ in the sharpness of these two roles regarding children, so must the classes differ in this respect regarding parents. That is exactly what others have found. (See Chapters 15 and 16.) These class differences in gender roles make it

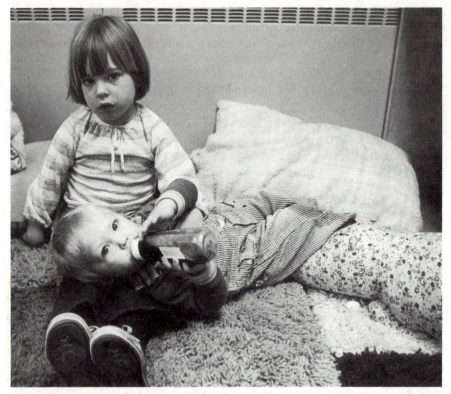

This young girl has already begun a role identification. Photo by Robert Olsgard, courtesy of The Minnesota Geographic Society, Project Coordinator, Tim Strick.

clear that although there may be some biological factors that underlie gender role differences, they are not rigidly fixed, for they do vary by social class training.

It is assumed by most researchers and theorists in the area of gender-role development that a strong identification with the same-gender parent at an early age helps greatly in the future establishment of an appropriate gender role (Mussen, 1970). For such identification to take place, a certain degree of nurturance between the parent and child must take place. According to this view, a father who was strictly authoritarian and not nurturant to his son would block his son from being able to identify with him. Mussen and Distler's earlier work (1959) lend some empirical support to this view. There are other views that add complexity to this simple view of gender role learning occurring with the same-gender parent. For example, Miriam Johnson (1963) proposes and Helbrun (1965) supports the view that it is the father rather than the mother that makes sharper distinctions between the relationships to male and female children. If this is so, then the learning of gender roles will often be more influenced by the father regardless of the gender of the child.

Money and Ehrhardt (1972) propose that there are two processes through which one learns a gender role. One process is the traditionally named one of identification with the person of the same gender. Money and Ehrhardt argue that in addition to that process there is the process of "complementation," which is learning one's own role by learning what the complementary role of the opposite gender consists of. Their theory is a most interesting one, and they assert that one learns gender roles much as one would learn two different languages, one of which is spoken and the other of which is understood but not spoken. By this view we learn both gender roles, but we code one set of roles negative in terms of action and the other set of roles positive in terms of what we shall act out. This view has much to offer in terms of explaining how it is that people who identify with one gender role may still act in particular ways in line with the opposite gender role. For example, the transvestite most often identifies as a male, and yet this doesn't prevent him from dressing on occasion as a female. Also, the homosexual male identifies most often with the masculine gender but has a sexual partner preference that is part of the female gender role. The mechanisms that trigger the acting out of aspects of the opposite gender-role behavior are not well known at present, but the Money–Ehrhardt theoretical approach can do much to help us specify and test ideas in this area.

One might hypothesize that the sharper the gender-role distinction in a society, the greater the likelihood that one will find people who act out role behaviors of the opposite gender. This would be expected because of the greater number of such behaviors that would be possible in a sharply distinguished gender role society and also because of the greater complexity in learning precisely the proper roles in such highly differentiated types of societies.

Gender roles play an important part in encouraging or discouraging other attitudes as one grows up. Kagan and Moss (1962) and Mussen (1961, 1962, 1970) report findings that attitudes and behaviors related to aggression tend to stay if the child is male and tend to be inhibited if the subject is female. Likewise, passive attitudes or behaviors tend to be inhibited if the child is a male. So the fit of a response with one's gender role is a key determinant of how stable that response will be. All of this selectivity resulting from cultural gender-role emphasis leads to considerable male–female difference in adult personality and interests.

A Brief History of Equalitarianism Trends in Gender Roles

Five centuries before the birth of Christ, Plato argued for greater female equality. In his *Republic* he set down the model of a society that would allow women to work alongside men and that would raise children communally without any knowledge of biological parenthood and, finally, would place them into the social positions for which they were best suited. This type of equality of the genders, then, is not new in terms of philosophy. What is relatively new in the Western world is the degree of achieving such equality. The Greeks never achieved it to any great degree, for they were "double standard" in their view of allowing men to run society and placing women in the home (if they were wives) or in the bed chamber for pleasure if they were hetaerae (Lecky, 1955). The Romans were coarser than the Greeks and continued the double-standard or sharply differentiated gender role treatment of women. But during the Punic Wars there was a period of increased female rights, and husbands were eventually barred from the right to kill members of their families if they disobeyed them. Despite such periodic gains, women remained very much second-class citizens. Christianity formerly professed belief in a single standard that would judge men and women alike on moral issues. However, this equality was not actually achieved, and during the Middle Ages the position of women reached an even lower level in terms of their legal, political, and marital positions (Queen and Habenstein, 1974).

The nineteenth-century feminist movement in America was not unique then in its demand for female equality. What was unique was the fact that women were destined in the Western world to achieve a far greater share of their demands than they ever had before. This achievement is important to grasp in order to understand our present-day Family System. The point most historians choose as the start of the modern movement was the 1848 feminist meeting in Seneca Falls, New York, where a "Declaration of Sentiments" was issued, starting with the familiar sounding words: "We hold these truths to be self-evident: that all men. . . ." But then they added *and women* are created equal" (Ditzion, 1953, 257–260). Seventy-two years later women had won the vote, were working by the millions, had more equalitarian marriages, and had established themselves as less of a corps of second-class citizens than ever before in the Western world. But they had only taken a few initial steps toward full equality (O'Neill, 1969).

The feminist movement in the nineteenth century, like most major social movements, was not a monolithic effort. There were many factions. On the "left" in the liberal wing was the famous Victoria Claflin (Woodhull). Victoria published a newspaper in New York City in which she advocated the rights of women to have sexual relations on an equal basis with men. The well-known Reverend Henry Ward Beecher was offended by her ideas and often criticized her. Fate led to an escalation of their conflict. Elizabeth Cady Stanton had been told by a Mr. Tilton that his wife was having an affair with the Reverend Beecher. Mrs. Stanton passed this information to Victoria. Victoria warned the reverend to stop picking on her and also warned his sister (Harriet Beecher Stowe) to cease and desist from annoying her. Since they did not comply, she published an account of Reverend Beecher's affair in her weekly newspaper. This eventually led to a trial, wherein the reverend was acquitted by a hung jury, but Mrs. Tilton was convicted of "indefensible conduct" by a church committee (Shaplen, 1954).

Such tumultuous doings were not typical of the feminists, for most of the feminists were not permissive regarding sexuality. They tended to favor sexual equality on the abstinence level rather than on the permissive level. By the 1870s the feminist movement had split into a conservative branch with women like Lucy Stone and Julia Ward Howe and a more liberal branch with women like Susan B. Anthony and Elizabeth Cady Stanton. The feminists split also on the prohibition plank. The adoption of this plank by Carrie Nation and other feminists led to the alienation of many male supporters. These men were willing to give women greater equality, but not willing to stop drinking alcohol in order to accomplish this.

The feminist movement was relatively successful. Surely there is today, in the

Victoria Woodhull, November 1871, asserting her right to vote. Courtesy of the New York Historical Society, New York City.

1980s, a good deal of differential treatment and differential evaluation of men and women, but much less than before. Why? What was it that made this revolutionary attempt to increase female rights more successful than the myriad previous attempts? Also, what stopped it from fully achieving its goals? Basically I believe the answer lies in the modern urban–industrial society with its economic opportunities. For the first time in the Western world millions of women could easily find paid employment and earn a living at something other than prostitution. At first, many of the female jobs were menial, but even these still offered women the chance to be self-supporting. In time jobs with somewhat more desirous working conditions came to be taken over by females. This was the case in the position of store sales workers who once were predominantly male and today are predominantly female. Telephone operators and secretaries, too, started out as male occupations and changed later on. By 1900, 5 million women were working, and by 1980 over 40 million women were working. Women had increased from 18 percent of the total labor force to over 40 percent. There are many more women working in America than ever before, but they have not until very recently made much headway in the key professions. For example, in 1910 about 19 percent of the college teachers were women; in 1960 about 19 percent of the college teachers were women. However, by 1970 the proportion had risen to 28 percent. The same type of comparison could be made in medicine, law, religion, politics, and the like. Table 3.3 gives some valuable information on this point for various occupations. Women have entered the labor market in unprecedented numbers, but they have largely entered specific positions that are heavily gender segregated such as sales and office clerks, stenographers, nurses, public school teachers, and so forth. Edward Gross's examination

TABLE 3.3

Women as Percentage of All Workers in Selected Professional Occupations (U.S.A., 1900–1977)

OCCUPATION	1977	1970	1960	1950	1940	1930	1920	1910	1900
College professors, president, instructors	31.7	28.4	19.0	23.0	27.0	32.0	30.0	19.0	
Doctors	11.2	9.2	6.8	6.1	4.6	4.0	5.0	6.0	
Lawyers	9.5	4.8	3.5	3.5	2.4	2.1	1.4	1.0	
Engineers	2.7	1.6	0.8	1.2	0.3				
Dentists	2.9	3.4	2.1	2.7	1.5	1.8	3.2	3.1	
Scientists	15.6	13.1	9.9	11.4					
Biologists	——	34.9	28.0	27.0					
Chemists	13.7	11.9	8.6	10.0					
Mathematicians	——	22.5	26.4	38.0					
Physicists	——	3.9	4.2	6.5					
Nurses	96.7	97.3	97.0	98.0	98.0	98.0	96.0	93.0	94.0
Social workers	——	62.7	57.0	66.0	67.0	68.0	62.0	52.0	
Librarians	79.8	81.9	85.0	89.0	89.0	91.0	88.0	79.0	
Clergy	——	2.9	5.8	8.5	2.2	4.3	2.6	1.0	4.4

Source: Cynthia F. Epstein (1970):967; 1970 data source: U.S. Bureau of the Census.
U.S. Census of Population 1970, Occupation by Industry, *Final Report PC (2)-7c*
(1974):241–242; 1977 data source: U.S. Bureau of the Census, 1978. Statistical
Abstracts of the United States: 419–420. *(A dash in the 1977 column indicates that
comparable data were not available.)*

revealed very little change from 1900 to 1960 in the degree to which occupations are by gender segregated (Gross, 1968). In the last thirty years, the new wave of women workers comprised mainly married women, and they entered occupations similar to those their mothers and grandmothers had entered before them. The first signs of any change in this are present in the 1970 data in Table 3.3.

However, the point still holds that despite the restriction on occupations that women could enter, the very fact that they could work and earn a supportive wage led to their ability to be more independent of men. This is particularly true at the low- and modest-income levels. At that level the woman's earning power is such that she can compete with that of the man. At the higher-income levels the situation is different, and most women could not keep themselves in "the style they are accustomed to" by their own work. This is perhaps one reason why divorce is lower at the higher levels. The important point is that this increase in available jobs in the late nineteenth century gave females a feeling of independence and males a realization of female economic potential. I believe this surely was one of the key factors in the successes that the feminists were able to achieve.

The occupations in which women work are heavily slanted toward what is culturally accepted as women's work such as public school teaching, secretarial work, sales work, nursing, hairdressing, and the like. The average income for women who work full time is about 60 percent that of the average income of men who work full time. In many ways women compared to men resemble blacks compared to whites. This is so despite the federal legislation passed in 1963 making it illegal to pay women less for the same work (Equal Pay Act, 1963, PL 88-38). It is estimated that less than 1 percent of all women are in white-collar governmental positions which determine policy or administer programs.

The biggest increase in female workers has come from married women who now make up over 60 percent of the working women, but in 1920 made up only 23 percent of the working women (U.S.Department of Labor, 1963, p. 29). Figure 3.1 shows a comparison of the genders within both black and white races, regarding median income for full-time employees. Surely, a good deal of the difference is because women occupy lower-paid jobs, but it must not be forgotten that one reason women have lower-paying jobs may be the discrimination against them in the higher-paying jobs. Also, even when the job is the same, females seem to at times earn less money.

Several important points can be ascertained in Figure 3.1. First, it is clear that

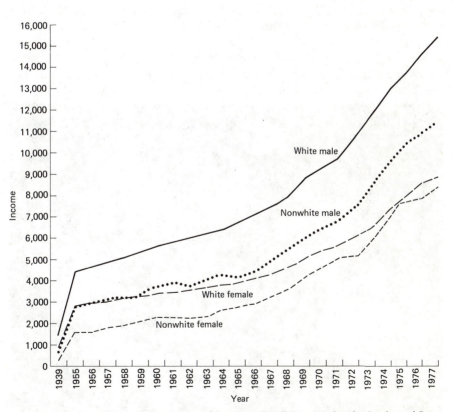

Figure 3.1. Median Wage or Salary Income of Year-Round Full-Time Workers by Gender and Race, 1939 and 1955-1977. (United States Bureau of the Census, Historical Statistics of the United States: Colonial Times to 1970, Part I, Washington, D.C., 1975; United States Bureau of the Census, Current Population Reports, Series P60, Nos. 80, 85, 90, 97, 101, 105, 114, 118. Table 56: Industry and Race.)

whites earn more than nonwhites. Second, white males are much better off compared to nonwhite males, but white females are only slightly better off compared to nonwhite females. Also, the male–female difference between whites is greater than it is between nonwhites. As far as trends go, there are tendencies for the differences between whites and nonwhites to become smaller only when one compares females. As of the present, the economic supremacy of white males is apparent.

The reader should be aware that the nineteenth-century feminist movement went into a relatively dormant stage after achieving the vote in 1920. It was in the early 1960s, around the time of the publication of *The Feminine Mystique* (Friedan, 1963) that the present feminist movement began to pick up momentum. It gained a great deal of its strength from females who participated in the New Left movements on the college campuses in the late 1960s. Such women found that females were not given equality in the New Left organizations, and they increasingly broke away and joined the feminist movement. The movement's numbers, even as recently as 1973, were estimated to be only about 75,000 members in the women's rights groups fighting for legal and other changes and perhaps 15,000 in the women's liberation groups raising the consciousness of their members (Carden, 1974).

One very important distinction needs to be made regarding the new feminist movement. Probably the most popular position is that much more is needed than

More women are entering the ranks of traditional male jobs—as this woman bus driver. Photo by Robert Olsgard, courtesy of The Minnesota Geographic Society, Project Coordinator, Tim Strick.

simply to give women equal opportunity to work in jobs that men now control. Rather, most feminists feel that the entire economic and political system needs renovation so that humanistic values take more hold and competitive and conflict relationships are reduced. Of course, women's movement people fall along a continuum on this issue, but it is well to keep in mind that they want more than a share of the male system; in many cases, they want to establish a new system. I will discuss this further in later chapters when we talk of the lack of fit of our occupational system with the dual-career family.

It is well to keep in mind at this point that the women's movement is largely staffed by highly educated females. In Carden's study of 104 members of women's groups, she found that over 90 percent had graduated from college. There have been some changes in the feminist movement in the last five years or so. Carden (in a personal communication in 1979) estimated that the grass roots basis of the movement has expanded rapidly. Small, local groups operate now in hundreds of American cities to aid in feminist issues on equal rights, abortion, rape counseling and such (Carden, 1977, 1978). On the other hand, consciousness raising groups have decreased because of the increase in public writing and discussion about gender equality. The largest organization for feminists is the National Organization for Women (NOW). It had grown to an estimated 100,000 members by 1979.

Why was it that the feminists did not gain the full equality that they sought? The basic reason, which will be elaborated in later chapters of this book, is that the traditional family-role differentiation was kept fundamentally intact. By this I mean that the female role in the family is still basically what it has been throughout our history, despite dramatic changes by small numbers. The female has the key responsibility for the home and for rearing children. While it may be common for women to be employed outside the home today, it is not common for men to stay home and care for the home and raise children. In short, women have taken on a second task without having discarded their homemaking task and, in fact, while still maintaining the clear primacy of the homemaking task. Women seem to work for two reasons mainly: (1) money and (2) to escape the cultural isolation of the home (Hoffman and Nye, 1974). The total career woman is very much a rare phenomenon even in the 1980s. Most women clearly have maintained their feeling of responsibility for the homemaker role despite their outside employment and despite the fact that they may expect some additional minor help from their husbands. Now, my contention is that as long as women have the homemaker role as their key role they are limited in the extent to which they can economically equal men. This is so because occupation, and not marriage and the family, is the male's key life role in our society. National surveys (Yankelovitch, 1974) have shown that although there is strong support for equal pay for equal work, there still is strong support for the female to stay home with her preschool children. How can the male and female be viewed the same as competitors for a job in business, or for a post in politics or religion, when their basic societal roles are so different? How can they themselves view these alternate roles the same when their backgrounds and life interests diverge significantly?

Gender Roles: Measures and Recent Changes

There are psychological and sociological approaches to the measure of gender roles. Several of the psychological measures can be found in the work of Broverman et al. (1972), Spence et al. (1975) and Bem (1974). The psychological measures focus upon what personality traits are "feminine" and/or "masculine." The feminine traits cluster about warmth and expressiveness and the masculine traits generally cluster around competence, rationality, and assertion (Broverman et al., 1972). The masculine traits are generally more highly valued in our society and this implies that the self-concepts of females should be more negative than that of males. Some of this literature also deals with "androgyny" or a mixture of femininity and masculinity. Bem (1974) defines androgyny as a *balance* of masculine and feminine traits whereas Spence et al. (1975) defines androgyny as a high score on *both* feminine and masculine traits. The reader can see that the emphasis here is on the personality of the individuals involved and not on the specific rights and duties that go with the various social role aspects of being male and female.

The sociological approach is the one more relevant to our interests. The measures of gender role here have focused heavily on equalitarianism or the extent to which males and females are judged equally in various life areas. The focus has been on two areas: (1) roles in marriage and the family; (2) roles in the occupational world. The connection of these two role areas is stressed in present-day feminist ideology as well as in sociological explanation. It should be clear by now that if females are assigned to child care and the power and prestige roles are outside the home, equality is not possible. One of the more interesting studies involving five different samples was done by Mason and Czajka (1976) and I will use it to illustrate some basic conclusions of sociological gender role analysis and to talk of some recent trends.

The Mason and Czajka study is of interest because it deals with trends in the crucial years of 1964–1974. These were the years when many other signs indicated that gender roles were undergoing radical changes in both the areas of family and marital roles and the area of occupational roles. Table 3.4 shows the reader some typical questions used to measure gender roles in both the family and occupational dimensions. Using such measures, Mason and Czajka examined five national studies that had been done between 1964 and 1974 and sought to discover if there was evidence of increasing equalitarianism in gender roles and if so, which groups were changing more than others.

Between 1964 and 1974 (the years examined by the five studies), there had been a vast amount of cultural change particularly in terms of the division of labor between the genders. More women divorced and maintained single-parent households than ever before and this presented an alternative to traditional role divisions. Wages for female employment rose sharply and attracted an unprecedented number of married women into the labor force and this too gave an alternative role model for women. The female labor force also grew because educational levels for females rose, and highly trained females are the most likely to seek employment. These

TABLE 3.4

Gender Role Items Used by Mason and Bumpass in 1970 National Study*

1. It is much better for everyone involved if the man is the achiever outside the home and the woman takes care of the home and family.
2. If anything happened to one of the children while the mother was working, she could never forgive herself.
3. A working mother can establish just as warm and secure a relationship with her children as a mother who does not work.
4. A preschool child is likely to suffer if his mother works.
5. Women are much happier if they stay at home and take care of their children.
6. Men and women should be paid the same money if they do the same work.
7. On the job, men should not refuse to work under women.
8. A woman should have exactly the same job opportunities as a man.
9. Women should be considered as seriously as men for jobs as executives or politicians or even president.

Mason and Bumpass (1975:1219). Questions 1, 3, and 4 were used in the 1977 National Opinion Research Center's annual General Social Survey and are likely to be repeated in future National Surveys by NORC. Questions 1 to 5 measure family role orientation and Questions 6 to 9 measure occupational role orientation.

general trends during this century afford a context for comprehending these more recent changes. The long-term trends are briefly presented in Tables 3.5, and 3.6.

The question raised by Mason and Czajka is: Given the changes in actual work and family relations that have occurred, is there evidence that attitudes toward gender roles have also basically changed in the 1964 to 1974 period? There are two major dimensions of gender roles measured in the questions they examined: (1) marriage and family roles and (2) labor market roles. A study done in 1970 (Mason and Bumpass, 1975) was one of the five studies examined (see Table 3.4 for the questions used) and the results showed that beliefs about possible harm to children of working women was an excellent predictor of the degree to which one would endorse traditional division of labor in the home. In short, if a woman believed that preschool children are psychologically harmed if their mother works, that woman would be likely to endorse traditional roles for all men and women and desire to stay at home herself. Interestingly, this national sample did not show strong relationships between such beliefs about maternal employment and attitudes toward female rights to equal pay and equal job opportunities in the labor market. Thus, one could believe that preschool mothers who are employed do not harm their children, but still not be any more likely than other women to endorse equal pay for women workers. This lack of association indicates that in 1970 there was no strong ideology favoring new gender roles that integrated attitudes related to possible harm to children with attitudes toward equal pay for women. If there was an integrated philosophy of equality in gender roles, such attitudes should go together more strongly than they did in this 1970 national survey. It is interesting to note that in the 1973 and 1974 national surveys examined, such attitudes were integrated to a greater extent. This would indicate that shortly after 1970 there did develop a more coherent and integrated philosophy concerning female work. This new integration is significant because it is evidence of a change in basic gender

TABLE 3.5

Number (in Thousands) of Persons in the Labor Force (Age Sixteen and Over)[a] by Gender, 1890–1979

Year	Total	MALE		FEMALE	
		Number	Percent	Number	Percent[b]
1890	21,815	18,218	83.5	3,597	16.5
1900	27,323	22,489	82.3	4,834	17.7
1910	35,749	28,738	80.4	7,011	19.6
1920	41,017	32,739	79.8	8,278	20.2
1930	48,163	37,617	78.1	10,546	21.9
1940	54,410	40,640	74.7	13,770	25.3
1950	62,221	44,426	71.4	17,795	28.6
1960	69,590	47,075	67.6	22,515	32.4
1970	85,332	54,099	63.4	31,233	36.7
1974	90,691	55,371	61.1	35,320	38.9
1979	96,842	56,559	58.4	40,283	41.6

[a]*1950–1960 data based on persons fourteen years and over.*
[b]*Total distribution may not equal 100 percent due to rounding of percentages.*
Source: 1890–1940 data: *U.S. Bureau of the Census, Historical Statistics of the United States 1789–1945* (1949:64). 1950–1974 data: U.S. *Department of Labor's Manpower Administration, Manpower Report of the President* (1974: 250–251, Table B–1). 1979 data: U.S. *Department of Labor, Bureau of Labor Statistics, 1979, REPORT 565*, No 1, First Quarter, p. 2; U.S. Department of Labor, Bureau of Labor Statistics, *News,* 1979: 2.

TABLE 3.6

Percent of Women in the Labor Force Who Are Married, 1890–1977

Year	Married (+ sep.)	Other (div., wid., single)
1890	13.9	86.1
1900	15.4	84.6
1910	24.7	75.3
1920	23.0	77.0
1930	28.9	71.1
1940	36.4	63.6
1950	52.1	47.9
1960	59.9	40.1
1970	63.4	36.6
1973	63.0	37.0
1977	61.3	38.7

SOURCE: *1890–1970 data: U.S. Bureau of the Census,* Historical Statistics of the United States: Colonial Times to 1970, Part 1 (1975: 133). 1970–1977 data: U.S. Bureau of the Census, *Statistical Abstract of the United States 1978* (1978: 404).

role attitudes. Such an acceptance of integrated equalitarian attitudes indicates that basic thinking on the question of roles is changing. The Mason and Czajka study of national samples then is helpful in supporting the view that there have been attitude changes in the 1964–1974 period, and more importantly, that these attitude changes seem integrated in ways that signal important changes in the shared female gender role conception. (See also Thornton and Freedman, 1979.)

Higher educated females have always been the most ardent supporters of greater female rights. The evidence today indicates that they still are the leaders in the feminist movement and are the strongest supporters of change. However, a related important question remains: Has the gap become larger between the college-educated females and others or have other women moved up in equalitarian views at about the same pace and thus kept the gap the same as in the past? Mason and Czajka's answer is that the gap stayed the same from 1964 to 1974. In that period, all educational subgroups of females increased in equalitarianism about the same amount. This information is also important because it allows us to conclude that there is not only increasing support for equalitarian tendencies but that the support is growing equally in all education groups. This conclusion would lead one to expect grass-roots as well as elite support for many of the equalitarian gender role changes (Carden, 1977; 1978). One of the factors that encourages equalitarian attitudes in all female groups is employment experience. Women who are employed are significantly more likely to favor equalitarian gender roles at the work place and also in the home. With over 40 million working women and with half of all married women working, such equalitarian pressures are indeed widespread. In fact, research in general would indicate that the two strongest predictors of gender role equality are educational level and employment status. The more education and employment of women, the greater the gender role equality. Figure 3.2 illustrates this relationship.

*Fig. 3.2 Some Basic Causes of Gender Role Equality**

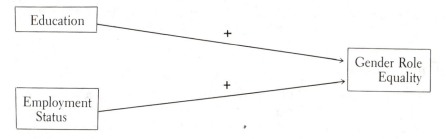

A line connecting two variables indicates a causal relation. The arrowhead shows the causal direction. A plus sign indicates a positive relation wherein as one variable goes up, so does the other and as one variable goes down, so does the other. A minus sign indicates a negative relation, i.e. as one variable goes up, the other goes down. See Appendix 4 for further explanation.

We will discuss the empirical evidence concerning the impact of maternal (and paternal) employment on preschool children in Part IV of this book, but it is still important here to stress that attitudes toward possible harm to preschoolers is one of the key indicators of crucial change in gender roles. As long as women believe that mothers of preschool children are harming those children by working outside the home, there will not be as wholehearted participation in such employment by women and this in turn will maintain male dominance in pay and power. In 1970 married females in America were split evenly on this question of "preschool children's damage" (Mason and Bumpass, 1975). More recent evidence indicates greater endorsement of preschool mothers working. (See U.S. Department of Labor, 1979, Report 575:2.)

In most Western countries there is a crucial drop at ages 25–34 in female employment. More equalitarian countries, like Sweden, show much less of a drop at ages 25–34 (Reiss, 1979). Even in Sweden, a higher proportion of women are in part-time work at that age. Relatives and day-care centers have entered in to free some preschool mothers for employment. Nevertheless, the key component in change seems to have been an attitudinal change endorsing preschool mothers as having the right to work. I would suggest that if you wish to discern how equalitarian a society is, the percentage of women employed is not as good an index as is the percentage of mothers of preschoolers who are employed. If a high proportion of the 25–34-year-old group of women are working, then one can conclude that the traditional gender roles hae been modified to accept mothers of preschoolers as employees, and the stress on motherhood has likely been reduced. (We will discuss this further in Chapter 15.)

As we shall see in Part IV in the United States the expectation of outside employment has an effect on one's desired number of children (Scanzoni, 1976a and 1976b; Waite and Stolzenberg, 1976). Thus, as employment becomes a basic part of the female role, related changes in the desired family size occurs. Obviously, such gender role changes which bear upon occupational participation and birth rates are of immense importance to the understanding of a society. We will refer back to such interrelationships in Chapter 15 but it is important here for the reader to grasp the broad outlines of this type of gender role change.

Summary and Conclusion

Virtually every segment of this book deals with areas where gender roles are centrally involved. The core distinctions made in gender roles have to do with courtship, marital, and family roles. Therefore, it is vital that we be clear on the meaning of this concept and on the current shared attitudes and behaviors that go to make up gender roles today. The modern-day conceptions of biosocial influences affords one an understanding of the alterability of the influences of whatever biological factors are operating. The processes of role socialization, as described by Mead and others, display the flexibility of learning and the interdependence of the various roles we play. It is conceivable to have a society in which males are heavily socialized to be as interested in nurturing the newborn infant as is the feamale today. What it would take to accomplish this, and whether we are willing to pay the price, is a separate set of questions which we will address later.

The importance of trends in this century toward equalitarian gender roles cannot be overemphasized. The impact on birth rates, on future occupational plans, and on marriage desires are but a few important consequences. I hasten to add that no Western society has achieved anything close to equality in gender roles (Holter, 1970). Even in Sweden (see Chapter 17) full-time employed females earn only 70 percent of what full-time employed males do—in America it is 60 percent and in the Soviet Union it is estimated to be about 65 percent (Swafford, 1978). China shows similar male–female differentials (Parish and Whyte, 1978).

The male advantage can be further seen in some recent work by McLaughlin (1978). McLaughlin found that the pay scale in an occupation was directly related to the percentage of males in that occupation. Female-dominated professions, although perhaps high in prestige, do not provide as much money as male-dominated occupations. Since over 75 percent of all males and females work in fields dominated by a single gender, this finding is quite important. One clear example of how female dominance affects the rewards in an occupation comes from the Soviet Union. Almost 80 percent of the medical doctors in Russia are now females. This was not always the case and certainly the loss of some 15 million Russian men in World War II was a key encouragement for the government to increase the proportion of female doctors. But as the percent of females in medicine rose, the pay for doctors fell. Today the medical doctor in the USSR earns about the same as a worker in industry. The top medical jobs (surgeons, administrators) still pay well but they are predominantly occupied by males. So the trends in pay for doctors in the Soviet Union follow McLaughlin's proposition that as the percent of females in an occupation rises, the pay falls. In a male-dominated culture, whatever women do will be thought of as less valuable than what men do. The reader thus should be aware that we surely have a "double standard" in our gender roles and that equalitarianism is only being approached.

References

Aronoff, Joel, and William D. Crano. 1975. A Re-examination of the Cross Cultural Principles of Task Segregation and Sex Role Differentiation in the Family," *American Sociological Review* 40 (February):12–20

Barry, Herbert, M.K. Bacon, and I.L. Child. 1957. "A Cross-Cultural Survey of Some Sex Differences in Socialization," *Journal of Abnormal and Social Psychology* 55 (November):327–332.

Bem, Sandra L. 1974. "The Measurement of Psychological Androgyny," *Journal of Consulting and Clinical Psychology* 42 (April):155–162.

Broverman, Inge K., S. R. Vogel, D. M. Broverman, F. E. Clarkson, and P. S. Rosenkrantz. 1972. "Sex Role Stereotypes: A Current Appraisal," *Journal of Social Issues* 28, No. 2:59–78.

Calhoun, Arthur W. 1945. *A Social History of the American Family*. New York: Barnes & Noble. (three vols; originally published in 1917.)

Carden, Maren L. 1974. *The New Feminist Movement*. New York: Russell Sage.

———. 1977. *Feminism in the Mid-1970s*. New York: Ford Foundation.

———. 1978. "The Proliferation of a Social Movement," pp. 179–196 in *Research in Social Movements, Conflicts and Change*. Vol. 1. Greenwich, Conn: JAI Press.

Center for the American Woman in Politics. 1979

Publication. 1521 New Hampshire Avenue, Washington, DC 20036.

Chase, Ivan D. 1975. "A Comparison of Men's and Women's Intergenerational Mobility in the U.S.," *American Sociological Review*, 40 (August): 483–505.

Coale, Ansley J., et al. 1965. *Aspects of the Analysis of Family Structure*. Princeton, NJ: Princeton University Press.

Davidson, Laurie, and Laura K. Gordon. 1979. *The Sociology of Gender*. Skokie, IL: Rand McNally.

Davis, Kingsley. 1940. "Extreme Social Isolation of a Child," *American Journal of Sociology* 45 (January): 544–564.

———. 1947. "Final Note on a Case of Extreme Isolation," *American Journal of Sociology* 50 (March): 432–437.

Ditzion, Sidney. 1953. *Marriage, Morals and Sex in America*. New York: Bookman Associates.

Duncan, Beverly, and Otis D. Duncan. 1978. *Sex Typing and Social Roles: A Research Project*. New York: Academic.

Duncan, Greg J., and James N. Morgan. 1978. "Five Thousand American Families: Patterns of Economic Progress," *Institute for Social Research* 6. Ann Arbor: University of Michigan Press.

Epstein, Cynthia F. 1970. "Encountering the Male Establishment: Sex Status Limits on Women's Careers in the Professions," *American Journal of Sociology* 75 (May): 965–982.

Featherman, David L., and R. M. Hauser. 1976. "Sexual Inequalities and Socio-Economic Achievement in the U.S., 1962–1973," *American Sociological Review*, 41 (June): 462–483.

Flavell, John H., et al. 1975. *The Development of Role-Taking and Communication Skills in Children*. New York: Wiley.

Friedan, Betty. 1963. *The Feminine Mystique*. New York: Dell.

Furstenberg, Frank F. 1966. "Industrialization and the American Family: A Look Backward," *American Sociological Review* 31 (June): 326–337.

Galenson, Marjorie. 1973. *Women and Work: An International Comparison*. Ithaca, NY: Cornell University Press.

Goldberg, Steven. 1973. *The Inevitability of Patriarchy*. New York Morrow.

Green, Richard. 1974. *Sexual Identity Conflict in Children and Adults*. New York: Basic Books.

Gross, Edward. 1968. "Plus ca change . . . ? The Sexual Structure of Occupations over Time," *Social Problems* 16 (Fall): 198–208.

Hammond, Dorothy, and Alta Jabow. 1975. "Women: Their Familial Roles in Traditional Societies," a Module of Cummings Publishing Company. Menlo Park, CA.

Hartley, Ruth E. 1960. "Children's Concepts of Male and Female Roles," *Merrill-Palmer Quarterly* 6 (January): 83–91.

Heilbrun, Alfred B. 1965. "An Empirical Test of the Modeling Theory of Sex Role Learning," *Child Development* 36 (September): 789–799.

Hill, Reuben, and Joan Aldous. 1969. "Socialization for Marriage and Parenthood," in David A. Goslin (ed.), *Handbook of Socialization Theory and Research*. Skokie, IL.: Rand McNally, pp. 885–950.

Hill, W. W. 1935. "The Status of the Hermaphrodite and Transvestite in Navaho Culture," *American Anthropologist* 37: 273–279.

Hoffman, Lois W., and F. Ivan Nye. 1974. *Working Mothers*. San Francisco: Jossey-Bass.

Holter, Harriet. 1970. *Sex Roles and Social Structure*. Oslo, Norway: University Publishers.

Johnson, Miriam. 1963. "Sex Role Learning in the Nuclear Family," *Child Development* 34 (June) pp. 319–333.

Kagan, Jerome. 1964. "Acquisition and Significance of Sex Typing and Sex Role Identity," in Martin L. Hoffman and Lois W. Hoffman (eds.), *Review of Child Development Research*. New York: Russell Sage, pp. 137–167.

———, and Howard A. Moss. 1962. *Birth to Maturity*. New York: Wiley.

Kiefer, Otto. 1934. *Sexual Life in Ancient Rome*. London: Routledge & Kegan Paul.

Kinsey, Alfred C. et al. 1953. *Sexual Behavior in the Human Female*. Phildelphia: Saunders.

Kohn, Melvin L. 1959. "Social Class and Parental Values," *American Journal of Sociology* 64 (January): 337–351

———. 1969. *Class and Conformity*. Homewood IL: Dorsey Press.

Komarovsky, Mirra. 1976. *Dilemmas of Masculinity*. New York: Norton.

Lecky, William E.H. 1955. *History of European Morals from Augustus to Charlemagne*. New York: Braziller.

Licht, Hans. 1953. *Sexual Life in Ancient Greece*. New York: Barnes & Noble.

Lopata, Helena. 1971. *Occupation: Housewife*. New York: Oxford University Press.

Lynn, David B., and William I. Sawrey. 1958. "The Effects of Father-Absence on Norwegian Boys and Girls," *Journal of Abnormal Social Psychology* 59 (September): 258–262.

Maccoby, Eleanor E. 1966. *The Development of Sex Differences.* Stanford, CA: Stanford University Press.

_____, and Carol Jacklin. 1974. *The Psychology of Sex Differences.* Stanford, CA: Stanford University Press.

Martin, M. Kay, and Barbara Voorhies. 1975. *Female of the Species.* New York: Columbia University Press. See Chap. 4, "Supernumerary Sexes," pp. 84–107.

Marwell, Gerald. 1975. "Why Ascription? Parts of a More or Less Formal Theory of the Functions and Dysfunctions of Sex Roles," *American Sociological Review* 40 (August): 445–455.

Mason, Karen, and Larry Bumpass. 1975. "U.S. Women's Sex Role Ideology, 1970," *American Journal of Sociology* 80 (March): 1212–1219.

_____, and J. L. Czajka. 1976. "Change and U. S. Women's Sex-Role Attitudes 1964–1974," *American Sociological Review* 41 (August): 573–596.

McLaughlin, Steven D. 1978. "Occupational Sex Identification and the Assessment of Male and Female Earnings Inequality," *American Sociological Review,* 43 (December): 909–921.

Mead, George H. 1934. *Mind, Self and Society.* Chicago: University of Chicago Press.

Money, John, and Anka Ehrhardt. 1972. *Man and Woman: Boy and Girl.* Baltimore: Johns Hopkins University Press.

Murdock, George P. 1967. "Ethnographic Atlas: A Summary," *Ethnology* 6 (April): 109–236.

Mussen, Paul H. 1961. "Some Antecedents and Consequents of Masculine Sex Typing in Adolescent Boys," *Psychological Monographs* 75 (No. 2): entire no. 506.

_____ 1962. "Long-Term Consequents of Masculinity of Interests in Adolescence," *Journal of Consulting Psychology* 26 (October): 435–440.

_____. (ed). 1970. *Carmichael's Manual of Child Psychology.* Vols. 1 and 2 (3rd ed.). New York: Wiley.

_____, and L. Distler. 1959. "Masculinity, Identification and Father-Son Relationships," *Journal of Abnormal Social Psychology* 59 (November): 350–356.

Nalbandov, A. V. 1964. *Reproductive Physiology.* San Francisco: W. H. Freeman.

Newton, N. 1967. "Psychological Aspects of Lactation," *New England Journal of Medicine* 277:4–12.

O'Neill, William L. 1969. *Everyone Was Brave: The Rise and Fall of Feminism in America.* Chicago: Quadrangle Books.

Osmond, Marie, and Pat Martin. 1975. "Sex and Sexism: A Comparison of Male and Female Sex-Role Attitudes," *Journal of Marriage and the Family* 37 (April): 744–758.

Parish, William L., and Martin King Whyte. 1978. *Village and Family in Contemporary China.* Chicago: University of Chicago Press.

Petros, John W. 1975. *Sex Male, Gender Masculine.* Port Washington, NY: Alfred Publishing Company.

Quadagno, David M., Robert Briscoe, and Jill S. Quadagno. 1977. "Effect of Perinatal Gonadal Hormones on Selected Nonsexual Behavior Patterns: A Critical Assessment of the Non-Human Literature," *Psychological Bulletin* 84, No. 1, : 62–80.

Queen, Stuart A., and Robert Habenstein. 1974. *The Family in Various Cultures.* (4th ed.). Philadelphia: Lippincott.

Reiss, Ira L. 1956. "The Double Standard in Premarital Sexual Intercourse: A Neglected Concept," *Social Forces* 34 (March): 224–230.

_____. 1967. *The Social Context of Premarital Sexual Permissiveness.* New York: Holt, Rinehart and Winston.

_____. 1979. "Sexuality and Gender Roles in Sweden and America: A Theoretical Perspective," in H. Lopata (ed.), *Research on the Interweave of Social Roles: Women and Men.* Greenwich, CT: JAI Press.

Rosenfeld, Rachel A. 1978. "Women's Intergenerational Occupational Mobility," *American Sociological Review,* 43 (February): 36–47.

Rossi, Alice S. 1977. "A Biosocial Perspective on Parenting," *Daedalus* (Spring): 1–31.

Scanzoni, John. 1976a. "Gender Roles and the Process of Fertility Control," *Journal of Marriage and the Family* 38 (November): 677–692.

_____. 1976b. "Sex Role Change and Influences on Birth Intentions," *Journal of Marriage and the Family,* 38 (February): 43–60.

Schlegel, Alice (ed). 1977. *Sexual Stratification: A Cross-Cultural View.* New York: Columbia University Press.

Schlesinger, Yaffa. 1977. "Sex Roles and Social Change in the Kibbutz," *Journal of Marriage and the Family* 38 (November): 771–780.

Schneider, David M., and Kathleen E. Gough (eds.). 1961. *Matrilineal Kinship.* Berkeley: University of California Press.

Shaplen, Robert. 1954. *Free Love and Heavenly Sinners.* New York: Knopf.

Spence, Janet T., Robert Helmreich, and Joy Stapp. 1975. "Ratings of Self and Peers on Sex

Role Attributes and Their Relation to Self-Esteem and Conceptions of Masculinity and Femininity," *Journal of Personality and Social Psychology* (32) No. 1:29–39.

Stryker, Sheldon. 1964. "The Interactional and Situational Approaches," in Harold T. Christensen (ed.), *Handbook on Marriage and the Family.* Skokie, IL: Rand McNally, pp. 125–170.

_____. 1968. "Identity Salience and Role Performance: the Relevence of Symbolic Interaction Theory for Family Research," *Journal of Marriage and the Family* 30 (November): 558–564.

Swafford, Michael. 1978. "Sex Differences in Soviet Earnings," *American Sociological Review,* 43 (October): 657–673.

Swedish National Bureau of Statistics, 1975. *Levnadsfërhollanden Arsbok* 1975. Stockholm: Liber Förlag, Almänna Forloget.

Thornton, Arland, and Deborah S. Freedman. 1979. "Changes in the Sex-Role Attitudes of Women: 1962–1977," *American Sociological Review* 44 (October):831–842.

U.S. Bureau of the Census. 1949. *Historical Statistics of the U.S. 1789–1945.* Washington, D.C.: Government Prnting Office.

_____. 1974. *U.S. Census of Population, 1970. Occupation by Industry.* Final Report PC (2)7c. Washington, DC: Government Printing Office.

_____. 1975. *Historical Statistics of the United States: Colonial Times to 1970, Part 1 and Part 2.* Washington, DC: Government Printing Office.

_____. 1978. *Statistical Abstract of the United States: 1978.* Washington, DC: Government Printing Office.

_____. 1979. "Money Income in 1977 of Families and Persons in the United States," *Current Population Reports* Series P-60, No. 118. Washington, DC: Government Printing Office. (See also earlier annual issues of this report.)

U.S. Department of Labor. 1963. *American Women.* Washington, DC: Government Printing Office.

_____. 1974. *Manpower Report of the President.* Washington DC: Government Printing Office.

U.S. Department of Labor, Employment & Training Administration. 1978. "Women in Traditionally Male Jobs: The Experience of Ten Public Utilities." R&D Monograph #65. Washington, D.C. Government Printing Office.

_____ Bureau of Labor Statistics. 1979. Report 565, No. 1 (First Quarter). Washington D.C.

_____, Bureau of Labor Statistics. 1979. *News.* (May 4). Government Printing Office. Washington, D.C.

U.S. Department of Labor. 1979. *Women in the Labor Force: Some New Data.* Series Report 575 (October). Washington, D.C., Government Printing Office.

Waite, Linda J., and R.M. Stolzenberg. 1976. "Intended Childbearing and Labor Force Participation of Young Women: Insights from Non-Recursive Models," *American Sociological Review* 41 (April): 235–252.

Weitz, Shirley. 1977. *Sex Roles.* New York: Oxford University Press.

Whyte, Martin K. 1978. *The Status of Women in Preindustrial Societies.* Princeton, NJ: Princeton University Press.

Wolf, Wendy C., and Neil D. Fligstein. 1979. "Sex and Authority in the Workplace: The Causes of Sexual Inequality," *American Sociological Review* 44 (April):235–252.

Yankelovich, Daniel. 1974. *The New Morality.* New York: McGraw-Hill.

Yorburg, Betty. 1974. *Sexual Identity.* New York: Wiley.

Part Two   THE GROWTH OF PARTICIPANT-RUN COURTSHIP

Courtship in the

New Land

FOUR

The Early Settlers

The earliest stories of courtship on the shores of America stress the high degree of autonomy and the participant-run quality of the system. "Speak for yourself, John," was not just what Priscilla said to John Alden when he spoke to her of another man's love; it was even more so the hallmark of the system of courtship in seventeenth century America (Calhoun, 1945, p. 52, vol. 1). Given the background of these early settlers, it is not surprising that their courtship system should have such high autonomy. The pilgrims were fleeing religious persecution. They were seeking a place where they could worship in their own fashion. They were, in a sense, rebels against the "establishment" in Europe. In addition, Protestantism in general seems to promote a more individualistic interpretation of Christianity and to stress the importance of the individual and his or her accomplishments in this world. I am sure many of the readers of this book are familiar with Max Weber's famous treatise on this topic: *The Protestant Ethic and the Spirit of Capitalism* (Weber, 1930). Weber argues that the growth of Protestantism disseminated an individualistic ethic and an emphasis on deeds, which helped promote the capitalistic economic system in Europe and America. This same individualistic ethic encouraged the growth of a relatively free courtship system.

Another factor that encouraged this freedom from parental controls on courtship was the nature of the migrations from Europe to America, from East to West, and from rural to urban areas. All three of these major types of migration were migrations of either single individuals or small nuclear families (Tibbits, 1965). Thus, the controls on courtship that go with a strong extended family never took hold here (Gordon, 1978: Chap. 7). The adventurous person who came to these shores and traveled across the country possessed a high degree of individualism, and the courtship institution reflected this in its relative freedom from parental controls.

In 1966 a young sociologist by the name of Furstenberg examined the historical evidence on the nature of the family in the first half of the nineteenth century. He found that the nineteenth-century male and female and their family relationships were remarkably high in female independence, a lack of extended family controls, and equalitarian relationships in courtship. In short, *before* industrialization really took root, there were present in America many of the characteristics of the modern-day courtship institution (for an earlier view, see Tocqueville, 1954).

Similar conclusions concerning the historical forms of American courtship can be found in other historical analyses of the family system (Greenfield, 1961). The older line of reasoning contended that we once had an extended family system in America, wherein three generations lived together in one household and farming was their means of livelihood. The Industrial Revolution in the mid-nineteenth century was viewed as the force which broke up this type of family system and replaced it with a family type more compatible with industrialization. Since industrialization demanded that workers be geographically mobile and willing to move where job opportunities existed, it meant that workers would have to be willing to leave their parents behind and thereby break up the extended family. This view is still probably very widely believed. However, Clark Tibbits (1965) examined the census data to see what year showed the greatest percent of three-generation families living together in one household. The answer was 1946, the year after World War II ended and the year of a severe housing shortage resulting from millions of returning veterans and high birth rates. Even then the percent of extended families was small. This indicates that the extended family was probably never the dominant family form in America. It probably was, and to some extent still is, a common family type among wealthy people, and perhaps because of this identification with power and prestige, it became idealized as our family form. It may be interesting for the reader to note that even in China, where the extended family had always been venerated, the best current evidence indicates that the extended family was common only among a minority of the population and usually among the wealthier groups (Coale *et al.*, 1965).

The more accurate view of the relation of industrialization to our present-day family, marital, and courtship institutions would be that many of the current characteristics of these Family Systems preceded the Industrial Revolution and helped to shape it (Laslett, 1977: Chap. 1; Seward, 1978) This is not to deny that the Industrial Revolution and the urban revolution that accompanied it were also having an impact on the entire Family System. Surely a free, autonomous dating system is encouraged by an urban setting, wherein parents do not know all the eligible mates, and by an industrial system that gives daughters and sons economic power that can be used to free themselves from parental domination. Such two-way feedback type of causation is an extremely common situation in human societies, and that is the view that is being put forth here.

To understand somewhat more fully the changes in courtship in this century, it may be best to briefly cover some older courtship customs. An interesting eighteenth-century custom called "bundling" may be a good place to start.

Gustav Vigeland "The Kiss," Vigeland-Musseet, Oslo.

Bundling to Cohabitation in Two Easy Centuries

In the mid-eighteenth century Boston was the largest city in America with a population of approximately 16,000 people. New York was second with 13,000 citizens. These statistics are important primarily for the clarity with which they show the rural nature of America 200 years ago. It may be difficult for Americans living in the 1980s, with only about 4 percent of the population living on farms, to realize that most people lived that way in the eighteenth century. In fact, the country as a whole did not pass the 50-percent urban mark until approximately 1920. Surely the styles of courting would have to adapt themselves to this change from a rural to an urban society.

One of the oldest forms of courting in rural eighteenth-century America was bundling, which flourished in New England and the mid-Atlantic states (Doten, 1938). Bundling affords an excellent illustration of how a courtship custom integrates with the basic type of social system in which it exists. Winters in New England were harsh and long, and the roads were few and difficult to travel in the winter. If a young man saw a woman who caught his eye in church, how could he get to see her during the winter months? He could with luck travel the few miles to her house on Saturday night. But to expect him to be able to return that same evening was too much. He could become lost or caught in a storm and, in any case, would arrive home quite late because no mechanical transportation was available. Thus, if courtship was to be encouraged, some method of allowing the male to stay over at the female's home was needed.

To obtain fuel in the eighteenth century meant cutting down trees and chopping up the wood. Thus, fuel could not be easily spent and was in short supply. This meant that the house that the man would visit would not be heated late into the night, and the man would therefore need blankets for warmth. The woman's parents wanted to leave the young couple alone to talk and get to know each other better, in the hope that matrimony might eventuate, but they did not have the fuel to allow them to stay up comfortably and talk. In addition, there was a shortage of beds in most households, so that the man could not be offered his own bed for the night. Very often the man would have to share a bed, and since the object was to allow him to talk to their daughter, the bed he shared would likely be hers. It was this sharing of a common bed during winter courtship in New England that came to be known as bundling.

Bundling was supposed to operate on an honor system. There were to be no intimate sexual embraces and certainly no sexual intercourse. Instead, it was a way to accommodate the man's need for lodging and to afford the couple time to talk to each other. The fuel and bed shortage thus pressured toward bundling as a courtship form. In actuality the honor system seemed to break down. At least after engagement there is good reason to suspect that sexual relations did occur in the bundling bed. This was not always easy, for the bed might be near the parents' or a sibling's bed. But the high percentage of pregnant brides in New England at this time testifies to the violation of the honor system. In Groton, Massachusetts, the Groton Church records examined by Arthur Calhoun show that of 200 weddings performed from 1761 through 1775, 66 involved confessions of fornication to the minister (Calhoun, 1945, p. 133, vol. 1). Thus, about one-third of the brides confessed their "indiscretion" at marriage, and probably more than one-third of the females had engaged in coitus because it is likely that predominantly those who were pregnant would confess fornication, since they could not otherwise have their babies baptized. Other females who were nonvirginal, but not pregnant, might well not confess fornication to the minister. For an overview of premarital pregnancy before the Twentieth century, I present Table 4.1

That this system of courtship worked to get people married is best evidenced by the fact that mothers would often defend the practice against the attacks of the clergy. One can be sure that mothers, who themselves had experienced bundling, were aware of the possibility of sexual relations. They therefore must have favored bundling because they felt it led to marriage, despite the sexual intercourse that may have occurred during engagement. One should remember that two centuries ago, engagement was a betrothal to marry and was very seldom broken. Intercourse during engagement has always been the most accepted form of sexuality outside of marriage, and the Puritans of the eighteenth century were no exception to this norm. One interpretation of this acceptance of coitus during engagement is that

TABLE 4.1
Premarital Pregnancy in America, 1680–1910

| Historical Period | TIME BETWEEN MARRIAGE AND BIRTH OF FIRST CHILD | | | | | |
	Under 6 Months		Under 8½ Months		Under 9 Months	
	%	N	%	N	%	N
–1680	3.3	511	6.8	511	8.1	663
1681–1720	6.7	445	14.1	518	12.1	1156
1721–1760	9.9	881	21.2	1146	22.5	1442
1761–1800	16.7	970	27.2	1266	33.0	1097
1801–1840	10.3	573	17.7	815	23.7	616
1841–1880	5.8	572	9.6	467	12.6	572
1881–1910	15.1	119	23.3	232	24.4	119

Source: Adapted from Smith and Hindus, 1975, p. 561. Reprinted by permission of
The Journal of Interdisciplinary History and the MIT Press, Cambridge, Mass. (See
Chapter 7 for more recent data.)

such coitus has the least likelihood of disturbing the chances for marriage or the
nature of the ongoing marital institution.

It is worth noting that the bundling custom was practiced only in winter, thus
further demonstrating that this was a custom that fit into the needs for courtship
during the rugged conditions of a New England winter. Such a custom was not
the only way to meet the courtship needs of a group during harsh winters. In the
nineteenth century people in the Midwest and Far West did not utilize such
customs, but worked out other ways of getting young people together. Many of the
settlers coming to New England and to the mid-Atlantic states came from areas
of Europe where customs similar to bundling existed, and this, too, may have
encouraged the growth of bundling there.

By the nineteenth century, as cities grew, the conditions supporting the custom
diminished. Also, the honor system seemed to break down even further, and some
parents resorted to bundling "boards" that were inserted in the middle of the bed
to separate the couple. However, if the couple wanted, such obstacles would not
be difficult to overcome. Finally, the parlor replaced the bundling bed, and by the
twentieth century, the automobile offered another place of privacy for young people.
However, it is interesting to note that Kinsey found that the most common place
for young people to have premarital coitus was the female's home (Kinsey et al.,
1953, p. 310). Thus, although many changes have occurred, the locale for sexual
intimacy has at least partially remained in the home.

The bundling custom illustrates a point that I shall make over and over in this
book, that is, that one way to understand a custom is to examine its fit with other
customs or parts of society. Such an examination of interrelationships affords one
an understanding of the factors that maintain a custom and the factors that are
likely to disrupt or change the custom. For example, with bundling one can state
that the fuel shortage, the weather, and travel conditions supported the custom as
did the desire to find a means of allowing the couple to court in private. Also, the

A nineteenth century dance hall at the "Wickedest Man's House." Photo courtesy of Harper's Weekly, *August 1868, Minnesota Historical Society, St. Paul.*

historical experience with such customs in the background of the early settlers helped support this custom. During the nineteenth century, as new settlers arrived and urbanization proceeded, these supports were weakened, and one could accurately predict the decline of such a custom. One can apply this same approach to the growth of casual dating during the 1920s, of the going-steady custom during the 1940s, and to the growth of cohabitation during the 1960s. Let us now turn to these twentieth-century changes in courtship.

Rating and Dating in the Roaring Twenties

One area where the influence of social and cultural backgrounds on dating can be examined is the area of dating on college campuses. Campus dating affords us a chance to see how societal forces impinge on the courtship processes. Over fifty years ago Willard Waller examined the way the then newer forms of courtship were operating on the campus of the Pennsylvania State University. Waller was particularly struck by the deterioration of the older forms of courtship, which led in predictable fashion to engagement and marriage. In place of this stable form of courtship he reported a "rating-dating" system. The rating-dating system consisted of mostly casual dating and was seen as largely exploitative and thrill-seeking and as not integrated with marriage. Waller felt that the old-new contrast was so sharp that he refused to call rating-dating "true" courtship, for he felt it was simply a system of dalliance and not likely to lead to engagement or marriage.

Waller discovered the rating-dating system as operating strongly in the fraternity system on the campus of the Pennsylvania State University (Waller, 1937). Each fraternity would have a ranking on campus, and people would date in accord with such a ranking. One key object in dating was to reassert one's status by showing off the high ranking of one's date. The key purpose, then, was to establish one's prestige on campus. What helped establish prestige were factors such as popularity, access to cars, money, dancing ability, and belonging to the best fraternity organizations. Serious marriage-oriented dating did occasionally occur, but when it did, it was thought not to involve these types of competitive and materialistic rating factors.

Waller's work began in the late 1920s and reflects the clash of an older with a newer form of dating. Such situations are always subject to gross misinterpretation because the observer may have a strong commitment to the older or newer system and therefore see the other one as "inadequate." Further, there is a tendency to exaggerate the nature of both the older and newer customs. Researchers who studied campus dating after Waller generally did not find support for all of his views (Lowrie, 1951). We need not conclude that Waller was one-sided and neglected to see the other characteristics of the new form of casual dating. It might be that for the campus he studied, at the time he studied it, what he found was true. But in any case, when Christensen and Johnsen (1971), Blood (1955), and Smith (1952) retested Waller's ideas, they found only minor support. All three of these researchers found that the "competitive-materialistic" basis of dating was not very powerful, and instead reported that personality factors were more important in choosing dates. The personality factors they stressed were a sense of humor, cheerfulness, being a good sport, naturalness, and considerateness. Blood did find some traces of Waller's type of ratings, but mostly among the Greek organizations, and even there they were not the dominant basis for rating or dating. Despite these changes in rating factors, it should be borne in mind that the presence of personality "rating" factors was found in all three of these replications. The replications were done on the campuses of Purdue University, the University of Michigan, and the Pennsylvania State University. Other research on specific values in mate selection was done by Hill, McGinnis, Hudson, and Henze in 1939, 1956, and 1967. The same questions were used in all three studies. They report (Hudson and Henze, 1969) a great deal of similarity in the values sought in mate selection during that twenty-eight-year period.

Then in 1960, in a study done on the campus of Iowa State University (Rogers and Havens), it was found that serious dating relationships seemed to be also in line with the same rating factors that influenced casual dating relations. It seemed that here again Waller's theory was not borne out, for Waller contended that serious dating was not based on the same rating factors as casual dating.

There is one other important point about which Waller may have been mistaken. Waller contended that the students at the Pennsylvania State University were from a very similar parental social-class background and, therefore, parental background was not a factor in the students' campus prestige rating. However, another study of an eastern technical college indicated that the Greek system selects the students from wealthier backgrounds (Levine and Sussman, 1960) and that various fraternities may compete to obtain the students from the "better" backgrounds.

A Newer Conception of Campus Dating

In 1959, after thinking about Waller's position and the new evidence that was coming in from more recent research, I decided to formulate a new conception of campus dating and to test it on the campus of the College of William and Mary (Reiss, 1965). The college was a coeducational state-supported campus with 1,800 single undergraduates. About half the students were in Greek organizations. Although one might argue that the students on this campus might differ from other campuses, it seemed to be a suitable campus to make a first test of some new ideas concerning campus dating.

The basic theoretical proposition that guided my thinking was that the dating patterns of a group will follow the social-class lines of that group and thereby encourage class endogamous dating and mating. Many earlier studies had given evidence of the validity of this proposition (Dinitz et al., 1960). One such well-known study was Hollingshead's (1949) *Elmtown's Youth*. Hollingshead found that the dating behavior of his high school sample was very much in line with social-class backgrounds; that is, the wealthier youngsters with fathers in the higher-rated occupations tended to date their own "kind" and, accordingly, the poorer youngsters dated other poor youngsters.

Now, one logical deduction from the above theoretical position is that young people on college campuses would also date in accordance with their parental social-class background. Furthermore, one could deduce that the campus social-class divisions that are formed will reflect the parental social-class background of the students. This follows, for if parental social class determines friendship and dating patterns, then it ought to determine the groups that one will be admitted into on campus, and thus the campus groups will tend to be homogeneous in respect to the parental social-class background of the members.

My position was that the rating factors, whether they be of the materialistic-competitive sort that Waller (1937) found or of the personality sort that Blood (1955) found, will reflect the social-class background of the students. In short, if one takes these rating factors only for their direct meaning as rating factors for choosing dates, then one misses the more important meaning they have as factors that help select people of the same social-class background. Certain characteristics such as possessing cars, money, or dancing ability and manners of dress and speech surely may be taken to reflect one's class background. Also, personality factors like naturalness, considerateness, and sense of humor can be conceptualized as indirectly reflecting social-class backgrounds. Different social classes place different emphasis on such personality traits. I am arguing that it is these class factors that enable one to understand the courtship system and perceive that it is more than just a rating-dating system of dalliance. I will elaborate on this as the results of my research are reviewed.

I was positing that both casual and serious dating would reflect campus and parental social class. Waller failed to see the tie to parental social class and thus thought the entire casual-dating system was aimless and would have to be distinguished from more serious dating. I am saying that even casual dating is tied in with social class and helps in making the selection of serious dates in accord with class lines. In summary, I was proposing two hypotheses: (1) Serious as well as casual dating will be in line with a campus class system; (2) the campus class system and the related dating will reflect parental class background.

METHODOLOGY OF THE STUDY

One reason I undertook this study was that the students in one of my Sociology of the Family classes did not believe that social and cultural factors had anything to do with dating. They thought dating was a purely individualistic matter. Perhaps some of you reading this book share that view. If so, this study will be of particular interest to you.

There were ten fraternities and nine sororities at William and Mary, with a total of 840 members and 151 pledges. There were 809 single, independent students. Females and males were equally represented in both the Greek and independent segments of the campus. I drew upon two groups of students to test my hypotheses. First, I obtained information on all the "Greek students" who were involved in serious-dating relationships. This was done in order to see if within such a highly organized Greek system one would find a pattern of class homogamous dating influencing serious dates. ("Serious" was defined as exclusive dating.) Second, I drew a random sample of *all* single students on campus and had them rank all the Greek organizations. I also used this sample to test the second hypothesis concerning the influence of parental social class on campus social class and campus dating. My all-Greek serious-dating sample consisted of 245 students, and my random total campus sample consisted of 144 students. Refusal rates were very low.

On the basis of the rankings by the 144 randomly chosen students, the fraternities were divided into five high- and five low-status groups and the sororities into five high- and four low-status groups. We dichotomized our rankings for simplicity's sake. The rankings of the sororities showed more agreement among the 144 total campus students than the rankings of the fraternities but both rankings were high on agreement.

FINDINGS OF THE STUDY

Table 4.2 shows the results of the basic examination of the association between the campus rankings of the males and females involved in serious-dating relationships. All 245 Greek members who were seriously dating are represented in this table. The table should be read across each row so that one notes that of the sixty high-ranked fraternity males in serious-dating relationships, 64 percent were dating females from high-ranked sororities; 12 percent were dating females from low-ranked sororities; 17 percent were dating females who were not going to

TABLE 4.2

Percentage Distribution of Types of Serious Dating Partners among Greeks in the All Greek Sample[a]

	PERCENTAGE OF EACH TYPE OF PARTNER				
	High-Ranked Greeks	Low-Ranked Greeks	Off-Campus	Independent	Number of Serious-Dating Relations[b]
High-ranked fraternities	63	12	17	8	(60)
Low-ranked fraternities	14	19	23	44	(52)
High-ranked sororities	44	8	48	0	(86)
Low-ranked sororities	15	21	45	19	(47)

[a]Significant differences exist between high- and low-ranked Greeks in their choice of a Greek dating partner and in the percent dating Greeks and in the percent dating independents. Also, a significant difference exists between fraternities and sororities in the percent dating off campus.
[b]The percent of total members involved in serious relations is not significantly different for these four groups. Going from top to bottom of the table, we find the percentages to be 31, 27, 32, 25.
Source: Reprinted from Ira L. Reiss, "Social Class and Campus Dating," Social Problems, 13:2 (Fall 1965), p. 198. Reprinted by permission of The Society for the Study of Social Problems.

this college and lived off campus, either in this town or in some other town; and 8 percent were involved in serious-dating relationships with students who were independents; that is, who were not members of Greek organizations. I mention in a footnote to the table what aspects of the table were far enough from chance results to be called statistically significant. (The reader who wants to gain a fuller understanding of statistical significance and related measures should see Appendix 2.)

As the reader studies this table, it should become clear that being high ranked goes with dating someone else high ranked and avoiding independent students. Being low ranked means that your serious-dating partner is much less likely to be a Greek and if a Greek, more likely to be low ranked. Note that while 75 percent of the high-ranked fraternity men and 52 percent of the high-ranked sorority women were seriously dating other Greeks, only 33 percent of the low-ranked fraternity men and 36 percent of the low-ranked sorority women were seriously dating other Greeks. It seems, therefore, that the Greek serious-dating system is dominated by the high-ranked Greeks, and the lower-ranked Greeks are pushed more toward dating students who are independents.

One can see in Table 4.2 that fraternity men seem more willing than sorority women to date independents. I suggest that this was due to our cultural norm that states that it is preferable for a woman to get serious with a man at her own prestige level or higher. This norm is rooted in the traditional belief that the man establishes the status level of a marriage and so women should strive to move up or remain stable by their selection of a mate. Thus, men can date independents even if the independent women are ranked below themselves, whereas women do not have normative support for such downward dating. Support for the belief that independents were generally ranked lower on campus than Greeks comes from the total campus sample of 144 students. This sample ranked independents lower than Greeks. Even the independents in the total campus sample were apt to rank themselves low!

The dating patterns seemed to indicate that independent females were ranked higher than independent males on this campus. In our total campus sample of 144 students, there were 30 independents who were seriously dating someone. Only one male independent was dating a sorority female, whereas seven female independents were dating fraternity males. Further, two-thirds of the serious dates of independent males were off campus, whereas only one-third of the serious dates of the independent females were off campus. This indicates, then, that the independent females have greater access to the higher-ranked Greek organizations and are in general more acceptable on campus. In sum then, it seems that there is a four-tiered campus class system consisting of (1) high-ranked Greeks, (2) low-ranked Greeks, (3) independent females, and (4) independent males. The dating patterns as shown in Table 4.2 are in accord with this sort of campus ranking system.

Checks were also made to see if dating in general (not just serious dating) was also in accord with this fourfold campus class system. The 144 students in the total campus sample were asked relevant questions. Two-thirds of the 144 students dated at some time in Greek organizations. Most of those who did not date in Greek organizations were independents; 60 percent of the independent males and 35 percent of the independent females did not date at all in Greek organizations. Casual dating of Greeks showed the same patterns as found for serious dating in Table 4.2.

This similar relation of both casual and serious dating to the campus rating system indicates that Waller was mistaken when he refused to call campus casual dating "true" courtship. It would appear that the same general class considerations operate in both types of dating. Casual dating may help select a general "field of eligibles" from which the individual further selects a person with whom he wishes to become serious. The basis for becoming more serious may also be class-related characteristics. Evidence for this is found in the results showing that the statistical relation of serious dating to campus social class is even stronger than the relation of casual dating to campus social class. In any case, it seems clear that casual dating is on the main track of a marriage-destined type of dating system. Even though the couple involved are not aiming at marriage, the very fact that they come from compatible groups increases their chances of finding someone with whom they will become serious.

The reasons why Greek organizations were judged high or low were probed. Sociability, intelligence, maturity, and campus activity were the most frequently mentioned ranking factors. Minor factors were good looks, good manners, dress, and dancing ability, and these were stressed more by the Greeks than by the independents. Note that these minor factors are the kind of things that Waller reported as major factors in his study at Pennsylvania State University fifty years ago. Note also that Blood and Smith found these to be minor factors in their studies during the early 1950s. However, the key point is that one would miss the real importance of any of these factors if they are taken at face value and thought to tell the entire story of dating on campus. I believe that all these factors merely reflect the overall social-class systems from which these young people come. The community social classes differ in their endorsement of these rating factors. Students may well be attracted to the campus organizations which endorse the rating factors they were brought up to value most. It is this unintended selectivity that should tend to make the various campus classes correspond to parental social classes. Thus, high parental social class increases the likelihood that one belongs to a high campus social class. This basically was the meaning of the second hypothesis, and some relevant data can be found in this research project.

I divided the fathers' occupations into low and high. High occupations were those defined as executive or professional. In the random sample, of the high Greek fraternity men, 69 percent had fathers in high-status occupations, whereas only 54 percent of the low-ranked fraternity men had such high-status fathers. Eighty percent of the high-ranked sorority women had high-ranked fathers versus 60 percent of the low-ranked sorority women. The independent male and female difference is too small (both around 40 percent) to mean anything. But the difference between the Greeks and the independents as total groups is quite large.

The sorority females have the highest-ranked father backgrounds. This may help explain their reluctance to date independent males. The data tend to support the hypothesis that parental social class determines campus social class. However, many questions are left unanswered, for one does not know exactly how this parental social-class background affects the choice of dating partners. Is it that parental social class determines both the offspring's class on campus and also directly influences the likelihood that the offspring will choose someone of a similar class? Or is it that parental social class determines campus social class and campus social class itself creates similar interests with others of the same campus class and thereby determines one's choice of a dating partner? In short, many of the details of the causal relationship are yet to be worked out. But general support for the second hypothesis does seem to be present.

SUMMARY ON RATING/DATING

I have had several purposes in going over the relation of social class and dating practices. One of them was to point out the difference between intended and unintended consequences. Note that Waller may well be correct that the intended consequences of much casual dating is exploitative, thrill centered, and prestige seeking. What Waller missed was the *unintended* consequence of defining one's social class on campus in ways that encourage the selection of dating partners with whom one may establish a serious relationship. Many women seem to realize this possible unintended consequence and, although they are interested in serious relationships, they will go out with men who are just seeking to have fun with the hope that the man will become interested, and the relationship will then become serious. In short, they realize the possibility of unintended consequences for such men. Another unintended consequence of the campus dating system may be to help increase the likelihood of class endogamy in marriage, that is, to ensure that people of similar class backgrounds will marry. If campus dating is in accord with parental social class, then it follows that it is bringing together people of similar social classes and encouraging serious relationships between them. In this fashion the "free" campus dating situation may well be indirectly controlled by parental wishes and may lead to social-class homogamy of those who fall in love and marry. For older evidence of indirect parental control see Bates (1942), Sussman (1953), and Coombs (1962). Parents usually want their children to marry someone of a similar (or higher) social class, and campus dating systems unintentionally achieve this because of the ways in which they reflect parental social class. The difference then between a parentally restricted system and our courtship institution is one of degree and not entirely one of kind.

There are difficulties in generalizing from one college in Virginia to all colleges in America. How do we know that these same findings would occur if we studied a representative group of colleges drawn at random from a listing of all colleges? The congruence of these results with other studies is one way to gain confidence in their generalizability. Krain, Cannon, and Bagford (1977) recently tested many of the same ideas on a University of Iowa sample and found support for our findings on prestige homogamy. But what about those millions of young people who are not on college campuses? Does their dating fit the same principles reflected in this study of college-student dating? What about campuses where there are no Greek organizations? The reader should be aware of the many qualifications that must be appended to any piece of research. There are no simple, unqualified answers to questions about social life, and the examination of this one small area of courtship should make the reader aware of that.

Finally, I hope this discussion has helped clarify the sociological level of analysis. Very briefly put, this level stresses that the parts of the social system (norms, values, behavior patterns, group pressures, and the like) are the key causal factors. Biological forces or psychological forces are not necessarily denied, but they are not of central concern. We utilized social factors such as parental social class and campus class as explanatory of the choice of casual and serious dates. This approach does not deny that biological and psychological factors may be involved in such choices. Rather, we simply are not directly concerned in such other factors at this point and are stressing social forces. It is this emphasis that makes this a sociological text rather than a biological or psychological one. We shall comment concerning these other levels of explanation, but our stress will remain on the social level.

Steady Dating

A steady-dating arrangement is nothing new in any courtship system that allows for dating. The bundling customs of the eighteenth century were part and parcel of a steady-dating type of relationship, which the parents hoped would lead to engagement and marriage. What is unusual in dating relations is to have people dating who do not know each other very well and who are not serious about marriage. So it is casual dating, not steady dating, that is unusual.

However, something did change in the "going-steady" area during the 1940s. Going steady became the thing to do, whereas before it was something that only a minority of people would be involved in at one time. Also, in earlier decades going steady had signified a strong commitment to matrimony and was a brief step in a couple's relationship that soon led to engagement. In the 1940s much of this changed. The middle classes adopted the going-steady custom, but not as an imminent step to engagement; rather, it was a sign of strong affection that might lead to nothing more than mutual enjoyment of each other's company. Even as recently as the early 1940s Hollingshead reported on the lack of widespread going steady in the Midwest high school he studied and the semicritical attitude many youngsters had toward such an arrangement (Hollingshead, 1949, p. 237):

> Many parents disapprove of young people keeping "steady company," for normally after they have been doing so for a few months they start to think about getting married. . . . The students deride the "steady daters" as "sappy," "moony," "sleepy," "in love," or "dopey." When people are afflicted with these emotional states, they separate themselves from their fellow students, lose interest in normal clique activity, the school, and the opposite sex except the "boy" or "girl" friend. For all practical purposes, they are lost to the adolescent world with its quixotic enthusiasms and varied group activities.

This statement makes much less sense in today's courtship world. Those who go steady or date exclusively do not think of marriage so quickly as the statement implies. There may be a social-class factor here, for going steady was more popular among teenagers of the lower classes before it became popular in the middle classes. The lower classes do marry earlier, and thus going steady is a more serious relationship in the lower classes. However, when the middle classes took over the custom in the 1940s, they took a more casual view of it; the high proportion of college-age people who are now single and have gone steady with one or more people in high school is testimony to the lack of matrimonial commitment in this custom.

Furthermore, the derisive terms given to "steady daters" no longer occur. However, as I shall shortly discuss, the term "going steady" has fallen out of use in many places and is replaced by the term "going with someone." Steady daters were once thought of as people without the courage to compete on a casual-dating basis—people who wanted a steady date for security. However, even if that were the case during World War II when there was a shortage of men, it seems less the case today when people very often go steady just out of conformity. Young people do not criticize others today for going steady. The above quote from Hollingshead indicates that going steady breaks up the ties to the peer group, but more recently going steady became a requirement of keeping ties to the peer group because so much of the dating was planned around steady couples.

What are the causes of the going-steady custom? One can name the psychological cause of security, but as a sociologist I prefer to look for causes related to group factors: social variables rather than psychological variables. On this level one is struck by the symmetry of steady dating with monogamous marriage. Steady dating involves intense and intimate contact with a person of the opposite gender. The exclusiveness seems almost imitative of our monogamous marriage system, and surely it may have been unintentionally encouraged by the young people viewing similar intimate interaction on the part of their parents. Furthermore, a going-steady custom that was not so closely tied to immediate marriage would afford a chance for a young person to legitimately try out his or her "fit" with a few individuals before having to choose a permanent life partner. As such, it seems to be a supportive custom to our monogamous marriage system in that it helps in anticipatory socialization for the marital role. Whether it helps more than some other way is a separate question.

It is rare to find any system of relationships involving courtship which would consist of only two customary forms: (1) casual dating, involving virtually no commitment to marriage with that person and (2) engagement, involving a very high commitment of marriage with that person. One would expect that intermediate forms of dating would develop in such courtship systems. Serious dating very closely tied to marriage had always been present in American society. The nineteenth and twentieth centuries introduced, via contacts made on the job and in coeducational systems, a vast increase in casual dating. The old system of largely serious dating was being modified by the addition of casual dating. Casual dating gave the individual contact with literally hundreds of dating partners. It is to be expected that some mechanism would have developed that helped in narrowing down this vast array of partners to one that you would marry. The mechanisms were the many customs such as going steady which grew up in the twentieth century. These dating forms serve as intermediate steps in commitment between casual dating and engaged dating. Such a change is what sociologists call the "restructuring" of a social situation. What happened here is that the courtship design of the nineteenth century was gradually redesigned to fit the twentieth century. I would predict that we shall find a similar series of changes occurring in some of the East European, Middle Eastern, and Asiatic countries that are now moving toward a more fully participant-run courtship institution. The very term "dating" sounds too stiff and formal for the unstructured courtship system of the 1980s. As noted earlier, the term "going steady" is not used as often today because it denotes too rigid a set of obligations. As far as I can perceive, the looser term "going with" is the most popular usage today. This term indicates that a couple are dating each other on a largely exclusive basis. However, it does not indicate the precise degree of commitment and can be used to cover a ninth grade couple who will likely "go with" each other for only a month or two, as well as a college senior couple who will likely get married to each other in a month or two. Modifiers in speech are the only hint that distinguishes the degree of commitment in "going with" couples. For example, one might indicate that a particular couple are "really" going with each other or that another couple is only "sort of" going with each other. The vagueness is deliberate, for the norms of the courtship system demand high levels of informality and of movement in and out of "going with" relationships.

Formal dating involving a male calling for a female at her dormitory or her

Photo by Shelly A. McIntire, courtesy of The Minnesota Geographic Society. Project Coordinator: Tim Strick.

home is not as common as it once was. Thus, the casual dating that goes on today is not just couple dating. What appears to be very common is a form of casual group dating, wherein a group of several males and females will be at a party, a dance, a "kegger," or a bowling alley together but not as couples. This activity is often called "going out" and not "dating" or "going with." As the evening wears on some of the males and females may pair off. Individual couples that know each other but haven't yet started to go with each other may check to be sure they will both be at a certain gathering spot. That sort of arrangement is reminiscent of the more informal forms of dating. Once couples reach the "going with each other" stage, the likelihood of more formal types of "dating" increases. However, even there the female's home figures less in today's dating because so many more young people, particularly of college age or older, have their own apartments. From 1960 to 1980 there was a vast increase in the number of households run by unmarried individuals. Thus, the parental control on courtship has noticeably altered, since so much less of it occurs within parentally visible areas.

Cohabitation: Courtship for the 1980s

All of you reading this book have lived through a dramatic change in American courtship. Starting in the late 1960s, couples who before would go home to their own rooms were now spending an increasing number of nights together. There was nothing new about having a sexual affair but there was something new in the number of couples who were not returning to their own living quarters. For college students, this was encouraged by the new rules allowing visitation in the dormitories and by the increasing number of students who rented their own apartments. The increase in age at marriage also supplied a larger number of young single adults who could cohabit. For example, in 1960 for people aged 20–24, about one quarter of the females and half the males were single. By 1978 about half the females that age and two-thirds of the males were single (U.S. Bureau of the Census, P20, 327, 1978). In addition, there was a rapid growth of young people in the late 1970s due to the postwar baby boom that began in the 1940s and went to the late 1950s.

The speed with which the popularity of this custom grew was rare indeed. Like so many of the changes in the family, cohabitation was growing in popularity not just in America but all over the Western world. Sweden has been the leader in this growth. Between 1966 and 1973 the marriage rate there dropped 40 percent. That is an almost unprecedentedly sharp drop. However, the rise in cohabiting couples more than made up the difference. Many of these couples do eventually get legally married and today such cohabiting couples make up about 15 percent of the marriage-like couples in Sweden (Trost, 1978). In America they make up only about 2 percent of the total marriage-like couples (Macklin, 1978).

Although cohabitation has grown much quicker in countries like Sweden and Denmark, it has grown at a vary rapid pace in America also. Using census data on unmarried people who reside together, one would arrive at an estimate of over 1.1 million couples living together in 1978 who are not legally married (there are 50 million legally married couples in America). Back in 1960 that estimated figure would have been 439,000 couples living together without legal marriage (Glick, 1977). In 1978, 272,000 of these cohabiting couples had children living with them. We do not know how many of these children were born into an earlier legal marriage. Over one-third of the total number of couples had shared their residence for over two years at any one time. Cohabiting individuals make up almost 4 percent of all unmarried adults (Glick and Norton, 1977:34). These government

TABLE 4.3
Unmarried Cross/Gender Couples Living Together: U.S., 1960 to 1978

YEAR	ALL UNMARRIED COUPLES	IN 2-PERSON HOUSEHOLDS	IN HOUSEHOLDS THAT INCLUDE CHILDREN
1960	439,000	242,000	197,000
1970	523,000	327,000	196,000
1977	957,000	753,000	204,000
1978	1,137,000	865,000	272,000

Source: Glick and Norton, 1977:33; and U.S. Bureau of the Census, P20, No. 336:19, 1979. Courtesy of the Population Reference Bureau.

estimates are not to be taken as precise indication of the popularity of cohabation. However, while they may include some male and female couples who are not really cohabitants (older women and boarders), they also miss some couples who live together but do not report that fact. Overall, they are the best national estimates we have.

Macklin (1978) estimates that on the basis of the various studies done on college campuses about 25 percent of all college students have cohabited. The rate varies considerably by campus and, of course, it would be higher if we examined only college seniors. Clayton and Voss (1977) examined a random sample of over 2,500 young men who registered for the draft between 1962 and 1972 and found 18 percent of them had cohabited for at least a period of six months. The rate for whites was 16 percent and for blacks was 29 percent. Most of these males were not college students and thus it is apparent that cohabitation is popular at all educational levels. In addition, studies have shown (Bower and Christopherson, 1977; Henze and Hudson, 1974) that about half of the students who have not cohabited would like to have the experience. That would leave about 25 percent who have not cohabited and would not want to. Figure 4.1 presents this overall estimate to afford the reader some overview on the popularity of this new custom among college students. In Sweden, for the general population, it is estimated that over 90 percent cohabit at some time (Trost, 1978).

Clearly, the percentage of people who have cohabited will depend on the definition one gives of cohabitation. Clayton and Voss (1977) reported 18 percent of their sample had a cohabitation experience of at least six months' duration. Had they asked their question using a three-month cutoff (as Macklin did in 1972), their rate would have been higher. Other studies (Peterman, et al., 1974) used a cutoff point of a week. It is difficult to settle upon a specific time dimension. It seems that it may be easier to ask about intentions, that is, "Did you intend to reside

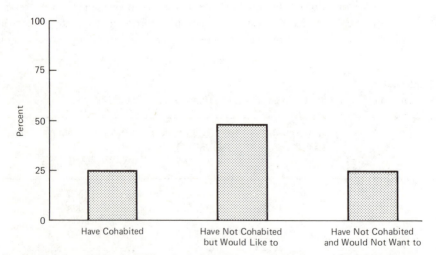

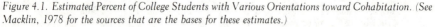

Figure 4.1. Estimated Percent of College Students with Various Orientations toward Cohabitation. (See Macklin, 1978 for the sources that are the bases for these estimates.)

together for at least several months or for an indefinite period of time? Such a question would afford us some measure of commitment to the relationship and distinguish it from a brief encounter wherein the couple expects to part shortly and is not setting up a stable relationship.

It is important to construct a typology of the cohabitation relationships. What subtypes exist and which are the most important to distinguish? One major distinction that I perceive in cohabitation concerns the attitudes of the participants toward having children while cohabiting. Most cohabiting couples do not want children and if pregnancy occurred they would abort or get legally married (Macklin, 1978). That orientation makes cohabitation simply another form of courtship. According to our definitions (see Chapter 2), for a custom to be considered a marital institution there must be legitimation of parenthood. In short, if cohabitants viewed themselves as participating in a marital institution then they would not feel that having a child must lead to a legal marriage or an abortion. It is true that they could accept having children but simply not want children and that would be different. But if they feel that having a child would *not* be acceptable and that the pregnancy must be made acceptable by performing a legal marriage, then clearly their cohabitation is not a marital type of relationship. Virtually all the studies of cohabitation from the first one done by Michael Johnson (1968) at the University of Iowa to the present day have found that cohabitants view their relationship as courtship and do not view it as an acceptable basis for having children. Cohabitants are generally by far the most efficient contraceptors of all copulating couples and thus their desire to avoid pregnancy is obvious (Johnson, 1968).

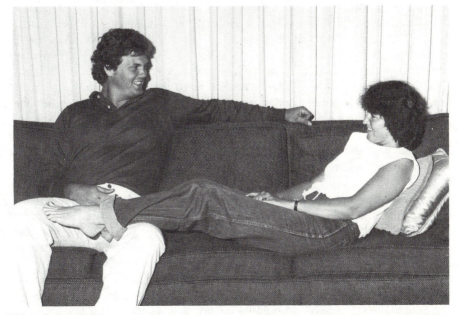

Photo by Ivan Kalman.

There is a second type of cohabitation wherein the couple do believe that it is acceptable to have a child if they so desire. Such couples would be in a marital type of relationship. For that relationship to be called part of a marital *institution* there would have to also be at least a subgroup of friends who thought alike and among whom the cohabitants lived. An institution is a social structure and necessitates more than just one couple's views. Surely, this type of nonlegal marital cohabitation occurs in our country although it is much less common than courtship cohabitation. One other difference between the nonlegal marital and courtship cohabitants would be in the expected length of time of the relationship. Courtship cohabitation would generally have expectations of shorter periods of time than the relationship would last. It is important to distinguish this type of nonlegal marital cohabitation from courtship cohabitation. Societal concerns become much stronger when children and longevity are involved and thus nonlegal marital cohabitation would be more likely to arouse legislative and judicial action. Table 4.3 indicated that almost a quarter of the cohabiting couples have children. However, many of these children were from a previous marriage and were not born to the cohabiting couple. In 1960, 45 percent of all cohabiting relations involved children, so clearly the increase in cohabitants have been largely without children. In summary, then, we would list two major types of cohabitation:

(1) Courtship cohabitation—where there is no desire for a lifelong union or any felt sanction for children to be born into the relationship;

(2) Nonlegal Marital cohabitation—where there may be a desire for a lifelong union and there is a felt sanction that children may be born into the relationship. The vast majority of cohabitation in America is of the courtship variety. For example, in a national study by Bower and Christopherson (1977), 95 percent of the cohabitants said that they desired to eventually legally marry someone. Clearly, then, those people did not view their cohabitation as an alternative to legal marriage.

Each of these types can be further subdivided if one desires. The courtship cohabitation can be divided by degree of affectionate commitment to each other. The non-legal marital cohabitation can be divided by the degree to which there is sub-group support for that sort of marital relationship. But the division into the above two basic types seems sound since it emphasizes the key distinction between courtship and marital cohabitation and thereby allows us to more clearly conceptualize the fit of this custom into the Family System.

Some of the research on cohabitation has compared the commitment of legally married people with that of cohabitants (Budd, 1976; Trost, 1978; Levine, 1979). In both America and Sweden it seems that married couples are more committed to the relationship than cohabiting couples. The rate of breakage also seems higher for cohabiting couples. Legal marriage does have a public support aspect to it that is greater than exists in most cohabiting relationships. Also, legal marriage has the deeper support of a wider range of kin and friends than does cohabitation. While this seems generally true for both types of cohabitation it would be even more the case for courtship cohabitation. Thus, if one were making comparisons between marriage and cohabitation, it would be important to specify which type of cohabitation you are talking about. So far none of the studies have done this and thus differences may be exaggerated because most of the cohabitants are of the courtship variety.

There have been even more studies comparing cohabiting people to people who are not cohabiting (Budd, 1976; Clayton and Voss, 1977; Peterman et al., 1974; Henze and Hudson, 1974; Bower and Christopherson, 1977; Macklin, 1978). Generally, the results indicate that there are many more similarities than differences between those who do and those who do not cohabit. Nevertheless, there are a few differences that consistently appear. Cohabitants are lower on measures of religiosity; cohabiting males are more emotionally supportive and cohabiting females are more assertive; and cohabitants seem higher on measures of interpersonal competence. The differences that are found generally indicate that the cohabitant is a more flexible, liberal person with high ability at establishing intimate relationships. However, the differences here are just a matter of degree and most cohabitants would overlap a great deal with more noncohabitants.

Given the kind of differences noted above one would expect that there would be less traditional division of labor in cohabiting relationships compared to legal marital relationships. Stafford et al. (1977), tested out this expectation and found that it did not hold up. They conclude that the reason for traditional division of labor in cohabiting couples is that the cohabitants had been exposed for so long to parental role models, which were traditional, that they had difficulty acting any other way. Perhaps, given a long-term commitment, cohabitants would work more at developing less traditional skills and interests. Cohabitants do display more androgynous types of personalities and interests, that is, they possess more of the traits that are traditional for the *opposite* gender and thus one would expect that they would be able to develop a nontraditional division of labor such as sharing cooking and financial responsibilities.

One interesting study done by Hill and his colleagues (1976) on four Boston colleges is worth commenting upon. One of the hypotheses checked in this study was the relative likelihood of cohabiting couples breaking up compared to couples who were having intercourse but not cohabiting and also to couples who were not having intercourse. This is of interest because there has been much speculation as to the consequences of cohabitation for a love relationship. Hill and his colleagues studied 231 couples going with each other in 1972 and restudied them six months, twelve months, and twenty-four months later. The sample was a volunteer sample from four Boston colleges. Without a randomly chosen, representative sample (see, for elaboration, Appendix 2) it is difficult to generalize to a larger group and, for example, to assume that the results hold in general for all four of the colleges that these studies come from. However, the study had the strong point of being a longitudinal study with four interviews over a two-year period. Eighty percent of the couples participated in all four interview waves. For examining change over time, this type of study is quite valuable for one can obtain measures before and after a change occurs and thus clarify cause and effect relationships (see Appendixes 3 and 4).

One hundred and three of the 231 couples broke up in the two-year period of the research project. This was a breakage rate of 45 percent in two years. For our purposes the interesting finding was that the cohabiting and noncohabiting groups all had roughly the same rate of breakage. Thus, it would seem that cohabitation does not affect the breakage rate in a love relationship. The intensity of love and intimacy were better predictors of breakups than whether one was cohabiting. A few studies have been done to see if cohabitation affects divorce rates. The results indicate that, analogous to Hill's findings, there is no association of cohabitation to divorce rates, one way or the other (Macklin, 1978).

Perhaps the most important finding of this study had to do with the male–female difference in the tendency to fall in and out of love. Which gender would you expect to be quicker to fall in and out of love? It was found that males were quicker to fall in love and males were also slower to break up a love relationship. One can "explain" this finding by asserting that women's primary role-training for marriage makes them more cautious about falling in love and also less hesitant to sever a love affair if there are serious doubts. Also, males are the aggressors in initiating a relationship and so they have in a sense chosen first and thus should fall in love first and perhaps strive more toward pursuing the goal they set for themselves. Thus, the male and female roles in our culture fit with this finding. However, one study doesn't make a theory and thus others will have to test this finding and the possible explanations of it before we can be confident about these male–female love differences. We can make sense out of any finding but not all that makes sense is true.

One other aspect of cohabitation and breakups needs to be commented upon here. The *Marvin* v. *Marvin* case (1976 and 1979) brings to the fore the issues of what obligations men and women who cohabit have to each other? Michelle and Lee Marvin lived together for seven years in a cohabiting relationship. After separating, Lee Marvin supported Michelle for eighteen months and then stopped. Michelle then sued Marvin for breach of what she asserted was a verbal contract stating that Lee would support her for life and share what wealth he earned during the seven years they lived together. The California Supreme Court ruled that if Michelle's allegation about an oral contract were true she was entitled to half the property Lee Marvin had amassed in the seven years they lived together. The case was sent back to the trial court for a hearing on the merits of Michelle's allegations. In April of 1979 the trial court ruled that Michelle should be paid $104,000 to help her reestablish herself in an occupation. Michelle had claimed she had given up her career to live with Lee Marvin. However, the judge also asserted that Michelle had not established that there was any explicit or implicit agreement such as she had claimed. The important part of this decision is not that either side won, for the verdict was a mixed victory for both parties. But rather, what is important is that the judicial decision does open up the way for cohabitation agreements having legal status. There were older rulings which argued that cohabitants have no legal rights for they haven't entered into a legal agreement and their sexual relationship is nonlegal. Now it seems that an oral promise can be considered (if proven) a basis for many types of legal rights (Lavori, 1976; MacNamara and Sagarin, 1977).

There will surely be other cases and the type of proof needed and the type of agreements that are enforceable will become clearer as judicial decisions are made.

The courts are not interested in the college cohabitation of six months—they are interested in those cohabitations that involve legal claims relevant to income and childbearing. Cohabitation involving wealthy people will likely be the substance of the cases that will be brought into court. The courts would be interested in cases involving paternity resulting from cohabitation.

The intrusion of the courts into cohabiting relationships is a fascinating development because it affords us insight into how our current legal marital system developed. Many centuries ago, our current legal marital customs arose due to the concern that children have stable adults to care for them. There was also concern for women who gave up their economic right to care for a man and then were deserted. So the current legal marriage system developed from concerns that are similar to those now confronting the courts. Our role conceptions today are changing and thus the legal precedents that will be set regarding cohabitation should differ from the older legal marital code.

In order to gain a perspective on cohabitation it is well to know something more about legal marriage. Legal marriage contracts have several essential provisions that are assumed to be in force even though they are not explicitly made known to the bride and groom. It is important to be aware of these. Most married people are not so informed. Four such legal assumptions are (Weitzman, 1978):

1. The husband is the head of the household;
2. The husband is responsible for family support;
3. The wife is responsible for domestic services; and
4. The wife is responsible for child care.

These are considered legally essential so that if a married couple formulated a written agreement that contradicted these provisions, it might well be considered illegal (Weitzman, 1978). Thus, one might have difficulty formulating an agreement that says the woman does not have to take care of the children or the man does not have to take economic responsibility. Those duties are legally implied by the marriage and cannot therefore be contradicted later by any written agreement. Now, it is possible that new decisions will be made due to changing gender roles but there is no clear indication of that as of now. If the Equal Rights Amendment were ratified, that would change these gender specific provisions of legal marriage. Also, an act of the legislature could change them. But short of such measures, these do continue to be legally valid. One can see our traditional gender roles embodied in these legal assumptions regarding marriage. Some of the older marriage codes had even stronger degrees of male dominance implied in them.

The related question then arises concerning what sort of contracts could cohabiting couples write that would be binding. It is possible that since they are not legally married, the above four legal assumptions related to a legal marriage would *not* apply. Thus, it may be that cohabitants could write many types of legally enforceable contracts, and need not abide by traditional gender role conceptions. The *Marvin* v. *Marvin* case seems to have established the possibility of the validity of such contracts. That in itself is a significant change. It is furthermore conceivable that the legal rulings on cohabiting relations will lead to changes in the legal assumptions regarding marriage.

Summary and Conclusions

The bundling and more formal courtship customs of the eighteenth and nineteenth century vanished in the twentieth century with the advent of casual dating as a mechanism for contacting potential mates. In a system that was no longer promoting formal engagements there was need for a custom such as going steady. Going steady afforded a step toward marriage but without the commitment of an engagement. Cohabitation was a further elaboration of the dating system to allow for the greater sexual openness that had developed. Like going steady it did not demand engagement and marriage but rather set a structure within which intimacy without marital commitment could occur. Both going steady and cohabitation seem to be congruent with our stress on intimate marital relationships. Such customs are one way to prepare for future marital intimacy. This is not to deny that one can remain virginal and prepare in other ways but rather it is to assert that many young people are sexually experienced today and so cohabitation seems to them a more acceptable choice.

The type of love that is involved in cohabitation may well be a more diffuse and less demanding love. If we accept that most cohabitants at any point in time are not going to marry each other and that the love they experience is therefore not necessarily viewed as the most fulfilling they are capable of, then it follows that such love relationships may be less romantic, less all demanding. It may also be that many of these cohabitants will come to accept and prefer this less demanding type of love due to the greater individual freedom it permits. Emphasis on individual freedom was a trait found to be more common among cohabitants than among those who did not cohabit (Macklin, 1978). Thus, one may surmise that the cohabitation experience may be altering our conceptions of love and developing adherents to newer love notions. Further, cohabitation may affect the nature of the husband–wife roles in marriage. Some of the changes that may follow from the cohabitation experience are more freedom to pursue separate careers and greater emphasis on outside roles as fulfilling. Whether this will lead to a change in levels of marital satisfaction is not clear. Nor is it clear how such changes may affect attitudes toward extramarital sexuality. We are in the midst of dramatic changes in our gender roles and it is well that we watch cohabitation carefully for signs of things to come.

References

Bates, Alan. 1942. "Parental Roles in Courtship," *Social Forces* 20 (May): 483–486

Blood Robert O., Jr. 1955. "A Retest of Waller's Rating Complex," *Marriage and Family Living* 17 (February):41–47.

Bower, Donald W., and Victor A. Christopherson. 1977. "University Student Cohabitation: A Regional Comparison of Selected Attitudes and Behavior," *Journal of Marriage and the Family* 39 (August):447–453.

Budd, L. S. 1976. "Problems, Disclosure, and Commitment of Cohabiting and Married Couples," unpublished doctoral dissertation. University of Minnesota.

Calhoun, Arthur W. 1945. *A Social History of the American Family;* 3 vols. New York: Barnes & Noble. (Originally published in 1917.)

Christensen, Harold T., and Kathryn Johnsen. 1971. *Marriage and the Family.* New York: Ronald.

Clayton, Richard R., and Harwin L. Voss. 1977. "Shacking Up: Cohabitation in the 1970's," *Journal of Marriage and the Family* 39.2 (May): 273–283.

Coale, Ansley J., et al. 1965. *Aspects of the Analysis of Family Structure*. Princeton, NJ.: Princeton University Press.

Coombs, Robert H. 1962. "Reinforcement of Values in the Parental Home as a Factor in Mate Selection," *Marriage and Family Living* 24 (May): 155–157.

Dinitz, Simon, et al. 1960. "Mate Selection and Social Class: Changes During the Past Quarter Century," *Marriage and Family Living* 22 (November): 348–351.

Doten, Dana. 1938. *The Art of Bundling*. New York: Holt, Rinehart and Winston.

Furstenberg, Frank F. 1966. "Industrialization and the American Family: A Look Backward," *American Sociological Review* 31 (June): 326–337.

Glick, Paul C. 1975. "A Demographer Looks at American Families," *Journal of Marriage and the Family* 37 (February):15–28.

_____, and Arthur J. Norton. 1977. "Marrying, Divorcing, and Living Together in the U.S. Today," *Population Bulletin* 32 (October):1–39.

Gordon, Michael. 1978. *The American Family: Past, Present and Future*. New York: Random House.

_____, and Tamara Haraven. 1973. "New Social History of the Family," *Journal of Marriage and the Family* 35 (special section) (August):393–495.

Greenfield, Sidney M. 1961. "Industrialization and the Family in Sociological Theory," *American Journal of Sociology* 67 (November):312–327.

Henze, Laura F., and John W. Hudson. 1974. "Personal and Family Characteristics of Cohabiting and Noncohabiting College Students," *Journal of Marriage and the Family* 36 (November): 722–737.

Hill, Charles T., Zick Rubin, and Letitia Anne Peplou. 1976. "Breakups Before Marriage: The End of 103 Affairs," *Journal of Social Issues* 32.1 (January):147–168.

Hollingshead, August B. 1949. *Elmtown's Youth*. New York: Wiley.

Hudson, John W., and Laura Henze. 1969. "Campus Values in Mate Selection: A Replication,"*Journal of Marriage and the Family* 31 (November):772–775.

Johnson, Michael P. 1968. "Courtship and Commitment: A Study of Cohabitation on a University Campus," Master's thesis, University of Iowa, Iowa City.

Kinsey, Alfred C., et al. 1953. *Sexual Behavior in the Human Female*. Philadelphia: Saunders.

Krain, M., et al. 1977. "Rating-Dating or Simply Prestige Homogamy?" *Journal of Marriage and the Family* 39 (November): 663–677.

Larson, Richard F., and Gerald R. Leslie. 1968. "Prestige Influences in Serious Dating Relationships of University Students," *Social Forces* 47 (December): 195–202.

Laslett, Peter. 1977. *Family Life and Illicit Love in Earlier Generations*. Cambridge, England: Cambridge University Press.

Lavori, N. 1976. *Living Together, Married or Single: Your Legal Rights*. New York: Harper & Row.

Lewin, Bo. 1979. *Om Ogift Samboende i Sverige* (On unmarried cohabitation in Sweden). Ph.D. dissertation, Uppsala University.

Levine, Gene N., and Leila A. Sussmann. 1960. "Social Change and Sociability in Fraternity Pledging," *American Journal of Sociology* 65 (January): 391–399.

Lowrie, Samuel H. 1951. "Dating Theories and Student Responses," *American Sociological Review* 16 (June):334–340

Macklin, Eleanor D. 1972. "Heterosexual Cohabitation Among Unmarried College Students," *Family Coordinator* 21 (October):463–473.

_____. 1976 "Unmarried Heterosexual Cohabitation on the University Campus." pp. 108–141 in J. Wiseman, *The Social Psychology of Sex*. New York: Harper & Row.

_____. 1978. "Nonmarital Heterosexual Cohabitation," *Marriage and Family Review* 1.2 (March/April):1–12.

MacNamara, Donald E. J., and Edward Sagarin. 1977. *Sex, Crime and the Law*. New York: Free Press.

Peterman, Don J., Carl A. Ridley, and Scott M. Anderson. 1974. "A Comparison of Cohabiting/Non-Cohabiting College Students," *Journal of Marriage and the Family* 36 (May): 344–354.

Rabb, Theodore K., and Robert I. Rotberg (eds.). 1971. *The Family in History: Interdisciplinary Essays*. New York: Harper Torchbooks.

Reiss, Ira L. 1965. "Social Class and Campus Dating," *Social Problems* 13 (Fall):193–205.

Ridley, Carl A., Dan J. Peterman, and Arthur W. Avery. 1978. "Cohabitation: Does It Make For a Better Marriage?" *Family Coordinator* 27 (April): 129–136.

Rogers, Everett M., and A. Eugene Havens. 1960. "Prestige Rating and Mate Selection on a College Campus," *Marriage and Family Living* 22 (February):55–59.

Seward, Rudy R. 1978. *The American Family: A Demographic History.* Beverly Hills, CA: Sage Publications.

Smith, Daniel Scott, and Michael S. Hindus. 1975. "Premarital Pregnancy in America, 1640–1971: An Overview and Interpretation," *Journal of Interdisciplinary History* 4 (Spring): 537–570.

Smith, William M., Jr. 1952. "Rating and Dating: A Restudy," *Marriage and Family Living* 14 (November):312–317.

Stafford, Rebecca, Elaine Backman, and Pamela V. Debona. 1977. "The Division of Labor Among Cohabiting and Married Couples," *Journal of Marriage and the Family* 39 (February):43–57.

Sussman, Marvin. 1953. "Parental Participation in Mate Selection and Its Effect Upon Family Continuity," *Social Forces* 32 (October): 77–81.

Tibbits, Clark. 1965. "The Older Family Member in American Society," pp. 1–11 in H. Lee Jacobs (ed.), *The Older Person in the Family: Challenges and Conflicts.* Iowa City: The Institute of Gerontology.

Tocqueville, Alexis de. 1954. *Democracy in America.* New York: Vintage Books. (Originally published as four volumes between 1835 and 1840.)

Trost, Jan. 1975. "Married and Unmarried Cohabitation: The Case of Sweden with Some Comparisons," *Journal of Marriage and the Family* 37 (August): 677–682.

_____. 1978. "Attitudes Toward and Occurrence of Cohabitation Without Marriage," *Journal of Marriage and the Family* 40 (May): 393–400.

U.S. Bureau of the Census. 1978. *Current Population Reports* P-20, No.327. Washington, DC: Government Printing Office.

_____. 1979. *Current Population Reports* P-20, No.336. Washington, DC: Government Printing Office.

Waller, Willard. 1937. "The Rating and Dating Complex," *American Sociological Review* 2 (October): 727–734.

Weber, Max. 1930. *The Protestant Ethic and the Spirit of Capitalism.* London: Allen and Unwin. (Originally published in 1904.)

Weitzman, Lenore J. 1978. *The Marriage Contract.* Englewood Cliffs, NJ: Prentice-Hall.

_____, et al. 1978. "Contracts for Intimate Relationships," *Alternative Lifestyles* 1.3 (August): 303–378.

Yllo, Kersti A. 1978. "Nonmarital Cohabitation," *Alternative Lifestyles* 1.1 (February):37–54.

Sociological Perspective on Love

FIVE

Introduction

Few phrases are more powerful influences on behavior than "I love you." Such a declaration can alter one's life plans, change one's sexual orientation, and affect one's self-esteem! But the question arises as to how common this love potential is, how it has changed over time, and how one falls in love in the first place. This chapter will focus on these concerns.

PLATO'S INFLUENCE ON WESTERN LOVE NOTIONS

One of the earliest sources of Western love conceptions is in the fifth-century B.C. writings of the Greek philosopher Plato. In the dialogue *Symposium* Plato develops his beliefs about love and thereby reveals what some members of the upper classes in Athens thought about love at that time. Plato felt that love, more than any other force, would inspire virtue (Plato, 1956, p. 178*b*):

> For the principle which ought to be the guide of men who would nobly live—that principle, I say, neither kindred, nor honor, nor wealth, nor any other motive is able to implant so well as love . . . a lover who is detected in doing any dishonorable act, or submitting through cowardice when any dishonor is done to him by another, will be more pained at being detected by his beloved than at being seen by his father, or by his companions, or by anyone else.

Love then is seen as a vital part of human society, for it is the best guarantee of human virtue. But Plato goes on and poses the question as to which type of love is the best and is most likely to spur man to virtuous deeds. He distinguishes two types, which he calls (1) common and (2) heavenly (Plato, 1956, pp. 180c, 181c).

> The Love who is the offspring of the *common* Aphrodite is essentially common, and has no discrimination, being such as the meaner sort of men feel, and is apt to be

Aphrodite. Photo by Michael Perry.

of women as well as of youths, and is of the body rather than of the soul . . . But the offspring of the *heavenly* Aphrodite is derived from a mother in whose birth the female has no part—she is from the male only; this is that love which is of youths, and the goddess being older, there is nothing of wantonness in her.

This may surprise Americans today but the preferred form of love to Plato was homosexual. Homosexual love was viewed as a love more involved with the soul, the intellect, and reason, than with the body. The common type of love can be heterosexual or homosexual, but is ranked lower because it stresses physical pleasure above spiritual pleasure. It is this emphasis on love of the soul and not the body that has brought the term "platonic" love, down even to our day, to mean a love without sexuality. But, as we can see above, it more correctly means a homosexual love wherein sexual pleasures are of secondary consideration. Plato felt "true" love was a lasting love and that time was its best test. Heavenly love fit those requirements best.

Later in the dialogue Plato offers a legend to support his conception of love. Whether he intended this literally is doubtful. I believe he intended it to be taken allegorically. He recounts a time in ancient days when there existed men, women, and hermaphrodites. But all three of these creatures had double the usual number of legs, arms, heads, and sex organs. Zeus became angry with these people and decided to punish them by cutting them all in half. This ancient division led to a constant yearning to be whole again, a vague malaise pressuring one to find one's other half. Love then is the desire to secure one's complementary part. Given an equal division of the ancient world into the three original creatures, then at least two-thirds of the people in the world, after the division by Zeus, should be homosexually inclined. This is so, for cutting the original man in half produced two men who would seek homosexual relations; cutting the original woman in half would produce two women who would seek homosexual relations; and cutting the original hermaphrodite in half would produce a man and a woman who would seek heterosexual relations. The hermaphrodite halves are the heterosexuals, and they are the people who seek the common variety of love. Some of the homosexual halves seek the preferred heavenly variety of love. As one can see, this allegory gives the basis for homosexuality and defines love as the seeking of what is missing in one's self. It is perhaps the oldest statement of the theory that people seek in love what they are lacking in themselves. It is well to note here that Plato's direct statement of heavenly love speaks only of male homosexual love. Since the dialogue is written from the male perspective, one can only assume that the same two types of love would apply also to females. The lower status of females in ancient Greek society helps explain this male orientation

Despite the fact that Plato was speaking of homosexual as well as heterosexual love, it is clear that his ideas about love are applicable to our present-day conception of love. In fact, the Platonic conception of love was quite influential in shaping present-day notions. Before we trace that influence, let us briefly turn to Rome and see how, several centuries after Plato, the Mediterranean world produced another major figure in the historical development of Western love notions.

OVID'S INFLUENCE ON WESTERN LOVE NOTIONS

Of course, it should be clear that just as Plato reflected predominantly upper-class Athenian cultures of the fifth century B.C., Ovid reflected the upper-class Roman culture of the first century after Christ. These men influenced future generations not solely by their own writings, but also by the force of the influence of the many other contemporaries who shared these same views with them.

Ovid's most famous work is his *Art of Love*. In that book he presented a view of love quite in contrast to that of Plato. Love to Ovid was sensual. It was not romantic or intellectual in any deep and lasting sense. It was not the fulfillment of one's wholeness. Love involved a type of warfare and jealousy. It was a game of mutual deceit in which one would often pretend to be pale, unable to sleep or to eat. One would try to win the attention of the other person for the physical pleasures involved. Love was also heterosexual to Ovid. What Ovid describes as his view of love is what Plato called common love and which Plato rejected as being of inferior quality to heavenly love.

The love affairs of which both Plato and Ovid wrote were largely adulterous love affairs. A free participant-run courtship institution was not present for the ruling classes, and parental control was much stronger than now. Thus, Ovid is talking of a man's love for a married woman. Here is a passage addressed to a married woman who must go to a party attended by both her husband and her lover. The lover advises her as follows (Ovid, 1957, *The Loves*, Book 1, Chap. 4, lines 12–54):

> . . . get there before him, and when he reclines, you beside him,
> Modestly on the couch, give my foot just a touch,
> Watch me for every nod, for every facial expression,
> Catch my signs and return them, never saying a word.
> I can talk with my eyebrows and spell out words with my fingers,
> I can make you a sign, dipping my finger in wine.
> When you think of the tumbles we've had in the hay together,
> Touch your cheek with your hand; then I will understand.
> If you're a little bit cross with the way I may be behaving,
> Let your finger-tip rest light on the lobe of an ear.
> If, on the other hand, what I am saying should please you,
> Darling, keep turning your ring; symbol enough that will be.
> . . . Let him drink all he wants; keep urging him, only don't kiss him.
> Keep on filling his glass, secretly, if you can.
> Once he passes out cold, perhaps we can figure out something—
> Time and circumstance maybe will give us a chance.

Beside the emphasis on the intrigues required to escape the confines of one's marriage, there is a good deal of advice as to how to make oneself more attractive. Here is what Ovid offers to the Roman woman of his day (Ovid, 1957, *The Art of Love*, Book 3, lines 255–286):

> Faults of the face or physique call for attempts at disguise.
> If you are short, sit down, lest, standing, you seem to be sitting,
> Little as you may be, stretch out full length on your couch
> Even here, if you fear some critic might notice your stature,
> See that a cover is thrown, hide yourself under a spread.
> If you're the lanky type, wear somewhat billowy garments,
> Loosely let the robe fall from the shoulders down.
> If you're inclined to be pale, wear stripes of scarlet or crimson,
> If you're inclined to be dark, white is an absolute must.
> Let an ugly foot hide in a snow-covered sandal.
> If your ankles are thick, don't be unlacing your shoes.
> Do your collarbones show? Then wear a clasp at each shoulder.
> Have you a bust too flat? Bandages ought to fix that.
> If your fingers are fat, or your fingernails brittle and ugly,
> Watch what you do when you talk; don't wave your hands in the air.
> Eat a lozenge or two if you think your breath is offensive,
> If you have something to say, speak from some distance away.
> If a tooth is too black or too large, or the least bit uneven,
> Pay no attention to jokes; laughter might give you away.
> Who would believe it? The girls must learn to govern their laughter.
> Even in this respect tact is required, and control.
> Do not open the mouth too wide, like a braying she-jackass,
> Show your dimples and teeth, hardly much more than a smile.
> Do not shake your sides or slap your thigh in amusement—
> Feminine, that's the idea; giggle or titter, no more.

Ovid goes further and gives advice on drinking when one is pursuing a love object (Ovid, 1957, *The Remedies for Love*, lines 804–810):

> Wine prepares the heart for love, if you don't overdo it,
> If your spirits are not deadened and buried in wine.
> Fire can be fanned by a wind, as fire, by a wind, is extinguished,
> A gentler breeze fans the flame, a heavier puts it to death.
> Either get thoroughly drunk, or be a teetotal abstainer:
> Anything in between causes the passions to rise.

Finally, the pleasure emphasis of the entire love "game" is clear in the following lines (Ovid, 1957, *The Loves*, Book 2, Chap. 10, lines 26–38):

> Show me the girl who can say I couldn't answer her need,
> More than once in the night I have risen to every occasion,
> Risen, again at dawn, a thoroughly competent man.
> Lucky the man who dies in duels with Venus as second.
> Grant me, gods, such an end, if I must die in my bed.
> Let the soldier expose his breast to the darts of the foeman,
> Let his crimson blood buy him a glorious name,
> Let the trader seek wealth, and die in the midst of a shipwreck,
> Thirsting for more than gain, drinking the salt of the sea.
> But as for me, let me go in the act of coming to Venus:
> In more senses than one, let my last dying be done.
> And at my funeral rites, let one of the mourners bear witness:
> "That was the way, we know, that he would have wanted to go."

Here, as in Plato's writings, the male perspective is clearly emphasized and the female viewpoint is only of secondary interest. This orientation reflects the male dominance in both Athens and Rome.

LOVE IN THE TWELFTH CENTURY

The union of the spiritual quality of Platonic love and the sensual quality of Ovidian love occurred in about the tenth century in Europe. The Platonic version of love entered Moslem Spain via wandering Spanish poets. Duke William IX of Aquitaine knew Spanish culture and became one of the first French troubadours. He introduced some of the Platonic and Ovidian aspects that were increasingly being circulated, with the revived interest at this time in studying Greek and Roman writings. William IX's granddaughter was the famous Queen of France and England, Eleanor of Aquitaine, and Eleanor's son was the equally renowned Richard the Lion Hearted. (For a popular historical account of romantic love see Hunt, 1959; Day, 1954, or Queen and Habenstein, 1974.) Richard's stepsister was Marie, the countess of Champagne, and it was she who had her chaplain write what has come down to us as the oldest document of European romantic love. The reader should note that there are very large gaps in our historical understanding of the love in the Western World over the past 25 centuries. I am merely touching upon some of the key writings and speculations as to how they interrelate.

Marie asked her chaplain, Andrew, to write down the twelfth-century conception of love that was present in the courts of France. This book, supposedly written about 1184 by Andreas Capellanus (Andrew the chaplain), is known as the *Art of Courtly Love*. The book is written as advice on the nature of love to a young man by the name of Walter. The elements of both Plato and Ovid are clearly present in this work, as are the elements of present-day romantic love. However, one should remember that in the twelfth century the love relationship was still extramarital and consisted usually of a married woman and a married (or single) knight. Love was not a basis for marriage. Marriages were largely economically based at this ruling-class level, and love affairs were therefore extramarital.

The Ovidian influence can be seen in Andreas's definition of love (Capellanus, 1959, p. 28):

> Love is a certain inborn suffering derived from the sight of and excessive meditation upon the beauty of the opposite sex, which causes each one to wish above all things the embraces of the other and by common desire to carry out all of love's precepts in the other's embrace.

Platonic influence is also present, for Andreas says (p. 61) ". . . love . . . the root and principal cause of everything good. . . ." So he, in some measure, agrees with Plato that love is the key cause of man's virtues, but unlike Plato he is talking of heterosexual love and unlike Plato he also is talking of love with a very strong and active sexual component.

Andreas believes that passion must be moderated, and too much passion can be a bar to love. The way to acquire love is fivefold: One must have (1) a beautiful figure, (2) ready speech, (3) excellent character, (4) great wealth, and (5) generosity. In a sense these are the "rating" factors of twelfth-century love relations, analogous to those found by Waller (1937) and others in the early twentieth century (see Chapter 4). The most important factor, Andreas states, is excellence of character. With a fine enough character, even class lines can be crossed. Here, too, we have a similarity to the courtship patterns of today. Social class was an important limiting factor to love affairs in the twelfth century—to an even greater extent than it is in the twentieth-century American society. However, it still was possible to cross class lines if one had some compensating factor, such as an excellent character. In fact, the bulk of the book of Andreas is devoted to nine sections, each one of which tells one how to carry out a love affair under a different social-class combination. Only three social classes were considered capable of experiencing love: the upper nobility, the lower nobility, and the middle or business classes. The lower classes and farmers were considered too animalistic to carry out love affairs. Now the three eligible classes were examined by Andreas in all nine logical ways that they can combine with one another. Andreas does recommend that one stay within his own social class, but six of his nine essays instruct one how to behave in case he violates the class homogamy norms. For example, if your partner is from a lower class than yourself, then you can be blunter and less formal, and it is suggested that the love will probably not last as long.

The love relationship itself proceeded in four stages that were titled by Andreas as (1) the giving of hope, (2) the granting of a kiss, (3) the enjoyment of an embrace, and (4) the yielding of the whole person. The female controls the speed of progress, and she can back out entirely at anytime before the last stage. It is clear from Andreas' description that romantic love was usually consummated by sexual intercourse. It is also true that there were places and times where romantic love stressed more the Platonic elements and sexual intercourse did not occur (Castiglione, 1959). This seems to have been the case in Barcelona, Spain, under King Juan of Aragon and his wife. There the love affair of the wife was approved by the husband and consisted of talking about the nature of love. Also, the thirteenth-century Italians had some nonsexual love affairs such as that of Dante Alighieri and Beatrice. However, at the time Dante was involved in an unconsummated love affair with Beatrice, he had a wife and a mistress.

Andreas does delineate two types of love. He calls the first "pure," and it is a type that does not involve sexual intercourse. The second is called "mixed love," and it does involve sexual intercourse. He calls both these types real love, but states that pure love lasts only a brief time until it changes into the mixed type of love, and he cynically comments that even the mixed love does not last long after it is consummated. There is a preference for some spiritual element being present in the love relationship of either the pure or mixed variety, but it is clear that both varieties have a sensual element. Even the pure lovers may kiss and pet and sleep nude with each other on occasion. While it is true that the discriminate female is valued, the indiscriminate female is valued more than the female who never engaged in a love affair. The myth of what the afterlife is like supports this ranking, for the female who has never loved suffers the worst fate in the next world.

The rules of love are laid down neatly in the form of thirty-one statements. I reproduce them here, for they clearly show the connections of twelfth-century romantic love to its past and to the present day (Capellanus, 1959, pp. 184–186):

1. Marriage is no real excuse for not loving [someone else besides one's mate].
2. He who is not jealous cannot love.
3. No one can be bound by a double love.
4. It is well known that love is always increasing or decreasing.
5. That which a lover takes against the will of his beloved has no relish.
6. Boys do not love until they arrive at the age of maturity [eighteen for boys and twelve for girls].
7. When one lover dies, a widowhood of two years is required of the survivor.
8. No one should be deprived of love without the very best of reasons.
9. No one can love unless he is impelled by the persuasion of love.
10. Love is always a stranger in the home of avarice.
11. It is not proper to love any woman whom one would be ashamed to seek to marry [such as a close relative].
12. A true lover does not desire to embrace in love anyone except his beloved.

13. When made public, love rarely endures.
14. The easy attainment of love makes it of little value; difficulty of attainment makes it prized.
15. Every lover regularly turns pale in the presence of his beloved.
16. When a lover suddenly catches sight of his beloved, his heart palpitates.
17. A new love puts to flight an old one.
18. Good character alone makes any man worthy of love.
19. If love diminishes, it quickly fails and rarely revives.
20. A man in love is always apprehensive.
21. Real jealousy always increases the feeling of love.
22. Jealousy, and therefore love, are increased when one suspects his beloved.
23. He whom the thought of love vexes eats and sleeps very little.
24. Every act of a lover ends in the thought of his beloved.
25. A true lover considers nothing good except what he thinks will please his beloved.
26. Love can deny nothing to love.
27. A lover can never have enough of the solaces of his beloved.
28. A slight presumption causes a lover to suspect his beloved.
29. A man who is vexed by too much passion usually does not love.
30. A true lover is constantly and without intermission possessed by the thought of his beloved.
31. Nothing forbids one woman being loved by two men or one man by two women [but not actively at the same time].

These rules supposedly came from the court of King Arthur, but more than likely they were a consolidation of rulings from the many courts of love which were held to debate the issue of what the rules of love were. These courts would be composed of noblewomen like the countess of Champagne and her lady friends. They would debate these matters at great length and issue formal decrees concerning the nature of love. It is likely that those debates led to this collection of thirty-one rules which Marie had Andreas put down in writing. One can detect clearly in these thirty-one rules the Platonic stress on spiritual qualities and just as clearly the Ovidian stress on the outward signs of love and the physical gratifications of love.

The reader should remember that these are rules composed by aristocratic females, and thus males likely stressed the physical aspects more in their own thoughts and behaviors. One should not be deceived into thinking that since there was romantic love, the double standard was absent and females were given, in love, the same rights as males. This was not the case as can be seen in many of the comments Andreas makes (Capellanus, 1959, pp. 161–162):

A woman must therefore be careful not to be tripped up by the snares of a deceitful lover, because so many of them do not desire to be loved, but merely to gratify their passions or to boast in company of their conquests over women.
    But what if the man should be unfaithful to his beloved—not with the idea of finding a new love, but because he has been driven to it by an irresistible passion for another woman? What for instance, if chance should present to him an unknown

woman in a convenient place or what if at a time when Venus is urging him on to that which I am talking about he should meet with a little strumpet or somebody's servant girl? Should he, just because he played with her in the grass, lose the love of his beloved? We can say without fear of contradiction that just for this a lover is not considered unworthy of the love of his beloved unless he indulges in so many excesses with a number of women that we may conclude that he is overpassionate.

. . . all things in this world which are by their nature immodest are more readily allowed to men, in the case of a woman they are, because of the decency of the modest sex, considered so disgraceful that after a woman has indulged the passions of several men everybody looks upon her as an unclean strumpet unfit to associate with other ladies.

It is clear from the above that the female must watch her reputation and control her sexuality much more than the male, even under the romantic love system. The male is allowed other sexual outlets; the female has to be cautious even when involved in love affairs. Andreas asserts that premarital love affairs are particularly forbidden, for they lead to the husband despising his nonvirginal wife, but extramarital love affairs are more tolerated, for the deceit can be more easily concealed since the female is already nonvirginal.

It is somewhat of a historical mystery as to what caused the rise of romantic love in the tenth through twelfth centuries in Europe. (For one point of view see De Rougemont, 1940.) Surely it was in part the rediscovery of the Greek and Roman writings; in part, a reaction to the brutality of the age; in part, a reaction to the scarcity of noblewomen in castles with many bachelor knights; and in part, perhaps an anti-church reaction. But whatever the causes were, the romantic love development of those centuries led to a tender, sexual relationship between men and women which was not so common in other contexts. It led to a legitimization of sexuality outside of marriage for the female. Female sexuality is historically most closely linked with affection, and the romantic love movement added an affectional motivation for female sexuality. This is a very important historical event if we are to understand present-day love and sexual customs.

From the twelfth to the twentieth century many changes in romantic love occurred. First the notion became more widely adopted. Perhaps imitation of the ruling classes, perhaps the presence of similar causal conditions led to this. In any case, as the romantic love notion spread, it created problems with the common man, for he wanted romantic love, but he did not want to allow his wife to engage in extramarital sexuality. The resolution of this dilemma was gradually worked out by shifting romantic love to the premarital period and making it the basis for marriage. This was a long and involved process, and I shall not go into the historical details here, except to note that the emphasis upon premarital love was a new conception. Since marriages were arranged, love was not the key basis of marriage and was not encouraged before engagement. Soon, though, couples began to demand more power in the choice of an engagement partner, for they now wanted to love that person. In this way romantic love helped bring about the freer courtship customs that, even in the seventeenth century, were widespread among the European settlers who came to America.

In the above fashion the originally extramarital romantic love became premarital. The spiritual and sensual elements in romantic love are still present, and Plato and Ovid are surely alive in their influence. There are those who stress an idealistic version of romantic love and argue that sexuality corrupts such pure feelings, and there are others (increasingly in the majority) who argue that it is precisely the presence of romantic love feelings that justifies sexual contact of various degrees (Reiss, 1967: Chap. 5). The idealistic, emotional qualities of romantic love are still present, but today's generation seems to have striven to give reason somewhat more control over the situation. We shall look at some evidence of this later.

Cross-cultural Views on Love

The brand of love described in Andreas's thirty-one rules of love is the Western variety of a universal species. Love is universally recognized in human society. The differences exist on two levels: (1) the conditions under which and the extent to which love is encouraged and (2) the cultural "dressing" given to love. Let it be clear that I am here talking only of heterosexual love and not of homosexual love, parental love, love of friends, love of God, and so forth. One could include these other types of love, but to simplify things, I will not do so at this point.

Our culture is distinct in its stress on encouraging love *before* marriage. Even considering only the Western world, American society encourages premarital love more than most Western cultures, although differences are diminishing. The encouragement of love as the basis for marriage means that direct parental control of courtship is minimized. A parent today cannot control with whom one's child will fall in love, except indirectly, by bringing up the child to be more compatible with people who hold certain values and come from certain backgrounds. There is no more precise way in a free courtship system to control love. South American countries and some Eastern European countries, where parental control of courtship is more valued, have less free courtship but still emphasize love as one basis for marriage.

Outside the Western world love is not premaritally stressed quite so much. The area in the Pacific called Polynesia is an exception to this, for love is highly valued as a basis for marriage in much of Polynesia. We saw this in part in our discussion of the Trobriand Islanders. In fact, William Goode (1959) classifies Polynesia, together with northwestern Europe and America, as the key places that today have the full romantic love complex. (For an account of Polynesia see Danielson, 1956.) Nevertheless, it should be clear that Goode is *not* implying a diffusion of European love ideas to Polynesia. Rather, he supports the view of an independent origin of love in Polynesia.

One of the major changes that occurred after the 1949 takeover of China by the Communists was the shift to a love-based marital system (see Chapter 18 for more details). Japan's westernization also produced less parental control and more love marriages, although there still is noticeable parental control today in both cultures.

In the rest of the world, love is known, but it is controlled more before marriage. The key difference may be that love in these other societies is expected to take place *after* marriage and not necessarily before. Quite a few years ago, Ralph Linton stated the case very clearly (Linton, 1936, p. 174):

> Practically all societies consider married life the most normal and desirable type of existence for adults. The spouses are expected to find in such relationships not merely regular satisfaction of sexual needs and cooperation in economic matters, but emotional response as well. There are a few societies where the claims of the consanguine group are so strong that it is taken for granted that spouses will not feel affection for each other, but in at least 90 percent of the world's cultures the ideal patterns for marriage do call for it. Even when marriages are arranged by the parents and the young people have no opportunity of knowing each other in advance, there is usually a sincere effort to bring together individuals who will have the potentialities of a happy life together.

Now it should be clear that in most of these non-Western societies, the concern is not with producing a romantic love match in accordance with the thirty-one rules of love from King Arthur's court. Rather the concern is with having two people who can get along emotionally, who are congenial, and who, in the broad meaning of the term, "love" each other. But the full-fledged romantic love of Andreas is considered in most societies as an abnormality or exaggeration. Love in the general sense of a deep emotional attachment is valued, but the cultural dressing is usually less ornate than that found in the full romantic love complex.

William Goode was one of the first to develop a theoretical explanation of why so many cultures try to control love relationships among single people (Goode, 1959). Goode's explanation was that love was potentially disruptive of mate choices in line with the existing stratification system. In short, he contends that to allow love as the basis for marriage means a higher risk of having marriages between people from different social classes—marriages that would disrupt the existing class structure and displease some of the parents involved. Goode lists five ways of controlling love:

1. child marriage
2. severe limits on the field of eligible mates
3. isolation of the sexes premaritally
4. chaperonage
5. indirect parental and peer controls

This is an interesting categorization of the ways of controlling premarital love relationships. American society clearly fits the fifth type of pattern. Many Latin American societies fit the fourth type of control. Looking at some of the cultures we examined in earlier chapters, we could say that the Nayar would fit the first pattern on the tali-rite marriage, but the subsequent marriages would be much freer. Thus, one society seemingly can have more than one type of love-control system operative. The Trobriand society would fit the fifth type except for the royalty who are expected to marry patrilateral cross cousins (father's sister's daughter) and they could be classified under the second type. Jamaica would be the fifth type, although some parents try to isolate the sexes (third type). The kibbutzim would be the fifth type.

Now Goode asserts that the upper classes will be most likely to control love, for they are most concerned with not disrupting class lines since they have the most wealth to lose. Some evidence in support of this comes from the cultures Goode examines such as Samoa (Mead, 1949). The Trobriand Islander supports this notion, since the royalty did place more restrictions on mate choice and love relationships (Malinowski, 1929). On the surface, Goode's proposition here makes sense; that is, it has what the sociologists call "face validity." The debutante balls, private schools, exclusive neighborhoods, and prestige colleges that the wealthy send their children to in this country would seem to be a control mechanism on their range of possible love partners which is more restrictive than that present in the social classes below them.

Finally, it should be noted that the shift to love-based marriage coincided with the increased freedom of young people in work and in geographic mobility. The duty-based marriage is weakened by economic independence and geographical distance. The forces promoting autonomy have continued throughout our history and have encouraged love as a basis for marriage more in America than anywhere in the West.

Sociological Explanations of Heterosexual Love Relationships

Love, as Senator Proxmire sees it, is a wonderful mystery, which he feels should remain as such, for he believes science has no business studying love relationships (Walster and Walster, 1975). Many people share that view because it serves their personal interests well. If one falls out of love, it is simpler just to label the old love as "infatuation" and not as "real" love. One can view oneself as a victim of this mysterious emotion: infatuation-love. If love can be scientifically analyzed, then one can avoid being a "victim" and may have to take responsibility for falling in love and that may be, to some people, more threatening and burdensome. Nevertheless, we can, if we want, learn to understand love just as we understand friendship. Love is no more mysterious than digestion—a process we remain unaware of until we have a problem. The sociologist starts with the assumption that to understand is worthwhile and love is no exception to that pursuit.

INTENSITY OF LOVE

How does one know he or she is in love? How intense does the feeling have to be? It is interesting to note that few people raise such issues concerning love for parents or even for friends. I believe that the reason the questions "How intense must it be?" and "Is it really love?" occur so frequently in courtship–love relationships is that one is supposed to make a major life decision on the basis of that love feeling. We have been trained to choose a lifelong mate on the basis of love, and that creates anxiety concerning the certainty of one's choice. No such important lifelong choice is involved in other love relationships, and thus, they are defined in a more relaxed fashion. One way to minimize such anxiety is to realize that love feelings are on a continuum from 0 to 100 percent. One can then accept the fact that what one feels to be love *is love of some degree* and thereby avoid the use of derogatory terms such as "puppy love" or "infatuation." Such terms are usually aimed at love relations that the labeler believes to be not good enough for marriage. The user of the term "infatuation" usually believes that either love is "real" love or it is not love at all. It seems more objectively true that love feelings, like other feelings, vary in intensity; the one key question most American youth want answered is not "Is this love?" but "Is this the kind of love on which I can build a lasting marriage?" Posing the question this way avoids getting hung up on the irrelevant question of whether it is "really" love and instead poses the relevant question of whether it is a lasting-marriage-type love.

We can no more go to a person who says she feels she is in love and tell her she is not feeling real love than we can go to a person who is feeling anger or hate and tell her that she is not feeling real anger or hate. Clearly feelings are subjective, and if one feels them, they are real in that sense. Whether one ought to feel these feelings or can feel them more intensely or more permanently with someone else is a separate question. Courtship love, then, by my definition, is a type of intense, positive, emotional feeling developed in a primary relationship involving a single male and female. The issue of multiple loves will be dealt with later. The question of how intense the relation must be before it is labeled love is one that the various subcultures in America answer in somewhat different ways. We have high school subcultures that define the intensity level in ways that make love occur much more frequently. College-age subgroups define the intensity level as higher and experience love less frequently. Also, college couples expect different traits to go with their loves than do high school couples. The same cultural variation is experienced regarding how similar the rights of single couples are to those of husbands and wives. Some groups accept intercourse before marriage and promote confidences among single couples as deep as those of married couples. Behavior varies by age, social class, religious background, ethnic group, and other social factors.

The basic types of love relationships may be divided into four major types. (1) *romantic love*, which would be love in line with many of the thirty-one tenets of love laid down by Andreas Capellanus 800 years ago; (2) *sexual-romantic love*, which is another variety of romantic love but one that stresses the sexual component as most important—compatibility of the couple in the sexual area is considered the key criterion of a good love relationship; (3) *rational-romantic love*, which modifies the emotionality factor by requiring the people involved to analyze the facts of their relationship and their likely future abilities to satisfy each other's needs; and (4) *mixed varieties* of the above elements. Type 1 is more common among younger teenagers (Reiss, 1967:76–81) whereas Type 3 seems more common among college-educated youth. Type 2 is a minor-type popular with some people from all parts of society. Elaine and William Walster's breakdown of love speaks of "passionate love," which is similar to our Types 1 and 2, for they stress the sexual and emotional qualities. The Walsters have a second type of love called "companionate love," which would overlap some with our Type 3 (rational-romantic love). (See Walster and Walster, 1978.) Other typologies exist but, generally, the emotional-rational elements are the key ingredients as they are in our typology.

During the past twenty-five years, several explanations of heterosexual love have been developed and partially tested. We are a long way from achieving an understanding in depth but we have made some inroads and have gained some understanding of how people fall in love. I will review some competing theories and try to arrive at a degree of integration of these views. I will start with the "Wheel Theory" because it takes the most general overview of the processes by which we fall in love.

THE WHEEL THEORY OF LOVE

The development of love can be conceptualized into four processes: (1) rapport, (2) self-revelation, (3) mutual dependency, and (4) need fulfillment. These processes are very closely interrelated in ways that I shall describe.

When two young people meet, a very quick assessment is made of felt rapport. To what extent does each person feel at ease with the other? To what extent do they feel they "understand" the other person? To what extent do they feel free to talk to the other person? The ease of communication is the first door that must be unlocked if love is to develop. All of us seem to strive, to one degree or another, to gain rapport with those who are in the mate-selecting process. People vary considerably in their ability to gain rapport with others and in the accuracy of their role-taking (i.e. feelings about others). Some are quite good at accurately sizing up a person they have just met and are able to feel at ease with a wide variety of types of people. Some are quite poor and inaccurate at understanding others and find it difficult to feel relaxed with most people. One's social and cultural background is a key basis upon which to predict the range of types of people for whom one could feel rapport. Broad factors such as religious upbringing and educational background would make one able to understand a person with similar religious and educational backgrounds, and thus make rapport more likely. The style of upbringing also affects the range of people for whom one can feel rapport. If one is brought up with a very strong "we" and "they" attitude, it would be more difficult to feel rapport for anyone who varied from the "we" type. Within some of these general-background factors, role definitions may further aid in predicting for whom one will feel rapport. For example, if two people are both relatively equalitarian about male–female rights to careers after marriage, or rights to choose what to do on a date, or control over money, then such people would be expected to feel rapport for each other more easily than if one person was equalitarian and the other believed in more segregated gender roles. These are some of the key factors that affect the feelings of rapport that males and females have for each other when they first meet. It is well to bear in mind that the sociologist is interested in finding overall generalizations about mating and not in predicting individual mating.

A feeling of rapport almost inevitably leads one to feeling relaxed and therefore

Photo by Michael Perry.

self-revelation can more easily occur. This is the second process in the love cycle, and I have labeled it simply "self-revelation." Here, too, one can see how social and cultural background affects the way a love relationship develops. One's background and related role conceptions are key determinants of the sort of things revealed by an individual to another person at a particular stage in a relationship. For example, some groups feel that talking about one's views on religion and politics is proper even on a first encounter, whereas other groups advise against discussing such topics on a first encounter because they feel it will lead only to conflict and ill feelings. Males are typically brought up and socialized to feel that sexual intimacies are proper to reveal at an earlier point in the courtship than are females. Much of the "battle of the sexes" results from such differences in cultural timing between male and female groups. Some groups, like the upper class, may socialize youngsters to be more formal in their revelations than would be the case for youngsters socialized in middle- or lower-class groups. In short, I am asserting here that in addition to the amount of rapport felt, one other factor that is a good predictor of self-revelation is the view on proper revelation which is present in one's socialization groups.

Rapport encourages revelation of self and this in turn builds up interdependent habit systems, that is, one gets used to doing things that require cooperation from the other person to accomplish. This is the third process in the development of a love relationship, and I call it *mutual dependency*. One needs the other person as an audience for one's jokes, as a confidant(e) for the expression of one's fears and wishes, as a partner for one's sexual needs, and so forth. Thus, habits of behaving develop which cannot be fulfilled alone, and in this way one becomes dependent on the other person. Here, too, social and cultural background is relevant, for clearly the type of habits that develop result from the type of revelation in the relationship, and that is dependent on one's conceptions of the ·courtship role.

The fourth and final process in the development of a love relationship is the one I have called *intimacy need fulfillment*. I am here referring to basic personality needs such as those Strauss (1947) used in his early research, that is, the need for someone to love, the need for someone to confide in, and the need for sympathetic understanding. These needs are of prime relevance to the important social role performances of the person. These are emotional needs related to family or occupational roles or both. The one common characteristic such needs have that is relevant to love is intimacy. That is, they are needs which, as they are fulfilled, express the closeness and privacy of the relationship. For example, the need for emotional support or sympathy are expressions of the underlying need for intimacy. We have other needs but they are not related to intimacy; they are less relevant for explaining love relationships. In my initial statement in 1960 I spoke of all personality needs. I am here revising this to focus more on intimacy needs. We need to carefully define this concept and develop specific measures of it (see Chapters 9 and 10).

By virtue of rapport, one reveals oneself and becomes dependent, and in the process of carrying out the relationship one fulfills certain basic intimacy needs. To the extent that these needs are fulfilled, one finds a love relationship developing. In fact, the initial rapport that a person feels on first meeting someone can be presumed to be a dim awareness of the potential intimacy need fulfillment of this other person for one's own needs. If one needs sympathy and support and senses these qualities in a date, rapport will be felt more easily; one will reveal more and become more dependent, and if the hunch was right and the person is sympathetic, one's intimacy needs will be fulfilled.

The basic overall conception that love develops through the processes of rapport, self-revelation, mutual dependency, and intimacy need fulfillment, I have labeled the "wheel theory" (Reiss, 1960). I chose this label because, as indicated in Figure 5.1, the processes are interdependent, and a reduction in any one of them will affect the development or maintenance of a love relationship. For example, if one reduced the amount of self-revelation due to an argument or because of a competing interest, that would affect the dependency and intimacy need-fulfillment processes, which would in turn weaken the rapport process, which would in turn tend to lower the revelation level even further. Thus, the processes flow into one another in one direction to develop love and can flow the other way to weaken a love relationship. I have marked the arrows "+" and "−" to indicate that the direction in which the processes increase can be reversed and all the processes thereby decrease the feelings of love.

The outer ring is labeled "sociocultural background." This general background is seen as producing the next ring of "role conceptions." Both of these rings are the context for the interpersonal processes described in the wheel theory. All four of the processes are influenced by role conceptions because role conceptions define

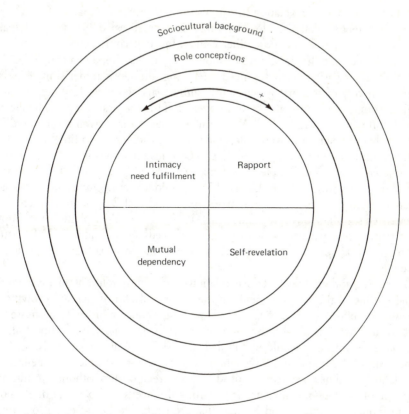

Figure 5.1. Graphic Presentation of the Wheel Theory of Love. (Revised, 1980.)

what one should do and expect in a love relationship. The sociocultural background in terms of education, religion, and such shapes the specific types of role conceptions that exist in a group. Figure 5.1 graphically presents these ideas and hopefully gives the reader the feeling of integration and interrelation which is being asserted.

Examine the graphic presentation of the wheel theory more closely and ask yourself if it applies *only* to love relationships. The answer clearly is no; it seems to be an explanatory schema that would apply to the development of primary (close, intimate, face-to-face and durable) relationships of any sort (friendship, love for parents, and so on). Thus, I am suggesting that love is simply one type of primary relationship and develops through the same general processes as do other types of primary relationships. So love may be defined as one type of an intimate, mutually need-fulfilling relationship. Courtship love in America is distinguishable from other primary relationships by its cultural dress. The norms defining expected role behavior in a courtship-love-relationship differ sharply from those defining role behavior in a parent-child relationship. The areas of expected rapport, revelation, mutual dependency, and need fulfillment are defined differently for various love and friendship relationships. Komarovsky (1974) reported that young people had quite different areas of revelation to parents (money problems) than to friends and lovers. She reports that the closest intimacies were revealed by men to female friends, but women often choose other women for their confidantes.

One should note that in all love relationships, the likelihood of a couple feeling that all of their basic personality needs are being fulfilled is rather slim. Anselm Strauss was one of the first to study this some years ago with 120 engaged and married couples and found that only 18 percent of his couples claimed 100 percent need fulfillment (Strauss, 1947). What this implies is that, given the complexity and number of needs of most people, one will love each person a little differently. Different intimacy needs may be fulfilled in each love relationship. Also, it follows that one could love two people simultaneously. Despite the fact that this violates the third rule of King Arthur's Court of Love, it does occur. Quite some time ago Albert Ellis checked 500 college females and found that 25 percent of them had experienced simultaneous love affairs (Ellis, 1949). One could explain this as simply the result of two partners satisfying different needs of an individual. It seems common during summer vacations where one of the love partners is not in the same city.

There is another aspect of love relationships that is relevant to present-day changes. One of the basic elements in the new family forms that are evolving is a new conception of love. The older, traditional conception of love stressed a relationship that was all-absorbing—a relationship in which all or almost all of one's *need for intimacy* would be fulfilled. I stress here "intimacy" needs, for that is the heart of the traditional love notion. The need, for example, for intellectual stimulation could be taken care of outside of a love relationship without diminishing the value of the love relationship. It is mainly the needs felt to reveal one's most private thoughts, actions, and feelings that are central to heterosexual love relationships (see Jourard, 1971). The romantic type of love (type 1) discussed above fits the traditional conception.

The new love beliefs differ, and they derive from the humanistic psychology movement and from leaders like Carl Rogers and Abe Maslow. Maslow states that the "self actualizing" person values love, but he does not need to have it. The individual's personal growth and development are the center, and love relations are viewed in terms of what they do for that central focus. Also, since the focus is on change and development of the individual, it is difficult to conceive that one other person could possibly satisfy all or most of the intimacy needs of such a dynamic individual. The intimate relationships of such a person involve a large element of allowing each other the right to new experience and personal growth possibilities. Thus, the amount of possessiveness or demands for need fulfillment or fixed role responsibilities are drastically reduced. In short, the new love conception spells out a love that satisfies only some intimacy needs and posits a belief that it will be necessary to have other intimate relationships with other individuals in order to satisfy other intimacy needs. This view contends that the excessive expectations and restrictions related to the traditional view of love leads to disillusionment and to resentment. What we called the rational-romantic type of love would in part fit into this new view of love.

One may visualize the focused, traditional, intimacy conception as a triangle wherein only one person is at the apex of the triangle. *Exclusivity* is thereby stressed. All intimacies may be revealed to that one person. But no intimacies shared with that person are to be revealed with people lower down the triangle. The intimacies at each lower level are sharable only with those at a higher level. The lower level intimacies would be more specialized to particular areas such as work intimacies, kin intimacies, and so forth. The diffuse love conception would have less focus on one person although one person would have the larger share, and thus other people might be quite close to the most intimate position. The diffuse position thus stresses *priority* of need fulfillment rather than *exclusivity* of need fulfillment and can be presented as a trapezoid figure. A totally diffuse intimacy conception would lack even the priority of any one person but have several equal people at the top level. Such an approach would be illustrated as a rectangle. Figure 5.2 illustrates these three types of intimacy conceptions.

There are degrees of endorsement within the traditional, focused, exclusive views of love, and the new diffuse, priority views of love. One could endorse the traditional view totally and demand that a lover have no primary relationships with any friends and none with any persons of the opposite sex at all. In short, one could demand to be the only person to whom one is close in their entire life space. On the other hand, in the new view, one could assert that a lover need not meet more than a portion of one's intimacy needs, for other lovers or friends can be enjoyed who will fill in the remaining intimacy needs, both sexual and nonsexual. There

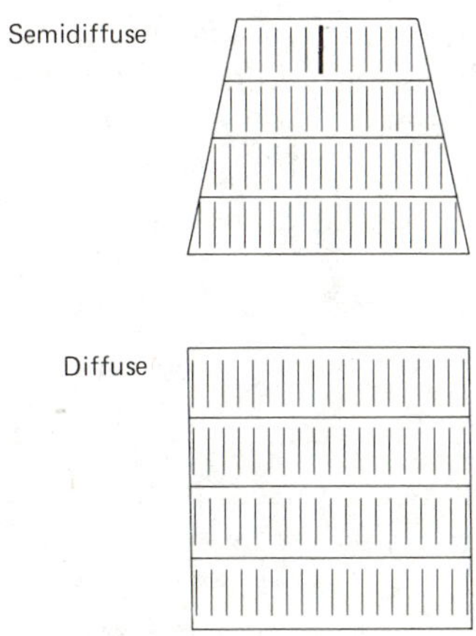

Figure 5.2. Focused and Diffuse Intimacy Conceptions.

is a point wherein the new and traditional views of love are quite similar. Moderate adherents of both views might well believe that for love to lead to marriage, it should satisfy *most* of one's intimacy needs but should leave one free to explore mutually agreed-upon ways of satisfying the remaining minority of intimacy needs. Thus, although the focused and diffuse views of love are different, there are areas of overlap. The reader should keep this new view of love in mind, for although it is not as popular as the focused traditional form, it is a key factor in encouraging the adoption of many alternative family forms, and we shall return to it often.

THE LEAP OF FAITH

There is no fully rational way on the basis of a year or so of knowing someone to predict the next fifty years, and yet this is exactly what our type of courtship institution demands. After "going with" a person for a period of time, we may feel that we are in love and decide to marry. How do we know that we could not feel a more intense form of love? We never know this for sure. In fact, if we have been in love more than once, then we know that what we once thought was a good love affair can turn out to be inferior to our next love affair. How do we know that we are not just being emotionally carried away when we decide that this present love affair is the best we are capable of and that marriage should come next? Experience and rational examination can help, but doubt is always possible.

What marriage in our type of courtship system involves, then, is a leap of faith, if I may borrow an existentialist term. We take this leap of faith despite the lack of scientific evidence because of our intense love feelings. We are socialized in anticipation of falling in love so that our motivations are built up over the years. When we do fall in love, we already know a good deal about how to act, what to say, and how to feel. This is the same sort of anticipatory role socialization that occurs in our occupational, educational, religious, political, and other domains.

In Western society romanticism became increasingly the motive to marriage, and with it marriage became more popular. America today has one of the highest marriage rates, and Americans marry at one of the youngest ages of any modern country. Part of this can be assumed to result from the popularity with both sexes of marriage for love. Perhaps the newer, more diffuse form of love may present less motivation to marry. In some ways this newer view of love can be an argument for not marrying in order to keep the greatest number of personal growth "options" open.

DO OPPOSITES ATTRACT?

We now have a way of conceptualizing how love develops and what are some of its varieties. Fulfillment of needs produces love feelings, but what about the persons who are able to fulfill our needs? Are they possessed of needs similar to our own or do they have needs opposite to our own? During the 1950s, Robert Winch of Northwestern University undertook extensive research in an attempt to answer this question (Winch, 1958). Let us now look at his work and at those who retested his ideas.

Robert Winch's classic study of love relationships was conducted on only twenty-five married couples at Northwestern University. In his book, *Mate Selection* (1958), Winch notes that he accepts the findings of Burgess and Wallin (1953) and those of many other authors which show that there is homogamy (like marrying like) when we talk of social and cultural characteristics such as place of residence, educational, and religious background. But although Winch accepts the research support for homogamy as valid for social and cultural traits, he raises the question of whether personality traits are likewise homogamous. He feels that *social and cultural* homogamy establishes the "field of eligibles" from which one will choose a mate, but that this choice is based on *psychological* heterogamy (opposites mating with each other). This position is somewhat at odds with Burgess and Wallin's position for some of their homogamy findings do bear on psychological homogamy. For example, Burgess and Wallin tested similarities on Thurstone's neurotic inventory (Burgess and Wallin, 1953, p. 208) and found support for homogamy.

Everyone agrees that being of the same social class does not make you fall in love. It may shape your needs for a style of life so that you will find each other compatible. The key question remaining however is, do personality needs have to be the same or opposite for compatibility? This is a question that Burgess and Wallin leave unanswered. Thus, when Winch asserts heterogamy of needs, he is putting forth a theoretical answer to this question. The wheel theory of the development of love does not specify whether the need structures of the two individuals falling in love will be homogamous or heterogamous. Thus, Winch is asserting a further specification of the love process by declaring that the presence of a heterogamous or complementary-need structure produces the feelings of love.

Winch posits two types of complementary needs: (1) where the degree of each need varies radically and (2) where the needs are opposite. The question of how to define the key personality needs is answered by borrowing Murray et al.'s (1938) twelve needs and basic characteristics. Table 5.1 presents a listing and definitions of these needs plus three general traits. The basic theory Winch contends is that we love those who gratify our needs. These twelve needs are, he believes, basic enough to cover the vital parts of most people's personality makeup. Winch then proceeds to test the notion on twenty-five couples at Northwestern University who were married less than two years.

Winch utilized three basic types of tests of his theory that complementary needs were the basis for mate selection. One test consisted of Thematic Apperception Tests (TAT). The respondent is presented with a picture and asked to say what is going on. The belief is that people will project their own needs onto the picture and see things in accordance with those needs. Thus, the prejudiced person sees any black in a picture as about to commit a crime; the striving person sees a person in the picture as striving toward some goal; and so on. The TAT test did not support Winch's theory, although it did not support the homogamy theory either.

A second test consisted of very lengthy life-history analyses. Many hours were spent talking and gaining details of the life histories of each respondent. The hope was that this in-depth probing would reveal the basic twelve needs and support Winch's complementary need theory. However, this check did not support the theory either, although it did not support the homogamy view either.

TABLE 5.1

The Twelve Needs and Three General Traits

VARIABLE	DEFINITION
	Needs
Abasement	To accept or invite blame, criticism, or punishment; to blame or harm the self.
Achievement	To work diligently to create something and/or to emulate others.
Approach	To draw near and enjoy interaction with another person(s).
Autonomy	To get rid of the constraint of other persons; to avoid or escape from domination; to be unattached and independent
Deference	To admire and praise a person.
Dominance	To influence and control the behavior of others.
Hostility	To fight, injure, or kill others.
Nurturance	To give sympathy and aid to a weak, helpless, ill, or dejected person or animal.
Recognition	To excite the admiration and approval of others.
Status aspiration	To desire a socioeconomic status considerably higher than one has (a *special case of achievement*).
Status striving	To work diligently to alter one's socioeconomic status (a *special case of achievement*).
Succorance	To be helped by a sympathetic person; to be nursed, loved, protected, indulged.
	General Traits
Anxiety	Fear, conscious or unconscious, of harm or misfortune arising from the hostility of others and/or social reaction to one's own behavior.
Emotionality	The show of affect in behavior.
Vicariousness	The gratification of a need derived from the perception that another person is deriving gratification.

Source: Robert F. Winch, 1958:90

The third check, which became the basis for Winch's book and most of his articles, consisted of asking forty-five rather open-ended questions of each respondent. The questions were worded so as to probe the general areas of the twelve needs. Of all the checks made as a result of the answers to these forty-five questions, about 20 percent came out sharply enough in the hypothesized direction predicted by Winch's theory to be called statistically significant. (See Appendix Two for further explanation of statistical significance.) In short, 20 percent came out sharply enough in the hypothesized direction so that "chance" could be ruled out. The other 80 percent again did not support the heterogamy view, but did not give support to the homogamy view either.

Let us go a little further into Winch's findings, despite some misgivings about the reliability and validity of his results. If we assume that there was some overall validity despite the crudeness of the measures, then it is worthwhile to look at his strongest findings and perhaps preserve them as the essence of the study. Winch did conclude that there were two key dimensions: nurturant-receptive and dominant-submissive. He assumes that these two dimensions can be summed up as indicating a tendency for assertive people and receptive people to mate. Winch thus concludes that the key single dimension that explains need complementarity in love relations is that of assertiveness-receptiveness. Although none of the twenty-five couples fits this complementary-needs schema fully, it was generally true that nurturant people married receptive people and dominant people married submissive people. Thus, there was a general sort of support for the existence of this key complementary-need dimension of assertiveness-receptiveness.

In the decades since Winch published his mate-selection book, there have been many repeat studies of his ideas. (For an early criticism see Roscow, 1957.) Most of these other studies did not support Winch's views. (See Bowerman and Day, 1956; see also the studies listed in Winch, 1967.) Winch himself in 1967 wrote that he felt that these replications did not use the exact same set of needs, or his exact way of measuring needs, for example they often used Edward's personal preference schedule to measure needs; thus their different results may be caused by such divergencies from the original study. His critics claim they used improved or equivalent measures. Here is a good example of a common controversy in sociology. It is this kind of debate and constant testing and retesting which is at the heart of science, and I hope that the reader gains some appreciation of the value of this process.

At this point I would like to state some of my own views on Winch's theory First, as a matter of sociological curiosity I would want to search beyond the personality needs to social and cultural forces that might sustain such needs. I expressed this interest in my discussion of the wheel theory. More recent research by Bermann (1966) concluded that the concept of role expectation was a better predictor of dyadic stability in a group of nurses than was need complementarity. Bermann said he found that those whose expectations of roles were compatible were likely to be stable in their dyadic choices. Now, one can combine role expectation and need complementarity to advantage, and Bermann and Winch were sympathetic to this idea. I think the key point here is that courtship and marital role expectations are important factors in the development of a love relationship. Also, such role expectations fit more directly with a sociological approach, whereas the focus solely on needs fit more directly with a psychological approach. (Murstein, 1967, and Trost, 1967, report on other key checks on Winch's conception.)

I believe that it is logically possible that two people with the same personality needs could simply take turns satisfying each other or they could specialize in the areas wherein they require such needs to be fulfilled. For example, two people can each have needs for dominance, succorance and nurturance. They can nurture each other in respect to their specialized roles by helping in role performance at home or at work. They can each dominate in regard to certain matters in the home or out of it. In short, it does not seem necessary to have complementary or different needs to be compatible. Further, it seems to me that some types of traits do not go well with homogamy, whereas others do. For example, having a bad temper is something best left to only one person in a marriage, whereas a need for nurturance would seem to be perfectly suitable for both mates to possess. In sum, I would conclude that there is little *a priori* basis upon which to assume that personality needs that are homogamous or heterogamous are, by those very facts, more conducive to a love relationship. I conclude that we ought to seek out the types of needs that do contribute to a love relationship when homogamous and the types that contribute when heterogamous. Such greater specification of expected results may make testing more easy to do and to interpret.

The question of types of needs brings up another very important point. While it is true that any need satisfaction will contribute to becoming attached emotionally to another person, it is also true that some particular needs may be the key element in the development of a heterosexual love relationship. One particular type of need I have in mind is the need for intimacy. An intimate relationship is one in which there is a high degree of self-revelation. The revelation would be of those aspects of oneself that are generally not revealed to acquaintances, that is basic hopes, fears, and self-feelings. Now, it surely is the case that the kind of needs Winch measures may be related to intimacy. For example, perhaps a particular person can be more intimate if he or she is in a dominant or in a submissive role relationship. Thus, dominance-submissiveness may be related to love, but mainly because it triggers different degrees of intimate self-revelation. In our society there are ways of satisfying needs for recognition by interacting with a wide number of other people. The love relationship is supposed to be the key place where needs for intimacy are satisfied. If, in addition, other needs are satisfied, that surely would be conceived as an asset, but the core needs in a heterosexual love relationship are, in my judgment, the intimacy needs related to the key area of self-revelation that are defined as "private" by the individuals.

I further think that when those intimacy needs are satisfied with others, problems of jealousy may arise but do not when other needs such as dominance, recognition, and so forth are satisfied with others. If I am correct in this, then what we need to do is investigate the intimacy-need fulfillment in love relationships and base our predictions on that specific inquiry. In effect, I would stress as in the wheel theory, that "intimacy need fulfillment" is the most central type of need fulfillment in terms of promoting love.

THE LOVE FILTERS

We can go somewhat further in our quest for an explanation of the development of love in American society with a discussion of an important research study conducted by Kerckhoff and Davis (1962). Their study utilized ninety-four engaged or seriously dating couples at Duke University. The basic purpose of the study was to discern how social and cultural homogamy, value consensus, and need complementariness related to progress toward mate selection.

The Kerckhoff and Davis study was a longitudinal one, involving two interviews, six months apart, with the same couples. The goal was to see just how social and cultural homogamy, value consensus, and need complementariness affected changes in intention to marry (progress in mate selection).

Kerckhoff and Davis found that three stages of selection seemed to occur in the movement toward more marital commitment. The first stage is no surprise and simply asserts that *social and cultural homogamy* is the earliest selective factor. People who do not match up on religion, educational background, and such are selected out early in the mate-selection process. All ninety-four couples were high on homogamous factors of this kind, indicating that the low-homogamy types never made it to the serious dating stage and thus were not even in this sample. *Value consensus* was the second filter in the mate-selection process. This was determined by noting that the couples who had been going with each other a long time were almost all high on value consensus thus indicating that value consensus was a filter in progress toward mate selection. The couples who knew each other a short time and were low on value consensus were not progressing toward mate selection while those who were high on this area were progressing. Thus it seemed that value consensus selected out couples after homogamy had made an initial selection. Finally, the *need-complementarity* factor seemed to operate. Among those couples who knew each other a long time, more of those with need complementarity were progressing toward marriage. Kerckhoff and Davis found that couples who knew each other a short time had more idealized views of each other, and such idealization may have kept them from fully realizing their degree of need complementarity. The needs tested were not fully in line with Winch's notions, and the issue of similar or different needs is not settled by this study. They used three complementary needs from Schutz's (1958) research. However, Kerckhoff and Davis' study does afford evidence of a three-stage selective process and affords a general framework within which to view the development of love relationships leading to marriage. Their approach is compatible with most of the ideas put forth in this chapter, and it helps to, at least tentatively, fit these notions together. Levinger et al. (1970) has raised some important qualifications of the Kerckhoff and Davis thesis of stages of increasing commitment. In a retest of Kerckhoff and Davis, Levinger found that the theory did not hold up in his sample. The best prediction of progress in a love relationship was the expectations of such progress by the individuals involved. Thus, although this area is important, we must ask for further testing before adopting any views as established.

One final point: In case the reader is wondering why Winch and Kerckhoff and Davis used college-student samples, the answer is quite simple. Students are a most available and cooperative set of respondents to sample and thus afford an inexpensive source of data. The samples used were not random probability-type samples of their campuses. They used mostly volunteers. This means that it is difficult to generalize beyond the couples in the sample and assert that these results apply to others. Also, what of the many millions of young people who never become college juniors and seniors? Noncollege people are in the majority of that age group. Are the findings from these nonrepresentative groups of college couples applicable to noncollege couples?

Further, we know that many engagements break up. Thus, when we study engaged couples and their attitudes, we should realize that such attitudes may be quite different for those couples destined for an early break up. Here again, the value of a follow-up study (a longitudinal study) is apparent, and that is why Burgess and Wallin's original 1,000 engaged couples were followed for over twenty years. The Kerckhoff and Davis study was longitudinal and that is a definite plus since it was studying change. A longitudinal study has the advantage of measuring change as it occurs, rather than having to guess about such changes. For example, if we studied freshmen and seniors at one point in time (cross-sectional study), we could assert that the freshmen would be like the seniors in three more years. However, that may not be accurate for many freshmen drop out and thus seniors are a select sample of all freshmen. Also, external pressures (war, depression) can change before these freshmen become seniors. Also if the seniors had higher I.Q.'s we would not know if that was due to the three years of education or to smarter students staying in college. Thus, to understand change, it is more valid to follow the freshmen through to their senior year and thereby understand changes more accurately. This is a more costly process but it also more fully reveals the intricacies of changes that are occurring.

There are also differences by social class that should be taken into consideration. In fact, one can argue that at the lower social-class levels, there is very little in the way of a formal engagement period. Check the engagement notices in the daily newspapers and you can quickly see that such notices help to maintain the status of middle-class and upper-class people. It is a way of telling the world what a good catch the female has made and what a nice background both she and her fiancé have. One rarely sees an announcement citing the fiancé as a ditch digger and the bride-to-be a tenth-grade dropout or her father a garbage collector. The lower-class groups decide to marry and do so with much less public fanfare. Thus, by studying college groups who are relatively well-off in background, we do not learn much about these out-of school young people from the lower socioeconomic classes.

As noted earlier, some of the more recent conceptualizations of the love process have stressed the concept of role compatibility, that is, compatible ideas about how males and females should act in courtship and marital roles (Lewis, 1973). Lewis's notion is congruent with the wheel theory and he does test it out in a longitudinal study. We still need to formulate specific hypotheses about particular aspects of one's role conceptions that are most central to falling in love. For example, is the equalitarian dimension or the flexibility dimension of roles of central importance? Even if we assume that those aspects of roles that relate most directly to intimacy needs are the most important, we still need to be able to specifically identify those aspects. Research by Lewis (1973) does bring in the idea of accuracy of role-taking as important, that is, how accurate is one in ascertaining what the role conceptions of the other person actually are. This is another crucial dimension. Such accuracy would affect the development of love by facilitating need fulfillment.

Emphasis on the role conception of the two persons is also found in a theory of love put forth by Bernard Murstein (1971). Murstein posits a three-stage theory which begins with a *stimulus* stage that is not unlike the rapport stage of the wheel theory. But Murstein does emphasize the importance of physical appearance in this initial stage more than other theorists in this area have done. It would be important to specify just how much more important sexual attraction is over other factors in establishing rapport in a new relationship (see also Mathes, 1975). Stage two in Murstein's theory deals with *value comparison*. This reminds one of the second stage in the Kerckhoff and Davis theory and is quite similar in meaning. It simply refers to a period during which the couple compares values to test for

Courtesy of the Minnesota Geographic Society. Project Coordinator: Tim Strick. Photo
by Shelly A. McIntire.

compatibility. Finally, the third stage is directly concerned with compatibility, particularly *compatible ideal self and ideal spouse images*. Burgess and Wallin (1953) had long ago stressed the importance of such ideal images. Surely these ideal images relate directly to one's role expectations and to one's need fulfillments. The extent to which such ideal images are mutually compatible is related to the role-fit concept of Lewis and to the need-fulfillment concept of the wheel theory.

The Walsters have put forth a related but somewhat different explanation of love. They posit an "equity theory," which is a form of "exchange theory" stressing that persons feel most comfortable when they are getting a "fair" return out of a relationship. People who are getting more than they feel they deserve, and especially those who feel they are getting less than they deserve, will not feel comfortable. Thus, one can predict who will fall in love by examining the particular qualities that produce equity in the matching of persons (Walster and Walster, 1978). This approach is a social-psychological alternative to the sociological approach which focuses heavily on role compatibility. One could put the equity and role ideas together and examine if the role compatibility relates to feelings of equity.

What seems to be needed now is not more theorizing but more empirical testing and refinement of these many overlapping ideas in carefully designed, longitudinal research projects. Sociologists are making headway in the search for an explanation of love, and with continued empirical work, we can make some major advances. Only with careful testing can we confidently clarify our concepts and select the most theoretically useful ideas.

Summary and Conclusions

For as long as we have any written record, we have found evidence of love conceptions. The specific types of people involved and how they were supposed to act has altered over time, but everywhere we find love conceptions as a part of human society. Philosophical discussions of the nature of love go back at least 2,500 years to Plato. But only recently has there been empirical testing of theories of love.

In the past decade some preliminary efforts at refining our theories of love have been put forth. For example, the general research on attraction, friendship, and liking has been related to the love process to a greater extent (Murstein, 1971, 1976; Berscheid and Walster, 1969; Rubin, 1973; Huston, 1974). In particular, psychological notions of *reinforcement, balance, exchange,* and *reward* have all been utilized to explain why people fall in love. Some have developed experimental methods of measuring love by observing the length of time people stare at each other (Rubin, 1973) and, oddly enough, this does correlate with other measures of love. Others research the physiological reactions that accompany "passionate love" (Walster and Walster, 1978). There are also numerous sociological theories such as those discussed (Wheel Theory, Filter Theory, and so on). It would seem that the level of data and theory is rapidly reaching the necessary "critical mass" for making important theoretical advances in our understanding of love.

References

Berman, E., and D. R. Miller. 1967. "The Matching of Mates," in R. Jesser and S. Fenschback (eds.), *Cognition, Personality and Clinical Psychology.* San Francisco: Jossey-Bass.

Berscheid, Ellen, and Elaine Walster. 1969. *Interpersonal Attraction.* Reading, MA: Addison-Wesley.

Borland, Dolores M. 1975. "An Alternative Model of the Wheel Theory," *The Family Coordinator* 24 (July): 289–292.

Bowerman, Charles E., and Barbara R. Day. 1956. "A Test of the Theory of Complementary Needs as Applied to Couples During Courtship," *American Sociological Review* 21 (October): 602–605.

Brain, Robert. 1976. *Friends and Lovers.* New York: Basic Books.

Burgess, Ernest W., and Paul Wallin. 1953. *Engagement and Marriage.* Philadelphia: Lippincott.

Capellanus, Andreas. 1959. *The Art of Courtly Love,* trans. by John Jay Parry. New York: Ungar.

Castiglione, Baldesar. 1959. *The Book of the Courtier,* trans. by Charles S. Singleton. New York: Doubleday.

Centers, Richard. 1975. *Sexual Attraction and Love.* Springfield, IL: Charles C Thomas.

Danielsson, Bengt. 1956. *Love in the South Seas.* New York: Reynal.

Day, Donald. 1954. *The Evolution of Love.* New York: Dial.

De Rougemont, Denis. 1940. *Love in the Western World,* trans. by Montgomery Belgion. New York: Harcourt, Brace & World.

Ellis, Albert. 1949. "A Study of Human Love Relationships," *The Journal of Genetic Psychology* 75 (September): 61–71.

Goode, William J. 1959. "The Theoretical Importance of Love," *American Sociological Review* 24 (February): 38–47.

_____. 1963. *World Revolution and Family Patterns.* New York: Free Press.

Heiss, Jerold W. 1962. "Degree of Intimacy and Male-Female Interaction," *Sociometry* 25 (June): 197–208

Hill, C.T., Z. Rubin, A. Peplau. 1976. "Breakups Before Marriage: The End of 103 Affairs," *Journal of Social Issues* 32 (Jan.):147–167.

Hinkle, Dennis E., and Michael J. Sporakowski. 1975. "Attitudes Toward Love: A Reexamination," *Journal of Marriage and the Family* 37 (November):764–768.

Hunt, Morton M. 1959. *The Natural History of Love.* New York: Knopf.

Huston, Ted L. (ed.). 1974. *Foundations of Inter-personal Attraction*. New York: Academic.

Jourard, Sidney M. 1971. *The Transparent Self*, 2nd ed. New York: Van Nostrand.

Kerckhoff, Alan C., and Keith E. Davis. 1962. "Value Consensus and Need Complementarity in Mate Selection," *American Sociological Review* 27 (June):295–303.

Kirkpatrick, Clifford, and Theodore Caplow. 1945. "Courtship in a Group of Minnesota Students," *American Journal of Sociology* 51 (September): 114–125.

Komarovsky, Mirra. 1974. "Patterns of Self-Disclosure of Male Undergraduates," *Journal of Marriage and the Family* 36 (November):677–686.

Krain, Mark. 1975. "Communication Among Premarital Couples at Three Stages of Dating," *Journal of Marriage and the Family* 37 (August):609–618.

Levinger, George, et al. 1970. "Progress Toward Permanence in Courtship: A Test of the Kerckhoff-Davis Hypothesis," *Sociometry* 33 (December): pp. 427–433.

Lee, John. 1974. *Colours of Love*. Toronto: New Press.

Lewis, Robert A. 1973. "A Longitudinal Test of a Developmental Framework for Premarital Dyadic Formation," *Journal of Marriage and the Family* 35 (February):16–27.

Linton, Ralph. 1936. *The Study of Man*. New York: Appleton.

Malinowski, Bronislaw. 1929. *The Sexual Lives of Savages in North-Western Melanesia*. New York: Harvest Books. (Published by Harcourt Brace Jovanovich.)

Maslow, Abraham. 1962. *Toward a Psychology of Being*. New York: Van Nostrand.

Mathes, Eugene W. 1975. "The Effects of Physical Attractiveness and Anxiety on Heterosexual Attraction Over a Series of Five Encounters,"*Journal of Marriage and the Family* 37 (November):769–773.

Mead, Margaret. 1928. *Coming of Age in Samoa*. New York: Morrow.

Murray, Henry A. et al. 1938. *Explorations in Personality*. New York: Oxford University Press.

Murstein, Bernard (ed.). 1967. "Empirical Tests of Role, Complementary Needs, and Homogamy Theories of Marital Choice," *Journal of Marriage and the Family* 29 (November):689–696.

_____. 1971. *Theories of Attraction and Love*. New York: Springel.

_____. 1976. *Who Will Marry Whom?* New York: Springer.

Ovid. 1957. *The Art of Love*, trans. by Rolfe Humphries. Bloomington: Indiana University Press.

Plato. 1956. *Symposium*, trans. by Benjamin Jowett. Indianapolis: Bobbs-Merrill.

Queen, Stuart A., and Robert Habenstein. 1974. *The Family in Various Cultures*. Philadelphia: Lippincott.

Reiss, Ira L. 1960. "Toward a Sociology of the Heterosexual Love Relationship," *Marriage and Family Living* 22 (May):139–145.

_____. 1967. *The Social Context of Premarital Sexual Permissiveness*. New York: Holt, Rinehart and Winston.

Rogers, Carl. 1972. *Becoming Partners: Marriage and Its Alternatives*. New York: Delacorte.

Roscow, Irving. 1957. "Issues in the Concept of Need-Complementarity," *Sociometry* 20 (September):216–233.

Rubin, Zick. 1973. *Liking and Loving*. New York: Holt, Rinehart and Winston.

Schutz, William C. 1958. *A Three-Dimensional Theory of Interpersonal Behavior*. New York: Holt, Rinehart and Winston.

Strauss, Anselm. 1947. "Personality Needs and Marital Choice," *Social Forces* 25 (March):332–335.

Theodorson, George A. 1965. "Romanticism and Motivation to Marry in the United States, Singapore, Burma and India," *Social Forces* 44 (September):17–28.

Trost, Jan. 1967. "Some Data on Mate-Selection: Complementarity," *Journal of Marriage and the Family* 29 (November):730–738.

Waller, Willard. 1937. "The Rating and Dating Complex," *American Sociological Review* 2 (October):727–734.

Walster, E., V. Aronson, D. Abrahams, and L. Rottman. 1966. "Importance of Physical Attractiveness in Dating Behavior," *Journal of Personality and Social Psychology* 4 (November):508–516.

Walster, Elaine, and G. W. Walster. 1978. *A New Look at Love*. Reading, MA: Addison-Wesley.

Winch, Robert F. 1958. *Mate-Selection: A Study of Complementary Needs*. New York: Harper & Row.

_____. 1967. "Another Look at the Theory of Complementary Needs in Mate Selection," *Journal of Marriage and the Family* 29 (November):756–762.

Sexuality and Sexual-

Partner Preferences

SIX

Introduction to the Study of Sexuality

No one reading this chapter is devoid of sexual experience and yet we are just beginning to learn the nature of human sexuality. The scientific study of human sexuality begins with the psychological literature of the late nineteenth and early twentieth centuries. Kraft-Ebing's *Psychopathia Sexualis* in 1886 is usually dated as the first work that attempted to arrive at a scientific understanding of human sexual behavior. Kraft-Ebing was a Viennese psychiatrist whose interest was in developing therapeutic techniques for treating what he defined as sexual pathology. Sadism, masochism, masturbation, and nocturnal emissions were some of the "pathological" areas he wrote about. In fact, it was he who coined the word *masochism* after the well-known Count Sacher-Masoch who wrote about sadistic females and masochistic males. Masturbation was viewed as dangerous and likely to lead to "other forms of pathology." Those with the more serious pathologies were known to masturbate frequently and it was assumed masturbation was pathological. What was not known to such writers as Kraft-Ebing was that masturbation was also quite common in the general population. It was not until recent decades that the stigma laid upon masturbation by Kraft-Ebing and his colleagues was even partially lifted.

Sigmund Freud built upon Kraft-Ebing's research on sexual pathology. One of his classic works was published in 1905, entitled *Three Contributions to the Theory of Sex*. In it Freud put forth the revolutionary doctrine that the child was naturally a sexual creature with sexual desires of many sorts. This conception laid the basis for Freud's view of the oedipal complex and of the causes of sexual disorders that resulted from the restrictions on libidinal sexuality imposed by human society. Shortly before this time (1891), Havelock Ellis, an Englishman, published his six volumes entitled *Studies in the Psychology of Sex*. In these volumes, Ellis put forth a "new" view of homosexuality which rejected the older "learning" theories and imposed a biological view of homosexuality. He had to publish this book in America because his books were viewed as "obscene" in England. So the study of human sexuality was born in the Victorian era of so-called sexual repression. (For further details on early development see: Money and Musaph, 1977: Section I.)

In addition to the psychological interest in human sexuality, there was an anthropological interest in sexuality in the late nineteenth century. We spoke of this briefly in Chapter 1 when we mentioned the debate between Lewis Henry Morgan and Edward Westermarck concerning the reality of an original state of sexual promiscuity as the beginning stage in the evolution of humanity. Later, during World War I, Bronislaw Malinowski spent several years in the Trobriand Islands near New Guinea and eventually wrote *The Sexual Life of Savages in Northwestern Melanesia* (1929) and many other works. This work and those discussed above were the beginning of the scientific study of sexuality. It began less than one hundred years ago and for the first fifty years, at least, it was completely dominated by psychological and anthropological researchers.

Why were the sociologists so late in studying human sexuality? The answer basically is that psychologists and anthropologists have more socially acceptable motives for such research. The psychological-medical study of sexuality is related to the treatment of what many people feel is pathological sexual behavior. Thus, the public views of "immoral" sexual behavior could be supported by the psychological labels of "abnormality," "disorder," and "pathology." During the past one hundred years these labels have been bestowed on masturbation, female orgasm, and intercourse for pleasure (Comfort, 1967). The anthropologists studied faraway primitive, pagan cultures that no one expected to have the "advanced" views of civilized society. Thus, anthropologists too could reinforce our superiority by showing us how far we had come from these savage customs of permissive premarital intercourse and masturbation (Reiss, 1967:Chap. 1).

The scientific research of the sociologist is not about an emotionally disturbed individual or a primitive hunting society—it is about our own society and thus it is far more likely to arouse hostile responses. The sociological approach is closer to home and therefore potentially more explosive. Sociologists study our behavior and attitudes and therefore they may weaken our faith in the conventional sexual morality. The sociologists' justifications for disturbing the peace and tranquility of the conventional citizen is less socially supported. Sociologists are seeking to understand, to explain, to gain insight into the nature of the world in which we live. At times the average citizen wonders how much of this effort will pay off in practical terms. When you add to that concern the risk of embarrassment, you find many sociologists in the past who felt that the study of sexuality was not a "safe" or a "prestigious" field of study. The lack of safety is backed up by history. When Hitler took over in 1933 the famous Magnus Hirschfeld Institute for Sexual Science in Berlin was closed and the field of sexual science in Germany was not to be revived until after the end of World War II. Sexologists such as Hirschfeld, Marcuse,

Reich, and Freud had to leave the country (Meyenburg and Sigusch, 1977; Money and Musaph, 1977).

When social scientists first started to write marriage and family textbooks for college students in the 1920s, they often took a moralistic approach. It was safer to criticize sexual behavior as immoral than to report objectively and analyze its meaning (Reiss, 1956 and 1957). Actually, it was a zoologist by the name of Alfred Kinsey who had the courage to undertake a nationwide scientific research on human sexuality. Kinsey had found that he could not answer the questions of his students regarding sexuality and decided he would undertake a national research project to seek out those answers (Christenson, 1971). With the publication of his first book, *Sexual Behavior in the Human Male* (1948), the modern era of scientific, socio-logical research was born. America took the leadership in such research and we still retain it today. The Institute for Sex Research at Indiana University survives today and now sponsors research predominantly by sociologists. Over a half dozen national studies have been done by other researchers since Kinsey (Reiss, 1967; Simon, Berger, and Gagnon, 1972; Hunt, 1974; Zelnik and Kantner, 1977; Levitt and Klassen, 1974; Sorensen, 1973). The scientific study of human sexuality is now an acceptable, even respectable, part of social science research and theory.

What Is This Thing Called Sexuality?

Before we proceed to look at the actual behavior and attitudes of people it is best to try to gain some clarity regarding the concept of sexuality. Our goal here is the same as it was in Chapter 2 when we defined the Family System; that is, we do not wish to simply arrive at an arbitrary definition that is convenient. Nor do we wish to promote the type of sexuality that one group or another may favor. We want to get at the essence of sexuality, at what is common to it under all conditions—premaritally, maritally, extramaritally, with a marriage partner, or with a prostitute, heterosexually as well as homosexually. In addition, we want a definition that is sociological, that is, that refers not only to its biological or psychological nature, but also to the *shared* or *social* nature of human sexuality.

Very few precise definitions of sexuality exist. Perhaps it is because of our past avoidance of direct discussion of sexuality. There are definitions in the popular press that treat sexuality in its broadest sense so as to include any esthetic appreciation as sexual. Kinsey used the term sexual to refer to behaviors that were on the path to orgasm. Some use sexual to refer to an inborn "drive." The vaguer one's defi-nition, the more easily everyone can fit their view to it and the less critical the response. However, vagueness hinders scientific research and understanding. Thus, I will strive to put forth a more specific definition. I offer the following definition as a suitable starting point for sociological inquiry. *Human sexuality consists of those shared patterns of belief and behavior that directly or indirectly relate to erotic stimulation.* Now let's analyze this definition. First, note that it starts by specifying "shared beliefs and behavior patterns." That phrase could be used if we were talking of any customary aspect of human society, e.g., political activity, religious activity, economic activity, and so forth. The shared aspect indicates that it is a suitable subject for sociologists to study—it is not simply the idiosyncratic behavior of a few individuals. Belief and behavior *patterns* are the two main ways that humans in society organize any area of their life.

The last phrase in the definition is one that more specifically zeroes in on the essence of sexuality. Here I am asserting that there must be an impact in some fashion (direct or indirect) on erotic stimulation. This is *not* a definition that puts sexual intercourse or "genital sex" at the heart of sexuality. On the contrary we are speaking of *any act or thought* that is erotically *stimulating*. Intercourse is not required to be the act. The stimulation can be the result of reading a romantic novel or of a kiss which excites us and thereby leads to some minor erotic stimulation. Some acts of kissing do not involve erotic stimulation. If we are kissing our grandmother it is unlikely to lead to any erotic stimulation and thus it is not sexual by our definition. A touch of a hand on our arm or a smile can be as sexual as direct genital touching. Love or affection can, of course, promote genital stimulation particularly if it comes from a person that our social group defines as a suitable stimulator. Of course, we can be stimulated by "unacceptable" others such as those in our own nuclear family or by those married to others and it would still be a sexual response. Genital contact alone is not enough to definitely indicate

Gustav Vigeland's "Young Man and Woman." Courtesy of Vigeland-Museet, Oslo.

erotic stimulation. A gynecologist can touch the clitoris of a female patient and this *may* not be felt as genital stimulation by either of them. In fact, husbands do not become jealous of gynecologists precisely for this reason—they assume that the examination is not sexual—if they suspected that one or both were enjoying it sexually, they would be much more likely to become jealous. Thus, I am not stressing genital contact in my definition but rather erotic stimulation from any source whatsoever. Now, of course, an erotic kiss or touch will ultimately show itself in some genital response such as lubrication of the vagina or erection of the penis. But even those who, due to some physical or psychological restriction, do not lubricate or get erections, can be erotically stimulated. So I choose to focus on the erotic aspect as central. The culture one is raised in teaches one how to respond to different actions or thoughts and defines some as proper bases for erotic response and some for nonerotic. Just the simple touching of a potentially erotic zone is not sufficient—one needs to have become sensitized to that situation as being part of an erotic script. We can innovate and elaborate, but we all have erotic scripts.

Rape is another act in which the victim is not erotically stimulated. The emotions of fear and anger predominate for the rape victim. The rapist is viewed as involved in an act which to himself is erotically stimulating. There are those that would stress the hostile aspects of the rapist act (Brownmiller, 1975) but even they would admit that erotic stimulation on the part of the rapist is usually also present.

Thus, to be sure we have a sexual act we need to know if it involves erotic stimulation, directly or indirectly. Each society teaches its members the proper conditions for sexual stimulation. Individuals may, of course, violate these social patterns in the sexual area as they may in the religious, political, educational, or any other area of common behavior. But the group has a defined way of genitally arousing its members and that is what sociologically constitutes eroticism or sexuality. The attitudes regarding these acceptable ways of erotic arousal are shared sexual attitudes and the actual behaviors are, of course, also sexual aspects of society. We will spell out many of these patterned ways of believing and behaving shortly.

Another way to grasp the essential qualities of human sexuality is to seek out the characteristic consequences of sexual acts. There are two consequences of all sexuality that would be recognized in any culture on this planet. To be sure, they do not always occur but they are probable outcomes and one would need to make an effort to be sure of avoiding either of them. The first consequence is *physical pleasure*. One can be certain that the various sexual positions and the time and energy spent in finding a partner willing to participate in them would not occur if one or both of the actors did not seek and obtain physical pleasure for such actions. Physical pleasure cannot be equated with orgasm. Orgasm is, of course, a very intense form of physical pleasure but there are many other pleasures involved in sexual relationships. Pleasure is connected to all the sexual acts such as oral and anal sexuality as well as manual, breast, and genital manipulation. *The definition being proposed is not centered on intercourse—it is centered on erotic response.* Many prostitutes have intercourse without erotic response and for them such an act has the structure of a sexual act but not the feelings and thus it is from our perspective a pseudosexual act for the prostitute, although a fully sexual act for the customer. It is analogous to two people acting as friends but one or both not feeling like a friend. Human acts most often require attention to the feelings and thoughts that accompany them, if they are to be understood.

Finally, intercourse is but one sexual act that can yield pleasure. As sociologists we make no assumptions regarding the normality of focusing on sexual intercourse as the source of one's erotic pleasure. Some psychiatrists make such assumptions but such views are irrelevant to sociological theories.

The second typical consequence of sexual relationships is *psychological intimacy*. Sexuality is a catalyst for the growth of intimate relationships. Surely the long history of prostitution indicates that sexual acts can be performed with physical satisfaction as the major goal. There are those who prefer to avoid emotional involvement and to avoid any psychological intimacy. Nevertheless, it is here suggested that there is a tendency for this physical pleasure of the sexual act and the physical and psychic revelation of that act to encourage both further pleasure seeking and further self-revelation. The sexual act is here viewed as setting a pleasurable and revealing context in which different types of pleasure and revelation can easily blossom forth. One of the most popular sexual standards in the Western world is called "permissiveness with affection" (Reiss, 1960: Chap. 5). This standard stresses the connections between affectionate feelings and sexual feelings. Although many enjoy sexuality without the addition of other psychological satisfactions, most all people seem to prefer sexuality when it occurs in an affectionate relationship. Affection can occur first and encourage the addition of physical pleasure or physical pleasure can occur first and encourage the addition of affectionate ties. In terms of the wheel theory of love presented in the last chapter, rapport, revelation, dependency and intimacy need fulfillment in one area of interaction encourage the growth of those processes in other areas. Thus, what we are asserting here is consistent with that theory. Sexuality is a common way of fulfilling intimacy needs.

Many people who are committed to one person seek to avoid emotional involvement with other people. Such individuals will deliberately seek to minimize the chances for a conflicting involvement—by limiting the frequency of interaction, by avoiding romantic situations, and by explicitly telling the other person of their limitations. (We shall further discuss some aspects of this process when we discuss marital and extramarital sexuality in Part III.) Actions of this sort indicate that people are aware of the intimacy encouraging aspects of sexuality and they occasionally strive to minimize that sort of outcome. Cultures differ in their encouragement of either the pleasure or intimacy components of sexual relationships. Some areas of the world, like Polynesia, endorse pleasure seeking. Other cultures with orthodox religious connections strive to restrict such activities (Kennedy, 1973).

Jealousy is the result of the conceptualization of sexual intimacy as indicating a very high degree of self-revelation. Thus, the exclusive, focused conception of love ties sexuality into love very closely, whereas the priority, diffuse conception of love views sexuality and love as more easily separable and therefore sexual exclusivity is not so strongly demanded. In terms of traditional gender roles discussed in Chapter 3, the exclusive, focused conception that ties love and sexuality together is the perspective that is taught by Western culture more to women and the priority, diffuse love conceptions that may separate love and sexuality, is the perspective taught more to males in Western culture. Clearly, there is much overlap here and today there are many females and males who simply do not endorse the traditional views taught to their gender.

Heterosexual and Homosexual Orientations: A Sociological Perspective

Each culture defines the context in which the pleasurable and the intimacy consequences of sexuality should and should not occur. One of the major impassable borders is the homosexual–heterosexual distinction. Homosexual behavior is reported in all major civilizations of the past and present day. We discussed in the last chapter the Greek position on both homosexual love and heterosexual love (see also Licht, 1953). The Romans were not so tolerant of homosexuals as the Greeks, and our own attitudes have been influenced by this tradition of intolerance toward homosexuality (Kiefer, 1934).

The debate in scientific circles regarding the etiology of homosexuality has gone on for generations. I noted earlier that Havelock Ellis, writing in the 1890s, spoke of rejecting the older view that homosexuality is learned and put forth instead a newer view that it is biologically inherited. Ellis states:

> Some authorities who started with the old view that sexual inversion is exclusively or chiefly an acquired condition [like Nacke and Bloch] later adopted the more modern view (1954, p. 165).

The situation today in sociology has come around full circle again and now favors the view that homosexuality is learned. Some psychologists, particularly those who are followers of Freud, tend to view homosexuality as a pathological condition (Gadpaille, 1972). They feel it is a fixation at an earlier state of sexual development and that it often is caused by a morbid fear of women. However, in December 1973, the American Psychiatric Association removed homosexuality from its list of pathologies. Thus, professional opinion today, particularly among the younger therapists, is more likely to assume that homosexuality is not an illness but a learned life-style.

The term "homosexual" includes both male and female homosexuals, but the research literature focuses more on male homosexuals. The concept of "homosexual" may be defined in many ways. It seems that the essence of homosexuality is preference for a sexual partner of the same sex, and thus we shall define a *homosexual as one whose preferred erotic imagery and sexual partner choice is of the same gender.* By simply changing the word "same" to "opposite" we would have an acceptable definition of a heterosexual. We have not specified the amount of sexual behavior because it seems clear that one can be celibate and still be either heterosexually or homosexually inclined. Also one may experience *heterosexual* behavior but be utilizing *homosexual* erotic imagery and/or strongly prefer homosexuality. Our judgment here is that the imagery and preference are the most important elements in being homosexual or heterosexual. This allows also for degrees of preference and imagery and makes bisexuality a state wherein both same and opposite sex objects are relatively equally valued. It is worth noting that female homosexuality seems more tolerated, and females are themselves more tolerant of homosexuality. Kinsey et al. (1953, p. 489) found evidence of such female tolerance, and more recently Steffensmeir (1970) and Levitt and Klassen (1974) found the same tendency. In all societies lesbianism is less common than male homosexuality (Churchill, 1967; West, 1968). Lesbians, in our culture at least, are more romantic and selective, and male homosexuals more sensate and promiscuous (Kinsey et al., 1953; Ward and Kassenbaum, 1965; Bell and Weinberg, 1978). In short, female homosexuals show "traditional" female-type orientations to sexuality, and male homosexuals show "traditional" male-type orientations to sexuality. There are roles within both groups of homosexuals which divide into "butches" and "femmes" or "bulls" and "queens." However, observers agree that most homosexuals play both roles. Hooker (1965) and Bell and Weinberg (1978) present data showing that men will be the passive partner in some cases and the active partner in others.

Kinsey et al. (1948, 1953) believed that heterosexuality was more common because it was advantageous in the following ways: (1) The female vagina is more easily penetrated than the male anus; (2) culturally taught male aggressiveness goes better with female submissiveness than with another aggressive male; and (3) the

Gay Rights Parade, San Francisco, 1978. Courtesy of the National Sex Forum. Photo by Laird Sutton.

lack of intromission in female homosexuality reduces interest. A society's stress on heterosexual conditioning because of its need to perpetuate itself through offspring is another factor that makes homosexuality less common than heterosexuality (Beach, 1965; 1977). In this sense the structure of society, which utilizes Family Systems to select mates, legitimize parents, and nurture children, makes it likely that homosexual behavior will be less fully promoted. It may be allowed as an added source of pleasure or romance, but it has usually not been promoted competitively to heterosexuality.

Now, some qualifications are needed here, for we do know that among the Siwans in Africa (Ford and Beach, 1951:131–132) every married man is expected to have a young teenage boy for homosexual relationships. Also, in the Trobriand case (Malinowski, 1929) the natives did not know that coitus led to pregnancy, so they would not consciously promote heterosexuality for that reason. However, the one factor that is present in both the Siwan and Trobriand cultures is the high importance placed upon the family and the relations of the individuals in the family. The individual's loyalty is defined as belonging more to the family than to any homosexual liaison. This type of societal stress on the family means that heterosexual ties are encouraged and that homosexual relations, when allowed, will not usually be permitted to interfere in the operation of the family. In short, I believe, it is the lack of a perceived integration of homosexual ties to the Family System that has led to the minimization of this type of relationship. Now, homosexual couples could raise children, and one could conceive of a society whereby the state distributed babies to couples (whether the couple was homosexual or heterosexual). Under such a system homosexuality might be much more widely accepted, for it would be more integrated with the Family System.

The extent to which family members in a society see homosexuality as a threat to their system of heterosexual family life depends on various factors. One such factor would be the degree to which such people were "uptight" about the adequacy of their heterosexual cultural paths. If such cultural paths to heterosexuality were emotionally accepted and perceived as achieving their goals, I would expect less opposition to homosexuality. The evidence from the cross-cultural work of Churchill (1967) and Ford and Beach (1951), and from studies of nonhuman animals (Beach, 1977), is that homosexual behavior is very common. This fact is of prime importance, for what it means is that we must explain the *lack* of homosexual relations in any group, more than we must its occurrence. If the organism is born relatively neutral in regard to heterosexuality or homosexuality, then cultural training must be involved in any control of either type of sexuality.

There is one finding in the nonhuman animal studies of homosexuality (Beach, 1977) that is of special relevance here. All species of animals seem to display homosexual behavior on the part of both males and females. The situation that provokes a homosexual response is the presentation by an animal of the same sex, of the sexual stimuli of the opposite sex (Beach, 1977:307). In short, if a male assumes the lordotic position (bending over with the rear up in the air), another male may try to mount and may attempt penetration. Relatedly, a female in estrous may be mounted by another female, particularly if that other female is also in estrous (Beach, 1977:309). Beach perceives these behaviors as illustrating the principle of "Stimulus-Response Complementarity." If this stimulus-response complementarity were all that were operating, there would be complete bisexuality in all animal species. But this is not the case because of what Beach calls the "sex-linked prepotency" in motor patterns and stimulus sensitivity. In other words, the physiology of each sex is such that they are much more likely to respond to an animal of the opposite sex. Hormonal manipulation during critical stages of sexual differentiation in nonhuman animals can lead to alterations which produce "homosexual behavior," that is the sexual behavior of the opposite genetic sex (Beach, 1977). Further, Beach reports that repeated injections of estrogen in nonhuman males induces them to exhibit lordosis (Beach, 1977:311). The relevance of this for humans is still an open question (Masters and Johnson, 1979:409–411). But without such deliberate hormonal manipulation, there does appear to be a preference for the opposite genetic sex in other animals.

Thus, in nonhuman animals there is an almost universal presence of *occasional* homosexual acts. However, one must add here that not all mounting of a male by a male can clearly be designated as a homosexual act. This is so because oftentimes there is no sign of an erection and no penetration. Some such mounting may be simply dominance behavior. Some of the mounting behavior does involve erection and thus would more easily be labeled as arousal by the same sex and thus, homosexual. Of greater importance is the fact that "exclusive" or "preferential" homosexuality is virtually unknown in other animal species (Beach, 1977:Chap. 11). Nonhuman homosexual behavior occurs occasionally but does not become the preferred pattern for a particular animal. Animal physiologists like Beach assume that it is the hormonal and brain structure which gives an advantage to the cross-sex attraction in nonhuman animals. Why is the human case different? Why do we find exclusive homosexuality and exclusive heterosexuality only in human societies? Let us look to the recent research for some insight into this question.

In the Bell and Weinberg study of matched groups of homosexuals and heterosexuals it was found that a large majority of the homosexual males and homosexual females had experienced *heterosexual intercourse* (Bell and Weinberg, 1978:286) (see Table 6.1). Furthermore, between 14 and 33 percent of the homosexual sample had heterosexual intercourse during the past year. These are results from a sample of 1,000 homosexuals who were almost all very high on the preference of homosexuality over heterosexuality (see Table 6.1). In addition, 13 to 47 percent had been married; about half of those who married used heterosexual erotic imagery (see Table 6.1). Thus, it is apparent that human homosexuals do experience heterosexual acts and as can be seen in Table 6.1, the majority had experienced heterosexual arousal and thus they were not just "going through the motions" when having heterosexual relationships. Thus, the homosexual, at least in the younger years, is not devoid of heterosexual experience but instead is someone who has experienced both forms of behavior and comes to prefer the homosexual form. Most homosexuals do have heterosexual experience but there still is a dif-

TABLE 6.1

Percentage of Homosexual Participation in Heterosexual Activities

	WHITE HOMOSEX- UAL MALES	BLACK HOMOSEX- UAL MALES	WHITE HOMOSEX- UAL FEMALES	BLACK HOMOSEX- UAL FEMALES
Current Kinsey Rating	(N = 575)	(N = 111)	(N = 228)	(N = 64)
6: Exclusively Homosexual	74	62	68	61
5: Almost Exclusively Homosexual	18	23	19	17
4: Bisexual	3	11	5	5
0–3: Bisexual to Exclusive Heterosexual	5	4	8	17
Ever Heterosexual Coitus?	(N = 573)	(N = 110)	(N = 229)	(N = 64)
No	36	27	17	12
Yes	64	73	83	88
Any Heterosexual Coitus in Past Year?	(N = 573)	(N = 110)	(N = 229)	(N = 64)
No	86	78	76	67
Yes	14	22	24	33
Ever Heterosexual Arousal?	(N = 575)	(N = 111)	(N = 229)	(N = 64)
No	28	16	21	20
Yes	72	84	79	80
Have You Ever Been Married?	(N = 575)	(N = 111)	(N = 229)	(N = 64)
No	80	87	65	53
Yes	20	13	35	47
Homosexual Erotic Imagery During Marital Intercourse - Sometimes or Often?	(N = 106)	(N = 14)	(N = 72)	(N = 29)
No	45	43	53	55
Yes	55	57	47	45

Source: Bell and Weinberg, 1978: 286, 289, 374, 385.

ference then between human and nonhuman homosexuality. Human homosexuals are the only homosexuals who *prefer* homosexual behavior to heterosexual behavior. In other species, homosexuality is simply an occasional activity.

It is interesting to note that in parts of Polynesia where sexual behavior is more openly accepted and encouraged, preferential homosexuality seems quite rare (Malinowski, 1929; Marshall and Suggs, 1971). Marshall (p. 161) describes the situation in Mangaia as follows:

There are boys and men who enjoy and excel at cooking and who like women's company, cutting out clothes for women to sew, sewing, and washing clothes. (Supposedly, there are women who enjoy doing men's work or taking the lead with girl partners in ballroom dancing.) Some of the men bear such stigmata of the hermaphrodite as a high voice, dainty ways, a woman's walk, and a characteristically feminine carriage. But they are hard workers, incredibly clean, and show no apparent wish for male sexual partners.

Reports such as the above make one speculate that perhaps our culture encourages homosexuality by its strong opposition to the common tendencies of some people to identify with specific aspects of the opposite gender's role. One may logically assume that there would be in the human situation homosexual acts just as there are in other animal species. But it still may be that the *degree of preference* is a result of the *degree of social condemnation* of homosexuality. The path to heterosexuality may be blocked by feelings that if one has any homosexual inclinations then one cannot be a heterosexual. The data in Table 6.1 show that homosexuals do have heterosexual interests and thus perhaps the societal condemnation shifted the balance toward homosexual erotic response.

There are other reasons which would explain the difference in sexual orientations in humans. Human sexuality in many ways seems less controlled by fixed hormonal structures than is the case for other animal species. One example of this is the human female's orgasmic capabilities. In other species it is much more likely that female orgasm will occur predominantly during estrous. This is not a fixed rule but it is a strong tendency. In the human female, there is a constant ability to be sexually aroused that seemingly far exceeds that of other female animals. The hormonal controls promoting receptivity at the time of the greatest likelihood of pregnancy (estrous) seems lacking or certainly very weak in human females. The most recent data on differences in erotic response and imagery between males and females indicates that these differences are today rather minor (Osborn and Pollack, 1977; Robbins and Jensen, 1978; Vance and Wagner, 1976; Schmidt, 1975; Schmidt and Sigusch 1970; Masters and Johnson, 1966). Kinsey reports larger differences for his 1940s sample (Kinsey et al., 1953:651–678). Thus, learning seems to play a much greater role in humans. The range of sexual patterns in other species is much smaller than it is in the multitude of human societies that comprise the human species. Here, too, the great diversity is testimony not of our biological differences but of our cultural and learned differences. Thus, if learning is so much more powerful in the human case, it follows that we may develop preferences that other species lack and our "innate bias toward heterosexuality" would thus be much weaker than in other species (Meyer-Bohlburg, 1977).

Kinsey developed a simple means of rating the degree of homosexual-heterosexual preference one possessed. His approach is presented in Figure 6.1. A zero on this scale indicates exclusive heterosexuality both in feelings and behavior and a six represents the same exclusivity for homosexuality. The data from Kinsey and his associates (1948:643; 1953:499) indicates that there is a high degree of types 5 and 6 at about age ten (15 percent of males and 8 percent of females) but that by age twenty types 5 and 6 make up only about 4 percent of the males and 2 percent

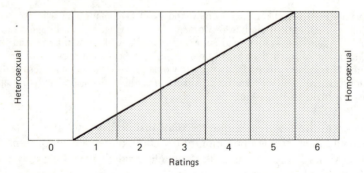

Figure 6.1. Heterosexual-Homosexual Rating Scale. (Alfred C. Kinsey et al., Sexual Behavior in the Human Male *(Philadelphia: Saunders, 1948), p. 63. Based on both psychologic reactions and overt experience, individuals rate as follows:*
0-exclusively heterosexual with no homosexual
1-predominantly heterosexual, only incidentally homosexual
2-predominantly heterosexual, but more than incidentally homosexual
3-equally heterosexual and homosexual
4-predominantly homosexual, but more than incidentally heterosexual
5-predominantly homosexual, but incidentally heterosexual
6-exclusively homosexual

of the females. For those who stay single into their late twenties and beyond (not more than 15 percent of all individuals), this percent does rise. Ultimately, Kinsey found that about 37 percent of the males and 13 percent of the females had at least one homosexual orgasm—in most cases this occurred in the teenage years and did not lead to preferred homosexuality (types 5 and 6). The precise figures cannot be taken as representative of the country because, as we shall shortly discuss, Kinsey did not use a probability type of representative sampling technique.

One of the most recent and extensive studies of homosexuality comes from the previously cited Bell and Weinberg (1978) research. They studied approximately 1,000 homosexual males and females and also 500 heterosexual males and females from the Bay Area of San Francisco. Their sample does not represent America. But it is not reasonable to require that one have a representative sample of homosexuals—there is no directory from which one can draw every one-hundredth name. So we must be content with samples of the sort utilized by Bell and Weinberg and we need to focus on relationships in the data rather than ask how representative of all homosexuals is the study. Some of the relationships found by Bell and Weinberg are presented in Table 6.2.

The table divides the respondents into five subtypes which Bell and Weinberg felt were a useful typology:

1. *Close-Coupleds*: Those involved in emotionally close relationships which focus upon each other for sexual and interpersonal satisfactions;
2. *Open-Coupleds*: Those involved in living with a special sexual partner but who tended to seek satisfaction outside the relationship;
3. *Functionals*: Those who organize their lives around their sexual experiences;

TABLE 6.2:
Percentage of Respondents in Each Homosexual Subgroup with Certain Sexual, Social, and Psychological Characteristics: Males and Females

	Close-Coupled		Open-Coupled		Functional		Dysfunctional		Asexual	
	(N=67) Male	(N=81) Female	(N=120) Male	(N=51) Female	(N=102) Male	(N=30) Female	(N=86) Male	(N=16) Female	(N=110) Male	(N=33) Female
					(See percents)					
1. Exclusively or predominantly homosexual in behavior	94	96	96	91	95	80	92	69	83	69
2. Has homosexual sex at least twice a week	69	43	60	51	100	60	47	31	0	0
3. Had at least 20 homosexual partners in past year	0	0	61	8	100	10	90	12	0	0
4. Had fewer than 6 homosexual partners in past year	69	100	15	53	0	33	5	50	46	100
5. Thinks somewhat or quite a bit about sexual matters	84	51	80	67	89	80	87	62	69	61
6. Does not at all regret being homosexual	69	68	54	59	78	100	0	0	37	73
7. Feels fairly happy or very happy	99	94	88	84	95	87	71	69	60	67
8. Seldom or never feels lonely	84	84	75	61	70	63	36	62	50	27
9. Relatively depressed	12	23	37	45	24	33	55	56	47	39

Source: Bell and Weinberg, 1978: 478–481.

4. *Dysfunctionals*: Those who are troubled and obtain little gratification from their lives; and

5. *Asexuals*: Those who lack involvement with others.

Between 70 and 75 percent of the 1,000 homosexuals in their sample fit into one or the other of these five subtypes. The subtypes help impress upon one the variety of people who are homosexual.

The male–female differences which have been cited widely in the literature are documented in Table 6.2. Most importantly, this difference is seen in the question on number of partners: even among the "functionals" only 10 percent of the female homosexuals had at least twenty partners in the last year whereas 100 percent of the male "functionals" had that many partners. Another major difference is one that exists among the five subgroups for both males and females. It is predominantly the "dysfunctional" and "asexual" subgroups that display a high level of psychological problems concerning questions of happiness and regret over their homosexuality. Those two subgroups make up about 40 percent of the males and 20 percent of the females in these five groups. Thus, the overall adjustment of females seems better than males. Also, if one were comparing homosexuals and heterosexuals in general, the homosexuals would come out with more problems but if one compared only those homosexuals in the first three subtypes, the heterosexual-homosexual difference would disappear. This makes it apparent why particular studies could come up with large differences and others with no differences when comparing homosexual and heterosexual groups (for references see Bell and Weinberg, 1978:197).

Similar comparative results come from studies by Saghir and Robbins (1973) who also compared matched groups of homosexual and heterosexual males and females; and from Schofield (1965) who compared English male homosexuals and male heterosexuals; and from Schafer (1977) who compared male and female West German homosexuals.

A study by Weinberg and Williams (1974) attempted to see if growing up homosexual in a more acceptant culture (Copenhagen and Amsterdam vs. New York and San Francisco) would make for differences in psychological problems and personal outlooks and perhaps affect the size of the dysfunctional and asexual subgroups. The psychological differences in problems were surprisingly small but there were differences. The European homosexual seemed less threatened by the heterosexual world and experienced and anticipated less intolerance. They were more open about their homosexuality and were more likely to have heterosexual friends. So the initial results indicate that cultural context of homosexuality does make a difference although more work with broader samples is needed to precisely specify the differences.

The evidence cited above would seem to support the perspective that our sexual preference (same gender or opposite gender) is learned. A significant finding is that male homosexuals seem influenced by the emphasis of the broader male gender role on separating sexuality and love and female homosexuals seem influenced by the broader female gender role emphasis on joining sexuality and love. In this sense homosexual behavior has a strong culturally learned stamp upon it. The large proportion of homosexuals who have had heterosexual experience and the early age of homosexual experience also backs up the idea that homosexuality is a sexual preference which comes out of the family and peer experience of youth, just as does the heterosexual partner choice. Let us now explore this in greater detail.

LEARNING SEXUAL MOTIVATION AND CHOICES

Being raised in a particular group develops sexual motivation in young people at the same time as the genetic sex of the object of that sexual motivation is being defined. There is an inborn tendency toward sexual behavior of some sort due to the fact that stimulation of the genitalia and other erotic areas is felt as a physical pleasure. All human groups have devised ways of obtaining such physical pleasure. More importantly, when one learns the accepted way to pursue sexual pleasure, one is learning a set of reasons for that pursuit. In short, I am *not* proposing a biological "drive" theory of sexuality but rather a learned view of sexuality. The child experiments and learns on its own some ways of gaining pleasure from genital sensations. Masturbation is quite common in infants and small children (Kinsey et al., 1948:53). But the culture has a master plan, so to speak, which it tries to impose on each generation regarding the proper ways of satisfying oneself and others sexually. The motivation is not necessarily there for carrying out the approved sexual acts but it is learned at the same time as one picks up the details of that society's structured way of achieving sexual satisfaction. For example, if an older peer shows one a picture of an attractive person of the opposite gender and states how wonderful it would be to kiss or hold that person, then one is being taught the expected sexual preference (opposite sex) and at the same time one is being taught that this is a wonderful and exciting thing to do. Thus, one's motivation to perform sexually is taught simultaneously with the teaching of the genetic sex that can produce that "wonderful" outcome. Like a rat learning a maze, having a reward at some path helps in learning to pursue that particular path.

Even today people exist who believe that sexuality springs forth full-blown at puberty like Athena from the head of Zeus. The notion of infant or childhood sexuality is rejected by many parents, as many young people cannot fully accept the idea that their middle-aged parents have strong sexual interests. Sigmund Freud in 1905 shocked much of the Western world with his assertions regarding childhood sexuality (1962:1):

> Popular conception makes definite assumptions concerning the nature and qualities of this sexual impulse. It is supposed to be absent during childhood and to commence about the time of and in connection with the maturing process of puberty; it is supposed that it manifests itself in irresistible attractions exerted by one sex upon the other and that its aim is sexual union or at least such actions as would lead to union. But we have every reason to see in these assumptions a very untrustworthy picture of reality. On closer examination they are found to abound in errors, inaccuracies, and hasty conclusions.

Group differences in prepubertal sexual behavior can be documented cross-culturally. Ford and Beach (1951:188–192) have some of the best evidence on this regarding a large number of societies. They report: "Adults in a large number of societies take a completely tolerant and permissive attitude toward sex expression in childhood" (Ford and Beach, 1951:188). In such societies masturbation by young children is very common. In fact, in some cultures, like the Hopi in our own Southwest, the parents will masturbate their young children to relax them. Other cultures do not encourage, but they tolerate, such childhood sexuality. Among the Trobrianders, about whom we have spoken several times earlier in this book, it is common for girls to start intercourse at about age eight and boys at about age ten. Thus, without going into further detail, it seems clear that prepubertal sexuality is a reality and that because of cultural training in one's socialization groups, variations occur both within one society and among societies.

The above supports Freud's position that children are sexual creatures. However, the same evidence contradicts some of his other views. For example, Freud believed that for the boy, at about ages four and five, there ensues an oedipal conflict in which the boy desires his mother sexually but fears his father's reprisals and, as a result, the boy enters a latency period in which he represses all sexual activity. The latency period ends at about age twelve with puberty, and then adult sexual behavior follows. Now, the evidence from other cultures and from our own makes it amply clear that between ages five and twelve there is a great deal of sexual activity going on. Perhaps the most striking evidence of this comes from the M.A. thesis of Boone Hammond (1965). Hammond studied lower-class black children in a St. Louis housing project. His report indicates that a good deal of sexual activity, including coitus, occurs during the so-called latency period. It occurs in this lower-class black housing project in a much more open and obvious way, but surely it also occurs elsewhere.

Perhaps the best way to show the extent of early childhood introduction to sexuality is to quote from Boone Hammond's thesis. This quote refers to the response a six-year-old girl gave to some pictures of men and women. Any picture could be interpreted in a large number of ways (nonsexual as well as sexual) (Hammond, 1965:36, 37):

> Finally we have . . . six-year-old Jane . . . who is making up stories about the pictures shown to her from the Thompson modification of the T.A.T. (a device used to get at the language structure of the children). Q: 'Tell me a story about these pictures.' A: 'A man he was fucking this lady. He was raping a lady. He made a lady pregnant. A man and a lady, they fucking. A lady's waiting for her husband to give him some pussy . . . .' The documented cases similar to those mentioned above are numerous in the data that have been collected but these few will suffice to show that there is an early awareness and socialization in matters concerning sex. It is not uncommon while walking up the steps to an apartment or while walking down a hall to have to step over a couple actively engaged in the act. You merely say, 'Excuse me, brother, I would just like to pass,' and continue on your way while the couple continue to 'take care of business'—uninterrupted by you. Having intercourse in the hallways is a commonplace occurrence and can be seen as an adaptation to a lack of privacy.

The above quote indicates some of the many opportunities for learning about sexuality in various subcultures of our country. It also indicates that in many respects the latency period is rather manifest.

Since there is a great deal of sexual activity and contact with sexual attitudes from birth onward, the learning opportunities in human sexuality are immense (Martinson, 1976). We have seen that many adults report extended experience with both homosexual and heterosexual activities and attitudes. The data on homosexuality we examined did indicate relatively early homosexual experience—before age ten. Perhaps one's sexual-partner preference is determined by how early one is exposed to heterosexual experiences that are satisfying as compared to homosexual experiences that are satisfying. (I prefer the term "sexual-partner preference" to the more conventional "sexual-object choice"—I think "partner" sounds more human than "object.") Our culture, as all Western cultures, asserts a sexual model which involves the goal of a heterosexual outcome. Broderick's study (1966) of 10–17-year-olds showed the ordered series of steps most young people go through to achieve this heterosexual outcome. Starting at very early ages one learns to fall in love (often without communicating this to the love object) and to have crushes on members of the opposite gender. Then one learns, by senior high school, to go to movies with someone of the opposite gender, to dance, and to date. Each step helps in the learning processes involved in the next step. Related to this overall process is a constant passing down from older and similar age peers of the lore of sexual and romantic relationships. Beliefs concerning the glories of romantic attachments are passed down more often in the female peer group and stories of the wonders of sexual excitement are more often passed down in the male group. These cultural attitudes also prepare one for choosing a partner of the opposite gender. Often, there is open ridicule or hostility toward homosexuality incorporated in the youth culture which further pressures toward heterosexual choices. Parents, too, pass down, often through indirect comments about sexuality, a perspective that supports heterosexual behavior. However, the parental message is clearly less sexually permissive than the one emanating from peers.

Many people experiment with a variety of sexual acts as young children. The degree to which we are included in the heterosexual peer pathways directly influence our acceptance of peer standards in place of our more personal learned satisfactions. As with other animals, there is every reason to believe that our own early childhood sexual acts would often include homosexual pleasures as well as heterosexual ones. If we are dealing with a child who has an early and strong interest in sexuality, then the pressure for deciding on a sexual-partner preference is increased. The ways in which one may be insulated from the major peer and parental cultural training in sexuality are multiple. One common way would be by relative isolation from peers. Another way would be by being frightened by parental horror stories of the risks of heterosexual relations. Another way would be if a child were not isolated from peers but peers were openly hostile. If, in addition to such experiences, one was able to gain satisfaction from experimenting with homosexual relations, then the choice of heterosexuality would become even less attractive.

The above is a socialization view of heterosexual–homosexual role learning.

There are virtually no parents who raise children to be homosexual. Thus, we must seek the causes of homosexuality at least in part in the very socialization processes that are aimed at reducing heterosexuality. Masturbation may well be one important influence on sexual-partner preference. One may develop in masturbation the erotic imagery of a particular gender and that can be incorporated into that person's erotic potential. In this way even isolated children can be socialized by literature which develops a particular erotic imagery. I have noted earlier in this chapter that in Polynesia one finds very little homosexuality of a preferred sort. Perhaps that indicates that a more open and positive perspective on heterosexuality is more successful in socializing young people into that sexual preference. Perhaps a lack of hostility toward homosexual behavior reduces the likelihood of homosexuality becoming a preference. The Western view of homosexuality has a strong element of fear, of homophobia. Perhaps this fear indicates an implied lack of social confidence in heterosexuality.

The ease with which our heterosexuality is seen as threatened by homosexuality may itself be productive of homosexuality. Perhaps those cultures that strive for exclusive heterosexuality in the most compulsive fashions are the very ones that will have the highest amounts of exclusive homosexuality. These are as yet still questions without firm answers but the literature we have examined so far in this chapter does lend support to these possible explanations.

There is other support for our socialization view of sexual orientation. Some of the psychological literature, such as Bieber et al.'s (1962) well-known study does indicate support. Bieber reported on a comparative study of 206 male psychiatric patients—106 of whom were homosexuals and 100 of whom were heterosexuals. The homosexual patients were less physically active during childhood, more isolated, and participated little in competitive sports. Homosexuals were less likely to have received heterosexual information and their mothers were more puritanical. Also, homosexuals reported more difficulties in their relations with their parents due to dominant mothers and absent or disinterested fathers. All of this fits in with our view of the importance of peers and parents in socialization regarding sexual preference choices. Of course, psychiatric patients do not represent all homosexuals and heterosexuals. Bell and Weinberg's work shows the great diversity of people who have homosexual partner preferences. But other studies do lend *some* support to the above findings (Saghir and Robbins, 1973; Schofield, 1965). Nevertheless, we have only a few pieces of the puzzle. For more definitive answers we will have to wait upon future research. Bell and Weinberg are planning to publish a second book on their 1970 sample of homosexuals and heterosexuals, analyzing the origins of sexual preference, and this work may move us closer to understanding such partner preferences.

SEXUAL-PARTNER PREFERENCE AND GENDER ROLES

After our discussion in Chapter 3 it should be apparent that the sexual-preference choice one makes is but one small feature of a person's total gender-role repertory. One may conform to the traditional conception of a male role in the occupational, religious, educational, and other spheres without having a heterosexual partner preference. We have seen how male and female roles differ in their relative stress on sexuality and affection. So the basic gender role training does make a major difference for homosexuals and heterosexuals. Certainly, in terms of basic gender identity, male and female homosexuals identify with their own gender. The stereotype of the male homosexual in female dress who thinks he is a woman is a distortion of reality. Male homosexuals do on occasion go "in drag." But they rarely think of their gender as being female. Relatedly, the male who is a *transvestite*, that is, dresses on occasion in women's clothing, is more often than not a heterosexual and not a homosexual. The transvestite and the homosexual illustrate the worth of John Money's notion of complementation as a process in gender role learning. Money asserted that as we grow up we learn both gender roles in detail but we code the role of the opposite gender with a negative sign saying "do not act upon." There are scores of behavioral attitudinal aspects to each gender role. The homosexual has taken the sexual-partner preference assigned to the opposite gender and acted upon it. The transvestite has taken the clothing style of the opposite gender and acted upon it. We now can raise the question as to why this particular aspect of gender role was altered by these people. But it is of equal importance to realize that it is but one aspect of a very complex gender role. We cannot assume that because that single aspect is altered, that all other parts of the gender role are altered and the basic gender identity is therefore changed. In fact, in a culture which had more overlap in male and female gender roles, homosexuality and transvestitism might not even be labeled as out of line with one's gender role. Notice that there are no women transvestites. Women are allowed to wear men's style clothing, and those who do so are not thereby labeled deviant nor are they seen as violating their gender role. Similarly, in parts of Polynesia, the male who engaged in a feminine occupation or made an occasional homosexual advance would not be exceeding his culture's gender role limits. In our own Western culture, the male and female gender roles are kept more distinct from each other and are therefore more subject to violation.

One other phenomenon related to sexual partner preference is transsexualism. A transsexual is a person who is attracted to someone of the same gender but, unlike the homosexual, a transsexual think's of himself as a member of the opposite genetic sex who happened to be "trapped in the wrong body." During the last twenty years several thousand such people have undergone surgery and related hormone treatment in order to have their body transformed into that of the opposite sex. In this way transsexuals can change their body to the one they believe is their "real" body. Again, I would suggest that if we had less distinct male/female gender role concepts many such people might feel more comfortable with the gender role of their own genetic sex. If the difference in gender roles were less, then it means less to be assigned to one role or the other. Also, as discussed in Chapter 3, if our culture had a third gender category, such individuals might accommodate to that gender without surgery. (The entire July 1978 issue of *Archives of Sexual Behavior* is devoted to transsexualism.)

The attitude we have toward homosexual choices can be seen in perspective in Table 6.3. Here it can be seen that 72 pecent of a national adult sample said that homosexuality is always wrong. Some perspective on this can be obtained by observing in the table that only 31 percent believe that premarital intercourse is always wrong. Finally, extramarital intercourse is seen as close to homosexuality in that 73 percent view it as always wrong. We have gone through a great many liberalizing changes in our sexual orientation in America but clearly we are still in many respects more restrictive than other Western countries, even on premarital coitus, let alone homosexuality. It is true that we now have about twenty states which have consenting adult laws that hold that whatever two adults do in private is not a matter of concern for the law. But equally clear is the fact that, compared to many other cultures, we have a rather narrow view of sexual-partner preference. Of course, one can find more restrictive societies (for example, the Irish) but there are also many less restrictive societies such as the Scandinavians (see Chapter 17).

TABLE 6.3

Attitudes Toward Various Sexual Acts in a National Sample of U.S. Adults, 1977

	PREMARITAL SEXUAL INTERCOURSE	HOMOSEXUAL RELATIONS Percentages	EXTRAMARITAL SEXUAL RELATIONS
Always Wrong:	31	72	73
Almost Always Wrong:	9.5	6	14
Only Sometimes Wrong:	23	7.5	10
Not Wrong at All:	36.5	15	3
	(N = 1,481)	(N = 1,453)	(N = 1,510)

Source: National Opinion Research Center, 1977: 131, 132.

Summary and Conclusions

There are obviously several ways in which one can approach the sociological questions related to human sexuality. Several theories about sexuality have been put forth (Hardy, 1964; Whalen, 1966; and Kelley, 1978). In one sense it is important that the reader be exposed to a range of perspectives and we have attempted to do that. But it is necessary, in order to clearly communicate, that we arrive at some consensus concerning the meaning of sexuality and the ways in which sexual-partner choices are made. I have expressed in this chapter some of the understanding gained from sociological research and theory. I have deliberately chosen to deal with homosexual and heterosexual partner choices at the same time. The understanding of these choices is so complex that to attempt to explain only one sexual partner choice would be to forego important insights that derive from the understanding of the opposite type of sexual partner choice. Human sexuality is an entity—it has a wholeness and unity to it. The recent work comparing homosexual and heterosexual responses by Masters and Johnson (1979) lends additional support to this view. The number of similarities in all areas of comparison far outweigh the differences present in the psychophysiology of sexual response. In sum, the process of developing a preference for a partner of the same or opposite sex is a single process of erotic sensitization and not two separate processes. The same is true of the processes that lead to having coitus or not, becoming pregnant or not, having an abortion or not, marrying while pregnant or not, and having a baby out of wedlock or not. None of these processes can be divided into a separate theory for those who do and those who do not. Ultimately, perhaps, we will arrive at a theory that will link together all these processes. The next two chapters attempt to build in that direction.

References

Acosta, Frank X. 1975. "Etiology and Treatment of Homosexuals: A Review," *Archives of Sexual Behavior* 4 (January): 9–29.

Archives of Sexual Behavior 7.4 (July 1978). This entire issue is on "Transsexualism." Based on the Fourth International Conference on Gender Identity.

Beach, Frank A. (ed.). 1965. *Sex and Behavior.* New York: Wiley.

———(ed.). 1977. *Human Sexuality in Four Perspectives.* Baltimore: Johns Hopkins University Press.

Bell, Alan P., and Martin S. Weinberg. 1978. *Homosexualities.* New York: Simon & Schuster.

Benjamin, Harry. 1966. *The Transsexual Phenomenon.* New York: Julian.

Bieber, Irving, et al. 1962. *Homosexuality: A Psychoanalytic Study.* New York: Basic Books.

Broderick, Carlfred. 1966. "Socio-sexual Development in a Suburban Community," *The Journal of Sex Research* 2 (April):1–24.

Brownmiller, Susan. 1975. *Against Our Will: Men, Women and Rape.* New York: Simon & Schuster.

Christenson, Cornelia V. 1971. *Kinsey: A Biography.* Bloomington: Indiana University Press.

Churchill, Wainwright. 1967. *Homosexual Behavior Among Males: A Cross-Cultural and Cross-Species Investigation.* New York: Hawthorn.

Clemmer, Donald. 1958. "Some Aspects of Sexual Behavior in the Prison Community," *Proceedings of the Eighty-Eighth Annual Congress of Correction of the American Correctional Association.* Detroit, MI, pp. 377–385.

Clinard, Marshall. 1978. *The Sociology of Deviant Behavior.* New York: Holt, Rinehart and Winston.

Comfort, Alex. 1967. *The Anxiety Makers.* London: Thomas Nelson.

Ellis, Havelock. 1954. *Psychology of Sex: A Manual for Students.* New York: New American Library of World Literature. (First published in 1891.)

Ford, Clellan S., and Frank A. Beach. 1951. *Patterns of Sexual Behavior.* New York: Harper & Row.

Freud, Sigmund. 1962. *Three Contributions to the Theory of Sex.* New York: Dutton. (Originally published in 1905.)

Gadpaille, Warren J. 1972. "Research into the Physiology of Maleness and Femaleness," *Archives of General Psychiatry* 26 (March):193–206.

Gebhard, Paul H., et al. 1965. *Sex Offenders; An Analysis of Types.* New York: Harper & Row.

Giallombardo, Rose. 1966. *Society of Women: A Study of a Women's Prison.* New York: Wiley.

Green, Richard. 1974. *Sexual Identity Conflict in Children and Adults.* New York: Basic Books.

Hammond, Boone. 1965. "The Contest System: A Survival Technique," unpublished Master's thesis, Washington University, St. Louis, MO.

Hardy, Kenneth R. 1964. "An Appetitional Theory of Sexual Motivation," *Psychological Review* 71, No. 1 (January):1–18.

Heilbrun, Alfred B. 1965. "An Empirical Test of the Modeling Theory of Sex Role Learning," *Child Development* 36 (September):789–799.

Hooker, Evelyn. 1965. "Male Homosexuals and Their 'Worlds,'" in Judd Marmor (ed.), *Sexual Inversion: The Multiple Roots of Homosexuality.* New York: Basic Books, pp. 83–107.

Humphreys, Laud. 1970. *Tearoom Trade.* Chicago: Aldine.

Hunt, Morton. 1974. *Sexual Behavior in the 1970's*. Chicago: Playboy Press.

Kelley, Jonathan. 1978. "Sexual Permissiveness: Evidence for a Theory," *Journal of Marriage and the Family* 40 (August):455–468.

Kennedy, Robert. 1973. *The Irish*. Berkeley: University of California Press.

Kiefer, Otto. 1934. *Sexual Life in Ancient Rome*. London: Routledge.

Kinsey, Alfred C., et al. 1948. *Sexual Behavior in the Human Male*. Philadelphia: Saunders.

_____. 1953. *Sexual Behavior in the Human Female*. Philadelphia: Saunders.

Kraft-Ebing, Richard von. 1965. *Psychopathia Sexualis: A Medico-Forensic Study*, trans. by Harry E. Wedeck. New York: Putnam. Originally published in 1886.

Levitt, Eugene E., and Albert D. Klassen, Jr. 1974. "Public Attitudes Toward Homosexuality: Part of the 1970 National Survey by the Institute for Sex Research," *Journal of Homosexuality* 1.1:29–43.

Licht, Hans. 1953. *Sexual Life in Ancient Greece*. New York: Barnes & Noble.

Malinowski, Bronislaw. 1929. *The Sexual Life of Savages in North-Western Melanesia*. New York: Harvest Books. (Published by Harcourt Brace Jovanovich.)

Manosevitz, Martin. 1974. "Early Sexual Behavior in Adult Homosexual and Heterosexual Males," in Nathaniel N. Wagner (ed.), *Perspectives on Human Sexuality*. New York: Behavioral Publications.

Marshall, Donald S., and Robert C. Suggs (eds.). 1971. *Human Sexual Behavior: Variations in the Ethnographic Spectrum*. New York: Basic Books.

Martinson, Floyd M. 1976. "Eroticism in Infancy and Childhood," *Journal of Sex Research* 12 (November):251–262

Masters, William, and Virginia Johnson. 1966. *Human Sexual Response*. Boston: Little, Brown.

_____. 1979. *Homosexuality in Perspective*. Boston: Little, Brown.

Meyenburg, Bernd, and Volkmar Sigusch. 1977. "Sexology in West Germany," *Journal of Sex Research* 13 (August):197–209.

Meyer-Bohlburg, Heino F. L. 1977. "Sex Hormones and Male Homosexuality in Comparative Perspective," *Archives of Sexual Behavior* 6 (July): 297–325.

Money, John, and Herman Musaph (eds.). 1977. *Handbook of Sexology*. New York: Elsevier-North Holland Co.

_____, and Anke Ehrhardt. 1972. *Man and Woman: Boy and Girl*. Baltimore: Johns Hopkins University Press.

National Opinion Research Center (NORC). 1977. "Cumulative Codebook for the 1972–1977 General Social Surveys." Chicago: University of Chicago.

Osborn, Candice A., and Robert H. Pollack. 1977. "The Effects of Two Types of Erotic Literature on Physiological and Verbal Measures of Female Sexual Arousal," *Journal of Sex Research* 13 (November): 250–256.

Reiss, Albert J., Jr. 1961. "The Social Integration of Queers and Peers," *Social Problems* 9 (Fall):102–120.

Reiss, Ira L. 1956. "The Double Standard in Premarital Sexual Intercourse: A Neglected Concept," *Social Forces* 34 (March):224–230.

_____. 1957. "The Treatment of Premarital Coitus in Marriage and Family Texts," *Social Problems* 4 (April):334–338.

_____. 1960. *Premarital Sexual Standards in America*. New York: Free Press.

_____. 1967. *The Social Context of Premarital Sexual Permissiveness*. New York: Holt, Rinehart and Winston.

Robbins, Mina B., and Gordon D. Jensen. 1978. "Multiple Orgasm in Males," *Journal of Sex Research* 14 (February):21–26.

Rosen, David H. 1974. *Lesbianism: A Study of Female Homosexuality*. Springfield, IL: Charles C. Thomas.

Saghir, Marcel T., and E. Robbins. 1973. *Male and Female Homosexuality*. Baltimore: Williams & Wilkins.

Schafer, Siegred. 1977. Sociosexual Behavior in Male and Female Homosexuals: A Study in Sex Differences," *Archives of Sexual Behavior* 6 (September):355–364.

Schmidt, Gunter. 1975. "Male-Female Differences in Sexual Arousal and Behavior During and After Exposure to Sexually Explicit Stimuli," *Archives of Sexual Behavior* 4 (July):353–365.

_____, and Volkmar Sigusch. 1970. "Sex Differences in Response to Psycho-sexual Stimulation by Films and Slides," *Journal of Sex Research* 6 (November): 268–283.

Schofield, Michael. 1965. *Sociological Aspects of Homosexuality: A Comparative Study of Three Types of Homosexuals*. Boston: Little, Brown.

Simon, William, and John H. Gagnon. 1967. "Homosexuality: The Formulation of a Sociological Perspective," *Journal of Health and Social Behavior* 8 (September):177–185.

Simon, William, Alan Berger, and John Gagnon. 1972. "Beyond Anxiety and Fantasy: The Coital Experiences of College Youth," *Journal of Youth and Adolescence* 1, No.3:203–222.

Sorensen, Robert. 1973. *Adolescent Sexuality in Contemporary America.* New York: World Publishing.

Steffensmeir, Darrell. 1970. "Male and Female Attitudes Toward Homosexuality," unpublished Master's thesis, University of Iowa, Iowa City.

Ullerstam, Lars. 1966. *The Erotic Minorities.* New York: Grove.

Vance, Ellen B., and Nathaniel N. Wagner. 1976. "Written Descriptions of Orgasm: A Study of Sex Differences," *Archives of Sexual Behavior* 5 (January):89–98.

Ward, David A., and Gene G. Kassenbaum. 1965. *Women's Prison: Sex and Social Structure.* Chicago: Aldine.

Weinberg, Martin S., and Collin J. Williams. 1974. *Male Homosexuals.* New York: Oxford University Press.

West, Donald J. 1968. *Homosexuality.* Chicago: Aldine.

Whalen, Richard E. 1966. "Sexual Motivation," *Psychological Review* 73, No.2 (March):151–163.

Zelnik, Melvin, and John F. Kantner. 1977. "Sexual and Contraceptive Experience of Young Unmarried Women in the United States, 1976 and 1971," *Family Planning Perspectives* 9 (March/April):55–71.

Premarital Sexual Permissiveness: Trends and Causes

SEVEN

Recent Trends in Premarital Sexuality

In the last fifteen years our historical knowledge of the Family System in America has increased vastly. For the most part, this has been due to the interest on the part of some historians in a behavioral science approach to recent American history. New journals have been formed to publish these results. For example, in 1976, *The Journal of Family History* was founded. Church records, cemetery records, census records, city officer's notebooks, and many other ingenious sources have been utilized. One of the outcomes of this new historical insight is a more balanced perspective on the Victorian era of the late nineteenth century.

Carl Degler's work (1974) is of particular interest to us here. He studied attitudes toward female sexuality in the late nineteenth century; the Victorian era had the reputation of being an extremely strict period in terms of sexual mores. Degler quotes the story of the nineteenth-century English mother who was asked by her daughter, just before she was to be married, how she should behave on her wedding night. The mother advised her daughter to "Lie still and think of the Empire" (Degler, 1974:1467). Medical doctors frequently wrote of female sexuality as follows: "The majority of women [happily for them] are not very much troubled with sexual feelings of any kind" (Acton, 1857:133). In an 1883 medical journal the American doctor Theophilus Parven told his medical class: "I do not believe one bride in a hundred, of delicate, educated, sensitive women, accepts matrimony from any desire for sexual gratification; when she thinks of this at all, it is with shrinking, or even with horror, rather than with desire" (Parven, 1883:607). This may seem amusing to those of you reading this today but the consequences of this view for nineteenth-century women were far from amusing. If a medical doctor assumes that the absence of sexual desire is the normal female state, then the presence of sexual desire would be defined as a disease. This was indeed the case for some doctors and clitoridectomies (the surgical removal of the clitoris) was at times the operation of choice to "cure" the disease (Comfort, 1967).

The above picture of the Victorian view of female sexuality is well-known among other historians. Degler set out to investigate whether these views were those of a vocal minority or whether they indeed represented the majority opinion of both the medical profession and of the urban middle class population. His careful search led him to find that many of the medical writers who were the most popular did *not* share the views concerning female sexuality quoted above. He found considerable evidence of medical writers advising that care be given to the "pleasure of both parties." There was advice concerning the value of simultaneous orgasm from authors in the late nineteenth century such as Dr. J. Marion Sims, the founding father of American gynecology. Evidence from many sources indicated that husbands complained to doctors about their wives' lack of passion and this can be taken as evidence that Victorian husbands *expected* their wives to be passionate. There were articles advising women not to masturbate because of the harm it was felt that produced. Here, too, such articles would be unnecessary if women were sexless and were not tempted to masturbate.

Degler concluded that previous historians were not as careful as they might have been in examining the literature. They had taken books that were normative and prescriptive and thought they described the status quo. The authors of the "sexless female" image were arguing for a state of affairs they *wanted* to exist, more than they were presenting evidence that such a state of affairs did indeed exist. A careful reading of the literature indicates that these conservative authors recognized that the Victorian world was not the way they wanted it to be. Many complained about married couples having intercourse for no other end but pleasure! So these authors were trying to persuade people to adopt a new standard, instead of describing accurately what was common in their day. Obviously, some people did share the conservative beliefs put forth—some did have clitoridectomies—but it is equally clear that many others felt quite differently about sexuality in the Victorian era.

One of the most interesting results of Degler's research was the discovery of a hitherto unknown research begun at the University of Wisconsin in 1890 by Dr. Clelia Duel Mosher. This was a pioneer study of married women's sexuality and it was discovered in the archives at Stanford University where Dr. Mosher taught later in her life. Dr. Mosher used a questionnaire consisting of twenty-five multiple-part questions. Questions were asked concerning the number of conceptions by choice or accident, frequency of intercourse, intercourse during pregnancy, occurrence of orgasms, purpose of intercourse, desire for intercourse, and contraception utilized. A most amazing set of questions for a research project that began in 1890!

Dr. Mosher gathered her information over many years; the last interview was in 1920. She had a total of forty-five different women that she studied. All but one woman was born before 1890; 70 percent were born before 1870. Thus the great majority of the women in the Mosher survey grew up and married in the nineteenth century. The respondents were far above average in education, with most of them attending college or normal school. Thus, they would be middle- or upper-middle-class women. About two-thirds of the women had worked before marriage, usually as school teachers.

The results are a fascinating insight into this segment of the nineteenth-century female population. Almost 80 percent testified that they felt desire for sexual intercourse independent of their husband's desires. About the same proportion said they had experienced orgasm in marital coitus. (For those women born before 1875, 82 percent experienced orgasm.) Two-thirds of the women listed reproduction as the primary purpose of sexual relationships but most of them felt pleasure was a goal as well. Only one woman thought sexual relations were exclusively a male pleasure. Clearly, the view of sexual intercourse as something that a woman tolerates or does as a duty was not dominant in this group of females. A common view of these women was that sexual intercourse was an expression of love and that love was its main justification. Pregnancy was clearly feared and many women stated their wish to avoid unwanted pregnancy.

Overall, then, the Mosher survey (as reported by Degler) indicated that there were many people who married during the Victorian era who did not endorse the view of woman as a sexless creature, nor did they overlook the importance of sexual pleasure in marriage.

We discussed in Chapter 4 that in the middle of the eighteenth century sexual intercourse before marriage seemed to be a rather common practice with about one-third of the brides pregnant at marriage (Calhoun, 1945; Smith, 1975). It now seems that even in the late nineteenth century, at least among the higher educated, married women were quite aware of their own sexual natures and most often enjoyed marital coitus. It still may be true that the late nineteenth century was an era of reduced sexual satisfaction and expression compared to the late eighteenth century but it is likely that this reduction has been overstated by some historians.

The question arises here as to what has changed since the late nineteenth century—particularly in the area of premarital sexual relationships. If we take the full century from 1880–1980 one can see an almost constant increase in the acceptance of sexuality, both within and outside of marriage. Few would dispute this—the question is not one of connecting the two lines joining 1880 to 1980—that without a doubt this is a sharp upward line on almost any measure of sexuality. The question rather is: Was the rate of growth relatively constant in all ten decades or were there particular times when change was dramatically increased or slowed?

My answer to the above question has to be an approximation—we lack the exact set of indices that would afford the precision needed for a complete answer. My conception of those ten decades of changes in premarital sexual permissiveness is contained in Figure 7.1. I would contend that there were two periods of exceptional change: (1) 1915–1925, and (2) 1965–1975. After each of these periods of rapid change there are signs of more gradual changes that indicate a consolidation of the increases. I believe that it has been sexual behavior which has changed first and sexual attitudes which have gradually caught up. Although clearly once the attitudes have caught up to the behavior, the attitudes themselves have helped precipitate another increase in sexual behavior. In this sense the feedback relationship makes the assignment of causal priority to behavior more problematic.

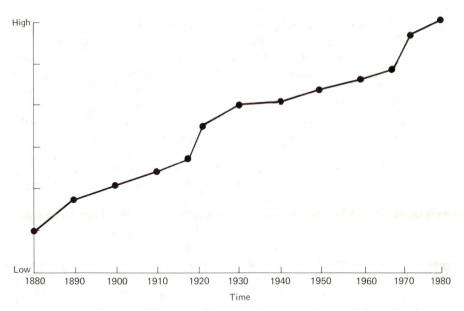

Figure 7.1. Rough Estimate of Rate of Changes in Premarital Sexual Permissiveness—1880–1980.

Smith (1978) argues for a somewhat earlier sexual increase than 1915–1925. He believes the sharper increase began about 1880 and was largely over by 1915. This is a complex point but the increase in divorce rates fits closely the pattern drawn in Figure 7.1 and supports a rapid general rise 1915–1925. Let us look at some of these research data.

There are studies of premarital sexuality throughout this one hundred-year time period, but the first one that is really impressive as a basis for broad overall understanding of trends is the work done by Alfred Kinsey and his colleagues. (For a complete list of studies on premarital sexuality see Bowman and Spanier, 1978: 88–91.) We have briefly touched upon Kinsey's work before. In 1937 Kinsey was a zoologist who, with help from the Rockefeller Foundation and Indiana University, began research into human sexual behavior. He was ably assisted by Wardell Pomeroy (a psychologist), Clyde Martin (a statistician), and later on by the current director of the Institute for Sex Research, Paul Gebhard (an anthropologist). These few researchers, in the years 1938 to 1950, interviewed over 16,000 respondents. They underwent extensive interview training for a period of a year in order to memorize the codes for the 300 to 500 questions they had to ask. Ideally, one would have hoped that Kinsey would choose a random sample of the American population. In that way he could have considered his results to be representative of the entire American population. However, he feared that there would be excessive refusal to cooperate in a random sample on the topic of sexuality. For this reason he chose to use a group sampling prcedure. So he selected a wide variety of groups (church, clerical, college, PTA, etc.) which he believed represented the nation. He then tried to persuade the leader of each group to cooperate and to be interviewed. Kinsey's hope was that if he could persuade the group leader to cooperate, then that person would help persuade the members of the group to cooperate. About one-fourth of all the groups he contacted did give 100-percent cooperation. The interviewers, years later, did retakes of the same interviews to see if the same results would be obtained. In addition, they would compare answers given by husbands and wives. These and other checks indicated support for the reliability and validity of their interviews. The problem of representativeness nevertheless remained. What broader group did those interviewed represent? Seventy-five percent of the female sample was composed of women who had been to college. A large proportion of the lower-class male group was composed of ex-convicts. Thus, Kinsey's study probably best represents the white, urban, Protestant, college-educated person from the northeastern quarter of the country. For other subgroups of Americans, Kinsey's findings are more subject to questioning.

Kinsey's study was the best up to that point in time. A group of respected statisticians evaluated it and judged it to be the best of studies done up to that time (Cochran, et al., 1954). Despite the above-mentioned sample limitations, it was superior in representativeness to studies of psychiatric patients or college sopho-mores. Kinsey focused upon behavior. He asked questions about the frequency of occurrence of a wide range of sexual behaviors. But he asked very little about attitudes toward those behaviors. The theoretical underpinnings of his study as-sumed that attitudes were epiphenomenon—they were rationalizations and the real explanations of behavior were rooted in the biological makeup of the male and female of the species. Given Kinsey's training as a zoologist this orientation is what one would expect. Still, in our search for trends, we can utilize his findings without his theoretical perspective.

TABLE 7.1
Premarital Coitus of Women by Decade of Birth (in percent)

	DECADE OF BIRTH			
	Before 1900	*1900–1909*	*1910–1919*	*1920–1929*
None	73.4	48.7	43.9	48.8
With fiancé only	10.4	24.4	23.3	27.3
With fiancé and others	10.4	21.0	25.6	17.4
With others only	5.5	5.4	7.0	6.5
Incomplete data	0.3	0.5	0.2	0.0
	100.0	100.0	100.0	100.0
Number of cases	(346)	(610)	(896)	(627)

Source: The data for this table were furnished to the author by the Institute for Sex Research, thanks to the kindness of Dr. Gebhard and Dr. Martin. It was contained in a letter to the author dated February 23, 1960. The word "fiancé" here means the man eventually married by the woman answering these questions. The table is based on 2,479 "ever married" women. Part of the data can be found in Alfred Kinsey, Sexual Behavior in the Human Male (Philadelphia: Saunders, 1948), Chap. 8, and all of the cases are from this volume. This table was first published in Ira L. Reiss,-1960:230.

Kinsey and his associates did most of their interviewing in the 1940s. They spoke with women who were born in four different birth decades. Table 7.1 compared the premarital coital rates of these women by decade of birth. This table is based upon only those women who were married, because with a sample of unmarried women one never knows how many more may eventually have premarital coitus. A sample of married women includes only those whose premarital sexuality is over. There is a clear trend in these data. Among women born before 1900 about one quarter were nonvirginal at marriage, whereas among those born in any of the first three decades of the twentieth century about 50 percent were nonvirginal at marriage. This same type of sharp increase holds up in the various educational and other subgroups in Kinsey's sample. Thus, even though the sample does not represent the entire country, such consistent results tend to suggest that a change was occurring, at least for a large segment of the population. Other studies by Burgess and Wallin (1953) and Terman (1938) gave further support to these Kinsey findings.

Females born in 1900 would be at the peak of their courtship activities between 1915 and 1925. This was the birth cohort that research indicated would first show the radical change from those born before 1900. This is one reason I have portrayed the 1915–1925 decade to indicate a sharp increase in premarital sexual relationships. The Kinsey data on males did not show any similar type of radical change. However, the Terman study of about 800 highly educated husbands and wives from California did indeed show a similar pattern for males as well as females (Terman, 1938:321). Terman, too, found the sharpest change in the birth cohort born 1900–1909 (see Table 7.2). Perhaps, all we can really conclude on the basis of these data is that the higher-educated groups in this country experienced a change at this time.

It is instructive to examine which categories of premarital relationships showed the greatest gains in Tables 7.1 and 7.2. The greatest increase was in "with fiancée only" and "with fiancée and others." These categories both indicate that "person-centered sexuality" was growing the most. The "with others only" category for males would indicate support for the double standard, which allows males to have intercourse but only with women they do not marry or love (Reiss, 1960: Chap. 4). Note how Terman's data indicates a dramatic drop in that category. The choice was never a major one for females. Relatedly, Kinsey notes that those males in his sample who were born in the twentieth century did have drastic reduction in the frequency of coitus with prostitutes when compared to males born in earlier decades (Kinsey et al., 1948:410). So all these findings tend to point to a dramatic change occurring to people who would be reaching physical maturity in the 1915–1925 decade. The exact percentage increase does not matter—what is important is the picture that emerges of a period of relatively rapid change in sexual relationships.

The Kinsey data on those females born in the first three decades of the twentieth century indicate little in the way of change in rates of virginity. Nevertheless, there is evidence from Kinsey's data that there was a large increase in petting to orgasm rates for those born in each of the first three decades of this century. For example, by age twenty, only 10 percent of the women born before 1900 had petted to orgasm; the comparable rate for the next three decades is 17 percent, 22 percent, and 28 percent (Kinsey et al., 1953:275). Thus, sexual intimacy was increasing in

TABLE 7.2

Premarital Coitus of Men and Women by Decade of Birth (in percentages)

	DECADE OF BIRTH		
Husbands	*Before 1890*	*1890–1899*	*1900–1909*
None	50.6	41.9	32.6
With fiancée* only	4.6	7.6	17.2
With fiancée* and others	9.2	23.0	33.7
With others only	35.6	27.5	16.5
Total	100.0	100.0	100.0
Number of cases (N)	(174)	(291)	(273)
Wives			
None	86.5	74.0	51.2
With fiancé only	8.7	17.7	32.7
With fiancé and others	2.9	5.8	14.0
With others only	1.9	2.5	2.1
Total	100.0	100.0	100.0
Number of cases (N)	(104)	(277)	(336)

The fiancé(e) referred to here is the person eventually married.
Source: Lewis M. Terman, 1938:321.

the petting area. Perhaps with a more representative sample we would have picked up coital changes as well. Nevertheless, it does seem that the data point to the 1915–1925 decade as significantly different than other decades at least in the *degree* of change in premarital coital rates.

One can substantiate the importance of the 1915–1925 decade by looking for other signs of radical social change. Sexual customs do not change in a vacuum. Large changes in sexual customs signal the occurrence of major changes in other areas of the society. There certainly were such major changes occurring in this decade. First, there was a world war. World War I began in 1914 and we entered it officially in 1917. The war brought our entire country into closer contact with European culture. Millions of our young men and smaller numbers of women went abroad and learned about ways of living other than those to which they were accustomed. On the home front, there was a significant increase in female employment—and that too instilled new ideas in young people. In addition, this period was the time, in part due to the war, that the United States entered the world scene as a major world power. It was the first military return to Europe of the upstart colonies. Lafayette had helped us in our war of independence and when General Pershing arrived in France he went to Lafayette's grave to tell the world: "Lafayette, we are here!" The industrial power of America helped win the day for the Allied cause. Our recognition as a key power in the world was one factor in the fantastic rate of economic growth of the twenties, which eventuated in the Great Depression. By 1920, the great waves of immigrants were slowing down considerably. This was the time which historians list as the achievement of our full urban-industrial development. In 1920 we passed the 50 percent urban mark for the first time. Such changes in sexuality, world contact, and urbanism had to be felt in the basic male–female gender roles and particularly in the part of those roles that involves sexual attitudes and behaviors.

Another index of the radical rate of change was in divorce rates. Between 1915 and 1920 our divorce rate increased over 50 percent (Jacobson, 1959:90). In the five years before that (1910–1915), it had increased only about 10 percent. Clearly, something new was happening. Such rise in divorce is usually a signal of a radical change in the rules by which men and women interact—i.e., a change in gender roles. That sort of change is congruent with the changes reported by Kinsey and Terman in sexual behavior.

The forty years from 1925 to 1965 are portrayed in Figure 7.1, as encompassing only moderate change. As we already noted, there is some evidence of change from the Kinsey research that shows a rise over the four birth decades in petting to orgasm. Also, between 1940 and 1960 the illegitimacy rate in this country tripled. We will say more about this in Chapter 8. Such a rise in illegitimacy should indicate a rise in female nonvirginity. However, it is possible that an increase in frequency of intercourse and number of partners could produce a rise in illegitimacy without an increase in nonvirginity. The Kinsey data show little evidence of an increase in nonvirginity at that time period and so we look for other explanations. However, we must remember that the Kinsey sample is not representative of the country. Perhaps the rise in illegitimacy came from the lower-educated groups not fully represented in Kinsey's sample. There is some evidence from other trend data supporting at least a modest rise in the 1940–1960 time period (Udry, 1975). I have taken a compromise position and in Figure 7.1 show a moderate rise in premaritial permissiveness in the 1940s and 1950s.

Although very few readers of this book were alive during the first period of radical change (1915–1925), most all of you were alive during the second period:1965 to 1975. The data from three National Opinion Research Center (NORC) representative samples of adult Americans support the view that there has been a major change in premarital sexual attitudes in that recent period. The first national sample was carried out in 1963 as part of my study of causes of premarital sexual attitudes (Reiss, 1967). The second national sample was part of the 1970 research project of Levitt and Klassen (1974). The third is the 1975 General Social Survey that the National Opinion Research Center carried out as part of its annual research program. The percentage of adults who stated that premarital intercourse was always wrong changed between 1963 and 1975 from approximately 80 percent to only 30 percent. That amount of change in a twelve-year period is most unusual. All three of these studies utilized probability type samples of the country and thus one can feel confident that dramatic changes in premarital sexual attitudes have occurred.

There is also a national sample source for changes in premarital sexual behavior. Zelnik and Kantner, two sociologists-demographers from Johns Hopkins University, undertook two national research projects—one in 1971 and one in 1976. Unfortunately, their focus was restricted to on fifteen to nineteen-year-old females. Virtually all the research to date indicates that female sexuality has changed far more

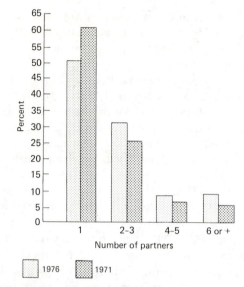

Figure 7.2. *Percent of Sexually Experienced Never-Married Women Aged 15 to 19, by Number of Partners Ever, 1976 and 1971. (Zelnick and Kantner, 1977:61.)*

than male sexuality and thus the female group is the better one to sample for evidence of change. Table 7.3 shows clear indications of change between 1971 and 1976 in teenage female premarital sexual intercourse rates. Twenty-seven percent of the teenage female group were nonvirginal in 1971 and 35 percent of that group were nonvirginal in 1976. That may seem like a minor increase but it is actually an increase of 30 percent in just a five-year period. These rates are considerably higher than Kinsey's findings of 20 percent nonvirginal by age 20. In the 1976 Zelnik and Kantner sample, 55 percent were nonvirginal by age 19. It is interesting to note in Figure 7.2 that about 60 percent of both black and white female teenagers said they had only one partner in 1971 and this decreased to about 50 percent in 1976. The rate in Kinsey's data was also about 50 percent. Of course, Zelnik and Kantner's sample consists only of teenage women and one would expect the percentage with only one partner to go down considerably by the time these women are married.

Once again, if we look for general changes occurring in the 1965–1975 decade we find a remarkable similarity to the 1915–1925 period. First, we were also involved in a major war—this one in Vietnam. Any war speeds up social change, but this particular war also had another catalyst operating toward change. Vietnam was the most unpopular war ever and millions of people challenged the government's right to draft men into service and to continue the war. Once people are angered enough to challenge the federal government, they are more likely able to challenge other aspects of their life-style. In this sense, an unpopular war bred greater change than a popular war such as World War II.

A second common indicator of social change in these two periods was the divorce rate. Beteen 1965 and 1975 the divorce rate in America doubled. This is

TABLE 7.3

Percent of Never-Married Women Aged 15–19 Who Have Ever Had Intercourse, by Age and Race, 1976 and 1971

AGE											
		STUDY YEAR AND RACE									
		1976				1971				% increase 1971–1976	
	ALL	WHITE		BLACK		ALL	WHITE		BLACK		ALL WHITE BLACK
		%	N	%	N		%	N	%	N	
15–19	34.9	30.8	1,232	62.7	654	26.8	21.4	2,633	51.2	1,339	30.2 43.9 22.5
15	18.0	13.8	276	38.4	133	13.8	10.9	642	30.5	344	30.4 26.6 25.9
16	25.4	22.6	301	52.6	135	21.2	16.9	662	46.2	320	19.8 33.7 13.9
17	40.9	36.1	277	68.4	139	26.6	21.8	646	58.8	296	53.8 65.6 16.3
18	45.2	43.6	220	74.1	143	36.8	32.3	396	62.7	228	22.8 35.0 18.2
19	55.2	48.7	158	83.6	104	46.8	39.4	287	76.2	151	17.9 23.6 9.7

Source: Zelnik and Kantner, 1977:56.

similar to the very rapid rise in divorce in the 1915–1925 period. Divorce, among other things, is an indicator of changes in gender roles. As gender roles change it becomes more difficult for males and females to know what to expect from each other and more relationship issues have to be personally worked out. In time new systems are constructed and divorce stabilizes—as it did after 1920 and as it now seems to be doing. (See Chapter 12.) The divorce rate itself is also affected by changes in what men and women do in society—the vast increase in female employment, particularly for young mothers, has added an expected employment dimension to the female role. Much of this increase also has occurred since 1965 (see Chapter 15). This increases the female's economic independence and perhaps her assertiveness in general. Such changes are likely to be reflected in sexual attitudes and behavior. Of course, there are other factors that affect sexual attitudes and behavior and we shall talk of those very shortly. But suffice it to say that the signs of a major social change were present in the 1965 to 1975 decade. Hunt's 1972 national study indicated that among married 18–25-year-olds, 95 percent of the men and 81 percent of the women had premarital coitus (Hunt, 1974:15). Tavris and Sadd (1977:34), in their 1974 *Redbook* reader survey reported that 80 percent of the wives experienced premarital intercourse. The percent nonvirginal was 96 percent for the respondents who were under twenty and 68 percent for those forty and over. Historians have called the 1965–1975 decade the start of the postindustrial period (Bell, 1973). The industrial society was concerned with the production of goods and services. The postindustrial society was concerned with the *equitable* division of the goods and services produced by a society. The civil rights legislation and the women's movement are but two indications of this recent increased concern with equity.

I am suggesting that the period of rapid change is over because the social indicators support this view. The divorce rate is leveling out. Since 1976 change in divorce rates has been quite minor. The marriage rate, which had gone down, is now rising. The birth rate, which had fallen since 1958, is now seemingly stabilized. Thus, there are many signs that rapid social change has ceased. I believe we are entering another period of consolidation, similar to the 1925–1965 period. In such a period of time attitudes and behavior come closer together and after trial-and-error consideration, relative priorities are given to the new social choices that have opened up. I believe we are now in a period of consolidation and will remain in it at least until the 1990s. There are those who view the current situation as a backlash and a countertrend. I will later discuss my reasons for viewing it as a consolidation. But I should note here that the increase in confrontations today may simply be an indication that things have changed and those who do not approve are voicing their disapproval. Beyond the verbal clashes there are very few signs of a reversal in sexual permissiveness. But more of this later.

Explanations of Premarital Sexual Permissiveness

When I took my first position as a college professor of sociology, I was asked to teach a course in sociology of the family. I had never taken a course in that area as a graduate student. However, I did have a strong interest in the study of human sexuality. I had written a paper on the topic in my senior year in college. Shortly after that the male volume of the Kinsey report appeared and that further increased my interest in that area. So, when a few years later I was asked to teach a family course, I decided I would choose a textbook on the basis of the quality of its chapter on sexuality. I found this to be a most difficult task. Many of the textbooks took a moralistic approach to human sexuality (Reiss, 1956; 1957). A few ignored any lengthy discussion of sexuality. The general textbook attitude was traditional and premarital intercourse was pictured in several of the leading texts as "lustful," "selfish," and "promiscuous." Intercourse was portrayed as leading to one or more of the following consequences: guilt, social condemnation, venereal disease, and pregnancy. There was little discussion of premarital intercourse between people in love; no discussion of contraceptive protection; and virtually no discussion of consequences such as physical pleasure or psychological intimacy. Several authors had either ignored the Kinsey data or used it selectively to backup their moral position. The textbook approach in many books was simply a moral treatise that proclaimed the evil of premarital intercourse. That was in 1953 and the situation today is radically changed—at least on premarital intercourse if not on other areas of sexuality. But that experience encourged me to do some careful thinking about just what could be said about premarital sexuality in America from a scientific as opposed to a moralistic view. In 1960 I published a book on that topic and then set about to undertake my own national research, which I published in book form in 1967. In 1974 and 1979 I, together with Brent Miller, published a refinement of the explanations I had put forth earlier (Reiss and Miller, 1974; 1979).

   The essence of my 1960 book was to point out that we have in America several premarital sexual standards—not just one—and that the consequences of premarital sexual intercourse vary depending on which of those standards one adheres to (for a later statement of a similar view see Christensen 1962). I delineated four premarital sexual standards:

1. *Abstinence:* Premarital intercourse is considered wrong for both men and women, regardless of circumstances;

2. *Double Standard:* Premarital intercourse is more acceptable for men than for women;

3. *Permissiveness with Affection:* Premarital intercourse is considered right for both men and women when a stable relationship with love or strong affection is present;

4. *Permissiveness With or Without Affection:* Premarital intercourse is considered right for both men and women if they are so inclined, regardless of the amount or stability of affection present (this was called Permissiveness Without Affection in my 1960 book—I feel the above new label is more precise as to the content of this standard).

The first standard is the formal sexual standard in the Western world—at least since the advent of Christianity. There is no record of any society achieving abstinence for even the majority of its males—although a few rare societies such as the early Puritans (seventeenth century) may have come close. In most all societies, the vast majority of males have been sexually experienced at marriage. The real variance in history has been in who the partners of the males would be. The double standard gave males greater sexual rights in amost every society. In some societies the partners for males were prostitutes and lower-class women; in others it was the girl next door, and in some, all of these. Rates of intercourse for small groups of males have varied; e.g. the Terman data we just examined shows changes for college-educated males but the rates of nonvirginity were much higher and, I suspect, more stable among the vast majority of males with less education. So throughout the past 2,000 years while abstinence was our *formal* standard the double standard was our *informal* standard.

There have always been adherents to "permissiveness with affection." We noted in Chapter 4 that in the late Puritan period (late eighteenth century) about a third of the brides were pregnant at marriage. Intercourse among couples who were seriously involved with each other and/or engaged has always been the least condemned type of premarital coitus. The Anglo-Saxons levied the lowest fine for this sort of "violation" (Queen and Habenstein, 1974). In addition, there have been those who have accepted such intercourse as fully proper. So the roots of the permissiveness with affection standard go back a long way in time. The entire romantic love movement discussed in Chapter 5 endorses the conception that affection justifies sexuality and that is also the underlying premise of this modern-day standard.

"Permissiveness with or without affection" is also of ancient heritage. It will be familiar to you as in line with Ovid's conception of love relationships, although Ovid was talking predominantly of extramarital relationships. This standard has not been strongly endorsed in the Western world. The tradition is that males can enjoy

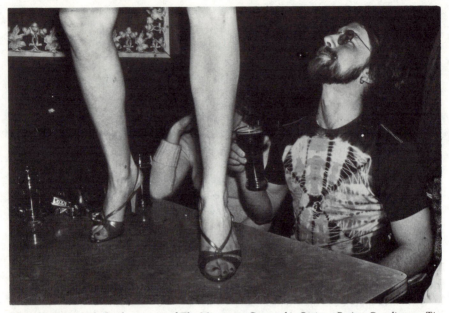

Photo by Craig Litherland, courtesy of The Minnesota Geographic Society. Project Coordinator: Tim Strick.

sexuality without affection, in accord with the double standard, but females have not often been granted equal privileges. The full endorsement of permissiveness with and without affection is more apt to be found in Polynesia, in some of the cultures we have spoken of such as the Trobriand (Malinowski, 1929) and Mangaia islands (Marshall, 1971).

The four standards can be further subdivided (Reiss, 1960; 1967): Abstinence into kissing and petting subtypes; the double standard into degree of acceptance of female sexuality; permissiveness with affection into degree of affection required; and permissiveness with or without affection into the degree to which affectionate sexuality is preferred.

These standards still seem applicable today as a way of categorizing the views of young people.

Back in 1959 we found that the endorsement of abstinence ranged from 20 to 80 percent depending on the particular school examined (Reiss, 1967: Chap. 2). Many schools today come out closer to the 20 percent endorsement. For the adult population twenty-one years old and above in 1963 the endorsement of abstinence averaged about 80 pecent. This, too, has changed dramatically. Today, as noted earlier, the adult endorsement would be only about 30 pecent (NOC, 1977).

The four standards are useful categories with which to conceptualize different belief systems regarding premarital sexual permissiveness. However, for research purposes it is simpler to have a single dimension, running from low to high, upon which to measure the degree of permissiveness of any one individual. Sexual permissiveness is in this sense viewed as the degree to which various sexual acts are accepted. Such a single dimension would allow an immediate comparison of everyone as to relative rank on this premarital sexual permissiveness dimension. In 1959 I developed a set of twelve questions that would allow for a ranking of all respondents. Table 7.4 lists the full set of twelve questions and Table 7.5 shows the logic of the scale. We broke up premarital sexual permissiveness into three behavioral categories of kissing, petting, and coitus. Then we cross-classified these three behavioral categories by four states of affection: engaged, love, strong affection, and no affection. The matrix created by these components (Table 7.5) comprises the twelve questions.

It was deemed necessary to ask respondents more than just if they believed a certain sexual behavior was acceptable. People judge such matters in terms of the amount of affection present. For example, some people would accept premarital intercourse but only if they were in love. The question on premarital intercourse would not be clear unless we specified whether love was present. So we classified each behavior by an affectionate state to guarantee that our questions would have precision and a singular meaning to the respondents. We included the kissing questions because we were planning to administer the scale to junior high school students. Actually, the first three kissing items were endorsed by almost everyone and so they can be dropped except for use on very young or very low permissive populations. For a college population, one could select out only the four coital questions.

It should be noted that the scale refers only to one gender. A second set of twelve questions is administered to everyone to ask about the other gender. Thus, the researcher then has a permissiveness score on the "male scale" and on the "female scale" for each person. These scores can be compared to measure the "equalitarianism" of the respondent. If one were interested in classifying people into one of the four premarital sexual standards, that, too, can be constructed from the answers to the male and female scales (for instructions see Reiss, 1964:197; 1967:Chap. 2).

In 1959 we drew representative samples from two Virginia senior high schools, two Virginia colleges, and one college in New York state. Then, in 1963, we contracted for the National Opinion Research Center (NORC) to draw a representative national sample of adults in America. One major goal was to test our scales on these varied samples. The scales came out in an ordered and cumulative fashion—so that the way one answered one question determined the way other questions were answered. In short, the scales met the full set of criteria for Guttman-type scaling (Guttman, 1950). Since that time these scales have been used in scores of research projects in this country and in many other countries (Rashke and Li, 1976; Hampe and Ruppel, 1974; Stillerman and Shapiro, 1979; Perlman et al., 1978). Table 7.6 presents the results in our student and national adult samples. It is interesting to note that although the level of acceptance has increased considerably today, recent testing indicates that the rank order of the questions remains the same (Walsh et al., 1976). The only questions whose rank order does significantly vary is question 4 and 8. These are two of the nonaffection items. A high permissive group endorses intercourse with affection (questions 9, 10, 11) more

TABLE 7.4

Reiss Male and Female Premarital Sexual-Permissiveness Scale

First decide whether you agree or disagree with the view expressed. Then circle the degree of your agreement or disagreement with the views expressed in each question. We are not interested in your tolerance of other people's beliefs. Please answer these questions on the basis of how YOU feel toward the views expressed. Your name will never be connected with these answers. Please be as honest as you can. Thank you.

We use the words below to mean just what they do to most people, but some may need definition:

Love means the emotional state which is more intense than strong affection and which you would define as love.

Strong affection means affection which is stronger than physical attraction, average fondness, or "liking"— but less strong than love.

Petting means sexually stimulating behavior more intimate than kissing and simple hugging, but not including full sexual relations.

Male Standards (Both Men and Women Check This Section)

1. I believe that kissing is acceptable for the male before marriage when he is engaged to be married.

    Agree: (a) Strong   (b) Medium   (c) Slight
    Disagree   (d) Strong   (e) Medium   (f) Slight

2. I believe that kissing is acceptable for the male before marriage when he is in love.
   (The same six-way choice found in Question 1 follows every question.)
3. I believe that kissing is acceptable for the male before marriage when he feels strong affection for his partner.
4. I believe that kissing is acceptable for the male before marriage even if he does not feel particularly affectionate toward his partner.
5. I believe that petting is acceptable for the male before marriage when he is engaged to be married.
6. I believe that petting is acceptable for the male before marriage when he is in love.
7. I believe that petting is acceptable for the male before marriage when he feels strong affection for his partner.
8. I believe that petting is acceptable for the male before marriage even if he does not feel particularly affectionate toward his partner.
9. I believe that full sexual relations are acceptable for the male before marriage when he is engaged to be married.
10. I believe that full sexual relations are acceptable for the male before marriage when he is in love.
11. I believe that full sexual relations are acceptable for the male before marriage when he feels strong affection for his partner.
12. I believe that full sexual relations are acceptable for the male before marriage even if he does not feel particularly affectionate toward his partner

(The 12 female questions are the same except the gender reference is changed.)

Source: Ira L. Reiss, 1967: 211–214. (Unless you are administering this scale to a very young and/or low permissive group, you can eliminate the kissing questions.) Scaling instructions can be found in appendix E of Reiss (1967) and in Reiss (1964).

than they endorse petting without affection (question 8). In a low permissive group this ranking is reversed. This knowledge of variation can be useful but to be able to obtain a "universal ordering" of items which would not vary by the group it was administered to, we dropped questions 4 and 8. We also dropped questions 1, 2, and 3 since virtually everyone accepted these questions. Then we combined the love and engaged questions (5 and 6; 9 and 10) because the responses were very

TABLE 7.5

The Basic Components in the Reiss Premarital Sexual Permissiveness Scale*

| | SEXUAL BEHAVIORS | | |
Affection States	Kissing	Petting	Coitus
Engaged	1	5	9
Love	2	6	10
Strong Affection	3	7	11
No Affection	4	8	12

* *The number in each cell corresponds to the Question Number in the scale. The precise questions are in Table 7.4*

similar to the condition of love and engagement. This left us with the universal order going from most accepted to least accepted of questions: (5 and 6), 7, (9 and 10), 11, 12. These five questions always have come out in this identical scale order and allows for comparison of very diverse groups.

Table 7.7 presents how our four race-gender groupings come out on this universal scale. There are large differences in these various race-gender groups in Table 7.7, but we can still rank them and compare them. The zero rank or "scale type" means that none of the five questions were agreed to by those respondents. The 5 rank means that all five questions in the universal scale were agreed to. The "cumulative" quality of this type of Guttman scale can be illustrated by noting that anyone who agreed to question 11 must have agreed to the three questions that rank above question 11 in acceptance ([5 and 6], 7, (9 & 10)). In short, to accept a question that has low acceptance means that you must also accept all those questions that are more acceptable. If actual choices fit this cumulative pattern we have a Guttman scale. Over 90 percent of the responses must fit these cumulative ranking predictions in order for the scale to be acceptable. In this universal form of the scale in Table 7.7, 98 percent of the answers fit the predicted pattern. Similar results have been obtained in the numerous recent uses of these scales in the United States and elsewhere. Finally, it is important to report that although the data presented in Tables 7.6 and 7.7 are about twenty years old, the rank order of questions today is still the same and, furthermore, the differences between whites and blacks and between males and females still appear. For example, Morton Hunt's (1974:117–119) data indicates that for the 18–25-year-olds in 1972, 86 percent of the males and 59 percent of the females would endorse question 11 and 71 percent of the males and 29 percent of the females would endorse question 12 for their own sex.

Once we had devised a reliable and valid measuring instrument for premarital sexual permissiveness, then we could explore the causes of changes in that important dimension. I will not present the findings in technical form. The interested reader can see the recent publication by Reiss and Miller (1979). Instead, I will present some of the basic factors which we believe to be causally involved in affecting the level of premarital sexual permissiveness.

The thirteen propositions in Table 7.8 are but a select list of the propositions that we found to be important in our research (Reiss, 1967; Reiss and Miller, 1974;

TABLE 7.6

Percentage Agreeing with Each Item in Male and Female Scales in the Adult and Student Samples

QUESTION NUMBER	NATIONAL ADULT SAMPLE (1963) TOTAL PERCENT	STUDENT SAMPLE (1959) TOTAL PERCENT
Male Scale		
1	95.3	97.5
2	93.6	98.9
3	90.2	97.2
4	58.6	64.2
5	60.8	85.0
6	59.4	80.4
7	54.3	67.0
8	28.6	34.3
9	19.5	52.2
10	17.6	47.6
11	16.3	36.9
12	11.7	20.8
N	(1,390)	(811)
Female Scale		
1	95.0	98.5
2	93.3	99.1
3	88.1	97.8
4	50.1	55.2
5	56.1	81.8
6	52.6	75.2
7	45.6	56.7
8	20.3	18.0
9	16.9	44.0
10	14.2	38.7
11	12.5	27.2
12	7.4	10.8
N	(1,411)	(806)

Source: Ira L. Reiss, 1967:29.

1979). The reader should note that the phrase "influencing in a positive direction" simply means that as one variable goes up, the other variables go up, and as one goes down, the others go down. So, in proposition one, the more the rewards outweigh the costs, the higher one's permissiveness. To "influence in a negative direction" means that as one variable goes up, the other variable goes down. For example, in proposition seven, the more responsibility you have for other family members (like younger siblings), the lower your premarital sexual permissiveness will be. (See Appendixes 2, 3, and 4 for further elaboration on propositions.) I have deliberately left out some qualifiers concerning the precise conditions under which

TABLE 7.7

Percentage Distribution of Guttman-Scale Types on Universal Five-Item Scale by Race
and Gender for the Student and Adult Samples*

| | PERMISSIVENESS SCALE TYPES | | | | | | |
| | Low | | | | | High | |
	0	1	2	3	4	5	N
	Percent of Student Sample						
White Male	7	11	20	18	19	25	(287
White female	26	27	20	14	10	2	(324)
Black male	4	4	7	17	31	37	(115)
Black female	14	16	25	30	11	4	(118)
Total	15	17	19	18	16	15	(844)
	Percent of Adult Sample						
White male	22	7	40	7	8	15	(607)
White female	54	15	25	2	2	3	(649)
Black male	18	5	13	15	21	29	(62)
Black female	32	17	21	7	10	12	(81)
Total	37	11	31	5	6	10	(1,399)

*The male-standards scale was used to compute scale types for men, and the female-
standards scale was used for women. Thus, this scale scores the individual on self-
permissiveness.
Source: Ira L. Reiss, 1967:36.

the proposition holds in order to simplify the picture. For example, propositions
five and six are much more likely to hold if one feels that parents and/or peers are
"important" reference groups. I have stated these thirteen propositions in a semi-
formal way to afford the reader more awareness of the need for precision in scientific
work. There is even greater clarity and precision gained when one presents such
propositions in diagram form. The act of diagraming forces one to be more precise
and explicit about what one is saying. It is more difficult to be vague and contradictory in diagram form than in thought or even in words alone. So the same
thirteen propositions are presented in Figure 7.3. They should be self-explanatory
but I will comment on some of them.

One of the basic explanations of premarital sexual permissiveness concerns the
tension between parental and courtship institutions. These are two sources of major
influence on premarital sexual standards. As the teenager gets older, there is evidence that the reference group of greatest importance switches from parents to
peers. The work of Walsh and his colleagues (Zey-Ferrell, Tolone, and Pocs) best
illustrates this with rare panel data on two cohorts of students followed through
four years of college between 1967 and 1974 (Walsh et al., 1976; Zey-Ferrell et
al., 1977). They document the shift toward peers as the reference group of greatest
importance and also show how that shift associates with an increase in sexual
permissiveness. This increase in permissiveness is congruent with propositions five

TABLE 7.8

Thirteen Selected Propositions Concerning Causes of Premarital Sexual Permissiveness

---

1. The extent to which one values the rewards (e.g. pleasure and intimacy) and devalues the costs (e.g. pregnancy and disease) of sexuality, influences in a positive direction the degree of one's premarital permissiveness.
2. The extent to which one values the rewards of love relationships and devalues the costs influences in a positive direction the degree of one's premarital sexual permissiveness.
3. The endorsement of equality in sexual rights for men and women influences in a positive direction one's premarital sexual permissiveness.
4. The degree to which one's parents are perceived as accepting nonsexual pleasures (e.g. eating, drinking) influences in a positive direction one's premarital sexual permissiveness.
5. Perceiving one's premarital sexual permissiveness as close to one's parent's premarital sexual permissiveness influences one's own permissiveness in a negative direction.
6. Perceiving one's premarital sexual permissiveness as close to those of one's peers influences one's premarital sexual permissiveness in a positive direction.
7. Responsibility for other family members (e.g., siblings) influences one's premarital sexual permissiveness in a negative direction.
8. Participating in courtship influences one's premarital sexual permissiveness in a positive direction.
9. The autonomy of the courtship group influences one's premarital sexual permissiveness in a positive direction.
10. The level of acceptance of premarital sexual permissiveness in the adult institutions (family, religious, political, etc.) in a community influences in a positive direction one's premarital sexual permissiveness.
11. The *traditional* level of premarital sexual permissiveness in the adult institutions in a community influences in a positive direction one's premarital sexual permissiveness. (Traditional refers to customs in existence for at least two or three generations.)
12. The perceived premarital sexual permissiveness of one's reference groups influences in a positive direction one's premarital sexual permissiveness.
13. The priority of marriage and family roles influences in a negative direction one's premarital sexual permissiveness.

Source: Derived from Reiss, 1967; Reiss and Miller, 1979.

and six in Figure 7.3. This is not to deny the power of parents as influences on premarital sexual standards (Libby, Gray, and White, 1978), but rather to assert that over time parental power becomes modified. Walsh (1970) found that there was no clear association between the premarital sexual permissiveness levels parents said they accepted and those their college-student children accepted. However, there was a positive correlation between the level of permissiveness that college students *perceived* their parents as accepting and their own permissiveness. In short, the students' *perception* of parental permissiveness is what is influential. The lack of communication between parent and child on sexuality is well documented even for today and that makes misunderstanding quite easy to occur (Harriet Reiss, 1973; Sorensen, 1974). These findings are congruent with Proposition twelve.

Proposition two brings out a causal pathway that many studies have supported, namely, the importance of love and commitment for the development of premarital sexual permissiveness. As has been mentioned, this is a factor that seems more potent for females than for males due to our gender role training. Also, there are other causal forces operating (see the other twelve propositions in Figure 7.3). Nonetheless, love and sexuality have a close interrelationship. In our discussion

Photo by Shelly A. McIntire, courtesy of The Minnesota Geographic Society. Project Coordinator: Tim Strick.

of sexuality earlier in this chapter, it was pointed out that sexual relationships can act as a catalyst in the development of love relationships. Of course, the reverse also occurs with love occurring first and then the sexual relationship encouraged to develop by affectionate feelings. The low number of partners reported for females (Zelnik and Kantner, 1972, 1977; Sorensen, 1973; Simon, Berger, Gagnon, 1972; Hunt, 1974; and Tavris and Sadd, 1977), also supports the importance of commitment and affection, especially to females. Nevertheless, the cohabitation custom discussed in Chapter 4 indicates that both genders appreciate stability.

Despite the notable increases in premarital sexual permissiveness in recent years, the evidence from several researchers indicates that increases in sexual permissiveness are not always made easily, quickly, and smoothly. In the 1967 book I report the fact that the majority of respondents reported some guilt or qualms about almost all the sexual behavior when they first began that behavior (Reiss, 1967: Chap. 7). This is likely due in part to the emphasis some people place on negative consequences like pregnancy and disease and the lack of emphasis on things like physical pleasure (see proposition one). The vast majority of people who felt guilty simply repeated the behavior until they came to accept it and then went on to more advanced behavior about which they again had some reservations. They went through the process of qualms, repeated behavior, and then experimenting with more intimate behavior over and over again. Individuals differed in the speed and

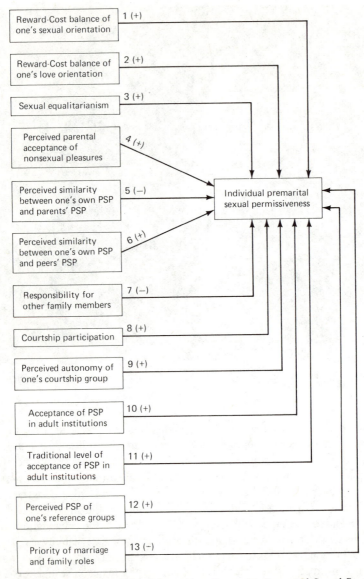

Figure 7.3. Diagram of Thirteen Selected Propositions Concerning Premarital Sexual Permissiveness (PSP). The number on each line corresponds to the number of the proposition in Table 7.8.

ease with which they moved through these processes and this likely was due to different background values. More recent studies support these early findings. Sorensen (1973) in his 1972 national study of 13–19-year-olds, reports that 63 percent of the females felt fear and 36 percent felt guilty and worried after their first coital experience (Sorensen, 1973:205). Hunt reports that in his sample of 18–25-year-olds, two-thirds of the females and over a third of the males felt regret after their first coital experience (Hunt, 1974:157). Premarital intercourse apparently is still viewed as an important act and for most young people it is not done casually. Having sexual relations with affection is one key means used to overcome guilt. In terms of our sexual standards, it would seem that "permissiveness with affection" has become the dominant standard. This is in line with my 1960 prediction (Reiss, 1960: Chap. 10).

Finally, we should discuss some basic demographic factors that are related to sexual permissiveness—specifically social class. Does it make any difference if one is lower, middle, or upper social class in terms of levels of premarital sexual permissiveness or sexual behavior? The old Kinsey findings on males showed much higher rates of premarital intercourse for the lower-educated males (Kinsey et al., 1948). College-educated males were the lowest on rates of nonvirginity and frequency of coitus. We have presented data earlier in this chapter indicating that college males may have changed toward more permissiveness in the early decades of this century. Thus, it is reasonable to expect this group to be less sexually active than the lower-educated males who have a longer tradition of high permissiveness. Regardless, by the early 1960s something had changed in the relationship of social class to sexual attitudes and behavior. In my 1963 national sample I found that the expected negative relationship of class and sexual permissiveness (lower class, more permissive) was present only for the blacks. The whites did not show any relationship when looked at as a total group. Finally, we discovered that when you divided the whites into those who were politically and religiously *liberal*, there was a remarkable change—in such a liberal group the higher-educated people were the *most* sexually permissive. This was a complete reversal of Kinsey's findings and was a great shock to us to find in our data. One of the most rewarding aspects of research is precisely this finding of an unexpected pattern in the data being examined. When we looked only at those who were politically and religiously *conservative*, we found Kinsey's old negative relationship of social class and sexual permissiveness. The importance of this finding is that it indicates that a liberal approach to politics and religion may be a key element in promoting premarital sexual permissiveness (see proposition one in Figure 7.3). By the early 1960s this new liberalism had evidently spread enough so that it counterbalanced the negative relationship of social class and permissiveness which the conservative sector displayed (for further evidence on liberalism see Staples, 1978). In more recent work (NORC, 1977) one finds that there is some evidence of even a small *positive* relation of social class to permissiveness for the *overall* adult culture. The liberal segment is now large enough to somewhat outbalance the conservative segment. It is interesting to note that blacks as a group come out more conservative on most nonsexual measures (Kohn, 1977; Lipset, 1960; Inkeles, 1960). In the research data blacks continue to display a negative relation of class and permissiveness.

A liberal group accepts permissiveness and thus the leaders, the highly educated element, can more easily be acceptant of sexual permissiveness and still be leaders in the group. The opposite is true in a conservative group. It is interesting to note that Zelnik and Kantner's findings from their 1971 national sample showed a negative relationship for black teenage women (58 percent nonvirginity for females from low-educated backgrounds and 37 percent for females from high-educated backgrounds). In their group of white females, the father's education made very little difference—the range was 25 percent to 22 percent nonvirginal (Zelnik and Kantner, 1972:11). Thus, the racial and class findings in Zelnik and Kantner's study is similar to what I found in my 1963 research.

In the years since the 1967 book I have done additional work on developing an explanation of the causes of changes in premarital sexual permissiveness levels. Together with Brent Miller, I strove to clarify the original ideas and interrelate them (Reiss and Miller, 1974; 1979). The thirteen causes in Figure 7.3 each have possible relationships to all other causes in the diagram. We specified the ways in which these thirteen variables (and a few others) related to one another and thereby developed a more complete theory of premarital sexual permissiveness. In this integrated set of causes, the ninth proposition, stressing the autonomy of one's courtship, became one key focus of the causal diagram. The degree to which one feels free from outside adult controls (e.g., religion, family) is considered to be a crucial determinant of one's level of premarital sexual permissiveness. Many of the other variables in Figure 7.3 were related to autonomy in various ways. Because of the centrality of this concept we have called the latest version of our theory the "autonomy theory of premarital sexual permissiveness." The interested reader can examine the more technical aspects of these views in Reiss and Miller (1979). For our purposes here it is sufficient to note that in this century, all thirteen causes in Figure 7.3 have changed in the direction which increases premarital sexual permissiveness.

Summary and Conclusions

We have covered a large amount of material in order to gain a better understanding of trends and causes of premarital sexual permissiveness. I have suggested that changes in sexuality are implicated in overall changes in gender roles (see Chapter 3). The two time periods of greatest change in sexuality (1915–1925 and 1965–1975) were also the occasion of overall social change that affected many other aspects of the masculine and feminine roles in our culture. The causal quest is the dominant one in all science—the search for explanation is the number one objective of science. Thus, we strove to gain some foothold on how and why some people become more sexually permissive than others. Before we close this chapter, one final point regarding overall social change in premarital sexual permissiveness needs to be made. We have in America moved toward a considerably more sexual permissive society in this century. Probably 75 percent of all women and 90 percent of all men are entering marriage nonvirginally in 1980. Females in particular have changed the most in many sexual attitudinal and behavioral areas. But the essence of the change in this century is not the growth of permissiveness but rather *the legitimation of choice*. An increase in sexual behavior and acceptance is one type of event. An increase in what choices are viewed as legitimate for people to make is a much more important societal event. An increase in permissiveness can be temporary. An increase in societal legitimation of choice is much more likely to last.

No sexual standard ever fit all Americans but it is only the recent generations of Americans who have made a public issue of this. They have proclaimed to the world that there are several legitimate choices of premarital sexual relationships. All Americans agree that force and fraud are not acceptable bases for a sexual relationship. Beyond these universal restrictions the scope of acceptable sexuality has vastly expanded. There still are many who cling to a single sexual code for all and wish that code were imposed on everyone. There are those who have established new ways and wish these more permissive ways to be imposed on everyone. But there are also those who are trying to legitimize choice in the sense of allowing for a number of alternative sexual life-styles that are all considered legitimate for those who choose them. This is a rare thing—to find people tolerating what they do not personally practice. We may well see the dogmatists on the traditional and the innovative sides in open battle on many issues. These more dogmatic groups may try to push aside those who favor open choice. The most crucial question is whether the people who believe in legitimacy of choice will hold to their position and gain popularity in the next generation or whether we shall simply move to some new unitary standard for all. I will return to this issue in the last chapter of the book.

References

Acton, William. 1857. *The Functions and Disorders of the Reproductive Organs in Youth, in Adult Age and in Advanced Life, Considered in Their Physiological, Sound & Moral Relations*. London: J. & A. Churchill.

Asayama Shin'ichi. 1975. "Adolescent Sex Development and Adult Sex Behavior in Japan," *Journal of Sex Research* 11 (May):91–112.

Bell, Daniel. 1973. *The Coming of Post-Industrial Society: A Venture in Social Forecasting*. New York: Basic Books.

Bell, Robert, and Jay B. Chaskes. 1970. "Premarital Sexual Experience Among Coeds, 1958 and 1968," *Journal of Marriage and the Family* 32:81–84.

Berscheid, Ellen, Elaine Walster, and George Bohrnstedt. 1972. "Your Body Image: A Questionnaire," *Psychology Today* 6 (July):57–64.

Bowman, Henry A., and Graham B. Spanier. 1978. *Modern Marriage*, 8th ed. New York:McGraw-Hill.

Broderick, Carlfred B. 1966. "Socio-Sexual Development in a Suburban Community," *Journal of Sex Research* 2 (April):1–24.

Broude, Gwen J., and Sarah J. Green. 1976. "Cross-Cultural Codes on Twenty Sexual Attitudes and Practices," *Ethnology* 15 (October):409–429.

Burgess, Ernest, and Paul Wallin. 1953. *Engagement and Marriage*. Philadelphia: Lippincott.

Calhoun, Arthur W. 1945. *A Social History of the American Family*. New York: Barnes & Noble.

Chesser, Eustace. 1957. *The Sexual, Marital, and Family Relationship of the English Woman*. New York: Roy.

Christensen, Harold T. 1962. "Value-Behavior Discrepancies Regarding Premarital Coitus in Three Western Cultures," *American Sociological Review* 27 (February):66–74.

———. 1978. "Recent Data Reflecting Upon the Sexual Revolution in America," paper presented at the International Sociological Association in Uppsala, Sweden, August 1978.

———, and Christina F. Gregg. 1970. "Changing Sex Norms in America and Scandinavia," *Journal of Marriage and the Family* 32 (November):616–627.

Cochran, William G., Frederick Mosteller, and John Tukey. 1954. *Statistical Problems of the Kinsey Report on Sexual Behavior in the Human Male*. Washington, DC: American Statistical Association.

Collins, John K., et al. 1976. "Insights into a Dating Partner's Expectations of How Behavior Should Ensue During the Courtship Process,"

Journal of Marriage and the Family 38 (May):373–378.

Comfort, Alex. 1967. *The Anxiety Makers: Some Curious Preoccupations of the Medical Profession.* London: Thomas Nelson.

Degler, Carl N. 1974. "What Ought to Be and What Was: Women's Sexuality in the Nineteenth Century," *American Historical Review* 79 (December): 1467–1490.

DeLamater, John, and Patricia MacCorquodale. 1979. *Premarital Sexuality.* Madison: University of Wisconsin Press.

Ehrmann, Winston W. 1959. *Premarital Dating Behavior.* New York: Holt, Rinehart and Winston.

Freedman, Mervin B. 1965. "The Sexual Behavior of American College Women: An Empirical Study and an Historical Survey," *Merrill-Palmer Quarterly of Behavior and Development* 11 (January):33–39.

French Institute of Public Opinion. 1961. *Patterns of Sex and Love.* New York: Crown.

Glenn, Norval D., and Charles N. Weaver. 1979. "Attitudes Toward Premarital, Extramarital and Homosexual Relations in the U.S. in the 1970's," *Journal of Sex Research,* 15 (May):108–118.

Gottlieb, David, et al. 1966. *The Emergence of Youth Societies: A Cross-Cultural Approach.* New York: Free Press.

Guttman, Louis. 1950. "The Bases for Scalogram Analysis," chap. 3 in Samuel A. Stouffer, et al., *Measurement and Prediction.* Princeton, NJ: Princeton University Press.

Hampe, Gary D., and Howard J. Ruppel, Jr. 1974. "The Measurement of Premarital Sexual Permissiveness: A Comparison of Two Guttman Scales," *Journal of Marriage and the Family* 36 (August):451–464.

Heise, David R. 1967. "Cultural Patterning of Sexual Socialization," *American Sociological Review* 32 (October):726–739.

Hornick, Joseph D. 1978. "Premarital Sexual Attitudes and Behavior," *The Sociological Quarterly* 19.4 (Autumn):534,544.

Hunt, Morton. 1974. *Sexual Behavior in the 1970's.* Chicago: Playboy Press.

Inkeles, Alex. 1960. "Industrial Man: The Relation of Status to Experience, Perception, and Value," *American Journal of Sociology* 66 (July):1–31.

Jacobson, Paul H. 1959. *American Marriage and Divorce.* New York: Rinehart and Co., Inc.

Jurich, Anthony P., and Julie A. Jurich. 1974.

"The Effect of Cognitive Moral Development Upon the Selection of Premarital Sexual Standards," *Journal of Marriage and the Family* 36 (November):736–741.

Kandel, Denise, and Gerald S. Lesser. 1969. "Parent-Adolescent Relationships and Adolescent Independence in the United States and Denmark," *Journal of Marriage and the Family* 31 (May):348–358.

Kantner, John F., and Melvin Zelnik. 1972. "Sexual Experience of Young Unmarried Women in the United States," *Family Planning Perspectives* 4 (October):9–18.

Katz, Joseph, et al. 1968. *No Time for Youth.* San Francisco: Jossey-Bass.

King, Karl, Jack O. Balswick, and Ira E. Robinson. 1977. "The Continuing Premarital Sexual Revolution Among College Females," *Journal of Marriage and the Family* 39 (August):455–459.

Kinsey, Alfred C., et al. 1948. *Sexual Behavior in the Human Male.* Philadelphia: Saunders.

———. 1953. *Sexual Behavior in the Human Female.* Philadelphia: Saunders.

Kohn, Melvin. 1977. *Class and Conformity,* 2nd ed. Chicago: University of Chicago Press.

Kraemer, Helena C., et al. 1976. "Orgasmic Frequency and Plasma Testosterone Levels in Normal Human Males," *Archives of Sexual Behavior* 5 (March):125–132.

Kuhn, Manford H. 1955. "Kinsey's View of Human Behavior," in Jerome Himelhoch and Sylvia F. Fava (eds.), *Sexual Behavior in American Society.* New York: Norton.

Levitt, Eugene, and Albert Klassen. 1974. "Public Attitudes Toward Homosexuality: Part of the 1970 National Survey by the Institute for Sex Research," *Journal of Homosexuality* 1.1:29–43.

Libby, Roger W., Louis Gray, and Mervin White. 1978. "A Test and Reformulation of Reference Groups and Role Correlates of Premarital Sexual Permissiveness Theory," *Journal of Marriage and the Family* 40 (February):79–92.

Lipset, Seymour M. 1960. *Political Man: The Social Bases of Politics.* New York: Doubleday.

Luckey, Eleanor B., and Gilbert D. Nass. 1969 "The Comparison of Sexual Attitudes and Behavior in an International Sample," *Journal of Marriage and the Family* 31 (May):348–359.

MacCorquodale, Patricia, and John DeLamater. 1979. "Self-Image and Premarital Sexuality," *Journal of Marriage and the Family,* 41 (May):327–339.

Malinowski, Bronislaw. 1929. *The Sexual Life of Savages in North Western Melanesia.* New York: Harvest Books. (Published by Harcourt Brace Jovanovich.)

Marshall, Donald S. 1971. "Sexual Behavior on Mangaia," in Donald S. Marshall and Robert C. Suggs (eds.), *Human Sexual Behavior: Variations in the Ethnographic Spectrum.* New York: Basic Books.

National Opinion Research Center (NORC). 1977. "Cumulative Codebook for the 1972–77 General Social Surveys." Chicago: NORC, University of Chicago.

Osborn, Candice A., and Robert H. Pollack. 1977. "The Effects of Two Types of Erotic Literature on Physiological and Verbal Measures of Female Sexual Arousal," *Journal of Sex Research* 13 (November): 250–256.

Parven, Theophilus. 1883–1884. "Hygiene of the Sexual Functions," *New Orleans Medical and Surgical Journal* 11:607.

Paxton, Anne Lee, and Edward J. Turner. 1978. "Self-Actualization and Sexual Permissiveness: Satisfaction, Prudishness and Drive Among Female Undergraduates," *Journal of Sex Research* 14 (May):65–80.

Perlman, Daniel. 1974. "Self-Esteem and Sexual Permissiveness," *Journal of Marriage and the Family* 36 (August):470–474.

_____, et al. 1978. "Cross-Cultural Analysis of Students' Sexual Standards," *Archives of Sexual Behavior* 7, (November):545–558.

Queen, Stuart, and Habenstein, Robert. 1974. *The Family in Various Cultures,* 4th ed. Philadelphia: Lippincott.

Rainwater, Lee. 1966. "Some Aspects of Lower-Class Sexual Behavior," *Journal of Social Issues* 22 (April):96–108.

Raschke, Vern, and Angelina Li. 1976. "Premarital Sexual Permissiveness of College Students in Hong Kong." *Journal of Comparative Family Studies* 7 (Spring): 65–74.

Reiss, Harriet M. 1973. "Contraception and Parental Communication," unpublished research paper.

Reiss, Ira L. 1956. "The Double Standard in Premarital Sexual Intercourse: A Neglected Concept," *Social Forces* 34 (March):224–230.

_____. 1957. "The Treatment of Premarital Coitus in 'Marriage and Family' Tests," *Social Problems* 4 (April):334–338.

_____. 1960. *Premarital Sexual Standards in America.* New York: Free Press.

_____. 1964. "The Scaling of Premarital Sexual Permissiveness," *Journal of Marriage and the Family* 26 (May):188,198.

_____. 1967. *The Social Context of Premarital Sexual Permissiveness.* New York: Holt, Rinehart and Winston.

_____. 1973. *Heterosexual Permissiveness Inside and Outside of Marriage.* Morristown, NJ: General Learning Press, pp. 1–29.

_____, and Brent C. Miller. 1974. "A Theoretical Analysis of Heterosexual Permissiveness," Technical Report No. 2. Minneapolis: University of Minnesota Family Study Center.

_____. 1979. "Heterosexual Permissiveness: A Theoretical Analysis," in W. Burr, R. Hill, I. Nye, and I. Reiss (eds.), *Contemporary Theories About the Family.* Vol. I New York: Free Press.

Robbins, Mina B., and Gordon D. Jensen. 1978. "Multiple Orgasm in Males," *Journal of Sex Research* 14 (February):21–26.

Schmidt, Gunter. 1975. "Male-Female Differences in Sexual Arousal and Behavior During and After Exposure to Sexually Explicit Stimuli," *Archives of Sexual Behavior* 4 (July):353–365.

_____, and Volkmar Sigusch. 1970. "Sex Differences in Responses to Psycho-Sexual Stimulation by Films and Slides," *Journal of Sex Research* 6 (November):268–283.

Schofield, Michael. 1965. *The Sexual Behavior of Young People.* Boston: Little, Brown.

Schulz, Barbara, George W. Bohrnstedt, Edgar F. Borgatta, and Robert E. Evans. 1977. "Explaining Premarital Sexual Intercourse Among College Students: A Causal Model," *Social Forces* 56 (September): 148–165.

Sigusch, Volkmar, et al. 1970. "Psychosexual Stimulation: Sex Differences," *Journal of Sex Research* 6 (February):10–24.

Simon, William, Alan Berger, and John Gagnon. 1972. "Beyond Anxiety and Fantasy: The Coital Experiences of College Youth," *Journal of Youth and Adolescence* 1.3:203–222.

Smith, Daniel Scott. 1978. "The Dating of the American Sexual Revolution: Evidence and Interpretation," in Michael Gordon (ed.), *The American Family in Social-Historical Perspective,* 2nd ed. New York: St. Martin's.

Sorenson, Robert. 1973. *Adolescent Sexuality in Contemporary America.* New York: World Publishing.

Staples, Robert. 1978. "Race, Liberalism-Conservatism and Premarital Sexual Permissiveness: A Bi-Racial Comparison," *Journal of Marriage and the Family* 40 (November):733–742.

Stillerman, Eric D., and Colin M. Shapiro. 1979. "Scaling Sex Attitudes and Behavior in South Africa," *Archives of Sexual Behavior* 8 (January):1–13.

Suggs, Robert C. 1966. *Marquesan Sexual Behavior: An Anthropological Study of Polynesian Practices*. New York: Harcourt, Brace & World.

Tavris, Carol, and Susan Sadd. 1977. *The Redbook Report on Female Sexuality*. New York: Delacorte.

Terman, Lewis M. 1938. *Psychological Factors in Marital Happiness*. New York: McGraw-Hill.

Udry, J. Richard, Karl E. Bauman, and Naomi M. Morris. 1975. "Changes in Premarital Coital Experiences of Recent Decade of Birth Cohorts of Urban American Women," *Journal of Marriage and the Family* (November):783–787.

Vance, Ellen Belle, and Nathaniel N. Wagner. 1976. "Written Descriptions of Orgasm: A Study of Sex Differences," *Archives of Sexual Behavior* 5 (January):87–98.

Walsh, Robert H. 1970. "A. Survey of Parents and Their Own Children's Sexual Attitudes," unpublished Ph.D. dissertation. University of Iowa, Iowa City.

———, Mary Zey-Ferrell, and William L. Tolone. 1976. "Selection of Reference Group, Perceived Reference Group Permissiveness, and Personal Permissiveness Attitudes and Behavior: A Study of Two Consecutive Panels (1967–71; 1970–74)," *Journal of Marriage and the Family* 38 (August):495–507.

Zelnik, M., and J. F. Kantner. 1972. "Sexuality, Contraception and Pregnancy Among Young Unwed Females in the United States," in U.S. Commission on Population Growth and the American Future. *Demographic and Social Aspects of Population Growth*. Washington, DC: Government Printing Office; 1:355–375.

———. 1977. "Sexual and Contraceptive Experience of Young Unmarried Women in the U.S., 1976 and 1971," *Family Planning Perspectives* 9 (March/April):55–71.

Zelnik, M., Y. J. Kim, and J. F. Kantner. 1979. "Probabilities of Intercourse and Conception Among U. S. Teenage Women 1971 & 1976" *Family Planning Perspectives*. V.II (May/June):177–183.

Zey-Ferrell, Mary, William L. Tolone, and Robert H. Walsh. 1977. "Maturational and Societal Changes in the Sexual Double-Standard: A Panel Analysis (1967–71; 1970–74)," *Journal of Marriage and the Family* 39 (May):255–271.

The Management of Premarital Pregnancy

EIGHT

Now that we have some grasp of trends and causes of premarital permissiveness, let us examine some of the consequences that are of interest to sociologists and lay lpeople alike. One major area of importance concerns the ways in which premarital pregnancy is dealt with in our society today.

Premarital Contraceptive Behavior

In primitive societies infanticide and abortion are ancient methods of controlling unwanted births (Himes, 1963; Noonan, 1966). In our Western heritage, coitus interruptus (withdrawal) was a well-known technique mentioned in the Old Testament (Genesis 38:7–10):

> And Er, Judah's first born, was wicked in the sight of the Lord; and the Lord slew him. And Judah said unto Onan: 'Go in unto thy brother's wife and perform the duty of a husband's brother unto her, and raise up seed to thy brother!' And Onan knew that the seed would not be his; and it came to pass, whenever he went in unto his brother's wife, that he used to spill it on the ground, lest he should give seed to his brother. And the thing which he did was evil in the sight of the Lord; and He slew him also.

The ancient Egyptians recommended putting crocodile dung against the cervix as a method of contraception. Animal membranes were at times used as crude coverings of the penis to prevent contraception. A sponge, placed against the cervix, was recommended by Francis Place in 1823 (Himes, 1963:214). In 1844 Goodyear invented the vulcanization of rubber. This permitted the development of a thinner, more flexible rubber condom which was destined to become very popular (Himes, 1963:201.) By the last decades of the nineteenth century, both the condom, the diaphragm, and the pessary cap were in use at least by the better-educated segments of Western society. The effectiveness of such methods can be seen by the fact that between 1876 and 1936 the British birthrate was cut in half, and the birth rates of Hungary, Austria, Germany, Italy, the Netherlands, Denmark, Sweden, Norway, Belgium, and France were similarly reduced (Himes, 1963:378). Thus, the nineteenth-century methods were very effective in reducing unwanted births. But there was still a great deal of opposition to their use in the Western world and it took pioneers like Margaret Sanger in America and Marie Stopes in England to spread the availability of birth control to the masses. In fact, it was Margaret Sanger who, in 1915, coined the term "birth control." By the 1960s the pill and the IUD were added to our common methods of contraception. There was still opposition though to unmarried teenagers using contraception. Family planning clinics especially designed for teenagers only came into being in the late 1960s. In 1970 Congress passed the Family Planning Services and Population Research Act and established an Office of Population Affairs. Expenditures in these services are now in the hundreds of millions of dollars.

Anyone reading this brief review of our contraceptive history might believe that contraceptive usage would be virtually universal among premarital couples today. The Zelnik and Kantner data on thousands of teenage women in 1971 and 1976 give the lie to this view. Table 8.1 shows that by 1976 there had occurred a noticeable shift to the use of the pill. In 1976, 31 percent had used the pill the last time they had had intercourse, whereas in 1971 the figure was 15 percent. One can also note from Figure 8.1 that the percent using contraception at last intercourse

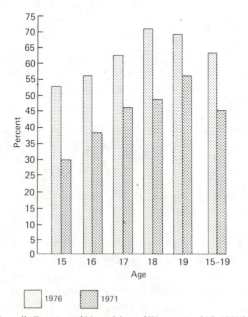

Figure 8.1. Percent of Sexually Experienced Never-Married Women Aged 15–19 Who Used Contraception at Last Intercourse, by Age, 1976 and 1971. (Zelnik and Kantner, 1977:62.)

rose considerably in that five-year period. It was 45 percent in 1971 and 63 percent in 1976. In both 1971 and 1976 younger females were less likely to use contraception. There still are some racial differences. In 1976, among the 15–17-year-old females, it seems that black females used the pill more and white females used withdrawal and the condom slightly more.

Knowledge of the time of greatest pregnancy risk during the menstrual cycle clearly supports the position that we are far from a fully contraceptively informed society. Overall, 41 percent of the females knew the times of greatest pregnancy risk. If one looks only at females who had intercourse, the percent with correct knowledge is 45 percent and among those who were virginal it was 32 percent. Even among 18- and 19-year-olds who were having intercourse the percent with accurate knowledge was only 51 percent. There was a sharp black–white difference with only 24 percent of the black teenagers knowledgeable about the time of highest risk of conception. There was only a small increase in overall knowledge of pregnancy risk between 1971 and 1976. This is surprising considering the presence of sex education in the schools, and in light of the improved contraceptive usage of the 1976 sample.

TABLE 8.1

Percent Distribution of Sexually Experienced Never-Married Women Aged 15–19, According to Method Used at Last Intercourse, by Age and Race, 1976 and 1971

METHOD				AGE AND RACE					
	All			*White*			*Black*		
	15-19	15-17	18-19	15-19	15-17	18-19	15-19	15-17	18-19
1976				(N= 378)	(N= 205)	(N= 173)	(N= 408)	(N= 215)	(N= 193)
Pill	31.2	21.6	42.9	30.4	21.9	40.5	35.3	30.7	40.4
IUD	2.2	1.3	3.4	2.9	2.0	4.0	2.5	0.9	4.1
Condom	12.6	15.2	9.3	13.2	14.2	12.1	9.8	13.5	5.7
Douche	2.3	2.4	2.3	1.1	1.5	0.6	5.1	4.6	5.7
Withdrawal	10.6	14.9	5.4	12.2	15.6	8.1	3.4	4.7	2.1
Other	4.5	3.0	6.3	5.0	2.9	7.5	2.2	1.4	3.1
None	36.6	41.6	30.4	35.2	41.9	27.2	41.7	44.2	38.9
Total	100.0	100.0	100.0	100.0	100.0	100.0	100.0	100.0	100.0
1971				(N= 551)	(N= 314)	(N= 237)	(N= 674)	(N= 420)	(N= 254)
Pill	15.1	7.7	23.0	13.4	6.0	23.2	13.6	9.5	20.5
IUD	0.8	0.2	1.4	0.4	0.0	0.9	2.1	1.2	3.5
Condom	14.4	17.3	11.2	14.7	18.2	10.1	16.0	16.0	16.1
Douche	1.7	2.1	1.3	0.5	0.6	0.4	3.1	3.8	2.0
Withdrawal	10.3	9.4	11.3	12.9	12.4	13.5	3.9	4.8	2.4
Other	2.9	2.4	3.4	2.9	2.6	3.4	2.5	2.1	3.1
None	54.8	60.9	48.4	55.2	60.2	48.5	58.8	62.6	52.4
Total	100.0	100.0	100.0	100.0	100.0	100.0	100.0	100.0	100.0

Source: Zelnik and Kantner, 1977:67.

The most obvious sociological question concerning contraception is: What are the factors that affect contraceptive use among single females and males? Given the increase in contraceptive use between 1971 and 1976, one could then examine any answer to see if the reasons for contraceptive use also increased in that five-year period. Let us take a brief look at the explanations for contraceptive usage that have been put forth in the research literature. Prudence Rains (1971) suggested an explanation of contraceptive usage based upon the degree to which the woman is free from moral ambivalence and accepts the correctness of her sexual behavior. If the woman is ambivalent and unsure of the rightness of her sexual behavior, then she will be less likely to protect herself contraceptively. Rains did not systematically test this thesis but rather impressionistically analyzed two unwed mother facilities which she felt supported her thesis.

At about the same time as Rains's book appeared, three of us had begun to test some ideas about contraceptive usage on a college female sample (Reiss, Banwart, and Foreman, 1975). We utilized a sample of about 500 females divided into those who (1) went to a contraceptive clinic on campus, (2) those who went to a private doctor for contraceptive advice, and (3) those who did not go to any professional. Our goal was to see if we could find the causes of contraceptive use by comparing the females who did not go for contraceptive help with those who did. We had five factors that we thought encouraged clinic attendance (or contraceptive usage):

1. Endorsement of the right to chose one's own sexual life style;
2. Self assurance;
3. Early sex information;
4. Congruency of sexual behavior and sexual standards; and
5. Degree of dyadic commitment.

All five hypothesized factors were thought to influence contraceptive usage in a positive direction; that is, the more one had of any one of them, the more likely one would use contraception. The reader will note that our first factor is similar to Prudence Rains's notions about lack of moral ambivalence. Our test supported this hypothesis and also hypotheses 2 and 5. Early sex education and the congruence of sexual standards and behavior did not seem to influence contraceptive usage.

In 1978 John Delamater and Patricia MacCorquodale published their research comparing the approach of Rains and of our five-factor approach. They used a representative college-student sample of some 450 nonvirgins (men and women) and also a town sample of some 300 men and women. They reported that the following *all promoted* contraceptive use:

1. Having had more than one intercourse partner;
2. The relative frequency with which intercourse was performed; with current partner;
3. The number of lifetime coital experiences; and
4. The extent to which contraception was discussed in advance.

All four of these fit with Rains's idea concerning lack of moral ambivalence and her view that long-term involvement in sexuality helped reduce moral ambivalence.

This, of course, also fits with the first hypothesis in the Reiss, Banwart, and Foreman study. The number of lifetime coital acts could indicate being with one or many partners and thus only partly fit with our fifth hypothesis regarding the importance of dyadic commitment. Delamater and MacCorquodale report support for our second hypothesis concerning self-assurance. Unlike our original findings, they also found support for our fourth hypothesis in that the congruence of behavior and standards did associate with contraceptive use. Thus, there is support for both our own view and that of Rains's, and there is some new information concerning the importance of discussing contraception in advance. One could take such discussion as an indication of acceptance of one's sexuality but it is a particularly important indicator. Discussion of contraception was one of the very few factors which also was a good predictor of male contraceptive effectiveness.

One other study is worth mentioning here—a research project by Thompson and Spanier (1978) done in 1977 on the campus of the Pennsylvania State University on over 400 male and female students. Unlike the Delamater and MacCorquodale study, this was not a random sample of the campus but it still may be heuristic in revealing basic factors connected to contraceptive use. Their results further support the major influence of discussion about contraception with the partner. Such discussion was likely to lead to the partner (of either gender) influencing in the direction of effective contraception. Most other factors seem to affect contraceptive use indirectly by acting upon contraceptive discussion. For example, frequency of intercourse makes it more likely that there will be discussion of contraception and thus indicates influence from the partner to use contraception. The same explanation fits the "involvement with partner" factor. The way that emotional involvement affects contraceptive use is by making it more likely that contraception will be discussed. Friends were also directly influential on female contraceptive use but not on male contraceptive use.

My conclusion on our current state of contraceptive use would be that acceptance of oneself as a sexual being with the right to sexual choice is one crucial determinant. This basic idea incorporates significant elements of all five of the hypotheses of the study I did with Banwart and Foreman. However, it seems apparent that the most crucial way this sexual self-acceptance affects contraceptive use is by promoting discussion about contraception. If this conclusion is correct, then the increase in contraceptive use reported by Zelnik and Kantner between 1971 and 1976 may be in part due to greater sexual self-acceptance which has encouraged more contraceptive discussion and use. This type of change may be more important in terms of effective contraception than knowledge of the high-risk pregnancy days. Figure 8.2 portrays the causal conception put forth here.

Premarital Pregnancy

Pregnancy out of wedlock is almost universally disliked. Even in very permissive cultures, such as the Trobrianders', marriage is arranged when a woman becomes premaritally pregnant (Malinowski, 1929). Since premarital intercourse in the Trob-

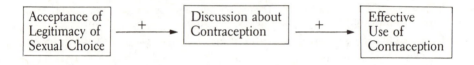

Figure 8.2. Proposed Model of Contraceptive Use

riand Islands is accepted and the connection between premarital intercourse and pregnancy is not known, marriage is not arranged to cover up the premarital coitus that has occurred. The preference around the world for childbirth to occur in marriage is, I believe, simply the result of a judgment that a marital setting is the "most effective" place to raise a child. The marital institution, as we defined it, has the key function of legitimizing parenthood and is a universal institution. Thus, it follows that every society has a social structure wherein childbirth is supposed to occur. When the limits of that accepted institution are violated by a birth out of wedlock, an attempt is made to bring the birth into the wedlock system in some fashion.

Mead (1928) reports that in Samoa premarital pregnancy is handled by allowing the pregnant girl to select one male to be her husband from among those males who have had intercourse with her. In our own society, which compared with Samoa is sexually restrictive, we have little in the way of institutionalized norms as to how one proceeds when a premarital pregnancy occurs. In good measure this is the case because our older, formal norms decreed that premarital coitus is not to occur, and thus one need not formulate norms to handle pregnancy outcomes. In more permissive societies these consequences are planned for, and in some ways they seem to have less disruptive effects. For example, Harold Christensen compared the impact of premarital pregnancy in the United States with its impact in Denmark—a more permissive society (Christensen, 1966). The Danish subjects in his study were more likely to have premarital coitus, more likely to become premaritally pregnant, and more likely to either marry or bear the child out of wedlock (Christensen, 1966:63). When the premarital pregnancy occurred, the Danish subjects were the slowest to get married (five months after conception). The American Midwest subjects married two months after conception, and the American Mormons often married before confirming the pregnancy (Christensen, 1966:65). The impact of premarital pregnancy on the marriage differed also. The Danish marriages that followed a premarital pregnancy had a much smaller increase of divorce over what was normal for their group. The American couples who married when the female was premaritally pregnant had a much higher rate of divorce over what was normal for their group. Thus, the more permissive a culture, the less disruptive is the impact of premarital pregnancy on a marriage.

It is well to gain an overview of premarital pregnancy and its outcome as a setting for the research and explanations to be covered here. More than illegitimacy rates need to be consulted; there are two other major outcomes of premarital pregnancy that require some examination: (1) abortion and (2) marriage. A group may be high on abortion, moderate on marriage, and low on illegitimacy when premarital pregnancy occurs. This seems common among college-educated young people. A different situation, wherein abortion rates are high and marriage rates are low and illegitimacy is high, is a common lower-class pattern. Thus, to really understand premarital pregnancy, we need to look at illegitimacy, abortion, and marriage outcomes of premarital pregnancy. There are other outcomes that are less common, such as spontaneous abortions, which we shall largely ignore.

The best source for detailed information on premarital pregnancy rates is the Zelnik and Kantner studies. These studies were, as noted before, national samples of several thousand 15–19-year-old females and were carried out in both 1971 and 1976. Table 8.2 contains the overall figures for pregnancy rates among females of this age group in the two different sample years.

The reader knows from our earlier discussion that there was an increase in the proportion of teenage females who were sexually involved and this shows up in Table 8.2 when one notes that 11.6 percent of all teenagers became pregnant in 1976 compared to 9 percent in 1971. However, when one looks at only those women who had premarital intercourse (the population at risk) the rates are almost identical for the two samples (29.8 percent and 28.3 percent). It remains to be specified why with improved contraception in 1976 there was not a decline in pregnancy rates. Of course, there can be changes in the number of partners and frequency of coitus and this increases the risk of pregnancy and perhaps is part of the answer.

Table 8.3 shows that about 36 percent of the white and 9 percent of the black premarital pregnancies lead to marriage *before* the child is born. A small proportion of both races marry shortly *after* the child is born (about 9 percent). Table 8.4 shows what happens to those women who did not marry by the time the pregnancy outcome occurred. Again, there is a large race difference with many more blacks producing a live birth and many more whites having an induced abortion. Note that for whites by 1976 there is a definite shift to fewer live births (44 percent to 27 percent) and higher use of abortion (33 percent to 45 percent). This shift to

TABLE 8.2

Percent of Women Aged 15–19 at Interview Who Experienced a First Premarital Pregnancy, Among All Women and Among Women Who Had Premarital Intercourse, by Race, 1976 and 1971

| WOMEN AGED 15–19 | PERCENT EXPERIENCING A FIRST PREMARITAL PREGNANCY | | | | | |
| | 1976 | | | 1971 | | |
	Total	White	Black	Total	White	Black
All	11.6	9.3	25.4	9.0	6.4	25.5
N	2,175	1,481	694	4,341	2,924	1,417
Had premarital intercourse	28.3	25.2	39.5	29.8	24.3	47.1
N	1,022	576	446	1,477	731	746

Source: Zelnik and Kantner, 1978a:12.

TABLE 8.3

Percent Distribution of Women Aged 15–19 at Interview Who Had a Premarital First Pregnancy, by Changes in Marital Status Before and After Pregnancy Outcome, According to Race, 1976 and 1971

TIMING OF CHANGE IN MARITAL STATUS	1976			1971		
	Total (N=336)	*White* (N=160)	*Black* (N=176)	*Total* (N=512)	*White* (N=178)	*Black* (N=334)
Total	100.0	100.0	100.0	100.0	100.0	100.0
Married before outcome*	28.0	36.5	8.8	35.4	52.2	8.5
Not married before outcome	72.0	63.5	91.2	64.6	47.8	91.5
Married after outcome	9.2	9.4	8.6	10.6	12.3	7.8
Never married*	62.8	54.1	82.6	54.0	35.5	83.7

Includes currently pregnant women.
Source: Zelnik and Kantner, 1978a:13.

abortion has led to a reduction in the total out-of-wedlock births that this teenage group produced.

It should be kept in mind that January 1973 was the date of the Supreme Court decision that liberalized abortion in the United States. Thus, the increased use of abortion in the 1976 sample reflects this increased availability. Why the black group has not had an equivalent increase in abortion is difficult to ascertain. It cannot be due to the Hyde Amendment, which restricted Medicaid funds for abortion use, because that occurred in 1977. Zelnik and Kantner (1978) and Sarvis and Rodman (1974) feel that abortion rates for blacks is underreported in part

TABLE 8.4

Percent Distribution of Premarital First Pregnancies to Women Aged 15–19 at Interview Who Were Unmarried at Outcome, by Type of Outcome and Race, 1976 and 1971

OUTCOME OF PREGNANCY	1976			1971		
	Total (N=249)	*White* (N=86)	*Black* (N=163)	*Total* (N=392)	*White* (N=86)	*Black* (N=306)
Total	100.0	100.0	100.0	100.0	100.0	100.0
Live birth	46.0	27.4	75.6	59.2	44.3	71.6
Stillbirth	1.3	1.4	1.2	0.3	0.0	0.5
Miscarriage	11.1	14.9	5.0	7.4	7.6	7.3
Induced abortion	30.6	44.9	7.9	17.7	32.9	5.0
Currently pregnant	11.0	11.4	10.3	15.4	15.2	15.6
Plans to marry before outcome	8.4	**	**	19.0	**	20.7
No plans to marry before outcome	91.6	**	**	81.0	**	79.3

Note: A double asterisk signifies N<20.
Source: Zelnik and Kantner, 1978a:13.

because of more negative attitudes by blacks toward abortion. We need more careful research here to obtain an accurate picture.

Abortion

The changes in abortion laws leading up to the january 1973 Supreme Court decision have been phenomenal. Until 1967 there was not a liberalized abortion law in any of the fifty states. In 1967 Colorado adopted a liberalized abortion law, and by 1970 a total of sixteen states had done the same, with some like New York having abortion-on-demand types of laws. The increase in the number of legal abortions rose sharply after 1969. Figure 8.3 diagrams this impressive change. There were vast public attitude changes occurring. In some cases, studies were undertaken (as in Colorado) to see if attitudes would become more acceptant after legalization. The findings supported the idea of legalization affecting attitudes in a positive direction. Abortion law reform had all the earmarks of a social movement whose time had come. The greater acceptance of sexuality in all its aspects was, no doubt, an aid to the abortion movement. The general strong feeling, especially among young people, that the individual had the right to choose his or her own sexual behavior and attitudes did a great deal to support the right of women to control the consequences of such behavior by having abortion available. It is no accident that the success of the abortion reform movement coincided with the sharp increase in sexual behavior in the late 1960s. These changes were both part and

Photo by Linda Bartlett, courtesy of the National Abortion Rights Action League.

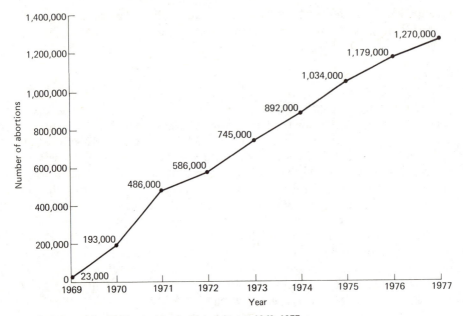

Figure 8.3. *Number of Abortions in the United States: 1969–1977.*
Source: Composed by author. 1969 to 1972 rates are from: U.S. Dept. of HEW,
Center for Disease Control, 1975. 1973–1974 figures are from Edward Weinstock et al.
(1975:23). Figures for 1975, 1976, and 1977 are from Forrest et al., 1978.

Photo by Olof Kallstrom, courtesy of The Minnesota Geographic Society. Project Coordinator: Tim Strick.

TABLE 8.5

Rate of Abortions per 1,000 Women Aged 15–44, and Ratio of Abortions per 1,000 Abortions Plus Live Births,* by Age, Race, Marital and Medicaid Status, 1976

CHARACTERISTIC	RATE	RATIO
Age		
<15	7.7†	563
15–19	34.5	386
(15–17)	(24.4)	(407)
(18–19)	(49.5)	(372)
20–24	40.1	259
25–29	24.8	180
30–34	15.0	214
35–39	9.5	322
>40	3.8‡	444
Race		
White	19.0	229
Black and other	58.0	389
Marital status		
Married	10.5	94
Unmarried	43.2	648
Medicaid status§		
Eligible	61.5	u
Ineligible	20.7	u

*Births six months later, applying 1976 characteristics.
†Numerator is abortions to girls under 15; denominator is number of 14-year-old females.
‡Numerator is abortions to women 40 and older; denominator is women 40–44.
§Numerator is abortions by Medicaid payment status; denominator is number of women 15–44, according to eligibility for Medicaid.
Note: u = unavailable.
Source: Forrest, et al., 1978: 275.

parcel of a multifaceted new morality that was making increasing inroads in America. It is also worth noting that higher-educated males were strong on supporting abortion reform, often more so than females. Finally, like many social movements, a powerful and sizable minority spearheaded this one (Blake, 1971).

I will rely on the Planned Parenthood data since the government uses only what is reported to them while Planned Parenthood actively seeks information from all facilities. The rates and ratios in Table 8.5 allow one to take account of how the number of abortions relates to the number of 15–44-year-old women and to the live birthrate. For example, table 8.5 shows that there are only 7.7 abortions for every 1,000 women under 15. However, for every 1000 abortions plus live births that do occur to such women, 563 of the 1000 are abortions and only 437 are live births.

Although data collection on abortion is quite new (starting in 1969), there are

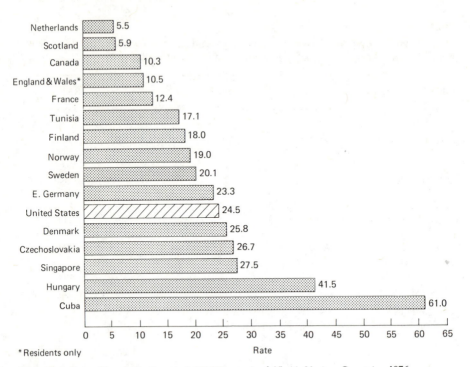

Figure 8.4. Rate of Legal Abortion per 1,000 Women Aged 15–44, Various Countries, 1976. Source: Forrest, et al., 1978:273.

already some consistencies that deserve mention. The older abortion literature (Gebhard et al., 1958; Calderone, 1958) stressed the fact that the majority of abortions were given to married women. The current scene does not support this view. Approximately 75 percent of the abortions in recent years have been performed on unmarried women. Unmarried includes divorced and widowed as well as single women. Abortions today are performed on a very youthful clientele. For example, approximately one-third of the females were in their teens; another third were twenty to twenty-four years old and the remaining third widely scattered in the twenty-five and older age groups. This means that in 1977, of the approximately 1,270,000 abortions, about 400,000 were given to teenagers. A July 1979 Supreme Court Decision struck down a law that demanded that women under eighteen obtain parental consent for an abortion. Thus age is not a barrier to obtaining abortion.

The abortion rates for each age group in part reflect effective contraceptive usage (see Table 8.5). Older females are much more effective in their contraceptive usage. This can also be seen in the Zelnik and Kantner data for 15–19-year-old women (Figure 8.1 and Table 8.1). Relatedly, whites are contraceptively more effective than blacks and married women more than unmarried.

I have included Figure 8.4 here to afford the reader some perspective on the abortion rate in the United States compared to other countries. Our abortion rate does appear high compared to countries like Sweden. We know that almost all females have premarital intercourse in Sweden (Zetterberg, 1969). Thus, when the Swedish abortion rate per 1,000 females comes out lower than ours it is a clear sign of the poorer effectiveness of our means of handling pregnancy (Furstenberg, 1976). We will speak further about Sweden in Chapter 17 of this book.

Pregnant Brides

Another choice when premarital pregnancy occurs is to marry. In terms of official records of legitimacy—even a child born one day after the parents marry is officially recorded as a legitimate birth. Some females expect marriage to follow if they become pregnant and therefore are not as active in trying to prevent pregnancy. Table 8.3 earlier in this chapter indicated that in 1976, 28 percent of those who became pregnant married before they gave birth and an additional 9 percent married after they gave birth. There is a large racial difference, with the total percent of pregnant teenagers who married (before or after birth) being 46 percent of the white females and 17 percent of the black females.

In 1978 the government released figures on trends in the proportion of women who either had a child when first married, or whose first child was born within eight months of their first marriage. Table 8.6 presents these figures for women married between the ages of 14 and 24. Of course, a few women who bear a child in eight or fewer months after marriage are giving birth prematurely. However, premature births account for only a small percent of the total of such births.

Reading across the "first child born before first marriage" row for all the groups indicates that there has been some recent increase in the percent of females who have a child prior to their first marriage. The increase is rather small in absolute percent (less than 3 percent) but still worth watching. It may indicate some increased tolerance of unmarried females who keep their child. There has been a trend in the direction of keeping one's premarital child rather than giving the child up for adoption and this data fits with that trend. Note that the next line: "pregnant with first child" shows a recent *decrease*. This type of event seems to have peaked in the 1960s and now may be declining a bit. Again the change is only on the order of 5 percent but considering the range of the percentages, that is also significant. Overall, adding these two types of premarital conceptions together, the trends over the time period covered are remarkably stable except for the rise from the low point for those married between 1952 and 1956. Thus, it would appear that such trends in premarital conceptions are not a good predictive base for understanding the radical changes in sexual attitudes and activities that have occurred since 1965.

Another important relationship that is revealed in this table is the great variation in premarital conceptions for different age groups. Clearly the 14–17-year-old group is far ahead of all other age groups. Also, this seems to be an area of great increases starting in those marriages made in the mid-1960s. These 14–17-year-old women comprise only about one-sixth of all wives but they are the only age groups that shows such radical trends over time. Looking at the overall group of women aged

TABLE 8.6

Fertility Status at Time of First Marriage, for Women Who Were First Married at Ages 14 to 24 Years, by Period of First Marriage

(Numbers in thousands)

RACE, AGE, AND FERTILITY STATUS AT FIRST MARRIAGE	TIME OF FIRST MARRIAGE (JULY 1 to JUNE 30)				
	1972 TO 1976	*1967 TO 1971*	*1962 TO 1966*	*1957 TO 1961*	*1952 TO 1956*
ALL RACES					
Women, 14 to 24 years	6,737	6,744	5,688	5,205	4,832
Percent, total	100.0	100.0	100.0	100.0	100.0
First child born before first marriage	9.4	7.8	6.7	7.4	6.8
Pregnant with first child*	14.4	18.8	19.6	15.8	12.4
All others	76.1	73.4	73.7	76.8	80.9
Women, 14 to 17 years	1,128	1,095	1,215	1,238	1,132
Percent, total	100.0	100.0	100.0	100.0	100.0
First child born before first marriage	8.7	6.3	4.3	4.4	5.7
Pregnant with first child*	32.4	34.2	30.6	24.0	18.2
All others	59.0	59.5	65.1	71.6	76.1
Women, 18 and 19 years	2,259	2,151	1,916	1,710	1,433
Percent, total	100.0	100.0	100.0	100.0	100.0
First child born before first marriage	8.5	7.4	5.7	5.1	5.2
Pregnant with first child*	16.8	23.4	22.9	14.9	13.9
All others	74.8	69.1	71.4	79.9	80.9
Women, 20 and 21 years	1,812	1,983	1,473	1,235	1,232
Percent, total	100.0	100.0	100.0	100.0	100.0
First child born before first marriage	9.5	7.4	7.0	9.9	6.5
Pregnant with first child*	7.3	13.7	14.7	12.6	8.8
All others	83.2	78.9	78.3	77.5	84.7
Women, 22 to 24 years	1,538	1,515	1,084	1,022	1,035
Percent, total	100.0	100.0	100.0	100.0	100.0
First child born before first marriage	11.2	10.0	10.6	11.9	10.4
Pregnant with first child*	6.2	7.9	8.2	11.0	8.2
All others	82.5	82.0	81.2	77.1	81.4
WHITE					
Women, 14 to 24 years	6,001	5,979	5,053	4,594	4,298
Percent, total	100.0	100.0	100.0	100.0	100.0
First child born before first marriage	6.6	5.1	4.5	4.7	4.5
Pregnant with first child*	14.3	18.4	18.7	14.8	11.5
All others	79.1	76.5	76.8	80.5	84.0
BLACK					
Women, 14 to 24 years	600	631	542	518	481
Percent, total	100.0	100.0	100.0	100.0	100.0
First child born before first marriage	37.7	32.0	26.8	30.1	26.6
Pregnant with first child*	16.8	22.3	28.2	25.1	20.2
All others	45.5	45.6	45.0	44.8	53.2

*Women whose first child was born 0 to 8 months after the time of first marriage.
Source: U.S. Bureau of the Census, 1978, P-20, No. 325:5. See p. 61 of this report for a complete breakdown within the white and black subgroups.

14–24, the same general pattern held for blacks and whites, but in the 1972–1976 marriage period the black group has 55 percent in these combined types of premarital conception and the white group only 21 percent. This difference fits wth the high proportion of black females who do not marry when premaritally pregnant (Table 8.3).

Additional government data indicates that college graduates were not as likely to give birth within eight months after marriage as less-educated mothers (U. S. Department of HEW, 1970, 18, No. 12). The most likely group to be pregnant at marriage was those mothers with one to three years of high school. Pregnancy, of course, may well be the reason that these females are high school dropouts. When college females become pregnant, they resort to abortion rather than marrying or bearing an illegitimate child. Teenage females seem high on all three premarital pregnancy outcomes: illegitimate birth, abortion, and marriage when pregnant.

A word or two should be added here of the writings of trends in premarital pregnancy before 1950 (see Chapter 3). Smith and Hindus (1975) argue for a rapid rise in premarital pregnancy, particularly as measured by pregnant brides, between 1750 and 1800. Edward Shorter (1975) also makes this case. In addition, some of Phillips Cutright's work (1972) fits with this thesis. We have discussed earlier how one-third of the brides in some areas of the United States in the late eighteenth century were pregnant at marriage (Chapter 4). Sexual activity in serious courtship relationships in this period then seems to be supported by several researchers. Smith and Hindus (1975) and Shorter (1975) disagreed on whether this rate fell in the nineteenth century and now is rising again. My own inclination is to side with Smith and Hindus (1975) and assert that the "pregnant bride" rate fell in the nineteenth century. We do know that contraception was much more effective in the late nineteenth century and that premarital births and illegitimacy declined then also. This could be taken as a sign that the percent of pregnant brides also declined. I have tried to keep the focus mainly on the twentieth century because certainty declines rapidly as we go back in time. For the years before 1850 there is no adequate census anywhere except for one or two countries and, thus, one must rely on bits and pieces of data found in a few small communities. For the twentieth century there is data indicating that premarital pregnancy was lower for women marrying prior to the 1950s (U. S. Bureau of the Census, 1965, P-20, No. 18).

Births Out of Wedlock

In 1977 there were 516,000 illegitimate births in the United States for a rate of about 26 illegitimate births for each 1,000 unmarried women aged 15–44. In that same year the overall number of births was 3,327,000 or a rate of 67.8 births per 1,000 women aged 15–44 (U. S. Department of HEW, 1979, 27, No. 11). Almost 16 percent of the total births were illegitimate. This 16 percent illegitimacy *ratio* is an increase over previous years, but clearly it is a result of the sharp fall in legitimate births that began to evidence itself as early as 1958. Such a decrease in

TABLE 8.7

Estimated Number of Illegitimate Births per 1,000 Unmarried Women 15–44, By Age and Race of Mother: United States, 1940–1977.

AGE AND RACE Total	1977	1973	1970	1965[a]	1960	1950	1940
		Rate per 1,000 Unmarried Women in Specified Group					
15–44 years	26.0	24.5	26.4	23.5	21.6	14.1	7.1
15–19 years	25.5	22.9	22.4	16.7	15.3	12.6	7.4
20–24 years	34.7	31.8	38.4	39.9	39.7	21.3	9.5
25–29 years	28.5	30.0	37.0	49.3	45.1	19.9	7.2
30–34 years	17.2	20.5	27.1	37.5	27.8	13.3	5.1
35–39 years	8.3	10.8	13.3	17.4	14.1	7.2	3.4
40–44 year	2.4	3.0	3.6	4.5	3.6	2.0	1.2
White							
15–44 years	13.7	11.9	13.8	11.6	9.2	6.1	3.6
15–19 years	13.6	10.7	10.9	7.9	6.6	5.1	3.3
20–24 years	17.7	15.6	22.5	22.1	18.2	10.0	5.7
25–29 years	14.7	16.1	21.1	24.3	18.2	8.7	4.0
30–34 years	9.5	10.7	14.2	16.6	10.8	5.9	2.5
35–39 years	4.8	5.9				3.2	1.7
40–44 years[b]	1.4	1.7	4.4	4.9	3.9	0.9	0.7
Nonwhite							
15–44 years	79.4	84.2	89.9	97.6	98.3	71.2	35.6
15–19 years	86.4	89.7	90.8	75.8	76.5	68.5	42.5
20–24 years	105.6	108.9	121.0	152.6	166.5	105.4	46.1
25–29 years	77.8	82.4	93.8	164.7	171.8	94.2	32.5
30–34 years	44.6	56.4	89.8	137.8	104.0	63.5	23.4
35–39 years	18.6	26.2				31.3	13.2
40–44 years[b]	6.6	7.2	21.7	39.0	35.6	8.7	5.0

[a]*Refers only to births occurring within the United States. Alaska and Hawaii are included beginning with 1960. Figures for age of mother not stated are distributed.*
[b]*Rates computed by relating illegitimate births to mothers aged thirty-five and over to unmarried women aged thirty-five to forty-four.*
1977 Data Source: U. S. Department of Health, Education, and Welfare, Monthly Vital Statistics Report, 27:11 (February 5, 1979):19.
1973 Data Source: U. S. Department of Health, Education, and Welfare, Monthly Vital Statistics Report 23, No. 11 (January 30, 1975): 11.
1970 Data Source: U. S. Department of Health, Education, and Welfare, Monthly Vital Statistics Report 22, No. 12, Supplement (March 20, 1974): 11.
1940–1965 Data Source: U. S. Department of Health, Education, and Welfare, National Center for Health Statistics, Trends in Illegitimacy: U. S. 1940–1965, Series 21, No. 15 (February 1968): 4.

legitimate births tends to raise the proportion of all births made up by illegitimate births. Perhaps the best way to gain insight into illegitimacy is to examine the illegitimacy *rate*, which is the number of illegitimate births per 1,000 unmarried women aged 15–44 in a particular year. This figure is preferable because it is not affected by the legitimate birthrate, and it takes into account the size of the population at risk (15–44-year-old women). This rate is also better than looking at raw numbers of illegitimate births in each age category. One easy illustration of this comes when one examines the 15–19-year-old situation. About half of all illegitimate births occur to females in this age group. But teenagers represent about two-thirds of the total unmarried female population, so having half the illegitimate births is not a high rate. Females aged 20–24 represent only about a quarter of the single female population, but have somewhat more than their share of the illegitimate births. Thus, looking only at the number of births out of wedlock, one can easily arrive at an erroneous conclusion as to the risk of illegitimacy for teenagers. It is necessary to examine the number of births *per 1,000 females in that age group*. Table 8.7 and Figure 8.5 present the illegitimacy rate from 1940 to the present time. From about 1880 to 1940 there was a general decline in illegitimacy from the high levels of the late eighteenth century. Table 8.7 and Figure 8.5 detail the trend since 1940.

One key trend visible in Table 8.7 is the sharp increase in illegitimacy rates from 1940 to 1960. In those twenty years the illegitimacy rate tripled from 7.1 to 21.6 births for every 1,000 unmarried women aged 15–44. This increase seemed just slightly more for whites than for nonwhites. Nonwhites comprise about 90 percent black and 10 percent all other racial groups. We use nonwhite rates because black rates were not separately available until 1969 and because the black and nonwhite rates are very similar.

A second feature of this trend is that from 1960 on, the white rate is the only one to show a significant increase. One other basic feature is the rise in illegitimacy among teenage mothers. This rise is particularly noticeable in the white group and particularly sharp in the 1965–1970 period. Finally, it should be clear to the reader that despite the rise in teenage illegitimacy, the illegitimacy rate is still higher for the 20–24-year-old group, and the 25–29-year-old group is also usually higher.[1]

[1]I will illustrate the possible confusion created by current methods of estimating illegitimacy rates. Note that in Table 8.7 the 15–19-year-old women in 1977 have an illegitimacy rate of 25.5 illegitimate births per 1,000 women. The comparable rate for 20–24-year-old women is 34.7 and thus they appear to have a higher illegitimacy rate. However, if we figure the rate using only those women who are "at risk," namely, those women who are nonvirginal, the situation changes dramatically. There were in 1977 roughly 10 million women aged 15–19 and 90 percent of them were single, that is, 9 million. Of the single women, Zelnik and Kantner estimate 35 percent are nonvirginal. That yields 3.1 million nonvirgins as the true "population at risk" among 15–19-year-olds. Among the 9.7 million 20–24-year-olds there are only 45 percent single or about 4.4 single women and we would estimate the nonvirginity rate at about 70 percent. This yields 3 million nonvirginal women as the "at risk" population. The number of illegitimate births to these 3 million 20–24-year-olds in 1977 was 169,000, which yields a rate of 55 illegitimate births per 1,000 nonvirgins. The comparable rate for 15–19-year-olds based on 240,000 illegitimate births is 76 illegitimate births per 1,000 nonvirgins. Thus, the teenage rate per 1,000 *nonvirgins* is indeed higher than the 20–24-year-old rate per 1,000 *nonvirgins*. That seems like a more

This basic trend in illegitimacy shows a sustained rise in all rates from 1940–1960 and a continued rise in the teenage rates. These trends require some explanation. Phillips Cutright has done extensive analyses of trends in illegitimacy, and he argues that for blacks a very large proportion of the rise in illegitimacy was a result of improved health that increased fecundity (ability to become pregnant) and decreased miscarriages (1972a; 1972b). This improvement in health consists of improved nutrition and reduction of venereal diseases that can lead to miscarriage.[2] (For general rates and trends in venereal disease see U. S. Center for Disease Control, 1979.) Both these factors increase the likelihood of becoming pregnant and carrying the child to term. Cutright calculates that gains in white health were much less in this time period, and thus such health improvements accounted for somewhat less than a quarter of the rise in white illegitimacy. A drop of about a year in average age at first menses (from thirteen and a half to twelve and a half) may account for part of the increase in that such a drop would indicate a higher proportion of fifteen- and sixteen-year-old females who would be fully capable of becoming pregnant. It is estimated that it takes about two and a half years from time of first menses to the time when a female is ovulating regularly during each menstrual cycle and thus is capable of becoming pregnant each month. This drop in age at first menses is also related to improved health in that it is believed to be caused by better nutrition.

Cutright rejects a decrease in contraceptive usage as a cause of higher illegitimacy. He argues that there is no reason to suppose a decline in the use of contraception in this time period since knowledge and availability were increasing. Thus, a conservative position would be that there was no decrease in premarital contraceptive usage in the 1940–1960 period.

On abortion there are, of course, no representative national data before legalization in January 1973, but there is no reason to assume a decline in use of abortion either. So here, too, one may assume no change. An examination of the proportion of pregnant brides indicates that there has been an increase in this type of outcome. This would make one expect a *decrease* in illegitimacy. This is so

---

reasonable basis to compute illegitimacy rates because the risk of the virginal women is zero and if they are included, any group with a large proportion of virgins will seem to have a low illegitimacy rate despite the presence of a high risk to nonvirginal women. In addition, the increase in the teen rate from 1970 to 1977 may well be illusory. According to Zelnik and Kantner, the nonvirginity rate from 1971 to 1976 increased by about 30 percent. This increase in the proportion of nonvirgins automatically raises the likelihood of illegitimate births going up in total numbers. If the base were only nonvirgins then the base would show an increase and the rate would be adjusted accordingly. The increase in illegitimacy rate from 1970–1977 is actually less than 30 percent and thus one can conclude that there has been no increase at all in the illegitimate rate per 1,000 *nonvirgins*. Again, the inclusion of virgins in the total number of females confuses comparison of rates by age groups and between years. Now that we have reliable nonvirginity data on 15–19-year-olds, it would be well to at least calculate their rates based on nonvirgins only and look for trends accordingly. Also, our data on older females is improving in reliability and should allow us to convert to nonvirginity basis for all females sometimes during the 1980s.

[2] It is important to note that teenage mothers in Sweden do not exhibit the higher health risks to themselves and their babies that U. S. teenagers do (Bremberg, 1977). This finding implies that our poorer health care for teenage American pregnant women may make the difference.

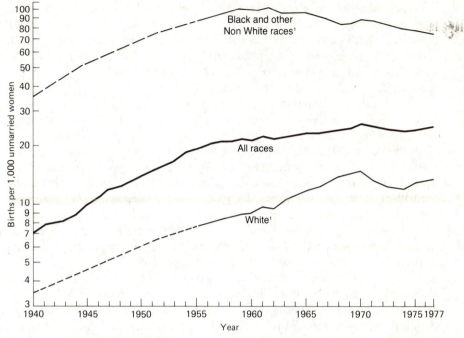

[1] Data for Whites and for Blacks and other races are for 1940, 1950, and 1955 through 1975. The broken lines indicate discontinuous series.

Figure 8.5. Illegitimate Births Per 1,000 Unmarried Women 15–44 Years Old, by Race: 1940 to 1977. Source: 1940 to 1975: U.S. Bureau of the Census, 1978, Series P-23, No. 70:4 (as corrected in Series P-23, No. 70, August 1978 Errata Sheet). 1977 Data Source: U.S. Department of Health, Education, and Welfare, Monthly Vital Statistics Report 27, No. 11 (February 5, 1979): 19.

because the increase in pregnant-when-married means more premarital pregnancies are being resolved by marriage, and thus fewer pregnancies should be eventuating in illegitimate births. Since data indicate an *increase* in illegitimacy in this 1940–1960 period, we face even more of a mystery as to how this rise in illegitimacy occurred. Increased births in hospitals, where illegitimate status could be discerned, may be part of the explanation, but especially for whites, hospital births were already quite high by 1940. Increased welfare benefits for AFDC has been proposed as a cause of more registration of illegitimate births, but Cutright examined illegitimacy rates in states with high and low benefits and looked for changes in trends and found no difference, so this explanation seems weak.

Cutright thus concludes that there has been an increase in female nonvirginity between 1940 and 1960 and this accounts for much of the rise in illegitimacy. This seems like a reasonable explanation except for the fact that, as the reader knows, the research on premarital intercourse indicates very little increase in female nonvirginity rates between 1940 and 1960. One can support Cutright by arguing that these studies were not likely to include representative groups of poor people and of black people. Almost 60 percent of the illegitimate births are to black females, and about 80 percent of the black females and 60 percent of the white females with illegitimate births are in the income bracket we would call "below the poverty line" (Cutright, 1972*b*). Thus there may have been a rise in sexual behavior for this segment of the population. One still needs an explanation as to why such a change occurred predominantly among the lower classes. In short, there are difficulties with the Cutright explanation also.

I would offer an additional possible explanation for the rise in illegitimacy between 1940–1960. One can increase pregnancy rates by increasing the frequency of coitus or the number of coital partners. There is no evidence that the number of partners rose during that period, but the frequency of coitus may well have increased. From the 1920s until the late 1960s there was a consolidation process going on, wherein the advances in sexual behavior that had occurred were becoming normatively accepted. If this was the case then a reduction in guilt may have occurred by the 1940s which may *not* have led to large increases in nonvirginity but *may* instead have encouraged those who were nonvirginal to relax and enjoy more what they were doing and thus increased their coital frequencies. The start of World War II may well have stepped up the speed of this change.

Finally I should add here that the illegitimacy rate is not the best index of changes in sexual relationships. The rate was low from 1880 to 1940 and that is precisely the period when radical changes were occurring in sexual relations. Also, the illegitimacy rate changed relatively little in the decade 1965–1975 during the dramatic changes in nonvirginity. Thus, the sharp rise in illegitimacy rates from 1940–1960 may also *not* reflect any large changes in overall nonvirginity but instead reflect factors such as increased frequency of sexual intercourse and increased fecundity. It is a long way from nonvirginity to births out of wedlock and many factors are involved.

By the late 1960s better contraceptive and abortion opportunities were making themselves felt. Thus, when the rise in female nonvirginity occurred in the late 1960s, it did not show itself in illegitimacy rates except for the teenage group (see Table 8.7). The teenage group is (as we know from Zelnik and Kantner) the poorest at contraceptive protection. The leveling off that is occurring in illegitimacy rates even for the teenage group indicates a change in contraceptive attitudes and skills.

Perspective on the trends may be gained by another look at Table 8.7. If one compares the 1940 with the 1977 data, one can see that despite the rapid rise in the late 1960s in teenage rates, the overall percent increase since 1940 for teenagers is smaller than for any age group up to thirty-five years of age. Teenage rates went from 7.4 to 25.5 percent a 245 percent increase, whereas the 20–24-year-old females showed a rise from 9.5 to 34.7 percent, which is a slightly higher rise, and the 25–29-year-old group went from 7.2 to 28.5 percent, an increase of almost 300 percent. Thus, on balance it appears that the teenagers did not increase their relative risk of pregnancy in the past generation, but rather were slower at achieving the final plateau level of current illegitimacy rates. The statistical picture leads one to posit a delayed following by the teenage population of their older sisters and brothers.

Cutright's overall conclusions are that the two best predictors of illegitimacy are the marital fertility rates and the economic prosperity in the country. The higher the marital fertility rates, the higher the illegitimacy rates; the higher the economic prosperity, the lower the illegitimacy rates. In general, the European data do support such overall correlations. For example, the illegitimacy rates seemed to rise sharply from 1750–1850, and so did marital fertility rates. Also from about 1880 to 1940 illegitimacy rates did not rise, and in some decades they declined. At that same time marital fertility rates were declining. The reasoning behind this relationship is in part based upon the use of contraceptives. If marital fertility rates fall, they do so largely due to changes in contraceptive usage. Also, if health factors are involved, they will affect all pregnancies and not only those that occur in marriage. The economic prosperity factor operates to indicate that in good times there is an increase of people who wish to control births and who are knowledgeble about contraception. This explanation still leaves much to be desired, for in the 1960s marital fertility was falling and economic prosperity was rising and thus the prediction would have been that illegitimacy should drop sharply—but instead there was a modest rise. Such an event does not mean that the predictive factors are erroneously identified; it simply means that other causal factors are involved and for a sound theoretical basis for prediction we must get to know more of these other factors. I would submit that changes in values concerning pleasure, risk-taking, and conformity are involved.

There is another important set of questions that we have not examined. Such questions deal with the consequences to women who have had a premarital pregnancy. For example, what are the economic consequences of such an experience? Furstenberg (1976) has reported that there are economic costs for those women who become mothers premaritally but that when parents support the unmarried mother, even the economic consequences can be minimized. Freedman and Thornton (1979) also report that in their longitudinal data the long-term consequences of pregnancy at marriage were not as dramatic as the short-term consequences. This entire area is a logical extension of this chapter's work which the interested reader can follow up on.

Summary and Conclusions

The reader should be aware that pleasure and intimacy are also key outcomes of premarital intercourse. We spoke of those outcomes at length elsewhere and so in this chapter we have examined the pregnancy outcomes of premarital sexuality. We followed out the potential consequences of sexual relationships by examining contraception, pregnancy, abortion, pregnant brides, and births out of wedlock. These all relate to the understanding of how premarital pregnancy is managed today in America. I presented some explanations that are pieces of the overall puzzle that we are seeking to grasp. The logical path we followed is graphically presented in Figure 8.6. This simple diagram lists the paths that must be followed if one is to arrive at some of the outcomes of premarital sexual relationships which we discussed. We can make rough estimates of how many people are involved at several of these different junctions, and Table 8.8 does just that for America in 1977.

Steps

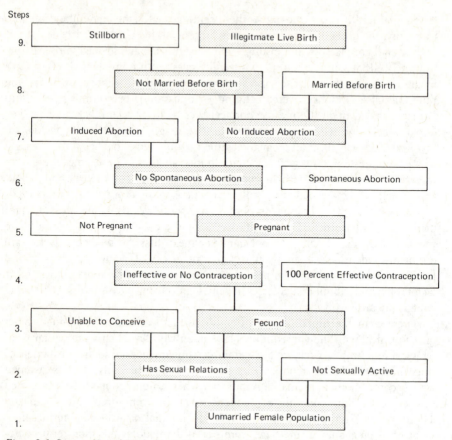

9. Stillborn   Illegitmate Live Birth

8. Not Married Before Birth   Married Before Birth

7. Induced Abortion   No Induced Abortion

6. No Spontaneous Abortion   Spontaneous Abortion

5. Not Pregnant   Pregnant

4. Ineffective or No Contraception   100 Percent Effective Contraception

3. Unable to Conceive   Fecund

2. Has Sexual Relations   Not Sexually Active

1. Unmarried Female Population

Figure 8.6. Steps to Unwed Motherhood. (Read diagram from the bottom up.)
*Source: Derived from K. Davis and J. Blake, 1956:211. The style of presentation above
is from Cutright (1972a).*

From a theoretical perspective, it is apparent from Figure 8.6 that the causes
of premarital intercourse are fundamental to the entire process (see Chapter 7).
Such causes may well affect later choices portrayed in this diagram by affecting
desire to marry, abort or use contraception. Thus it is vital to further develop our
theoretical understanding of factors that are the basic influence on premarital sexual
permissiveness. Thirteen such factors were discussed in a preliminary way in Chapter 7. The ultimate linkage of the causal factors in Chapter 7 with the outcomes
of Chapter 8 is a prerequisite for understanding sexual trends in America.

One such linkage that can be asserted concerns proposition ten from Chapter
7, which hypothesized that the acceptance of premarital sexual permissiveness in
the adult institutions (economic, political, religious, educational, etc.) was a direct
cause of greater acceptance on the part of young people. This same adult acceptance
would likely lead to more open discussion and utilization of contraception and thus
reduce premarital pregnancy rates. One might also assume that the amount of
equalitarianism (Proposition 3–Chap. 7) would encourage males to be concerned
about pregnancy and thus reduce pregnancy risks. Also, if one had friends who

TABLE 8.8

Estimated Total Pregnancies for 1977 in the United States*

Total = 5,800,000

Outcome:
  Live Births: 3,300,000
      (a) Legitimate 2,800,000
      (b) Illegitimate 500,000
  Abortions: 1,300,000
  Miscarriages and Stillbirths: 1,200,000

*Tietze (1978) estimates the teenage share of these total pregnancies. In 1976 there were (in round numbers 1.1 million teenage pregnancies with 570,000 ending in live births (56% legitimate 44% illegitimate); 380,000 pregnancies ended in abortion and 150,000 in miscarriages. Miscarriages and stillbirths are estimated as equal to 20% of the live births and 10% of the abortions for teenagers and 30% of live births and 15% of abortions for the total group, in accord with Tietze's suggestions.

were also having sexual relationships (Proposition 12–Chap. 7) these friends might well discuss contraceptive methods that were available and thereby decrease the risk of pregnancy. Thus, one can examine which propositions that are causes of premarital sexual permissiveness might also be hypothesized to have a causal impact on pregnancy.

The importance of marriage to a person (Proposition 13–Chap. 7) may relate in a different way to pregnancy outcomes. It may affect one's willingness to abort or marry when pregnant. Some other causes of premarital sexual permissiveness do not so clearly relate to pregnancy outcomes; for example, how much one participates in courtship (Proposition 8–Chapter 7) is not related to pregnancy in as obvious a way as the other propositions discussed above. We need to hypothesize linkages such as I have done above but in a systematic way, in line with one's own theory of how sexual relationships and their outcomes develop.

Any explanation of pregnancy outcomes would have to include more than just the factors discussed in Chapter 7 but utilizing those factors would be a way to integrate our explanations. We have mentioned other causal factors in this chapter. Pregnancy and its outcomes is not a simple area of behavior to explain. Our progress will depend on our willingness to formulate explanations and to test them carefully. The beginning of such explanations of human sexual relationships has been presented in Chapters 6, 7, and in this chapter. Perhaps some of you reading this book will be among those who will be motivated to become involved in research concerning this fascinating puzzle of human sexuality.

References

Blake, Judith. 1971. "Abortion and Public Opinion: The 1960–1970 Decade," *Science* 171 (February):540–549.

Bracken, Michael, et al. 1972. "Correlates of Repeat Induced Abortions," *Journal of Obstetrics and Gynecology* 40 (December):816–825.

Bremberg, Sven. 1977. "Pregnancy in Swedish Teenagers," *Scandinavian Journal of Social Medicine* 5:15–19.

Calzderone, Mary. 1958. *Abortion in the U.S.* New York: Harper & Row.

Christensen, Harold T. 1966. "Scandinavian and

American Sex Norms: Some Comparisons with Sociological Implications," *Journal of Social Issues* 22 (April): 60–75.

Cutright, Phillip. 1972*a*. "The Teenage Sexual Revolution and the Myth of an Abstinent Past," *Family Planning Perspectives* 4 (January): 24–31.

_____. 1972*b*. "Illegitimacy in the U. S.: 1920–1968," in Charles Westoff and Robert Parke (eds.), *Demographic and Social Aspects of Population Growth*. Washington, DC: Government Printing Office.

Davis, Kingsley, and Judith Blake. 1956. "Social Structure and Fertility: An Analytic Framework," *Economic Development and Cultural Change* 4 (April):211–235.

Delamater, John, and Patricia MacCorquodale. 1978. "Premarital Contraceptive Use: A Test of Two Models," *Journal of Marriage and the Family* 40 (May):235–247.

Devereux, George. 1955. A *Study of Abortion in Primitive Societies*. New York: Julian.

Diamond, Milton, et al. 1973. "Sexuality, Birth Control and Abortion: A Decision-Making Sequence," *Journal of Biosocial Science* 15 (July):347–361.

Ford, Kathleen. 1978. "Contraceptive Use in the U.S., 1973–1976," *Family Planning Perspectives* 10 (September/October):264–269.

Forrest, Jacqueline D., Christopher Tietze, and Ellen Sullivan. 1978. "Abortion in the U. S., 1976–1977," *Family Planning Perspectives* 10 (September/October):271–279.

Freedman, Deborah S., and Arland Thornton. 1979. "The Long-term Import of Pregnancy at Marriage on the Family's Economic Circumstances," *Family Planning Perspectives*, 11 (January/February):6–21.

Furstenberg, Frank F., Jr. 1976. *Unplanned Parenthood*. New York: Free Press.

Gebhard, Paul H., et al. 1958. *Pregnancy, Birth, and Abortion*. New York: Harper & Row.

Hartley, Shirley F. 1975. *Illegitimacy*. Berkeley: University of California Press.

Himes, Norman E. 1963. *Medical History of Contraception*. New York: Gamut Press.

Hornick, Joseph D., Louise Doran, and Susan H. Crawford. 1979. "Premarital Contraceptive Usage Among Male and Female Adolescents," *Family Coordinator* 28 (April):181–190.

Malinowski, Bronislaw. 1929. *The Sexual Life of Savages in North Western Melanesia*. New York: Harvest Books. (Published by Harcourt Brace Jovanovich).

Mead, Margaret. 1928. *The Coming of Age in Samoa*. New York: Morrow.

Moore, Kristin A., and Steven B. Caldwell. 1976. "Out of Wedlock Pregnancy and Childbearing," Working Paper 992–02. Washington, DC: Urban Institute.

_____. 1977. "The Effect of Government Policies on Out of Wedlock Sex and Pregnancy," *Family Planning Perspectives* 9 (July/August): 164–169.

_____., Sandra L. Hofferth, Steven B. Caldwell, Linda J. Waite. 1979. *Teenage Motherhood: Social and Economic Consequences*. Washington, Urban Institute, 1979.

Noonan, John T., Jr. 1966. *Contraception*. Cambridge, MA: Harvard University Press.

Pope, Hallowell. 1967. "Unwed Mothers and Their Sex Partners," *Journal of Marriage and the Family* 30 (August):555–567.

Rains, Prudence M. 1971. *Becoming an Unwed Mother*. Chicago: Aldine.

Reichelt, Paul A. 1978. "Changes in Sexual Behavior Among Unmarried Teenage Women Utilizing Oral Contraception," *Journal of Population* 1:57.

Reiss, Ira L. 1973. *Heterosexual Permissiveness Inside and Outside of Marriage*. Morristown, NJ: General Learning Press, pp. 1–29.

_____, Albert Banwart, and Harry Foreman. 1975. "Premarital Contraceptive Usage: A Study and Some Theoretical Explorations," *Journal of Marriage and the Family* 37 (August):619–630.

Sarvis, Betty, and Hyman Rodman. 1974. *The Abortion Controversy*, 2nd ed. New York: Columbia University Press.

Shorter, Edward. 1975. *The Making of the Modern Family*. New York: Basic Books.

Sklar, June, and Beth Berkov. 1974. "Abortion, Illegitimacy, and the American Birth Rate," *Science* 185 (September 13):909–915.

Smith, Daniel S., and Michael S. Hendus. 1975. "Premarital Pregnancy in America, 1640–1971: An Overview and Interpretation," *Journal of Interdisciplinary History* 4 (Spring):537–570.

Thompson, Linda, and Graham B. Spanier. 1978. "Influence of Parents, Peers and Partners on the Contraceptive Use of College Men and Women," *Journal of Marriage and the Family* 40 (August):481–492.

Tietze, Christopher. 1978. "Teenage Pregnancies: Looking Ahead to 1984," *Family Planning Perspective* 10 (July/August): 205–207.

U. S Bureau of the Census. 1969. "Marriage, Fertility and Childspacing: June 1965," *Current*

Population Reports Series P-20, No. 186. Washington, DC: Government Printing Office.

———.1978. "Fertility of American Women: June, 1977," *Current* Population Reports Series P-20, No. 325 (September). Washington, DC: Government Printing Office.

———. 1978. "Fertility of American Women: June, 1977," *Current Population Reports* Series P-20, No. 325 (September). Washington, DC: Government Printing Office.

———. 1978. "Perspectives on American Fertility, *Current Population Reports* Series P-23, No. 70 (July). Washington, DC: Government Printing Office.

U. S. Department of Health, Education, and Welfare, Center for Disease Control. 1974. "Venereal Disease Statistical Letter: August 1974." No. 120 (October), Bureau of State Services, Atlanta, GA.

———. 1975. "Abortion Surveillance, 1973," (May) Atlanta, GA.

———. 1978. "Abortion Surveillance, 1976," (August) Atlanta, GA.

———. 1978. "Reported Morbidity and Mortality in the U.S.," 26, No. 53 (September). Atlanta, GA.

U.S. Department of Health, Education and Welfare, National Center for Health Statistics. 1964. *Natality Statistics Analysis: United States, 1962.* Series 21, No. 1 (October). Washington, DC: Government Printing Office.

———. 1968. *Trends in Illegitimacy: United States 1940–1965.* Series 21, No. 15 (February). Washington, DC: Government Printing Office.

———. 1970. *Monthly Vital Statistics Report,* Vol. 18, No. 12 (March 27). Washington, DC: Government Printing Office.

———. 1974. *Monthly Vital Statistics Report,* Vol. 22, No. 12 (March 20). Washington, DC: Government Printing Office.

———. 1975. *Monthly Vital Statistics Report,* Vol. 23, No. 11 (January 30). Washington, DC: Government Printing Office.

———. 1979. "Final Natality Statistics, 1977," *Monthly Vital Statistics Report,* Vol. 27, No. 11 (February 5, 1979) Washington, D.C.: Government Printing Office.

Vincent, Clark E. 1961. *Unmarried Mothers.* New York: Free Press.

Weinstock, Edward, Christopher Tietze, Frederick S. Jaffe, and Joy S. Dryfoos. 1975. "Legal Abortions in the United States Since the 1973 Supreme Court Decisions," *Family Planning Perspective* 7 (January/February):23–31.

Zelnik, M., and J. F. Kantner. 1972. "Sexuality, Contraception and Pregnancy Among Young Unwed Females in the United States," in U.S. Commission on Population Growth and the American Future, *Demographic and Social Aspects of Population Growth.* Washington, DC: Government Printing Office; 1:355–375.

———. 1974. "The Resolution of Teenage First Pregnancies," *Family Planning Perspective* 6 (Spring): 74–80.

———. 1977. "Sexual and Contraceptive Experience of Young Unmarried Women in the U.S., 1976 and 1971," *Family Planning Perspectives* 9 (March/April): 55–71.

———. 1978a. "First Pregnancies to Women Aged 15–19: 1976 and 1971," *Family Planning Perspectives* 10 (January/February): 11–20.

———. 1978b. "Contraceptive Patterns and Premarital Pregnancy Among Women Aged 15–19 in 1976," *Family Planning Perspective* 10 (May/June):135–142.

Zetterberg, Hans. 1969. *Om Sexual livet i Sverige (On Sexuality in Sweden).* Stockholm: Statens Offentliga Utredningar.

Part Three THE MARITAL INSTITUTION

The Marital Relationship: Roles, Power, and Communication

NINE

A Demographic Overview of Marriage

Marriage is a part of our social life that very few Americans fail to experience. Even in this day of increased popularity of cohabitation, marriage is still a very popular institution. In the United States only about 6 percent of the men and 4 percent of the women who reach the 45–54-year age bracket have never been married. Figure 9.1 indicates this rapid induction of young Americans into marriage—by the early thirties, over 90 percent have been married. Compared to other Western countries we marry at an earlier age and in very high proportions. For example, Swedes marry about three years later than we do and roughly 20 percent never marry (Reiss, 1979). The long-range trend in age at first marriage can be seen in Table 9.1. The age at marriage for males during a thirty-year period went from 23.3 in 1948 to 24.2 in 1978. In between these years, the lowest age was 22.5, reached in the late 1950s during one of the historical high points of our marriage rate. The 1978 median age of 24.2 was not surpassed during that thirty-year period. The median age for females was 20.4 in 1948 and 21.8 in 1978. The low point for female median age at marriage was also during the late 1950s. The 1978 age of 21.8 is also the highest in that thirty-year period. I have deliberately taken this thirty-year perspective so that the reader does not overestimate the amount of change in age at first marriage. A closer look at Table 9.1 indicates that in the five years from 1973 to 1978 there was a rise of about one year in the median age for both genders. It is really about the time of the late 1960s that any noticeable change in age at first marriage occurred. A change of just one year can make significant differences in the proportion of young people at any particular age who are single. Table 9.2 indicates, for example, that in 1960 only 28 percent of all the 20–24-

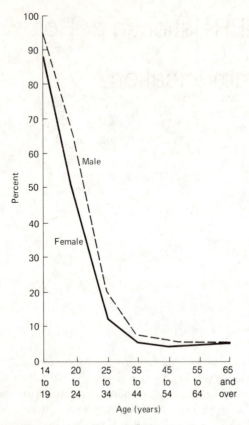

Figure 9.1. Never-Married Persons, by Age: March, 1977. (U.S. Bureau of the Census, 1978, p. 23, No. 77:3.)

year-old females were single; by 1978 that percentage had risen to 48 percent (U. S. Bureau of the Census, 1978, P-20, No. 327). By the late twenties, even in 1978, the percent single was down to 18 percent and by the early thirties, only eight percent had never married. So, as of now, the change in average age at marriage appears as a delay rather than a rejection of marriage. However, it is too early to be sure for it is possible that those who now are twenty years old will end up with a higher never married percent by the time they are in their thirties. The current percent married in their twenties is at a low point compared to 1960, but it should be kept in mind that the percent single at particular ages from 1890 to 1940 was quite similar to the 1978 rates reported in Table 9.2 (Jacobson, 1959). It is interesting to note that the percentage of people who never married in the 1890–1940 period was *higher* than today. Perhaps the delay of marriage is the first sign of an increase in the percentage of people who never marry. If that percent rose to just 10 percent, it would be double what it is today.

TABLE 9.1

Median Age at First Marriage, by Gender: 1890–1978

YEAR	MALE*	FEMALE	YEAR	MALE*	FEMALE
1978	24.2	21.8	1959	22.5	20.2
1977	24.0	21.6	1958	22.6	20.2
1976	23.8	21.3	1957	22.6	20.3
1975	23.5	21.1	1956	22.5	20.1
1974	23.1	21.1	1955	22.6	20.2
1973	23.2	21.0	1954	23.0	20.3
1972	23.3	20.9	1953	22.8	20.2
1971	23.1	20.9	1952	23.0	20.2
1970	23.2	20.8	1951	22.9	20.4
1969	23.2	20.8	1950	22.8	20.3
1968	23.1	20.8	1949	22.7	20.3
1967	23.1	20.6	1948	23.3	20.4
1966	22.8	20.5	1947	23.7	20.5
1965	22.8	20.6	1940	24.3	21.5
1964	23.1	20.5	1930	24.3	21.3
1963	22.8	20.5	1920	24.6	21.2
1962	22.7	20.3	1910	25.1	21.6
1961	22.8	20.3	1900	25.9	21.9
1960	22.8	20.3	1890	26.1	22.0

*Figures for 1947–1977 are based on Current Population Survey data supplemented by data from the Department of Defense on marital status by age for men in the Armed Forces. Figures for earlier dates are from decennial censuses.
Source: 1890 to 1977 data: U. S. Bureau of the Census, 1978, P-23, No. 77:4. Data: U. S. Bureau of the Census, 1979. P-20, No. 338:1.

TABLE 9.2

Women and Men Remaining Single (Never Married) 1960–1978

	(in percent)		
Women Single:	1960	1970	1978
Ages 20–24	28.4	35.8	47.6
25–29	10.5	10.5	18.0
Men Single:			
Ages 20–24	53.1	54.7	65.8
25–29	20.8	19.1	27.8

Source: U. S. Bureau of the Census, 1978, P-20, No. 327:4 and 1977, P-20, No. 306:3.

Figure 9.2 affords one a comparative view of marriage rates from 1870 to date. Note that Figure 9.2 shows the total current marriage rate (first marriages and remarriages combined). This figure does not show the decline in the first marriage rate because the remarriage rate makes up for some of the decline in the first marriage rate. Almost 30 percent of the marriages that occur in any one year today are to previously married people. Most of these previously married people are divorced. Remarriage rates after about 1970 started to decline, and together with the declining first marriage rate, pulled down the overall marriage rate. In very recent years, this overall rate has started to level out, but it is well below the peak years of the 1940s when World War II and the prosperity it brought raised our marriage rate to all time highs. We may well be entering into a stable period. We will discuss this further in Chapter 12 on divorce and remarriage. Surely, marriage is still a very popular institution but the speed with which people enter it has slowed down and we may well find that its overall popularity will decrease some in the decade of the 1980s.

One way to further gain an overview on marriage in America is to examine some of the important general characteristics of husbands and wives. Table 9.3 presents some valuable data in this regard. Note that in March 1977 there were an estimated 49,940,000 husbands and 51,115,000 wives. Where did the 1,175,000 wives come from? It is instructive to examine this question because it makes one

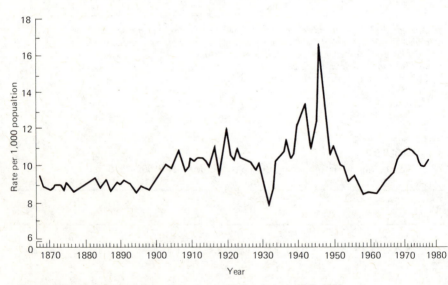

Figure 9.2. United States Marriage Rates (per 1,000 Population): 1867–1978.
Source: 1867–1969 data: U. S. Department of HEW, Vital and Health Statistics,
Series 21, No. 21 (September 1971): 2.
1970–1977 data: U. S. Bureau of the Census, 1978, Statistical Abstract of the United
States: 1978: 79.
1978 data: U. S. Department of HEW, Monthly Vital Statistics Report 28, No. 2
(May 15, 1979):2.

aware of the limitations of the data we are working with here. The actual number of husbands and wives is obtained by asking people about their marital status. People can lie and people can be mistaken. For example, a male who is about to get divorced in a few weeks may report himself as already divorced while his wife who is interviewed in her home may report herself as married. Some husbands may be deserting their families and deliberately lie about their marital status. Some women may be embarrassed to admit having children born out of wedlock and so list themselves as "separated." In addition, some people may be married to a mate who is not a citizen of this country. Too often we take data in tables as if it were written in stone—this comparison of husbands and wives should increase our willingness to look further and examine carefully the basis for any set of data. We cannot throw out all data that have flaws or we will end up with nothing to analyze. But we can be aware of the limitations present and seek improvement on the next research project.

I would like to use Table 9.3 as a small exercise in how to get the most out of a table. There is an opportunity in Table 9.3 to derive a great deal of information. Note, for example, line three under Wives' Characteristics—"percent of all women in age group"—how the percent rises to a peak in the thirties. It does not go beyond 83 percent, despite the fact that 96 percent of all women eventually marry, because women are constantly divorcing and being widowed. Therefore, no one age group has 96 percent *currently* married, even though that percent do eventually marry. Note that about 39 percent of the women sixty-five and over are married and then glance at the same line for husbands and you will see that 77 percent of the husbands sixty-five and over are married. This is due to the greater longevity of women so that most women live beyond their husbands' lifetime. Now drop down to the percent of nonwhite over sixty-five for both husbands and wives and note that nonwhites at that age have become a smaller proportion of the total number because they divorce more and have a shorter life expectancy.

Now look at the Living Arrangement section of wife and husband. Here we see that 93.9 percent of wives and 96.1 percent of husbands are living with their mates. If we take that percentage of the respective number of husbands and wives, we get almost exactly 48 million husbands and wives living together as of March 1977. This then tells us that the excess number of women over men who claim to be married (1,175,000) must also assert that they are not living with their husbands. So we have about 3,115,000 wives and only 1,940,000 husbands who say they are married but separated from their mates. Just how many other men who are legally married are missing, and how many women who are not married say they are, is impossible to know. Depending on your view of men and women, you will estimate differently and no one has bothered to investigate this question. In this same section of Table 9.3 one can see just how rare it is for a married couple to be living with someone else. Only 1.1 percent of all those married couples are not living in their own household and almost all of these are living with relatives. Note that this proportion is by far the greatest in the 14–24 age group—indicating that such housing is likely a temporary arrangement for newly married couples. Further, in

TABLE 9.3
Characteristics of Husbands and Wives in the United States, March 1977

Characteristic	AGE OF HUSBAND, IN YEARS							
	14 and over	14–24	25–29	30–34	35–44	45–54	55–64	65 and over
Husbands—Number in thousands	49,940	3,549	5,888	5,960	9,643	9,784	8,109	7,007
—Percent distribution	100.0	7.1	11.8	11.9	19.3	19.6	16.3	14.0
—Percent of all men in age group	63.4	16.2	68.5	82.0	86.2	86.9	85.6	76.7
Race—percent	100.0	100.0	100.0	100.0	100.0	100.0	100.0	100.0
White	90.4	90.5	90.1	89.5	89.2	90.5	91.6	91.4
Nonwhite	9.6	9.5	9.9	10.5	10.8	9.5	8.4	8.6
Living arrangement—percent	100.0	100.0	100.0	100.0	100.0	100.0	100.0	100.0
Living with wife	96.1	91.8	95.7	95.7	96.7	96.7	96.8	96.7
Own household	95.0	87.0	93.7	94.9	96.2	96.3	96.4	95.6
Relative's household	1.0	4.6	1.9	.8	.5	.4	.4	1.0
Nonrelative's household	.1	.2	.1	▼	▼	▼	▼	.1
Not living with wife	3.9	8.2	4.3	4.3	3.3	3.3	3.2	3.3
Own household	2.3	2.8	2.3	2.7	2.1	2.3	2.2	2.2
Other	1.6	5.4	2.0	1.6	1.2	1.0	1.0	1.1
Labor force participation in 1976—percent	100.0†	100.0†	100.0	100.0	100.0	100.0	100.0	100.0
In labor force	80.4	87.9	93.7	94.8	94.6	92.3	76.5	22.2
Not in labor force	19.6	12.1	6.3	5.2	5.4	7.7	23.5	77.8

Characteristic	AGE OF WIFE, IN YEARS							
	14 and over	14–24	25–29	30–34	35–44	45–54	55–64	65 and over
Wives—Number in thousands	51,115	6,063	6,725	6,256	9,908	9,700	7,434	5,029
—Percent distribution	100.0	11.9	13.2	12.2	19.4	19.0	14.5	9.8
—Percent of all women in age group	59.3	27.3	75.8	82.8	83.1	80.5	70.1	38.8
Race—percent	100.0	100.0	100.0	100.0	100.0	100.0	100.0	100.0
White	89.6	89.5	87.9	88.3	88.2	89.9	91.8	92.1
Nonwhite	10.4	10.5	12.1	11.7	11.8	10.1	8.2	7.9
Living arrangement—percent	100.0	100.0	100.0	100.0	100.0	100.0	100.0	100.0
Living with husband	93.9	90.5	92.9	93.6	94.0	95.0	95.4	95.4
Own household	92.8	86.6	91.6	93.0	93.7	94.6	94.9	94.1
Relative's household	1.0	3.7	1.2	.6	.3	.4	.5	1.2
Nonrelative's household	.1	.2	.1	¶	¶	¶	¶	.1
Not living with husband	6.1	9.5	7.1	6.4	6.0	5.0	4.6	4.6
Own household	4.6	4.1	5.3	5.3	5.4	4.3	3.7	3.5
Other	1.5	5.4	1.8	1.1	.6	.7	.9	1.1
Labor force participation in 1976—percent	100.0†	100.0†	100.0	100.0	100.0	100.0	100.0	100.0
In labor force	45.8	54.0	52.1	49.3	54.8	50.6	37.1	7.5
Not in labor force	54.2	46.0	47.9	50.7	45.2	49.4	62.9	92.5

† Excludes husbands and/or wives under age 16.
¶ Less than 0.05.
Note: Data relate to the civilian noninstitutionalized population and members of the Armed Forces who live with their families on or off post.
Source: Statistical Bulletin: Metropolitan Life Insurance Co., Vol. 59, No. 4. Oct.-Dec. 1978: 12 and 15. Based on reports of the Bureau of the Census and Department of Labor.

the sixty-five and over age group, this percent rises above what it was for couples thirty-five to sixty-four years of age. Here, of course, we have elderly parents living with their children.

Finally, labor force participation enlightens us further about male and female roles in marriage. From age twenty-five until age fifty-five males average over 90 percent in the labor force while females average only 50 percent in the labor force (and have a much higher part-time proportion as well).

All in all Table 9.3 affords the careful reader a wealth of information on husbands and wives in America. Many of these initial insights will be dealt with in greater depth in other parts of the book but this table will assist the reader in obtaining an overall grasp of the "approximately" 50 million married couples in America.

Husband–Wife Role Differentiation in Marriage: Fact or Fancy?

The previous section should have afforded a macro, large-scale view of marriage in America. Now let us move in closer and develop a micro or small-scale view of marriage. The first step in this perspective is to analyze the ways in which husband and wife roles are distinguished in our culture and elsewhere. One of the most widespread beliefs, even today, is that there is a need for specialization in the family group and this involves one person being the expressive leader (taking care of emotional needs) and one person being the instrumental leader (taking care of decision making and problem solving). Parsons and Bales (1955) is the major source of this view. Zelditch (1955) extended the view to other cultures and asserted that the male would be the instrumental leader in a marriage and the female the expressive leader. The reason for this gender assignment was, according to Zelditch, based on the biological attachment of the mother to the child, which led her to become the emotional support of the child and the family unit in general. Let us follow briefly the way in which this proposition developed and its current status. This will help show the process by which scientific concepts develop and change.

Back in the early years after World War II, a series of experiments was carried out at Harvard University under the supervision of Bales and Slater (1955). Similar work was being conducted at the University of Michigan and other schools. The apparatus at Harvard comprised, first of all, a small room with a table and six chairs. At one end of this room was a one-way mirror. On the "see through" side of the one-way mirror was another room with tape recorders and other instruments. Small groups of Harvard undergraduate males previously unknown to one another would be sent into the experimental room and given an administrative problem of some sort to read about, discuss, and arrive at a decision within forty minutes. In the observation room the tape recorders were taking down every word, and these were being classified according to a set of categories that Robert Bales had developed. There were four major types of responses which the men could make, and each of these types was broken into three subtypes (see Table 9.4). Bales and Slater tested fourteen different groups and found that the four major types of response were distributed as follows:

positive reactions—26 percent

problem-solving attempts—56 percent

questions—7 percent

negative reactions—11 percent

After each 40-minute session the participants would be asked several questions. Two of these questions interest us here. They were asked which of the group members they would choose as the best-liked person and which person had the best ideas. One could choose the same person as best liked and as having the best ideas. In fact, one could choose himself for one, or both, of these positions. First, it is well to note that in most cases the best-idea man and the best-liked man were different people. The typical group did not choose one person as both best-liked and best-idea man. Further, the best-idea and best-liked choices differed in their communication patterns. The men chosen as best-liked were typically high on the percent of their response which was listed in the "positive reactions" category. In short, the best-liked person was a supportive person who praised the ideas of others. The best-idea man had an unusually high proportion of his responses in the "problem-solving attempts" category. In short, the best-idea man spent much of his time putting forth ideas. A further difference was that the "idea" man was not so responsive to the ideas of others—in fact, he responded mostly to his own ideas and elaborated upon them. The "liked" man, on the other hand, was more responsive

TABLE 9.4

Categories for the Classification of Acts of Communication

A. Positive reactions	1. Shows solidarity; raises others' status; jokes; gives help; rewards 2. Shows tension release; shows satisfaction; laughs 3. Agrees; shows passive acceptance; understands; concurs; complies
B. Problem-solving attempts	4. Gives suggestion, direction, implying autonomy for others 5. Gives opinion, evaluation, analysis; expresses feelings, wishes 6. Gives orientation, information; repeats; clarifies; confirms
C. Questions	7. Asks for orientation information; repetition, confirmation 8. Asks for opinion, evaluation, analysis, expression of feeling 9. Asks for suggestion, direction, possible ways of action
D. Negative reactions	10. Disagrees; shows passive rejection, formality; withholds help 11. Shows tension increase; asks for help; withdraws "out of field" 12. Shows antagonism; deflates others' status; defends or asserts self

Source: Robert F. Bales and Philip E Slater, 1955:267.

to the ideas of others, and what he had to say was mostly in response to what someone else said.

Bales took these results and speculated on their meaning. It seemed that in small groups there was role specialization. Roles seemed to differentiate into an idea or task leader and a liked or emotional leader. They named these roles, respectively, "instrumental role" and "expressive role" and concluded that all small groups would differentiate roles in this manner. These two types of roles seemed essential in the organization of any social system or group. Specialization was assumed necessary in order to develop adequate skill at the particular role. Talcott Parsons, also at Harvard University, was another key figure in the development of these ideas (Parsons and Bales, 1955). It was at this point that Slater parted company with the formulation of these ideas. He did not accept the necessity of having separate persons perform instrumental and expressive roles (Slater, 1961).

It remained for Morris Zelditch, Jr. (1955) to test the proposition that if roles differentiated into instrumental and expressive leaders in small groups, and the family is a small group, then roles ought to differentiate in the family. Zelditch was speaking of the nuclear family composed of husband, wife, and child. He chose to test this idea out cross-culturally and see if nuclear families did differentiate roles into instrumental and expressive in all cultures around the world. He expected to find that this was the case and that the male was always the instrumental leader and the female the expressive leader. Nothing in the Bales and Slater work supports the idea that a particular gender would associate with a particular role. Zelditch based this upon some assumed biological factors. He reasoned that it was the female who carried the child for nine months, was able to nurse the newborn, and would be temporarily disabled by pregnancy and childbirth. Thus, he concluded males would be better suited to the demands of problem solving, for they would not so often be disabled or so attached to infants. Some qualifications of this type of reasoning have been discussed in Chapter 3.

Zelditch defined the instrumental role in the nuclear family as including responsibility for the solution of group tasks, for skills and decisions, and for being the ultimate source of discipline of children. The expressive role included responsibility for emotional solidarity, management of tensions, emotional care, and support. He examined fifty-six societies around the world by utilization of the Human Relations Area Files developed by George Peter Murdock at Yale University. He found that forty-six of the fifty-six cultures did fit his notions of role differentiation and also his notions of which gender would fit with each role. The most common situation in the ten societies where his theoretical propositions did *not* work out was the presence of a matrilineal kinship system. In such a kinship system the female line is important. We have seen among the Nayars and Trobriand Islanders that this means a man's role, in relation to his wife, will be minimized in comparison with his role in his sister's family. Thus, within the nuclear family, husbands may not play the instrumental role so much because their wives' brothers may be doing just that. A wife's brother would frequent his sister's house and train her children in the ways of the lineage to which they belong. Thus, the uncle and not the father, might well be the chief disciplinarian and decision maker for the family group.

Females were thus more likely to fit the hypothesized role differentiation than were males. This does not mean that males are any less attached to the family, however. It merely means that males were more attached to their sister's families, in some instances, than to their own. It should also be noted that in the case of the Marquesan Islanders, the female role specialization is not as predicted (Suggs, 1966) for a different reason. In the classical Marquesan case the female has several husbands, and the youngest husband is often given the task of nurturing the children. The wife is very busy primping to be attractive for her husbands. Her key role is defined in terms of being sensually attractive and not in terms of nurturance. In this case, then, the husbands are involved in both the instrumental and the expressive roles, and no particular combination of one husband and wife contained both roles. For a full analysis of other exceptions the reader is referred to Zelditch's article (1955).

Now, these studies by Bales, Slater, Parsons, and Zelditch raise some very interesting questions. Are we being blinded by our own cultural values regarding what is important? For instance, why is decision making regarding what meals to make, when a child needs a doctor, when to clean the house, and such not thought of as decision making? Why are only those decisions that males have traditionally been assigned thought of as "real" decision making? Does the father's decision that Johnny cannot go out to play after supper make him more of an instrumental leader than the mother's decision as to what they shall eat for supper? In our society at least, it seems apparent that both husbands and wives are making decisions, and therefore it is extremely difficult to call only one person an instrumental leader. Rather, it seems more accurate to speak of specialization of decision making in various areas of family living.

Further, I wonder if fathers are not expressive leaders in some areas of family life? A study done by Payne and Mussen (1956) found that 87 percent of a group of adolescent boys saw their fathers as more "rewarding" than their mothers. Clearly, it would be difficult for children to identify with a father who was purely instrumental and did nothing to aid in their emotional care and support. Surely, in relation to his mate, the husband in America (like a wife) has an expressive role in that he is culturally expected to help his wife manage tensions and give emotional care and support. Here too, it might well be more accurate to say that our society defines certain areas as ones in which women are expected to be expressive leaders.

What is it, then, that makes the Zelditch notion so popular? Many people feel convinced that men are more instrumental leaders than women, and thus Zelditch must be ultimately right. The reason for this underlying feeling, I believe, is that the male is still today more the instrumental leader *outside* the family. The distinction between power outside and power inside the family needs to be made. Leik (1963) ran an interesting experiment that pointed to this very distinction. He used nine family groups, each one containing a mother, father, and daughter. He analyzed their interaction patterns when they were divided up as family groups and when they were divided up into pseudofamily groups of a mother, father, and daughter, but all from different real families. When in the pseudofamily groups the males did do more of the decision making, but when divided into real family groups the mothers shared the instrumental role with the fathers. In short, it seemed that because of their leadership in business and politics, males often will gain leadership in interaction with females. However, in any intimate family group such outside power may mean much less and may be sharply curtailed by the intimate and affectionate bonds involved in the marital and family relationships. It is our awareness of this male power *outside* the family that makes us feel that the male is the instrumental leader *in* the family. However, in the family the male's leadership seems much more circumscribed and limited to specific spheres. Thus, we must question whether Zelditch adequately measured task and emotional leadership in his cross-cultural search. It also seems that instead of an overall rating on these two roles, it may be best to spell out the areas in which each gender operates as task or emotional leader.

George Levinger (1964) adds further information to this area of role specialization in the family. Levinger studied sixty married couples in Cleveland, Ohio. He found that, although *in general* husbands did rate higher on their needs for autonomy and lower than wives on needs for affiliation, nurturance, and succorance, *within the marriage* husbands and wives expressed very similar needs. *In public* the male's needs for nurturance may be suppressed in order to fit the male-role image or perhaps because of the irrelevance of such needs in his work. Levinger did find that most family tasks were specialized as either the husband's or the wife's. But in the socioemotional realm, in the realm of expressive behavior, Levinger believes that there must be reciprocity. The wife cannot be an expressive person to a husband who does not respond expressively to her. Both husbands and wives in the majority of these sixty Cleveland couples valued the emotional satisfaction that goes with the expressive role as more important to marital satisfaction than task performance. After the arrival of children, more role specialization occurs, for then the wife, more than the husband, may for a time be the expressive leader with the children. But with each other there still may be greater equality in expressiveness. So here is another complicating factor. We must note whether the role specialization we are speaking of is said to occur between the husband and wife or between parents and their children. A man may be the instrumental leader with his children, share instrumental and expressive roles equally with his wife, and be an instrumental leader in his occupational work. It should be clear by now that we must specify which social context we are speaking about if we are to obtain meaningful answers. The research of Leik and Levinger, although based upon small samples, has contributed greatly to the level of sophistication with which we approach this area today. Further, the increase in male–female equality and reduction in gender-role differentiation should make the current similarities between the genders even greater than found in the Leik and Levinger studies.

Clearly the Harvard undergraduate male groups that Bales and Slater experimented with are not the same as families. For one thing, families face many other decisions besides the administrative type of decisions given to the students for discussion. For another, families have an age and gender difference within them that does not occur in male student groups. Finally, there is a wide set of traditions concerning role performance in the family, whereas there is little tradition concerning how students should act in small-group research laboratories. More careful research on families, perhaps in small-group laboratories, is called for here.

In just the past few years some important research in the area of marital-role differentiation has been carried out. This research has focused on cross-cultural data and is relevant to the applicability of the role differentiation thesis to cultures around the world. Aronoff and Crano (1975, 1978) first tested the notion that males are the instrumental leaders and thus their task would be to produce the vast majority of the subsistence production of any culture. They tested this idea out on 862 societies available in Murdock's *Ethnographic Atlas* (1967). Their results indicated that females contributed 44 percent of the subsistence production. The range went from 32 percent to 51 percent in different cultural areas of the world. Thus, there is evidence that females participate in a major way in the subsistence production of cultures around the world (including gathering, hunting, fishing, animal husbandry, and agricultural societies). So, at the very least, we would have to qualify any notion of task specialization in the subsistence area.

Crano and Aronoff (1978) also attempted a check on the task specialization in the area of expressive roles, particularly in child care. For this check Crano and Aronoff utilized 186 cultures from the Standard Cross-Cultural Sample as coded by Barry and Paxson (1971). The data was divided into care for infants (up to nine months of age) and care for children (one to five years of age). There were radical differences in child care for these two age groups. In the case of infant care, in 90 percent of the sample of 186 cultures, the mother was the principal caretaker. However, for the young child (ages 1–5), in only 24 percent of the sample was the mother the principal caretaker. Fathers in 32 percent of the societies maintained a "regular close relationship" or "frequent close proximity" (the two highest expressive contribution categories) with an infant. For young children ages 1–5, 55 percent of the sample showed fathers in such close relationships.

A check of complementary involvement (of both mothers and fathers) was also made. This indicated that with infants there was a tendency for societies wherein mothers were the principal caretakers to not have as much paternal involvement with the care of the infant. Nevertheless, in societies where the mother was heavily involved in the care of a child (ages 1–5), there was *no tendency* for this to reduce the care given by fathers. Thus, the role of child care does seem specialized in one parent predominantly during infancy. Crano and Aronoff speculate that perhaps this is due to the urgent need for special attention at this time, and in order to ensure survival, one parent is given chief responsibility and the other parent is expected to be available to help when needed. In childhood, the survival issue is less central and if either parent is low on care, this is less likely to influence the care given by the other parent.

One final check in the Crano and Aronoff (1978) study was to examine how the participation of the female in the caretaking role related to her participation in the subsistence contribution to that society. No significant relationship appeared.

This means that even when the female has the principal share of child care, she is just as likely to contribute to the subsistence needs of the economy. Of course, such a comparison does not indicate how much power the female has in each society. It may be that females contribute the same proportion of subsistence in societies where their child care varies considerably, but that only in societies where their child care is minimized do they have high political power. These are additional questions that future research will have to answer. But for now, we can conclude by asserting that the cross-cultural examination of the role-differentiation thesis in dicates the need for serious qualifications. There appears to be a great deal of role sharing, although the highest role differentiation occurs in hunting societies and when dealing with individuals who have newborn infants. In all societies, the sharing tended to increase after infancy, and females would continue to contribute to subsistence activities. Thus, we arrive at a modified role differentiation perspective which seems in line with the facts in our own society as well as elsewhere. These cross-cultural findings also are congruent with the perspective put forth earlier concerning the importance of specifying the division of roles by specific tasks.

Husbands, Wives, and Power

Now that we have some insight into husband and wife task division, let us examine the crucial area of husband–wife power relationships. First, it is important to clarify what is meant by the concept of power. I would judge the definitions offered by Cromwell and Olson (1975) and Scanzoni (1979) to be the most agreed upon ones in sociology today (Rollins and Bahr, 1976). These definitions stress that power is the ability or potential of an individual to influence the behavior of other members of a social group. Power in this sense is not conceived as an attribute of an individual per se but rather as a characteristic that can be measured between any two individuals who are interacting. Power is not a fixed trait for it depends upon the particular other person to whom one is relating. Further, power may vary according to the particular situation. For example, a person may be more powerful in decisions regarding children than in decisions regarding car purchases.

One of the most widely shared approaches to power was put forth by French and Raven (1959) and Raven, Centers, and Rodrigues (1975). According to this view, power is related to the perception others have of you. If others perceive you as able to help them in their goals, then you will have the ability to influence their behavior and therefore you will possess power. In this sense a judgment concerning power must be made from the perspective of the individuals who are interacting. An outside observer can, of course, add much information, but such an observer may be witnessing actions with little importance to the actors in that social group. For example, you may not care what TV show is selected and therefore agreeing to someone else's choice is hardly a test of power. It is when the issue is important to each person, and there is conflict in goals, that power can best be measured. Only the individuals themselves can inform the observer about such importance and conflict. This is not said to minimize the value of objective observation of

Photo by Ivan Kalman.

marital interaction but rather to stress the importance of self-report type of studies (Cromwell and Olson, 1975: Chap. 8). Distortion can also occur in a self-report study of power. The following illustrates this point. The normative structure in our society has stressed that wives should not be dominant, and such normative expectations do affect people's self-report (Turk and Bell, 1972). Despite increased acceptance of equalitarian relationships, traditional normative pressures make husbands more likely to overestimate their power and wives more likely to underestimate theirs (Cromwell and Olson, 1975). So there are clear limits to self-report studies. However, observational studies of marital power usually involve taking married couples into a laboratory setting and giving them some topic to discuss or some game to play that will reveal who is the more powerful. There are also limits to this approach because the laboratory is not the home and the artificial task is not a real-life situation to the couple. Thus, one cannot fully rely on the results of either self-report or observational studies. It should be obvious now as to why most sociologists seem to favor using both self-report *and* observational measures to judge the nature of marital power.

Raven, Centers, and Rodrigues (1975) have put forth and tested a conception concerning the bases of marital power. According to French and Raven's (1959) theory, there are six bases of power:

1. *Coercive Power:* based on the belief that the other person will punish one for noncompliance.
2. *Reward Power:* based on the expectation that the other person will do something in return—reward one for compliance.
3. *Expert Power:* based on the belief that the other person has superior knowledge and can help one achieve one's desires.
4. *Legitimate Power:* based on the acceptance of a particular role structure giving the other person the right to request compliance and giving one the duty to comply.
5. *Referent Power:* based on identification with the other person and therefore obtaining satisfaction by behaving in a similar way to the other person.
6. *Informational Power:* based on the other person's careful and successful explanation of the need to do something.

In the mid-1960s a sample was drawn from Los Angeles to test the validity of these bases of power for marital interaction. One additional purpose was to test some older ideas concerning marital power derived from a study of Detroit wives by Blood and Wolfe (1960). A multiclass sample was drawn in Los Angeles and 776 respondents interviewed (55% were wives and 45% husbands). Raven and his colleagues checked to see how common were the different bases of power. They found it difficult to measure informational power but they did test the other five bases. The results of their check is reported in Table 9.5. Note that wives attribute expertness as the basis of husband power much more than do husbands. Also, husbands attribute referent power more to their wives (that is, power based on feeling that one should see eye to eye with the other person because of identification with the other person).

There were differences by social class. The higher social classes were less likely to attribute reward or coercion as the basis of the other person's power. But more

TABLE 9.5

Percentages of Husbands and Wives Attributing Each Basis of Power to Respective Spouses

Sex of Respondent	PREDOMINANT BASIS OF POWER ATTRIBUTED TO SPOUSE				
	Reward	*Coercion*	*Expert*	*Legitimate*	*Referent*
Male (331)[a]	6	3	21	22	48
Female (342)	4	4	37	18	36
Total[b] (746)	4	3	26	19	48

[a]*Ns. In comparing percentages for males and females a difference greater than 7.5% is significant at the .05 level. (See Appendix 2 for meaning of significance levels.)*
[b]*Discrepancy in N due to failure of some interviewers to indicate gender of respondent.*
Source: Raven, et al., 1975:223

important were differences found by areas of specific activities. These results are seen in Table 9.6 and are very important for they show that the answer to the question of power will vary by the domain that is asked about. This was one criticism of the Blood and Wolfe (1960) research. Blood and Wolfe used questions on eight decision areas to measure power. Raven et al. demonstrated that if different areas were asked about, the distribution of power would change.

The explanation of how the five bases of power differ can be seen in that expert power is the key basis of the decision to see a doctor whereas legitimate power is the basis of visiting a friend or relative. There is a face validity to such findings. Further, since husbands and wives differ in the type of power they wield (see Table 9.5), it is important to define power by specific situations because each type of situation tends to activate a different power base. Scores could be added up on a variety of situations to arrive at an overall score, but this would involve obscuring a number of differences in power within specific areas.

The reasons why a mate has power were found to vary by how satisfied one was with the marriage. Table 9.7 shows the relationship. This table points out that those who are not at all satisfied with their marriages attribute a high percentage of their spouse's power to coercion. The very satisfied married couples attribute their mate's power most to referent power and least to reward or coercion power.

The five bases or causes of power were meaningful to the Los Angeles husbands and wives who were interviewed by Raven and his colleagues. They understood the different power types and had no difficulty answering the questions. Do these types cover all bases of power? How do husbands and wives differ on the use of

TABLE 9.6
Percentage Attributing Each Basis of Power to Spouse as a Function of Domain of Power

| Domain of Power | N | PREDOMINANT BASIS OF POWER ATTRIBUTED TO SPOUSE | | | | |
		Reward	Coercion	Expert (in percent)	Legitimate	Referent
"Visit some friend or relative"	768	7	8	15	43	27
"Change some personal habit"	758	6	9	35	30	20
"Repair or clean something around house"	766	5	13	28	35	19
"Change station on TV or radio"	766	14	13	8	30	35
"Go somewhere for outing or vacation"	760	10	3	10	37	40
"Go see a doctor"	768	1	2	55	22	20

Note: In comparing percentages between domains, any difference in percentage greater than 5% is significant at the .05 level of confidence.
Source: Raven, et al. 1975: 226.

TABLE 9.7

Percentage Attributing Each Basis of Power to Spouse as Related to Satisfaction in Marriage

Degree of Satisfaction with Marriage	n	PREDOMINANT BASIS OF POWER ATTRIBUTED TO SPOUSE				
		Reward	Coercion	Expert (in percent)	Legitimate	Referent
Very satisfied	537	3	2	27	20	49
Fairly satisfied	172	8	3	27	19	42
Not at all satisfied	19	0	42	26	10	21
No response	28	0	4	22	14	60

Source: Raven, et al., 1975: 229

these forms of power? Other researchers, like Johnson (1974), have shown that men were more prone to use expert, legitimate, and informational power. Women were more prone to use referent power, informational power, and helplessness. Helplessness was not included in the original list of six unless one views this as an appeal for identification and, therefore, a type of referent power. It clearly is a tactic utilized by someone in an underdog status. As gender roles change, one would expect that the types of power bases employed by husbands and wives will converge more than before (Nye, 1974).

MALE POWER AND SOCIAL CLASS

Let us turn now to an important issue concerning marital power and then try to see how we can integrate it with Raven's approach to power. There is a widespread belief that the lower-class husband is more dominant in his marriage than the upper-class husband. As is often the case, there is an alternate public belief that the lower-class husband is dominated by his wife because of his poor economic abilities and that the upper-class husband is the most dominant type of male. One would think that with two such beliefs present, no matter which was true, the man in the street could argue for the insight shown by common sense. But the findings from Blood and Wolfe (1960) and others (Komarovsky, 1964; Rodman, 1967 and 1972) indicate that both positions are somewhat in error.

If we look at American lower blue-collar workers (unskilled and semiskilled), we find that husband dominance seems to be higher in this category than among upper blue-collar skilled workers (Blood and Wolfe, 1960; Komarovsky, 1964). However, from there on, ascending in social class leads to an increase in husband power; that is, lower white-collar workers have more husband dominance than both types of blue-collar workers; upper white-collar workers in turn have more husband dominance than lower white-collar workers (Ericksen et al., 1979). Research from France (Michel, 1967) indicates a relatively similar association, with a general tendency for the upper occupational, educational, and income groups to display more husband dominance. However, similar studies in Yugoslavia (Buric and

Zecevic, 1967) and Greece (Safilios-Rothschild, 1967) have found almost completely opposite results. They found that the upper classes have the least husband dominance in marriage. (These studies were instigated by Reuben Hill, former director of the University of Minnesota Family Study Center.) How can we make sense of such contradictory findings? One important service that a sociologist can perform is to take a set of diverse research findings and make sense of them in terms of some general theory. Such an explanation may well be in error, but at least it starts us in the direction of making sense out of our findings. Hyman Rodman has suggested a way to make sense of the seemingly contradictory findings on how social class and husband dominance relate to each other (Rodman, 1967 and 1972).

Rodman thinks that the reason that the United States and France show the *most* male dominance in the higher social classes and Yugoslavia and Greece show the *least* male dominance in the higher social classes is closely related to the cultural traditions in each country regarding male–female equality. Rodman believes that France and the United States have a stronger tradition of male–female equality, whereas Greece and Yugoslavia have a stronger tradition of male dominance, that is, a patriarchal tradition. In patriarchal societies it is the upper classes that are most likely to be changing toward the newer equalitarian customs. Thus, in such a society it would be the upper classes who would most likely have weakened the patriarchal tradition and be more likely to give wives increased power. In relatively more equalitarian societies, as the United States and France, equalitarian emphasis has increased to the point where male dominance is not strongly guaranteed by custom alone at most class levels. Men are more in need of some "resources" of their own in order to support their cultural dominance. Upper-class men are most likely to have resources in the way of educational background, professional prestige, income, and such; thus they dominate the most. The case of the lower blue-collar males having more power than the upper blue-collar males fits very well with this type of explanation. The lower blue-collar males embody the last remnant of a strong patriarchal tradition—a tradition that the upper blue-collar males have not held onto quite so tenaciously. Thus, the lower blue-collar males' power comes from this tradition of patriarchy, whereas the upper blue-collar male, being more equalitarian in tradition, must earn his male dominance by his income, educational, and other resources. The result is that the lower blue-collar male is more dominant in marriage.

What Rodman has shown us is the importance of first knowing the general cultural background of a group before you predict which social class is more likely to be male dominant. We can see this within our own society in the above comparison of lower and upper blue-collar workers. We can see it also in black–white comparisons which show that at the same social-class level, white males are more dominant over their wives than are black males (Blood and Wolfe, 1960).

This discussion can be put in terms of the theoretical approach of Raven et al. (1975) which we discussed earlier. The point Rodman is making regarding the importance of the patriarchal tradition is what Raven et al. would call "legitimate power." When Rodman talks of resources which one mate can use to obtain power over the other, we are reminded of "expert power" and "reward power." The insights afforded by Rodman are important and they point up the limits of the simple "resources" approach used by Blood and Wolfe and many other earlier writers. These other approaches stress resources as the key element and take what is called an "exchange theory" approach (Emerson, 1976); that is, they stress that people act on the basis of how to maximize rewards and minimize costs. The balance of rewards and costs is the profit or value of the action. However, it is difficult to discern how "legitimate power" would fit the resource or exchange model. Raven's approach to power focuses on six different types of causes and thereby affords us a broad base within which to strive to integrate the important explanations of sociologists like Rodman. With Raven's approach, there is the virtue of not entering into the debate over whether exchange or other orientations have the "best" approach. One is thereby free to choose explanations that seem valid regardless of which approach they fit.

Communication and Marital Relationships

Communication patterns are vitally affected by the power dimensions of husband and wife roles and by changes in those dimensions. It is no accident that the divorce rate rose dramatically in the 1915–1925 decade and doubled in the decade from 1965–1975. This rise was in part a sign of radical changes that were occurring in gender roles. Such changes add areas of potential dispute and tend to change the balance of power in various social settings between males and females.

Social change is visible in many institutional settings. One can see it in the economic, political, religious, educational, and family institutions. One example would be the change toward increased female employment and, more importantly, the trend toward demands for greater equality in pay and greater opportunity for female promotion in industry (Kanter, 1977). Those changes became visible in the 1960s and 1970s and are one major cause of other rapid changes occurring in our society. In another sense those occupational changes are also an effect of changes in our political system which helped promote greater movement toward equality for blacks and females. The Supreme Court decisions on civil rights, segregation, and abortion were one element of that political change. The relevant result of such changes, for our interests, is visible in the impact on gender roles. If opportunities for females in occupations are increasing and more women are working and moving ahead, then there is likely to develop, however slowly, a change in the gender role of females to include these occupational endeavors as part of the feminine role. Such a change means that the emphasis on wife–mother roles will be decreased and that means that the traditional role of the female will change. If the male gender role changed exactly in accord with the female role and if male expectations of females in wife–mother roles therefore changed, there would be no conflict. But that does not typically occur. Instead, what occurs are conflicts of expectations in marital roles. Husbands feel that wives are not focused enough on the husband's career, but instead are increasingly thinking of their own career. Wives feel that husbands are insensitive to their needs and are demanding that the wife remain

Photo by Pam Reiss.

"trapped" in the restricted role of the traditional wife–mother. Thus, in periods of rapid role changes we should expect increases in marital tensions and in divorce rates. Role changes may threaten some males' sense of power, and conflict may result from the attempt to preserve and/or change the traditional male advantage. We shall discuss in Chapter 12 the implications of this for long-term divorce trends. At this point our interest focuses on communication conflict in marriage, and the above affords the reader one major social cause of such communication conflict.

There has been a series of studies on marital communication and conflict that may well be worth touching upon here. This type of research affords us deeper insight into the specific interactional processes that help explain the results of national studies of marital satisfaction rates or reports of divorce rates. One major center for studies of marital communication was at the University of Oregon. Much has been done there by Robert L. Weiss in collaboration with colleagues and former students. Birchler and Vincent both did their dissertation under Weiss on an analysis of maritally distressed and maritally nondistressed couples (1975). Patterson's work is also of first importance and will be touched upon here also. These professionals are ultimately interested in intervention and therapy, but their work is also central for a scientific understanding of marital interaction, and thus I include it here. Their orientation is one emphasizing social learning. This approach stresses the "exchange" perspective and the "reinforcement" perspective as important elements in behavior modification (Homans, 1961; Skinner, 1953). In brief, the stress is on the married pair utilizing a balance of costs and rewards in their relationship. They assume that when action leads to a favorable balance of rewards, that particular action will be more likely to occur again; that is, it will be reinforced. The cost–reward balance aspect (exchange theory) should be familiar to the reader since it was just discussed in relation to marital power.

The study by Birchler, Weiss, and Vincent consisted of twenty-four couples who responded to a newspaper advertisement asking for couples experiencing marital stress or couples who were happily married. The subjects were paid a small fee and were offered treatment after the study. In support of the validity of difference between these two groups of twelve couples, it was found that each of the twelve couples who reported themselves as experiencing stress utilized the offer of treatment, and none of the couples who reported themselves as happily married did so. The laboratory setting involved having each couple interact as a marital dyad and then as a stranger dyad with an opposite-sex distressed partner and a second stranger dyad with an opposite-sex happily married person (nondistressed). In addition, the twenty-four couples were asked to keep daily records of all the pleasing and displeasing behaviors engaged in by one's spouse for a period of fourteen days. The laboratory interaction consisted of four minutes of "just talking about anything" and ten minutes of resolving differences of opinions in typical marital conflicts. In the marital-conflict situation each partner was given contradictory information so that they would disagree on the issue presented (Olson and Ryder, 1970).

One important hypothesis concerned the expectation that distressed couples would give each other fewer positive reinforcement responses and more negative reinforcement responses. That result was precisely what was found in their tests of marital interaction. A second finding of some interest is that when the marital pair were interacting, there was considerably more negative reinforcement and less positive reinforcement than when the same individuals were interacting with strangers. This result held for distressed and nondistressed couples. In other words, it seems that married couples in general treat each other in more negative and less positive ways than they do strangers. This fits with Robert Leik's findings discussed earlier in this chapter, which noted differences in the way people act in their own families and outside. The authors posit a long-term trend within intimate dyadic relationships which is toward a decrease in positive reinforcements and an increase in negative reinforcements. They have no longitudinal data to support this view. Long-term trends in marriage will be examined in Chapter 10.

In regard to the spouse's record keeping of the ratio of "pleases" to "displeases," there were also some theoretically valuable results. Controlling for the amount of time spent together, the nondistressed couples had a ratio of almost 30 to 1 (pleases to displeases), and the distressed couples had a ratio of just a little more than 4 to 1. This is a most impressive difference in interactive patterns. Note that both sets of couples displayed more pleases than displeases. Perhaps there is a minimum ratio that is necessary for marital interaction to continue at all. Further analysis revealed that the distressed couples relied more heavily on coercion and aversive control than did the nondistressed couples. The distressed couples tried to force the outcomes they wanted and used negative means of controlling their spouses' behavior. This finding fits with the results reported above in Raven et al.'s (1975) study of marital power (see Table 9.7). The laboratory experiment covered all of the above points and led to the same conclusions regarding differences between these two types of couples. This is a rather important aspect of the study because it showed similarity in results in self-report and experimental means of investigation. A common criticism of experimental research had been that it did not reflect what happened in the real world. One could act one way in the laboratory and a different way at home. Here is evidence that there is a high correlation between measures in the laboratory and measures taken at home, at least in this area of research.

Further checks showed the distressed couples spent less time with each other and more time with other people, as compared to the nondistressed couples. Such avoidance tactics may be a means of escaping unpleasant contact and a way of handling by compensation the strains of the marital relationship. However, the distressed couples seemed to be on a track toward increased marital conflict despite such attempts to adjust.

Another study that Robert L. Weiss and some of his colleagues undertook (Wills et al., 1974) reported other relevant data. They found in a small sample that most of the marital-satisfaction scores could be accounted for by the "displeasurable" behavior that was occurring in the marriage. Perhaps of even greater interest was the finding by Weiss that displeasurable behaviors were more likely to be recip- rocated than were pleasurable behaviors. If this finding can be substantiated, it gives an important insight into the progressive deterioration processes of marriage and other close intimate dyads. Displeasurable behaviors carried strong weight in the overall judgments that mates made concerning the quality of their marital interaction. It is worth reporting that Bradburn's (1969) findings, to be discussed in the next chapter, also showed that displeasurable behaviors carried the most weight in predicting marital unhappiness. The need to view happiness as composed of two separate dimensions (rewards–tensions) is apparent.

On pleasurable behavior, a gender difference appeared that throws light on the place of gender roles in marital interaction. Males tended to give more importance to instrumental or task behaviors (like a wife who helped balance the checkbook), and females gave most importance to affectional, pleasurable behaviors (like show- ing sympathy and support for one's mate). Clearly gender-role preparation in our culture supports such emphasis on two different types of valued outcomes. Of equal significance is the conclusion that each gender is handicapped by this gender training in that each knows the least how to give the other gender what is valued the most. For example, males are not trained in giving affectionate responses, and yet that is what females find most satisfying.

One other study in this area that is relevant to Weiss's work was done by Harold L. Rausch and his colleagues at the University of Massachusetts. Rausch and his colleagues also worked with a clinical emphasis on studying communication and conflict. They utilized a sample of forty-eight couples (again, white and middle class) and not married very long. They had them improvise and problem solve in terms of a problem description given to the wife and husband. The problem description was altered for each person so as to guarantee disagreement. They reported a striking stability in the couple's patterns of interaction that began very early in marriage and maintained itself thereafter. They report that avoidance was a common pattern of dealing with conflict, and interestingly, they found that "avoidance" couples would report equal amounts of marital satisfaction when compared to those couples who dealt more directly and openly with their conflicts. This indicates that, from a subjective view at least, there are many ways to satisfactorily handle marital conflict.

At the current time there is a series of research projects reaching fruition under the leadership of David Olson (1981) at the University of Minnesota. These projects involve the use of measuring instruments such as the Inventory of Marital Conflict (Olson and Ryder, 1970). This inventory presents a couple with a short story and then asks them to discuss the specifics of that story. (For the origin of this approach, see Strodtbeck, 1951.) Some of the accounts are altered so as to create conflict by giving different versions of the story to each mate. The interaction of the couple is then coded into a 20-category code which is collapsed into three major communication categories:

1. Task Leadership
2. Actual Conflict
3. Expression of Affect (mostly negative)

Then by cluster analysis the scores of both husband and wife are recorded and a matrix of possible combinations of these three major types of interactive communication is composed (Miller, 1975; Druckman, 1979; Norem, 1979). This is an empirical way to arrive at couple-types of interaction. The several research projects that have been conducted have found some differences in the types of combinations of the three major categories that actually occur (Olson, 1981). Further, the Inventory of Marital Conflict does not measure the positive effect and the rewards of interaction as well as other instruments do. Thus, clearly more work is needed, but this is a promising approach. There were nine types selected by cluster analysis in a test utilizing 396 couples. Only 26 percent were wife-led types, 12 percent shared leadership, while 58 percent were husband-led types. The 396 couples were from the Washington, D. C. area and had been married two to three years. The nine types were selected by cluster analysis from 27 possible types. With the help of such empirically based typologies, we can perhaps better qualify the outcomes of specific events, like the birth of a child, or the loss of a child, or the assumption of a career by both partners. Such events may well have quite different impacts on couples who communicate and interact in different ways. Some forms of interaction may aid or impede the handling of such common events.

VIOLENCE AND MARRIAGE

When the ability to obtain desired results by talking is lacking, violence at times occurs. Violence in the family is an ancient custom. The Roman husband was by law allowed to kill any members of his family. The early records of the settlers in America indicate no lack of violence between all possible combinations of family members. Infanticide in history is common—with mothers being the usual persons to carry out the act. There is widespread acceptance of "minor" forms of "violence" in the family, e.g., spanking of children. But much of the violence that happens is of a more severe sort. For example, in 1975 more than 3,000 husbands or wives killed their spouses. At about that same time, some 2,000 children were killed by their parents (Steinmetz, 1978). Studies of siblings indicate that about 5 percent were attacked by a sibling wielding either a gun or a knife. Steinmetz (1978) reports that the national estimate is that about 7 percent of wives and more than one half of one percent of husbands had received "severe beatings" from their mates at some time in their current marriage. Steinmetz feels that the proportion of husbands beaten up is much closer to that for wives but that husbands do not report such incidents as often. The homicide figures back up the greater equality notion in that husband–wife homicides (the single most likely type of homicide) account for more than 15 percent of all murders committed in a year and are evenly divided between husbands and wives as the victims (see FBI Uniform Crime Reports).

Clearly, if we were to take more moderate forms of violence we would find much higher proportions of married couples involved. Why is violence as common as it is in marriages of people who "married for love?" No precise answer can be given to this with our current state of knowledge. It has only been since the late 1960s that interest in marital and family violence has risen and led to research being undertaken. The November 1971 issue of the *Journal of Marriage and the Family* was one of the first devoted entirely to family violence. This then is a new area of investigation. We have some hints here and there and recently a scale has been developed and tested on a national sample to measure the use of reasoning, verbal aggression, and violence within a family (Straus, 1979). Also, there are some valuable attempts to begin the search for causes (Gelles and Straus, 1979). We do find that people who themselves were abused are more likely to physically abuse others. But not everyone fits this category. We also find that people of lower education and poorer communication skills are more likely to be recorded as husband or wife beaters. Nevertheless, many wealthy people are also involved in marital violence and perhaps more of them are able to escape being listed in the official statistics (Steinmetz, 1978). It also appears that marital violence is focused on younger women, particularly women under thirty-five years of age. Of course, there are instances at all ages. These younger women, in the great majority of cases, have children. The stress of parenthood, both in the form of economic and of parental pressure, is relevant to the occurrence of violence.

Our culture, more than many others, does tolerate violence. For example, in 1977 the Supreme Court upheld the teacher's right to use corporal punishment on students. Thus, some violence is legitimate and sanctioned by society. I would judge that we are in a period when we are starting to become more restrictive regarding the amount of violence we will tolerate in marriage and family relationships. We have not approached the Swedish level, where it is against the law for parents to strike their children. Nevertheless, the very fact that in the last decade this issue has become central to our concerns indicates that the amount of family violence has surpassed the tolerance limits of many Americans. We have seen, earlier in this chapter, that as a means of control, coercion occurs most often among those who are dissatisfied in their marriages. Perhaps our greater willingness to divorce and break a marriage has made us less tolerant of violence in marriage. Today more men, and especially more women, seem willing to report violence, and shelters are multiplying all over the country for such individuals. If we tolerate less strain and stress in an ongoing marriage today, then it follows that this itself would make marital violence more likely to be labeled a "social problem."

Summary and Conclusions

This chapter was intended to afford the student an overview of marital relationships. Since we are dealing with 50 million married couples, there obviously is need to have some basic explanations that help us make sense of the myriad of day to day patterns that occur among those couples. We did this first by the use of demographic data that allowed us to see the major patterns in trends regarding age at marriage, gender and race differences, and typical living and working arrangements. Then we examined the degree to which expressive and instrumental roles are applied respectively to females and males. This too should help in understanding the variety of patterns in role relationships in marriage.

I chose two crucial dimensions in marital relationships to focus upon in the balance of the chapter: (1) power and (2) communication. These are two of the most important areas to understand if one hopes to comprehend marital relationships in America. We have some baseline data from Raven and his colleagues (1975) on five reasons for marital power. It will be interesting to watch and discern if "legitimate power" of husbands is now declining due to moves toward greater gender equality. Communication is the means by which power is exercised as well as the means by which many of the felt needs and desires of individuals are made known and possibly satisfied. This power and communication perspective leads naturally into a concern with marital commitment. That is the subject of the next chapter.

References

Aldous, Joan, Thomas Condon, Reuben Hill, Murray Straus, and Irving Tallman (eds.). 1971. *Family Problem Solving*. Hinsdale, IL: Dryden Press.

Aronoff, Joel, and William D. Crano. 1975. "A Re-Examination of the Cross-Cultural Principal of Task Segregation and Sex-Role Differentiation in the Family," *American Sociological Review* 40 (February): 12–20.

Bales, Robert F., and Philip E. Slater. 1955. "Role Differentiation in Small Decision-Making Groups," in Talcott Parsons (ed.), *The Family: Socialization and Interaction Process*. New York: Free Press, pp. 259–306.

Bane, Mary Jo. 1976. *Here to Stay: American Families in the Twentieth Century*. New York: Basic Books.

Barry, H., and L. M. Paxson. 1971. "Infancy and Early Childhood:Cross-Cultural Codes," *Ethnology* 10:466–508.

Birchler, Gary R., Robert L. Weiss, and John P. Vincent. 1975. "Multidimensional Analyses of Social Reinforcement Exchange Between Maritally Distressed and Nondistressed Spouse and Stranger Dyads," *Journal of Personality and Social Psychology* 31 (February): 348–360.

Blood, Robert O., and Donald M. Wolfe. 1960. *Husbands and Wives: The Dynamics of Married Living*. New York: Macmillan.

Bott, Elizabeth. 1957. Family and Social Network. London: Tavistock.

Bradburn, Norman M. 1969. *The Structure of Psychological Well-Being*. Chicago: Aldine.

Burgess, Ernest, and Paul Wallin. 1953. *Engagement and Marriage*. Philadelphia: Lippincott.

Buric, Olivera, and Andjelka Zecevic. 1967. "Family Authority, Material Satisfaction and the Social Network in Yugoslavia," *Journal of Marriage and the Family* 29 (May):325–337.

Centers, Richard, Bertram H. Raven, and Aroldo Rodrigues. 1971. "Conjugal Power Structure: A Re-examination," *The American Sociological Review* 36 (April):264–278.

Crano, William D., and Joel Aronoff. 1978. "A Cross-Cultural Study of Expressive and Instrumental Role Complementarity in the Family," *American Sociological Review* 43 (August): 463–471.

Cromwell, Ronald E., and David H. Olson (eds.). 1975. *Power in Families*. New York: Halsted.

Druckman, Joan. 1979. "Premarital Relationships: Interaction Types and Processes," University of Minnesota Ph.D. dissertation. Unpublished.

Emerson, R. M. 1976. "Social Exchange Theory," in A. Inkeles, J. Coleman, and N. Smelser (eds.), *Annual Review of Sociology*. Palo Alto, CA: Annual Reviews, Inc., pp. 335–362.

Ericksen, Julia A., William L. Yancey, and Eugene P. Ericksen. 1979. "The Division of Family Roles," *Journal of Marriage and the Family* 41 (May): 301–313.

French, J. R. P., and B. H. Raven. 1959. "The Bases of Social Power" in D. Cartwright (ed), *Studies in Social Power*. Ann Arbor: University of Michigan Press.

Gelles, Richard J., and Murray A. Straus. 1979. "Determinants of Violence in the Family: Towards a Theoretical Integration," in W. Burr, R. Hill, I. Nye, and I. Reiss (eds.), *Contemporary Theories About the Family*. Vol. I New York: Free Press.

Glick, Paul C. 1977. "Updating the Life Cycle of the Family," *Journal of Marriage and the Family* 39 (February):5–13.

———, and Arthur J. Norton. 1977. "Marrying, Divorcing and Living Together in the U. S. Today," *Population Bulletin* 32 (October):1–41.

Heer, David M. 1958. "Dominance and the Working Wife," *Social Forces* 36 (May):341–347.

———. 1963. "The Measurement and Basis of Family Power: An Overview," *Journal of Marriage and the Family* 25 (May):133–139.

Herbst, P. G. 1952. "The Measurement of Family Relationships," *Human Relations* 5:3–35.

Homans, George. 1961. *Social Behavior: Its Elementary Forms*. New York: Harcourt, Brace & World.

Jacobsen, Paul. 1959. *American Marriage and Divorce*. New York: Holt, Rinehart and Winston.

Johnson, P. B. 1974. "Social Power and Sex-Role Stereotyping," Ph.D. Dissertation. University of California, Los Angeles.

Kanter, Rosabeth M. 1977. *Men and Women of the Corporation*. New York: Basic Books.

Kinsey, Alfred C. et al., 1953. *Sexual Behavior in the Human Female*. Philadelphia: Saunders.

Kobrin, Frances E. 1976. "The Primary Individual and the Family: Changes in Living Arrangements in the U. S. Since 1940," *Journal of Marriage and the Family* 39 (May):233–239.

———, and Gerry E. Hendershot. 1977. "Do Family Ties Reduce Mortality? Evidence from the United States, 1966–68," *Journal of Marriage and the Family* 39 (November):737–745.

Kolb, Trudy M., and Murray A. Straus. 1974. "Marital Power and Marital Happiness in Relation to Problem-Solving Ability," *Journal of Marriage and the Family* 36 (November):756–766.

Komarovsky, Mirra. 1964. *Blue-Collar Marriage*. New York: Random House.

Leik, Robert K. 1963. "Instrumentality and Emotionality in Family Interaction," *Sociometry* 26 (June):131–145.

Levinger, George. 1964. "Task and Social Behavior in Marriage," *Sociometry* 27 (December):433–448.

Marini, Margaret M. 1978. "The Transition to Adulthood: Sex Differences in Educational Attainment and Age at Marriage," *American Sociological Review* 43 (August): 483–507.

Michel, Andrée, 1967. "Comparative Data Concerning the Interaction in French and American Families," *Journal of Marriage and the Family* 29 (May): 337–345.

Miller, Brent C. 1975. "Types of Marriage Interaction and Their Relation to Contextual Characteristics in a Sample of Young Married Couples," University of Minnesota Ph.D. dissertation. Unpublished.

Murdock, George P. 1967. "Ethnographic Atlas: A Summary," *Ethnology* 6 (April): 109–236.

Norem, Rosalie. 1979. "A Longitudinal Study of Premarital Couple Interaction," University of Minnesota Ph.D. dissertation. Unpublished.

Nye, F. Ivan. 1974. Emerging and Declining Family Roles," *Journal of Marriage and the Family* 36 (May):238–245.

Olson, D. H., and R. G. Ryder. 1970. "Inventory of Marital Conflicts (IMC): An Experimental Interaction Procedure," *Journal of Marriage and the Family* 32 (August): 443–448.

Olson, David. Forthcoming, 1981. *Typologies of Marriage and Family Systems.*

Parsons, Talcott, and Robert F. Bales (eds.). 1955. *Family, Socialization and Interaction Process.* New York: Free Press.

Payne, Donald E., and Paul H. Mussen. 1956. "Parent–Child Relations and Father Identification Among Adolescent Boys," *Journal of Abnormal and Social Psychology* 52 (May):358–362.

Rainwater, Lee. 1966. "Some Aspects of Lower-Class Sexual Behavior," *Journal of Social Issues* 22 (April):96–109.

Rausch, Harold L., William A. Barry, Richard K. Hertel, and Mary Ann Swain. 1974. *Communication, Conflict and Marriage.* San Francisco: Jossey Bass.

———, Ann C. Grief, and Jane Nugent. 1979. "Communication in Couples and Families," Chap. 19 in W. Burr, R. Hill, I. Nye, and I. Reiss (eds.), *Contemporary Theories About the Family.* Vol. I New York: Free Press.

Raven, Bertram H., Richard Centers, and Aroldo Rodrigues. 1975. "The Bases of Conjugal Power," in Ronald E. Cromwell and David Olson (eds.), *Power in Families.* New York: Halsted.

Reiss, Ira L. 1979. "Sexual Customs and Gender Roles in Sweden and America: An Analysis and Interpretation," in Helena Lopata (ed.), *The Interweave of Social Roles: Women and Men.* Greenwich, CT: JAI Press.

Rodman, Hyman. 1967. "Marital Power in France, Greece, Yugoslavia, and the United States: A Cross-National Discussion," *Journal of Marriage and the Family* 29 (May):320–325.

———. 1972. "Marital Power and the Theory of Resources in Cultural Context," *Journal of Comparative Family Studies* 3 (Spring):50–69.

Rollins, Boyd, and Stephen Bahn. 1976. "A Theory of Power Relationships in Marriage," *Journal of Marriage and the Family* 38 (November): 619–627.

Safilios-Rothschild, Constantina. 1967. "A Comparison of Power Structure and Marital Satisfaction in Urban Greek and French Families," *Journal of Marriage and the Family* 29 (May):345–353.

———. 1970. "The Study of Family Power Structure: A Review 1960–1969," *Journal of Marriage and the Family* 32 (November):539–552.

Scanzoni, John. 1979. "Social Processes and Power in Families," Chap. 13 in W. Burr, R. Hill, I. Nye, and I. Reiss (eds.), *Contemporary Theories About the Family.* Vol. I New York: Free Press.

Skinner, B. F. 1959. *Science and Human Behavior.* New York: Macmillan.

Slater, Philip. 1961. "Parental Role Differentiation," *American Journal of Sociology* 67 (November):296–311.

Sprenkle, Douglas H., and David H. Olson. 1978. "Circumplex Model of Marital Systems: An Empirical Study of Clinic and Non-Clinic Couples," *Journal of Marriage and Family Counseling* (April):59–74.

Statistical Bulletin: Metropolitan Life Insurance Co., Vol. 59, No. 4. October–December 1978.

Steinmetz, Suzanne K. 1978. "Violence Between Family Members," *Marriage and Family Review* 1, No. 3 (May):1–16.

Straus, Murray A. 1979. "Measuring Intrafamily Conflict and Violence: The Conflict Tactics (CT) Scales," *Journal of Marriage and the Family* 41 (February):75–88.

Strodtbeck, Fred L. 1951. "Husband–Wife Interaction over Revealed Differences," *American Sociological Review* 16 (December):468–473.

Suggs, Robert C. 1966. *Marquesan Sexual Behavior: An Anthropological Study of Polynesian Practices.* New York: Harcourt, Brace & World.

Taylor, Patricia A., and N. D. Glenn. 1976. "The Utility of Education and Attraction for Females' Status Attainment Through Marriage," *American Sociological Review* 41 (June):484–498.

Turk, James L., and Norman W. Bell. 1972. "Measuring Power in Families," *Journal of Marriage and the Family* 34 (May):215–222.

U. S. Bureau of the Census. 1977. "Marital Status and Living Arrangements: March, 1976." Current Population Reports. Series P-20, No. 306 (January). Washington, DC: Government Printing Office.

———. 1978. "Households and Families by Type:

March 1978 (Advance Report)," Current Population Reports. Series P-20, No. 327 (August). Washington, DC: Government Printing Office.

———. 1978. "Perspectives on American Husbands and Wives," Current Population Reports. Series P-23, No. 77 (December). Washington, DC: Government Printing Office.

———. 1978. *Statistical Abstracts of the United States: 1978*. Washington, DC: Government Printing Office.

——— 1979. "Marital Status and Living Arrangements: March 1978." Current Population Reports. Series P-20, No. 338 (May). Washington, DC: Government Printing Office.

U. S. Department of Health, Education, and Welfare. 1971. "Marriage: Trends and Characteristics, United States," Series 21, No. 21 (September). Washington D.C.: Government Printing Office.

———. 1979. *Monthly Vital Statistics Report* 28, No. 2 (May 15, 1979). Washington, D.C.: Government Printing Office.

Wills, Thomas A., Robert L. Weiss, and Gerald R. Patterson. 1974. "A Behavioral Analysis of the Determinants of Marital Satisfaction," *Journal of Consulting and Clinical Psychology* 42 (December):802–811.

Wolfe, D. M. 1959. "Power and Authority in the Family," in D. Cartwright (ed.), *Studies in Social Power*. Ann Arbor: University of Michigan, Institute for Social Research, pp. 99–117.

Zelditch, Morris Jr. 1955. "Role Differentiation in the Nuclear Family: A Comparative Study," in Talcott Parsons and Robert F. Bales (eds.), *The Family: Socialization and Interaction Process*. New York: Free Press, pp. 307–352.

Dyadic Commitment in Marriage

TEN

Introduction

A crucial question often asked regarding marital relationships is: What are the factors that affect the degree of commitment to the relationship by husbands and wives? For two years, from the fall of 1969 to the fall of 1971, a total of nine faculty members and graduate students at the University of Minnesota held an informal seminar on the overall topic of dyadic commitment. The seminar met about twenty-five times for several hours each time, and we all gained a great deal of understanding of dyadic commitment. Four faculty and five graduate sociology students were in the group (Professors Reiss, Tallman, Levy, and Bohrnstedt and graduate students Klein, Lee, Troost, H. Raschke, and Cogdill). Much of what follows builds upon that seminar experience.

Basically, our seminar group started out with a desire to understand the processes involved in marriage that led to some unions ending up in divorce and others seemingly remaining rewarding and stable. We wanted more than simply a divorce study, for we were well aware that many unhappy couples do not divorce and that some couples who appear adjusted do divorce. In short, it seemed that commitment to marriage was not based just on factors that promote happiness but on a broader set of variables. We called this "marital dyadic commitment." The term "dyadic" simply emphasizes the two-person nature of the group, and the term "commitment" here refers to the "determination to continue" something, in this case, a marital relationship.

There is a pair quality to dyadic commitment (Otto and Featherman, 1972). Both individuals may be equally committed, or one may be more committed than the other. Also, the commitment is to a relationship and not to an object or a cause, and in that sense there is a pair or interactive quality to dyadic commitment.

This pair quality may alter in either direction after marriage, and our basic concern here is to delineate the key causal factors that might produce this alteration.

There are three factors that we felt were the key variables in affecting dyadic commitment in a marriage: (1) interaction reward-tension balance, (2) normative inputs, and (3) structural constraints. Let us now go over these in order.

Interaction Reward–Tension Balance

This is the most obvious of the forces that might affect one's determination to stay in a particular dyadic relationship. However, the way to operationalize this broad variable is not so apparent. Previous researchers in this area often assumed that a negative relationship existed between marital tensions and marital rewards. That is, if one was high on tensions, then one was assumed to be low on rewards and vice versa. Norman Bradburn (1969) questioned this assumed relationship and in his study measured both tensions and rewards and checked the correlation between these two areas. He found very little relationship. Bradburn's study involved five separate well-chosen samples with good response rates (about 80 percent). One of the interesting things he measured was self-reported happiness. This is of value because his results show that both married males and females (compared to singles), in the total sample of over 2,700 respondents, reported significantly higher degrees of happiness. Those who had been married but were not married at the time of the interview (they were separated, divorced, or widowed) were clearly the most unhappy within both male and female groups. Male–female differences were slight but in the direction of other studies which showed single and divorced men less happy than their female counterparts. Similar results were found in a more recent national study by Campbell and his colleagues (1976, Chap. 10). (See also Glenn, 1975, for some interesting questions about male–female comparisons.) Table 10.1 shows the specific findings from Bradburn.

Bradburn found further that lower social-class groups reported somewhat less marital happiness than the higher social-class groups. One most impressive finding was that there was a strong relationship between personal happiness and marital happiness. It was so strong that virtually no one who was "not too happy" in their marriage reported being personally happy (Bradburn, 1969:158).

The next question concerned how measures of the tensions and rewards in marriage would correlate with the general happiness ratings given to these marriages. These findings are presented in Table 10.2. This table shows that marital happiness relates as one would expect, that is, in a positive direction to companionship and sociability and in a negative direction to tensions. Companionship and sociability are the two measures of the rewards of the marital relationship, and it can be seen that they correlate very little with marital tensions. Thus, marital rewards and marital tensions are seen as largely independent qualities of a marital relationship. One can be high on one of these, and there is no way to predict that person's position on the other one from knowing this. Bradburn found that marital companionship and sociability correlate with overall positive-affect qualities of the

TABLE 10.1

Marital Status and Avowed Happiness, by Gender

(in percent)

MARITAL STATUS	"VERY HAPPY"	"PRETTY HAPPY"	"NOT TOO HAPPY"	TOTAL PERCENT	N
				Men	
Married	35	56	9	100	(1,009)
Never married	18	63	19	100	(150)
Separated	7	55	38	100	(42)
Divorced	12	53	35	100	(34)
Widowed	7	56	37	100	(27)
				Women	
Married	38	55	7	100	(1,171)
Never married	18	68	14	100	(79)
Separated	12	45	44	101*	(98)
Divorced	11	66	23	100	(64)
Widowed	14	54	32	100	(90)
				N	(2,764)
				NA	(23)
				Total N	(2,787)

Not 100 percent because of rounding.
Source: Norman M. Bradburn (1969): 149.

TABLE 10.2

Coefficients of Association among Measures of Marriage Adjustment, (gammas)*

MEASURE	COMPANION- SHIP	SOCIABILITY	TENSIONS	HAPPINESS
Companionship		0.34	−0.08	0.44
Sociability	0.37		−0.01	0.20
Tensions	−0.15	0.02		−0.36
Happiness	0.40	0.26	−0.41	

Gammas for men (N = 781) are above the diagonal; gammas for women (N = 957) are below the diagonal.
Source: Norman M. Bradburn (1969): 163.

marriage and tensions correlate with the overall negative-affect qualities of the marriage. Thus, the quality of a marriage is the balance between the rewards and tensions, and these must be separately estimated for they do not correlate with each other. The precise questions used to measure these two dimensions are found in Table 10.3.

Bradburn further found that marital happiness affected personal happiness for both sexes, but more for females than for males. He followed couples over time and found that changes in overall marital happiness seemed to result more from changes in marital tensions than from changes in marital companionship and sociability. This was true for both males and females. This fits with the research reported in Chapter 9 which showed that "displeasing" was more likely to be reciprocated than "pleasing." Thus, the tension dimension seemed to have more centrality for measuring changes in marital and personal happiness. However, it should be clear that both rewards and tensions affect marital happiness. For example, Bradburn found that the higher social classes were more likely to have higher scores on companionship and sociability, the reward measures of his study. Higher social classes evidently have life-styles that encourage companionship and sociability experiences. This is due partly to having more money to engage in a greater variety of companionship and sociability experiences. However, the negative association of social class and tensions was weaker. This indicated that although status can increase the rewards, it is more difficult for status to decrease the tensions involved in a marital relationship. Nevertheless, the presence of high status does enhance a relationship, and this shows up in a lower divorce rate for the higher social classes. Table 10.4 presents the overall association of marital happiness with social class and affords the reader a general overview. The table is divided by males and females and also by the first interview wave and the third interview wave to show the stability of this association over the several months separating interviews one and three. This adds to our confidence in the stability of this finding.

The Bradburn study should afford us some feeling for the elements that enter into basic rewards and tensions in a marriage. Actually, this approach is but a beginning. One would have to study the effect of one mate's reward–tension balance on the other mate's reward–tension balance. One could not simply average the husband and wife scores and get a marital score—the interaction of the two would have to be considered. Otto and Featherman (1972) made this point a few years ago and carried out research to show that it was the husband's success at his job that most affected the degree of satisfaction he felt with his marriage, and it was the husband's marital satisfaction that most affected the wife's marital satisfaction. The interrelation of husband and wife satisfaction (as well as job satisfaction) was clearly brought out in Otto and Featherman's work (1972). This necessity to consider the couple and not two separate individuals has been brought out earlier in Chapter 9 in our discussion of the new couple interaction typologies that are being developed (Olson, 1981).

TABLE 10.3
Questions Used To Measure Marital Tensions and Rewards

MARITAL TENSIONS

I am going to read you some things about which husbands and wives sometimes agree and sometimes disagree. Would you tell me which ones caused differences of opinion or were problems in your marriage *during the past few weeks?*

First, how about—	Yes	No
A. Time spent with friends?	—	—
How about—		
B. Household expenses?	—	—
C. Being tired?	—	—
D. Being away from home too much?	—	—
E. Disciplining children?	—	—
F. In-laws?	—	—
G. Not showing love?	—	—
H. Your husband's job?	—	—
I. How to spend leisure time?	—	—
J. Religion?	—	—
K. Irritating personal habits?	—	—

MARITAL REWARDS

I'm going to read you some things that married couples often do together. Tell me which ones you and your (husband/wife) have done together *in the past few weeks.*

	Yes	No
A. Visited friends together.	—	—
B. Gone out together to a movie, bowling, sporting event, or some other entertainment.	—	—
C. Spent an evening just chatting with each other.	—	—
D. Worked on some household project together.	—	—
E. Entertained friends in your home.	—	—
F. Gone shopping together.	—	—
G. Had a good laugh together or shared a joke.	—	—

H. Ate out in a restaurant together.   —   —

I. Been affectionate toward each other.   —   —

J. Taken a drive or gone for a walk just for pleasure.   —   —

K. Did something that the other one particularly appreciated.   —   —

L. Helped the other solve some problem   —   —

Source: Norman M. Bradburn (1969): 275, 297.

OTHER REWARDS AND TENSIONS IN MARRIAGE

A word or two needs to be said here to be sure the reader is aware that Bradburn's measures of rewards and tensions are not all-inclusive. For example, in Chapter 5 we discussed the love relationship. It seems apparent that some measure of love would be important in order to ensure that the reward potential of love is included in the total reward–tension balance of a marriage. Some elements of love are caught in any questions on the quality of marital interaction, but it is felt that others need special measurement. For example, one of the key variables in a love relationship is self-revelation (see Chapter 5). It would be helpful to utilize a special set of questions that would get at the degree of self-revelation in a relationship. There are scales to measure self-revelation such as those devised by Sidney Jourard (1968). I developed a self-revelation scale for our seminar group and I include that on the following page. It would also be necessary to ask the respondents to indicate how important each area of self-disclosure is to themselves—that is, how highly do they value the opportunity to disclose in each area (see Table 10.5).

TABLE 10.4.

Marriage Happiness by Gender and Socioeconomic Status, for Waves I and III (Percent "Very Happy")

		SOCIOECONOMIC LEVEL		
Sex	*Wave*	*Low*	*Medium*	*High*
Men	I	59 (360)*	62 (330)	65 (307)
	III	58 (266)	61 (257)	65 (253)
Women	I	50 (430)	62 (464)	72 (288)
	III	47 (332)	66 (370)	66 (250)

*The numbers in parentheses are the base for the percentage.
Source: Norman M. Bradburn (1969): 156.

TABLE 10.5
Self-Disclosure Scale

Check the degree to which the following statements characterize your relationship with your mate (very much to very little, six choices):

 1. I tell my mate a great deal about the things that happen during the day while we are apart.
 2. If I am even slightly concerned about my health, I tell my mate about it.
 3. I discuss my urinating and defecating habits with my mate.
 4. I tell my mate fully what my parents or siblings are doing and thinking.
 5. I allow my mate to see me when I look the worst.
 6. I am not embarrassed to be seen nude by my mate.
 7. If I am planning something in connection with my job or the home, I will confide in my mate and talk it over with my mate.
 8. If my mate has some habit which irks me, I will tell my mate about it.
 9. If I am afriad of something that might happen, I will confide this fear to my mate.
10. If I do something that I feel bad about, I confide it to my mate.
11. I discuss my personal feelings about sex fully with my mate.
12. There is no topic of a personal nature about which I reveal more to any person than I do to my mate.
13. If I am attracted to a person of the opposite sex, I let my mate know it.
14. If I am depressed about something, I let my mate know it.
15. If I am angry about something, I let my mate know it.

Source: Composed by Ira L. Reiss in 1971. The respondent should be asked about the importance (high, medium, or low) of each of the 15 areas in this scale.

The reader will recall that in our discussion of love, we also stressed the importance of the compatibility of the role conception of the two people involved. Role compatibility would be a major source of need fulfillment, or the lack of it could be a source of marital tension. Measures of such compatibility are available (Tharp, 1963; Lewis, 1973), and this, too, would need to be developed in any study of overall reward–tension balance.

The above factors of role fit, self-revelation, and Bradburn's reward–tension scales make up a set of measures that should enable one to measure more completely the total nature of the reward–tension balance in the interaction in a particular marriage. One could then assign an overall positive score depending on the degree to which rewards exceeded tensions and a negative score if tensions outweighed rewards.

Normative Inputs

The second major factor that is believed to be causally involved with dyadic commitment is normative inputs. The clearest example of this factor would be a belief system that supported the idea of marriage being a union for life and of divorce and remarriage being unacceptable. Some religious groups hold to such beliefs. The position here is that if one believed in such norms, that would increase dyadic commitment in and of itself. Such normative support would exert pressure on dyadic commitment independently of the reward–tension balance. It would be one key foundation of the continuation of a marriage even if it was not interpersonally rewarding. This viewpoint has a good deal of face validity, but very little direct research on it has been done.

Another form of normative support would be measured in the degree to which significant others, like kin and friends, define the couple as possessing an ideal or normatively prescribed type of marital relationship. Ackerman's research (1963) on a cross-cultural sample showed that divorce rates were higher in those groups where there was little support for existing marriages by nearby friends and kin. This finding would be congruent with the view that such support of the marriage by friends and kin is a type of normative support and that it would contribute to dyadic commitment. (See also the more recent work by Lewis, 1973.) The above gives some idea of two types of normative support that could operate as a causal force on dyadic commitment; now let's turn to our third and last source of dyadic commitment.

Structural Constraints: Parenthood, Occupation, and Relationships

Structure refers to the patterned ways in which our social roles relate and pressure each other. For example, to study the way in which our role in the occupational sphere affects our role in the marital sphere is an investigation of structure. We are particularly interested here in such role relationships in terms of how they may restrict the ways in which one carries out the marital role. Thus, we shall focus on nonmarital roles that appear to have a direct impact on marital roles. The expectations and role performances tied to one role may well place limits on what one may do in another role, and it is to this which the concept of structural constraint sensitizes us.

PARENTAL DUTIES

Many people fail to separate parental roles from marital roles, but strictly speaking the two roles are conceptually distinct. The marital roles are focused upon the husband-and-wife interactions, whereas the parental roles are focused upon the parent-and-child interactions. Thus, strictly speaking the parental role is *outside* of the marital role, but it can well have an impact upon the way one carries out the rights and duties that go with a married status. There have been several important studies done which have investigated the extent to which taking on parenthood duties affects one's satisfaction with the marital roles of husband and wife (Dumon, 1978).

There are basically eight family-life stages: (1) beginning families; (2) child-bearing families; (3) families with preschool children; (4) families with school-age children; (5) families with teenage children; (6) families as launching centers; (7) families in the middle years; and (8) aging families (see Duvall, 1975). Blood and Wolfe's 1960 study of Detroit homemakers utilized a representative sample of 800 women and measured their marital satisfaction levels at their particular family-life-cycle stages. Their findings showed a general decline in marital satisfaction, particularly from Stage 1 through Stages 5 and 6.

A different study done by Rollins and Feldman (1970) focused upon middle-class families in Syracuse, New York. They used a sample of some 400 wives and also found that Stage 5 was the low point of marital satisfaction but that Stages 6, 7, and 8 showed an increase in marital satisfaction such that Stage 8 was about equal in marital satisfaction to Stage 1. In other words, Rollins and Feldman found a clear-cut curvilinear type of relationship of marital satisfaction and stage in the family life cycle. In order to clarify these findings, Rollins and Cannon (1974) designed a study of almost 500 Mormon families and used both the measures of marital satisfaction that Blood and Wolfe employed as well as the Rollins and Feldman measures. In addition, they added a third measure (the Locke–Wallace measure of marital satisfaction). In this way they hoped to see what shape the relationship of marital satisfaction would take using these three measures. The Locke–Wallace scale was used for it is the most widely utilized instrument to measure marital satisfaction, and thus, one could feel that the shape of the relationship with this measurement instrument would be the most reliable and valid finding. (For a newer instrument, see Spanier, 1976.) Also Rollins and Cannon used both males and females in their study—an additional improvement over some of the older studies and a way of checking if males experienced different changes in marital satisfaction than did females.

Figure 10.1 shows the results of using the three measures of marital satisfaction on the Mormon sample. It is interesting to note that all three measures showed general agreement, indicating that Stage 5 (teenage children) was the low point of marital satisfaction and they also agreed in indicating a curvilinear relationship. It appears that as the children pass the teen years and leave home, there is an increase in marital satisfaction. One can speculate that the lack of stress and strain which was associated with child rearing is a key force in raising marital satisfaction in Stages 6, 7 and 8.

A rather important point needs to be made concerning the degree of change in marital satisfaction. Figure 10.1 shows that most of the variation covers the range from 46 to 56. This is out of a possible range of scores from 14 to 70. Thus, it is apparent that even if we agree on the nature of the change in marital satisfaction, it is still quite clear that the change covers only a small range of response. In short, marital satisfaction does not decrease to the point where scores close to the low point of 14 would occur. In fact, when analyzing changes in marital satisfaction, Rollins and Cannon (1974) found that less than 10 percent of the changes in marital satisfaction are due to changes in the family-life-cycle stages. So not only do family-life stages not create large changes in marital satisfaction, but *other factors* seem much more important in changing marital satisfaction besides stage of family-life cycle (Schram, 1979; Harry, 1976). Some of these may relate to occupational and other roles soon to be discussed.

Rollins and Cannon (1974) suggest that one factor that is more important in gaining insight into marital satisfaction is role strain. They refer here to the potential

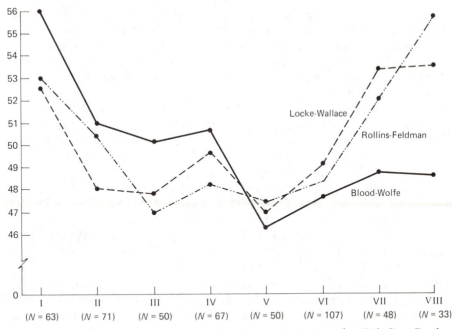

Figure 10.1. *Mean Standard Scores on Marital Satisfaction at Each Stage of an Eight-Stage Family Life Cycle Measured by Three Instruments. Scores are standardized with a mean of 50 and standard deviation of 10 to facilitate visual comparisons of trends. Male and female scores are combined. Source: Boyd C. Rollins and Kenneth L. Cannon (1974):275.*

conflict among roles and the complexity of roles that an individual is involved in. It may well be that by middle age this role complexity in terms of activities in the family as well as in activities outside of the family in work and in community activities with kin and friends may have raised the level of role strain considerably and thereby decreased marital satisfaction. After middle age the gradual reduction in the complexity of roles one is involved in would tend to reduce role strains, and this would help account for the rise in marital satisfaction. Of course, the stage of the family life cycle would be one factor that could affect role strain, but it would be only one such factor. The situation is difficult to fully evaluate with the present data. One could, for example, contend that marital satisfaction rises after middle age because by that time most of the couples who could not get along have divorced or separated from each other.

The above discussion should afford the reader some feel for the complexity of interpreting research findings. Questions have come up concerning the importance of the amount of change in marital satisfaction, also the relative advantage of focusing on role strains to explain changes in marital satisfaction over focusing on stage of family life cycle, and finally the question of whether the changes that are found in these cross-sectional (done at one point in time) studies would be supported by a study that was longitudinal (studied over time). For example, would we find that those couples who were lowest on marital satisfaction and most drastically affected by having children (or by role strains from other sources) would drop out of marriage and thus make those remaining couples who were married longer seem to be increasing in satisfaction? We need to follow individual couples through in time to be able to really know what happens in the area of marital satisfaction. (For new suggestions, see Schram, 1979; Spanier, 1979; Campbell et al., 1976; and Gifford and Bengtson, 1979.)

The basic idea of studying role strains is directly in line with our search for structural constraints relevant to dyadic commitment in marriage. The data we have discussed above on changes in family life stages seem to indicate that activities associated with the parental role are, to some degree, negatively related to marital dyadic commitment. It appears that children lessen marital satisfaction, and with their departure some of this loss is restored. We should bear in mind that the drop in marital satisfaction may not be enough to destroy the marriage, but it is none-theless present. We need careful research that would spell out more clearly the specific types of situations in which the addition of children is most or least likely to lower marital satisfaction.

We also, of course, need a measure of parental satisfaction. While it is true that marital satisfaction may be reduced by the presence of children, it may be equally true that parental satisfaction is increased by that same presence. Very little has been done toward measuring parental satisfaction. We are interested here predominantly in marital commitment and thus we shall not pursue this point at this time.

Photo by Ivan Kalman.

OCCUPATIONAL SUCCESS

A second major type of structural constraint is the occupational role. Does occupational success increase the likelihood of dyadic commitment in a marital relationship because of the economic and other rewards it brings or does the effort of achieving occupational success lead to alienation from one's mate and thereby lessen dyadic commitment in marriage? Does a wife take pride in her husband's success or does she feel less important by comparison? All of these lines of reasoning are logical and plausible. Only careful examination of research will allow us to choose among them.

The research studies present contradictory images of the impact of occupational success on dyadic commitment. Cuber and Harroff's classic research is a good study to begin the search for helpful findings in this area. Cuber and Harroff's study is impressionistic—they did not have a specific set of questions that they asked a representative group of married couples. Rather, they selected a sample of some 400 individuals who were at the top of their respective professions, such as bank presidents, army generals, full professors, corporation presidents, and so on. They then spent many hours over the next five years talking with each individual. They probed in many ways to get at the quality of life of these individuals and particularly at their feelings and behaviors in the area of marriage. The sample was composed of both males and females. The results of this study can hardly be taken as definitive, but they are surely stimulating, and they have inspired much new thinking. One of the most provocative aspects of their report was the typology of marriages they put forth. They took only those individuals who had been married at least ten years and who had never seriously thought of divorce and then developed a typology of five types of marriage from their examination of these couples. Keep in mind that these results apply to the most stable of the married people in the sample. The five types of marriage were:

1. conflict-habituated marriages
2. passive-congenial marriages
3. devitalized marriages
4. vital marriages
5. total marriages

The first three types of marriage they thought of as comprising *utilitarian types* of marriage, that is, marriages based upon convenience and staying together because of lack of better alternatives, rather than marriages which were held together by very high intrinsic rewards. Of course, one must be getting something out of a marriage to remain in it, but that something may include things like a good cook or entertainer, social acceptance as a married person, a good wage earner, and on occasion a convenient sex partner. The "vital" and "total" types of relationships were conceived of as belonging to the general category of *intrinsic marriages*. By "intrinsic" Cuber and Harroff meant that the basic interaction of the two people in these marriages was rewarding. The *vital* subtype differs from the *total* subtype in that vital involves fewer areas of need fulfillment. The total subtype of marriage satisfies most, if not all, of an individual's intimacy needs. The vital subtype fulfills a few of an individual's key intimacy needs but by no means all of them. It is interesting to note that extramarital coitus was common in all subtypes except the total one. We shall discuss this later in Chapter 11 on extramarital sexuality but we can note here that there is a suggestion of a positive relationship between sexual exclusivity and intimacy need fulfillment. It is also worth pointing out that Cuber and Harroff estimate that roughly 80 percent of the marriages they examined were the utilitarian type; about 15 percent were vital and about 5 percent were total. Thus, the American ideal of a high degree of intimacy-need satisfaction in marriage seems achieved by only a small minority of these highly successful individuals.

These findings make one conclude that the relationship between occupational success and dyadic commitment would be negative; that is, the successful individuals fall heavily into utilitarian marriages, and such marriages seem to involve rather low degrees of dyadic commitment. Now one can argue that although only 20 percent of the successful individuals are in intrinsic marriages, that the percent would be even lower if we were to look at only moderately successful individuals. There is no way to test that idea out in the Cuber and Harroff data since they have no comparison group, and no other data exist that utilize the typology they put forth. Thus, we are left with a provocative set of findings but with little in the way of firm conclusions regarding the relation of occupational success to dyadic commitment. It is quite possible that Cuber and Harroff studied a group that diverges from the general pattern. It may well be that the more successful one is, the *more* one is likely to be committed to continue the marriage, *but* when one reaches the very highest successful group the relationship reverses itself, and it is that very successful group that Cuber and Harroff focused upon. This would illustrate a curvilinear relationship of success and commitment. The difficulty involved in settling this issue should show the reader the worth of thinking carefully about the type of sample one selects so as to be best able to answer key theoretical questions. See the four appendixes for a further elaboration on this point.

What other evidence is there on this question? There is the basic evidence from divorce statistics (to be discussed in depth in Chapter 12) which indicates that the poorer one is, the more likely a divorce is to occur. This would seem to argue for a positive relationship between occupational success and dyadic commitment. But that sort of overall correlation does not tell us much about how occupational success can affect dyadic commitment. One relevant research is reported by John Scanzoni in his book *Opportunity and the Family* (1970). Using a representative sample of people from the Indianapolis area, Scanzoni investigated a wide variety of marital processes. One of his findings is directly relevant to our interests here. Scanzoni reported higher rates of marital satisfaction for couples wherein the husband was moving in an upward direction occupationally. Scanzoni explains this by reference to an interactional process. He believes that as the wife sees that her husband is succeeding at his occupational role, then she feels more motivated to work at her homemaker and mother role. Further, as the husband then perceives the wife as succeeding at her homemaker role, he strives even more to succeed at his occupational role. The husband and wife thus are involved in a mutually reinforcing process. Of course, we are speaking here of traditional husband and wife roles. This process would not work if the wife and husband felt that they each shared equally the responsibility for occupational and household successes. In such a nontraditional marriage a similar process could occur, but it would involve a starting mechanism of one person showing skill at the variety of tasks he or she performed and the other person then being encouraged to do the same. In short, it could be a more competitive process of people involved in the same roles rather than in complementary roles. Scanzoni talks of this alternative in a later book (1972).

The work of Macke, Bohrnstedt, and Bernstein (1979) adds a further qualification to Scanzoni's research. These researchers utilized part of the sample from a *Psychology Today* survey of readers. That magazine attracts a highly educated group of readers. They reasoned that among such people, a husband's success would reduce the self-esteem of a housewife. Further, they hypothesized that if the wife were professionally employed, then the husband's success would not reduce her self-esteem. The economic benefits of the husband's job, they believed, would generally raise the feelings of marital success, but if the woman had no job herself, she would still feel belittled by her husband's success. In short, they rejected the idea of a housewife having a vicarious involvement with her husband's success in his work. They selected two groups of women from the *Psychology Today* respondents—one was a housewife group and the other a group of wives professionally employed. The results basically indicated support for their ideas. The housewife whose husband was successful had lower self-esteem although his success increased the feeling of marital success. On the other hand, for the professional wives, neither of these processes were operating. Now, of course, if we were to take a group of lower-educated wives, these results might not occur. The findings may well be due to the felt pressures by higher educated wives to prove their own worth by having a career. Under such pressure, when a husband succeeds, the comparison makes the wife feel more like a failure, even though the resultant income and prestige improves her conception of the marriage.

One other important study is a longitudinal study of 900 marriages in the Detroit area carried out by Freedman and Coombs (1970). This study ties together some of the concerns we dealt with in the preceding section regarding the effect of children on dyadic commitment and the concerns we have here with the effect of occupational success on dyadic commitment. One of the important findings of the Freedman and Coombs study was that the *timing* of births, as much as the number of births was important for the economic future of a family. In short, they found that couples who had their first child (conceived premaritally or not) within the first year of marriage were couples who would space their children very close together and who would not advance economically as much as those couples who started out economically the same but who delayed having children until after the first year of marriage and spaced them further apart. Thus, birth patterns can affect occupational success just as occupational success can affect birth patterns (more on this in Chapter 15).

We also know from other studies that premaritally pregnant couples who marry have an above-average chance of divorce (Glick, 1975). Thus, overall it would seem that occupational advancement may well be part of an overall ability to plan and carry out ideas related to advancing one's economic position. The ability to regulate birth may well be part of a more general planning ability which is relevant to occupational success. In short, it may be that the number of children per se is only one factor affecting the quality of a marriage. The second factor is the lack of planning ability indicated by the occurrence of a large number of children spaced close together. That lack of planning ability may affect dyadic commitment by lessening chances of occupational success as well as by increasing strains due to large numbers of children. Of course, there are people who plan to have children close together and to have many children. However, studies by Westoff (1971) and others indicate that more often a high number of births indicates unwanted pregnancies and poor planning abilities due to low marital communication (Hill, 1966) or to other factors.

We have found then two causal processes that Scanzoni and Freedman and Coombs point to and which may lead us to conclude that occupational success is related in a positive direction to dyadic commitment. Scanzoni points to the mutual reinforcement of occupational and household success, and Freedman and Coombs lead us to speculate that planning abilities which go with occupational success may well be important in maintaining a marriage. Otto and Featherman's (1972) work, previously cited, also supports a positive relationship between occupational success and dyadic commitment. However, the work of Macke and her colleagues (1979) specifies that this positive relationship probably holds best for more traditional and noncareer wives, but they seem to pay a price in lowered self-esteem and that could eventually lead to resentment and weaken the marriage. Nonetheless, until more data is in, we will assume that, on balance, occupational success raises dyadic commitment.

SHARED TIES TO KIN AND FRIENDS

A third area of structural constraints that clearly relates to dyadic commitment involves relationships with kin of the husband or wife and with close friends. Here we are in an area based on very little research knowledge. We spoke earlier in this chapter about the work of Ackerman and Lewis which implied that normative support by kin and friends binds the couple more to their marital relationship. Beyond that we really know very little. A reasonable hypothesis would be that where husband and wife share ties to a particular kin or friend, that should strengthen the dyadic commitment of their marriage. The reasoning here is that such ties held in common would lead to additional sources of interpersonal satisfaction and to the likely development of more shared norms and thus contribute to dyadic commitment in these ways. Ties to kin and friends that are not shared may well be divisive in that they can be sources of dispute regarding visiting and help given to such kin or friends.

An Overview of Dyadic Commitment

A few causal diagrams will present parts of our theory of the three main factors that impact upon dyadic commitment in marriage. Figure 10.2 represents the basic causal conception that is being discussed in this chapter. It points out the three causes of dyadic commitment and also shows some specific paths of influence that the three variables have on dyadic commitment. I have deliberately been very general in this diagram and have not divided the three major causal variables into their subparts—nor have I indicated anything specific about the causal relationships (negative, positive, or curvilinear).

The diagram does, however, show some interesting types of relationships. For example, structural constraint is viewed as having a direct effect on dyadic commitment, just as the other two major variables do. But structural constraint, unlike the other two variables, is shown to have indirect effects on dyadic commitment as well. The diagram posits that structural constraints will affect total reward–tension balance and that variable will, in turn, impact on dyadic commitment. Also, the diagram shows that structural constraints will affect normative inputs and that variable will, in turn, impact on dyadic commitment. The reasoning here has been touched on above and basically involves the position that constraints such as re-lationships with children or with one's work will lead to a change in interaction with one's mate and thus alter the reward–tension balance. Secondly, these con-straints will also tend to change one's views relevant to such normative beliefs as marriage is for life. Depending on the constraints we are speaking of, the effect can be to increase or decrease these two other key variables. Overall then we view structural constraints as the key dynamic element in our theory since it has the potential of introducing a great deal of change which originates in roles outside of the marriage. The reward–tension balance and the normative inputs are dynamic in their own right, and they do vary in line with the day-to-day marital interaction. Nevertheless, many of the key elements that may dramatically change that reward–tension balance or the normative input lie in the structural constraints that occur over time in areas like parenthood, occupation, and kinship ties.

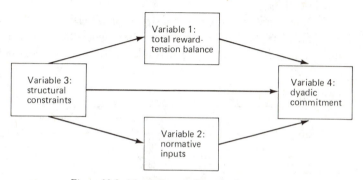

Figure 10.2. Major Causes of Dyadic Commitment.

Figure 10.3 presents, in simple diagram form, the ideas we spoke of regarding parenthood duties as a structural constraint. Note that this variable is seen as having a direct effect on dyadic commitment and also an indirect effect on it via the key variable of "total reward–tension balance." Parenthood is seen as a structural constraint affecting both these variables. By lowering the reward–tension balance, parenthood duties will indirectly lessen the level of dyadic commitment. This is so because the level of the reward–tension balance influences in a positive direction dyadic commitment, and thus the lower that balance is, the lower the dyadic commitment will be. The reader by now should be becoming more sophisticated in reading these causal diagrams, and hopefully, will recall that a positive relation is one in which, as one variable goes up or down, so does the other variable; a negative relation is one in which, as one variable goes up, the other variable goes down. (See Appendix 4 for elaboration.)

Figure 10.4 presents two relationships we discussed under the general topic of structural constraint: (1) occupational success and (2) parenthood duties, and shows how they interrelate. Note that without the diagram, it would be easy to talk only about these two variables separarately. Once one presents them in diagram form, the option of connecting the two variables in some causal fashion is made apparent. That is one of the major values of presenting ideas in diagrammatic form—one is forced to make decisions about potential connections among variables. The figure shows the relationship between these two variables to be in a negative direction. I could have added an arrow from occupational success to parenthood duties, showing a positive relationship based on the belief that money from being successful would increase the ability to handle parenthood duties by hiring help, taking vacations, and so forth. This would lessen parenthood duties for that couple. However, that idea did not seem sufficiently firmly empirically planted and thus was not posited. Instead, I illustrated the position that as parenthood duties increase the chances for occupational success decreases. This is basically in line with the data from Freedman and Coombs (1970) discussed above. Here as elsewhere such general and unqualified associations between two variables are not likely to be empirically true without some specifications of the conditions under which it would hold. Future empirical testing of the posited relationship will inform us regarding any needed qualifications.

Figure 10.5 shows another structural constraint of which we spoke, namely, shared kin ties. This variable is also related to parenthood duties. This diagram affords a more specific view of the causal network involved in the ideas put forth

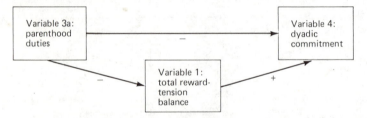

Figure 10.3. Parenthood Duties, Reward-Tension Balance, and Dyadic Commitment.

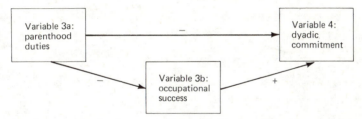

Figure 10.4. Occupational Success, Parenthood Duties, and Dyadic Commitment.

in this chapter. The underlying reasoning is that as parenthood duties increase, one is more likely to seek out kin ties to help in those duties and these ties to kin are likely to increase one's dyadic commitment. This is so despite the fact that parenthood duties are also viewed as lowering dyadic commitment due to factors that go along with it. This demonstrates the multiple effects possible from one variable, particularly when the variable is as complex as parenthood duties.

Figure 10.6 puts together the three preceding diagrams and also gives more of an overall causal perspective on dyadic commitment. It is by no means a complete causal diagram of our ideas. That would be too complex to present in one diagram, but it does include the three main structural constraint subtypes and the overall variable of reward–tension balance.

The overall worth of diagramming should by now be apparent. This approach forces one to make decisions regarding relationships that become obvious only when one has diagrammed them. It makes one aware of the necessity of specifying how one will measure a particular concept and whether that measurement will vary in a positive, negative, or curvilinear direction with some other variable. The specificity demanded by the diagram, in other words, forces one to become more precise in one's own thinking. Also, by making a specific choice regarding how two variables relate, it becomes more obvious what choices were not elected—one could have posited a feedback relationship; one could have posited a second causal relationship to another variable, and on and on. Thus, alternative theoretical explanations also become more apparent, and this encourages research. Thus, the reader would be well advised to test some of his or her own ideas by use of these simple diagramming conventions. The reader can also try to diagram ideas put forth in other chapters of this book. (For theory books in the family area which develop causal analyses see Burr, 1973; and Burr, Hill, Nye, and Reiss, 1979.)

The area of dyadic commitment may have at first seemed like a relatively simple

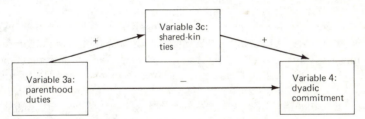

Figure 10.5. Kin Ties, Parenthood Duties, and Dyadic Commitment.

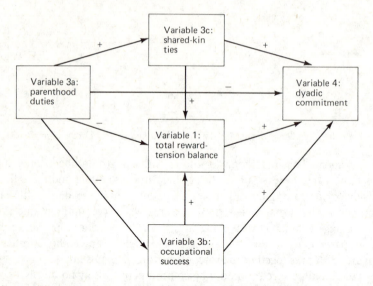

Figure 10.6. Structural Constraints, Reward-Tension Balance and Dyadic Commitment.

area which one could very briefly deal with. I hope the discussion in this chapter has dissuaded most of you from a such an idea. Clearly this is a most complex area. Equally clear is the fact that it is a crucial area to study. It is quite possible that the high divorce rate today is due to a lessening of the normative support for lifelong commitment and an increase in the types of structural constraints that lessen commitment. Nevertheless, it is also possible that the reward–tension balance may be no lower than in earlier periods. Only if we measure these three key inputs to dyadic commitment shall we be able to more accurately know what the quality of American marriage is like in the last two decades of the twentieth century. This knowledge may be useful for cohabiting as well as marital dyads. We may also learn how to alter these inputs more intentionally rather than simply be the unknowing recipients of such influences.

Summary and Conclusions

Dyadic commitment is probably the ultimate mystery in marital relationships. We studied role differentiation, power relations, and communication problems in the last chapter, and, of course, there are many unknowns there as well. But one key interest in most of the marital processes is to discern how they affect the determination of a married couple to stay together, that is, their dyadic commitment. We delineated three major causes of the level of dyadic commitment in a relationship: (1) reward–tension balance, (2) normative inputs, and (3) structural constraints. My own interests are in the structural constraint area. I feel particularly that parenthood duties and occupational success are the keys to understanding dyadic commitment in the 1980s. This is so because these two areas touch the pulse of social change brought about by more equalitarian gender roles. The entire impact of parenthood on marital commitment may well be different if husbands have a larger share of these duties than they have had in the past. Such a change could work either way — to increase or decrease the reward–tension balance, but it seems to be a central issue in either case. With dual earner marriages increasingly common, the impact of occupational success becomes more complex as the research of Macke and her colleagues (1979) indicates. The effect of a husband's success on the self-esteem of his wife may well depend on the wife's conception of what she *should* be doing at home and outside the home. Also, although the husband's success in work does increase the sense of marital success—would that also be true of the wife's success at work? Macke et al. reported that when the wife is also employed, the husband's success is not strongly related to felt marital success. So there is here the possibility that many of the causes of dyadic commitment may well differ for couples espousing equalitarian gender roles. Structural constraints refer to roles outside the marital role, but nonetheless, these constraints are some of the key factors that relate to changes toward more equalitarian marital roles. We will have more to say about constraints like parenthood and occupation in Part Four of this book.

References

Ackerman, Charles. 1963. "Affiliations: Structural Determinants of Differential Divorce Rates," *American Journal of Sociology* 69 (July):13–21.

Blood, Robert O., and Donald Wolfe. 1960. *Husbands and Wives: The Dynamics of Married Living.* New York: Free Press.

Bradburn, Norman M. 1969. *The Structure of Psychological Well-Being.* Chicago: Aldine.

Burr, Wesley R. 1970. "Satisfaction With Various Aspects of Marriage over the Life Cycle," *Journal of Marriage and the Family* 32 (February): 29–37.

———. 1973. *Theory Construction and the Sociology of the Family.* New York: Wiley.

———. Reuben Hill, Ivan Nye, and Ira L. Reiss (eds.). 1979. *Contemporary Theories About the Family.* 2 vols. New York: Free Press.

Campbell, Angus. 1975. "The American Way of Mating: Marriage Si, Children Only Maybe," *Psychology Today* 8 (May):37–43.

———, Philip E. Converse, and Willard L. Rodgers. 1976. *The Quality of American Life.* New York: Russell Sage.

Cuber, John E., and Peggy Haroff. 1965. *The Significant Americans.* New York: Appleton.

Dumon, Wilfried A. 1978. "When Two Become Three." Paper presented to the International Union of Family Organizations in Vienna (June).

Duvall, Evelyn. 1975. *Family Development,* 5th ed. Philadelphia: Lippincott.

Freedman, Ronald, and L. Coombs. 1970. "Social and Economic Correlates of Family Building Patterns in Detroit," Unpublished Final Report Project No. 312–6–207, U.S. Department of Health, Education, and Welfare (plus Appendixes A through F).

Gilford, Rosalie, and Vern Bengtson. 1979. "Measuring Marital Satisfaction in Three Generations: Positive and Negative Dimensions," *Journal of Marriage and the Family* 41 (May):387–398.

Glenn, Norval D. 1975. "The Contribution of Marriage to the Psychological Well-Being of Males and Females," *Journal of Marriage and the Family* 37 (August):594–601.

Glick, Paul. 1975. "A Demographer Looks at American Families," *Journal of Marriage and the Family* 37 (February):15–28.

Harry, Joseph. 1976. "Evolving Sources of Happiness for Men Over the Life Cycle: A Structural Analysis," *Journal of Marriage and the Family* 38 (May):289–296.

Hicks, Mary, and Marilyn Platt. 1970. "Marital Happiness and Stability: A Review of Research in the Sixties," *Journal of Marriage and the Family* 32 (November):553–575.

Hill, Reuben. 1966. "The Significance of the Family in Population Research," in William T. Liu (ed.), *Family and Fertility*. Notre Dame, IN: University of Notre Dame Press.

Johnson, Michael P. 1968. "Courtship and Commitment: A Study of Cohabitation on a University Campus." Master's thesis, unpublished, University of Iowa, Iowa City.

Jourard, Sidney M. 1968. *Self-Disclosure: An Experimental Analysis of the Transparent Self.* New York: Wiley.

———. 1971. *The Transparent Self*, 2nd ed. New York: Van Nostrand.

Levinger, George. 1975. "Marital Cohesiveness and Dissolution: An Integrative Review, " *Journal of Marriage and the Family* 27 (February): 19–28.

Lewis, Robert A. 1973. "Social Reaction and the Formation of Dyads: An Interational Approach to Mate Selection," *Sociometry* 36 (September):409–419.

Macke, Anne S., George W. Bohrstedt, and Ilene N. Bernstein. 1979. "Housewives' Self-Esteem and Their Husbands' Success: The Myth of Vicarious Involvement," *Journal of Marriage and the Family* 41 (February):51–57.

Olson, David. 1981. *Typologies of Marriage and Family Systems*. (Forthcoming)

Otto, Luther, and David L. Featherman. 1972. "On the Measurement of Marital Adjustment Among Spouses." Unpublished working paper 72–74, University of Wisconsin Center for Demography and Ecology, Madison.

Pineo, Peter C. 1961. "Disenchantment in the Later Years of Marriage," *Marriage and Family Living* 23 (February):3–11.

Renne, Karen. 1970. "Correlates of Dissatisfaction in Marriage," *Journal of Marriage and the Family* 32 (February):54–67.

Rollins, Boyd C., and Kenneth L. Cannon. 1974. "Marital Satisfaction over the Family Life Cycle: A Reevaluation," *Journal of Marriage and the Family* 36 (May):271–284.

———, and Harold Feldman. 1970. "Marital Satisfaction over the Family Life Cycle," *Journal of Marriage and the Family* 32 (February): 20–28.

Scanzoni, John H. 1970. *Opportunity and the Family*. New York: Free Press.

———. 1972. *Sexual Bargaining*. Englewood Cliffs, NJ: Prentice-Hall.

Schram, Rosalyn W. 1979. "Marital Satisfaction Over the Family Life Cycle: A Critique and Proposal," *Journal of Marriage and the Family* 41 (February):7–12.

Spanier, Graham B. 1976. "Measuring Dyadic Adjustment," *Journal of Marriage and the Family* 38 (February):15–28.

———, Robert A. Lewis, and Charles L. Cole 1975. "Marital Adjustment over the Family Life Cycle: The Issue of Curvilinearity," *Journal of Marriage and the Family* 37 (May):263–277.

———, William Sauer, and Robert Larzelere. 1979. "An Empirical Evaluation of the Family Life Cycle," *Journal of Marriage and the Family* 41 (February):27–38.

Tharp, B.F. 1963. "Dimensions of Marriage Roles," *Journal of Marriage and the Family* 25 (November):389–404.

Westoff, Leslie A., and Charles F. Westoff. 1971. *From Now to Zero*. Boston: Little, Brown.

The Sexual Lives of Married People:

Inside and Outside of Marriage

ELEVEN

One almost universal aspect of marital interaction is the sexual relationship between the husband and the wife (see Chapter 2 for some rare exceptions). The sexual relationship both affects and is affected by other aspects of the marital tie. In terms of our discussion of dyadic commitment we can here stress the importance of marital sexual satisfaction as a component of the overall reward–tension balance in marital interaction. From a theoretical perspective we would be interested to observe if marital sexuality has been altering in ways that are similar to changes occurring in premarital sexuality as discussed in Chapter 7. Also, our interest will center on how marital sexuality reflects the type of gender-role differentiation that exists in a group. For example, we would expect marital sexuality to be different in groups that differ on the degree of male dominance present in the major institutional life areas.

Unfortunately, the amount of research that has been expended on marital sexuality is quite small. The reader has seen that there is a good amount of quality research on *premarital* sexuality. For marital sexuality, we shall generally have to utilize studies on fertility that have asked questions about the sexual lives of the respondents and a few other studies that investigated marital-coital rates and orgasmic frequencies. We shall gather what we can and try to paint as complete a picture as possible, but there will be many gaps. There is a very recent body of data on *extramarital* sexuality and in the second part of this chapter we shall strive to integrate this with our discussion of marital sexuality. In this way we hope to be able to develop a perspective of the sexual lives of married people both inside and outside of marriage.

Overview of Marital Sexuality

The Polynesian area is one that is well known for studies of its sexuality. Malinowski's work on the Trobrianders, Margaret Mead's work on the Samoans, Marshall's work on the Mangaians, and Suggs's work on the Marquesans are but a few of the anthropological accounts of the sexual life of Polynesians. In most of these accounts some analysis of marital sexuality is included. Sexuality in marriage and before marriage is considerably more permissive in Polynesia than it has been in America. Some ethnographic reports point up the emphasis on female marital sexual satisfaction. In parts of Polynesia if the husband does not have intercourse at least once each night with his wife, this fact will be transmitted to the women in the marketplace, and the husband will be teased for his low sexual performance. In short, wives expect this nightly lovemaking and will let their disappointment be known when this expectation is not met. Average frequency of intercourse in America, as we shall see, would be only about twice a week. In Mangaia the young boy is taught that it is proper to bring the woman to two or three climaxes before he allows himself to have an orgasm (Marshall and Suggs, 1971:Chap. 5). This sort of behavior is expected to occur in marital sexuality as well as outside of marriage.

In other ways groups like the Trobrianders of Polynesia are quite conservative. It is rare to see a husband and wife display affection in public, and typically the wife will walk behind the husband. During the wife's menstrual period the male will view her as unclean and will not have coitus with her. In these and other ways the Trobrianders show a sexually more restrictive orientation than is found in America.

TRENDS IN THE TWENTIETH CENTURY

In the twentieth century expectations have moved in the direction of more open acceptance and encouragement of female sexual response in marriage. One of the famous sex manuals of the early twentieth century was by T. H. Van Der Velde. His approach was to encourage the husband to carefully arouse his wife and to try to achieve simultaneous orgasm with her. He stressed the importance of patience, care, and concern. One can still detect here, then, the strong elements of male dominance in sexuality. The male, through his greater experience, is supposed to know more about sexual performance, and he thus should act as the instructor for the female who is presumably innocent and not cognizant of how to be sexually aroused. This is a particularly interesting view since the male's sexual experience in this type of double-standard setting will likely be with females for whom he has little affection. Yet this type of experience supposedly makes him capable of teaching his wife how to have sexual relations in a loving relationship. It seems clear that the underlying logic derives from male dominance and control of sexuality and not from careful reasoning.

The trend toward greater concern for the wife's orgasm is visible in the research data of Kinsey presented in Table 11.1. It is apparent that the percentage of women experiencing orgasm started to rise among women born in the first decade of this century, or in other words, those entering marriage during the 1920s. Note that there was no increase in the frequency of marital coitus and in fact a slight decrease in frequency occurred. This may indicate that male concern for female sexual satisfaction was increasing to the point where coitus was performed more due to mutual interest and with stronger commitment to female orgasm. However, it is still the case today that "frequency of intercourse" is most often defined by the number of male orgasms and not in terms of female orgasm. For example, suppose that a husband and wife have intercourse and only she reaches a climax and then a half hour later they have intercourse again and this time both reach orgasm. How many times have they had intercourse? Frequently, the single orgasm of the male is considered the end of the sexual act and only one act of intercourse is reported. If the male had reached orgasm each time, two acts of intercourse might well be reported regardless of the wife's orgasmic response. Despite the greater concern today for female orgasm, the male perspective is still dominant.

TABLE 11.1

Active Incidence and Frequency of Marital Coitus for Wives, by Decade of Birth

Age During Activity	Decade of Birth	COITAL EXPERIENCE		COITUS to ORGASM	Cases In Total Sample
		Active Incidence (percent)	Active Median Frequency per Week	Active Incidence (percent)	
16–20	Bf. 1900	100	3.2	61	(61)
	1900–1909	99	2.6	64	(114)
	1910–1919	99	2.8	66	(173)
	1920–1929	100	2.8	80	(230)
21–25	Bf. 1900	99	2.8	72	(207)
	1900–1909	99	2.5	80	(378)
	1910–1919	100	2.5	87	(625)
	1920–1929	100	2.4	89	(447)
26–30	Bf. 1900	100	2.5	80	(274)
	1900–1909	99	2.2	86	(507)
	1910–1919	99	2.1	91	(731)
	1920–1929	100	2.0	93	(153)
31–35	Bf. 1900	98	2.2	85	(292)
	1900–1909	98	1.9	92	(508)
	1910–1919	99	1.7	92	(448)
36–40	Bf. 1900	98	1.9	86	(285)
	1900–1909	98	1.3	92	(463)
	1910–1919	98	1.5	91	(105)
41–45	Bf. 1900	93	1.6	84	(275)
	1900–1909	94	0.9	88	(225)

Source: Alfred C. Kinsey et al. (1953): 397.

Note that the 1920 period is the same time period during which we found a rapid rise in female nonvirginity before marriage (see Chapter 7). This is further evidence that the changes that were occurring in sexual behavior were part and parcel of overall broad changes in gender roles. When a society undergoes radical social changes, the expectations of males and females in the occupational, educational, religious, political, and family areas will all evidence these changes. These gender-role components were visible in changes in female participation in the labor force, in females obtaining the vote, in greater participation in higher education, and in modified marital and family-role expectations. Directly and indirectly such changes also affect the sexuality component of gender roles. In short, the institutional changes affected sexual relationships by changing the basic determinants of such sexual expectations. For example, as increasing proportions of women worked, it became more apparent to women that there were ways they could exist independent of male economic support. In addition, working women would come in contact with more males under rather open sexual opportunity conditions, away from home and parents or kin. Contact with the world outside the home also increased the likelihood that women would learn of the latest contraceptive methods and also meet other women who like them were becoming more aware of alternatives to the traditional female role. In these ways then the occupational changes were bound to affect sexual relationships and to do so not only in the premarital area but also in the marital and, as we shall see, in the extramarital area also. What affected female sexuality in this century more than anything else were the changes in the female priority weighting of wife-mother roles in the direction of more weight being given to female jobs and career roles.

Further support for the overall changes comes from recent national data indicating a rise in marital coital frequency occurring between 1965 and 1970. Note that this time period also coincides with the second period of rapid sexual change in the area of premarital relationships. The Westoff data (Table 11.2) come from two probability-type national samples of women aged fifteen to forty-four. The rise is from an average of 6.8 times in four weeks to 8.2 times in four weeks—an increase of 21 percent.

There are reasons for believing that the rise was due to more than sampling variability and is a real increase. One convincing bit of evidence concerns the time taken to become pregnant. Westoff reported that the time period was shorter in 1970 than in 1965. One could conclude that the added frequency of coitus would be the key factor that increased the likelihood of pregnancy occurring in a short period of time. The effectiveness of contraceptive methods increased during this period of time, with the pill becoming more popular, and thus one cannot assume that faster pregnancy is due to poorer contraceptive usage. Faster pregnancy occurred regardless of the contraceptive method used. Westoff further notes that those women with traditional female-role orientations have lower rates of marital coitus, and such women decreased between 1965 and 1970. Also, women who work (not for money alone, but for career reasons) have higher coital frequencies, and such women also increased in this five-year interval. Higher-educated females also have higher frequencies, and they, too, increased in this time period. Finally, women

TABLE 11.2

Percent Distribution of Coital Frequency in Four Weeks Prior to Interview, 1965 and 1970*

| | PERCENT | |
Coital Frequency	1965 (N=4,603)	1970 (N=5,432)
Total	100.0	100.0
0	7.0	6.1
1–2	12.8	9.9
3–4	20.9	17.0
5–6	15.6	14.6
7–8	16.6	15.2
9–10	9.3	10.4
11–12	8.3	9.9
13–14	1.5	1.5
15–16	3.8	6.2
17–18	0.6	1.0
19–20	2.1	4.2
21 or more	1.7	3.9
Median	5.8	7.5
Mean	6.8	8.2
Standard deviation	5.2	6.2

*In this table the analysis is of currently married women under age forty-five living with their husbands.
Note: Percents may not add to 100 because of rounding.
Source: Charles F. Westoff (1974): 136.

using the pill increased, and such wives have the highest rates of coitus—ten times in the last four-week period. Thus, all these relationships would make one expect an increase of the sort that Westoff found. It is also worth emphasizing that women of all age groups were involved in this rise in frequency of marital coitus. Thus, it was not just a youth phenomenon. All of this evidence adds up to a persuasive argument that a real change in frequency of marital coitus has occurred. Here is additional strong support for the view that there was a major change in gender roles occurring in the late 1960s–a change comparable only to that which occurred in the 1920s. Like the 1920s, this change was occurring in both premarital and marital sexuality.

Coital Frequency and Orgasm Rates

Evidence is needed regarding married female orgasm rates for this same period of 1965–1970. Only one such study has these rates for married women, and that is Morton Hunt's 1972 study of sexual relationships. This study does not have a true representative sample but instead has a volunteer sample with a high (80 percent) refusal rate. But since Hunt does report rare data, his study is worth examining. Hunt compared the orgasm rate of the approximately 700 wives in his sample with

Photo by Ivan Kalman.

the orgasm rate reported by Kinsey. It appears that the orgasm rate has risen somewhat when we make this comparison (see Table 11.3). Also, one notes that the frequency of marital coitus has even clearer signs of increase (see Table 11.4). In fact, the frequency is somewhat higher than that reported by Westoff. However, the Westoff sample is far superior, and since it was taken only two years before the Hunt sample, I would personally conclude that we should stick with the frequency figures of Westoff as representative of women fifteen to forty-five and view Hunt's and Kinsey's figures as representative of perhaps the more highly educated segments of our population. Hunt, like Westoff, reported changes in marital coital and orgasm rates to be occurring in all age groups. This gives further support to the view that the changes were part of a widespread social movement involving basic alterations in gender roles.

The respondents Hunt spoke to also reported a much greater variety of positions used in marital coitus. For example, about 15 percent of Kinsey's sample used rear-entry vaginal intercourse, but about 40 percent of Hunt's sample used that position. The Kinsey findings showed greater variation in position in the higher-educated groups and that difference is still present, but it is much smaller than in Kinsey's day. The male-above position is still the most popular, but there is a much greater proportion of the population now trying alternative positions. Oral sex was more common in Hunt's sample with approximately three-quarters of the couples having tried both cunnilingus and fellatio. Here, too, the higher-educated people are more

TABLE 11.3

Proportion of Marital Coitus Resulting in Orgasm: Married White Females, 1938–1949 and 1972

1938–1949 (KINSEY) FEMALES IN 15th YEAR OF MARRIAGE		1972 (HUNT SURVEY) FEMALES WITH 15 YEARS MEDIAN DURATION OF MARRIAGE	
Orgasm Frequency	*Percent of Wives*	*Orgasm Frequency*	*Percent of Wives*
90–100	45	All or almost all of the time	53
30–89	27	About 3/4 to about 1/2 of the time	32
1–29	16	About 1/4 of the time	8
None of the time	12	Almost none or none of the time	7

Source: Morton Hunt (1974): 212.

TABLE 11.4

Marital Coitus: Frequency Per Week as Estimated by Husbands and Wives

HUSBANDS, 1938–1946 AND 1972

	1938–1946 (Kinsey)			1972 (Hunt Survey)	
Age	*Mean*	*Median*	*Age*	*Mean*	*Median*
16–25	3.3	2.3	18–24	3.7	3.5
26–35	2.5	1.9	25–34	2.8	3.0
36–45	1.8	1.4	35–44	2.2	2.0
46–55	1.3	0.8	45–54	1.5	1.0
56–60	0.8	0.6	55 & over	1.0	1.0

WIVES, 1938–1949 AND 1972

	1938–1949 (Kinsey)			1972 (Hunt Survey)	
Age	*Mean*	*Median*	*Age*	*Mean*	*Median*
16–25	3.2	2.6	18–24	3.3	3.0
26–35	2.5	2.0	25–34	2.6	2.1
36–45	1.9	1.4	35–44	2.0	2.0
46–55	1.3	0.9	45–54	1.5	1.0
56–60	0.8	0.4	55 & over	1.0	1.0

Note: In both tables (Tables 11.3 and 11.4) Kinsey's data have been adapted by recalculating his five-year cohorts into ten-year cohorts to facilitate comparison with Hunt's data. The dates 1938–1946 and 1938–1949 refer to the years during which the interviews were conducted on which Kinsey's data are based; the Hunt fieldwork was done, as indicated, in 1972. The Hunt data are based on the white sample, since the Kinsey data are only for whites.
Source: Morton Hunt (1974): 190.

involved, but the lower-educated people are much more similar to them than they were when Kinsey gathered his data in the 1940s. The buttocks seem to be becoming increasingly sexually exciting, particularly to younger couples. Hunt found that about one quarter of the married couples under age thirty-five had tried anal intercourse, and a higher percent had tried manual–anal foreplay. Foreplay itself has been extended in time—a fact that supports the validity of the reported higher female orgasm rates. Hunt also reports longer intromission time in coitus (10 minutes versus 4 or 5 minutes in Kinsey's data), and this, too, would make us expect higher orgasm rates (Gebhard, 1966).

In 1974 *Redbook* magazine published a questionnaire and 100,000 women answered it. Again, it would be difficult to know just who these women represent but until a better-designed study comes along, we can still use the results that are of interest to us. Even nonrepresentative samples may yield insight into relationships among social factors of interest to us. We will also examine some findings regarding rates of behavior and here we must be aware of the difficulty of generalizing to the larger population. The frequency of marital coitus reported is very similar to that reported in the other studies we have commented upon. Table 11.5 presents this information. It seems that about twice a week or about nine times a month would be the average for this group of wives. Over three-quarters of their sample was under thirty-five years of age. Table 11.5 also reports the orgasmic behavior of the *Redbook* wives. The 7 percent who never experience orgasm is the same percent reported by Hunt. The *Redbook* wives do seem similar to Hunt's sample also in the proportion who always or most of the time experience orgasm.

There is an indication in the *Redbook* study of a high degree of acceptance of sexual experimentation. For example, 43 percent of the wives had tried anal intercourse and over 90 percent had experienced oral sexuality. Kinsey reported only about 50 percent with oral sexual experience. Table 11.6 presents the information on oral sexuality and on the reaction to it. Clearly wives enjoyed both forms of oral sexuality but strongly preferred cunnilingus to fellatio. One additional finding on marital sexuality that is of importance concerns the discussion of sexual feelings with husbands. Fifty-six percent of those who *always* discussed their sexual feelings with their husbands rated their sexual lives as very good whereas only 9 percent of those who *never* discussed their sexual feelings with their husbands rated their sexual lives as very good (Tavris and Sadd, 1977:107).

Both the Hunt and *Redbook* studies support the view that marital sexuality has increased somewhat in frequency and even more so in the variety of sexual acts that occur. I believe we can accept these conclusions as supported for those who have at least finished high school—for it is that group which is best represented in these studies. Also, there is evidence in Hunt and elsewhere that college- and noncollege-educated people are becoming more alike (Yankelovitch, 1974). The Westoff study does utilize a representative sample and it fits in several ways with these two studies and that lends further credence to our conclusions here. Westoff did report that the less traditional women had higher marital coital frequencies and this would argue for the importance of female gender-role changes as one cause of increases in marital sexual experimentation (Whitley and Poulsen, 1975).

It is important to have some way to measure marital sexual permissiveness. One

TABLE 11.5

Frequency of Coitus and Orgasm in Redbook Sample Wives

NUMBER OF COITAL ACTS PER MONTH						
0	1–5	6–10	11–15 (in percent)	16–20	21+	=
2	26	32	21	11	8	

PERCENT WHO REACH COITAL ORGASM				
All the time	Most of the time	Sometimes	Once in a while	Never
15	48	19	11	7

Source: Tavris and Sadd (1977):67, 74.

way to measure "permissiveness" regarding marital sexuality is to look at the variety of sexual acts that are viewed as acceptable for married couples. This approach would give us a scale that would measure degree of marital sexual permissiveness. I have developed such questions so as to get general normative responses. However, one could ask the same questions in a personal way by changing the reference of the question to the individual person. The suggested questions are in Table 11.7. This scale was tested by Vernon Raschke (1972) in his doctoral dissertation, and it was found to meet all the requirements of Guttman scales. Such a scale would allow us to test the idea that greater sexual satisfaction in marriage will occur as greater sexual permissiveness in marriage occurs. The *Redbook* study indicates that as marital sexual permissiveness increases so does sexual satisfaction. It would be worthwhile to examine this relationship in greater detail.

TABLE 11.6

Proportion of Wives with Experience of Cunnilingus and Fellatio and Their Reactions

	CUNNILINGUS (in percent)	FELLATIO
FREQUENCY		
Often	39	40
Occasionally	48	45
Once	6	6
Never	7	9
REACTION		
Very enjoyable	62	34
Somewhat enjoyable	28	38
No feelings	4	13
Unpleasant	4	12
Repulsive	2	3

Source: Tavris and Sadd (1977):88.

Quality of Marriage and Coitus

Hunt reports that marital coitus was 50 percent more frequent in marriages that were affectionately close compared to more "distant" type of marriages. Hunt feels that perhaps marital sexuality is more generally satisfying and has become more elaborate because marriages in general are closer. One might mention the high divorce rate, but that indicates that those who are unhappy have an easier and quicker exit to utilize and thus those who remain may well be on the average happier. Table 11.8 shows Hunt's findings relating marital closeness and sexual pleasure derived from marital sexuality. It is important to notice that even though both husbands and wives report the same positive association between pleasurable sex and marital closeness, the relationship is considerably stronger for females. In the "not-too-close" marriages, 62 percent of the females found sexuality to fall in the two "low pleasure" categories, whereas among males having "not-too-close" marriages, only 41 percent of the males' pleasure was so classified.

Similar findings on marital happiness affecting pleasure were reported by Paul Gebhard (1966) using the Kinsey data. Gebhard found that those marriages that were reported as "very happy" had considerably higher proportions of marital orgasm. However, all other marriages (from happy to unhappy) showed little variance—so it seems that only very high degrees of happiness make a difference. However, about 60 percent of the couples reported themselves as "very happy."

TABLE 11.7
Reiss Marital Sexual Permissiveness Scale

Please indicate the degree of agreement you have with the following items concerning sex practices for husbands and wives. We are not interested in what you would "tolerate," or "forgive," or "understand." Answer in terms of what you personally would find acceptable.

1. It is acceptable for a husband and wife to have intercourse only if they are willing to accept the possibility of pregnancy occurring.

> Strongly agree   Slightly disagree
> Moderately agree   Moderately disagree
> Slightly agree   Strongly disagree
> (These choices follow each question.)

2. It is acceptable for the husband and wife to have intercourse even when the motivation is primarily pleasure.
3. It is acceptable for a husband and wife to have intercourse only when in the position where the husband is on top.
4. It is acceptable for a husband and wife to have intercourse in other positions in addition to the husband on top.
5. It is acceptable for the wife to make oral love to her husband (that is, mouth-penis contact).
6. It is acceptable for the husband to make oral love to his wife (that is, mouth-vagina contact).
7. It is acceptable to stimulate the anal area as part of one's marital lovemaking.
8. Anything that the married couple agree upon as sexual practice is acceptable.

Source: Composed in 1971 by Ira L. Reiss.

TABLE 11.8

Sexual Pleasure by Marital Closeness: Total Sample, Percents

MARRIED MALES

	_____ Marital Relationship _____		
	Very Close (in percent)	Fairly Close	Not Too Close, or Very Distant
Marital sex life in past year was:			
Very pleasurable	79	45	12
Mostly pleasurable	20	50	47
Neither pleasurable nor nonpleasurable	1	2	17
Mostly or very nonpleasurable	—	3	24
	100%	100%	100%

MARRIED FEMALES

	_____ Marital Relationship _____		
	Very Close	Fairly Close	Not Too Close, or Very Distant
Marital sex life in past year was:			
Very pleasurable	70	30	10
Mostly pleasurable	26	58	28
Neither pleasurable nor nonpleasurable	1	8	45
Mostly or very nonpleasurable	3	4	17
	100%	100%	100%

Source: Morton Hunt (1974):231.

Further evidence on the determinants of female orgasmic responses come from work done by Clark and Wallin (1958a, 1964, 1965) and Levinger (1966). Clark and Wallin (1965) report that where the marital quality was "positive" during the first five years of marriage, then the sexual responsiveness of the wife increased over that five-year period. Where marital quality was "negative," then the sexual responsiveness of the wife did not change much in those first five years. After the first five years of a marriage that was qualitatively negative, it was difficult to raise sexual responsiveness even if the quality of the marriage improved in later years. This information is significant because it points out the importance of the quality of marriage in the early years in terms of female sexual responsiveness. Kinsey had indicated a general increase in the wife's sexual responsiveness the longer she was married. If we accept the findings of Clark and Wallin, then we must specify Kinsey's finding of a steady increase in female satisfaction and say it holds mostly for marriages that have an overall positive quality in the early years.

The Clark and Wallin data came from the original Burgess and Wallin data which we have used in earlier chapters. Their sample was not a representative sample, but rather consisted of 1,000 engaged couples in Chicago, most of whom married and have been followed up to the late 1960s. The data are valuable because of the longitudinal aspect—although the nonrandomness of the sample makes generalization hazardous. We can still utilize such findings to stimulate further testing and can derive fruitful hypotheses about relationships from such analyses.

One other study that throws light on factors productive of female orgasm and of sexual satisfaction of both husband and wife can be found in some of Lee Rainwater's (1966) work. Rainwater looked at lower-class husbands and wives who were in marriages where housework was jointly taken care of by sharing of chores and compared them with married couples who played more segregated roles wherein the wife did the traditional housework and the husband did the traditional male work of breadwinning and repairs around the house. The findings indicated that couples in joint-role relationships reported more female orgasm and more male *and* female sexual satisfaction in marriage than did couples involved in segregated roles. Further, the segregated couples viewed sexual relationships more in terms of a means of achieving "relief," and joint-role couples viewed sexual relationships more as an expression of closeness.

Here again, then, one sees the necessity to view sexuality in the context of the overall marriage. Of course, one can argue that it is marital happiness that produces both the desire to share roles and the ability to have more sexual enjoyment. My

Photo by Ivan Kalman.

own position is that it is a two-way street with marital satisfaction in general being the first important causal factor to affect sexual enjoyment (this fits with Clark and Wallin's findings on the early years of marriage) and then sexual enjoyment reacting back on marital satisfaction.

There may well be significant social-class differences in not only the quality and quantity of marital sexuality but in the ways in which sexuality relates to the overall quality of the marriage. We know from Kinsey, and more recently from Westoff and Hunt, that the higher-educated groups do have higher frequencies of coitus and more female orgasm. The image of the lower classes as being a haven of sexual orgies and high levels of satisfactions does not seem correct (Rubin, 1976). Rainwater compared lower and middle classes and found significantly higher levels of sexual satisfaction in the middle classes. What leads the general public astray in this judgment is the early age at which premarital sexuality can occur. In poverty areas one can find ten-year-olds copulating and five- or six-year-olds whose vocabulary includes as many sexual terms as some college students'. It is this openness of sexuality and the early beginning that lead to the conclusion of high levels of marital satisfaction in coitus. That does not follow because, as we have seen, the quality of a marriage is a key determinant of marital sexual satisfaction, and we know that the lower classes have more marital problems than the higher-educated classes. This is due in part to their lack of financial resources to handle health problems and to the discrimination that makes getting jobs difficult. Divorce, desertion, and separation rates are much higher as we approach poverty levels (see Chapter 12). The social context and the marital context of the lower-class life-style make sexual satisfaction more problematic than it is at higher educational levels.

The old familiar double standard can be clearly seen in the area of marital sexuality. The differential gender-role requirements for male and female sexuality increase the likelihood of females more than males reporting indifference to sexuality. Reporting on data gathered in the 1940s Burgess and Wallin (1953) indicated that 26 percent of the wives and 10 percent of the husbands (married about five years) reported that their premarital sexual attitude was one of disgust, aversion, or indifference. About half the married people said the husband was more passionate than the wife. Only between 8 and 17 percent said the wife was more passionate than the husband. (It is interesting that more husbands said this than did wives.) About 80 percent of the husbands said their wives had at times refused coitus, and only 27 percent of the wives said husbands refused coitus; 27 percent of the wives and 7 percent of the husbands said they never or only sometimes had orgasm. One should keep in mind that the husbands' lower refusal of intercourse and higher orgasm rates may well be due to the fact that they initiate coitus when they are in the mood. Wives generally respond to their husbands' initiative more often than openly initiating sexuality themselves. If the initiative were reversed, I would expect more male refusal and more male orgasmic failure.

Hunt's (1974) more recent data would argue for more similarity in recent years between husbands and wives, and also would indicate more positive orientation to sexuality by females. But the significant point is that there is still a gender difference that reflects the double-standard upbringing that is part of American gender roles. Even in Hunt's data we find about four-fifths of the husbands saying they would like more frequent marital coitus and only about one-third of the wives saying this (Hunt, 1974:217). Some of this difference may be due to people wanting to conform to presumed cultural norms (Levinger, 1966; Wallin and Clark, 1958a). Nevertheless, we should not fool ourselves into believing that because we now realize that females can be encouraged to be as interested in sexuality as are males, we thus have achieved that state of equality. It would be valuable to examine couples that are most similar in sexual desires and overall orientations and see how distinct they are from couples with large female male differences. One factor that appears to account for perceived similarity in sexual desire and performance in a marriage is marital happiness. Happier couples perceive more similarity in preferred frequency of coitus (Wallin and Clark, 1958b). There are still many sexually maladjusted couples, and sex therapy is now one of the most rapidly growing occupations in the country (Kaplan, 1974; Masters, Johnson, and Kolodny, 1977, 1980).

The reader might have noticed that although some of the studies do talk of male sexual enjoyment, the study of orgasm focuses almost exclusively upon the female. In part this may be a reflection of the interest of the almost exclusively male researchers, and in part it may reflect the cultural emphasis upon female orgasmic performance as problematic and male orgasmic performance as nonproblematic. According to our culture, males are not supposed to have orgasmic difficulties. Only in recent years have the facts of male orgasmic problems become better known (Masters and Johnson, 1970; Kaplan, 1974). It now appears that males quite commonly have at least occasional failures of erection and orgasm. As noted above, Burgess and Wallin reported 7 percent of the husbands with serious orgasmic problems during the first five years of marriage.

Our culture stresses a "tough" male attitude to sexuality. A male is not encouraged to talk about being scared during his first act of intercourse, about erection difficulties, or about premature ejaculation problems. The male is supposed to be relaxed, cavalier, confident, and hedonistic. Fear, anxiety, and performance difficulties are not discussed. The female role is quite different since her role has been, in the past, defined as a more submissive one. Thus, she is supposed to be less aggressive, and she can display fear and anxiety and performance difficulties. Most research has used the gender-role differences as if they represented reality, rather than as stereotypes to be investigated to see how commonly people fit them. Perhaps in the next few years we shall begin to see more complete studies designed to better understand male-female sexual differences and similarities. We can make a start in this direction by studies that integrate findings like those on the importance of husband's occupational success for marital satisfaction and the influence of marital satisfaction on sexual satisfaction. Thus, interestingly, a man's job and his wife's orgasm can be related! How does a woman's job affect her own and her husband's sexual life? This type of integration of ideas regarding both genders and the place of occupational influence is what we need to investigate.

One interesting aspect of marital sexuality is the increased emphasis on the sexual rights of wives. Some people have argued that marriage is a form of prostitution and that women sell their bodies for room and board. The importance of love in marriage, the evidence of greater sexual equality within marriage than outside of marriage, and the coital refusal rate by females all point to the exaggeration of such a view. Nevertheless, there is strong emphasis on the need for sexual equality in marriage. I recall attending a conference in California in the summer of 1972, where a woman presented the argument that wives should take a break each day and set aside 45 minutes for a relaxed session of masturbation. The emphasis here was on the right to self-enjoyment and the need for a break from household chores. Some women at this conference pointed out that they had several small children around the house and that this would present difficulties in being able to set aside a 45-minute period each day for masturbation. The point here is not the practicality of that situation but the fact that such proposals are one of many signs of a movement toward sexual equalitarianism both inside and outside of marriage (see Schwartz, 1973; and Laws and Schwartz, 1977).

There is also a point to be grasped here regarding the potential of new sexual tyrannies or dogmas. The demand that all wives have daily masturbation sessions or that they experiment with certain other types of sexuality can be just as narrow and dogmatic as the older view that wives should not enjoy sexuality too much. In both cases there is a singular model that is set down, and there is pressure for all to conform to one model. Those who for one reason or another do not conform are often viewed as "uptight." This is a far cry from freedom to find one's own sexual life-style even if that entails a different approach than what is in vogue. I shall comment further on this in the concluding chapter of this book.

Finally, we should bear in mind that the trends of increased sexual activity in marriage coincided quite closely with the trends we previously discussed regarding increased premarital sexual activity. The time of World War I and the time of the Vietnam War seemed to be the two key periods. Milder changes were occurring at the time of World War II. This similarity in marital and premarital sexual trends supports our basic position that such changes in sexuality reflect basic societal changes which impact on gender roles in the areas of male–female occupational participation, male–female political power, male–female educational activities, and male–female family life. The basic institutional changes produce gender-role changes in what is expected of a man and a woman, and some of these basic gender-role aspects influence, among other things, the sexuality aspect of gender roles. This simple causal picture should afford one a paradigm for gender-role changes that may help to better understand the causal pathways of change in our society in this century.

Extramarital Sexual Relationships

The emotional and intimate aspects of marital sexuality ensure that the occurrence of extramarital sexuality will be viewed by most people as a serious threat to the marital relationship. Extramarital intercourse is perceived by many as a possible beginning of a competitive relationship and as a penetration of the intimate boundaries of the marriage. Thus it is not surprising that many people assert that extramarital sexuality is always "bad" for marriage. But little account is taken of the type of marriage or of the type of extramarital relationship one is evaluating. Also, consequences are not carefully examined as to probability of their occurrence under various circumstances. The reaction to extramarital sexuality is more emotional than cognitive. Extramarital sexuality, in most societies, is more strongly condemned than is premarital sexuality. The National Opinion Research Center (NORC) sample (1977) and the Levitt and Klassen (1974) national sample indicated that over 70 percent of adult Americans feel extramarital coitus is "always wrong," and about another 15 percent believe it is "almost always wrong."

BASIC RESEARCH FINDINGS

Kinsey's research affords us some baseline figures on extramarital coitus. Table 11.9 presents the overall trend data. The data on females indicate that in the 1940s over one quarter of the females had at least one extramarital affair before they were forty years old. The data on males are not as precisely broken down, but they do indicate that about half the males had one extramarital affair by the time they were forty. There was a social-class difference with lower-educated males starting extramarital coitus sooner after marriage and then declining in this activity over the years. Higher-educated males waited ten years to become fully involved, but by that time they were the most active. Hunt (1974) reports similar findings.

One must remember that most of the Kinsey interviews were taken in the 1940s and the people who were forty or over at the time of the interview (and thus made up the subjects on whom the above statistics were calculated) were born sometime around 1900 and would today be about eighty years old. This raises the question

TABLE 11.9
Accumulative Incidence of Extramarital Coitus for Females

AGE	BORN BEFORE 1900	BORN 1900–1909	BORN 1910–1919	BORN 1920–1929
		(percentage)		
18			10	9
19		4	7	10
20	2	3	5	9
25	4	8	10	12
30	10	16	19	
35	18	26	25	
40	22	30		
45	21	40		

Note: To compare husbands and wives, one can observe that during ages 36 to 40, 28% of the husbands and 17% of the wives had extramarital coitus. For Kinsey's sample this was one of the high rate five-year periods of a marriage (Kinsey et al. (1948):412; 585; Kinsey et al. (1953):439)
Source: Alfred C. Kinsey et al. (1953):442.

of trends—do the trends in extramarital coitus match those in premarital and marital coitus? Is there more extramarital coitus today?

Table 11.9 indicates that there was a rise in extramarital coitus among those born in the first decade of the twentieth century. This is comparable to the premarital and marital sexuality trends. If such trends reflect basic overall changes in gender roles, these changes should be evidenced in all types of human sexual interaction. It is significant that, although the Kinsey trends began in the same birth decade on all three types of heterosexual behavior, in the case of marital and extramarital rates the rise seems to have continued on into later birth decades unlike the case of premarital coitus.

There are correlations between premarital and extramarital rates for females. Kinsey et al. (1953:Chap. 10) reports that 29 percent of the female nonvirgins experienced extramarital coitus, while only 13 percent of the premarital virgins did so. If premarital experiences influence extramarital experiences, it is reasonable to expect that process to take time to allow for those with premarital experience to marry and then gradually become extramaritally involved. Thus the rates for extramarital coitus may well rise later and at a different pace than those for premarital coitus.

The question of more recent trends in extramarital coitus in the late 1960s is more difficult to answer. When we consider the rise in divorce that occurred beginning in 1963 and continued up to date, we have reason to expect a rise in extramarital coitus. The evidence indicates that particularly after physical separation has occurred but before the official divorce decree, it is quite likely that extramarital intercourse will occur. Hunt (1974:260) reports that 52 percent of the divorced and only 17 percent of the currently married females have had extramarital coitus, and these higher rates for divorced females in part involve affairs after the marriage was broken but before the official divorce. Such intercourse is technically extramarital and thus would raise the overall percentage of married people with that experience. However, if we confine ourselves to extramarital coitus occurring in ongoing marriages where a decision to divorce has not occurred, then the rise is more problematical. There seems little evidence of change in the number of partners wives report. Kinsey et al. (1953) found 41 percent of the wives reported only one extramarital partner and the *Redbook* study (Tavris and Sadd, 1977: Chap. 4) lists 50 percent with only one partner. But Bell et al. (1975) reports a lower proportion with just one partner. Bell had a highly educated sample and this may be the reason for the greater number of partners. Judging by the outpouring of books on extramarital relationships, we have surely become more open in our discussion of this area of life. Our willingness to discuss the pro and con of an issue means that the issue is no longer sacred. There are few sacred areas left in our society today. For many generations it was assumed that extramarital sexuality was "bad" and no extensive debate on this issue occurred. Now we see clear signs that the debate is going on (Ellis, 1972; Hunt, 1969; Neubeck, 1969; Libby, 1973; Mazur, 1973; Ziskin and Ziskin, 1973). Such attitudinal debates on *premarital* coitus were common in the decades preceding the increase in premarital female nonvirginity.

Regarding actual increases in extramarital coitus, the Hunt (1974: Chap. 5) study is one of the few with relevant recent data. Hunt finds an increase in extra-marital coitus, predominantly for younger females under age twenty-five. This increase tends toward greater similarity in male and female rates in this under twenty-five group. He does not find any changes in older couples. However, the Hunt sample is not one to inspire confidence, and thus we must take his findings with a grain of salt. The *Redbook* study (Tavris and Sadd, 1977:116) reported that 30 percent of the wives were experienced by age thirty, and 40 percent by age forty. This is higher than the Kinsey rates in Table 11.9. The research work by Pietropinto and Simenauer (1977) displays a male rate of extramarital intercourse similar to that of Kinsey. Christensen (1973) studied college-student attitudes in nine cultures. He reports high acceptance in Denmark and Sweden compared to the United States. Denmark and Sweden also experienced an earlier public debate on these issues (see Chapter 17). I think it is fair to assert that extramarital coitus is today more opened up to public debate, and the likelihood is that a rise either has occurred or will shortly occur in extramarital behavior, particularly for college educated wives.

THE DOUBLE STANDARD IN EXTRAMARITAL COITUS

The question arises regarding why females are more restricted in extramarital sexuality than are males. Starting with the code of Hammurabi, it has been clear that males are granted greater sexual privileges outside of marriage than are females. In good measure the explanation we discussed for such a general double standard in Chapter 3 applies equally well here. We pointed out that males have been in power in most societies, and thus social codes will enhance their sexual op-portunities and privileges, rather than those of the female. In this vein it seems quite possible that the attachment of the female to the child-rearing role is a key basis of the double standard. This is perhaps most vividly demonstrated in the Trobriand Islands (Malinowski, 1929). The reader will recall that the Trobrianders have an equalitarian approach to premarital sexuality, but after marriage the male may kill his wife if she has extramarital coitus, and the wife can do very little if her husband has extramarital coitus. What causes this radical change after marriage?

One common answer that historians and others have offered is that it was fear of illegitimate offspring that supported the double standard in extramarital coitus. The Trobrianders are an excellent case for testing this idea because they did not know that sexual intercourse was causally related to pregnancy. They believed that pregnancy occurred when a spirit entered an opening in the woman's body, and this usually occurred while she was swimming. Males who had been away on fishing and other expeditions for a year or more would not react to the pregnancy of their wives. It will be recalled that children of eight or ten years of age often copulate in the Trobriand Islands. The natives would view this as proof that coitus has no causal relation to pregnancy because these children never became pregnant. So we have here an example of a society that is double standard (extramaritally) and yet does not believe in the causal relation of sexual intercourse to pregnancy;

thus, the fear of illegitimate offspring cannot be the reason for this situation. What then is the explanation?

My explanation would involve the tie of the female to the child-rearing role. The culture defines that role as demanding close attention and supervision, and thus extramarital relationships may be viewed as disruptive. In addition, it is a role that is outside of the high-prestige and high-power positions in the society. Thus, conformity pressures and expectations of loyalty are strong. These two aspects of the child-rearing role then reinforce the restrictions on the female's extramarital coitus. The power differential prevents the same logic of "essential tasks" being used to restrict males. After all, one could argue that since males do the essential economic work in the society, that any extramarital sexuality would have to be excluded for it might interfere with their important role performance. That is a logical position, but it is not part of the culture because males are in power, and thus it is they who restrict others and not vice versa.

If our reasoning is sound here, then it should follow that as females move into other roles than the parental one, the restrictions on their extramarital coitus should be modified. The same should occur as they gain in societal prestige and power. There is evidence that working women are more dominant in their marriages, and that career women have higher rates of extramarital coitus (Tavris and Sadd, 1977). But no conclusive test of this idea has been carried out. A check of just the percentage of females working would not be sufficient. For a particular group one would need to know how powerful was the female part of the population, how prestigious were their jobs, and whether they were freed from child-rearing tasks or were merely taking on additional work roles.

PERSPECTIVES ON EXTRAMARITAL SEXUALITY

Murdock's (1949) cross-cultural work affords some understanding of extra-marital coitus in other societies. Murdock found that only 20 percent of the societies allowed extramarital coitus. However, a closer examination revealed that about two-thirds of the societies allowed extramarital coitus if the partner was a potential future mate. For example, a husband could have intercourse with his wife's sister because she could become his second wife or she could become his only wife (if his present wife died). Thus, the general proposition that Kingsley Davis put forth decades ago (1939) still seems valid. A sexual custom is accepted to the degree that it is perceived as supporting the marriage and family institutions in that society. Having extramarital intercourse with a possible future mate can on occasion act as an integrative and stabilizing element in the marital institution. Nevertheless, there does appear to be more caution in most cultures regarding extramarital sexuality compared to premarital sexuality. There is general agreement that one must take care not to disrupt the ongoing marriage, for that is important not only to the married individuals but also to their kin and children. It is this greater involvement of others that I believe is one of the major reasons for the greater reluctance to accept extramarital coitus. Surely premarital sexuality also involves others, but there is no existing marriage nor any children involved that one must consider, and thus a more permissive air generally prevails. I do not mean to imply any justification for the greater censure of extramarital coitus; rather, I am pointing out that it is a more complex act in that it involves the lives of a greater number of people both directly and indirectly.

A word or two in the definition and measurement of extramarital sexuality may well be helpful at this point. Commonly, one thinks of extramarital sexuality as meaning only sexual intercourse involving a married person with someone other than their marital partner. However, a good deal of extramarital sexuality involves only petting and kissing. Kinsey (1953) accidentally found that extramarital petting was quite common, but since it was unexpected, he made no systematic investigation. I am suggesting that there is in extramarital sexuality an analogous situation to the "technical virginity" situation that still somewhat exists premaritally (see Reiss 1960; Chap. 9). Premaritally, we note that some females will tend to view themselves as virgins despite the fact that they have had extensive noncoital experience involving breast and genital petting. The stress on the importance of virginity, together with the presence of high temptation, encourages the development of such behavior patterns as "technical virginity." Extramaritally, I believe the same situation prevails. There is a stress on avoiding extramarital intercourse, and yet there are many opportunities that may be present to tempt one. This analogous set of cross pressures produces an analogous outcome where married people may engage in sensuous dancing, in erotic kissing, in breast and genital manipulation, but may still view themselves as "faithful" and not "adulterous." A total of 10 percent of Hunt's (1974:275) married sample reported extramarital petting but not coitus.

It would be most valuable to measure extramarital sexuality by a scale similar to my premarital scale. Such a scale could ask for the degree of acceptance of sexual behaviors under conditions of little or strong affection for the extramarital partner, under conditions of a happy or unhappy marriage, and with or without consent of the marital partner. It may well be that for extramarital sexuality one will find that the lack of strong affection for the extramarital partner will promote *greater* acceptance—in short, a reversal of what we found on premarital sexuality. This would fit with the emphasis that societies tend to place on protecting the marital relationship. In premarital sexuality the presence of affection helps ensure that marriage may result and thus is considered a favorable feature; in extramarital coitus the presence of affection may be considered an added risk that may break the existing marriage and may thus decrease the acceptability of the act. Christensen's research gives support to this view (1962, 1973).

Another important feature that distinguishes extramarital intercourse is the happiness of the current marriage. It would seem advisable to ask people what they feel is acceptable extramaritally, separately under the condition of a happy marriage and separately under the condition of an unhappy marriage. Sponaugle (1976), in a 1975 study of 117 married individuals representative of the city of Minneapolis, found that one of the most important factors in the acceptance of extramarital sexuality was the happiness of the marriage. Eighty-seven percent of the happiest persons were against extramarital sexuality and 57 percent of the moderately and less satisfied persons were against it. In a study of behavior Bell et al. (1975) found in an higher-educated sample that 20 percent of the happily married and 55 percent of the unhappily married females experienced extramarital coitus.

One other distinction is important to make at the outset. Extramarital sexuality not only covers a broad range of sexual behaviors and types of marriages, but it involves at least two major types of marital involvement in the extramarital relationship. First is the traditional variety of extramarital sexuality, that is, secretive and nonconsensual. Second is the extramarital relation which is known and perhaps consensual. Kinsey et al. (1953) reports that 40 percent of the females who were having extramarital coitus either knew their husbands were aware of that fact or believed they were. Hunt (1974:269) reports that 20 percent were sure their husbands knew of their affairs. Thus, the past is not confined to only nonconsensual or secretive extramarital sexuality. Granted it is not fully consensual just because one believes that a mate knows about the affair. Before it can be called fully consensual the couple should have arrived at what are the acceptable guidelines for an extramarital relationship (Ziskin and Ziskin, 1973). Consensual extramarital coitus involves only a small proportion of married couples. Nevertheless, it is a crucial dimension in evaluating extramarital relationships.

Table 11.10 illustrates four major types of extramarital relationships classified by the divisions of affection and consensuality. The happiness of the marriage can be taken into account by placing an A or a B after each type. Thus, one can measure extramarital sexual permissiveness by asking which, if any, of the four

TABLE 11.10

Types of Extramarital Sexual Relationships*

	LOVE EMPHASIS	PLEASURE EMPHASIS
CONSENSUAL (Acceptable to husband and wife)	1	2
NON-CONSENSUAL (No agreement between husband and wife)	3	4

*One should add the letter "A" to each of the four types when they occur in a happy marriage and the letter "B" if they occur in an unhappy marriage.
The questions which allow one to classify respondents would read as follows: Under which of the following conditions is extramarital coitus acceptable:
A Husband is involved in a happy marriage, and in the extramarital relationship there is:

  (a) a love emphasis and the relation is approved by his mate.
  (b) a pleasure emphasis and the relation is approved by his mate.
  (c) a love emphasis and the relation is not revealed to his mate.
  (d) a pleasure emphasis and the relation is not revealed to his mate.
Answer the same four questions if the husband is involved in an unhappy marriage.
Answer all the same questions for a wife.
The questions can also be asked for "oneself" and "one's mate."
Source: Composed by Ira L. Reiss (1978)—a revision of Reiss (1973).

types within a happy or an unhappy marriage is acceptable. The eight questions should form a Guttman-type scale similar to the one used in premarital sexual permissiveness.

Four Types of Extramarital Relationships

Table 11.10 presents four basic types of extramarital relationships. Let us look at them in sequence.

TYPE ONE: CONSENSUAL AND LOVE-ORIENTED

This is probably the rarest of the four types. This is so because it involves a consensual extramarital love relationship. The proportion of the 50 million married couples who have discussed extramarital sexual relationships *and* have agreed upon some set of conditions under which they are acceptable must be rather small. There are no accurate figures but I would estimate that it is probably somewhere between 5 and 10 percent of all married couples. In a 1976 national survey of some 2,000 males aged eighteen to forty-nine, 21 percent approved of a sexually open marriage—14 percent approved "somewhat," and 7 percent approved "strongly" (*Playboy* Report, 1979:5). I believe this percent would be less if one examined only married men and asked them only about their own marriage.

Now we must subdivide this small segment into those who would accept an extramarital love relationship and those who would restrict the agreement to only pleasure relationships. While I do think that many people would understand that a sexual relationship might occur if one fell in love—I do not think very many of these understanding people would accept it or want it in their own marriage. Generally, an extramarital love relationship would be felt as considerably more threatening than a pleasure-centered extramarital relationship. I believe it would take someone who accepted a "diffuse" conception of love to react differently. One would have to accept the reality of loving more than one sexual partner. As we discussed in Chapter 5, we do traditionally accept multiple, simultaneous love for parents and children but not for heterosexual partners. The folk wisdom is that multiple heterosexual love creates problems of competition that are more difficult to manage than multiple love of parents and children. Whether true or not, this is a popular perspective and would further limit the number of people who would be able to accept extramarital relationships that involved love.

If a person is in love with his or her mate, but feels that intimacy needs are not being satisfied in the relationship, then I believe that the lack of intimacy-need fulfillment would increase the possibility of an extramarital love relationship. Under such a condition, one could then fall in love and more easily have a relationship that would satisfy a different set of intimacy needs. In a sense, in such a case, there is more "room" for another love relationship to occur. In Chapter 5 we divided love into the categories of diffuse and focused and noted that diffuse love involved smaller amounts of intimacy needs being satisfied by one's mate. I am asserting here that those with a diffuse love relationship with their mate (compared to those with a focused love) would be more willing to accept a second love relationship.

Let us now briefly examine two kinds of extramarital affairs that fit our Type One extramarital relationship by being both consensual and loving: (1) intimate friendship and (2) group marriage.

Ramey coined the term "intimate friendship." He (1972, 1976) defines intimate friendship as basically friendship plus sexuality. Ramey has an evolutionary view of dyadic forms. He believes that traditional male-dominated marriage changes first to swinging (to be discussed shortly) and more equalitarian marital forms, and later develops into intimate friendship which in turn evolves into communal living and group marriage. He feels the level of trust and responsibility is highest in group marriages.

In simple terms, an intimate friendship develops when two couples who are friends either deliberately, or more likely accidentally, become sexually involved with each other's mates. This may happen at the end of a long evening of partying or spontaneously in other situations. Intimate friendship differs from swinging in that it is much more of a person-centered type of behavior than the usual recreational swinging. However, it should be noted that there are sizable minorities of swingers who also prefer person-centered affectionate relationships (Gilmartin, 1978).

One common way that group marriage develops can be seen in the following case study, based upon the experiences of a graduate student. This student and his wife met another couple with whom they got along very well. Both couples had children, and they interacted with each other as families and as couples. One night after an evening of partying, the two couples were dancing with each other's mates. They drifted into separate rooms and became involved sexually with each other. Such sexual encounters have occurred throughout history. What has changed is the range of choices now available. Formerly, there were several conventional choices available. The couples could fight physically and verbally and never see each other again. Secondly, the two couples could divorce and either go their own way or remarry the other person. They could discuss the issue and plan to continue their friendship but never let that happen again. Another choice would be to establish an intimate-friendship relation and continue the sexual exchanges but live in separate homes. Today there is one other logical alternative that has rarely been acted upon and this is: The two couples can live together in one household and share each other's mates sexually. This was the outcome in the case cited above. When that alternative is elected, one has created a group marriage. Thus a simple sexual encounter at a party may be part of a more general process possibly leading to intimate-friendship arrangements and perhaps ultimately to group marriage.

The above is not the only way to enter into a group marriage, but it is one common way. A courtship phase is part of entering group marriage just as it is part of entering monogamous marriage. Most group marriages involve two couples and so four people have to get along before group marriage is possible. Some testing of that tetradic relationship is needed. Some people today consciously examine other couples with group marriage in mind. Others, like the case cited, accidentally drift into such a relationship. Let us look further now at the nature of group marriage, its life-style, its longevity, and its likely future. Group marriage involves a type of extramarital sexuality that is unique. Nevertheless, it may well throw light on the larger society that gave birth to it.

The most ambitious and the only major study of group marriage was carried out by Larry and Joan Constantine (1973). They define marriage in general as involving intimacy and commitment to another with the assumption of continuance over time. They studied unions of three or more partners which had the qualities of intimacy, commitment, and expectation of continuance. They estimated that in the entire country there probably are not more than 1,000 group marriages. This rarity of group marriage is not peculiar to the United States. As we noted in Part I of the book, polygamous marriages are not rare if one means a single male and multiple females. There are also a few cultures with a single female and multiple male partners. But if one is speaking of multiple mates of both genders involved in one marriage, then we indeed have a very unusual type of union.

Murdock (1949), in his examination of 250 societies, reports none of them with such group marriages as the common form. In fact only one, the Kaingang in Brazil, had group marriages (between brothers from one family and sisters from another family) as a rare but acceptable form. The reason why marriages with multiple mates of both genders are rare is basically a matter of complexity. Going from a two-person group to a four-person group increases the number of relationships (going each way) from two to twelve, and that sixfold increase in complexity is a major hurdle to a stable existence. We noted in Part I that in polygynous cultures very often each wife would live in her own house with her own children, and one wife would often be a love choice who would help select the additional wives. In short, we saw the high degree of regulation that seemed to be required to make the complex polygynous relationships work.

In a group marriage of two females and two males, the situation is far more complex than a polygynous marriage of one male and three females. In the group marriage each individual has access to each other, and thus the segregation solution adopted in polygyny is nowhere near as workable. The equalitarian group marriage as occurs in America adds even more complexity, for there cannot be any single person who organizes or dominates the group. In a two-person group equality is difficult to achieve, but it can be done. In a four-person group, the lack of structure adds strains to the group's continuance. The questions arise as to who makes which decisions and who does which tasks and who has access to whom and for what. An additional complexity is the presence of children. About 80 percent of the Constantines' groups had children. When, in addition to all this, a high degree of intimacy is sought among all members of the group, the difficulty becomes even more apparent.

It is interesting to note that in the thirty-four group marriages that the Constantines studied, there were tendencies for a structure to develop which was similar to that of the polygamous societies we have discussed. For example, in the area of sexuality one most common structure was to take turns sleeping with the various partners. This solution avoids a personal choice constantly being made and minimizes jealousy. It is a common solution in polygynous societies.

Another organizing principle was seen in the fact that of the six triads (three-person groups) only one consisted of two men and one woman. The other five were two females and one male. This reflects our culture and probably results from the fact that males who are trained to be dominant and possessive find it more difficult to share one mate than do females who are trained to be more submissive and adaptable.

Another structural factor is that two-thirds of the groups consisted of two couples, and very often each of these couples was legally married before meeting the other couple. The dyadic emphasis of our culture shows through this common type of group marriage. Also, if the judgment that group marriage often results from "intimate friendships" is sound, then this emphasis on tetrads is what one would expect.

Let's look at some of the characteristics and problems of group marriage in the Constantines' report. First and foremost was the fragility of the group marriage. The Constantines might have had 100 groups instead of 34 if group marriage had been more stable. They had their own trailer and were ready to travel to interview the people involved in a group marriage as soon as they heard about such a union. Nevertheless, they were often unable to arrive quickly enough. Two-thirds of the group marriages broke up before they could get their interviewing completed. Using the group marriages that they did contact, which may well be a long-lived set of group marriages, the Constantines report that after one year only 44 percent of the group marriages were intact and after three years only 17 percent were intact. Thus, the average life span of a group marriage is between six and twelve months.

The people who enter into group marriage come from a nonreligious background and are liberal on politics and high on education and income. They are inner-directed and autonomous people who are desirous of increasing their experience of intimacy with people. The main reasons for seeking out group marriage were a desire for personal fulfillment and growth and a seeking of companionship. Four out of five of these people had been in encounter groups before, and thus their seeking of ways of getting in touch with their feelings and to grow was not a new thing.

One difficulty encountered was the tendency of the two dyads to resist a full blending into a tetrad. In short, each of the original dyads seemed to give their original mates preference and seemed to express deeper love for them. In this regard it is interesting to note that in 60 percent of the cases when a tetrad broke up, the original dyads stayed intact. This sort of "pair bonding," as it is called in animal studies, has strong parallels in many of our close animal relatives (Money and Ehrhardt, 1972).

The structuring of the group causes many difficulties. Because so many people are involved, frequent group meetings to set down explicit guidelines were needed. The need to get four people to agree to a solution instead of just two people was one major difficulty. The Constantines' respondents believed in a "no-lose" method (Gordon, 1970), which meant that everyone must agree on the solution. The high value placed on revealing feelings to each other also placed a strain on the group. Group members did advocate making "I" statements concerning how one felt, rather than "you" statements which place blame on others for one's feelings. For example: "I feel upset when there is loud music playing and I am trying to read" rather than "Shut the damn radio off, you idiot! Can't you see I'm trying to read!" These approaches no doubt reflect their psychological background which comes out of the "humanistic psychology" school (Child, 1973; Back, 1972) and follow the lines of thinkers like Abraham Maslow (1962) and Carl Rogers (1972).

As one might expect, jealousy was a major problem, and sexuality was often the center of it. Even in cultures with a tradition of polygamous marriages jealousy is present, and thus it is no surprise to find it here in a group with a monogamous tradition. More than half the respondents had extramarital coitus before getting involved with group marriage, so they were not a sexually naive group. Desire for sexual variety was listed as one important reason for getting involved in group marriage. Half the groups used the fixed-partner rotation schema as a way of handling jealousy. Frequent discussion of the sexual problem seemed to help in gaining more flexible arrangements. Group sexuality was rare, and dyadic sexuality was the rule. Nevertheless, it is important to state that sexual involvements outside of the group partners were very common. This fits with cross-cultural findings. Most polygamous cultures find that the predominant basis for multiple mates is *not* sexual variety but need for economic cooperation. In most such societies outside affairs are the source of sexual variety. In group marriage the aim was to gain sexual variety within a multiple-mate marriage, but that also often seemed to fail to satisfy sufficiently. The achievement of more pleasure may increase the desire for pleasure and thereby maintain the same gap between desire and achievement.

The Constantines have their own theory of jealousy and how to control it (1973:Chap. 16). They view jealousy as a result of fear of loss of control over the other person. They argue that if one has multiple sources of sexuality, the fear of loss will be reduced. Also, they suggest a reduction of the possessive approach to one's mate. Basically, they feel that we should each view ourselves as unique and thus realize that we can never really be replaced by another person. The Constantines offer no empirical evidence of the validity of their theory, and I for one have serious doubts about its efficacy. Without going into great depth it seems to me that although one may indeed be unique and irreplaceable, someone else may be viewed as *better*. Thus, I fail to see how fear of loss can be relieved by this conception of uniqueness. Also, while it is true that jealousy can be contained by reducing dependency (such as for sexual needs) on one's mate, to the extent that one does that, one may well reduce the need for the relationship itself. Jealousy is a complex emotion. We need to do some very careful thinking and some strategic research in this area. Judging from the almost universal presence of the jealous response (Maison, 1974), it is likely that we shall find it difficult to do more than contain and minimize this reaction as long as we have close interpersonal relationships (Mazur, 1973; Clanton and Smith, 1977). Even in cultures that bring women up to expect that there will be other wives, one finds jealous responses common. In Iran an insult to a married woman may involve a wish that she have a *havou*. A havou is a second wife and is often the wife a husband loves. Such competition is viewed as something negative even when expected.

One final point on group marriage concerns the impact on children. How do children react to such complex unions? Children lived with the adults in the same house and knew about the sexual sharing that occurred. The children reflected the dominance of the original dyad. They viewed themselves as having a family within a family. Their biological parents and themselves made up in the *inner* family, and the second dyad and their children made up the *outside* family. Again, the similarity to preliterate groups is striking. In preliterate groups, children may call all those of one's parents' age "Mother" and "Father" but still think differently of the mother and father who reared them. In terms of psychological effects, the Constantines found no striking benefits or costs. The children seemed able to take in stride group-marriage living.

The group-marriage form of Type One extramarital sexual relationships seems unlikely to become widespread. My judgment is that intimate friendships would also be restricted to a small number of couples. I would estimate that only about 1 or 2 percent of all married couples would ever be involved in intimate friendships.

TYPE TWO: CONSENSUAL AND PLEASURE-CENTERED

Here, too, we are speaking of a small percent of all extramarital affairs. Although I do believe that Type Two is a larger group than Type One, I would estimate that only about 5 percent of all the couples would ever be so involved. I assume Type Two to be more popular because it does not have the competitive threat of a second love relationship. But I assume it to be rare because it does involve consensuality, and thus involves the difficult process of getting both mates to agree. In the early 1970s two lawyers interviewed some 300 married couples who had reached consensual agreement on extramarital relationships (Ziskin and Ziskin, 1973). They found that the most common type of agreement was that the extramarital relationship should not involve love and that it should not interfere with the married couple's day-to-day lives. This sort of agreement aims at giving additional sources of satisfaction to one or both partners but in a fashion that does not alter the basic marital relationship. Most such couples do not want any reporting back about affairs, even though they accept that affairs may occur. Some psychological therapists present this as the type of affair with the lowest risk (Livsey, 1979).

Given our double-standard culture, it is likely that more wives would give their husbands permission of this sort than vice versa. Even when agreements are equalitarian, husbands may well be more possessive of their wives than vice versa. Table 11.11 on page 298 gives some data in support of this perspective. This is Kinsey data but I suspect it still has much validity today. Note that twice as high a percent of women said their spouse's extramarital affair was important in the divorce than said their own affair had a major effect on getting a divorce (27 percent vs. 14 percent). For men the difference is even more dramatic (51 percent vs. 18 percent). Note also that almost twice as many men as women said their spouse's extramarital affair was a major factor in the divorce (51 percent vs. 27 percent).

Another subgroup of Type Two people involves "swinging." This phenomenon has received so much attention that it should be stressed here that I assume that private extramarital affairs (such as described above) are more common among Type Two people than are swinging affairs. I believe this is so because the private affair is easier to compartmentalize and keep separate from one's marriage and such "distance" is what most people seem to want.

Basically, swinging entails an exchange of mates between two or more married couples. In actuality single couples may also be involved in a swing, but we are not interested in that here. The location is usually one of the couple's homes, and the sexual encounters may take place separately in private rooms or together in one room. There have been many small studies of swinging, but two major studies stand out as important. One is by Gilbert Bartell (1971) and consists largely of Chicago suburban swingers, and the other is by Brian Gilmartin (1978) and consists of California swingers. Using mainly these studies, let us start by describing the typical way that couples become involved in swinging.

The Gilmartin data indicate that the couples that enter into swinging have a history of extensive premarital sexuality and often are in their second marriages. Usually, both partners have been involved in traditional extramarital affairs before entering swinging. Thus, it should be clear that two virgins who marry and who have not had extramarital coitus do not typically decide to enter swinging. In short, it is a highly permissive and very experienced group who enter swinging. The husband is most often the initiator and usually proposes swinging as a way of protecting the marriage. The argument put forth contends that traditional extramarital coitus is private and personal and therefore can lead to emotional involvements that may threaten the marriage. Swinging is public and impersonal and thus does not run such high risks. Usually the wife will not immediately accept swinging

TABLE 11.11

Reported Significant Effect of Extramarital Coitus on Divorce

Significance of Affairs in Divorce	SUBJECT'S ESTIMATE OF SIGNIFICANCE OF OWN EXTRAMARITAL EXPERIENCE		SUBJECT'S ESTIMATE OF SIGNIFICANCE OF SPOUSE'S EXTRAMARITAL EXPERIENCE	
	Reported By		*Reported By*	
	Females	*Males*	*Females*	*Males*
	Percent		Percent	
Major	14	18	27	51
Moderate	15	9	49	32
Minor	10	12	24	17
None	61	61	—	—
Number of Cases	(234)	(181)	(181)	(82)

Source: Kinsey (1953):445.

because it is quite alien to the female person-centered type of sexual upbringing. But her concern for the marriage and the persuasiveness of her husband pressure her to try it.

Both Bartell and Gilmartin report that females ultimately seem to be able to enjoy swinging more than males despite their initial hesitation. The reasons for this are multiple. Most wives do not realize that they are capable of five or six orgasms a night, and the realization of this potential is exhilarating. By the same token, their husbands realize that they themselves are capable of only two or three orgasms an evening, and this is disappointing to them. The husbands further note that most of the females are not as attractive as their fantasies had led them to believe, and they are in competition with other males for the most attractive females.

Their wives meanwhile are also learning that they can respond to orgasm with other women. This results from the fact that while the husbands are resting up, they encourage the women to bring each other to orgasm so as to help restimulate themselves. The majority of wives successfully try homosexual orgasmic experience. After a period of several months, many of the same husbands who dragged their wives into swinging find that they have to drag them out of swinging.

The above is a general description of how married couples get involved in swinging. Nevertheless, it seems there are a variety of types of people who get involved in swinging. One way of seeing this variation is to compare the Bartell sample of suburban Chicago couples with the Gilmartin California sample.

Bartell's main sample consisted of 280 swinger couples from near Chicago. Bartell and his wife used special in-depth interviews on twenty of the couples and five of the single swingers. His swingers were generally about thirty years old and almost all white. Salesmen and lawyers were the most common occupations. Overall, they were a surprisingly "conservative" group in other aspects of their life-style. For example, 40 percent admired George Wallace. They were generally strongly against marijuana. About 85 percent of them had two or three children and sent them to Sunday school. Thus, in many ways these people were typical of other suburbanites, and one would have hardly deduced that they were swingers.

One key method of contacting other swingers is to advertise in the swinger magazines that are on the newsstands today. Two-thirds of Bartell's informants made contacts that way. Bars and personal references were also used to contact swingers. Particular bars come to have a reputation for being the place to meet other swingers. Bartell points out that there is a kind of courtship process among swingers. Often there is no sexual behavior at the first meeting, and all four people must feel positive for a relationship to continue. One of the major motivations that swingers assert is the desire to improve their own sexual lives. Most swingers will say that swinging did improve their sexual life and in general did help their marriage.

Almost all the female swingers studied were on the pill, and so pregnancy was not a likely outcome. There was fear of venereal disease, but few respondents reported contracting disease during swinging. Swinging comes to be a central feature of these people's lives, and they talk endlessly about it and plan for the weekend adventure with relish. The dropout rate rises after about two years of experience. Even those who remain in were found to reduce their activity. Reasons for dropping out were varied but included fear of VD, the excessive amount of time swinging took, loss of self-esteem due to promiscuity, and many other reasons (Denfield, 1974). Boredom with marriage was given by the dropouts as one primary motive for entering swinging.

It also seemed that swinging was a way of substituting for a lack of friends. This could indicate a general lack of close friends, and perhaps boredom relates to this isolation. Of course, studying dropouts, though valuable, is not an effective way to learn what the nondropouts are like. For that let's turn to Gilmartin's study.

Gilmartin's study (1973, 1974, 1975, 1978) took place in California. It was in many ways a more carefully designed project than was the Bartell study. Gilmartin had a control group of 100 nonswinger couples, matched by age, neighborhood, income, education, and number of children with his 100 swinger couples. A total of 70 percent of both groups came from the Los Angeles area (San Fernando Valley) and the rest from the San Francisco area (East Bay). The average age was about thirty-five years old. Gilmartin located most of his couples through swinging clubs, and the rest were people known to the club members. The matched group was chosen from the exact street on which the swingers lived. The presence of a control group is a major advantage, for it affords one a basis for knowing how unusual the swinger group was. For example, when Bartell reported that 40 percent of his swingers favored George Wallace, we would be better informed if we knew what that percent was in the general neighborhoods of these people. If it was also close to 40 percent, then we would know that characteristic is not peculiar to swingers.

Gilmartin found that one of the major differences between swingers and non-swingers was in the area of permissive values. Swingers were much more likely to favor abortion reform, legalization of marijuana, and premarital coitus for their children. Thus, Gilmartin's swingers were quite a bit different from Bartell's conservative swingers. Swingers did *not* differ from the controls in terms of personal happiness scores, personal anomie, marital happiness, boredom, or drinking habits. Gilmartin checked out such possible differences because many people believe that swingers must be unhappily married or they would never try anything as far out as swinging. The evidence indicates no significant difference.

From an objective perspective, that is not surprising. We really learn very little about alternative lifestyles by simply checking happiness levels. After all, it is probably true that if we were able to compare two famous nineteenth-century figures like Jesse James and William James, we would likely find them equally happy. The important element in a life-style is what one is happy *about*, and Jesse would have been happy about being a successful robber and William about being a successful writer of psychology books. Knowing what they are happy about is surely more informative than just knowing they are equally happy. No one has probed this important area, but I suspect that one major difference between swingers and nonswingers would be that pleasure and comfort of a physical sort, in nonsexual as well as sexual areas, make up a much greater part of the happiness of swingers.

Probably the most important characteristic of Gilmartin's swingers as compared to his controls was the very high degree of autonomy of the swinger group. Swingers had fewer kin in the area, knew fewer neighbors, joined fewer organizations, were less likely to belong to a religious group, and in all these ways indicated a higher degree of independence or what we could call autonomy. It is precisely such autonomy that may provide the freedom from outside constraint necessary to feel able to get involved in swinging. Swingers need not be concerned about the possibility of kin, neighbors, or church members disapproving or discovering their activities because swingers are not part of such groups. Gilmartin (1974) ties in this important autonomy factor with my own conclusions on the importance of autonomy as an influence on premarital sexual permissiveness (see Chapter 7). Here is an example of a general proposition that may explain in part the occurrence of premarital intercourse and also extramarital intercourse of the swinging variety.

There were some interesting differences in conceptions of love and marriage in the two groups. For example, only about 20 percent of the swingers said adultery is a sign of a poor marriage, but over 60 percent of the controls said that was true. In the control group, those marriages wherein traditional extramarital sexuality was occurring were reported low on marital happiness. However, the swinger marriages were a great deal higher on marital happiness than these conventional "adulterous" control marriages. Thus, not only do the swingers think extramarital sexuality is not a factor in poor marriages, but in their case they report no loss of marital satisfaction due to swinging. They almost universally claim that "the couple that swings together clings together."

To follow out this differential conception, Gilmartin notes that swingers were much more likely than controls to view sexuality as different from love. They saw sexual relationships as something that could be enjoyed as a good in itself even though on occasion it could be combined with love. Controls were more likely to see sexuality as only justifiable if love was present in a relationship. In this same vein, casual extramarital sexuality would lead only 4 percent of the swingers to consider a divorce, whereas it would lead almost half of the controls to consider a divorce.

There are background differences that Gilmartin also comments upon. Swingers started premarital coitus earlier, and almost three times as many swinger wives were pregnant when married (39 versus 14 percent). Swingers were more likely to have been divorced. About half the swinging husbands and a third of their wives had been previously divorced, compared to less than 15 percent of the nonswingers. About one-third of the swinging couples first met each other at a "swinging singles" gathering. More swingers also reported that their parents' marriages were not happy as did the controls'. Swingers also disagreed more with their parents' basic values. Here again we find clear evidence of the strong strain toward autonomy. Swinger wives also evidence this autonomy in their higher rate of holding a job outside the home (62 to 30 percent).

It seems apparent that the swingers whom Gilmartin studied are quite a bit different from the swingers whom Bartell studied. It is not necessary to conclude that one of the studies must be invalid. My conclusion would be that there are many types of swingers. Carolyn Symonds (1968), in one of the early researches in this area, described two types of swingers. She distinguished "utopian" swingers from "recreational" swingers. Utopian swingers were more likely to be single and city people, and recreational swingers were more likely to be suburban and married people. The utopian swingers engaged in swinging because they felt it was part of personal growth and a more meaningful life-style. The recreational swingers engaged in swinging more as a means of having fun and pleasure. It seems that both Gilmartin and Bartell were dealing with largely recreational swingers. However, Bartell's group was more of a "closet" type of secret swinger, and Gilmartin's group was more of an "open" type of swinger.

How widespread is swinging? Hunt found 2 percent of his sample had at some time participated in swinging as a married couple (Hunt, 1974, p. 271), and a much smaller percent were currently participating in it. Given the heavy volunteer nature of Hunt's sample, the national average is probably lower. Gilmartin (1978:472) also estimates that about 2 percent of all married couples is the top percent likely to have tried swinging. I would agree that swingers are a small group and would add that nonswinging, private affairs make up the majority of Type Two sexual encounters. I doubt if swinging will become much more popular because it does so blatantly go against the very powerful association of sexuality with affection, and it does go against the jealousy norms of our culture due to its openness. Interestingly, males seem to be more bothered by jealousy in swinging than are females. That is what one would expect since the idea of "possessiveness" is more common for the group in power. In any case, it would be difficult for most American couples to adapt to this form of extramarital coitus. That surely does not mean that it will disappear. Judging by literary accounts, swinging in one form or another has been a feature of our society for generations—only its visibility and popularity have changed (see Wiley, 1935). In our choice-conscious society, it will remain an alternative that small proportions of the married population will elect for at least a part of their married life. How long they will stay with it is difficult to say. About two-thirds of Gilmartin's swingers had been into swinging for over two years.

One final but very important point concerns the double-standard aspects of swinging. Many people view swinging as an equalitarian activity. Both the wife and the husband enjoy freedom in sexual adventures at the swing, and both are primarily concerned with their own marriage. However, this appearance is deceptive. The first evidence of a double standard is in the entré to swinging groups. It seems that a physically attractive female is always welcome, whereas the requirement for males is mainly that they bring an attractive female. Males are the instigators in most swinging activities and also are the ones who decide whether to get out of swinging. Perhaps the most obvious evidence of the emphasis on male sexual pleasure is in the area of homosexuality. The majority of wives in both Bartell's and Gilmartin's studies became involved in homosexual orgasm. As discussed earlier, lesbian behavior is encouraged by the males for their own sexual pleasure. But note that no male homosexual behavior is allowed. In fact, to move in the direction of male homosexuality is probably the best way to be excluded from a swinging group. Now, females might enjoy watching two males bring each other to orgasm, but males do not erotically enjoy viewing this and therefore the behavior does not occur. Thus, overall it is a male-focused type of sexuality despite the fact that the females involved are given participatory roles.

TYPE THREE: NONCONSENSUAL AND LOVE-FOCUSED

This is a secretive type of extramarital affair and I suspect is the least likely to be approved by our married population today. It involves both deception and a competitive love relationship and these are two highly negative factors in our culture. Many people fear that individuals who enter into extramarital affairs for pleasure will eventually end up in serious love relationships. People who believe this the most would be those who stress the power of love and sexuality. Such people feel that love cannot be controlled once it begins to develop. They therefore try to restrict all intimacy (sexual or otherwise) with the opposite gender. They feel that sexual motivations are also very powerful, and once given into will lead to the development of affectionate ties and to constant seeking of further sexual pleasure. The reader may recall that in Chapter 6 we defined pleasure and intimacy as the two main characteristics of sexual relationships. The question, then, is not whether there is a risk of intimacy and pleasure developing in sexual relationships—it is rather, how much control can one exercise over such intimacy and pleasure. In Type One affairs we encounter people who wish to see the intimacy of the relationship increase and in Type Two affairs we have people who wish to see the physical pleasure from the relationship increase. So such adherents do feel that they can manage the intimacy and pleasure aspects of sexuality. On the other hand, Type Three adherents may in part be composed of people who feel they had no control over the development of the love-based affair. In this sense, they may be romanticists. In addition, Type Three could be sought deliberately by an unhappily married person. In general, Type Three would not be a popular choice with those who are happily married. This is so because it is widely believed that a secret love affair may become so important that the marriage may be broken.

TYPE FOUR: NONCONSENSUAL AND PLEASURE-CENTERED

This is by far the most common type of affair for husbands, and I suspect a large proportion of wives as well (Tavris and Sadd, 1977:118; Hunt, 1969). The rationalization for this type asserts that since the affair is pleasure-focused, it does little harm to the marriage. Further, it is argued that since the mate would be threatened by even a pleasure-centered affair, the best thing is to keep the affair secret. I would expect that with the equalization of gender roles, more females will elect this type of affair (Atwater, 1979). Many females have husbands who would not accept extramarital relationships for their wives (even though they themselves may be so involved). The wife who believes in gender-role equality may resent this type of restriction and venture into her own Type Four affair. There is little extant data indicating the consequences of such affairs on marriage. Table 11.11 on page 298 indicated what divorced people *believe* about extramarital affairs in general but these are only divorced people and we have no information on what type of affairs they are speaking of. Hunt (1969), in a study of eighty affairs, states that marital breakage was very low.

The reader should make note of the fact that Types Three and Four are the most common types of affairs and yet have the least amount of research. Researchers often choose types that interest themselves and this often involves a focus on a minority pattern of behavior.

Causes of Extramarital Sexual Permissiveness: Some Recent Research

Research studies on extramarital sexuality is very largely a product of the 1970s. Prior to that time very little data exist outside of Kinsey's descriptive statistics. In recent years there have been a few studies that have begun to improve our insight into explanations of extramarital sexual permissiveness (Singh, et al., 1976). In the summer of 1978 three of us (G. C. Sponaugle, Ronald Anderson, and myself—all of the University of Minnesota) decided to utilize the samples of the National Opinion Research Center to help in building an explanation of extramarital sexual permissiveness.

Since 1972 the National Opinion Research Center (NORC) has undertaken a national sample each year that is representative of the country. For four of the years they had asked one question about attitudes toward extramarital intercourse. They also asked each year a large number of questions on many other characteristics of each respondent. These surveys are available for any researcher who wishes to use them. Sponaugle Anderson, and I decided that it was time for someone to try to develop an overall theoretical approach to extramarital sexual permissiveness. With the help of these national samples we were able to examine a number of propositions regarding causes of extramarital sexual permissiveness. Although we did not deal with behavior, we can always at a later time test the relationship of these attitudes to behavior. Extramarital sexual permissiveness is being defined here as the extent to which one accepted extramarital intercourse as proper under various conditions (Types One, Two, Three, and Four). We used the 1977 national sample for our basic check and also checked our findings on the 1976, 1974, and 1973 national samples. I will present below only some highlights of our results.

Figure 11.1 sums up our findings in the NORC national samples and also presents some new ideas we are putting forth (Reiss, Anderson, Sponaugle, 1980). I am presenting the material in the simplest fashion. There are many interrelationships among the variables in this diagram. Not all of them have an independent and direct influence on extramarital sexual permissiveness but this presentation will not elaborate on our multivariate analysis. The interested reader can refer to our research report (Reiss, Anderson, and Sponaugle, 1980).

Our analysis yielded eight key predictors. The most widely believed cause of a person accepting extramarital affairs is supposed to be an unhappy marriage. So the first variable in Figure 11.1 is: (1) *Happiness in Marriage*. As the sign indicates, we expected a negative relationship, i.e. the higher the marital happiness, the lower the extramarital sexual permissiveness. That was precisely what we found. However, as you can see from the diagram, that was but one of many variables that helped explain changes in extramarital sexual permissiveness. In addition, it turned out

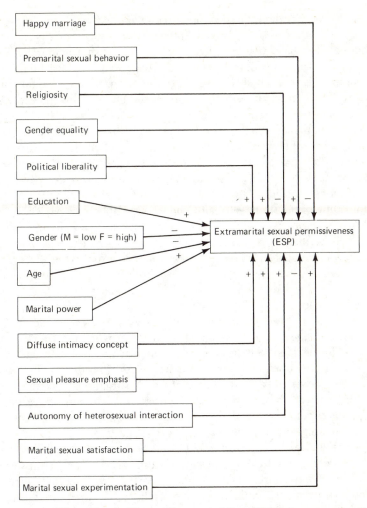

Figure 11.1. Predictors of Extramarital Sexual Permissiveness.

not to be the strongest. So we concluded that happiness of marriage was a cause of extramarital permissiveness but by no means the dominant cause. Bell et al. (1975) reported that 55 percent of his unhappily married wives and 20 percent of his happily married wives experienced extramarital intercourse (he measured behavior and not attitudes). Tavris and Sadd (1977:122) found 51 percent of the unhappy and 24 percent of the happy women in the *Redbook* study had had an affair. Sponaugle's 1975 study of Minneapolis (1976) reported that 43 percent of the unhappily married people and 13 percent of the happily married people accepted extramarital coitus. Glass and Wright (1977) state that the negative relationship of happiness of marriage and extramarital coitus held mainly for couples married less than twelve years. For those married more than twelve years this relationship was quite weak. This is a most interesting finding for it suggests that perhaps these longer-term couples have more security about their reationship and further perhaps they have other reasons, besides the happiness of their marriage, for getting involved extramaritally. It is precisely these types of qualifications which show the value of empirical research—through research we gain precision regarding the operation of causal factors.

The next causal factor that we examined was one that is familiar to us by now: (2) *Premarital Sexual Permissiveness.* We reasoned that if one learned the physical and psychological enjoyments of sexuality before marriage, then one would be more likely to seek such enjoyments after marriage. Several studies have presented such correlations—including Kinsey. In the NORC national sample, this factor proved to be one of the strongest of all those we were able to check.

(3) *Religiosity* is an obvious causal factor for we know how negative most religious groups are concerning extramarital sexual permissiveness. This factor proved to display a strong negative relationship to extramarital sexual permissiveness. We noted in Chapter 7 that this variable was negatively related to premarital sexual permissiveness and it here shows itself to have the same relationship to extramarital sexual permissiveness.

One of the more interesting potential causes was (4) *Gender Equality.* This variable measures the degree to which equal roles for males and females are endorsed. It is based upon four separate questions that ask about attitudes toward working mothers and division of labor in the home. As can be seen in Figure 11.1, the higher the gender equality, the higher the extramarital sexual permissiveness. This finding fits with the research which indicates that women into careers and women who are more assertive in their marriages are more likely to accept higher levels of extramarital sexual permissiveness (Tavris and Sadd, 1977).

(5) *Political Liberality* also worked out as predicted and those who were more liberal (by self-definition) were also higher on extramarital sexual permissiveness.

(6) *Education* was a surprisingly powerful predi tor. We expected higher-educated groups to be more permissive but the results were more powerful than we anticipated. It may well be that in higher-educated groups one can legitimately discuss the decision regarding extramarital sexual permissiveness, whereas in lower-educated groups, although people surely engage in extramarital relations, they do not feel it is a proper topic for discussion. In fact, one of the distinguishing aspects of many new forms of extramarital relationships such as swinging and intimate friendships is that they are heavily a custom of the college-educated group.

(7) *Gender* was a predictor of extramarital sexual permissiveness in that females were less permissive than males. This is true for all types of sexuality except homosexuality. Studies from Kinsey to date have indicated that females are more tolerant of homosexuality than are males. But on heterosexual areas, females are less acceptant.

Another rather obvious predictor is (8) *Age.* Older people did indeed come out less permissive than younger people.

Now, these first eight variables all came out as good predictors and as statistically significant in the NORC national studies. We did test out other factors that did not come out strong enough (Reiss, Anderson, and Sponaugle, 1980). These are eight important variables but we felt that there were other variables that would also be important but were not asked about in the NORC samples.

There were six such variables and they are the last six listed in Figure 11.1. (I will use a letter prefix to distinguish them from the eight empirically established factors.) (A) *Marital power* is one we have commented upon often. One key basis of males having greater sexual rights is their general dominance in marriage. Type Four extramarital relationship is the typical nonconsensual, pleasure relation that men are involved in due to greater opportunity and due also to the greater social sanction for such behavior. As women gain in marital power they should increasingly become involved extramaritally. Some of the other original eight variables (for example, gender equality) indirectly get at part of the dimension of power. Glass and Wright (1977) did report that wives who were more powerful in their marriages were more likely to accept extramarital coitus.

The next new variable is (B) *Endorsement of diffuse intimacy conception*. We have discussed this before. If one does not endorse a focused intimacy view then exclusivity is less important and extramarital relationships may well be more acceptable. (C) *Sexual pleasure emphasis* is another rather obvious factor—if one ranks sexual pleasure high on the scale of life satisfactions then extramarital relationships would seem to be more likely.

The (D) *Autonomy of heterosexual interaction* is our measure of opportunity. The degree to which one's work involves one with sexually attractive people of the opposite gender is an opportunity measure. So would be the degree to which one travels away from home and has leisure time to meet other people. It seemed to us that such an "autonomy" or opportunity measure was important.

One of the most crucial variables missing from the NORC study is a measure of (E) *Marital sexual satisfaction*. Our reasoning was that everything else equal (always the assumption), the more marital sexual satisfaction, the less the desire for extramarital relationships. Sponaugle (1976) found support for this as did Tavris and Sadd (1977:125) and Bell et al. (1975). The close relationship of marital sexual satisfaction to other areas of marital satisfaction has been long established (Burgess and Wallin, 1953). It seems worthy of inclusion in any list of causes of levels of extramarital sexual permissiveness.

The last predictor is (F) *Marital sexual experimentation*. Here we are talking about the degree to which married couples are open to trying new sexual forms for themselves. The data from the Tavris and Sadd (1977) *Redbook* study would indicate that there is considerably more such sexual experimentation in marriage today (see Table 11.6), and that those who experiment more are more sexually satisfied. There are two positions one can assume regarding the consequences of marital sexual experimentation. First, one can assert that such experimentation will enhance the marital satisfaction, open up communication, and satiate the couple and thereby decrease the degree to which one would endorse extramarital sexual permissiveness.

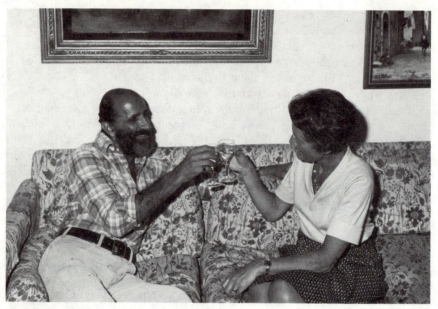

Photo by Ivan Kalman.

The second position is that such experimentation, although it may increase marital sexual satisfaction, will in turn raise the desire for additional pleasure. The theoretical position here is that pleasure does not lead to more than temporary satiation and in the long run leads to desire for an increment in the level of pleasurable satisfaction. This was our explanation, in part, of the connection between premarital and extramarital sexual permissiveness. We therefore endorse the "pleasure begets more pleasure" view rather than the "pleasure begets satiation" view. So we assert that marital sexual experimentation influences in a positive direction extramarital sexual permissiveness.

We organized these fourteen causal variables around two foci. The first focus was on the *quality of marital satisfaction*. Although this factor is not the only influence, it is clearly a powerful one. Almost every study found that those who were less happy were more acceptant of extramarital sexual permissiveness—particularly in the first decade of marriage. Several of the empirically tested predictor variables (religiosity, gender equality, gender, and education) have implications for marital happiness. These variables were found to influence extramarital sexual permissiveness *indirectly* by influencing marital satisfaction which in turn would influence extramarital sexual permissiveness. The second focus is around the overall *level of sexual permissiveness* accepted prior to marriage. Several of the original eight predictor variables were found to *indirectly* influence extramarital sexual permissiveness by affecting our measure of sexual permissiveness before marriage (religiosity, gender equality, political liberality, gender, and age). In short, we found that two of our variables—happiness of marriage and premarital sexual permissiveness) had the strongest *direct* influences on extramarital sexual permissiveness. The other variables generally worked on extramarital sexual permissiveness indirectly, by affecting one or both of these vital direct influences. Thus, we generalize these two types of variables as the key direct causes of changes in our dependent variable. Further, the six new variables can be conceptualized as related measures of these two basic concepts (A, B, E, F relate to happiness of marriage and C, D to sexual permissiveness). These six remain to be carefully empirically tested, whereas the first eight have been tested on four national samples and they do generally fit our above stated theoretical approach. One final comment—the college-educated group in our research data showed itself to be the most likely one to evidence rapid change in the near future. A research which focused in on that group would be valuable in gaining further clarity on trends for they are most likely to be the leaders in any changes in the 1980s.

Summary and Conclusions

There are a few threads that tie together the sexual lives of married people both inside and outside of marriage. One that strikes me as dominant in any explanation is the central place of psychological intimacy in acts of human sexuality. Clearly, both husbands and wives have tied in their affectionate feelings with their sexual relationships. This has more support in our tradition for wives than for husbands but both genders display the importance of affection as a context for sexual relationships in marriage. With this in mind, it then becomes not at all surprising that extramarital sexual relationships take on a special significance that is not present in other types of nonsexual extramarital friendships. As we discussed in Chapter 6, the physical intimacy of sexual acts tends to reveal basic personality traits of the people involved. One can work at controlling this—the prostitute-customer relationship is an extreme example. But it takes an effort and even prostitutes report learning a great deal about their customers. So emotional intimacy is a very possible outcome of sexual relationships and one which in turn may encourage and combine with increases in physical intimacy. This characteristic lends a special quality to sexual relationships outside of marriage and makes it a sensitive and threatening area to most spouses. Jealousy, defined as a fear of loss of something or someone valuable, is thus an expected reaction to extramarital sexual relationships. Of course, one can consciously work at reducing the sense of possessiveness, affirming the priority of the marriage, and increasing one's sense of trust. I would suggest that although this will lessen the problems of jealousy, it will not for most people eliminate it.

A key *control* on extramarital sexual relationships is the concern one has for one's spouse's feelings. One of the major *motivations* for extramarital sexual relationships is the excitement of a new sexual partner and a new intimate relationship. The concern for one's mate often conflicts with such motivations. Sponaugle's (1976) research in Minneapolis did indeed show the power of the concern for one's spouse's feelings. He listed fourteen possible conditions for the acceptance of extramarital sexual intercourse. The one condition that drew more acceptance than all others was: "If my spouse approves of extramarital sexual intercourse." About half of both the husbands and wives in the sample said they would accept extramarital sexual intercourse if their spouse approved. The condition of the spouse having a physical handicap which made marital coitus impossible only received about 40 percent endorsement as a basis for accepting extramarital coitus. Even a husband or wife being unable to satisfy his or her spouse sexually received only about 30 percent endorsement. The remaining eleven possibilities received less support. These responses indicate that the feelings of one's marital partner are of vital concern in any acceptance of extramarital sexuality. Note that half the couples would not accept extramarital intercourse even if their partner approved! Possibly, these people felt that the extramarital affair would injure their marital relationship despite their mate's approval. National surveys indicate that only 30 percent accept extramarital coitus and 70 percent say it is "always wrong." Apparently most respondents are not answering in terms of an acceptant spouse. If Minneapolis couples are at all typical, some 50 percent of all married couples would approve under such conditions.

Thus there is a dyadic quality to any one married person's decision about an extramarital affair and this distinguishes that decision from premarital sexual decisions. The dyadic quality also helps us to realize why the acceptance level of extramarital sexual relationships is below the behavioral level of extramarital permissiveness. There is a much closer relationship of attitudes and behavior in premarital sexuality. We saw in Chapter 7 how the opportunity to repeat any sexual act with an acceptant partner was a key factor in overcoming guilt and eventually coming to accept that sexual act. Extramarital coitus is more difficult to repeat due to the greater complexity in arranging for such behavior. The necessity for secrecy and the lack of subgroup support in most extramarital relationships must exact a price in anxiety and self-doubt that is much higher than in premarital relationships. Thus, the extinction of guilt and doubt by repetition and peer-group support is less likely to occur in extramarital affairs. This may lead to extramarital experience being more sporadic—perhaps related to a particular life crisis that one is facing.

It is precisely the low visibility level of extramarital affairs that makes autonomy such an important variable. The degree to which one is free, for example, to travel to another city is directly relevant to the degree to which one need not be so concerned about secrecy. The same would be true regarding separate vacations for husbands and wives. Gilmartin's (1978) swingers were very high on lack of involvement with community institutions, kin, and neighbors. This detachment increases the ability to regulate one's own life without controls from others.

I would hypothesize that freedom from other groups might also increase one's *marital* sexual permissiveness because there would be less social restraints influencing one's marital sexual choices. I would expect that the greater the autonomy the greater the congruence between one's sexual attitudes and sexual behaviors. Of course, no one is completely autonomous or they would not belong to a human society but there is a wide range of autonomy that is possible in human society.

In regard to extramarital sexual permissiveness, many of the variables in Figure 11.1 are indirect measures of autonomy. For example, those with higher education are more likely to endorse autonomy as a key life component (Kohn, 1977; and see Chapter 15). Younger people, politically liberal people, gender-equal people, and nonreligious people all are more likely to endorse autonomy. So these predictor variables are in some ways related to the general concept of autonomy. On an abstract level, autonomy appears to be a major causal factor for sexual permissiveness of all kinds.

The heart of the felt problem with extramarital sexuality is balance. The problem is how to maintain the clear dominance of the centripetal forces holding the marital dyad together and, at the same time, keep the centrifugal forces of the extramarital relationship from pulling one out of the marital dyad. In a general sense this problem was discussed in the last chapter under the rubric of structural constraints. One's occupation or even one's children can take the focus away from the marital relationship just as extramarital relationships can. But there are conventional norms that support the importance of such occupational and familial interests and this reduces the fear of disruption from such sources. This is not to say that such activities do not disrupt marriages but it is to say that our culture plays down this possibility. In relation to extramarital affairs our culture plays up the possible disruption. We have no adequate research data with which to decide the relative impact of these several "extramarital" roles.

Elaine and William Walster (1978) more than other writers have clearly put the issue regarding extramarital sexual relationships in terms of the wish for security vs. the wish for excitement. This is analogous to our position that the quality of the marriage and the overall sexual permissiveness are the two key determinants. The recent emphasis in our society has been on the individual's self-growth and self-pleasuring. This strengthens the "excitement" motivation to extramarital sexuality. There is in addition a growth of qualifications of the focused view of love and intimacy. More people seem to assert that one must expect that there will be important needs left unsatisfied by the marriage and that outsiders can take care of such needs. This qualification of need satisfaction in marriage also tends to aid in the acceptance of extramarital sexuality.

If I read the basic trends in American culture correctly, we should be entering a time of increased extramarital sexual permissiveness. Those individuals who raised the premarital sexual permissiveness during the 1965 to 1975 time period are now married or getting married. They are also the people who are raising the marital sexual experimentation rates reported in this chapter. I find it difficult to believe that they will not also increase the extramarital sexual permissiveness rates during the decade of the 1980s.

This increase will, I believe, be more gradual than the dramatic increase experienced in premarital and marital sexual permissiveness. This will be so because of the "dyadic decision" quality to extramarital affairs. Extramaritally, there is always the excluded mate (or mates) that increase risks and impede acceptance of extramarital affairs. Even in those few marriages where consensual agreements are arrived at—the typical agreement is very restrictive as to affection and frequency and time allowed for extramarital relations. The marital focus—the desire to be number one to your mate—restricts even those who are the most acceptant. In sum, due to marital dyadic commitment there are blocks to any rapid growth of extramarital sexual permissiveness. I suspect that the increase will be gradual and will involve more *tolerance* of affairs of a noncompetitive type rather than *endorsement* of affairs in general.

There are cultures such as the Turu in Tanzania where extramarital sexual affairs are informally institutionalized (Schneider, 1971). In this society, each husband and each wife picks a *Mbuya,* or romantic friend, who becomes a lover. Everyone knows this to be the case, even though it is considered poor form to be fully public about such lovers. But what of the marriage relationships—why do they not block such affairs as we contend they do in the Western world? The marriage relationships are lacking in love and are largely based on economic considerations. So romantic love must be satisfied outside of marriage. The case of the Turu should remind the reader of our own romantic love heritage which we discussed in Chapter 5. The affairs in the European courts of love in the twelfth century were also extramarital, and marriages in those days were also thought to be devoid of deep love feelings. I conclude from such examples that the less the emotional investment in marriage is in a culture, the more easily extramarital relations will be accepted.

What many in America are seeking today is a combination of a deep love relationship in marriage and some lesser level of intimacy outside of marriage. There is difficulty even in such a hierarchical blend. But there are difficulties also due to resentment at not being free to have such secondary pleasures. There are no easy solutions and one's personal values are the final arbiter.

References

Atwater, Lynn. 1979. "Getting Involved: Women's Transition to First Extramarital Sex," *Alternative Lifestyles* 2 (February):33–68.

Back, Kurt. 1972. *Beyond Words.* New York: Russell Sage.

Bartell, Gilbert. 1970. "Group Sex Among the Mid-Americans," *Journal of Sex Research* 6 (May):113–130.

———. 1971. *Group Sex.* New York: Wyden Books.

Bell, Robert R., And Dorothyann Peltz. 1974. "Extramarital Sex Among Women," *Medical Aspects of Human Sexuality* 5 (March):10–31.

———, Stanley Turner, and Lawrence Rosen. 1975. "A Multivariate Analysis of Female Extramarital Coitus," *Journal of Marriage and the Family* 36 (May):375–384.

Berger, Bennett et al. 1972. "Child Rearing Practices of the Communal Family," in Ira L. Reiss (ed.), *Readings on the Family System.* New York: Holt, Rinehart and Winston, pp. 582–594.

Bukstel, Lee H., Gregory D. Rolder, Peter R. Kilmann, James Laughlin, and Wayne M. Scotell. 1978. "Projected Extramarital Sexual Involvement in Unmarried College Students," *Journal of Marriage and the Family* 40 (May):337–340.

Burgess, Ernest, and Paul Wallin. 1953. *Engagement and Marriage.* Philadelphia: Lippincott.

Bernard, Jessie. 1974. "Infidelity: Some Moral and Social Issues," in James and Lynn Smith (eds.), *Beyond Monogamy.* Baltimore: Johns Hopkins University Press.

Child, Irvin L. 1973. *Humanistic Psychology and the Research Tradition: Their General Virtues.* New York: Wiley.

Christensen, Harold T. 1962. "A Cross-Cultural Comparison of Attitudes Toward Marital Infidelity," *International Journal of Comparative Sociology* 3:124–137.

_____. 1973. "Attitudes Toward Marital Infidelity: A Nine Culture Sample," *Journal of Comparative Family Studies* 4 (Autumn):197–214.

Clanton, G., and L. Smith. (eds). 1977. *Jealousy*. Englewood Cliffs, NJ: Prentice-Hall.

Clark, Alexander L., and Paul Wallin. 1964. "The Accuracy of Husbands' and Wives' Reports of Frequency of Marital Coitus," *Population Studies* 18 (November):165–173.

_____. 1965. "Women's Sexual Responsiveness and the Duration and Quality of Their Marriages," *American Journal of Sociology* 21 (September): 187–196.

Constantine, Larry L., and Joan M. Constantine. 1973. *Group Marriage: A Study of Contemporary Multilateral Marriage*. New York: Macmillan.

Cuber, John, and Peggy Harroff. 1965. *The Significant Americans*. New York: Penguin.

Davis, Kingsley. 1939. "Illegitimacy and the Social Structure," *American Journal of Sociology* 45 (September):215–233.

Denfield, Duane. 1974. "Dropouts from Swinging," *The Family Coordinator* 23 (January): 45–49.

Edwards, John. 1973. "Extramarital Involvement: Fact and Theory," *Journal of Sex Research* 9 (August): 210–226.

Ellis, Albert, 1972. *The Civilized Couple's Guide to Extramarital Adventure*. New York: Pinnacle Books.

Ford, Clelland, and Frank Beach. 1953. *Patterns of Sexual Behavior*. New York: Harper & Row.

Gebhard, Paul H. 1966. "Factors in Marital Orgasm," *Journal of Social Issue* 22(April):88–95.

Gilmartin, Brian. 1974. "Sexual Deviance and Social Networks," in James Smith and Lynn Smith (eds.), *Beyond Monogamy*. Baltimore: Johns Hopkins University Press, pp. 291–323.

_____. 1975. "That Swinging Couple down the Block," *Psychology Today* 8 (February):55–58.

_____. 1978. *The Gilmartin Report*. Secaucus, NJ: Citadel Press.

_____, and D. V. Kusisto. 1973. "Some Personal and Social Characteristics of Mate-Sharing Swingers," in R. Libby and R. Whitehurst (eds.), *Renovating Marriage*. San Francisco: Consensus Publishers, pp. 146–166.

Glass, Shirley P., and Thomas L.Wright. 1977. "The Relationship of Extramarital Sex, Length of Marriage, and Sex Differences on Marital Satisfaction and Romanticism: Athanasiou's Data Reanalyzed," *Journal of Marriage and the Family* 39 (November): 691–703.

Gordon, Thomas. 1970. *Parent Effectiveness Training*. New York: Wyden Books.

Hunt, Morton. 1969. *The Affair*. New York: World Publishers.

_____. 1974. *Sexual Behavior in the 1970's*. Chicago: Playboy Press.

Johnson, Ralph E. 1970*a*. "Extramarital Coitus," *Journal of Marriage and the Family* 32 (May):279–2830.

_____. 1970*b*. "Some Correlates of Extramarital Coitus," *Journal of Marriage and the Family* 32 (August): 449–457.

Kanter, Rosabeth. 1972. *Commitment and Community*. Cambridge, MA: Harvard University Press.

Kaplan, Helen Singer. 1974. *The New Sex Therapy*. New York: Brunner/Mazel.

Kinsey Alfred C., et al. 1948. *Sexual Behavior in the Human Male*. Philadelphia: Saunders.

_____. 1953. *Sexual Behavior in the Human Female*. Philadelphia: Saunders.

Kohn, Melvin. 1977. *Class and Conformity: A Study in Values*, 2nd ed. Chicago: University of Chicago Press.

Laws, Judith Long, and Pepper Schwartz. 1977. *Sexual Scripts: The Social Construction of Female Sexuality*. New York: Holt, Rinehart and Winston.

Levinger, George. 1966. "Systematic Distortion in Spouses' Reports of Preferred and Actual Sexual Behavior," *Sociometry* 29 (September):291–299.

Levitt, Eugene E., and Albert D. Klassen. 1974. "Public Attitudes Toward Homosexuality: Part of the 1970 National Survey by the Institute for Sex Research," *Journal of Homosexuality* 1 (1): 29–43.

Libby, Roger. 1973. "Extramarital and Comarital Sex," in R. Libby and R. Whitehurst (eds.), *Renovating Marriage*. San Francisco: Consensus Publishers.

_____, and Robert Whitehurst (eds.). 1973. *Renovating Marriage*. San Francisco: Consensus Publishers.

_____, and _____ (eds.). 1977. *Marriage and Alternatives*. Glenview, IL: Scott, Foresman.

Livsey, Clara G. 1979. "Coping with Adultery That Threatens Marriage," *Medical Aspects of Human Sexuality* (April):8–23.

Maison, Sally. 1974. "Jealousy: A Theoretical and Cross-Cultural Review." Unpublished research paper, University of Minnesota.

Malinowski, Bronislaw. 1929. *The Sexual Life of*

Savages in North-Western Melanesia. New York: Harvest Books. (Published by Harcourt Brace Jovanovich.)

Mancini, Joy A., and Dennis K. Orthner. 1978. "Recreational Sexuality Preferences Among Middle-Class Husbands and Wives," *Journal of Sex Research* 14 (May):96–106.

Marshall, Donald. 1971. "Sexual Behavior on Mangaia." Ch. 5 in Donald Marshall and Robert Suggs (eds.), *Human Sexual Behavior.* New York: Basic Books.

———, and Robert Suggs (eds.). 1971. *Human Sexual Behavior.* New York: Basic Books.

Maslow, Abraham. 1962. *Toward a Psychology of Being.* New York: Van Nostrand.

Masters, William, and Virginia Johnson. 1970. *Human Sexual Inadequacy.* Boston: Little, Brown.

———, ———, and Robert Kolodny (eds.). 1977. *Ethical Issues in Sex Therapy and Research.* Boston: Little, Brown.

———, ———, and ——— (eds.). 1980. *Ethical Guidelines for Sex Therapy and Research.* Boston: Little, Brown.

Mazur, Ronald. 1973. *The New Intimacy.* Boston: Beacon Press.

Mead, Margaret. 1928. *Coming of Age in Samoa.* New York: Morrow.

Money, John, and Anke Ehrhardt. 1972. *Man and Woman: Boy and Girl.* Baltimore: Johns Hopkins University Press.

Murdock, George P. 1949. *Social Structure.* New York: Macmillan.

National Opinion Research Center Codebook, 1972–1977. NORC (October 1977).

Neubeck, Gerhard (ed.). 1969. *Extramarital Relations.* Englewood Cliffs, NJ: Prentice-Hall.

Pietropinto, Anthony, and Jacqueline Simenauer. 1977. *Beyond the Male Myth.* New York: Times Books.

Playboy Report on American Men. 1979. Chicago: Playboy Enterprises. (Analyzed by William Simon and Patricia Miller)

Rainwater, Lee. 1966. "Some Aspects of Lower-Class Sexual Behavior," *Journal of Social Issues* 22 (April):96–108.

Ramey, James W. 1972. "Communes, Group Marriage and the Upper Middle Class," *Journal of Marriage and the Family* 34 (November 1972):647–655.

———. 1976. *Intimate Friendship.* Englewood Cliffs, NJ: Prentice-Hall.

Raschke, Vernon. 1972. "Religiosity and Sexual Permissiveness." Unpublished Ph.D. dissertation, University of Minnesota.

Reiss, Ira L. 1960. *Premarital Sexual Standards in America.* New York: Free Press.

———. 1973. *Heterosexual Permissiveness: Inside and Outside of Marriage.* Morristown, NJ: General Learning Press, pp. 1–29.

———, Ronald Anderson, and G. C. Sponaugle. 1980. "A Multivariate Model of the Determinants of Extramarital Sexual Permissiveness," *Journal of Marriage and the Family* (May).

Roebuck, J., and S. L. Spray. 1967. "The Cocktail Lounge: A Study of Heterosexual Relations in a Public Organization," *American Journal of Sociology* 72 (January):388–395.

Rogers, Carl. 1972. *Becoming Partners.* New York: Delacorte.

Rubin, Lillian. 1976. *Worlds of Pain: Life in the Working Class Family.* New York: Basic Books.

Schneider, Harold K. 1971. "Romantic Love Among the Turu." Ch. 3 in Donald Marshall and Robert Suggs (eds.), *Human Sexual Behavior.* New York: Basic Books.

Schwartz, Pepper. 1973. "Female Sexuality and Monogamy," in R. W. Libby and R. N. Whitehurst (eds.), *Renovating Marriage: Toward New Sexual Life Styles.* Danville, CA: Consensus Publishers, 211–226.

Singh, B. Krishna, Bonnie L. Walton, and J. Sherwood Williams. 1976. "Extramarital Sexual Permissiveness: Conditions and Contingencies," *Journal of Marriage and the Family* 38 (November):701–712.

Smith, James R., and Lynn G. Smith (eds.). 1974. *Beyond Monogamy.* Baltimore: Johns Hopkins University Press.

Safilios-Rothschild, Constantine. 1977. *Love, Sex and Sex Roles.* Englewood Cliffs, NJ: Prentice-Hall.

Sponaugle, G. C. 1976. "Extramarital Sexual Relations." Unpublished paper, University of Minnesota.

Suggs, Robert C. 1966. *Marquesan Sexual Behavior: An Anthropological Study of Polynesian Practices.* New York: Harcourt, Brace & World.

Symonds, Carolyn. 1968. "Pilot Study of the Peripheral Behavior of Sexual Mate Swappers." Unpublished Master's thesis, Riverside College, University of California.

Tavris, Carol, and Susan Sadd. 1977. *The Redbook Report on Female Sexuality.* New York: Delacorte.

Van Der Velde, T. H. 1929. *Ideal Marriage: Its Physiology and Techniques*. New York: Random House.

Wallin, Paul, and Alexander L. Clark. 1958a. "Cultural Norms and Husbands' and Wives' Reports of Their Marital Partner's Preferred Frequency of Coitus Relative to Their Own," *Sociometry* 21 (September):247–254.

———. 1958b. "Marital Satisfaction and Husbands' and Wives' Perception of Similarity in Their Preferred Frequency of Coitus," *Journal of Abnormal and Social Psychology* 47 (November):370–373.

Walshok, Mary L. 1971. "The Emergence of Middle-Class Deviant Subcultures: The Case of Swingers," *Social Problems* 18 (Spring): 488–496.

Walster, Elaine, and G. William Walster. 1978. *A New Look at Love*. Reading, MA: Addison-Wesley.

Westoff, Charles F. 1974. "Coital Frequency and Contraception," *Family Planning Perspectives* 3 (Summer):136–141.

Whitehurst, Robert. 1969. "Extramarital Sex: Alienation or Extension of Normal Behavior," in Gerhard Neubeck (ed.), *Extramarital Relations*. Englewood Cliffs, NJ: Prentice-Hall, pp. 129–146.

Whitley, Marily P., and Susan B. Poulsen. 1975. "Assertiveness and Sexual Satisfaction in Employed Professional Women," *Journal of Marriage and the Family* 37 (August):573–582.

Wiley, Philip. 1935. *As They Reveled*. New York: Avon.

Wise, Jeff. 1975. "The Relationship Between Extramarital Coitus and Marital Happiness." Unpublished graduate paper, University of Minnesota, Minneapolis.

Yankelovitch, Daniel. 1974. *The New Morality*. New York: McGraw-Hill.

Zetterberg, Hans. 1969. *Om Sexuallivet i Sverige*. (About Sexuality in Sweden) Stockholm: SOU (State Public Report).

Ziskin, J., and M. Ziskin. 1973. *The Extramarital Sex Contract*. Los Angeles: Nash Publications.

If at First You Don't Succeed:
Divorce and Remarriage in America

T W E L V E

Divorce: An Overview

An essential feature of human marriage in all societies is its vulnerability. Marriages can, for a variety of reasons, dissolve, and all societies have one or more ways to handle marital stress situations. Some societies have tried to restrict divorce by making it illegal. Marriages in such societies are often dissolved by the husband or wife leaving and taking residence in another city and becoming a bigamist. Male-dominant societies allow males to have mistresses as a way of making married life more attractive, even under stress. Desertion is another alternative that becomes prevalent in cases where other ways out of marital strain are not readily available. These are illustrations of the principle that some system of escaping from an unpleasant marriage will be found by every human group. Now let us look more closely at one very popular way of handling marital strain in American culture: divorce.

The annual number of couples divorcing was 1,122,000 in 1978. The notion is commonplace that divorce rates in America are a constantly increasing phenomenon. (Annulments can be ignored. They number only about 3 percent of all divorces, and most occur in New York and California.) The popular press tends to speak of divorce rates in terms of the ratio of divorces decreed in a particular year to marriages performed in that year. Thus, in 1978 there were roughly 1.1 million divorces and 2.2 million marriages (U.S. Department of HEW, 1979. *Monthly Vital Statistics Report* 27, No. 12). The divorce "rate" is then given as 50 percent because that is the percentage that divorces constitute of all marriages made in that year. This is a faulty way to look at divorce because very few of those 1.1 million divorces in 1978 came from those 2.2 million marriages that commenced in 1978. Most all of those divorces came from marriages begun in earlier

316

years. The average duration of first marriages that end in divorce is now about seven years. Figure 12.1 shows the relation of divorce to years married. One can see that the highest percentage of divorces does occur in the first few years after marriage, but it is not until after approximately seven years of marriage that 50 percent of those who are going to divorce have actually done so. This has been shortened slightly in recent years. Note also that there is no marked increase at any point after the decline begins at three years duration.

If one wanted a more meaningful rate of divorce, one should look at the percentage of all existing marriages that break up in any one year. By using such a comparison we find that in 1978 there were over 1.1 million divorces among a total of 51.1 million married women or a rate of almost 22 divorces for every 1,000 marriages in existence that year. Note that using the rate per 1,000 married women does not necessitate making any assumptions about future years. The best current estimate is that roughly four out of every ten marriages made in recent years will end in divorce (Glick and Norton, 1977).

We all know that the raw number of divorces each year has been steadily rising. But that does not tell us much about the *rate* of divorce per 1,000 married women because the population has increased, and the number of married women has steadily increased. Thus, an increase in the number of divorced people in any year is, in part, simply due to the overall population increase. To see if the divorce rate has risen we need the divorce statistics per 1,000 married women and must compare them for different years. This can be seen in Figure 12.2 for the years 1920 through 1980. It is interesting to note that the divorce rate in 1920 was 8 per 1,000 wives,

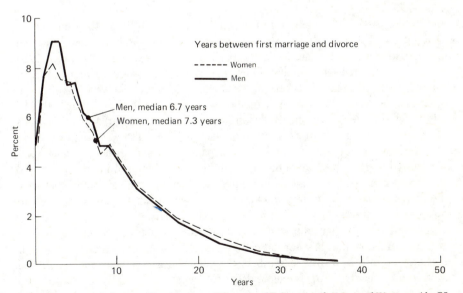

Figure 12.1. *Intervals between First Marriage, Divorce, and Remarriage for Men and Women under 75 Years Old in 1975.*
Source: *U.S. Bureau of the Census (1976), Series P–20, No. 297:15.*

and by the early 1940s the rate has risen to about 10 per 1,000; then during the 1950s it had actually fallen under 10. Since the early 1960s the rate has been clearly rising and by the late 1960s the rise began to increase sharply. From 1965 to 1975 the divorce rate doubled. One important thing to note in Figure 12.2 is the very small difference between the 1920 and 1960 rates. The very high peak in the mid-1940s is due to the high divorce rates associated with World War II (1941–1945) and with the years immediately following the end of that war. Many thousands of marriages were made in haste during that war. There also was a natural strain on marriage then because of the years of separation. Finally, there were couples who stayed together because of the crises of the Great Depression of the 1930s and were then breaking up in the 1940s. These are some of the key factors that gave the 1940s an increase in divorce rates and that gave 1946 in particular a record divorce rate that was not equalled for almost thirty years.

Looking over the figures presented so far in this chapter, one notes that divorce is a phenomenon that has not radically increased during the 1920–1965 period. A sharp increase in divorce came before 1920. The debate over the morality of divorce also occurred largely before 1920 (O'Neill, 1967). Divorce is associated with economic conditions in part; during good times the overall divorce rate increases, as can be seen in Figure 12.2 by comparing the 1930s with the 1940s. In part, this is a result of more people being able to afford going through the legal

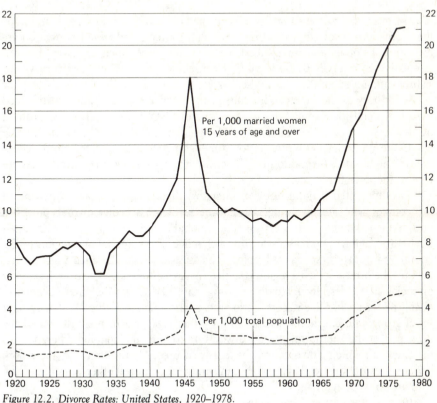

Figure 12.2. Divorce Rates: United States, 1920–1978.
Source: U.S. Department of HEW, May 16, 1979, Vol. 28, No. 2:1. The 1978 rate is estimated from government reports.

process of divorce instead of simply deserting or separating. In part, it is also a result of the feeling that it would be undesirable to break up a marriage during an economic crisis when family members are in greater need of mutual support (Preston and McDonald, 1979).

Variations in Divorce Rates

Before we get more specific about comparative divorce rates, it is well to warn the reader that divorce statistics are far from perfect. The reader may not know that it was only during the 1930s that even birth and death statistics became available in accurate form for the entire country. Before that time, estimates had to be made from existing data. Divorce data are quite a bit behind birth and death statistics. The National Office of Vital Statistics began improving the marriage and divorce statistics in 1946. At the present time, although all states report the number of divorces, only somewhat over half the fifty states report full information to the federal government on the characteristics of divorces granted. The reader should bear in mind that all we can do is present the best available information and hope the estimations involved are accurate. A major source of valuable information are the Current Population Surveys that the government conducts each year on representative samples of 40,000 to 50,000 households. Because of these surveys our statistics improved greatly during the 1970s.

As far back as the nineteenth century, the divorce data on America indicated a general trend for divorce rates to increase from East to West (U.S. Department of HEW, Series 21, No. 13: 1967:7). This situation still exists, and the divorce rate in the Western states is three or four times as high as the rate in the Northeastern states. The South is second to the Western states, and the North Central states are next to the lowest in divorce rates.

This differential is not a result of migratory divorces. Only about 5 percent of the couples who are divorcing take advantage of the speedier divorce processes outside their state of residence; thus, the regional differences cannot be accounted for by this factor. The reasons for this difference in divorce rate by region of the country can only be speculated upon. The East-to-West difference suggests that perhaps the time at which a region is settled makes a difference. The overall stability of social life is less in a rapidly growing state like California than in an old, established state like New York. Also, those who migrate to the West may be a select group who are more unstable in their marriages. Such instability may have been part of the motivation to move westward. There also may be differences in the ease with which a divorce may be legally secured. Up until recently New York had a very strict divorce law, and that may have encouraged other ways of dealing with an unhappy marriage.

From a cross-cultural perspective, one notes that from 1930 to 1965 the rest of the industrialized world increased their divorce rates more rapidly than we did (United Nations, 1979). One key factor that relates to the faster increase in divorce rates in most other Western countries is the concomitant increase in the growth of a "free," autonomous courtship system in those same countries. In short, I am positing that a key factor that promotes divorce in marriage is a courtship system that stresses choice by the young people who are courting rather than by their parents. One can surely find historical evidence to support this in America. Although we have always had strong elements of free mate choice, these forces were strengthened as our country industrialized and urbanized during the nineteenth century. It may be difficult to realize that it was only in 1920 that the urban population became the majority in America. In the fifty years between the Civil War and World War I, this country underwent very rapid urban and industrial growth, and at the exact same time our divorce rate per 1,000 married women increased from 1 per 1,000 married women to 8 per 1,000 married women per year. In the years from 1920 to 1963, it had gone only from eight to nine. From 1963 to 1978 the increase was dramatic—from nine to twenty-two. Thus, one key increase in divorce occurred at the time of our greatest urban industrial growth around World War I. Such growth encourages a free, autonomous courtship system for reasons that we have examined in Chapter 4. The second key increase occurred during another period of radical change toward more courtship autonomy as a result of the criticism of the Vietnam War and the increased rights given to young people such as the right to vote at age eighteen.

An autonomous courtship system where the participants choose their own mates is conducive to high divorce rates. In such a system the bases of choice are the factors that are important to the young people who are doing the choosing. The factors important to youth are typically the qualities of the interpersonal relationship. How much affection and concern or love exist between the couple becomes of first importance. Love becomes a key basis for marriage. A sense of duty to reproduce, or to marry within one's own class or religion, becomes of secondary importance. Love is a quality in a relationship that can be lost more easily than can a sense of duty dictating that one should be married and raise a family. This being the case, the basis for marriage can be lost more easily when that basis is love. In such a case, the individuals involved will seek a divorce because marriage has been defined by them as involving a love relationship.

Now, let me qualify and point out that, surely, young people in our society do not fully control the choice of their mates, and they do not fully lack a sense of duty toward marriage and parenthood, and they do not always divorce when they feel love has left their union. But—and this is the crucial point—compared with a culture wherein parents make the choice of mate, they are more likely to divorce if the interpersonal relationship is viewed as of a poor quality. In Western cultures where mate choice is more parentally controlled, I would expect the lack of love to lead not so much to divorce as to adultery, separation, or other compensatory activities that would still allow the marital union to remain technically intact. The more one is culturally taught to seek love as the basis for marriage, the more likely it is that one will break up the marriage entirely and seek another love when the original love relationship deteriorates.

Now, if love-based marriage promotes high divorce rates and if urban industrial growth promotes love-based marriages, then it follows that divorce rates will increase as a society increases its urban industrial development. Such an increase can be documented for almost all European countries between 1930 and 1965. Of course, other factors control divorce rates—factors like Catholicism and strict divorce laws (Stetson and Wright, 1975). The United States achieved a high degree of urban industrial growth before 1930, and many of the European countries achieved a faster rate of increase after 1930; therefore, the divorce rate in the United States has increased from 1930 to 1965 at a slower rate than in most of the outer countries. After 1965 virtually all the European countries experienced the same rapid rise in divorce as occurred in America (Chester, 1977). In part, this is due to similar trends toward economic prosperity but it is also true that a general increase in the autonomy of young people was occurring throughout the Western world.

The above explanation fits the existing data in at least an overall fashion, but some additional qualifications are needed. If, for reasons other than love-based marriage, there is an extremely high divorce rate in a nonindustrialized society, then *after* industrialization, the divorce rate may decrease rather than increase. Japan is one of the few countries that showed a *smaller* increase in divorce from 1930 to 1965 than the United States and is a perfect example of this situation.

Photo by Michael Perry.

Japan *before* industrialization in the nineteenth century had a very high divorce rate. There was kin support for a divorced woman with children, and divorce was allowed quite freely. Divorce then often resulted from incompatibility of a wife with her mother-in-law. *After* industrialization the divorce rate *decreased*. The common people in Japan had a system of free mate choice before industrialization and, with industrialization and the attempt to raise the standard of living, many of these freedoms were reduced rather than increased. It was the upper class in Japan that had stricter parental control over mate choice, and this upper-class pattern became more widespread after industrialization around the turn of the century (Goode, 1963: Chap. 7). Then, starting in the 1930s, a new movement began that allowed young people more freedom of choice in mate selection. The trend in recent decades is toward greater freedom of mate choice for young people, and there is in evidence a slowly rising divorce rate. The gradual trend in Japan toward love marriages and autonomous choices is found in Dore's (1958) finding that before 1921 only 11 percent of his sample had love marriages, but 23 percent had love marriages in the 1920s, 33 percent in 1941 through 1945, and 46 percent in 1945 through 1951. This gradual increase in love marriages has led to an increase in divorce rates, although the rate is small compared to most other countries (Dore, 1958:166).

Perhaps, then, the more general conclusion on this one important cause of high divorce rates would be that the higher the emphasis on the importance of the affectionate tie between husband and wife, the higher will be the divorce rate in a society *wherein husband-wife stability is a key value.* One key factor in promoting such emphasis on husband-wife stability is a courtship system that gives autonomy to the young people. Traditional duty-based marriage societies may also, of course, value husband-wife stability. But some traditional societies that do not give autonomy can nevertheless have a high divorce rate, because they do not value the stability of husband-wife relationships and because of the emphasis they place on other kinship ties. We saw this possibility very clearly in the case of the Nayar, where the husband-wife tie is deemphasized and the stable, stressed tie is through the matrilineage. Outside the Western world one finds societies that do not value the husband-wife tie as much as we do, and that in itself can lead to a high divorce rate. With industrialization, such a divorce rate can be decreased because of the increased stress on husband-wife relationships. But as the love-based marriage system comes into style, the divorce rate may increase again somewhat, as is now happening in Japan.

Divorce and Teenage Marriage

Besides factors such as love-based marriage and emphasis on husband-wife stability, there are many forces that relate to divorce. Within the United States it seems that teenage marriage goes with high divorce rates. But a careful look at the situation indicates that once again qualification is necessary. The risk of divorce varies greatly depending on what one means by "teenage marriage." If only one of the mates need be under twenty to warrant that label, then the divorce rate is not so high as when both are under twenty, and if one or both need be under eighteen to warrant that label, then the divorce rate is again increased. The increase in teenage marriage was a part of the general drop in age at marriage. Divorce rates by age at marriage as can be seen in Figure 12.3. Note that those who married in their teens had about twice the percent divorced in the three to five years after marriage period and the six to ten years after marriage period. In addition, it is interesting to see that those who married in their late twenties or later also show a rise in divorce. This latter group is quite small because about 90 percent of all women are married by age thirty.

Does the young age of the couple account for the high divorce rates? It is difficult to decide, for it could well be that the high premarital pregnancy rates (Chapter 8) placed a burden upon the marriage that helped to terminate it. The pregnancy and their youth may have impelled the parents to encourage marriage when the couple was not desirous of getting married. Also, dropping out of school may have lowered their ability to obtain well-paying employment and so added financial strain to the marriage (see Chapter 10). Finally, we know that the lower economic classes have less knowledge of contraception and, thus, are more likely to get premaritally pregnant. Also, we know that the lower classes traditionally marry at earlier ages. Thus, it is quite possible that teenage marriages fail not because of the young age of the female, but because they are mainly lower-class marriages and lower-class marriages generally have a high divorce rate because of

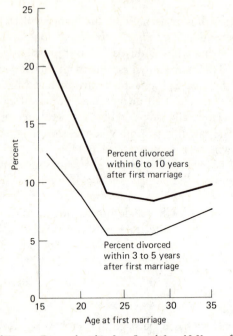

Figure 12.3. Percent of Women Divorced within 3 to 5 and 6 to 10 Years after First Marriage: U.S. 1970.
Source: U.S. Bureau of the Census, 1972 Census of Population: 1970, 4D, Age at First Marriage, Table 4 and diagramed in Glick and Norton, 1977:16.

the strains and stresses of the lower-class style of life. Thus, age itself may not be the only key issue although Bumpass and Sweet (1972) argue that it is the most important single variable. Those people who are likely to get pregnant, quit school, and live under great financial strain, have somewhat greater likelihoods of getting divorced no matter at what age they marry. The exact power of each variable in predicting divorce and the explanation of how they fit together remain to be investigated.

The basic trend toward earlier age at marriage in the 1940s was visible outside the United States. It became clear after World War II that almost all the countries that had gained economically from the war were experiencing a drop in the age of marriage. We have noted earlier that prosperity tends to encourage marriage (as well as divorce). In the United States the group that showed the most rapid decrease in age at marriage was the college educated. Before 1940 about one-third of the females who graduated from college never married. By 1950 this had been drastically reduced, and now over 90 percent of college graduates and 80 percent of the graduate-degree females marry (Glick, 1975:18). This is still a lower rate than for the overall population, where about 96 percent of the females marry, but it was a sharp increase over previous generations.

One reason for this low marriage rate among college-educated females is the tendency toward hypergamy (females "marrying up") among college-educated females. A male may marry a female less-educated than himself, and the majority of college-educated males do just that. But a female is more reluctant to marry down educationally. This is particularly true for college-educated females. High-school-educated females are more willing to marry down educationally. Even in 1977 only about 27 percent of the males and 21 percent of the females aged twenty-five to twenty-nine were college graduates (U.S. Bureau of Census, 1977. Series P-20, No. 314:10), and thus a college-graduate female has eliminated 73 percent of the males of her age if she refuses to marry a lower-educated person. Accordingly, the females who never marry cluster in the highest-educated groups. The males who never marry cluster in the lowest-educated groups.

There is a compensatory factor involved here in that college-educated groups generally have a low divorce rate. Here, too, one can argue that this low rate is a consequence of their age (they marry several years *above* the average for the country), so that they are therefore better prepared and more "mature." However, we have seen in Figure 12.3 that those who marry in their late twenties and above are *higher* on divorce. Thus, if age lowers the risk of divorce, it does so only up to the late twenties. Finally, one should add that the low rate might result from the fact that college-educated people come from a style of life that involves less economic strain and more rational control over their environment regardless of their age at marriage.

Social Class and Divorce

For a long time it was believed that wealthier people had higher divorce rates. Perhaps the Hollywood image of movie stars with high divorce rates and, in the past, publicity on wealthy men like Tommy Manville kept this notion alive. The sociologist who, more than anyone, has unraveled the association of social class and divorce rates is William J. Goode. He studied 425 divorced mothers in Detroit (Goode, 1951; 1956), and also studied divorce cross-culturally (1963).

In his classic 1948 study of divorced mothers, Goode found that his divorced sample differed from a married sample in that the divorced women were younger when they married by about one year and that the occupations of the husbands were toward the lower incomes—such as semiskilled factory workers. He also found that more of the divorced women had encountered parental disapproval of their marriages and that they had had shorter engagements than married women in general (Goode, 1956: Chap. 7). All these factors are interrelated. A person's overall social-class position is associated with the age at which one marries, how long one is engaged, how much consensus on values exists, and what occupation one is in (see Adams's 1968 study discussed in Chapter 16). The lower the social class, the younger the age at marriage; the shorter the engagement (if it is present at all), and the lower the consensus on values between parents and their children. Thus, the key questions that keeps coming up is: "Does social class determine the divorce rate and these other factors that associate with divorce?" Goode's data tend to place importance on the role of social class in divorce. Semiskilled operators had twice the divorce proneness of those at the upper end of the income scale (Goode, 1956:53). National census data support, with some qualifications, this general relationship of class and divorce and are presented in Table 12.1.

There are some exceptions to the expected negative relationships of educational level and divorce rate. First, in both the 1960 and 1975 calculations, for those who started but did not finish college, there is the same proportions in intact first marriages as there is among high school graduates. Thus, the extra years of education that these college dropouts have does not increase the proportion in intact first marriages. This is not a reversal of the expected finding but merely a weakening of the expected relationship. However, for females we can actually see a reversal in Table 12.1. Those who have seventeen or more years of education, that is, those females who go to graduate school, show about the same percent living in intact first marriages as do women who did not finish high school. This is true for both the 1960 and 1975 checks, although by 1975 the percent in intact first marriages had increased considerably from about 55 percent to 63 percent. In 1975 there were over 900,000 women with graduate education and thus this is a sizable group and one that doubled in numbers from 1960 to 1975.

It is interesting to speculate as to why this group of highly educated females should have so much lower "intact" rates than those women who completed only four years of college. The most obvious reason that comes to mind is that they are the best suited to take care of themselves financially, and perhaps this increases their unwillingness to tolerate an unhappy relationship. In addition, such career women are high on gender equality (see Chapter 3) and this means they will not be as willing to alter their lives to cater to their husband's career demands—as most traditional wives do. As we shall see in Chapter 15, dual-career marriages are complex and have high breakage rates. There are few new norms to regulate dual-career marriages and that lack of institutionalized guidance increases the likelihood

TABLE 12.1

Percent of Persons Aged 35–54 in Intact First Marriages, by Education: U.S., 1960 and 1975.

| Years of School Completed | PERCENT MARRIED ONCE, SPOUSE PRESENT | | | |
| | Men 35–54 | | Women 35–54 | |
	1960	1975	1960	1975
Total	72.8	72.5	67.4	66.0
0–11 years	67.6	64.6	62.5	57.1
12 years	74.6	72.2	69.8	66.4
13–15 years	75.5	72.1	70.8	69.1
16 years	81.3	78.6	73.0	77.3
17 or more	80.2	81.8	54.8	63.4

Source: U.S. Bureau of the Census, 1977, Series P–20, No. 312, Tables F and 3; and U.S. Census of Population: 1960, Vol. 2, 4D. Marital Status, Table 4, 1966, as reproduced and organized in Glick and Norton (1977):9.

of interpersonal conflict. Also, Cherlin (1979) reports that wives who earn closer to their husband's level of income are more likely to divorce.

Notice that the males with graduate education are quite different—they have the greatest likelihood of being in an intact first marriage. There are many more males with a graduate education, and thus most of these men marry women without graduate education. Such highly educated men are at the top of the prestige hierarchy in our culture and most often their lower-educated wives cater to their career needs. There still is considerable traditional cultural support for both the wife and the husband to focus on the husband's career. The situation then of graduate-trained males is almost the opposite of that of graduate-trained females—strong cultural support versus weak cultural support and this is one of the key reasons, I would suggest, for the difference in marital stability.

One factor that helps explain the low divorce rate for women and men with Bachelor's degrees is age at marriage. The reader will remember that Figure 12.3 indicated that those who marry in their twenties have lower divorce rates than those who marry in their teens. College-educated people do marry about two or three years older than the median and thus even without other differences their divorce rate would be low (Bumpass and Sweet, 1972). I do believe education has an independent influence beyond just increasing the age at marriage but age at marriage is a factor worth exploring.

Table 12.2 presents additional data on the association of marital stability and educational level. Table 12.1 showed what proportion of people in their middle years (35–54) were still in their first marriage. Table 12.2 indicates the likelihood of people who were in their late twenties in 1975 to eventually divorce. The first two columns in Table 12.2 show the proportion already divorced for the various educational backgrounds and the second two columns show the proportion who

TABLE 12.2

Likelihood of Divorce for Persons Aged 25–29 in 1975, by Educational Level: U.S., 1975

Years of School Completed	PERCENT OF PERSONS WHOSE FIRST MARRIAGE HAD ENDED IN DIVORCE BY 1975		PERCENT OF PERSONS WHOSE FIRST MARRIAGE MAY EVENTUALLY END IN DIVORCE	
	Men	Women	Men	Women
All ever-married persons born 1945–1949	13	17	34	38
0–11 years	15	24	34	44
12 years	15	17	36	37
13–15 years	15	19	42	49
16 years	8	8	29	29
17 or more	8	9	30	33

Source: U.S. Bureau of the Census, 1977, Series P–20, No. 312. Table H. Data rearranged and presented in Glick and Norton (1977):19.

may eventually divorce. The assumption is made that the future divorce experience of this group of 25–29-year-olds will be similar to that experienced by older adults in recent years. Note that for both males and females the prediction (based on recent cohort experience) is that the college dropout group will have the highest divorce rate. Perhaps those who do not finish one endeavor possess life-styles that interfere with finishing other endeavors. We note also that the same lack of stability found earlier in Table 12.1 is present here for graduate-educated women. The difference is not large but the estimation is that 33 percent of graduate-educated women and only 29 percent of four-year-college women will eventually divorce. Of course, these estimations need to be corrected as the actual divorces occur. But we need to rely on the experience of the immediate past cohort in order to predict. It is possible that these rates will be higher since the divorce rate has risen so rapidly since the mid-1960s. Figure 12.4 illustrates the overall prediction for this age group and affords a grasp of the outcomes of the divorce rate as of 1975. Note that of those who enter second marriages, it is estimated that 45 percent (thirteen of twenty-nine) will divorce a second time. This is somewhat higher than ther 38 percent estimated for first marriages. The risk of divorce increases with each marriage. Finally, it should be borne in mind that in second marriages, educational background affects the risk of divorce in the same way as we discussed for first marriages. If one were to derive estimates for 1980, the divorce rate would be slightly higher and the remarriage rate (twenty-nine of thirty-eight, or 76 percent) not much different.

Overall, then, upper-educated people, if they finish college do have a lower divorce rate. There are many reasons for this situation. The stresses in the lower-

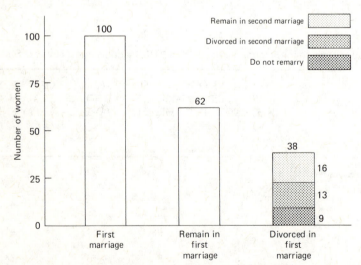

Figure 12.4. Marriage and Divorce Projections for Women Aged 25–29: 1975.
Source: Paul C. Glick and Arthur J. Norton (1977):36–37 (as diagramed in Kelley, 1979:597)

class style of life promotes the highest degree of marital strain and maladjustment, but whether or not the maladjustment shows itself in divorce rates depends on a variety of factors. One such factor would be the ease with which one can obtain a divorce in a society. When divorce is difficult and expensive to obtain, the upper classes will display the highest divorce rates *despite the fact* that the lower classes have the greatest marital maladjustment. Under such conditions, the lower classes will utilize separation, desertion, bigamy, and cohabitation to ease the strain of a tight-divorce situation. It may be that at the beginning of this century, when divorce was more difficult to obtain, the lower classes did not then have the highest divorce rates. As divorce became cheaper and more readily obtained, the lower class divorce rates rose. Since the 1930s, if not earlier, the lower classes in America have evidenced the highest divorce rate.

Another factor that leads to high instability in the lower classes is their weaker kinship structure. We shall see in Chapter 16 some support for this notion. Although Adams (1968) reports that the lower classes had more kin living nearby and visited them more, he also reported that the white-collar (middle) classes were more likely to have affectionate ties to kin and to have value consensus with their kin. This situation was, in turn, related to the greater occupational success of the middle-class fathers.

Zimmerman (1956), Ackerman (1963), and Lewis (1973) have presented evidence from America and from other societies that tends to agree with the importance of group support in preventing divorce. Part of this group support would be in the form of kinship backing, and such support seems stronger emotionally and economically in the middle classes. These researchers also found that if the wife has friends who are similar in values to herself this tends to keep her marriage intact. If one compared two groups of marriages that were identical in interpersonal quality, but one was supported by kin and friends and the other was not, one could wager that the group lacking such outside support would have higher divorce rates. This fits with our discussion in Chapter 10 concerning the role of normative support as a factor in dyadic commitment. The attitudes of others, as perceived by oneself, have a major impact on us. Here is further evidence of that same proposition. The attitudes of kin and friends that define a marriage as stable can help make that marriage last by strengthening a stable marital view on the part of the married pair. Just as we saw that courtship is not strictly an individual matter, so it would seem that marriage and divorce are also not strictly individual matters. The social context has a powerful influence in both instances.

How is it that divorce rates drop during a depression and yet the life-style of poverty seems to go with high divorce rates? The answer is that poor economic conditions go with a high degree of marital problems and maladjustment, but whether these lead to divorce depends on the ease of obtaining a divorce. In depressions divorce may be too expensive. Also, in depressions other factors, such as a sense of loyalty when under strain, may prevent one from getting a divorce. I mentioned earlier that many Great Depression marriages broke up later during the 1940s and contributed to that decade's high divorce rate. The reader should bear in mind, also, that during the Great Depression the lower classes still had the highest divorce rate. The only change was that the divorce rate for all classes was somewhat reduced (see Figure 12.2).

Intermarriage and Divorce

INTERFAITH MARRIAGE

The assertion has often been made that interfaith marriage is one cause of divorce, and therefore such marriages should display higher divorce rates. Older studies in the past by Bell (1938), Weeks (1943), and Landis (1949) supported that assertion. The most astute students reading this book should have some questions in their minds about this overall relation of divorce and interfaith marriage. We know that divorce rates are generally higher for the lower classes and for females who marry very young. Thus, before we can accept the findings that divorce is higher in interfaith marriages, we must "control" on social class and age at marriage. What I mean by this is that we must look at people who are of the *same* social class and the *same* age at marriage and see if, *within* a group alike in social class and age at marriage, those who are involved in interfaith marriages have higher divorce rates. If we do not check this out and simply look at some overall finding that lumps all classes and ages at marriage together, then it is always possible that the interfaith couples display a higher divorce rate, *not* because of their different faiths, but because such couples are more likely to be lower class and to marry early. The only way to check this out is to divide the total group into subgroups of the same social class and the same age at marriage and see if the difference in divorce rates still holds up. (See Appendix 3 for a more detailed statement of this common type of causal reasoning.)

One key study which made a check such as I suggest above is Burchinal and Chancellor's study of divorce and interfaith marriage in Iowa (1962). Iowa is one of two states that ask one's religion when one applies for a license to marry and when one is divorced. (The other state is Indiana.) Burchinal and Chancellor took the marriage and divorce data for the years 1953 to 1959 and calculated the "survival" rate for each type of religious marriage. In other words if during those years there were 10,000 homogamous Catholic marriages and 1,000 divorces were granted to marriages of two Catholics, then the divorce rate is 10 percent and the "survival rate" is 90 percent. Survival rates give a more objective picture of the situation than do failure or divorce rates. A failure rate of 10 percent for one group and 5 percent for another could lead to one's concluding that there is a great deal more failure in one group. Whereas a success rate of 90 percent for one group and 95 percent for the other group gives a more objective appreciation of the magnitude of the difference involved.

Table 12.3 presents the basic findings for the various subgroups in their sample. Note that Protestants were classified into those who are "church Protestants"—and

TABLE 12.3

Marital Survival Rates among Four Types of Religiously Homogamous or Interreligious Marriages by the Age of Brides and the Status of Husbands at Divorce

Spousal Religious Affiliation Types	Total	AGE OF BRIDES AND STATUS OF HUSBANDS							
		Nineteen or Younger				Twenty or Older			
		Low	Middle	High	Total	Low	Middle	High	Total
Catholic-Catholic	96.2	88.3	92.6	97.2	92.9	95.5	97.6	99.4	97.9
Church-Protestant or Protestant with/church Protestant or Protestant	86.2	68.1	81.5	93.2	80.9	83.1	92.0	96.3	92.7
Catholic-interreligious									
Catholic wife	79.8	63.9	74.3	86.7	73.0	77.4	89.4	91.1	86.9
Catholic husband	74.8	56.3	68.3	84.2	67.0	77.7	82.4	91.0	84.5
Total	77.6	60.3	71.2	85.5	70.1	77.6	86.1	91.0	85.8
Total	87.6	70.0	82.8	93.3	81.8	86.1	93.0	96.7	93.5

Source: Lee G. Burchinal and Loren E. Chancellor (December 1962): 753.

this means they gave the name of a specific denomination— and "other" Protestants, who are those people who simply wrote "Protestant" when asked their religion. The impact of the social class of the groom and the age of the bride can be seen by reading any one row of statistics across the table. For example, in Catholic-Catholic marriages between a bride nineteen or younger and a groom of low status, the seven-year survival rate (marriages still intact) was 88.3 percent. In the same Catholic-Catholic marriages, if the bride was twenty or older and the groom of high status, the survival rate was 99.4 percent. Or look at Catholic interreligious marriages and the figures would be 60.3 and 91.0 percent, respectively, for the same control categories. The range in these figures makes it clear that the age of the bride and the social class of the groom do make a difference in estimating divorce rates for interfaith marriages. However, religious mixture itself still seems to make a difference in survival rates. To see this, simply read down any column such as "bride twenty or older and groom high status" and one finds that the Catholic-Catholic survival is 99.4 percent, and the mixed marriage survival under the same age and status conditions is 91.0 percent. Thus, even with age and status controlled, the religious mixture makes a difference. However, and this is the key point, the difference is severely reduced and is considerably greater for some age and status combinations than for others. The difference is the least for the groups used above in my example, being only 8.4 percentage points. This type of mixed-faith marriage with a female twenty or older and a male of high status is a typical mixed-faith marriage of college-educated people. The extra divorce risk for this mixed-faith marriage group is small compared with that of the group with a female nineteen or younger and a low-status groom—in such a case the difference between a Catholic-Catholic and a mixed marriage is 88.3 and 60.3 percent, or 28 percent. Thus, for such people, a mixed-faith marriage entails much higher risks.

During the 1960s Christensen and Barber (1967) lent support to the findings of Burchinal and Chancellor. Finally, more recent evidence comes from a 1970 national sample of ever-married women under age forty-five. In this sample Bumpass and Sweet (1972) also found that even with age at marriage and other factors controlled, interfaith marriages still had higher divorce rates. Their method of analysis did not allow for discerning the specific differences we've discussed in Table 12.3. But it does indicate that even with the increase in interfaith marriage, there still seems to be some additional risk. Of course, this finding is not sufficient to either frighten one off from interfaith marriage or to encourage one. The value decision regarding any form of marriage is a personal one (see Appendix 1).

One ought to be aware of other possible interpretations of these findings. Any set of findings is tentative, for it is always possible that someone can come along and formulate a different and equally plausible explanation of what has been discovered. For example, instead of saying that the Burchinal and Chancellor findings lead one to conclude that religious mixture is one cause of divorce, I could conclude that there is a third factor responsible for these findings. A general nonconformist attitude might make one more willing to break the traditional barrier to interfaith marriage and also make one more likely to break the barrier to divorce. Thus, persons who intermarry might be more nonconformist and, because of this trait, have a likelihood to marry out of their religion and also to divorce. In such cases, the interfaith marriage might not be at all causally related to divorce. Only careful research will enable us to examine such alternate explanations. Interfaith marriages have increased throughout this century (Goldstein and Goldscheider, 1968; Thomas, 1956; Heer, 1962; Massarik and Chenkin, 1973). This is clearly seen in the Jewish group where, in 1900, 2 percent of the Jewish individuals were involved in a mixed-faith marriage and by 1972 this percent was 32 percent (Massarek and Chenkin, 1973:295). These trends should encourage future research.

INTERRACIAL MARRIAGE

In 1967 the Supreme Court invalidated the miscegenation laws that had been in effect for over two hundred years in many states. There was some increase in interracial marriages in the 1960s and even more in the 1970s (Carter and Glick, 1976:412). Nevertheless, today in 1980 less than one percent of all marriages are interracial. Table 12.4 presents data about the total number of interracial marriages in existence in 1970. Note that less than one percent of white and black wives are interracially married. The percent for other racial groups was considerably higher: 39 percent of American Indian wives; 33 percent of Japanese wives; 12 percent of Chinese wives; and 27 percent of Filipino wives. Since black-white interracial marriages have increased since 1960, those percents would be somewhat higher for those married since 1960.

In 1960 there was a total of 148,000 interracial marriages in existence. By 1970 this had increased to 330,000 as shown in Table 12.4. The 1977 total of interracial marriages was 421,000 (U.S. Bureau of the Census, 1978, P–23, No. 77:7). Only a minority of this total of interracial marriages consists of black/white marriages. For example, in 1960 there were 51,000 black/white marriages in existence; in 1970 the total black/white marriages in existence rose to 65,000 and by 1977 to 125,000. Table 12.4 will afford the reader a general appreciation of the overall variety of interracial marriages that exist. The trend seems to be toward more interracial marriages although such unions, particularly for blacks and whites, obviously still comprise a very small proportion of all marriages.

One characteristic of black/white marriages is that about three-quarters of the 125,000 black/white marriages in existence in 1977 were black males and white females. Note that the reverse situation traditionally prevails in white/Japanese marriages! In white/Chinese marriages and white/American Indian marriages the ratio seems almost even. The reasons for these different patterns are not at all understood. We do know that a large proportion of black/white marriages are among highly educated persons, i.e. those who graduate or at least attend college. Interracial marriage is the highest for those black males who go to graduate school (Carter and Glick, 1976:414). There is not a large difference in the percent of black females and males who attend college. Of those 25–29 years of age in 1977, 34 percent of black males and 29 percent of black females had attended college and about 13 percent of both genders graduated (U.S. Bureau of the Census, 1977, Series P–20, No. 314, Table 1). It is possible that a higher proportion of black

TABLE 12.4
Race of Husband by Race of Wife: 1970 U.S.A.

			RACE OF WIFE				
	White	Negro	American Indian	Japanese	Chinese	Filipino	Other race
Number by Race of husband:							
White	40,578,427	23,566	44,903	44,138	6,941	12,238	30,434
Negro	41,223	3,334,292	2,835	1,793	316	1,187	1,907
American Indian	40,039	1,527	76,867	235	95	241	779
Japanese	9,872	137	130	105,493	1,294	608	1,535
Chinese	7,188	324	55	2,418	74,853	552	1,191
Filipino	15,674	712	457	1,995	525	42,718	2,152
Other race	21,706	904	733	1,779	1,215	1,147	46,222
	40,714,129	3,371,464	125,980	157,851	85,239	58,691	84,220
Percent by race of Husband:							
White	99.7	0.7	35.6	28.0	8.1	20.9	36.1
Negro	0.1	99.2	2.3	1.1	0.4	2.0	2.3
American Indian	0.1	—	61.0	0.1	0.1	0.4	0.9
Japanese	—*	—	0.1	66.8	1.5	1.0	1.8
Chinese	—	—	—	1.5	87.8	0.9	1.4
Filipino	—	—	0.4	1.3	0.6	72.8	2.6
Other race	0.1	—	0.6	1.1	1.4	2.0	54.9
	100.0	100.0	100.0	100.0	100.0	100.0	100.0

Number by Race of husband (totals): White 40,740,647; Negro 3,393,555; American Indian 119,783; Japanese 119,069; Chinese 86,581; Filipino 64,233; Other race 73,706.

Source: U.S. Bureau of the Census; 1972. 1970 Census of Population PC(2)4c, Marital Status, Table 12, p. 262.

Percents below a tenth of one percent are indicated by a dash. Percents are rounded to the nearest tenth of one percent.

Photo by Leon Sokolsky.

males compared to black females attend predominantly white colleges and if so then that would help account for the higher likelihood of marriage of black males and white females. It is also possible that white females and black males have more favorable attitudes toward the other race than do white males and black females. At the moment these are purely hunches and obviously need to be examined along with other possible explanations. Some have suggested that interracial marriages increase in proportion to the equality of the racial groups involved. We do know that homogamy in background enhances the likelihood of marriage (see Chapter 5). Opportunity is another variable that seems important—generally the smaller the size of the group the greater the likelihood of an out marriage (Thomas, 1956). Gender imbalance has been found in interreligious marriages where among Jews it is the male and among Catholics it is the female who is most likely to marry outside their faith. These regularities have also not been adequately explained.

From the point of view of numbers, there are twelve black females for every ten black males. Thus, black females are concerned over interracial marriages for there already is a shortage of black males. This gender ratio could be brought closer into balance if more black females than black males married out but just the opposite is the case. Obviously, the motivation for interracial marriage is not to balance the gender ratio. There are other pieces to the black/white interracial marital puzzle. Government statistics indicate that those who do not fit the pattern of black groom and white wife have higher divorce rates than those who do fit that pattern. Divorce rates appear to be higher for both types but they are the highest for white husband

and black wife combinations. Data from the 1960 and 1970 censuses report that 90 percent of the white/white marriages and 78 percent of the black/black marriages contracted in the 1950s were still intact in 1970; and this compared with 63 percent of the black husband/white wife marriages and only 47 percent of the white husband/ black wife marriages (Carter and Glick, 1976:415).

One interesting indicator of the rates of interracial marriage is the proportion of children living with one or both parents who are of a race different from that of one or both parents. The percent was .5 percent for white children, 1 percent for black children, 11 percent for Chinese, 13 percent for Japanese, and 24 percent for American Indian children. Clearly, the focus on black/white interracial marriage is not because of its prevalence. Of all interracial marriages over 80 percent in 1970 and over 70 percent in 1977 were *not* black/white marriages. The reasons, I suspect, are that this is the largest nonwhite racial group and that there still are strong prejudices dating from slavery against black/white marriages. Other interracial marriages, although also viewed with prejudice, lack this same historical background and represent smaller population groups (Blackwell, 1975; Bilingsley, 1968; Miller, 1973). Although opposition appears to be lessening to black/white marriages, it is surely far from fully dissolved.

Children and Divorce

One of the most interesting questions concerning divorce revolves about the number of children involved and the impact of the divorce upon them. The question of the number of children involved in divorce can be easily answered. Figure 12.5 clearly shows how the number of children involved in divorce has tripled since 1953 and, until 1964, rose at a much more rapid rate than that of divorce itself. About 55 percent of divorces now involve children. The average number of children per divorce has ranged from 1.2 to 1.3, from 1960 to 1975 and in 1977 fell to just 1.0. Over one million children have been involved in divorce every year since 1972. Even in 1970 only about 70 percent of the children below eighteen were living with both their, only once married, natural parents (Glick, 1975: 21–22).

There seems to be an increased willingness since the 1950s to get divorced when children are present. One might interpret the greater number of children per divorce to be simply due to the increased birthrates following World War II. However, the birthrate has been declining since the late 1950s and is now at the lowest level in our history, and the number of children per divorce is still about what it was in 1960. Thus, it would seem that at least part of the reason for the increased presence of children in divorce is a real increase in acceptance of divorce when children are present.

One possible explanation for this change is that people today are more likely to believe that divorce will not harm a child psychologically any more than will an unhappy marriage and thus they are more willing to resort to divorce when they are unhappy. What is the evidence on the impact of divorce on children? (For a recent review see Longfellow, 1979.) It is interesting that at the same time as the

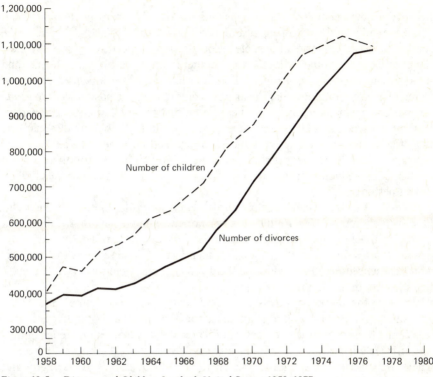

Figure 12.5.   Divorces and Children Involved: United States, 1958–1977.
Source: U.S. Department of HEW, May 16, 1979, Vol. 28,
No. 2:2.

number of children per divorce was rising, there was a notable increase in research into the question of the impact on them of divorce. Perhaps the researchers were caught up in some mood of the nation and were also wondering about the validity of the old norms that stressed the importance of "staying together for the sake of the children."

To get some indication of the impact of divorce on children, let us look at Goode's early study of divorced mothers in Detroit (Goode, 1956). This is a study dating from 1948 and since divorce was less acceptable then, this would tend to increase the likelihood that divorce would have a damaging impact on children. So, whatever negative effects we find here should probably be reduced at least somewhat. There are some comparable recent studies (Longfellow, 1979). In re-sponse to Goode's questioning, most of the mothers indicated concern about the possible damage to the child, but felt they had to get the divorce anyway. In later checks, only 14 percent of the mothers reported that the children were harder to handle after the divorce, and 55 percent saw little impact of the divorce process on the difficulty of handling their children (Goode, 1956:318). The mothers' view of the impact of divorce on their children was more optimistic if they had remarried. Of the remarried women in Goode's sample, 75 percent thought their children's lives were now better than in the previous marriage; 15 percent thought it was about the same; and only 8 percent thought it was worse (Goode, 1956:318). One should, however, be aware of possible rationalization in the answers given by these divorced women. Some of them may be attempting to justify their divorce and their present position. In addition, a study of children from divorced homes by Rosenberg (1965) indicates that remarriage seems to have the possibility of *lowering* the self-esteem of the child. Rosenberg found that those children whose parents had *not* remarried had higher self-esteem. We will shortly talk more of remarriage but clearly there are many types of remarriage and they need to be looked at separately in any assessment of their consequences on children. Also there may be a different consequence of remarriage for the divorced person than for the children of that person.

Another factor relevant to impact on children would be the age of the child. One would suppose that a child of a year or two should have less difficulty in getting adjusted to a new life-style than a child of nine or ten. The impact of the divorce process on the mother is another such factor. Goode reports that mothers who experienced high trauma during the divorce process were most likely to report that their children were not too happy.

What is the proper comparison for a child in a divorced home? Should we compare such a child to a child in an intact home, in an intact but unhappy home, in a home broken by death or separation? These choices make a difference in how one answers the question we are now discussing concerning the impact of divorce. There are a variety of studies in this area (Nye, 1957; Landis, 1962; Perry and Pfuhl, 1963; Burchinal, 1964; Rosenberg, 1965; Longfellow, 1979; Raschke and Raschke, 1979) which can be cited. There is a general similarity of findings.

Burchinal (1964) compared five family types: unbroken, mother only, mother and stepfather, both parents remarried, and father and stepmother. He checked over 1,800 adolescent boys and girls from all the seventh and eleventh grades in Cedar Rapids, Iowa. Burchinal reports that there were no statistically significant differences in personality characteristics of these adolescents in any of the five family types. There were also no significant differences among youngsters from these five family types in grades, participation in school or community activities, number of friends, attitudes toward school, and such.

Before Burchinal's study, Judson Landis (1962) and Ivan Nye (1957) reported similar findings indicating little difference in children from broken and unbroken homes. Nye (1957) compared children from intact but unhappy homes with children from broken homes and found little personality differences in adjustment measures. Perry and Pfuhl compared children from unbroken homes, broken homes, and "remarriage homes" and found little significant difference (Perry and Pfuhl, 1963).

Generally, then, the findings here indicate that there is little basis for concluding that divorce inevitably does lasting psychological damage to children. Now, of course, one must qualify this and note that it is possible that there was severe trauma at the time of divorce, but that the youngsters overcame it and showed no lasting effect. A check of children years later would never reveal such a situation.

Also, the studies I have mentioned above are local studies and far from adequate in terms of controlling on social class and other variables. It is possible that the impact on children differs for people in the different social classes. Perhaps the wealthier families have more money to ease the strain with vacations, psychological help, kinship support, and such. Equally possible is a hypothesis that states that the upper classes would show the most effect on children because a divorced woman of the upper classes would be least able to maintain her former standard of living by herself, and this would add an additional strain to the situation. A carefully done study by Rosenberg (1965:105) shows that emotional disturbance is more likely when the child is Catholic or Jewish, the mother young, and when the mother has remarried. Perhaps the greater sense of normative violation by Catholics and Jews is the explanation for the religious difference. Similar findings have recently been reported by Duberman (1975). The most recent study is by Raschke and Raschke (1979) who tested schoolchildren in a fashion similar to Burchinal's earlier study. Their results indicated that whether they came from an intact or a one-parent home was not a major factor. The differences in the child's self-concept depended on the amount of conflict in the home, regardless of what type it was. This was also the conclusion reached by Longfellow (1979) in her review of this area.

Let me caution the reader that the impact of divorce on children need not be only psychologically disturbing. It may well be that divorce produces more imaginative, more self-reliant types of personalities *because of* the lack of two parents as guides. We need not assume that if divorce has any consequence on children it must be "detrimental." Even if we do not like a behavior we must, in the interest of fairness, be willing to admit that it may have consequences that we do like and we should be willing to look for such consequences.

Divorce and Remarriage

One final important question concerning divorce is its relation to remarriage. Sociologists as far back as Emile Durkheim (1897) in the nineteenth century have considered divorce rates to be an index of social disorganization. The rate at which a home broken by divorce is reorganized by a remarriage is an important factor. If remarriage is common, then the notion that divorce is a measure of social disorganization is surely weakened. William Goode (1956) presents the viewpoint that remarriage rates are high when divorce rates are high and that divorce is simply a temporary break in family life and not a sign of social disorganization. Figure 12.6 shows the trend in remarriage, first marriage, and divorce rates from 1921 to 1977. There is a general congruence of remarriage and divorce rates except for the period after 1965 when divorce was rising and the remarriage rate started to fall.

Goode asserts that the role of being divorced is ambiguous. There is no clear-cut accepted way for divorced people to behave. There is no institutionalized role of divorced persons that states the rights and duties of that person in relation to others. For example, should one go to a new town to live, maintain the same

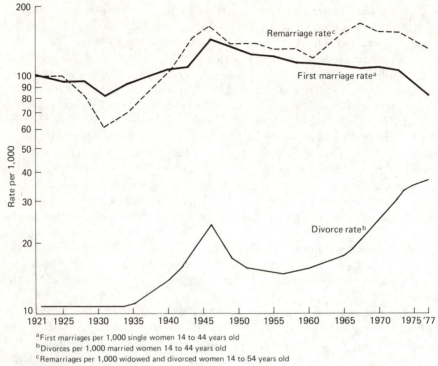

^aFirst marriages per 1,000 single women 14 to 44 years old
^bDivorces per 1,000 married women 14 to 44 years old
^cRemarriages per 1,000 widowed and divorced women 14 to 54 years old

*Figure 12.6. Rates of First Marriage, Divorce, and Remarriage for U.S. Women: 1921–1977.
Source: Glick and Norton (1977):5.*

married friends, and so on? The norms are not clear on many of these issues, and there are other norms that directly pressure toward remarriage. Remarriage is the easy way out of the ill-defined role of the divorced person and this may be one reason why high divorce rates go with high remarriage rates. Thus, although divorce does involve personal disorganization in its emotional stresses, it need not involve social disorganization because of the rapid remarriage of the divorced person. In this sense it is similar to broken engagements which also are not good measures of social disorganization.

These trends toward higher remarriage rates in the 1960s were largely confined to the white population where the percentage of all marriages in a particular year involving remarriage went up from 20 to 25 percent between 1960 and 1969. This rise in the proportion of remarriages has continued and in 1973, 28 percent of the marriages were remarriages (U.S. Department of HEW, Vol. 24, No. 5, 1975:3).

This proportion of remarriage prevails today. It is this rise in remarriage that partially balanced the drop in first marriages and thereby kept the overall marriage rate from dropping even more than it did in the 1970s. First marriage and remarriage rates now seem to be leveling out.

Most persons marry those of like status; for example, over 90 percent of the single men and women will marry another single person, whereas over half of the divorced men and women will remarry a divorced person and about half of the widowed population will marry people who have been widowed. The second most popular choice for widowed people is a divorced person, whereas the second most popular choice for the single group was a divorced person. In general, the choice in remarriages favored marriage to someone who had been divorced (U.S. Department of HEW, 1973, Series 21, No. 25:11). The high remarriage rate of this group is reflected in this choice pattern. The precise reasons for the above patterns can only be speculated about since no substantial research has been done on this point. Nevertheless, one obvious reason for the homogamy tendencies that comes to mind is that people who have gone through a similar type of break in their marriage have some common basis upon which to start a new relationship. Also, age is likely the reason that only divorced people choose single people as their second choice of future mate. Divorced people are younger than the widowed and thus there is a larger single population available to them. However, age and homogamy explain only part of the reasons, and we sorely need research on this type of "previously married courtship" experience.

The speed of remarriage also rose during the 1960s. In the 1950s the divorced person remarrying would have been divorced about four years on the average (U.S. Bureau of the Census, 1972). Remarriage now takes about three years on the average as can be seen in Figure 12.7.

Figure 12.7 points out that of those who remarry, over 15 percent do so within just months of the divorce and fully 50 percent do so in about three years. While it is true that more males who divorce remarry than do females, it is clear from

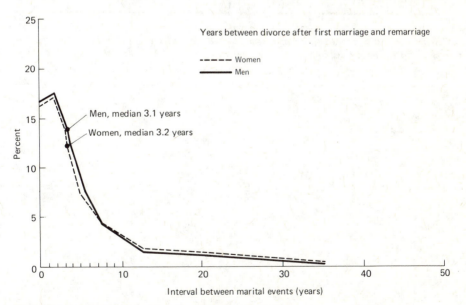

Figure 12.7. Median Number of Years from Divorce to Remarriage.
Source: U.S. Bureau of the Census, 1976, Series P-20, No. 297:15. *The estimates for the graph are based on all people born between 1900 and 1949.*

Figure 12.7 that, for those males and females who do remarry, there is little difference in the speed of the process. Comparing Figure 12.7 with Figure 12.1 indicates that the speed of exit from the first marriage is much slower than the speed of entry into the second marriage. It takes an average of seven years for those who divorce to leave the first marriage, but only three years after the divorce for those who remarry to enter their second marriage. For those who break the second marriage, the speed of exit increases. The average length of second marriage for those who divorce is about five years, some two years less than the average length of the first marriage (U.S. Bureau of the Census, 1976, P–20, No. 297:14). We saw in Figure 12.4 that an estimated 45 percent of second marriages will break compared to an estimated 38 percent of first marriages. Thus, there is a somewhat higher risk of divorce in second marriages. Third and higher-order marriages are quite rare but it is true that the divorce rate rises with each order of marriage.

I have added Table 12.5 to afford the reader more precise insight into remarriage rates and how they are affected by the age at divorce and number of children one has. Reading across the first row of figures you will note at the far right the 3.2 median years divorced for remarried women which is present in Figure 12.7. Note that for those "still divorced" the average time since the divorce is 4.7 years. The

TABLE 12.5

Characteristics of Divorced Women: U.S., 1975 (Women whose first marriage ended in divorce, by age at divorce, number of children born before divorce, duration of divorce, and whether remarried)

Age at divorce and number of children born before divorce	All women with first marriage ended in divorce		Percent remarried by survey date	MEDIAN YEARS DIVORCED* At survey date		
	Number	Percent		Total	Divorced	Remarried
Total aged 14–75 with fewer than 6 children born before divorce	9,068	100.0	66.0	3.6	4.7	3.2
Aged 14–29 at divorce	5,845	64.5	76.3	3.1	3.4	3.1
No children	1,932		79.6	2.9	2.6	2.9
1 child	1,947		75.0	3.1	3.6	3.0
2 children	1,233		74.9	3.1	3.4	3.0
3–5 children	732		73.6	4.0	5.2	3.8
Aged 30–39 at divorce	2,202	24.3	56.2	4.5	5.8	3.8
Aged 40–75 at divorce	1,021	11.3	28.1	5.5	6.5	2.9

*Number of years between divorce and survey date for those still divorced; number of years between divorce and second marriage for those remarried.
Source: U.S. Bureau of the Census, 1977, Series P–20, No. 312, Tables I, J, and K as organized and presented in Glick and Norton (1977):20.

3.6 figure on this line is simply the average number of divorced years for the total number of women, remarried or not. Looking at the findings regarding the impact of children on remarriage, it appears that this impact is quite small unless one has three to five children—then it does seem to go with a somewhat longer time to remarry (3.8 years). It is interesting that the percent remarried by the survey date (1975) doesn't vary very much according to how many children one has. Between 73.6 and 79.6 percent were remarried regardless of the number of children. Of course, one does not know if the range of choice and number of chances for remarriage was greater for those with fewer children. Those with no children do show the highest rate remarried and the quickest remarriage time but the differences are not great. One final aspect brought out by this table is that the younger one is at the time of divorce, the greater the chance for remarriage (76.3 percent to 28.1 percent). Now, these are not final figures for the women in the table—some of them will remarry after the survey date of 1975. About 75 percent of all divorced women (and 85 percent of divorced men) do remarry and in this total table only 66 percent of the divorced women did remarry by the survey date—so some additional remarriages will occur but these are unlikely to change the general type of relationships upon which we have focused.

When I spoke of courtship in Part II of this book, I spoke predominantly of the courtship of two individuals who were never previously married. Now, given the fact that between 25 and 30 percent of all marriages in any year involve at least one person who has been previously married, it is apparent that much courtship occurs among such people. Over three-quarters of the previously married who remarry are divorced people, for divorced people are more likely to remarry than widowed people. The courtship of previously married people is different. For example, whereas 80 percent of first marriages involve a religious ceremony, less than 60 percent of remarriages involve a religious ceremony (U.S. Department of HEW, 1973c, Series 21, No. 25:14). The likelihood of sexual intercourse before marriage is higher for divorced people (Gebhard, et al., 1958; Reiss, 1967; Hunt, 1974). Bernard (1956) has shown that such formalities as engagement announcements, honeymoon trips, and such are less likely in second marriages.

We have here then a type of courtship among previously married people that has hardly been touched upon by researchers. The "second marriage" courtship makes a fascinating comparison with the "first marriage" courtship that most all studies focus upon. Due to low divorce rates, the highest-educated group has usually had about half the proportion remarried as does the lowest-educated group in both races. Perhaps the fact that those who go to college and write college textbooks are least likely to be involved in a remarriage type of courtship accounts for the lack of research and interest in this important phenomenon. Perhaps now that our divorce rates have risen so dramatically, this situation will change. Perhaps we should systematically talk of "first marriage courtship" and "second marriage courtship" to encourage the distinction between these types of courtship.

Not only is courtship different in second marriages, but the family and marital relationships are also different (Walker, et al., 1977; Furstenberg, 1978; Duberman, 1975; Westoff, 1977). We are beginning to see a trickle of research reported here. For example, one key difference is in the number of parents, grandparents, and

Photo by David Sherman.

step-kin of all types involved in remarriages. A ten-year-old girl living with her remarried mother would have a stepfather and a biological father and an extra set of grandparents via the stepfather; and if her stepfather has children of his own she will have step-siblings. I could go on to illustrate the complexity by referring to the visits by her biological father as a major event in her life as distinct from children from once married homes. Stepparent relationships are complex and not clearly delineated in our culture. Duberman reports that stepmothers, in particular, have a difficult time in reconstituted families (Duberman, 1975). Marital relations cannot escape the impact of such a different set of relationships with children and other kin. Westoff reports that sexual relations are more satisfying and more frequent in the second marriage and national statistics do back up this finding (Westoff, 1977:126). Surely, the possibilities for exceptional rewards are present in reconstituted families but there is no denying the complexity of such families.

The function of marriage, we stated in Chapter 2, is the legitimization of parenthood. What about couples fifty years of age or older who marry, but all of whose children are grown and away, and who have no intention (and in most cases the females are postmenopausal) of having children? Does their marriage have the consequence of legitimizing parenthood? It would seem not to be the case. If any form of marriage deserves the name "companionship marriage," it would be this sort of union. It does not fully fit our conception of marriage as a transition to the family either; nor does the courtship involved fit our conception of parental influence on courtship. I would suggest that what we have in this type of marriage is socially and psychologically distinct. It is a relationship that, unlike younger marriage, comes from a different type of courtship and leads to a different type of family. It is, therefore, a very special part of the integrated set of institutions that we have called the Family Systems. I should like to think of it as a branch of the marital institution, an alternative type of marriage, which is not a central part of the dominant Family System. Perhaps the term "postparental marriage" would be appropriate. Such a marriage has its own type of courtship and its own type of family linkages. To further chart the interrelations between this type of marriage and the dominant Family System in America would be of great importance to our thinking in this area. It represents marriage with relatively weak ties to one's parents (who are usually deceased) and to one's children (who usually live separately). It fits what some writers have in mind as the ideal lovers' union with a minimal amount of responsibility. This type of marriage helps to make us aware of how much more than a simple "companionship marriage" is involved in most other American marriages. It is analogous to a youthful marriage wherein a deliberate plan to avoid having children is actually carried out. Both marriage types are "nonparental." We will talk further of such marriages in the next chapter.

Summary and Conclusions

Statistics in and of themselves have little value—but statistics that help one grasp a broad conceptual schema are of utmost value. I hope the reader feels that the statistics here have been of the latter variety. In 1978 over 1 million marriages were broken by divorce, and over 625,000 new marriages were contracted with at least one party who had been divorced or widowed. Perhaps 500,000 of these remarriages involved divorced people. These simple statistics lend force to William Goode's argument that divorce is not a sign of social disorganization, for we have a system that promotes remarriage for almost 80 percent of the divorced people and does so in a very short time. Thus, divorce for the majority of people seems to be a temporary break in their married years rather than a permanent one. In the majority of cases divorce does not seem to lead to the abandonment of children or to economic chaos. There is a psychological price involved, of course, but the overall system of marriage and the family seems to stay intact. Glick and Norton (1977) report evidence of a recent decline in the remarriage rate and it may reduce the proportion who remarry from 80 percent to perhaps 75 percent, and extend the period of time from divorce to remarriage. There is an increase in cohabitation among divorced people and this may be part of the reason for the reduction in the remarriage rate.

Death is also a major breaker of marriages, with about as many marriages breaking each year from death as from divorce. This is a radical change from a hundred years ago when divorce accounted for only 3 percent of marital breakage and death accounted for 97 percent (Jacobson, 1959; Thwing and Thwing, 1887). The impact of death on the remaining spouse and on children is another area in need of research.

At present, divorce seems a rather expected part of our Family Systems. Most of the states in the union have a "no fault" type of divorce law today (Wright and Stetson, 1978). Given a great deal of power in choosing mates on the part of young people and given interpersonal affectional attraction as the basis for marriage choice, the wonder is that the divorce rates are not higher. No social scientist would try to predict the next fifty years of interaction between two people and hope for such a low rate of inaccurate prediction. I have tried to point out how other countries are experiencing rising divorce rates as they adopt our type of participant-run courtship system. Also, the relatively early age at marriage is probably in good part a result of a participant-run system. Where people marry because they are in love and not primarily out of duty or for social/class reasons, one would expect them to be more desirous of marriage and, thus, marriage should occur earlier. The early age at marriage makes divorce and remarriage a more likely occurrence and probably encourages people to feel that a second chance can still be taken. Even with our rising age at first marriage, we still marry at relatively young ages. With love as the basis for marriage, young people who find they are no longer "in love" feel justified in divorcing and seeking to find a basis for a lasting marriage with another individual.

Many key questions remain unanswered. We know from the chapters on courtship that homogamy is a key factor in mate choice. How does it operate in remarriages as compared to first marriages? What is the full impact of divorce on children? And what is the impact of children on remarriage? How does the presence of one or more children affect courtship? What is the difference for children and for the father in the 10 percent of cases where the father receives custody (Gersick, 1979)? What type of man considers a woman with children a ready-made family and thus an advantage? How do these findings vary by the social class of the people involved? Do religious and economic factors play roles in remarriage that have not been commented upon at present? What is the impact of the increasing number of children involved in divorce on the adult roles of these children? Will their courtship differ because of this experience with more than one parental set or with only one parent? Will their marital stability differ (Mueller and Pope, 1977)? Will they be better equipped for self-reliant types of work in the economy? What about fertility between marriages? We know that over 10 percent of our births occur after a divorce and before a remarriage (Rindfuss and Bumpass, 1977; Glick and Norton, 1977). What are the social meanings and implications of such births?

Many chapters in Part Three are relevant to the understanding of the processes of interaction and social pressures that lead to divorce. In Chapter 9 we discussed the place of power and communication in marital conflict. In Chapter 10 we discussed our notions of how the reward-tension balance, norms, and structural constraints all operate to affect the determination to continue a relationship. In Chapter 11 the place of sexual attitudes and behavior in marriage was discussed in ways relevant to the understanding of divorce. Surely, the dynamic changes in male-female gender roles make prediction of one's mate's behavior much more difficult and thereby increases marital conflict and divorce. In addition, the earlier chapters pointed out in more depth the nature of gender roles and of our participant-run courtship in ways that should aid in understanding divorce.

One final point. Granted that in all Family Systems some breakage is inevitable and granted that remarriage mitigates the disturbance of such breakage, still one can raise the questions: "How much breakage is beyond the 'inevitable'? And to what extent does remarriage make divorce less 'disruptive' to the Family Systems?" I raise these questions because it is important that the reader not leave this topic thinking that social scientists have a metric system by which they can presently measure the level of divorce and remarriage that is compatible with what we value in our social lives. One should keep in mind that, with respect to a scientific understanding of human society, almost all laymen are blind. The sociologist can lead here only because "in the kingdom of the blind, the one-eyed man is king."

References

Ackerman, Charles. 1963. "Affiliations: Structural Determinants of Differential Divorce Rates," *American Journal of Sociology* 69 (July):13–21.

Adams, Bert N. 1968. *Kinship in an Urban Setting*. Chicago: Markham.

Albrecht, Stan L. 1979. "Reactions and Adjustments to Divorce: Differences in the Openness of Males and Females," *Family Coordinator*, Vol. 28 (in press).

Bell, Howard W. 1938. *Youth Tell Their Story*. Washington, DC: American Council on Education.

Bernard, Jessie. 1956. *Remarriage: A Study of Marriage*. New York: Holt, Rinehart and Winston.

Billingsley, Andrew. 1968. *Black Families in White America*. Englewood Cliffs, NJ: Prentice-Hall.

Blackwell, James E. 1975. *The Black Community*. New York: Dodd, Mead.

Brown, Prudence, Lorraine Perry, and Ernest Harburg. 1977. "Sex Role Attitudes and Psychological Outcomes for Black and White Women Experiencing Marital Dissolution," *Journal of Marriage and the Family* 39 (August):549–561.

Bumpass, Larry L., and James A. Sweet. 1972. "Differentials in Marital Instability: 1970," *American Sociological Review* 37 (December):754–767.

Burchinal, Lee G. 1964. "Characteristics of Adolescents from Unbroken, Broken, and Reconstituted Families," *Journal of Marriage and the Family* 26 (February):44–51.

————, and Loren E. Chancellor. 1962. "Survival Rates Among Religiously Homogamous and Interreligious Marriages," *Iowa Agricultural and Home Economics Experiment Station Research Bulletin* 512 (December):743–770.

Carter, Hugh, and Paul C. Glick. 1976. *Marriage and Divorce: A Social and Economic Study*, rev. ed. Cambridge, MA: Harvard University Press.

Cherlin, Andrew. 1978. "Remarriage as an Incomplete Institution," *American Journal of Sociology* 84 (November):634–650.

————. 1979. "Worklife and Marital Dissolution," Chap. 9 in George Levinger and Oliver C. Moles (eds.), *Divorce and Separation: Context, Causes and Consequences*. New York: Basic books.

Chester, Robert (ed.). 1977. *Divorce in Europe*. Leiden, The Netherlands: Martinus Nyhoff.

Christensen, Harold T., and Kenneth E. Barber. 1967. "Interfaith versus Intrafaith Marriage in Indiana," *Journal of Marriage and the Family* 29 (August):461–469.

Cutright, Phillips. 1971. "Income and Family Events: Marital Stability," *Journal of Marriage and the Family* 33 (May):291–306.

Dean, Gillian, and Douglas T. Gurak. 1978. "Marital Homogamy the Second Time Around," *Journal of Marriage and the Family* 40 (August):559–570.

Dore, Ronald P. 1958. *City Life in Japan*. Berkeley: University of California Press.

Duberman, Lucile. 1975. *The Reconstituted Fam-*

ily: A Study of Remarried Couples and Their Children. Chicago: Nelson-Hall.

Durkheim, Emile. 1897. Suicide. Paris: Felix Alcan.

Feldman, Harold, and Margaret Feldman. 1978. "The Effect of Father Absence on Adolescents." Unpublished Manuscript.

Furstenberg, Frank F., Jr. 1978. "Recycling the Family: Perspectives for Researching a Neglected Family Form." Paper presented at the American Sociological Association Meeting in San Francisco.

Gebhard, Paul H. 1958. Pregnancy, Birth and Abortion. New York: Harper & Row.

Gersick, Kelin E. 1979. "Divorced Men Who Receive Custody of Their Children," Chap. 18 in George Levinger and Oliver C. Moles (eds.), Divorce and Separation: Context, Causes and Consequences. New York: Basic Books.

Glick, Paul C. 1975. "A Demographer Looks at American Families," Journal of Marriage and the Family 37 (February):15–26.

———. 1973. "Perspectives on the Recent Upturn in Divorce and Remarriage," Demography 10 (August):301–314.

———, and Arthur J. Norton. 1977. "Marrying, Divorcing, and Living Together in the U.S. Today," Population Bulletin 32 (October):1–39.

Glock, Charles Y., and Rodney Stark. 1966. Christian Beliefs and Anti-Semitism. New York: Harper & Row.

Goldstein, Sidney, and Calvin Goldscheider. 1968. Jewish Americans: Three Generations in a Jewish Community. Englewood Cliffs, NJ: Prentice-Hall.

Goode, William J. 1951. "Economic Factor and Marital Stability," American Sociology Review 16 (December):802–812.

———. 1956. After Divorce. New York: Free Press.

———. 1963. World Revolution and Family Patterns. New York: Free Press.

Heer, David M. 1962. "The Trend of Interfaith Marriages in Canada, 1922–1957," American Sociological Review 27 (April):245–250.

———. 1966. "Negro-White Marriage in the United States," Journal of Marriage and the Family 28 (August):262–273.

———. 1974. "The Prevalence of Black/White Marriage in the U. S., 1960 and 1970," Journal of Marriage and the Family 36 (May):246–258.

Heiss, Jerold. 1960. "Premarital Characteristics of the Intermarried," American Sociological Review 25 (February):47–55.

Herberg, Will. 1956. Protestant-Catholic-Jew. New York: Doubleday.

Hill, Reuben. 1949. Families Under Stress. New York: Harper & Row.

Hunt, Morton. 1974. Sexual Behavior in the 1970's. Chicago: Playboy Press.

Jacobson, Paul H. 1959. American Marriage and Divorce. New York: Holt, Rinehart and Winston.

Kelley, Robert K. 1979. Courtship, Marriage and the Family, 3rd ed. New York: Harcourt Brace Jovanovich.

Komarovsky, Mirra. 1964. Blue Collar Marriage. New York: Random House.

Kramer, Judith R., and Seymour Leventman. 1961. Children of the Gilded Ghetto. New Haven, CT: Yale University Press.

Landis, Judson T. 1949. "Marriages of Mixed and Non-Mixed Religious Faith," American Sociological Review 14 (August):401–407.

———.1962. "A Comparison of Children from Divorced and Nondivorced Unhappy Marriages," Family Life Coordinator 21 (July):61–65.

Lee, David. 1968. "Marital Disruption Among Medical Faculty and Liberal Arts Faculty." Ph. D. dissertation, University of Iowa, Iowa City.

Lenski, Gerhard. 1961. The Religious Factor: A Sociological Study of Religion's Impact on Politics, Economics, and the Family Life. New York: Doubleday.

Levinger, George, and Oliver C. Moles (eds.). 1979. Divorce and Separation: Context, Causes and Consequences. New York: Basic Books.

Lewis, Robert A. 1973. "Social Reaction and the Formation of Dyads: An Interactional Approach to Mate Selection," Sociometry 36 (September):409–419.

Longfellow, Cynthia. 1979. "Divorce in Context: Its Impact on Children," Chap. 17 in George Levinger and Oliver C. Moles (eds.), Divorce and Separation: Context, Causes and Consequences. New York: Basic Books.

Massarik, Fred. 1974. "National Jewish Population Study: A New U.S. Estimate," 75:296–304. In American Jewish Yearbook 1974–75. Philadelphia: Jewish Publication Society of America.

———, and Alvin Chenkin. 1973. "United States' National Jewish Population Study: A First Report." 75:264–306. In American Jewish Yearbook, 1973. Philadelphia: Jewish Publication Society of America.

Mayer, John E. 1961. Jewish-Gentile Courtships. New York: Free Press.

McDowell, Sophia F. 1971. "Black-White Intermarriage in the U.S.," *International Journal of Sociology of the Family* (Special Issue):49–58.

Miller, Kent S., and Ralph M. Dreger (eds.). 1973. *Comparative Studies of Blacks and Whites in the U.S.* New York: Seminar Press.

Monahan, Thomas P., and William M. Kephart. 1954. "Divorce and Desertion by Religious and Mixed Religious Groups," *American Journal of Sociology* 59 (March):454–465.

Mueller, Charles W., and Hallowell Pope. 1977. "Marital Instability: The Study of Its Transmission Between Generations," *Journal of Marriage and the Family* 39 (February):83–92.

Nye, F. Ivan. 1957. "Child Adjustment in Broken and in Unhappy Unbroken Homes," *Marriage and Family Living* 19 (August):356–361.

O'Neill, William L. 1967. *Divorce in the Progressive Era.* New Haven, CT: Yale University Press.

Perry, Joseph B., and Erdwin H. Pfuhl. 1963. "Adjustment of Children in Solo and Remarriage Homes," *Marriage and Family Living* 25 (May):221–224.

Preston, Samuel H., and John McDonald. 1979. "The Incidence of Divorce Within Cohorts of American Marriages Contracted Since the Civil War," *Demography* 16 (February):1–25.

Quinley, Harold E., and Charles Y. Glock. 1979. *Anti-Semitism in America.* New York: Free Press.

Raschke, Helen, and Vern Raschke. 1979. "Family Conflict and Children's Self-Concept: A Comparison of Intact and Single-Parent Families," *Journal of Marriage and the Family* 41 (May): 367–374.

Reiss, Ira L. 1967. *The Social Context of Premarital Sexual Permissiveness.* New York: Holt, Rinehart and Winston.

Rindfuss, Ronald R., and Larry L. Bumpass. 1977. "Fertility During Marital Disruption," *Journal of Marriage and the Family* 39 (August):517–528.

Rosenberg, Morris. 1965. *Society and the Adolescent Self-Image.* Princeton, NJ: Princeton University Press.

Rosow, Irving, and K. Daniel Rose. 1972. "Divorce Among Doctors," *Journal of Marriage and the Family* 34 (November):587–598.

Scanzoni, John. 1979. "A Historical Perspective on Husband-Wife Bargaining Power and Marital Dissolution," Chap. 2 in George Levinger and Oliver C. Moles (eds.), *Divorce and Separation: Context, Causes and Consequences.* New York: Basic Books.

Schoen, Robert. 1975. "California Divorce Rates by Age at First Marriage and Duration of First Marriage," *Journal of Marriage and the Family* 37 (August):548–555.

Stetson, Dorothy M., and Gerald C. Wright, Jr. 1975. "The Effects of Laws on Divorce in American States," *Journal of Marriage and the Family* 37 (August):537–547.

Thomas, John L. 1956. *The American Catholic Family.* Englewood Cliffs, NJ: Prentice-Hall.

Thwing, C. F., and C. F. B. Thwing. 1887. *The Family: An Historical and Social Study.* Boston: Lee and Shepard.

United Nations. 1979. *Demographic Yearbook 1978.* New York: United Nations Publishers.

U.S. Bureau of the Census. 1958. *Current Population Reports.* Series P–20, No. 79 (February 2). Washington, DC: Government Printing Office.

———. 1966. *1960 Census of Population.* Vol. 2, 4D, "Marital Status." Washington, DC: Government Printing Office.

———. 1972. *1970 Census of Population.* PC(2)–4C: "Marital Status." Washington, DC: Government Printing Office.

———. 1976. *Current Population Reports.* Series P–20, No. 297 (October): "Number, Timing and Duration of Marriages and Divorces in the U.S.: June 1975." Washington, DC: Government Printing Office.

———. 1977. *Current Population Reports.* Series P–20, No. 307 (April): "Population, Profile of the U.S.: 1976." Washington, DC: Government Printing Office.

———. 1977. *Current Population Reports.* Series P–20, No. 312 (August): "Marriage, Divorce, Widowhood and Remarriage by Family Characteristics: June 1975." Washington, DC: Government Printing Office.

———. 1977. *Current Population Reports.* Series P–20, No. 314 (December): "Educational Attainment in the U.S.: March 1977 and 1976." Washington, DC: Government Printing Office.

———. 1978. *Current Population Reports.* Series P–23, No. 77 (December): "Perspectives on American Husbands and Wives." Washington, DC: Government Printing Office.

U.S. Department of Health, Education, and Welfare. National Center for Health Statistics. 1967. *Divorce Statistics Analysis: United States, 1963.* Series 21, No. 13. Washington, DC: Government Printing Office.

———. 1971. "Marriages: Trends and Characteristics," *National Center for Vital Statistics.* Series 21, No. 21 (September). Washington, DC: Government Printing Office.

_____. 1973 "Divorces: Analysis of Changes in U.S.: 1969," *Vital and Health Statistics.* Series 21, No. 22 (April). Washington, DC: Government Printing Office.

_____. 1973 "Teenagers: Marriage, Divorce, Parenthood and Mortality," *Vital and Health Statistics.* Series 21, No. 23 (August). Washington, DC: Government Printing Office.

_____. 1973 "Remarriages: United States," *Vital and Health Statistics.* Series 21, No. 25 (December). Washington, DC: Government Printing Office.

_____. 1975. *Monthly Vital Statistics Reports.* Vol. 24, No. 5 (July 30) Washington, DC: Government Printing Office.

_____. 1978. "Final Divorce Statistics, 1976," *Monthly Vital Statistics Report* 27.5 (August 16). Washington, DC: Government Printing Office.

_____. 1979a "Final Divorce Statistics, 1977," *Monthly Vital Statistics Report* 28.2 (May 16). Washington, DC: Government Printing Office.

_____. 1979b "Births, Marriages, Divorces and Deaths for 1978," *Monthly Vital Statistics Report* 27.12 (March 15). Washington, DC: Government Printing Office.

Walker, Kenneth N., Joy Rogers, and William Messinger. 1977. "Remarriage After Divorce: A Review," *Social Casework* (May):276–285.

Weeks, H. Ashley. 1943. "Differential Divorce Rates by Occupation," *Social Forces* 21 (July):334–337.

Weiss, Robert S. 1975. *Marital Separation.* New York: Basic Books.

Westoff, Leslie Aldridge. 1977. *The Second Time Around.* New York: Viking.

Wright, Gerald C., Jr., and Dorothy M. Stetson. 1978. "The Impact of No-Fault Divorce Law Reform on Divorce in American States," *Journal of Marriage and the Family* (August):575–580.

Zimmerman, Carle C., and Lucius F. Cervantes. 1956. *Marriage and the Family: A Text for Moderns.* Chicago: Regnery.

Part Four THE FAMILY INSTITUTION

The Parental Choice

THIRTEEN

Child-Free Marriages

As the birthrate dropped during the 1960s, the pros and cons of parenthood were increasingly debated. During the baby boom of the 1940s and 1950s, there was much less attention paid to the decision-making or rewards vs. costs aspects of parenthood. By the 1960s contraceptive usage improved, family planning entered into the birth choices of more and more couples, and the ultimate decision not to have children began to be discussed more openly (Bram, 1978). Virtually all the research on childless or "child-free" couples was done in the 1970s (Veevers, 1973, 1974; Houseknecht, 1977, 1978, 1979; Nason and Poloma, 1976; Beckman, 1978, 1979; Silka and Kiesler, 1977). It seems appropriate to first discuss child-free marriages and then proceed to discuss child-present marriages. The causal processes in these two types of marriages should be mutually enlightening.

Less than 5 percent of wives in the late 1970s expected to be childless (U. S. Bureau of the Census, 1977, P–20, No. 308, Tables 2, 12, 13). This was an increase, for in 1967 only 3 percent said they expected to be childless. The actual percent of wives who have been childless ranged from about 20 percent of those who married in the 1920s to about 5 percent of those who married about 1940. One of the reasons for the increased proportion of wives with children in this time period was the improvement in medical methods and better dietary habits and medical care (Glick, 1977). The desire for children on the part of virtually all married couples has long been taken for granted (Hoffman and Hoffman, 1973). In 1973 the Gallup Poll showed that only 1 percent of Americans viewed the childless family as "ideal." But despite this preference for children, there has been a downward trend in birthrates from the beginning of this country two hundred years ago. The only major interruption in that downward direction occurred in the

1940s and 1950s. Figure 13.1 illustrates this pattern since 1860 for both black and white groups.

Figure 13.1 also shows quite clearly that in the 1960s and 1970s we resumed the downward trend and we are now at the lowest birthrate in our history. Our current rate is roughly fifteen births a year for every 1,000 people in the country and it is holding steady. We saw in earlier chapters how the age at first marriage has risen and this, of course, delays childbirth in marriage and helps reduce the total birthrate by reducing the number of years in marriage when one is in the prime reproductive period. This delay can be graphically seen in Figure 13.2. It was around 1960 that the percent of wives in their twenties who were childless began to increase as the age at marriage rose and the birthrate fell. A glance at Figure 13.2 makes it clear why there is such interest in the question of childless marriages. There are now millions of wives postponing childbirth. So far only about 5 percent of them state that they intend to remain childless. But over 15 percent of the women in such "expectation" surveys do not answer this question and so there is much room for speculation. Are we experiencing a delay or will there be a dramatic growth in the proportion of married couples who choose not

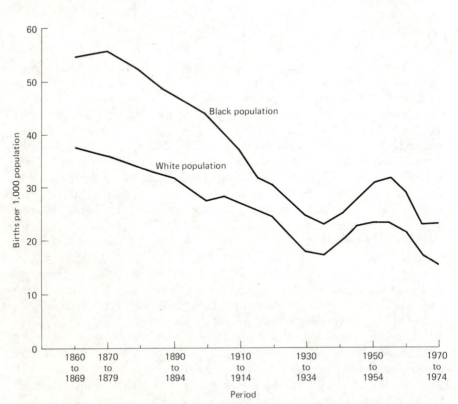

Figure 13.1. Crude Birth Rate of the White and Black Population: 10-Year Averages, 1860–69 and 1870–79 and 5-Year Averages, 1880–84 to 1970–74.
Source: U.S. Bureau of the Census (1978), P–23, No. 70:3.

to become parents? One way to move toward an answer to this question is to examine the new research on childless couples and discern if such couples seem to be on the rise.

There are no national studies of childless marriages and therefore we must base our conclusions on small studies of usually from 20–100 couples. These studies have examined aspects such as parenthood values, occupational goals of wives, happiness in one's own family of orientation, social pressures to have children, and degree of autonomy of the couple. Let us look at a few of the findings.

One well-designed study was carried out in 1975 by Silka and Kiesler (1977). Their study was comprised of sixty-one couples under the age of thirty who had no children. The study was carried out in Lawrence, Kansas. The respondents answered advertisements soliciting couples under thirty without children. The sixty-one couples divided almost exactly into three groups: (1) twenty-one couples where both mates agreed on the intention to never have children; (2) twenty-one couples who did intend to have children at a later date; and (3) nineteen couples who were unsure about having children.

One hypothesis to be investigated was whether those who did not intend to have

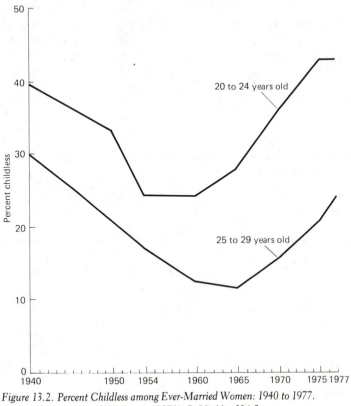

Figure 13.2. Percent Childless among Ever-Married Women: 1940 to 1977.
Source: U.S. Bureau of the Census (1978), P–20, No. 324:5.

children had thought about and discussed the issue of parenthood over a longer period of time. This was found to be the case. The "intend no children" group thought about this decision for five years and discussed it for three years. On the average this took about a year longer than any discussion about having children took among those who "intended to have children." The "unsure" group fell in between in both comparisons.

Silka and Kiesler also compared the three groups on nine questions concerning reasons for not having children. These results are presented in Table 13.1. Clearly, the "do not intend" group gave the greatest support to these nine reasons for not having children. The "unsure" group again came out in between but somewhat closer to the "do not intend" group. These results fit with Veevers research (1973) and Beckman's study (1979). Nason and Poloma (1976) also stressed the importance to child-free couples of marital dyadic satisfaction and their fear that a child would weaken that source of happiness. It is interesting to note that the decision to have or to not have children was much more likely to be central to the wife and the wife was more likely to have made that decision. Half the husbands who did not intend to have children said they would change their minds if their wives decided to have children. None of the wives who did not intend to have children said they would alter their plans if their husbands changed their minds. There is no mystery regarding the greater centrality of childbirth to females. This is due to the fact that the gender role of the female makes it clear, even in 1980, that there is a very high likelihood that the woman will have the major responsibility for any children that are born. Husbands may "help out" but the very term "help out" clearly indicates whose responsibility is the child rearing. Thus, the birth of a child is seen by wives as a major alteration of their current life-style. This is less the case for a husband.

TABLE 13.1

Percent of Married Women Citing Particular Reasons for Not Having Children

REASON FOR NOT HAVING CHILDREN	INTENTIONS FOR HAVING CHILDREN		
	Do Not Intend	Intend	Unsure
More time with spouse	100	48	74
Opportunities and freedom	90	43	89
Wife's job or career	81	43	74
Avoid responsibility	71	14	47
Leisure, travel	62	38	58
Worry, social problems	52	24	37
Economic concerns	48	33	53
Manage work load	43	9	68
Dislike for children, not sure good parent	29	5	16

Source: Silka and Kiesler (1977):21.

As we shall see in chapter 15, even in dual career marriages, it is still the wife who most often has the child-rearing responsibilities.

The couples who did not intend to have children were neither more nor less happy than the other two groups. They did have somewhat higher scores on preference for being alone and the wives in particular were more likely to describe themselves as independent. They also lived further from their parents. There is evidence then that those who intend to have no children may be high on autonomy (see also Houseknecht, 1978). Such autonomy would enable them to better handle any pressures toward conformity to the parental role. Surprisingly, there is no evidence presented by Silka and Kiesler that the "do not intend" couples have different attitudes about gender roles or marital roles. This is surprising because one would have thought that since childless couples were violating traditional parental roles, they would be more likely to endorse equalitarian roles. Nevertheless, there was no difference in gender-role attitude among any of the three groups. Houseknecht (1978) does report differences in gender-role attitudes in her study. Perhaps if we examined the couples in Silka and Kiesler's study in five years, we would find that those with children had become less equalitarian and those without children more equalitarian. It is after the birth of a child that husband and wife roles segregate noticeably. Such a longitudinal check would be necessary to clarify this question.

There was an indication that wives who intended not to have children were more successful at their jobs, were more into professional work, and were in better-paying positions (see also Veevers, 1974). Thus, success in the occupational world may well have encouraged their child-free decision. Beckman (1979) found that professional women as compared to nonprofessional women were more likely to want no children. Career plans may well encourage one to see child-planning decisions as important since they can affect one's future career. Furthermore, those who intended no children showed their seriousness by using the most effective means of contraception.

The decision not to become parents seems to be made after marriage and not before. Nason and Paloma's sample of thirty midwestern couples found only four who had decided against children before they married. Twelve couples took two to three years and the remaining fourteen couples took even longer to reach that decision. Of course, those who were more effective contraceptors would have more time for making this decision. The Nason and Paloma sample was congruent with the Silka and Kiesler study in finding that the commitment of wives to the child-free life-style was considerably stronger than that of husbands. This is a particularly important point because it implies that the key explanation of changes in childlessness will depend upon understanding forces that affect the female role. This in turn implicates the outside employment opportunities as a major potential cause. If our society is increasing the motivation for females to pursue careers and also increasing the opportunity for such careers, then it would seem that childless marriages should increase in frequency.

Beckman (1979) in a larger study has examined the causal relationship between desire for children and employment intentions. Her conclusions are that desire for children did affect one's employment intentions but that employment had little effect on desire for children. Of course, it may be that as the female gender role changes to include career aspirations, more women will grow up with less pressure to accept motherhood as essential to their feminine role. In this way the actual occupational experience will change the general expectations regarding children. I would like to see additional testing of this crucial causal relationship. I find it difficult to believe that the experience of being successful at a job and enjoying that line of work would not increase the likelihood of a woman concluding that parenthood might conflict with that occupational pursuit and therefore should be controlled in some fashion.

The relationship of childlessness to career orientation is worth pursuing one step further. College-educated wives are the most likely to end up in what we call "careers," that is, jobs that involve high commitment and a lifetime endeavor to advance in a particular type of work. Thus, if career goals affect desire for children in some fashion, then college-educated women should be overrepresented in the childless category. Table 13.2 deals with this precise point. This table presents "expectations" of married women ages 18–34 regarding childbearing. The expectations of the total sample fits the prediction that college women will be higher on childlessness: between 7.3 and 14.3 percent of college-educated woman expected no births ever, while 4.9 percent of the high-school educated and 2.6 percent of those with less than a high school education expected no births ever. This same relationship holds up at all age levels from 18 to 34. The fact that women in their thirties still show this relationship indicates that the expectations are realities, for such women are at the end of their childbearing years. Only a small proportion of women have children after age thirty-five. The average woman today has completed her childbearing by the time she is thirty years old (Glick, 1977:6).

The bottom of the table presents a black/white racial comparison. The positive relationship of child-free expectations and educational level seems weaker among blacks as compared to whites. At each educational level, the percent of black wives who expect no children is smaller than the comparable percent for white wives. For the college-educated group, 6.6% of the blacks and an average of 8.3% of the whites, expect no births. Birthrates (see Figure 13.1) are higher in the black group and perhaps the emphasis on births lowers the popularity of child-free marriages among all black groups. Note that about 21 percent of the black group expect four or more children while only about 10 percent of the white group expect that many. To further check out this finding, one should examine the data for blacks broken down by the various age groups—perhaps among younger blacks the pattern is different.

At this time we can say that there is evidence that highly educated females are the most likely to be part of a child-free marriage. This tends to support the view that career goals affect fertility, as well as vice versa. The size of this child-free group is still quite small (5.6%) and it seems likely that even if it grows, it will remain well under 10 percent of *all* marriages at least for the decade of the 1980s (Blake, 1979).

TABLE 13.2
Number of Lifetime Births Expected, by Years of School Completed, for Wives 18 to 34 Years Old: June 1978

(Percent distribution. Civilian noninstitutional population. Data limited to currently married women reporting on birth expectations.)

Race, Age and Years of School Completed	NUMBER OF WIVES (thousands)	NUMBER OF LIFETIME BIRTHS EXPECTED							
		Total	None	1	2	3	4	5 or 6	7 or more
ALL RACES									
Total, 18 to 34 years old	14,940	100.0	5.6	11.7	49.2	22.5	7.3	3.1	0.5
Not a high school graduate	2,602	100.0	2.6	11.1	38.7	26.1	12.5	7.5	1.5
High school, 4 years	7,354	100.0	4.9	12.2	49.4	23.8	7.2	2.2	0.3
College: 1 to 3 years	2,735	100.0	7.3	13.0	51.5	19.6	5.7	2.6	0.4
4 years	1,609	100.0	7.5	8.5	58.4	19.1	4.2	2.0	0.4
5 years or more	639	100.0	14.3	10.5	58.0	13.3	3.3	0.6	0.3
WHITE									
Total, 18 to 34 years old	13,585	100.0	5.6	11.7	50.2	22.3	7.0	2.7	0.4
Not a high school graduate	2,307	100.0	2.7	11.4	40.3	26.5	12.0	6.1	1.1
High school, 4 years	6,768	100.0	4.8	12.4	50.1	23.5	7.0	2.1	0.2
College: 1 to 3 years	2,461	100.0	7.5	12.4	52.4	19.3	5.6	2.5	0.4
4 years	1,471	100.0	7.5	8.2	59.7	18.6	3.8	2.0	0.3
5 years or more	577	100.0	14.0	10.6	58.7	13.5	2.8	0.5	-
BLACK									
Total, 18, to 34 years old	1,048	100.0	4.5	13.1	36.2	25.5	10.9	7.7	2.1
Not a high school graduate	236	100.0	2.1	9.8	22.6	22.6	17.9	20.0	5.1
High school, 4 years	492	100.0	4.3	10.8	39.2	29.5	10.8	4.1	1.4
College, 1 year or more	320	100.0	6.6	19.4	41.6	21.6	5.9	4.4	0.6

Source: U.S. Bureau of the Census (1979), P–20, No.341:27

Contraception and Marriage

We have discussed contraceptive usage among unmarried couples. We mentioned then that the improved contraceptive usage premaritally during the 1970s occurred at the same time as improved contraceptive usage in marriage. Let us look more closely now at marital contraceptive usage since it is vital to any increase in child-free or small families.

In 1976, in 30 percent of all married couples, with wives aged 15–44, either the wife or the husband had been sterilized. The sterilization procedures were about equally divided between husbands and wives, particularly at the higher income levels. Sterilization was particularly popular with couples 35–44 years of age where fully 50 percent of the couples had a wife or a husband who had been sterilized. Table 13.3 presents data from the 1976 National Survey of Family Growth consisting of several thousand white and black women aged 15–44 (Ford, 1978). It is important to note that the use of the pill, although still the most popular method (other than sterilization), has begun to fall off. Twenty-two percent of the wives used the pill and this was down from 25 percent reported just three years prior to that in another National Survey of Family Growth. From 1960 to 1973 the pill grew in popularity but the current evidence is that its popularity is now leveling off. Among younger wives (15–24 years old), 43 percent were on the pill, but even in this group, that figure was 45 percent in 1973.

If we examine the figures for black wives we do note some differences. Sterilization is somewhat less popular—only 24 percent of the couples use it as their method compared to 31 percent of the white couples. But an even more significant difference is in the "other nonusers" row. Note that 13.5 percent of the black wives and only 7.2 percent of the white wives are in this category. These are wives who do not want to become pregnant but are not using any contraceptive methods. This fits with the higher percent of black wives who report unwanted births (Weller and Hobbs, 1978).

When one examines contraceptive usage in America, the question often comes up: What about Catholic contraceptive practices—are they different because of religious doctrines? Westoff and Jones (1977b), using the 1975 National Fertility Study sample (a national representative sample of women ages 15–44) did check out Catholic contraceptive practices. Table 13.4 offers some idea of trends in this area. This table is for Catholics who receive communion at least once a month. If a table for all Catholics were presented the results would have been even more extreme. Note that in all four lengths of marriage columns there is a strong tendency toward not conforming with the birth-control teachings of the Catholic Church. The tendency has accelerated since the 1968 Encyclical, *Humanae Vitae*, denouncing the use of any birth-control methods other than rhythm. Andrew Greeley and his colleagues feel that the decline in Catholic religious attendance and confession in the last decade was due heavily to a negative response to the birth-control encyclical (Greeley, et al., 1976). With only 12 percent of even those Catholics who receive communion following the birth-control position of the church, the similarity to Protestant contraceptive usage is apparent. An examination by specific

TABLE 13.3

Percentage Distribution of Currently Married Women Aged 15–44 by Contraceptive Status, According to Age All Races, United States, 1976

CONTRACEPTIVE STATUS	AGES 15–44 1976		
	Total	White	Black
Number (in 000s)	27,185	24,518	2,144
(Unweighted N)	(6,414)	(4,764)	(1,557)
Total	100.0	100.0	100.0
Sterile	**30.2**	**31.0**	**24.3**
Nonsurgical	1.9	1.9	2.6
Surgical	28.3	29.1	21.7
Noncontraceptive	9.0	9.0	8.8
Female	8.2	8.2	8.7
Male	0.8	0.8	(0.0)
Contraceptive	19.3	20.1	12.9
Female	9.6	9.6	11.0
Male	9.7	10.5	1.9
Fecund	**69.8**	**69.0**	**75.6**
Noncontraceptors	21.1	20.0	30.2
Pregnant, postpartum	6.9	6.8	6.9
Seeking pregnancy	6.5	6.0	9.7
Other nonusers	7.7	7.2	13.5
Contraceptors	48.6	49.0	45.4
Pill	22.3	22.5	22.0
IUD	6.1	6.1	6.1
Diaphragm	2.9	3.0	1.8
Condom	7.2	7.4	4.5
Foam	3.0	2.9	3.8
Rhythm	3.4	3.5	1.4
Withdrawal	2.0	2.0	1.8
Douche	0.7	0.5	2.7
Other	0.9	0.9	1.2

Source: Ford (1978):265–267

type of contraceptive methods for Catholic and non-Catholic wives in 1975 indicates a high degree of similarity. Even on sterilization the proportions were quite similar (33 percent non-Catholics to 26 percent Catholics). Regarding rhythm, 5.9 percent of Catholics used that method and 1.7 percent of non-Catholics. All other methods were very similar in percentage usage. By the early 1980s even these small differences are likely to have vanished. The subgroups of Catholics who abide the most by the Church's teachings are the college-educated, many of whom have attended Catholic schools and colleges (Westoff and Jones, 1977*b*: 206). Only 17 percent of the college-educated were sterilized and 7 percent used the rhythm method.

The general evidence indicates that in the last two decades we have undergone a contraceptive revolution. Our ability to control or minimize unwanted births is

TABLE 13.4

Percentage of White, U.S. Catholic Married Women Aged 18–39 Receiving Communion at Least Once a Month who Conformed with Church Teaching on Birth Control by Never Using Any Form of Contraception or by Using the Rhythm Method Only

MARRIAGE COHORT	YEARS OF MARRIAGE			
	< 5	5–9	10–14	15–19
1941–1945				72.9
1946–1950			75.6	56.8
1951–1955		72.1	65.3	51.3
1956–1960	77.7	60.7	47.4	24.6
1961–1965	65.3	40.0	19.5	
1966–1970	24.3	4.1		
1971–1975	12.1			

Source: Westoff and Jones (1977b):204.

at an all-time high. In 1973 the National Survey of Family Growth (a representative national sample of thousands of women aged 15–44) attempted to evaluate the effectiveness of various methods of contraception. Table 13.5 presents data on effectiveness divided by whether the couples were trying to *prevent* any birth from occurring or whether they wanted more children but were trying to *delay* a birth until later. The table covers contraceptive use from 1970 to 1973. One interesting finding reported in Table 13.5 was that all methods (except the pill) work more effectively for those who wish to prevent any future births than for those who wish only to delay a birth. This comparison makes obvious the importance of motivation in the use of contraceptive methods. It was also true that most of the methods were more effective for couples married a longer period of time. For example, the condom had a failure of 9.8 percent for the youngest marriage group and only 2.2

TABLE 13.5

Percent of Couples Who Fail To Prevent an Unwanted Pregnancy or To Delay Their Next Wanted Pregnancy within the First Year of Contraceptive Use, 1970–1973.

CONTRACEPTIVE METHOD	CONTRACEPTIVE INTENTION	
	Prevent	*Delay*
	(Percent failing)	
All methods	3.7	7.3
Pill	2.0	2.0
IUD	2.9	5.6
Condom	6.6	13.7
Foam/Cream/Jelly	13.1	16.7
Diaphragm	10.3	15.9
Rhythm	9.5	28.8
Remainder	6.5	15.1

Source: Vaughan, et al. (1977): adapted from data in Table 2, p. 254.

percent for the oldest marriage group. Here again, motivation may be the important factor—the younger couples may feel more able to change their mind about having a child and thus are not quite as careful in contraceptive usage. Even the pill shows some variation in failure by age group (2.8 percent to 1.2 percent) (Vaughan, et al., 1977:254).

Using this same 1973 National Survey of Family Growth, a check was made on wives aged 15–44 in their first marriage to discern what percent of their pregnancies was wanted. Figure 13.3 graphically presents the findings. Note that the figure is divided to further indicate what proportion of children were wanted sooner than they arrived and what proportion later. This information applies to the success rates for those who simply wanted to plan the time of a birth. The unwanted percent, of course, applies to those who did not want another child at any time. The racial comparison is instructive. Due to government and private family-planning clinics, the difference in contraceptive practice and in unwanted births between the poor and the nonpoor has greatly diminished (Weller and Hobbs, 1978). But there still is a difference and part of that is reflected in the black/white comparisons in Figure 13.3

Overall for these first-married women (white and black together) only about 9 percent had an unwanted birth. Just two decades ago that figure would have been about twice as high. Overall, then, the picture in America at the start of the 1980s is one of a society that has become quite effective in its contraceptive usage. Over

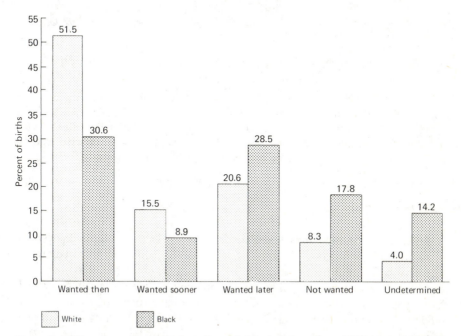

Figure 13.3. Wantedness status of births to Currently Married, Once-Married Women Aged 15-44, by Race, 1973.
Source: Weller and Hobbs (1978):170.

Gustav Vigeland
"Woman and Children,"
Vigeland Sculpture Park, Oslo.

92 percent of those who do not want to get pregnant are using contraception, 30 percent are sterilized, and about an equal percent are on the pill or using the IUD. These are the three most effective methods available today.

All three major religious groups and both races have greatly increased the effectiveness of contraceptive usage. It may well be that a goodly portion of the reduction in birthrates since the 1960s is due to this increase in effective contraceptive usage and only partly due to a decrease in desired family size.

One- and Two-Parent Families

Just what types of family units do our children live in? Table 13.6 gives an overview of all 76 million households in America and points out some very important trends that have been occurring in the past twenty years. One of the trends to note is that since 1960 the proportion of all households in America that are family households has decreased from 85 percent to 75 percent. A large part of this drop in the proportion of family households is accounted for by the concomitant rise in one-person households (13 percent to 22 percent). In part this rise is the result of affluence that allows us the luxury of living apart from our family and relatives at young and old ages. It also results from the increase in the age at first marriage because such an increase means that more young people who are old enough to live alone are not yet married. A major increase here includes those who are divorced and have no children and have not yet remarried. Another significant increase is in the number of female households with no husband present. From 1960 to 1978 these increased from 4.4 million to over 8 million.

The popular press often makes the point that the so-called typical American family of a married couple with children is a rarity today. It is true that only about 25 million households out of the over 76 million compose the traditional nuclear family. That percent looks small because we are taking as the base all households including the over 19 million nonfamily households. Nevertheless, we can easily show the prominence of the traditional nuclear family by simply taking as our base only those households involving a married couple. Figure 13.4 illustrates the proportion of such households with children. The overall average of 52 percent of married couple households with children under eighteen is an average of several different age groups. Married couples aged thirty-five to forty-four are almost all involved in households with children under 18 and over 70 percent of the households of younger couples also fit the traditional nuclear family pattern. Older married couples do show rapid declines in nuclear family households. The point was made earlier in this chapter that well over 90 percent of all married couples have children. Thus, the real change is not that so many fewer people marry or

TABLE 13.6

Households by Type and Size: 1978, 1970, and 1960
(Numbers in thousands. Noninstitutional population.)

Subject	1978 Number	1978 Percent	1970 Number	1970 Percent	1960 Number	1960 Percent
HOUSEHOLDS						
Total households	76,030	100.0	63,401	100.0	52,799	100.0
Family households	56,958	74.9	51,456	81.2	44,905	85.0
Husband-wife	47,357	62.3	44,728	70.5	39,254	74.3
Male householder, no wife present	1,564	2.1	1,228	1.9	1,228	2.3
Female householder, no husband present	8,037	10.6	5,500	8.7	4,422	8.4
Nonfamily households	19,071	25.1	11,945	18.8	7,895	15.0
Householder living alone*	16,715	22.0	10,851	17.1	6,896	13.1
Householder with nonrelative(s) present	2,356	3.1	1,094	1.7	999	1.9
AVERAGE HOUSEHOLD SIZE						
All ages	2.81	—	3.14	—	3.33	—
Members under 18 years	0.83	—	1.09	—	1.21	—
Members 18 years and over	1.97	—	2.05	—	2.12	—

*One-person household.
Source: U.S. Bureau of the Census (1979), P-20, No. 336:18.

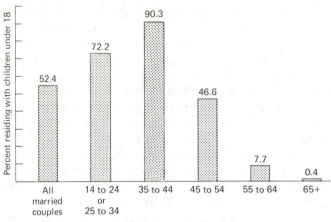

Figure 13.4. *Percent of Married Couples with Children under 18 by Age of Husband and Wife, March 1977).*

Source: U.S. Bureau of the Census. (1978): P–23, No. 77 20 (Graph composed from data on p. 20).

Photo by Ivan Kalman.

that more people are childless, but rather that *the total set of households today consists of many more people who are temporarily living alone.* Most of these people were married at one time (if they are elderly or divorced or widowed) and many of them will be married again (if they are young or recently divorced or single). Thus, the nuclear family is not going out of style, rather it is increasingly accompanied by people who for a period of time are living apart from a family situation (Korbin, 1976). That is a significant change but it is hardly the death knell of the nuclear family.

Some indication of the sources for the one-parent family can be seen in Figure 13.5. Of the over 8 million women in a family household with no husband present, 5,206,000 are mothers with children of their own under eighteen years of age. Many of the others are families according to the census bureau definition: "Two or more people living together, related by blood, marriage, or adoption." Thus, they could be two sisters, a mother and an older child, and so on. There is a dramatic growth in the divorced group of mothers visible in Figure 13.5—from 496,000 in 1960 to 2,227,000 in 1978. Another very sharp upward trend is visible in the "single, never married" group of mothers (from 83,000 to 836,000). The widowed group shows virtually no change and the "married, husband absent" group has about doubled in the eighteen-year period under examination. Overall, the number of mother-child one-parent families grew from 1,891,000 in 1960 to

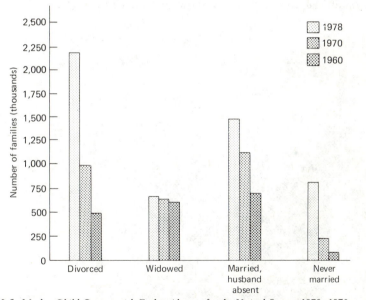

Figure 13.5. Mother-Child Groups with Father Absent, for the United States: 1978, 1970, and 1960. Mothers with one or more own children under 18 in the house.
Source: U.S. Bureau of the Census, Current Population Reports, Series P–20, *data in forthcoming reports. (These data were sent to me in a letter from Paul C. Glick, Senior Demographer, Population Division, Bureau of the Census, June 6, 1979).*

5,206,000 in 1978. Blacks comprise about 30 percent of all these one-parent families. The trends are comparable for both whites and blacks. The major difference is that of the total group of white mothers, the largest single group is divorced (43 percent), whereas for blacks the largest single group is the never married (34 percent). The trends discussed in earlier chapters help to make sense out of these findings. For example, we discussed the increase in "never married" mothers in Chapter 8 and the rise in divorced mothers in Chapter 12. Finally, the great majority of women who are "married, husband absent" are women who are separated from their husbands.

In 1978 there were 539,000 male-headed households with children under eighteen and no wife present, an increase from 301,000 in 1960. Over 92 percent of all children living with one parent were living with their mother (over 10 million in one-parent mother-headed households and fewer than one million in one-parent father-headed households). The tendency to give child custody to mothers has not changed greatly since 1960. There have been modifications, allowing more visiting privileges and joint custody for periods of time, but the mother still has priority. In part this is by default—for our gender-role training makes it more likely that fathers will agree that the child is "better off" with the mother. Fathers have little training in how to combine child care with employment whereas women have a great deal more experience in this double effort situation. There are some recent indications of males demanding more equality in custody and asking for an end to the traditional presumption that the wife is the best custodian for the child. It

Photo by Michael Perry.

will be interesting to see how successful is this effort. Finally, it surely is worthwhile to investigate the one-parent families that are headed by men and compare them to those headed by women.

Part of the growth of one-parent families is a trend toward fewer children living with both parents. Figure 13.6 details this trend. In 1976 only 80 percent of children under eighteen were living with both parents. For whites this percent was 85 percent and for blacks it was 50 percent. The higher divorce rate and the much higher separation rate and single-motherhood rate for blacks are key bases for this higher proportion of black children living with one parent. There are signs that the divorce rate is leveling off and that the premarital pregnancy rate is stabilizing. These factors would lead one to expect the trends toward one-parent families will also stabilize in the 1980s.

The characteristics and consequences of one-parent families are difficult to grasp. One factor that needs to be examined is the cultural tradition regarding the acceptability of the one-parent family. In black culture, where the one-parent

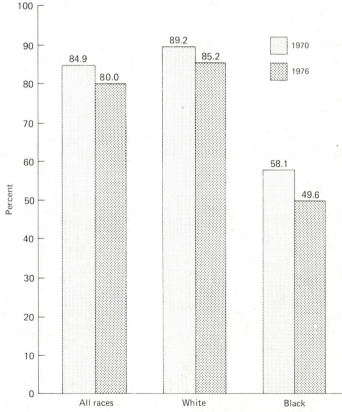

Figure 13.6. Percent of Persons under 18 Years Old Living with Both Parents, by Race: 1970 and 1976.
Excludes persons under 18 years old who were heads or wives in families or subfamilies.
Source: U.S. Bureau of the Census (1978) P–23, No. 66:23.

family is seemingly more accepted, the psychological costs of a woman entering into a one-parent family after a divorce may be considerably less (Savage et al., 1978). Also, the reason for single parenthood makes a difference (divorce, desertion, widowhood, imprisonment, and so forth). Finally, it is very important to consider family income. For example, the black/white difference noted in Figure 13.6 regarding proportion of children in two-parent families would disappear if we talked of people whose income was above the median. Figure 13.7 presents this graphically. The differences in the percent of black/white children in two-parent homes is quite small for those families earning $8,000 or more a year. Overall, about 60 percent of all black families are two-parent families and about 87 percent of all white families are two-parent families (U.S. Bureau of the Census, 1975, P–23, No. 54:107). However, if we looked only at those families with above average income, the black proportion would rise to about 85 percent of all families being two-parent families. There are strong stereotypes regarding the black family and so it is particularly important that we be clear that the majority of black families are two-parent families. Even though the overall proportion of children who live in two-parent families is 50 percent, Figure 13.7 makes it quite clear that the proportion of children in two-parent families rises above 80 percent in families earning above the median income.

The interrelationship of single-parent and two-parent families should not be lost sight of. One can belong to a two-parent family in one year and to a one-parent

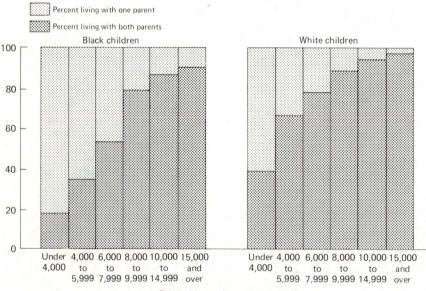

Figure 13.7. Own Children Under 18 by Presence of Parents and Family Income in 1973.
Source: U.S. Bureau of the Census (1975), P–23, No. 54:105.

family the next year. Conversely, many of those who today are in single-parent families will marry and become part of a two-parent family. Today particularly there is very rapid turnover in the various social roles related to the family. It is likely that about 45 percent of the children born in 1980 will live at least for a short period of time in a one-parent family during their childhood (Glick and Norton, 1977:29). Those who stay for life in a one-parent family are a distinct minority and those children and adults who stay for life in a two-parent family are becoming a smaller and smaller majority.

Summary and Conclusions

The degree to which the American married population has its birth process under control is unmatched in our history. This makes the choice of having children and of spacing them much more of a reality. I would expect to see these contraceptive skills increasingly visible in the *premarital* realm in the 1980s and thus I would predict a drop in the illegitimacy rate in this decade. It is important to bear in mind that the drop in the birthrate during the 1960s and the 1970s was due to a drop only in the legitimate birthrate. The illegitimate birthrate did not drop and, in fact, rose during this time period. So our total births were reduced because of drastic decreases in legitimate births. It is interesting to speculate what will happen if I am correct and the illegitimate rate does drop. We are now at zero population growth. The average number of births expected by women eighteen to thirty-four years old in 1978 was 2.1 and for women eighteen to twenty-four it was 2.0 (U.S. Bureau of the Census, Series P–20, No.330, 1978). Considering that at least 6 percent of all women will not marry and another 5 percent or more will marry but remain childless, these birth expectations would mean that women aged eighteen to twenty-four would not even replace themselves in the next generation. If we develop better premarital contraception, then the birthrates would be pulled down even further. It will be interesting to watch for these developments and see the political and economic reactions to such possible changes in our birthrates. We have become so accustomed to a growing population that many of us are unclear as to how to respond to a stable or declining population size.

The major overall change in our family institution in recent decades is the greater tolerance for a variety of forms. This is not a situation in which the traditional nuclear family has been discarded in favor of the single parent family. But we do seem more acceptant or at least tolerant of one-parent families (and of reconstituted families discussed in the last chapter). We also have more people living alone than ever before. This spreading out of many forms and breaking away from the family home has dropped the average household from about five persons in 1890 to less than three persons in 1980. I think it is still valid to say that most young people want to marry for life and want to have children but they accept the possibility of alternatives to this life plan more than did their parents or grandparents, and this is a significant addition to our cultural milieux.

References

Beckman, Linda J. 1978. "The Relative Rewards and Costs of Parenthood and Employment for Employed Women," *Psychology of Women Quarterly* 2, No. 3 (Spring):215–234.

———. 1979. "Fertility Preferences and Social Exchange Theory," *Journal of Applied Social Psychology* (in press).

Blake, Judith. 1979. "Is Zero Preferred? American Attitudes Towards Childlessness in the 1970's," *Journal of Marriage and the Family*, 41 (May): 245–257.

Bram, Susan. 1978. "Through the Looking Glass: Voluntary Childlessness as a Mirror of Contemporary Changes in the Meaning of Parenthood," Chap. 24 in Warren B. Miller and Lucile F. Newman (eds.), *The First Child and Family Formation*. Chapel Hill, NC: Carolina Population Center.

Bumpass, Larry, and Ronald Rindfuss, 1979. "Children's Experience of Marital Disruption," *American Journal of Sociology:* 85 (July) 49–65.

Cogswell, Betty E., and Marvin B. Sussman. 1979. "Family and Fertility: The Effects of Heterogeneous Experience," in Wes Burr, R. Hill, I. Nye, and I. L. Reiss (eds.), *Contemporary Theories About the Family*. New York: Free Press.

Farley, Reynolds. 1971. "Family Types and Family Headship: A Comparison of Trends Among Blacks and Whites," *Journal of Human Resources* 6(3):275–296.

Ford, Kathleen. 1978. "Contraceptive Use in the U.S., 1973–1976," *Family Planning Perspectives* 10 (September/October):264–269.

Gersick, Kelin E. 1979. "Divorced Men Who Receive Custody of Their Children," Chap. 18 in George Levinger and Oliver C. Moles (eds.), *Divorce and Separation: Context, Causes and Consequences*. New York: Basic Books.

Glick, Paul C. 1977. "Updating the Life Cycle of the Family," *Journal of Marriage and the Family* 39 (February):5–13.

———, "Who Are the Children in One-Parent Households?" (1980) Unpublished Manuscript.

———, and Arthur J. Norton. 1977. "Marrying, Divorcing and Living Together in the U.S. Today," *Population Bulletin* 32 (October):1–39.

Goldscheider, Calvin. 1971. "Religion, Minority Group Status and Fertility," in *Population, Modernization and Social Structure*. Boston: Little, Brown.

Greeley, Andrew M., W. C. McCready, and K. McCourt. 1976. *Catholic Schools in a Declining Church*. Kansas City, MO: Sheed and Ward.

Hoffman, Lois W., and Martin L. Hoffman. 1973. "The Value of Children to Parents," Chap. 2 in James T. Fawcett (ed.), *Psychological Perspectives on Population*. New York: Basic Books.

Houseknecht, Sharon K. 1977. "Reference Group Support for Voluntary Childlessness: Evidence for Conformity," *Journal of Marriage and the Family* 38 (May):285–292.

———. 1978. "Voluntary Childlessness," *Alternative Lifestyles* 1.3 (August):379–402.

———. 1979. "Childlessness and Marital Adjustment," *Journal of Marriage and the Family* 41 (May): 259–265.

Journal of Marriage and the Family. November 1978. This entire issue is devoted to studies of the black family.

Kobrin, Frances E. 1976. "The Fall of Household Size and the Rise of the Primary Individual in the U.S.," *Demography* 13 (February):127–138.

Nason, Ellen M., and Margaret M. Poloma. 1976. *Voluntary Childless Couples: The Emergence of a Variant Lifestyle*. Beverly Hills, CA: Sage Publications.

Pinkney, Alphonso. 1975. *Black Americans*. Englewood Cliffs, NJ: Prentice-Hall.

Rainwater, Lee, and William L. Yancey. 1967. *The Moynihan Report and the Politics of Controversy*. Cambridge: The Massachusetts Institute of Technology Press.

Rindfuss, Ronald, and Charles F. Westoff. 1974. "The Initiation of Contraception," *Demography* 11 (February):75–87.

———, and James A. Sweet. 1977. *Postwar Fertility Trends and Differentials in the U.S.* New York: Academic Press.

Savage, James E., Jr., Alvis V. Adair, and Philip Friedman. 1978. "Community-Social Variable Related to Black Parent-Absent Families," *Journal of Marriage and the Family* 40 (November): 779–785.

Scanzoni, John H. 1971. *The Black Family in Modern Society*. Boston: Allyn & Bacon.

Silka, Linda, and Sara Kiesler. 1977. "Couples Who Choose to Remain Childless," *Family Planning Perspectives* 9 (January/February): 16–25.

U.S. Bureau of the Census. 1975. "The Social and Economic Status of the Black Population in the U.S., 1974," *Current Population Reports* (July) Series P–23, No.54. Washington, DC: Government Printing Office.

———. 1976. "Fertility History and Prospects of American Women: June 1975," *Current Population Reports* (January), Series P–20, No.288. Washington, DC: Government Printing Office.

———. 1977. "Fertility of American Women: June 1976." *Current Population Reports* (June), Series P–20, No.308. Washington, DC: Government Printing Office.

———. 1978. "Marital Status and Living Arrangements, March 1977." *Current Population Reports* (April), Series P–20, No.323. Washington, DC: Government Printing Office.

———. 1978. "Population Profile of the U.S.: 1977." *Current Population Reports* (April), Series P–20, No.324. Washington, DC: Government Printing Office.

———. 1978. "Household and Family Characteristics: March 1977." *Current Population Reports* (August), Series P–20, No. 326. Washington, DC: Government Printing Office.

———. 1978. "Fertility of American Women: June 1978 (Advance Report)." *Current Population Reports* (November), Series P–20, No.330. Washington, DC: Government Printing Office.

———. 1978. "Characteristics of American Children and Youth: 1976." *Current Population Reports* (January), Series P–23, No.66. Washington, DC: Government Printing Office.

———. 1978. "Perspectives on American Husbands and Wives." *Current Population Reports* (December), Series P–23, No.77. Washington, DC: Government Printing Office.

———. 1978. "Perspectives on American Fertility." *Current Population Reports* (July) Series P–23, No. 70. Washington, DC: Government Printing Office.

———. 1979. "Population Profile of the U.S., 1978." *Current Population Reports* (April), Series P–20, No. 336. Washington, DC: Government Printing Office.

———. 1979. "Fertility of American Women: June 1978." *Current Population Reports* (October), Series P-20 No.341. Washington, D.C.: Government Printing Office.

Vaughan, Barbara, James Trusell, Jane Menken, and Elise F. Jones. 1977. "Contraceptive Failure Among Married Women in the U.S., 1970–73," *Family Planning Perspectives* 9 (November/December):251–258.

Veevers, Jean E. 1973. "Voluntary Childless Wives: An Exploratory Study," *Sociology and Social Research* 57 (April):356–366.

———. 1974. "The Life-Style of Voluntary Childless Couples," in L. Larson (ed.), *The Canadian Family in Comparative Perspective*. Toronto: Prentice-Hall.

Weller, Robert H., and Frank B. Hobbs. 1978. "Unwanted and Mistimed Births in the U.S.:1968–1973," *Family Planning Perspectives* 10 (May/June):168–172.

Westoff, Charles F., and Elise F. Jones. 1977a. "Contraception and Sterilization in the U. S., 1965–1975," *Family Planning Perspectives* 9 (July/August):153–157.

———, and ———. 1977b. "The Secularization of U.S. Catholics Birth Control Practices," *Family Planning Perspectives* 9 (September/October):203–207.

Willie, Charles V., and Susan L. Greenblatt. 1978. "Four 'Classic' Studies of Power Relationships in Black Families: A Review and Look to the Future," *Journal of Marriage and the Family* 40 (November):691–694.

The Interweave of Children and Parents

FOURTEEN

The Impact of the First Child

The previous chapter gave us a broad overview of trends in birthrates, contraception, and household composition. Now let us turn to the internal roles of the family institution. For over twenty years there has been research and debate as to whether the birth of the first child is a crisis for the parents. The mother in particular is expected to be ecstatic at giving birth to a child. Research indicates (LeMasters, 1957; Dyer, 1963; Hobbs, 1965) that this is at times not the case. "Cabin fever," a feeling of exhaustion, and "postpartum blues" are but a few not uncommon reactions to the birth of a first child. Although more women today may have realistic expectations, many women who have these negative reactions still often feel guilty because of their exposure to the romantic views about the joys of motherhood. The birth of a child often leaves the woman physically worn out for a period of weeks or longer. An infant's need for constant attention adds to the mother's lack of energy, especially in a traditional role-segregated home. To have to wake up to feed a baby once or twice a night can wear out even a new father who has not gone through the childbirth experience.

To further complicate the situation, mothers having their first babies often lack even basic information about infants. Perhaps this lack of knowledge in a society that stresses the importance of rational understanding accounts for the tremendous past popularity of Dr. Spock's book on baby care. Even today this book is still selling. Our ancestors a hundred years ago may have been no better prepared and may well have had no more assistance available either. I have earlier in this book (Chapter 4) dissected the myth in this country that we once lived in three-generation households, with grandparents and other relatives available to help out in child rearing and other areas. The high rates of migration from Europe, and from East to West, and from rural to urban places consisted predominantly of young people and not of three-generation households. In short, there was little opportunity to develop extended family households in this country. Thus, Dr. Spock has been popular not because the relatives that used to help are now gone but primarily because today we have the affluence and leisure to be concerned and to want to raise children in the most advantageous fashion. Among the very poor, the daily battle for food, shelter, and clothing occupies much more time, and fewer copies of Dr. Spock or other similar books are seen around the house.

The very fundamental character of the information in Dr. Spock's book illustrates the tremendous lack of knowledge concerning infancy among new mothers. Spock, for example, resolves the mother's fears regarding the navel. The cutting of the umbilical cord at birth leaves a stub attached to the navel that takes about a week to dry up, turn black, and fall off. Many new mothers who do not know what the stub is are often anxiety ridden and fearful of excessive bleeding when it falls off. Spock comforts such mothers with his straightforward description and his playing down of the importance of this occurrence. Another source of anxiety is the soft spot on the newborn infant's head. The skull at birth is not fully formed (which helps allow for plasticity during birth). There is an area, triangular in shape, toward the top front of the skull which is only scalp, with no bone underneath. This soft spot is called the "fontanel," and many mothers are anxious about this also. Dr. Spock once more comes to the rescue with a simple, straightforward

Gustav Vigeland "The Family,"
Vigeland Sculpture Park, Oslo.

statement that the spot is stronger than it seems and will be gone in eighteen to twenty-four months.

If I am correct about the romanticization of parenthood and about our lack of fundamental knowledge—in short, if our culture's anticipatory socialization for parenthood is inadequate—then the birth of the first child may well be at least a mild crisis for many parents. Even with a good deal of realism, knowledge, and preparation, one might argue that changing a dyad to a triad (a two-person to a three-person group) is such a major structural change that adjustment can be difficult. The addition of a key person like the loss of a key person, is likely to promote a crisis in the family regardless of the cultural setting.

Researchers like LeMasters (1957), Dyer (1963), Hobbs (1965), Feldman (1966), Russell (1974), and Hobbs and Cole (1976) investigated the impact of the birth of the first child on the parents. The first three researchers utilized small samples ranging from thirty-two to fifty couples. LeMasters (1957) found the greatest number of crises, with thirty-eight of his forty-six couples saying that the first child precipitated an extreme or severe crisis. The mothers reported loss of sleep, loss of social activity, loss of jobs, additional work, and increased worry. The fathers reported less sexual response from their wives, more economic pressures, and more work. Despite all these factors, almost all the couples eventually adjusted to the transition to parenthood—but not without a price.

Dyer (1963) found that much of the crisis feeling which LeMasters noted was not present. His thirty-two couples from Houston were interviewed within two years after birth and expressed less crisis response than did LeMasters' respondents. Dyer reported that the strength of the marriage helped avert crisis responses, but that 62 percent of the husbands said they felt neglected by their wives since the baby arrived.

Hobbs (1965) had the best sample of the three: fifty-three randomly chosen couples from Greensboro, North Carolina. He checked on crisis response ten weeks after childbirth. Hobbs found that mothers experienced more crisis response than fathers, but that only 13 percent reported even moderate crisis experience. This is radically different from LeMasters' 83 percent experiencing severe or extreme crisis and Dyer's 53 percent finding. Hobbs and Cole (1976) repeated their check on a similar sample ten years later and arrived at a similar conclusion. LeMasters asked about crisis response five years after birth; Dyer two years after birth, and Hobbs ten weeks after birth. The closer the questioning was to the birth, the less was the crisis reported. Perhaps the realization of the strain one has been under and the consequences of such strain on the marriage are not felt by many couples until a few years later. It could be argued that during the early months after childbirth one is too busy to realize the full extent of the impact of the birth. Also, perhaps it is easier to recognize a crisis intellectually after one is out of danger. To do so in the middle of it may be too emotionally upsetting. None of the three studies mentioned utilized research designs that are likely to settle this controversy. What is needed is a more carefully done study, preferably a longitudinal one carried out for a five- or ten-year period of time utilizing a more broadly based sample. Hobbs has done additional work questioning the findings of earlier studies and points to the importance of marital adjustment in handling this type of crisis (Hobbs, 1968).

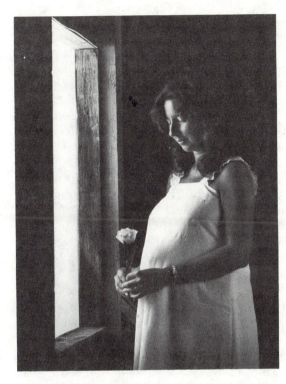

Photo by Cindy Knowlton.

Harold Feldman utilized a larger sample of mostly white-collar couples in an eastern city. He reports (Feldman, 1966:151–153) that the advent of children led to a disruption of marital communication and marital satisfaction. He arrived at this conclusion by comparing couples married the same length of time, some of whom had children and some of whom did not. Here, too, is evidence that for many couples the advent of a child, even if not considered a crisis of grave importance, does alter the basic interaction pattern of the husband and wife in ways that are potentially disturbing. Russell's research (1974) found only slight or moderate crises in a large urban sample. Russell points out the importance of balancing parental frustrations against parental gains in order to understand the variability in adjustment to first parenthood. Trends in marital satisfaction were discussed at length in connection with dyadic commitment in Chapter 10. It seems clear that children do lead to some diminishment of *marital* satisfaction. However, we must be aware of the possible additions in *parental* satisfactions that may also result.

The more one examines the evidence, the more one senses the full meaning and relevance of Bernard Farber's definition of the family as "a set of mutually contingent careers" (Farber, 1964). Farber's approach makes one aware of the multiple roles of men and women other than as husband and wife. These other roles of father and mother and the changing demands that result in all roles over time are important considerations. The "family development" approach most fully considers such variables (Hill and Rodgers, 1964; Aldous, 1978).

What this entire discussion should do is make clear to the reader that marital satisfaction and family satisfaction are not the same thing. While it does seem unlikely that one would be high on one and low on the other, it is quite possible that one might be high on one of these factors and only moderate on the other. The point is that these are in many ways distinct roles. In relation to the children, the father may be dominant; in relation to his wife, he may be submissive. A person may spend the greatest part of his or her time at home focusing on either the marital or the parental role. In fact, Farber (1964) has suggested that we classify families as child-centered versus mate-centered. A good deal of marital conflict may derive from such differences in focus on children and mates.

The thrust of my remarks on marital and family satisfaction is that this is a much more complex area than was once thought. There is a need to separate and examine the interrelation of marital and family satisfaction, and there is the ever-present need to test popular folklore that contends that children strengthen marriage. As in so many other areas, the answers are inevitably going to specify the conditions under which children do, and do not, strengthen a marriage and thereby delineate the conditions under which marital and family satisfaction may, or may not, be mutually reinforcing. A search for the sources of strain in the marital dyad, and particularly in such a dyad when it is placed in a family context consisting of several children, is of top research importance. We have only the glimmerings of such answers in the research we have examined in this chapter on the impact of the first child. Finally, I should add here that there are millions of single-parent households and it is a legitimate inquiry to ask how the birth of a child affects such households. Very little research has been done on such families and thus in this section and

Photo by Michael Perry.

elsewhere we speak primarily of the traditional two-parent family. Part of the reason for this gap in research may well be that the one-parent family has been viewed as a "deviant" form and therefore the research on it it has focused on its relation to other types of deviance such as crime and illness.

Sibling Roles in the Family

Part of the understanding of the impact of children on a marriage is recognition of the ways in which siblings affect one another. I shall not burden the reader with a vast number of studies, but instead will select what I consider to be a key study and utilize it to illustrate some basic notions regarding sibling relations in early childhood. (Sibling relationships at older ages will be dealt with in Chapter 16 when we speak of general kin ties.)

Orvill Brim (1968) took the information obtained by Helen Koch and examined it for his own interest in sibling relations. This type of "secondary analysis" of other people's research is becoming increasingly common. Brim applied some notions of role-taking and role-playing that come straight from the ideas of George Herbert Mead which we examined in Chapter 3. Brim starts with the reasoning that one learns how to perform one's own role by role-taking with others such as siblings. The more powerful the other person is, the more influential will be the role-taking. From these two notions he posits, first, that children with siblings of the opposite

Courtesy of Minnesota Geographic Society, Project Director: Tim Strick.
Photo by Olaf Kallstrom.

Photo by Michael Perry.

gender will display more traits of the opposite gender than will children who have siblings of the same gender. Second, he maintains that children who have siblings of the opposite gender who are older, will display the highest amount of the traits of the opposite gender. This is a rather neat, logical set of hypotheses, which follows closely from the notions of George Herbert Mead.

The sample Brim used consisted of almost four hundred five- and six-year-old children from two-child families. He had measures that indicated to what extent the child had expressive or instrumental traits (see Chapter 9). Male children were expected to display instrumental traits and female children expressive traits. Brim then looked to see if boys with sisters showed more expressive traits, if girls with brothers had more instrumental traits, and if children with older siblings of the opposite gender showed the greatest amount of traits of the opposite gender. The results come out mainly as predicted, and boys with older sisters were the most expressive of all boys. For girls, the relationships that were expected did not appear quite so clearly. Perhaps because of the constant presence of the mother as a model for girls, the impact of brothers—older and younger—is reduced. Perhaps, also, the greater speed with which girls mature physically makes them less easily influenced by boys.

In my national study of premarital sexual attitudes, I discovered that in families of two siblings of the same gender, the younger sibling was more permissive than the older sibling. One can apply Brim's explanation to my findings and contend that the younger sibling is influenced by the older sibling and thus has a source of higher permissiveness to imitate, which the older sibling lacks. The younger sibling thus learns about sexual motivations earlier and becomes relatively higher on permissiveness. Of course, other explanations are possible. But the point seems clear that the age and gender of one's siblings may well affect the attitudes and behaviors one will accept. The source of explanation most readily available is the one we have utilized, namely, the notions of Mead concerning role-taking and role-playing. Others have chosen to utilize "exchange theory" notions (see Chapter 10) and stress the rewards and costs of interaction (Schvaneveldt and Ihinger, 1979). In general, sibling research has been neglected although it is one of the three basic types of role relationships in the family institution. The other two are parent-child and husband-wife role relationships and they have received much more attention.

Impact of Parents upon Children

We have briefly discussed the impact of first children upon the parents' marriage and the impact of siblings upon each other. It is important also to comment upon what we know about the impact of parents upon their children. (For recent research see Ihinger, 1975). The socialization literature is a vast one, and I shall cover only a few highlights of it. Clearly, parents and their children form a primary group in the full sense that Cooley had in mind when he formulated the term "primary group" (1909). Cooley meant a group that was primary in the sense of influencing the individual first and having an impact of first importance. The parent-child group is the best example of such a group. There is no question that the emotional and intellectual makeup of the child is dramatically affected by the nature of the parent-child interaction. We stressed the importance of looking to this early interaction for sources of gender identity and for sources of love conceptions. I would like to focus here upon adolescent children and see the effects of parent-child relations upon them.

An impressive set of four doctoral dissertations by Darwin Thomas, Andrew Weigert, Viktor Gecas, and Elizabeth Rooney was undertaken in the late 1960s and early 1970s at the University of Minnesota. All focused upon the impact of family socialization upon the adolescent (Thomas, et al.,1974). The focus was upon four different adolescent characteristics: self-esteem (Gecas), conformity (Thomas), religiosity (Weigert), and deviant life-styles (Rooney). The basic theoretical question concerned the relationships of parental "support" and parental "control" to these four outcomes. Parental support was defined as that quality of the parent-child interaction that is perceived by the child as establishing a positive affectionate relationship. This basically involves the parents promoting the feeling in the child of self-worth and thereby encouraging competent activity. Parental control refers here to that quality of interaction perceived by adolescents as constraining them to do what the parent wants done.

Since the reader will see the meaning more clearly if the exact questions used to measure support and control are presented, this is done in Table 14.1. It is also well to note that the support measures have considerable overlap with the concept of nurturance, which I posited as the essential function of the family institution. Also, the support and control variables are quite similar in meaning to the expressive and instrumental roles which have been considered as two essential social tasks found in all human groups (see Chapter 9). Thus, these concepts are of central concern to the sociological understanding of parent-child relationships and are not just two minor dimensions of that relationship. The measures that Thomas and

TABLE 14.1

Questions Used To Measure Parental Support and Control

Control:

If I don't do what is expected of me, she/he is very strict about it.
  (very often, fairly often, sometimes, hardly ever, or never are the response categories)
She/he keeps pushing me to do my best in whatever I do.
She/he expects me to keep my things in good order.
She/he keeps after me to do well in school.

Support:

If I have any kind of a problem, I can count on her/him to help me out.
  (same response categories as control)
She/he says nice things about me.
She/he teaches me things I want to learn.
She/he makes me feel she is there if I need her/him.

Source: Darwin Thomas et al. (1974):12.

his colleagues used were originated by the Cornell Parent Behavior Description Study; they have been tested for validity and reliability and have stood up well. The samples for the four different dissertations came from six cities: San Francisco, Minneapolis, St. Paul, New York, San Juan, and Merida. The respondents were of high school age except for the use of college students in the San Francisco sample. They all came from intact families of the middle socioeconomic strata. They were not probability-type samples, however.

Looking at all four studies, there were some differences, but I shall focus on the common findings. It is interesting to note that male adolescents reported receiving more parental *control* than did females. Female adolescents reported receiving more parental *support* than did males. White-collar respondents were found to be given more parental support than blue-collar respondents. Females turned out to be higher than males on self-esteem and also to be more conforming than males. In this same vein females identified less with the counterculture (hippie culture was tested) than males. One very impressive finding was that parental support was much more powerful than parental control in predicting relationships with the four dependent variables. That is, high parental support was the best predictor of high self-esteem, high conformity, high religiosity, and high resistance to counterculture identification. It is interesting to note that parental support did produce adolescent self-esteem in family and adult contexts, but it was not related to self-esteem in peer contexts. In short, the adolescent's self-esteem in his or her relationships with peers was not affected by parental support. This would indicate the separateness of the peer world from that of the family world as well as the multidimensionality of self-esteem.

Thomas and his colleagues tried to discern how the relationship of parental support to these four dependent variables would vary under conditions of high or low parental control. (See Appendix 3 for a discussion of the logic involved here.) In short, would the degree of parental control affect the relationship of parental support to the four dependent variables of esteem, conformity, religiosity, and identification with the counterculture? The findings indicated that overall the parental control variable worked the same as the support variable, and thus when an adolescent was reported high on both, he usually had the strongest relationship to the four dependent variables.

There was one interesting exception that is worth mentioning. One might expect identification with a counterculture to be greatest when one was low on parental support and also low on parental control. That generally was the case for females. However, for males the strongest identification with the counterculture occurred when one was low on parental support and high on parental control. In short, when parents tried to restrict behavior but offered no emotional support in return for abiding by such restrictions, then the male adolescent was most likely to revolt. I mention this finding because it is precisely this kind of qualification that is a valuable payoff of research. It is always easy to make sense of such findings once they occur, but it is very difficult to know what one will find before carrying out the research. For example, one could argue that those adolescents who had high support and low control would be most likely to identify with a counterculture like the hippie movement because they would have the emotional stability and esteem to set out on their own and would lack parental restraints to such counterculture activity. The results did not support such an interpretation. One value then of research is that it affords checks on the scientific truth of the multitude of logical and "reasonable" explanations.

In some later writing, Rollins and Thomas distinguish between two types of control: (1) coercive and (2) inductive. By coercive they mean that the parents turn the situation into a contest of wills and demand conformity and threaten punishment

Photo by Ivan Kalman.

of various sorts if they are not obeyed. By inductive they mean that the parents *avoid* a contest of wills and try to reason out a solution to the problem which is satisfactory to all concerned. In short, the attempt is to obtain voluntary compliance. Rollins and Thomas report on a variety of research projects which indicate that coercive control lessens the likelihood of "social competence" in children. By social competence they include some of the variables discussed before, such as self-esteem and conformity, but they add additional indices of competence such as cognitive development, instrumental effectiveness, and creativity. When they examine inductive control they find it works opposite to coercive control, that is, the more inductive control, the *more* social competence in children. Thus, they are suggesting that it is necessary to refine our notions of control into these two subtypes in order to gain a more precise insight into the operation of parental control. Their recent examination of the research literature continues to uphold the positive relationship of parental support to the general social competence of children (Rollins and Thomas, 1979).

The question of parental control and support as factors in "nonconforming behavior," such as the delinquent behavior of adolescent children, is one that has received attention in the research literature. One of the classic studies was done by Sheldon and Elenor Glueck (1968). They studied a matched sample of five hundred delinquent and five hundred nondelinquent boys aged nine to seventeen. Both groups were from the greater Boston area and were matched on age, intelligence, ethnicity, race, and residence in an underprivileged urban neighborhood with a high delinquency rate. Between 1948 and 1963 the Gluecks did a follow-up study on these two groups taking them up to age thirty-one. One key area they examined was parent-child relationships. Overall, they report that the delinquent boys' families displayed weaker ties to one another, less stability, and fewer affectionate displays. Parental control was harsher and more likely to involve physical punishment in the delinquent boys' homes—in short, there was more coercive control (Glueck and Glueck, 1968). Thus, we have a situation with low support and high coercive control which is precisely the setting for producing a nonconformity reaction, or what Rollins and Thomas call a lack of general social competence (low on self-esteem, conformity, and so on).

The importance of parental support for avoiding delinquent behavior can perhaps best be seen in the results of Ivan Nye's study (1958). The sample Nye utilized consisted of several hundred high school students from the state of Washington. Despite its age, the findings are of such importance that the study has recently been reissued and other research has supported its conclusions. Figure 14.1 shows the rate of delinquent behavior to vary from 14 percent to 48 percent directly in accord with the degree of mutual acceptance of the child and the mother. This finding holds for relationships with fathers as well as with mothers. The results tend to uphold the importance of parental support for conforming behavior.

We have spoken of single-parent families in Chapter 13 and thus it is important to clarify the role of "broken homes" in the etiology of delinquency. Many studies have indicated that delinquents are more likely to come from homes broken by divorce, separation, desertion, or death (Wilkinson, 1974). But what does this mean causally? It is quite possible that delinquents come from broken homes because

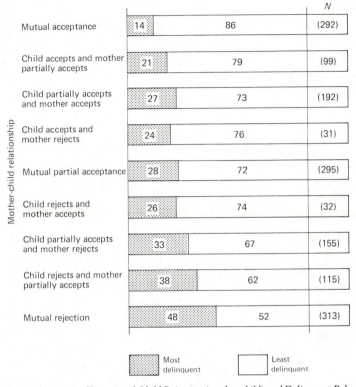

Figure 14.1. *Combinations of Parent and Child Rejection (mother-child) and Delinquent Behavior.*
Source: *F. Ivan Nye, (1958), p. 75.*

those arrested for delinquency are more likely to be in poverty areas and it is the pressures of poverty that raise both the crime rate and the broken-home rate. This view would argue that causally it may well not be the breaking of a home that leads to delinquency but the unhappiness in a home. There is no monopoly on unhappiness in broken homes and thus if happiness is the key factor, then when we examine *within* those who come from broken homes and *within* those who come from unbroken homes, we should find that those who are unhappy *within* each group will show the greatest tendency toward delinquency. This sort of check is precisely what Ivan Nye carried out and the results are presented in Table 14.2. Within those homes that were unbroken there is a difference of some 25 percent, depending if the home is happy or not (23 percent vs. 48 percent). Within the broken homes there is a difference of 19 percent depending on whether the home is happy or not (54 percent vs. 35 percent). The difference between broken and unbroken homes is only 8 percent (28 percent vs. 36 percent). Thus, clearly there is much greater predictability of delinquency by knowing whether one is in a happy home than by knowing if one is in a broken home. The small difference between broken and unbroken homes in delinquency may be due to greater economic stress in the broken homes. The proportion unhappy in these two groups is very similar— 19.4 percent of the broken homes and 18.6 percent of the unbroken homes are

TABLE 14.2

Happy and Unhappy, Broken and Unbroken Homes, and Delinquent Behavior

FAMILY STATUS	MOST DELINQUENT (Percent)	LEAST DELINQUENT (Percent)	N
All unbroken	28	72	(602)
Happy-unbroken	23	77	(490)
Unhappy-unbroken	48	52	(112)
All broken	36	64	(124)
Happy-broken	35	65	(100)
Unhappy-broken	54	46	(24)

Source: F. Ivan Nye (1958):46.

listed as unhappy. These overall findings are rather good evidence that whether the home is broken or not is only a minor factor in understanding delinquency. By far the more important factor is knowing if the home is happy or unhappy.

The happiness in a home would seem to be closely related to what Rollins and Thomas call parental support and thus we have additional evidence that parental support increased child conformity. Figure 14.2 affords an overview of Rollins and Thomas's view on causes of social competence (a composite of self-esteem, conformity, cognitive development, creativity, and instrumental competence). Note that parental coercion and parental induction are viewed to have opposite affects on social competence in children. This is in line with our earlier discussion. This causal diagram affords one a simple starting point for developing a more intricate conception of parent-child relationships.

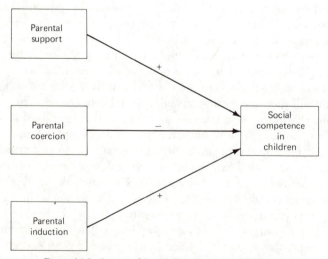

Figure 14.2. Causes of Social Competence in Children.
Source: Rollins & Thomas, 1979:334

Before leaving this topic, I want to add that there are many other causes of conformity or delinquency than simply the type of parent-child relationship. Some sociologists have stressed causes of delinquency such as association with those who are delinquent or nonconformist (Sutherland, 1960) and other sociologists have stressed the importance of opportunity to commit the delinquent act (Cloward and Ohlin, 1960). Still others have attributed the cause to the emphasis on financial success in our culture and noted that when opportunity to achieve success is blocked, it will provoke delinquency (Merton, 1938). Daniel Bell (1960) and others have pointed out that crime is a form of class warfare—the "have nots" try to take from the "haves." Rodman and Grams (1967), in an interesting summary of the literature on delinquency and the family, conclude that economic stress is the key cause of family disruption that may lead to delinquency. The reader should be aware that we are selecting out of a large matrix only those causes related directly to the family. A full analysis of nonconformity would obviously include many more.

Summary and Conclusions

The parental role is a complex one—in my judgment, it is more complex than the marital role. The skills involved in the formation of an individual's personality from birth to adulthood are greater than the skills involved in the mutual adjustment of two adults. Perhaps the greater complexity of the parental role stems in part from the much greater dependency of the child on the parent as compared to the dependency of one mate on the other. For at least the first few years of life the child's universe revolves about the parent. In marriage there are other sources of need fulfillment: in work, in friends, in relatives, and in hobbies. Thus the range of dependency in marriage appears to be less, although obviously being in love has a dependent aspect to it. One cannot help but become dependent on that which one values—even if there are alternative sources of need fulfillment. It may well be that those who choose to be childless are aware of the complexity and dependency involved in parenthood and reject it for just those reasons, while others rise to what they perceive as the challenge and the promise of parenthood.

References

Aldous, Joan. 1978. *Family Careers: Developmental Changes in Families.* New York: Wiley.

Bartz, Karen W., and Elaine S. Levine. 1978. "Child Rearing by Black Parents: A Description and Comparison to Anglo and Chicano Parents," *Journal of Marriage and the Family* 40 (November):709–721.

Bell, Daniel. 1960. "Crime as an American Way of Life: A Queer Ladder of Social Mobility," in Daniel Bell (ed.), *The End of Ideology.* New York: Free Press.

Brim, Orville G., Jr. 1968. "Family Structure and Sex-Role Learning by Children," in Norman W. Bell and Ezra F. Vogel (eds.), *A Modern Introduction to the Family,* 2nd ed. New York: Free Press.

Clark, John P., and Eugene Wenninger. 1962. "Socio-economic Class and Area as Correlates of Illegal Behavior Among Juveniles," *American Sociological Review* 27 (December):826–834.

Cloward, Richard A., and Lloyd E. Ohlin. 1960. *Delinquency and Opportunity.* New York: Free Press.

Cohen, Albert K. 1955. *Delinquent Boys*. New York: Free Press.

Cooley, Charles H. 1909. *Social Organization*. New York: Schocken.

Duncan, Beverly, and Otis Dudley Duncan. 1969. "Family Stability and Occupational Success," *Social Problems* 16 (Winter):273–285.

Dyer, Everett D. 1963. "Parenthood as Crises: A Re-study," *Marriage and Family Living* 25 (May):196–201.

Farber, Bernard. 1964. *Family: Organization and Interaction*. San Francisco: Chandler.

Feldman, Harold. 1966. "Development of the Husband-Wife Relationship." Research report, unpublished, Cornell University, Ithaca, NY.

Glick, Paul C. 1979. "Children of Divorced Parents in Demographic Perspective," *Journal of Social Issues* (in press).

Glueck, Sheldon, and Eleanor Glueck. 1968. *Delinquents and Nondelinquents in Perspective*. Cambridge, MA: Harvard University Press.

Hill, Reuben, and Roy H. Rodgers. 1964. "The Developmental Approach," in Harold T. Christensen (ed.), *Handbook of Marriage and the Family*. Chicago: Rand McNally.

Hirschi, Travis, and Hanan C. Selvin. 1967. *Delinquency Research: An Appraisal of Analytic Methods*. New York: Free Press.

Hobbs, Daniel F. 1965. "Parenthood as Crisis: A Third Study," *Journal of Marriage and the Family* 27 (August):367–372.

———. 1968. "Transition to Parenthood: A Replication and an Extension," *Journal of Marriage and the Family* 30 (August):413–418.

———, and Sue Peck Cole. 1976. "Transition to Parenthood: A Decade Replication," *Journal of Marriage and the Family* 38 (November):723–731.

Ihinger, Marilyn. 1975. "The Referee Role and Norms of Equity: A Contribution Toward a Theory of Sibling Conflict," *Journal of Marriage and the Family* 37 (August):515–525.

Johnson, Nan E., and C. Shannon Stokes. 1976. "Family Size in Successive Generations: The Effects of Birth Order, Intergenerational Change in Lifestyle and Familial Satisfaction," *Demography* 13 (May):175–187.

Journal of Marriage and the Family. November 1978. This entire issue is devoted to studies of the black family.

Kirkpatrick, Clifford, and Charles Hobart. 1954. "Disagreement, Disagreement Estimate, and Nonempathetic Imputations for Intimacy Groups Varying from Favorite Date to Married," *American Sociological Review* 19 (February):10–19.

LeMasters, Ersel E. 1957. "Parenthood as Crises," *Marriage and Family Living* 19 (November):352–355.

Lemert, Edwin M. 1967. *Human Deviance, Social Problems, and Social Control*. Englewood Cliffs, NJ: Prentice-Hall.

Matza, David. 1964. *Delinquency and Drift*. New York: Wiley.

McCord, Joan, and William McCord. 1958. "The Effects of Parental Role Models on Criminality." *Journal of Social Issues* 14 (July):66–75.

Merton, Robert K. 1938. "Social Structure and Anomie," *American Sociological Review* 3 (October):672–682.

Monahan, Thomas P. 1957. "Family Status and the Delinquent Child: A Reappraisal and Some New Findings," *Social Forces* 35 (March): 250–258.

Moynihan, Daniel P. 1965. *The Negro Family: The Case for National Action*. Washington, DC: Government Printing Office.

Nye, F. Ivan. 1958. *Family Relationships and Delinquent Behavior*. New York: Wiley.

Parsons, Talcott. 1959. "The Social Structure of the Family," in Ruth N. Anshen (ed.), *The Family: Its Function and Destiny*. New York: Harper & Row.

Pinkney, Alphonso. 1975. *Black Americans*. Englewood Cliffs, NJ: Prentice-Hall.

Rainwater, Lee, and William L. Yancey. 1967. *The Moynihan Report and the Politics of Controversy*. Cambridge: The Massachusetts Institute of Technology Press.

Rodman, Hyman. 1963. "The Lower-Class Value Stretch," *Social Forces* 42 (December):205–215.

———, and Paul Grams. 1967. "Juvenile Delinquency and the Family: A Review and Discussion." In *Task Force Report: Juvenile Delinquency and Youth Crime*. The President's Commission on Law Enforcement and Administration of Justice. Washington, DC: Government Printing Office.

Rollins, Boyd C., and Kenneth L. Cannon. "Marital Satisfaction over the Family Life Cycle," *Journal of Marriage and the Family* 32 (February):20–38.

Rollins, Boyd C., and Kenneth L. Cormanon. 1974. "Marital Satisfaction Over the Family Life Cycle: A Reevaluation," *Journal of Marriage and the Family* 35 (May):271–284.

———, and Darwin L. Thomas. 1975. "A Theory of Parental Power and Child Compliance." In Ronald E. Cromwell and David H.

Olson (eds.). *Power in Families*. New York: Halsted Press Division.

———. and Darwin L. Thomas. 1979. "Parental Support, Power and Control Techniques in the Socialization of Children." In Wes Burr, R. Hill, I. Nye, and I. L. Reiss (eds.), *Contemporary Theories About the Family*, Vol. I. New York: Free press.

Russell, Candyce S. 1974. "Transition to Parenthood: Problems and Gratifications," *Journal of Marriage and the Family* 36 (May):294–302.

Scanzoni, John H. 1971. *The Black Family in Modern Society*. Boston: Allyn & Bacon.

———. 1975. "Sex Roles, Economic Factors, and Marital Solidarity in Black and White Marriages," *Journal of Marriage and the Family* 37 (February):130–144.

Schvaneveldt, Jay D., and Marilyn Ihinger. 1979. "Sibling Relationships in the Family." In Wes Burr, R. Hill, I. Nye, and I. L. Reiss (eds.), *Contemporary Theories About the Family*, Vol. I. New York: Free Press.

Sewell, William H. 1961. "Social Class and Childhood Personality," *Sociometry* 24 (December):340–356.

Short, James F., Jr., and Fred L. Strodtbeck. 1965. *Group Process and Gang Delinquency*. Chicago: University of Chicago Press.

Spock, Benjamin. 1947. *Child and Baby Care*. New York: Pocket Books.

Sutherland, Edwin H., and Donald R. Cressey. 1960. *Principles of Criminology*. Philadelphia: Lippincott.

Thomas, Darwin, Viktor Gecas, Andrew Weigert, and Elizabeth Rooney. 1974. *Family Socialization and the Adolescent*. Lexington, MA: Heath.

Veroff, Joseph, and Sheila Feld. 1970. *Marriage and Work in America: A Study of Motives and Roles*. New York: Van Nostrand.

Wilkinson, Karen. 1974. "The Broken Family and Juvenile Delinquency: Scientific Explanation or Ideology," *Social Problems* 21 (June):726–739.

Willie, Charles V., and Susan L. Greenblatt. 1978. "Four 'Classic' Studies of Power Relationships in Black Families: A Review and Look to the Future," *Journal of Marriage and the Family* 40 (November):691–694.

Occupation and Parenthood

FIFTEEN

The occupational role, more than any other, has been singled out as a key influence on roles in the family institution. We will explore various facets of that influence in this chapter.

The Impact of Outside Employment on Fatherhood

There are fads and fashions in child rearing as in all social activities. Urie Bronfenbrenner (1958) contends that there is evidence that a general change in child-rearing patterns occurred shortly after World War II. The middle class became more acceptant of demand- and breast-feeding, more tolerant of toilet accidents, and more permissive about oral behavior, sexuality, and aggression against parents. Over the entire period since the 1920s the middle class has been stressing educational goals, and has been equalitarian and likely to utilize psychological rather than physical punishment. Then, as noted, after World War II the middle class also shifted to a more permissive position on the specifics of child rearing involving sexuality, aggression, and oral behavior. This change has brought middle-class child rearing to a position of higher general permissiveness than lower-class child rearing. Why this shift occurred is somewhat unclear, although the greater accessibility by the middle classes of advice from experts like Dr. Spock and the increased affluence of the middle classes have been cited as relevant factors.

The shift toward more general acceptance of infant sexuality, aggression, and acts like thumb sucking can be conceptually linked to the increased premarital sexual permissiveness of the college-educated population. We discussed this trend in Chapter 7, and pointed out how, by at least the early 1960s, the college-educated population had come to be as attitudinally acceptant of premarital sexuality as people with less education. Perhaps the more permissive child rearing of the middle classes since World War II was a factor in this change.

Much of the child-rearing literature prior to 1960 was based on Freudian notions of the importance of early infant training. Freud had asserted that the length of nursing, the speed of weaning, the age of toilet training, all tended to shape the adult personality. Many researchers assumed that parents' values were expressed by the infant feeding and toilet-training schedules. For example, if one weaned the infant slowly this might be assumed to indicate a generous and loving personality. Research would measure such parent-infant behavior and assume parental values and future child personality on that basis. All this is not very sociological for it stresses the unconscious and the psychological processes. By the late 1950s a sociological approach was forming and it was most lucidly articulated by Melvin Kohn.

KOHN'S RESEARCH

Melvin Kohn started his inquiry by studying two hundred white-collar and two hundred blue-collar families in Washington, D.C., during the late 1950s (1959). His work has continued right up to the present day. One reason for our interest in Kohn's work is his rejection of early child-rearing practices as the key to parental values and to the type of adult that will be produced. Kohn feels that age at toilet training and breast-versus-bottle feeding are customs subject to change *without* any basic change in values. In short, he feels that parents might well change from early to late weaning simply because a respected expert advised this, and parents therefore believe it would be good for their child. Such a change would not, Kohn believes, indicate that the parents had shifted from an emphasis on self-control to a more permissive set of values. Kohn contends that if we are interested in parental values that affect child rearing, then we should ask parents directly about their values, instead of trying to get indirect indicators of values from early child-rearing practices.

He conceives of each social class as having a distinct value orientation that affects parental behavior. The distinct value orientation is in good part a result of the conditions of work that go with the kind of occupations which are part of that social class. But instead of looking at early child-rearing practices as indicators of such class-linked values, Kohn asked his mothers and fathers what three characteristics they felt were most desirable in a fifth-grade child. All members of his sample had a fifth-grade child. Tables 15.1 and 15.2 present the proportions of mothers and fathers who have chosen the various traits as most desirable in their fifth-grade child. The tables are further broken down by gender and class. The class and gender breakdown seems to make a difference. Looking at the statistically significant differences (see Appendix 2), it seems that middle-class mothers of sons stressed happiness and curiosity *more* and obedience to parents *less* than did working-class mothers of sons. For girls the biggest differences seem to be the middle-class mothers' stressed consideration of others *more* and neatness and cleanliness *less*. The findings regarding fathers are generally similar. Table 15.2 shows that middle-class fathers stress obedience *less* for boys than do working-class fathers and dependability *more* than do working-class fathers. For girls, middle-class fathers put *more* emphasis on dependability and *less* on ability to defend oneself. Many other differences that are not quite large enough to be statistically significant can be seen in these two tables.

Overall, there seems to be a good deal of similarity between the choices made by middle-class and working-class parents. But there are differences worth discussing. Middle-class parents stressed things like happiness, curiosity, and dependability, whereas the working-class parents stressed things like obedience, neatness and cleanliness, and ability to defend oneself. Middle-class differences could be summarized by generalizing that such parents emphasize those factors that go with autonomy or self-direction. That is, they stress that a child be happy, curious, and dependable, all of which are traits that have a self-directive or "thinking for oneself" quality to them. The working-class parents, more than the middle-class parents, stress factors that go with conformity or general obedience to authority. This is surely the case for the traits of obedience and cleanliness that working-class parents were prone to emphasize.

In fact, this basic class difference of self-direction versus conformity seems to

TABLE 15.1

Proportion of Mothers Who Select Each Characteristic as One of Three "Most Desirable" in the Ten- or Eleven-Year-Old Child

	FOR BOYS		FOR GIRLS		COMBINED	
Characteristics	Middle Class	Working Class	Middle Class	Working Class	Middle Class	Working Class
1. That he is honest	.44	.57	.44	.48	.44	.53
2. That he is happy	.44*	.27	.48	.45	.46*	.36
3. That he is considerate of others	.40	.30	.38*	.24	.39*	.27
4. That he obeys his parents well	.18*	.37	.23	.30	.20*	.33
5. That he is dependable	.27	.27	.20	.14	.24	.21
6. That he has good manners	.16	.17	.23	.32	.19	.24
7. That he has self-control	.24	.14	.20	.13	.22*	.13
8. That he is popular with other children	.13	.15	.17	.20	.15	.18
9. That he is a good student	.17	.23	.13	.11	.15	.17
10. That he is neat and clean	.07	.13	.15*	.28	.11*	.20
11. That he is curious about things	.20*	.06	.15	.07	.18*	.06
12. That he is ambitious	.09	.18	.06	.08	.07	.13
13. That he is able to defend himself	.13	.05	.06	.08	.10	.06
14. That he is affectionate	.03	.05	.07	.04	.05	.04
15. That he is liked by adults	.03	.05	.07	.04	.05	.04
16. That he is able to play by himself	.01	.02	.00	.03	.01	.02
17. That he acts in a serious way	.00	.01	.00	.00	.00	.01
N	(90)	(85)	(84)	(80)	(174)	(165)

*Indicates social-class differences are statistically significant, at the 0.05 level or better, using the chi-square test.
Source: Melvin L. Kohn (1959):339.

fit very well with the conditions of life in these two classes. The case can particularly be made, and Kohn makes it very well, that the emphasis in child rearing in each social class is a direct reflection of those areas of life that are most problematic, most unresolved, for each class. The working class cannot take respectability for granted, so cleanliness is more important to promote in order to show what they stand for. The working-class occupations involve being supervised by foremen and managers, and thus obedience is a key feature of such work. Accordingly, the working-class parents stress obedience to external authority and this acts as antic-ipatory socialization for the type of work which later will be required of their children. The middle-class occupations involve more professional and managerial work that stresses interpersonal skills. Relatedly, one finds that child rearing, too, points up the need to develop self-reliance and dependability. Since many tasks of the middle classes involve deciding things for oneself, they involve the need for curiosity and self-control.

Kohn recognizes that there are two possible explanations for this association of occupational style and child rearing. One is that people with the appropriate ori-entation chose that occupation, and the other is that the occupation one enters

TABLE 15.2

Proportion of Fathers Who Select Each Characteristic as One of Three "Most Desirable" in a Ten- or Eleven-Year-Old Child[a]

Characteristics	FOR BOYS		FOR GIRLS		COMBINED	
	Middle Class	Working Class	Middle Class	Working Class	Middle Class	Working Class
1. That he is honest	.60	.60	.43	.55	.52	.58
2. That he is happy	.48	.24	.24	.18	.37	.22
3. That he is considerate of others	.32	.16	.38	.09	.35[b]	.14
4. That he obeys his parents well	.12[b]	.40	.14	.36	.13[b]	.39
5. That he is dependable	.36[b]	.12	.29[b]	.00	.33[b]	.08
6. That he has good manners	.24	.28	.24	.18	.24	.25
7. That he has self-control	.20	.08	.19	.00	.20[b]	.06
8. That he is popular with other children	.08	.16	.24	.45	.15	.25
9. That he is a good student	.04	.12	.10	.36	.07	.19
10. That he is neat and clean	.16	.20	.14	.09	.15	.17
11. That he is curious about things	.16	.12	.10	.00	.13	.08
12. That he is ambitious	.20	.12	.14	.00	.17	.08
13. That he is able to defend himself	.04	.16	.00[b]	.18	.02[b]	.17
14. That he is affectionate	.00	.04	.05	.18	.02	.08
15. That he is liked by adults	.00	.08	.00	.09	.00	.08
16. That he is able to play by himself	.00	.08	.05	.00	.02	.06
17. That he acts in a serious way	.00	.04	.00	.00	.00	.03
N	(25)	(25)	(21)	(11)	(46)	(36)

[a]*Fathers were interviewed in one-fourth of all the families in the study.*
[b]*Indicates statistically significant social-class differences at the 0.05 level or better using the chi-square test.*
Source: Melvin L. Kohn (1959):340.

shapes one's values. Kohn leans toward the latter explanation. He does so because he believes that individuals do not have that much range in their choice of occupations. A child born into the working class will typically remain in the working class, and the same is true for a child born into the middle class. The demands of the occupation that one remains in gradually tend to affect one's values and, consciously or not, cause one to further develop the crucial type of values related to the occupation. Kohn and Schooler (1973; 1978) examined these ideas and found them to be supported in the careful tests they conducted. Thus, it does indeed appear that the stress on conformity and related values in the working class and self-direction and related values in the middle class is the end result of the individual's being in a certain position in the social-class structure and, therefore, having a certain type of occupational work.

Support of Kohn's overall position is not hard to come by. First, we know from many studies that the working classes tend to be more authoritarian, more acceptant of obedience as a proper response than are other classes (Lipset, 1960). Such findings support the class differences posited by Kohn. Also, we can examine groups like Catholics and rural people, which we would expect to stress conformity, and see that Kohn reports that these groups tend to place more emphasis on working-class values like conformity. Also, the higher educated place more value on self-direction.

When wives work at white-collar jobs, they come to value self-direction more than wives of the same class background who do not have such jobs. In short, there seems to be evidence that one's position in a social organization, (occupation, and the like) does seriously affect one's values and in ways similar to those put forth by Melvin Kohn.

Kohn's data obtain further credence by their fit with other research such as that done by Rainwater (1966), by Bott (1957), and by Blood and Wolfe (1960). Kohn found that husbands and wives in the middle classes agree more on child rearing and display less role segregation in general than do mates in the working classes. Komarovsky's (1964) findings also support the position of greater role segregation among mates in the lower classes. In 1966 Kohn checked out this finding (Pearlin and Kohn, 1966) in Italy and found it held up. The values of wives were most like their husbands' in the middle classes. This recheck in Italy also found that the middle classes stressed self-direction and the working classes stressed conformity in their child rearing.

The three key aspects of the occupation that seemed to produce these value differences were: (1) closeness of supervision; (2) substantive complexity of the work; and (3) routinization of the work.

The Italian sample was examined to discern how important these three conditions of work were in terms of producing self-directed or conformity values. The data are presented in two parts in Table 15.3. The left-hand side of the table, under the heading "original comparison," is a straight percentage breakdown of the middle and working classes according to the values of self-direction and conformity (plus an intermediate value position). Note that the theory is supported in that 52 percent of the middle class versus 35 percent of the working class support self-direction values and 22 percent of the middle class versus 40 percent of the working class support conformity values. The right-hand side of the table is "standardized on conditions of work." That phrase means that the comparison is made as if one were only comparing those people in the two social classes whose jobs involved the same conditions of work (in terms of supervision, complexity, and routinization). Thus, the conditions of work are being equalized or "standardized" in this examination of the data. To the extent that the conditions of work caused the middle and working classes to display different values, the differences between the two classes will disappear in this standardized portion of the table. That will occur because the presumed cause (conditions of work) has been equalized in the two social classes, so it *cannot* produce any differences. Whatever differences appear in the standardized portion of the table then would have to be due to something other than conditions of work. Kohn has stressed conditions of work as the key causal factor in producing different values, so he would expect the differences to become quite small when standardization comparisons are made. A glance at the standardized part of the table shows that Kohn was largely correct. There is now no difference in self-direction (41 percent in both classes). There is a difference in conformity (25 percent versus 35 percent), but it is smaller than before the standardization. About two-thirds of the difference between the classes has disappeared due to controlling the conditions of work and therefore those conditions of work have been shown to be of great importance in determining self-directed or conformity values. The conclusion then is that if the two classes normally had the same conditions of work, value differences on self-direction and conformity would be greatly reduced. (See Appendix 3 for further discussion of this type of analysis of causes.)

In 1964 Kohn used a national sample of 1,500 fathers to test out his ideas on a sample that represented the entire country. He used a revised set of questions

TABLE 15.3

Father's Valuation of Self-Direction and Conformity by Social Class (Original and Standardized Comparisons)

Proportion of Fathers Who:	ORIGINAL COMPARISON		STANDARDIZED ON CONDITIONS OF WORK	
	Middle Class	Working Class	Middle Class	Working Class
Value self-direction	.52	.35	.41	.41
(Intermediate)	.26	.25	.34	.24
Value conformity	.22	.40	.25	.35
Total	1.00	1.00	1.00	1.00
Number of cases	(144)	(141)	(144)	(141)

Source: Melvin L. Kohn (1969):149.

TABLE 15.4

Parental Values, by Social Class

	MEAN SCORES FOR				
	Social Class 1 (High)	Social Class 2	Social Class 3 (Medium)	Social Class 4	Social Class 5 (Low)
Considerate of others	3.40*	3.36	3.24	3.06	2.95
Interested in how and why things happen	3.12	3.00	2.69	2.56	2.39
Responsible	3.07	3.05	2.85	2.72	2.72
Self-control	2.95	2.90	2.87	2.84	2.77
Good manners	2.84	2.94	3.13	3.26	3.40
Neat and clean	2.23	2.40	2.70	2.84	2.90
Good student	2.53	2.47	2.54	2.70	2.85
Honest	3.58	3.54	3.81	3.87	3.76
Obeys his parents	3.43	3.61	3.64	3.68	3.70
Good sense and sound judgment	3.16	3.09	3.12	3.03	3.01
Acts as a boy (girl) should	2.81	2.77	2.74	2.82	2.74
Tries to succeed	2.92	2.71	2.65	2.75	2.92
Gets along with other children	3.07	3.32	3.21	3.16	3.20
Numbers of cases	(74)	(192)	(431)	(580)	(222)

*High valuation is indicated by a score of 5, low by a score of 1. Social class 1 is high and social class 5 is low.
Source: Melvin L. Kohn (1969):50.

(see Table 15.4). The same social-class differences in values appeared in this sample. The children of the fathers in this sample ranged in age from three to fifteen. Thus the generalizability of Kohn's theory to parents of children of all ages was further established by this check. Then, in 1973 and again in 1975, the National Opinion Research Center (NORC) included Kohn's questions in their annual national survey. The results of these two national tests also were congruent with Kohn's theory (Kohn, 1977). Thus, we have here a set of ideas that has been tested many times over a twenty-year period and has consistently held up.

Kohn's theory and research have several advantages. First, in his Washington study he used a probability type of sample that included both fathers and mothers. Almost all the other previous studies used only mothers as respondents. Kohn tested and supported his notions on a national sample as well as on local samples. Also, Kohn's logic involves fewer assumptions than the early child-rearing theories. Instead of assuming that early child-rearing practices concerned with breast feeding or toilet training *reflect* parents' values, Kohn *directly* asked his parents about their values. Of course, the advantage of this direct approach depends on your psychological position. If you believe that people cannot tell you what their key values are and that they are unknowingly influenced by their own early childhood experiences, then you may be less willing than Kohn to ask the direct questions. As a sociologist, I minimize the assumptions I make about the importance of the unconscious and of early childhood practices. Kohn's position is more purely sociological and thus more attractive to a sociologist (such as myself). Of course, psychological explanations may be compatible with sociological explanations. But for simplicity, I have kept the focus upon sociological explanations.

Figure 15.1 sums up in diagram form Kohn's theory of how parental values are influenced by occupational conditions. Note that Kohn introduces three other factors into this diagram to complete his perspective. Education is a key influence on "intellectual flexibility," "occupational status," and "occupational conditions" (see lines in diagram). Education also comes earliest in time—the variables proceed in time from the left of the diagram to the right. Kohn views education as important because of its impact on these three variables. The development of intellectual flexibility is of crucial importance in enhancing one's ability to perform self-directed types of jobs. Occupational status (or the prestige of a job) is seen as a determinant of occupational conditions because the higher prestige jobs usually are higher on self-directive type of work conditions. Note that intellectual flexibility has an influence independent of occupation on one's values and orientations. The relationship between intellectual flexibility and values and orientations is diagrammed as a two-way relationship wherein each variable influences the other in feedback fashion; that is, intellectual flexibility changes values and orientations, and those new values and orientations then influence intellectual flexibility to change, and so on around and around. The same sort of feedback relationship is pictured with values and orientations and the major variable of occupational conditions and also between occupational conditions and intellectual flexibility. The diagram thus allows one to see the crucial role of occupational conditions, which is one of Kohn's major propositions, and which we analyzed in Table 15.3. But, in addition, one can see how other factors also are involved in the ultimate shaping of an individual's values and orientations. The worth of diagraming should be appreciated now by the reader, and I hope this diagram has added clarity to the words we have used to describe Kohn's theory. We have not put direction signs (positive, negative) between variables because some of the variables do not vary from high to low: for example, values and orientations (see Appendix 4 for a discussion of diagrams such as this).

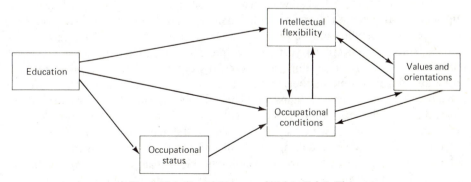

Figure 15.1. Causal Diagram of Melvin Kohn's Theory.

The Impact of Outside Employment on Motherhood

The above discussion makes the point that the father's occupation has an important influence on the values a parent will utilize in child rearing. What about the occupation of the mother? Does a mother who works outside the home have a different impact on her family than a nonworking mother? We have seen from Kohn's work that a woman who works in a white-collar (as opposed to a blue-collar) occupation tends to accept more values of self-direction for her children (similar to those which a man who works in such an occupation would come to accept). But this leaves unanswered many questions about the impact of working on the mother's care of her children and on the quality of her marriage and on the gender-role conceptions of her children. We shall discuss some of these factors now.

FEMALE LABOR FORCE PARTICIPATION

In Chapter 3, when talking about gender roles, we pointed out the vast growth in female labor force participation in the twentieth century. In 1900, 18 percent of the labor force was female and only 15 percent of those females were married. By 1980, 42 percent of the labor force was female and about 60 percent were married (U.S. Department of Labor, 1977; 1979a and 1979b). The enormity of that change in labor force participation marks this as a rare historical event that must have dramatic impact on the family institution. The present-day labor force participation rate involves about half of all women and about 80 percent of all men. During recent decades the participation rate of males has fallen while that of females has risen. Figure 15.2 illustrates this trend starting from 1950 and projected to 1990. Actually, the male labor force participation rate is well above 90 percent from age sixteen to age fifty-five. The female rate for those years would average about 55 percent. Both the male and female overall rate is pulled down by the low participation in employment of people after age fifty-five and especially after age sixty-five (U.S. Bureau of the Census, 1978, Series P–23, No. 77:25, p. 25). In Figure 15.3 the male rate is predicted to level out by 1990 while the female rate climbs to slightly above 50 percent of all women working.

The fact that about half of all women age sixteen and above are employed covers up more than it reveals. For one thing, there are vast differences in labor force participation depending on the presence of children. Figure 15.3 makes this obvious. Note that the critical years, where presence of children makes a major difference, is the sixteen- to thirty-four-year-old groupings. This is the time when most all women become mothers and the traditional gender-role tie to infant care greatly reduces labor force participation. The difference in labor force participation for women in this age group with and without children would be an excellent measure of the extent to which a culture endorsed the traditional tie of women to newborn children. There is no comparable alteration in the labor force participation of men at these ages. The advent of children affects male employment in the opposite fashion by increasing the need for financial support from them in line

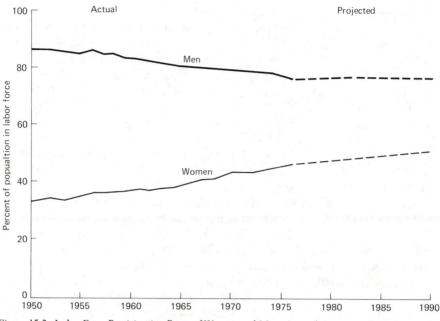

Figure 15.2. Labor Force Participation Rates of Women and Men, Annual Averages, 1950–1976, and Projected Rates for 1980, 1985, and 1990.
Source: U.S. Department of Labor (1977):63.

with the traditional male gender role and thus *increases* their labor force participation.

We should qualify the restrictive impact of childbirth on female labor force participation. There has been a dramatic change in the proportion of mothers who

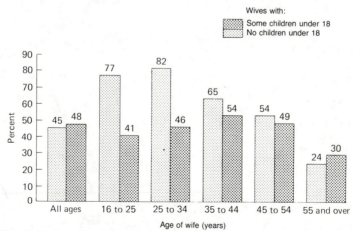

Figure 15.3. Labor Force Participation Rates of Wives
Source: U.S. Bureau of the Census (1978), P–23, No. 77:24.

are employed during the past thirty years. This is most sharply seen in the rise from 12-percent of mothers of preschool children employed in 1950 to 42 percent of such mothers employed in 1980 (see Figure 15.4). This type of change is of great significance for, as noted above, it is precisely here in the motherhood role that there is the strongest public opposition to female employment (see Chapter 3). If this resistance is changing, then it is worthy of note. Most of this increase in employed mothers of preschoolers is from women living with their husbands, but about 20 percent of preschool mothers are divorced, widowed, separated, or never married (U.S. Department of Labor. 1979b).

Here, too, though, we must add a further qualification. A large proportion of women do not work full-time year round. Much of the increase in female employment is due to part-time and not year-round employment. In 1977, for example, of all husbands and wives aged sixteen and over, 22 percent of the wives worked full-time year round and 65 percent of the husbands worked full-time year round. (U.S. Bureau of the Census, 1978, Series P–23, No. 77:25). Thus, of those wives who work, somewhat less than half are working full-time year round. The proportion working part-time would be higher if we dealt only with women who had preschool children. One of the reasons that women are heavily into part-time work is that they cannot obtain much help with their child and home duties when they go out to work. Thus, rather than taking on full-time work, many women choose to work part-time.

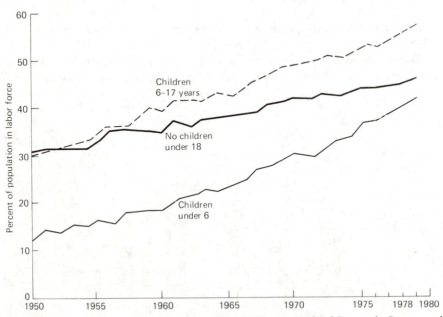

Figure 15.4. *Labor Force Participation Rates of Married Women, Husband Present, by Presence and Age of Own Children, 1950–76.*
Source: *U.S. Department of Labor, (1977):17 and U.S. Bureau of the Census (1979), P–20, No. 336:42.*

More women than ever before are in the full-time labor force. Photo by Randy Croce, courtesy of the Minnesota Geographic Society; Project Coordinator, Tim Strick.

Given our traditional gender roles, the marital status of a woman should make a considerable difference in the likelihood of outside employment. Figure 15.5 shows the reality of this expectation. Over 70 percent of the divorced women work, while only about half of the married women with a husband present are employed. The trend toward increased employment of the never-married is also instructive. This rise may well indicate that more women are entering the job market prior to marriage. This change could lead some women to reject marriage because it interferes with their already started career. Further, it could lead to lower birth expectations due to career plans (see Chapter 13). Of course, some of these never-married women are heads of one-parent families, just as are many of the divorced, separated, or even widowed group. We spoke in Chapter 13 at length about the millions of female-headed, one-parent families and so I will not go into this further here.

We saw in our discussion of gender roles that there have been increases in the proportion of women who are in medicine, law, and other professions (look back at Table 3.3). But we should not be misled by this into thinking that therefore the gap between male and female pay has closed. For about the last twenty years, full-time, year-round employed women have earned roughly 60 percent as much as men (U.S. Bureau of the Census, 1978, Series P–20, No. 324). Thus, the gains made by this small proportion of women in the top-ranked professions involve such a tiny fraction of the 40 million employed women that it does not alter the relative pay of women compared to men. The employment market is a gender-

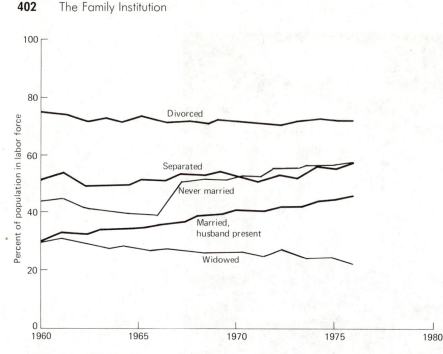

NOTE: Before 1967, data are for women 14 years and over; for 1967 and later years, data are for women 16 years
and over.

*Figure 15.5. Labor Force Participation Rates of Women by Marital Status, March 1960 to March 1976.
Source: U.S. Department of Labor (1977):16.*

segregated market (MacLaughlin, 1978). Women have always worked at very specific types of work and that continues to be the case. Since female work consists
generally of lesser-paying jobs, women continue to earn less than men. It is difficult
to escape the relatively low-paying female job market holds even for those women
who have a college education. College-educated women are now the most likely
to seek employment. Table 15.5 shows that the proportion of dual-work couples
goes up as education increases. Income is highly correlated with education, and
so it no longer is the case that poor women dominate the work force. The higher-
educated females surely have aspirations for higher standards of living and they may
feel that they must work in order to live at the level they desire. In addition, many
women work to escape the cultural isolation of the home. College-educated women
probably have this as a major motivation (Hoffman and Nye, 1974).

About a third of the wives who are employed earn as much or more than their
husbands (U.S. Bureau of the Census, 1978, Series P–23, No. 77:33). Since
about half the wives do not work, this means that about one in every six wives
earns as much or more than her husband. In 1977 the average husband earned a
little more than $12,000, and the average working wife earned a little less than
$4,000. The husband at the low end of the income scale and the husband at the
high end of the income scale were most likely to have a working wife whose income
equaled or exceeded his own. It would be valuable to discern what effect such
equal or superior earnings by the wife has on the marital relationship. We men-

TABLE 15.5

Labor Force Participation and Family Income, by Joint Educational Level of the Husband and Wife: March 1977

Labor Force Participation and Family Income	All Married- Couple Families	YEARS OF SCHOOL COMPLETED BY BOTH HUSBAND AND WIFE			
		Less Than 4 Years of High School	High School, 4 Years	College, 1 to 3 Years	College 4 Years or More
Total .... (thousands)	47,497	10,387	11,479	2,180	1,066
Percent	100.0	100.0	100.0	100.0	100.0
LABOR FORCE PARTICIPATION					
In labor force:					
Husband and wife	42.2	26.8	48.2	53.1	62.1
Husband only	38.5	37.4	39.7	35.4	29.5
Wife only	4.5	5.9	3.4	3.7	2.7
Neither spouse	14.9	29.9	8.7	7.8	5.6
Median income ....(dollars)	$16,013	$10,434	$16,800	$18,142	$26,645

Source: U.S. Bureau of Census (1978), P–23, No. 77:17

tioned in Chapter 12 that divorce rates are higher when wives earn as much as husbands. However, we have little idea of why this is so. Oppenheimer's (1977) research would seem to suggest that the status enhancement would outweigh any competitive threats in such a situation and thus there may be a felt reward for many equal-earning couples.

MARITAL AND PARENTAL SATISFACTION AND EMPLOYMENT

Ivan Nye (Hoffman and Nye, 1974:Chap. 8) examined the evidence concerning the impact of a wife's employment on marital satisfaction and on the child being raised. Nye reports that most of the studies (with the exception of Blood and Wolfe, 1960) indicated that in the blue-collar group's working mothers more than nonworking mothers seemed to undergo the most stress (Feldman and Feldman, 1973), although there was no indication of any higher divorce rates. Nye concludes that perhaps there are rewards from employment that balance out the added stresses and thus prevent divorce. There is some help from husbands in housework but generally not enough to make a great deal of difference. Employment to most women is comparable to taking on a second job in addition to that of being a wife and mother. In fact, it would seem that the public acceptance of mothers working is premised on the belief that such women would continue to also put forth a major effort as a mother. If a woman does not do that, then the public might think she is "neglecting" her maternal role (Mason and Bumpass, 1975). Public opinion stresses sharing, but it does not seem to demand that the husband take his full half share of the homemaker activities—rather, it demands that the woman fulfill her domestic responsibilities as well as those in her outside job. It should therefore be no surprise if stresses increase when women work outside the home. The surprise is that such stress occurs more in the blue-collar group; perhaps white-collar husbands are more supportive.

We spoke of Bradburn's work in connection with dyadic commitment (Chapter 10). That research is relevant here, too, for Bradburn does distinguish rewards and tensions in his measure of marital adjustment, so it is useful to take another look at his findings here. Orden and Bradburn (1969) distinguished between women who worked by their own choice and those who worked out of economic necessity. Their findings indicate that women who worked out of choice and not out of economic necessity were more likely to evaluate their marriages favorably. However, when there were preschool-age children at home, the nonemployed homemakers evaluated their marriages more favorably than even the employed mothers who liked their work. When the children were in grade school, the situation was reversed, and employed mothers who worked by choice reported more favorable marriages than did homemakers who did not have paid employment.

There is need for careful checking of such comparisons of working and nonworking groups because fully employed wives are older, have fewer children, and have more education. Therefore, we need to have controls on these differences to see if we shall still find differences in marital satisfaction by wives' employment status. No study has held all of these variables constant simultaneously. Overall, we have evidence indicating that age of children, work satisfaction, and social-class level all affect the relationship of paid employment to marital satisfaction. Lower-class mothers of preschool children who are working out of necessity report the lowest marital satisfaction. But exactly how these factors operate and how they relate to other variables are not known today.

Recently, Wright (1978) examined six national samples taken between 1971 and 1976 to seek out the differences in overall marital and other life satisfactions between wives who were employed and those who were not employed. His overall conclusion was that there is no consistent, significant difference between these two large groups. But what about some specific subgroup of wives, divided by age, social class, and type of job? Clearly, we are going to have to devise—and test—theories about variations in levels of marital satisfactions for specific groups of wives. As we have seen in Nye's and Bradburn's reports, there may be sharp subgroup differences that are being overlooked when we lump all employed and all unemployed wives together.

Evidence on the effect of maternal employment on children is much more scarce than that on marital satisfaction. Yarrow's classic work (1962) pointed out little overall differences in "quality of child care" between housewives and employed mothers. Differences were found in how satisfied the mother was with whatever she was doing at home or at a job. The satisfied mother (in either role) performed better in child care most of the time. Here, too, then, there are no simple yes or no answers.

The evidence on husbands' satisfaction by whether the wife is employed or not employed is also inconclusive (Burke, 1976; Booth, 1977). Here, too, we must divide husbands by their degree of equalitarianism, by the value they place on income, by their own occupational position, and so forth. Only in that way will we unravel the causal complexities of employment and marital satisfaction. We know from marital interaction studies (see Chapter 9) that a husband's occupational success can lead to resentment and to loss of self-esteem on the part of his wife if she is not employed (Macke, Bohrnstedt, and Bernstein, 1979). I would suspect that some husbands would be similarly affected if their wives' occupational success exceeded theirs. Perhaps marriages in which both parties are employed at relatively equal prestige and income levels would have the highest potential of satisfaction for both partners, particularly if there were no strains from preschool children. These are the types of theoretical notions that need to be spelled out and then empirically examined by future researchers.

DUAL-EARNER MARRIAGES

There are three basic types of dual-earner marriages: (1) dual career workers, (2) dual noncareer workers for both mates, and (3) dual combination of career and noncareer workers. These distinctions are worth making. A career involves an occupation to which one is highly committed and in which one hopes to advance to an ever-higher status over the years. A job that is noncareer involves less commitment and less lifelong loyalty. This distinction should be applied to male as well as female employment. The vast majority of male jobs are not career-type jobs. But this is even more the case for female jobs since careers cluster toward the top of the status hierarchy and female jobs cluster toward the middle and bottom of the status hierarchy. There is obviously more strain placed on a marriage if one or both workers are in careers. This is so because the time and energy demands of careers are so much greater than noncareer employment (Rapoport and Rapoport, 1978).

Research into dual-career marriages began in the late 1960s with the work of Rapoport (Rapoport and Rapoport, 1965). The term "dual-career" marriage was coined by Rapoport in 1969. Since then there have been several important studies carried out (Paloma and Garland, 1971a and 1971b; Mortimer, 1976, 1978; Holmstrom, 1972; Epstein, 1971). All these authors point out the stresses involved in dual-career families. The traditional male career has been called by Papanek (1973) a "two-person career." The male's career involved considerable assistance from his wife in the form of taking responsibility for child care and homemaking, entertaining his colleagues, talking over and helping with the work he brings home, and so on. Thus, a single career is premised on the basis that there will be a backup person and because of this, the career person can commit himself more completely to his career.

Such two-person careers are almost exclusively male roles. There are very few males who will do the backup work for their wives' careers. There is therefore little chance of women competing with men for the top career jobs given the present situation. The dual-career marriage is a compromise with that situation, in that

Two types of dual earners: (1) a shared business and (2) separate professional careers. Photo (left) by Craig Litherland, courtesy of the Minnesota Geographic Society; Project Director, Tim Strick. Photo (right) by Ivan Kalman.

it affords the possibility of equality for the husband and wife in a dual-career marriage. However, people in a dual-career marriage lack the backup system of the traditional two-person career. Thus, dual-career mates participate in an occupational system that demands high commitment but they lack the type of support available to males in traditional marriages (Ferber and Huber, 1979). The pressures on time and energy are immense and negotiation regarding how to manage the marital relationship is essential (Mortimer, 1978). It is not therefore surprising that many women in careers are single or divorced. The difficulties of a dual-career marriage make some women hesitate to marry and add strains that lead others to divorce.

Holmstrom's study of twenty dual-career families indicates the difficulties involved in such a marriage. All twenty marriages involved a wife with a Ph.D. degree and thus one might expect a high degree of equality. The husband's career comes first in most of these dual-career families. Thus, when a career opportunity opens up for the husband, the wife will often go with him, and her career may thereby suffer (Holmstrom, 1972:Chap. 4). The dominance of the male role in our society permeates even into dual-career families and thereby adds to the burdens of the female who elects to have both a career and a family.

The combination of career and family has been a male prerogative for most of the nineteenth and twentieth centuries. Prior to the nineteenth century, family enterprises (farms, businesses, and so on) were common and women shared more in the out-of-home activity than they have in the past 150 years.

The mid-nineteenth-century feminists accomplished more for the right to work outside the home than they did for the right to vote (Demos, 1977). As we discussed in Chapter 3 on gender roles, women around the world are actively involved in out-of-home work even though they also have strong role ties to the rearing of children. The change in the nineteenth century toward restricting middle-class women closer to the home was an unusual historical event. The nineteenth- and twentieth-century wife was taught to orient her role toward making the husband's career possible. If a woman works part-time, or if she still considers that her husband's job has higher priority than her own, then the types of changes required to support his career are minimized. Lotte Bailyn's work in England (1970) indicated that career women's marriages were happiest when the husband was family centered and supportive of his wife's career. If the husband himself was career oriented and gave his family low priority, then the career wife was least happy in her marriage. Thus, the cooperation of the husband appears to be a major factor in the success of dual-career marriages.

Even without traditional opposition to the changes demanded, there is greater complexity in dual-career marriages. There is less time for many household chores and organization becomes more imperative (Holmstrom, 1972:Chap. 6). Most jobs for females do not accommodate to the hours of public schools, and thus getting children to school before going to work is another common difficulty in dual-career marriages. Some countries, like Switzerland, have experimented with a flexible time plan, wherein the worker picks which forty hours in the week to work rather than being bound by a fixed schedule. Some such experiments are occurring in America. In any case, the domestic chores performed by the homemaker normally have to be added to the full-time outside work of both husband and wife. No matter how one organizes such a division of labor, it means expenditures of more time and energy and thus adds to the burdens of a dual-career union unless outside help can be afforded and arranged (Bronfenbrenner, 1977).

It should be clear that dual-career individuals are not necessarily people who want to change the traditional system. Holmstrom and others have reported that often such unions occur between two people who are traditional but who happen to each have a career they want to pursue. This helps explain why the traditional male role often dominates in such a marriage.

One final question that comes up in discussions of dual-earner marriages, and especially dual-career marriages, is whether such marriages tend to decrease the number of children. We spoke about this in Chapter 13. There is evidence that women in dual-work marriages have fewer children. The question, then, is whether the experience of working lowers the desire for children or whether those with low desire for children are more likely to move toward jobs and careers. From Chapter 13 we know that the decision, by most couples, to control the number of children is not made quickly. Those couples who decide to have no children take several years to reach that decision. Thus, it does not seem that a decision on number of children occurs early and leads to wives becoming employed if they decide in favor of a small family. We also know from Chapter 13 that college-educated females, in college and after, are the most likely to decide that they want no children or at most, only a small family. This can be taken as evidence that the college culture, with its emphasis on the choice of a life-style to suit the individual and its stress on female careers, may have an influence on one's fertility plans. This is evidence to support the view that value changes and employment experience change one's parental desires.

Some of the recent research literature bears on this question. Waite and Stolzenberg (1976) researched the question of whether the employment experience affects births or vice-versa. They decided that the *intended* number of children was affected by whether one was employed. So they conceptualized employment as the independent (causal) variable and births as the dependent (effect) variable. In 1978 Smith-Lovin and Tickamyer published their own examination of this question. Their data indicated that the *actual number of children* one has determined ones employment more than vice-versa. They recognized that Waite and Stolzenberg were talking of "intended births" and that they were focusing on "actual births." So both positions could be correct. It may be true that intended births are influenced by employment, but it may also be true that once one has a child (intended or not) that birth is a critical influence on one's willingness to seek outside employment. My own conclusion would be that there is a feedback loop between births and employment. The development of values in college or in one's home in favor of female employment would decrease birth desires. But this does not deny that the actual occurrence of a birth will decrease employment desires. As our contraceptive practices become more efficient—and they are moving that way rapidly—there should be fewer accidental births. More planned births would seem to strengthen the view that the desire to work outside the home would enter into the planning decisions and affect the number of births in a downward direction.

Summary and Conclusions

This chapter has pointed to the importance of the larger social structures in our society in determining the types of existing family institutions. For example, Kohn's work stressed that one's social-class, and the job conditions that are likely to go with that position, determine the type of values (self-direction versus conformity) which we pass on to our children. We also noted that one's educational background, marital status, and age of children are crucial determinants of one's employment situation. Again, the broader social structure seems implicated in determining our family relationships. Surely, other factors like our communication skills, our empathy, our personal value on parenthood are also relevant to the types of families in which we live (Hoffman and Hoffman, 1973). Nevertheless, the broader social structure in which we exist seems of first importance for understanding the family institution. Actually, we have found this to be true for the courtship and marital institutions as well but it seems that the research on the family makes the impact of social structure on our private lives even more obvious.

It is interesting that the differences between middle and working classes are analogous to the male-female differences in our society. By this I mean that women are generally taught more along the lines of conformity-type values and men along the lines of self-reliance-type values. In one cross-cultural study of 110 societies,

Barry and his colleagues (1957:269) stated: "Pressure toward nurturance, obedience, and responsibility is most often stronger for girls, whereas pressure toward achievement and self-reliance is most often stronger for boys." Thus, there is evidence that in many cultures females are trained in ways similar to the blue-collar working classes and males in ways similar to the white-collar middle class.

The question of equality between the genders thus resolves itself into a question similar to that of social-class equality. It is difficult to conceive of equality of the genders as long as females are trained more in terms of values that do not suit them for the higher-power positions in the society. Here, then, is further evidence of the roots of nonequality between the genders. Obviously, the particular differences in values that are taught to females are directly related to the fact that the female role in the family system is defined to include values like nurturance, obedience, and responsibility. The male role in our society is defined more in terms of achievement and self-reliance. Until such key-role differences are changed, one can hardly expect equality of males and females in the occupational system because the male is clearly being better prepared for the key-occupational positions.

Some change is occurring. Daughters of working mothers display more independence and achievement orientations. People today increasingly feel that the wife's occupation is an important determinant of the social status of the family (Sampson and Rossi, 1975). Thus, working wives and mothers have changed the basic gender role of the female, and this, too, will likely continue.

The worth of this overall discussion of the values involved in socializing children should be apparent. It explains not only different family patterns of child rearing but also affords us a basis for understanding inequality among the classes, the races, and between the genders. One key value of studying the family institution is exactly this—it throws a great deal of light on the broader social and cultural context in which the family is functionally integrated.

References

Bailyn, Lotte. 1970. "Career and Family Orientations of Husbands and Wives in Relation to Marital Happiness," *Human Relations* 23 (April):97–114.

Barry, Herbert, et al. 1957. "A Cross-Cultural Survey of Some Sex Differences in Socialization," *Journal of Abnormal and Social Psychology* 55 (November):327–332.

Blood, Robert O., and Donald M. Wolfe. 1960. *Husbands and Wives: The Dynamics of Married Living.* New York: Free Press.

Booth, Alan. 1977. "Wife's Employment and Husband's Stress: A Replication and Refutation," *Journal of Marriage and the Family* 39 (November):645–650.

Bott, Elizabeth. 1957. *Family and Social Network.* London: Tavistock.

Bronfenbrenner, Urie. 1958. "Socialization and Social Class Through Time and Space," in Eleanor Maccoby, et al. (eds.), *Readings in Social Psychology.* New York: Holt, Rinehart and Winston.

_____. 1977. "Toward an Experimental Ecology of Human Development," *American Psychologist* (July):513–531.

Burke, Ronald J., and Tamara Weir. 1976. "Relationship of Wives' Employment Status to Husband, Wife and Pair Satisfaction and Performance," *Journal of Marriage and the Family* 38 (May):279–287.

_____. 1976. "Some Personality Differences Between Members of One-Career and Two-Career Families," *Journal of Marriage and the Family* 38 (August):453–459.

Clark, Robert A., F. Ivan Nye, and Viktor Gecas. 1978. "Husbands' Work Involvement and Marital Role Performance," *Journal of Marriage and the Family* 40 (February):9–21.

Demos, John. 1977. "The American Family in Past Time," Chap. 2 in A. S. Skolnick and J. H. Skolnick (eds.), *Family in Transition.* Boston: Little, Brown.

Epstein, Cynthia F. 1971. "Law Partners and Marital Partners: Strains and Solutions in the Dual-Career Family Enterprise. " *Human Relations* 24:549–563.

Evans-Pritchard, E. E. 1965. *The Position of Women in Primitive Societies and Other Essays in Social Anthropology.* New York: Free Press.

Feldman, H., and M. Feldman. 1973. *The Relationship Between the Family and Occupational Functioning in a Sample of Rural Women.* Ithaca, NY: Department of Human Development and Family Studies, Cornell University.

Ferber, Marianne, and Joan Huber. 1979. "Husbands, Wives and Careers," *Journal of Marriage and the Family* 41 (May): 315–325.

Ferriss, Abbott L. 1971. *Indicators of Trends in the Status of American Women.* New York: Russell Sage.

Gecas, Viktor, and F. Ivan Nye. 1974. "Sex and Class Differences in Parent-Child Interaction: A Test of Kohn's Hypothesis," *Journal of Marriage and the Family* 36 (November): 742–749.

Havens, Elizabeth M. 1973. "Women, Work and Wedlock: A Note on Female Marital Patterns in the U.S.," *American Journal of Sociology* 78 (January):975–981.

Heckman, Norma A., Rebecca Bryson, and Jeff B. Bryson. 1977. "Problems of Professional Couples: A Content Analysis," *Journal of Marriage and the Family* 39 (May):323–330.

Heer, David M. 1963. "Dominance and the Working Wife," in F. Ivan Nye and Lois W. Hoffman (eds.), *The Employed Mother in America.* Skokie, IL: Rand McNally.

Hoffman, Lois W., and Martin L. Hoffman. 1973. "The Value of Children to Parents," Chap. 2 in James T. Fawcette (ed.), *Psychological Perspectives on Population.* New York: Basic Books.

———, and F. Ivan Nye. 1974. *Working Mothers.* San Francisco: Jossey-Bass.

Holmstrom, Lynda L. 1972. *The Two Career Family.* Cambridge, MA: Schenkman.

Kerckoff, Alan C. 1972. *Socialization and Social Class.* Englewood Cliffs, NJ: Prentice-Hall.

Kohn, Melvin L. 1959. "Social Class and Parental Values," *American Journal of Sociology* 64 (January):337–351.

———. 1963. "Social Class and Parent-Child Relationships: An Interpretation," *American Journal of Sociology* 68 (January):471–480.

———. 1969. *Class and Conformity.* Homewood, IL: Dorsey Press.

———. 1971. "Bureaucratic Man: A Portrait and an Interpretation," *American Sociological Review* 36 (June):461–474.

———. 1977. *Class and Conformity: A Study in Values,* 2nd ed. Chicago: University of Chicago Press.

———, and Carmi Schooler. 1973. "Occupational Experience and Psychological Functioning: An Assessment of Reciprocal Effects," *American Sociological Review* 38 (February): 97–118.

———, and ———. 1978. "The Reciprocal Effects of the Substantive Complexity of Work and Intellectual Flexibility: A Longitudinal Assessment," *American Journal of Sociology* 84 (July):24–52.

Komarovsky, Mirra. 1964. *Blue-Collar Marriage.* New York: Random House.

Lipset, Seymour Martin. 1960. *Political Man: The Social Bases of Politics.* New York: Doubleday.

Lopata, Helena Z. 1971. *Occupation: Housewife.* New York: Oxford University Press.

Maccoby, Eleanor E. 1960. "Effects Upon Children of Their Mothers' Outside Employment," in Norman W. Bell and Ezra F. Vogel (eds.), *A Modern Introduction to the Family.* New York: Free Press.

Macke, Anne S., George W. Bohrnstedt, and Ilene N. Bernstein. 1979. "Housewives' Self Esteem and Their Husbands' Success: The Myth of Vicarious Involvement," *Journal of Marriage and the Family* 41 (February):51–57.

Martin, Thomas W., Kenneth J. Berry, and R. Brooke Jacobson. 1975. "The Impact of Dual-Career Marriages on Female Professional Careers: An Empirical Test of a Parsonian Hypothesis," *Journal of Marriage and the Family* 37 (November):734–742.

Mason, Karen, and Larry Bumpass. 1975. "U.S. Women's Sex Role Ideology, 1970," *American Journal of Sociology* 80 (March):1212–1220.

McLaughlin, Steven D. 1978. "Occupational Sex Identification and the Assessment of Male and Female Earning Inequality," *American Sociological Review* 43 (December):909–921.

Mead, Margaret, and Frances B. Kaplan (eds.). 1965. *American Women:The Report of the Pres-*

ident's Commission on the Status of Women. New York: Scribner.

Miller, Daniel R., and Guy E. Swanson. 1958. *The Changing American Parent.* New York: Wiley.

Miller, Joanne, C. Schooler, M. Kohn, and K. Miller. 1979. "Women and Work: The Psychological Effects of Occupational Conditions," *American Journal of Sociology* 85 (July):66–94.

Mortimer, Jeylan. 1976. "Social Class, Work and the Family: Some Implications of the Father's Occupation for Familial Relationships and Sons' Career Decisions," *Journal of Marriage and the Family* 38 (May):241–256.

———. 1978. "Dual-Career Families—A Sociological Perspective," in S. S. Peterson, J. M. Richardson, and G. V. Kreuter (eds.), *The Two-Career Family: Issues and Alternatives.* Washington, DC: University Press of America.

Mueller, Charles W., and Blair G. Campbell. 1977. "Female Occupational Achievement and Marital Status: A Research Note," *Journal of Marriage and the Family* 39 (August):587–593.

Nye, F. Ivan, and Lois W. Hoffman (eds.). 1963. *The Employed Mother in America.* Skokie, IL: Rand McNally.

Oppenheimer, Valerie K. 1977. "The Sociology of Women's Economic Role in the Family," *American Sociological Review* 42 (June):387–406.

Orden, S. R., and N. M. Bradburn. 1969. "Working Wives and Marital Happiness," *American Journal of Sociology* 74 (January):392–408.

Papanek, Hanna. 1973. "Men, Women and Work: Reflections on the Two-Person Career," *American Journal of Sociology* 78 (January):852–872.

Pearlin, Leonard L., and Melvin L. Kohn. 1966. "Social Class, Occupation, and Parental Values: A Cross National Study," *American Sociological Review* 31 (August):466–479.

Poloma, Margaret. 1971. "The Married Professional Woman: A Study on the Tolerance of Domestication," *Journal of Marriage and the Family* 33 (August):531–540.

———, and Neal Garland. 1971."The Myth of the Egalitarian Family: Familial Roles and the Professionally Employed Wife," in A. Theodore (ed.), *The Professional Woman.* Cambridge, MA: Schenkman.

Psychology of Women Quarterly 3.1 (Fall 1978). This entire issue is on dual-career couples.

Rainwater, Lee. 1966. "Some Aspects of Lower-Class Sexual Behavior," *Journal of Social Issues* 22 (April):96–108.

Rapoport, Robert, and R. Rapoport. 1965. "Work and Family in Contemporary Society," *American Sociological Review* 30 (June):381–394.

———, and ———. 1978. "Dual Career Families: Progress and Prospects." *Marriage and Family Review* 1.5 (September/October):1–12.

Ridley, J. C. 1969. "The Changing Position of American Women: Education, Labor Force Participation, and Fertility," in *The Family in Transition.* Fogarty International Proceedings 3. Washington, DC: Government Printing Office.

Sampson, William A., and Peter H. Rossi. 1975. "Race and Family Social Standing," *American Sociological Review* 40 (April):201–214.

Scanzoni, John H. 1975. *Sex Roles, Life Styles, and Childbearing.* New York: Free Press.

Sears, Robert T., Eleanor E. Maccoby, and Harry Levin. 1957. *Patterns of Child Rearing.* White Plains, NY: Row Peterson.

Smith-Lovin, Lynn, and Ann R. Tickamyer. 1978. "Nonrecursive Models of Labor Force Participation, Fertility Behavior and Sex Role Attitudes," *American Sociological Review* 43 (August):541–557.

Sobol, Marion G. 1963. "Commitment to Work," in F. Ivan Nye and Lois W. Hoffman (eds.), *The Employed Mother in America.* Skokie, IL: Rand McNally.

Sweet, James A. 1973. *Women in the Labor Force.* New York: Seminar Press.

U.S. Bureau of the Census. 1973. *Occupational Characteristics.* Census of Population, 1970. Subject Reports, Final Report PC (2)–7a. Washington, DC: Government Printing Office.

———. 1978. "Population Profile of the U.S.: 1977."*Current Population Reports*, Series P–20, No.324. Washington, DC: Government Printing Office.

———. 1978. "Perspectives on American Husbands and Wives," *Current Population Reports* Series P–23, No.77. Washington, DC: Government Printing Office.

———. 1979. "Population Profile of the U.S.: 1978." *Current Population Reports*, Series P–20, No.336. Washington, DC: Government Printing Office.

U.S. Department of Labor. Bureau of Labor Statistics. 1974. *Special Labor Force Report 164.* Washington, DC: Government Printing Office.

———. 1977. *U.S. Working Women: A Databook.* Washington, DC: Government Printing Office.

———. 1979a. "The Employment Situation:April

1979." *News* (May 4). Washington, DC: Government Printing Office.

———. 1979*b*. "Employment in Perspective: Working Women." Report 565, No. 1, First Quarter 1979. Washington, DC: Government Printing Office.

———. 1979*c*. "Employment and Unemployment During 1978: An Analysis." Special Labor Force. Report 218. Washington, DC: Government Printing Office.

U.S. Department of Labor's Manpower Administration and U.S. Department of Health, Education, and Welfare. 1975. *Manpower Report of the President*. Transmitted to the Congress (April). Washington, DC: Government Printing Office.

Waite, L. J., and R. M. Stolzenberg. 1976. "Intended Childbearing and Labor Force Participation of Young Women: Insights from Nonrecursive Models," *American Sociological Review* 41(April):235–251.

Wright, James D. 1978. "Are Working Women Really More Satisfied? Evidence from Several National Surveys," *Journal of Marriage and the Family* 40 (May):301–313.

Yarrow, Marion, et al. 1962. "Child Rearing in Families of Working and Nonworking Mothers," *Sociometry* 25 (June):122–140.

Kinship Ties: From the Cradle

to the Grave

SIXTEEN

Until the 1950s the entire question of kinship ties in modern-day urban society was largely ignored. Kinship was viewed as worth studying in small primitive societies but not in modern industrial societies. It was believed that the impact of kinship was minimal in modern society. In some measure the work of the late Talcott Parsons, a Harvard sociologist, contributed to the view that in modern societies the family is not a key causal factor.

Parsons (1953) viewed the American society as stressing what he called "universalism" and "achievement." Universalism is the opposite of particularism—it is the use of standards which apply to all and which do not take into account individual, situational, and other specific factors. An example would be to give a job to the most efficient lathe operator rather than to the boss's son. To give it to the boss's son would be an illustration of particularism. Achievement is a relatively clear term referring to actual performances that accomplish goal seeking. The part of our society that best embodies both universalism and achievement is our occupational system. The occupational system deals with adaptive problems and is supposed to stress the avoidance of particularistic reasons for hiring and, instead, stress the fundamental importance of achievement. In short, our occupational system structures roles and defines the relations among people in ways most clearly in accord with our primary societal emphasis on universalistic and achievement values.

Parsons saw the family, or the kinship system in general, as stressing quite different values. The family stresses particularistic values. According to tradition, one is supposed to treat an older child, a younger child, a girl, all differently. That is, in the family one is supposed to be particularistic and consider differences such as gender and age. Basic differences between children of the same age and gender are also supposed to be considered. In short, there are no simple, straightforward, universalistic standards or skills required that can be applied to all individual family members. In addition, intrinsic individual worth and not achievement is stressed. Other differences show up in the diffuse, rather than specific, interests which family members have in one another. Employees have a very specific interest in one another in relation to work, whereas family members are interested in one another across a much broader range of life space.

The occupational and kinship systems, Parsons asserted are distinct, but they have an integrative factor: The same man who is father in the family unit is the man who is working in the occupational system. This integrates the family and occupational system, but also puts certain limits on the ways the two can work together. Parsons's conception was that the father gives all the members of his family the amount of social prestige he derives from his own occupation. All members of the family start with this initial status. (Other societies have not used occupation to assign status. For example, in the Indian caste system, status is assigned by virtue of the caste into which one is born.) The occupational system, then, is determinative in Parsons's thinking, and the kinship system must be compliant. If our occupational system demands that workers be willing to travel to new locations then the kinship ties cannot be of an extended family type that demand kin to stay in one locality. If the occupational system gives rewards by accomplishments, then the kinship system must not be one that demands that relatives give employment to one another regardless of accomplishments. The potential for conflict is great, Parsons believes, because the family operates on particularistic standards, and the occupational system operates on universalistic standards. Since the occupational system incorporates our dominant values, it will shape and control the type of kinship system. Thus, this view posits that when industrialization occurred in this country, the extended family broke down, and the isolated nuclear family came into being. This occurred as an adaptation of the family to the changing occupational system. This view is still widespread and popular, but let us look at what some of its critics have to say.

Kinship in the Urban Setting

We have dealt earlier with the question of the extended family prior to industrialization. The evidence from America and other cultures is that the extended family was chiefly the family of the wealthier people in a given society (Coale, et al., 1965; Burch, 1967; Laslett, et al., 1972). In our society the rapid migration waves prevented the extended family from being very common. The likelihood is that the presence of the nuclear family in America *before* industrialization was probably one factor that encouraged the development of industrialization (Seward, 1978). To be fair, one would also have to admit that the geographic mobility required by industrialization probably also reduced the likelihood of extended families becoming common and, in some cases, encouraged them to break up. However, since the extended family is common mostly among the wealthy few, it is questionable how many extended families ever existed. Also, we do know that in countries like Japan, industrialization and a modified form of the extended family, called the "stem family," coexist (Plath, 1964; Vogel, 1963; Dore, 1958). The stem family consists of the parents and one of their sons sharing a home. It is not a fully extended family, for not all children live with their parents after they marry. In any case, Japan is a highly industrialized country and yet has managed to combine the stem family with industrialization. Workers will often stay with one job for life in order to live with their parents. Sidney Greenfield (1961) reports that in Brazil an extended family will adapt to urban industrial life by renting an entire floor of an apartment building. Here, too, is evidence that industrialization need not "destroy" the extended family.

Although it seems that the majority of Americans never lived in an extended family, there is a traditional emphasis on the value of maintaining ties between married children and their parents. The extended family remains as an ideal in many people's minds. This is so despite the fact that most studies have shown that the vast majority of both married children and their parents do *not* want to live with one another (Shanas, et al., 1968; Shanas, 1973). But despite that fact, attachment between parents and children is an expected enough outcome, given the fact that parents nurture their children. Actually, the surprising thing would be to find a society in which parents and their married children were *not* emotionally attached to one another. Thus, Parsons's assertion that the nuclear family today can be called "isolated" from the parental family can be misleading. Parsons did not mean to imply total isolation, but even a high degree of isolation is doubtful

A 1922 family portrait. Photo by Sylvia Eisman.

and, more importantly, the term does imply alienation or a lack of emotional significance. Does the existing evidence support such a high degree of physical and emotional isolation of married people from their parents?

The answer to this question comes from research on kinship ties in urban settings. Shanas and her colleagues (1968) did a valuable study of how parents and their married children interact in Denmark, England, and the United States. In all three countries, the trends toward earlier ages at marriage, earlier childbirth, and few large families all contribute toward a narrowing of the age difference of the generations and a greater likelihood of married children having living parents. The Shanas study indicates that kin live remarkably close to one another in all three societies examined.

Shanas, more recently, added two Eastern European countries—Poland and Yugoslavia—and also added Israel to make a total of six societies. The data consisted of nationwide area probability samples, with each sample consisting of approximately 2,500 elderly persons in Denmark, Britain, the United States, Poland, and Yugoslavia. In Israel she utilized a probability sample of 1,142 older Jewish residents living in towns and cities. The data were collected between 1962 and 1969. Only about 4 or 5 percent of the elderly in each country are in institutional care and would not be included in this sample design.

In these six countries about four out of every five elderly people have at least one living child. In the three Western countries (United States, Britain, Denmark), 68 to 82 percent of the married elderly live only with their spouse (see Table 16.1). This is similar to what is found for Israelis of Western origin. But Israelis of Eastern origin and people in Poland and Yugoslavia have only about half of the married elderly living with only their spouse. This greater tendency to live with children and others in these countries is in part due to acute housing shortages and to the large agricultural populations in the Eastern European countries. For unmarried elderly people (widowed, divorced) there is a greater tendency to share a household with a child, another relative, or another person. A higher proportion of the unmarried elderly share a household with kin than is the case for the married elderly. Thus, shared household arrangements and, in this sense, greater dependency upon kin, is more usual for the elderly unmarried than for the elderly married population (Gibson, 1972).

This low proportion of elderly, particularly married elderly, who live with their children, should not lead us to conclude that the elderly are isolated from their kin. Table 16.2 clearly shows that from 52 to 84 percent of all old people are either living with a child or are within ten minutes of that child. In addition, visiting seems quite common. Table 16.3 shows that about half the elderly, not living with a child, saw a child within the last twenty-four hours, and over three-fourths saw a child within the last week. It is, of course, arbitrary to define what is a high or low amount of contact. However, by almost any definition the type of contact reported in Table 16.3 would *not* be called "low" and it evidences the lack of isolation of the elderly and of the nuclear family. The highest rate of isolation from kin of the elderly exists in Britain and Yugoslavia, where about one of every ten elderly persons who is not living with children is also without any children or other

TABLE 16.1

The Living Arrangements of Persons Aged Sixty-Five and Over in Six Countries by Marital Status[a]

Household Composition[b]	MARITAL STATUS and COUNTRY					Israel	
	Denmark	Britain	U.S.	Poland	Yugoslavia	Western	Oriental
				(percentages)			
Married Persons							
Percentage of persons living with:							
Spouse only	82	68	79	50	49	82	47
Plus married child	1	5	2	22	33	4	10
Plus unmarried child	14	23	15	19	11	12	41
Plus other relative	—	3	3	3	5	—	—
Plus others	3	1	1	6	2	2	2
(Number of persons)	(1,399)	(1,211)	(1,335)	(1,263)	(1,392)	(508)	(204)
Unmarried Persons							
Percentage of persons living:							
Alone	61	43	48	30	32	50	23
With married child	7	19	14	38	44	35	47
With unmarried child	15	18	20	16	8	9	21
With other relatives	7	13	12	9	8	—	—
With others	10	6	6	7	8	6	9
(Number of persons)	(1,107)	(1,289)	(1,107)	(1,451)	(1,192)	(285)	(145)

[a]Percentages in this table are based on all persons whether or not they have children.
[b]This is a priority code, that is, households with married children may also include unmarried children, and so on.
Source: Ethel Shanas (1973):507

TABLE 16.2

The Proportion of Elderly Persons in Six Countries Whose Nearest Child Lives Either in the Same Household or Within Ten Minutes' Distance*

COUNTRY		PERCENT
Denmark		52
Britain		66
United States		61
Poland		70
Yugoslavia		73
Israel	Western Origin	55
	Oriental origin	84

*Percentages in this table are based on number of persons with children.
Source: Ethel Shanas (1973):508.

TABLE 16.3

The Proportion of Elderly Persons in Six Countries Not Living with a Child Who Saw a Child Within the Last 24 Hours and Within the Last Week*

COUNTRY	SAW CHILD WITHIN LAST 24 HOURS (*percent*)	SAW CHILD WITHIN LAST WEEK (*percent*)
Denmark	53	80
Britain	47	77
United States	52	78
Poland	64	77
Yugoslavia	51	71
Israel	48	76

*Percentages in this table are based on number of persons with children.
Source: Ethel Shanas (1973):509.

relatives nearby. This figure is only 10 percent because in many cases where children are not present, the elderly have other relatives with whom they keep in contact. Finally, I should note that a study by Sauer (1975) indicates that one of the key determinants of older white people's "morale" is their family ties. Nevertheless, there is recent evidence that friendship is also of considerable importance to the elderly. In many cases, friends may be more likely than kin to promote morale and satisfaction. Arling (1976) and Wood and Robertson (1978) report that the importance of friends for the morale of the elderly *exceeds* the importance of kin. This is an interesting finding and we need to specify the conditions of this relationship in future work.

In general, findings supporting the close ties and interactions with kin have also been reported by many other researchers (Firth, 1956; Wilmott and Young, 1960; Young and Wilmott, 1964; Hill, 1970). In America, two research works elaborate nicely upon the findings of Shanas. The first of these is the work done by Eugene Litwak (1960a; 1960b). Marvin Sussman was examining the existence of extended-kin ties in American urban areas years before Litwak's work was published (Sussman and Burchinal, 1962, have good early references). But it was the work of Litwak, published in 1960, which jarred sociologists into the realization that we have been mistaken in our contention that extended-kin ties were unimportant in modern urban areas. Litwak accepts parts of Parsons' notions concerning the older forms of the American family being more in line with three generations living in one household, but he disagrees in that he believes that industrialism did not change this to the isolated nuclear family but rather changed the extended family into a *modified* extended family. In short, Litwak argues that (as was done in Japan and Brazil), our extended-family values have been preserved through a compromise with the classic extended-family form. To Litwak, the modified extended family is a family institution wherein close emotional ties are maintained between parents and married children, but geographical mobility occurs and children typically do

The nurturant role gets full play in the grandparent–grandchild relationship. Photo by Harriet Reiss.

not live in the same household with their parents. Litwak argues that extended-family ties do not conflict with a modern industrial bureaucratic system. He checked out his ideas (in his Ph.D. dissertation) by studying 920 white Buffalo mothers, all of whom were under forty-five years of age.

Litwak found support for his position through several checks. First, he classified his sample as extended family, nuclear family, or nonfamily-oriented. He did this by the responses to four statements (Litwak, 1960a:16):

1. Generally I like the whole family to spend evenings together;
2. I want a house where family members can spend time together;
3. I want a location that would make it easy for relatives to get together; and
4. I want a house with enough room for our parents to feel free to move in.

Those who agreed with items 3 and 4 were called "extended-family-oriented;" those who agreed to only items 1 and 2 were "nuclear-family-oriented;" and those who disagreed with all four questions were called "nonfamily-oriented." Litwak compared these three different family-orientation groups to see if the extended-family-oriented group would consist more of those people who had relatives living in the same town. He found this *not* to be the case. Roughly, the same percentage of people were extended-family oriented among those with relatives in town as among those with relatives living out of town (Litwak, 1960*b*:389). Thus, geographic mobility did not seem to destroy one's extended-family orientation. An even more interesting check is made in Table 16.4, where one can see that those with an extended-family orientation are the *most* likely to think they will take a job out of town. Here is rather strong evidence that extended-family orientations, Parsons notwithstanding, do not inhibit geographic mobility. In fact, the opposite may be the case. This same point was illustrated in an ingenious study by Strodtbeck (1958). He compared the Jewish family and the Italian family in New Haven. The Jewish family had just as strong feelings of family as the Italian, but they were more likely to encourage their children to leave home if that was necessary to getting ahead. The extended-family orientation thus may lead to support for leaving home.

A second important check was to see if the occupational group already at the top and the one that was moving up differed in their extended-family orientation from the downwardly mobile group or the stationary manual class. If the upwardly mobile are more extended-family oriented, then it would indicate support for the notion that such identification helps, rather than hinders, one's upward mobility. Table 16.5 shows that the upwardly mobile are more extended-family oriented (22 percent) than any group except the stationary upper class. Incidentally, the reader should note that this high extended-family orientation in the upper class fits with the thesis that the extended family is strongest in the upper-class segments of society.

All in all, these basic findings of Litwak bring into question Parsons's position that we have an isolated nuclear family. Perhaps more important, these data question Parsons's additional thesis that the isolated nuclear family is best integrated with the democratic industrial society. Litwak's data show that the extended-family orientation seems best integrated with our modern-day society. The modified version of the extended family does not demand geographic stability, nor does it demand that all family members work in the same enterprise, and because of this it is well integrated with the demands of modern industrial society. Such a family

TABLE 16.4
Strong Identification with Relatives Does Not Prevent People from Taking Jobs Elsewhere

	AMONG THOSE WITH RELATIVES IN THE CITY THE PERCENTAGE SAYING GOOD CHANCE HUSBAND WILL TAKE JOB OUT OF TOWN *Percent*	*Number of Cases*
Extended-family orientation	23	(128)
Nuclear-family orientation	18	(336)
Nonfamily orientation	14	(184)

Source: Eugene Litwak (1960b):390.

TABLE 16.5

Occupationally Mobile Groups are Moderately Identified with Their Extended Family

	PERCENTAGE EXTENDED-FAMILY ORIENTATION	PERCENTAGE NUCLEAR-FAMILY ORIENTATION	PERCENTAGE NONFAMILY ORIENTATION	POPULATION
Stationary upper class	26	55	19	100 (247)
Upwardly mobile class	22	55	23	100 (284)
Downwardly mobile class	17	52	31	100 (147)
Stationary manual class	15	51	34	100 (242)

Source: Eugene Litwak (1960a):17.

institution seems well suited to help individual members succeed in our type of society. However, in fairness to Parsons, I should add that we are *not* sure just how different his conception of the "isolated" nuclear family would be from Litwak's conception of the "modified" extended family. It is quite possible that Parsons viewed reality in the same way as Litwak, but simply chose terms that gave an unintended stress to the "isolated" qualities of the nuclear family even though he accepted the fact that such families have meaningful ties to other families. In any case, the ensuing debate added to our factual knowledge of the family institution. It also made us aware of the importance of the clear definition of concepts.

Kinship Interaction, Affection, and Values

Now that we have laid out the basic outlines of kinship ties in urban societies, it is necessary to fill in some of the details. I will do this by referring to another important study—this one done by Bert Adams (1968). Adams studied the city of Greensboro, North Carolina, during the summers of 1963 and 1964 and interviewed 799 people, all of whom were white, married only once and for not more than twenty years. He spoke to 467 females and 332 males. The sample divided into 62 percent white-collar respondents and 38 percent blue-collar respondents. Here, as elsewhere, one can raise the question of how typical the results from this sample would be for other cities in America and whether things have changed since then. I fully agree with the ideal of current, national, representative samples, but I caution the reader not to "throw the baby out with the bathwater." We must utilize the best available studies even if such studies are not perfect. The only other choice is to forget entirely about social science research and rely only upon our subjective experience. I think we have much to gain by following the former and not the latter path.

Several questions raised by Litwak's work are answered by the careful research of Bert Adams. For example, Adams uses both a measure of interaction frequency with kin and measures of affection and value closeness. By using both the objective measure of frequency of interaction and the subjective measures of affectional and value closeness of kin, Adams gives more breadth to our understanding of kinship relationships. He also breaks down his analysis into blue- and white-collar social classes, and that presents us with knowledge of whether the findings hold for both social classes or for just one. Adams started out by asking his respondents how many kin they would recognize if they saw them on the street. They were allowed to name the spouses of their kin but not their in-laws or their own wives and children. The average (median) number of kin named was twenty-eight. Females named somewhat more than males (30 versus 26). If both parents were living, the number named was considerably higher than if both parents were deceased (31 versus 20).

Knowledge of kin affords us some idea of the size of the kinship system with which urban Americans are involved. There are suggestions that females may somehow be more involved in this kinship system than males (they know more kin on the average). Also, the death of one's parents appears to have a major effect on maintaining the kinship system. Such death subtracts only two parents, but the loss lowers the known kin by eleven, and thus it seems that married couples with living parents are, in part, maintaining kin contacts for reasons connected to their parents. Perhaps they see their kin at their parents' home or during the time they visit their parents' city. Perhaps their parents encourage contact with other kin. In any case, this simple matter of assessing how many kin one would recognize leads to many initial insights about the kinship system.

Adams followed up this question by asking his respondents if relatives were *unimportant* in their lives. To this query, 11 percent said yes (8 percent females, 14 percent males). The respondents whose present occupation was lower than that of their parents—in other words, those who were downwardly mobile—were the most likely to say that relatives were not important in their lives, and they also were the most likely not to know many of their relatives. It is probable that the downward mobility and the lack of ties to relatives encouraged each other, and as one factor increased, it tended to increase the other. We know from Litwak that ties to relatives can affect one's mobility, and here, from Adams, is some evidence that the converse is perhaps also true. (For other relevant data see Klatzky, 1972.)

What about those who are upwardly mobile? Does their upward mobility tend to isolate them from their parents because of the achieved class difference? Parsons (1953), Schneider (1968), and Schneider and Homans (1955) have argued that such upward mobility would tend to separate the generations because of class differences. Litwak (1960a) has argued that this does not occur because the upwardly mobile youngsters receive deference and admiration from their parents, and the parents, in turn, are proud of their children's progress for they have probably helped in their achievements. Adams's check is more complete than the others, and thus it is important in answering this question. As far as knowledge of kin is concerned, the upwardly mobile know more kin than anyone else. The upwardly mobile in Adams's study are those whose fathers are blue-collar workers but who themselves are (or are married to) white-collar workers. Blue-collar people tend to be less geographically mobile over long distances and relatedly they tend to have more kin in the immediate area. The upwardly mobile white-collar people show a pattern somewhat in between the stable white- and blue-collar groups concerning geographic nearness to kin. The downwardly mobile group is, as expected, the least likely to have relatives nearby.

Now let us look at the interaction patterns with parents as well as the affection and value similarity with parents for those who are upwardly mobile. Does upward mobility have a deleterious effect on such relations? Table 16.6 gives part of the answer. Since 60 percent of the blue-collar group, but only 45 percent of the white-collar group have either their own or their mate's parents residing in Greensboro, one would expect higher rates of visiting by blue-collar workers. That is roughly what is found in these data. However, the upwardly mobile are somewhat less likely than the stable blue-collar people to visit their parents monthly or more often, although they are more likely to make such visits than are the stable white-collar people. Looking also at the breakdown in the other columns in the table, we see clearly then that being upwardly mobile (moving from the blue- to the white-collar class) does not dramatically break the interaction patterns with parents, and this is evidence in favor of Litwak's views that upward mobility does not break ties with extended kin. The reader may be interested to know that Elizabeth Bott, in her well-known study of twenty London families, also asserted that mobility does not affect family ties because parents feel they share in their children's accomplishments (1957). Similarly, Klatzky's study (1972) of father-son ties under mobility conditions showed no loss of contact.

Whereas the blue-collar people are closer to their parents and, therefore, interact with them more, the white-collar class dominates in other forms of communication such as letter writing and telephoning even when they are no farther away than the blue-collar class (Adams, 1968:47). The upwardly mobile once again seem to fall in between the stable blue-collar and stable white-collar classes.

TABLE 16.6

Frequency of Interaction with Parents According to the Gender and Occupational Stratum and Mobility of the Young Adults

			FREQUENCY OF INTERACTION (percent)			
Gender	Occupational Stratum and Mobility	Number of Respondents	Weekly or More	Monthly- Weekly	Less Than Monthly	Total Percent
	Upward white collar	(52)	31	40	29	100
	Stable white collar	(66)	27	29	44	100
Males	Stable blue collar	(53)	49	25	26	100
	Downward blue collar	(10)	60	30	10	100
	Upward white collar	(72)	26	35	39	100
	Stable white collar	(90)	30	26	44	100
Females	Stable blue collar	(72)	42	29	29	100
	Downward blue collar	(19)	26	26	47	99

Source: Bert N. Adams (1968):44.

One additional important check on the impact of upward mobility can be seen in Table 16.7, which shows the affectionate closeness to and value consensus with parents in Adams's sample. For males the pattern seems clear: The upwardly mobile males are more affectionately tied to their parents and have more value consensus than the stable blue-collar males, but somewhat less than the stable white-collar males. There are many possible explanations for this closeness and consensus of the upwardly mobile male, but the findings reveal that on a large number of checks the upwardly mobile male does not fit the stereotype of someone who is breaking off kin ties. In fact, in many ways he has more kin ties than the group he comes from, and thus one can hardly argue that mobility weakens those ties. The results fit very nicely with Litwak's position that extended-family ties help in mobility. The results for females in Table 16.7 indicate a much smaller difference between upwardly mobile and stable blue-collar females. Generally daughters are affectionately closer to their parents than are sons. Perhaps this greater attachment to the family mitigates against a large variation in affection due to upward mobility.

One can look over the preceding tables to distinguish the blue- and white-collar classes. We know from earlier chapters that blue-collar classes have greater segregation of roles between males and females. This also shows up in our tables from Adams in that white-collar males and females respond with more similarity to most questions than do blue-collar males and females. We know from Kohn (1977) and other studies that white-collar fathers participate more in the socialization of their children because of their more equalitarian roles. We noted how the blue-collar father may handicap his children for white-collar jobs because of the stress he places on conformity as opposed to autonomy. One can conclude that white-collar chil-

TABLE 16.7

Expression of Affectional Closeness to, or Value Consensus with, Parents According to the Gender and Occupational Stratum and Mobility of the Young Adult

Gender	Occupational Stratum and Mobility	Number of Respondents	AFFECTIONALLY CLOSE (PERCENT)		VALUE CONSENSUS (PERCENT)	
			To Father	To Mother	To Father	To Mother
Males	Upward white collar	(52)	54	60	52	52
	Stable white collar	(66)	65	62	68	58
	Stable blue collar	(53)	42	57	34	45
	Downward blue collar	(10)	50	40	50	30
	Total	(181)	54	59	52	51
Females	Upward white collar	(72)	58	83	39	65
	Stable white collar	(90)	71	83	58	64
	Stable blue collar	(72)	61	72	44	63
	Downward blue collar	(19)	68	68	58	63
	Total	(253)	64	79	49	64

Source: Bert N. Adams (1968):70.

dren feel closer to their parents (particularly fathers) because such fathers embody the success values of American society more than do blue-collar fathers. The white-collar father works in occupations that are more symbolic of success and thus he serves more as a model; therefore, value consensus and affection are more likely to occur. The upwardly mobile male is closer to his family despite his father's lower status because he himself has been able to advance and feels that his parents were somehow helpful in that advance.

An inspection of Table 16.7 shows that females generally are affectionately closer and have more value consensus with their parents than do males. Adams also reports that females have more mutual help relations with parents and more of a sense of obligation (1968:38). Adams found that males interact with parents more in accord with their affection and consensus for those parents. Females are not so strongly influenced by *the degree of* parental affection and consensus and interact about the same with parents regardless of how they feel. This supports the position that females have a greater sense of familial obligation. Sweetser's (1966) view is that modern industrial societies weaken male work-sharing kin ties and thus, by default, strengthen the female expressive kin ties.

The Aging Family

We have looked at kinship ties mainly from the point of view of married children and their parents. Let us shift the focus a bit now to the older generation and see how those who are sixty-five and above fit into the structure of our society. The older population is a rapidly growing group and will continue to be until about 1990. This is so because of large birth cohorts in the first twenty-five years of this century that are now aging into large numbers of older people (U.S. Bureau of the Census, 1976 Series P–23, No. 59). In 1900 the percentage of the population that was sixty-five or above was about 4 percent; in 1980 it reached 11 percent. By 1980 there were 9.8 million males and about 14.5 million females aged sixty-five and above. That is roughly two males for every three females. Females have an average life expectancy some eight years more than males (77 to 69).[1] It is interesting to

[1]Average life expectancy can be a confusing concept. In 1900 our life expectancy was a little over forty-nine years; it is now about seventy-three years. Some believe that this means that at age forty-nine, people in the year 1900 were in the same physical condition as people at seventy-three are today. This is not so. Life expectancy is estimated from the experience of a cohort of babies born at a particular time. Thus, life expectancy is greatly affected by infant mortality in the first year of life. In some areas of the world today 20 or 30 percent of the infants born could be deceased one year later. Maternal death rates are also quite high. Children in general have high death rates from illness and accidents. Thus, the primary way that a culture increases its average life expectancy is to reduce infant death rates, maternal death rates, and childhood death rates. Such a reduction permits a larger proportion of a birth cohort to reach older ages and raises considerably the average life expectancy. To illustrate the importance of death rates at young ages it can be pointed out that the number of additional years that a person of sixty-five could expect to live in 1900 was twelve and in 1977 it was sixteen. This is an increase of only four years. Clearly much of the twenty-four-year increase in life expectancy since 1900 has occurred at younger ages.

note that the life expectancy difference was only four years in 1940. Thus, the greater integration of the female into the world outside the home in the last forty years has not decreased female longevity—in reality such outside participation may be causally involved in the increase of female life expectancy. Perhaps the greater variety of tasks open to females has promoted more activity and interest in life.

The greater longevity of women means that their marital and living arrangements are quite different from those of men especially after age sixty-five. Figure 16.1 presents the dramatic differences. Almost eight out of every ten males sixty-five and over are married, whereas only four out of every ten females of that age are married. Again, over half the women that age are widowed whereas only one man in seven is widowed. Of course, the fact that men usually marry women two or three years younger than themselves, together with the fact that women usually outlive men by some eight years, means that males will be much less exposed to the probability of outliving their mates than will females.

In addition, the remarriage rate for males sixty-five and over is seven times that of females the same age (U.S. Bureau of the Census, 1976, Series P–23, No. 59:47). The proportion of unmarried women age sixty-five and above is three times that of the proportion of unmarried men in that age group, and this means that elderly males have a larger marriage market in which to operate. The traditional custom of older men marrying younger women further expands the marriage opportunities for elderly males above those of elderly females.

The difference in marital status affects the living arrangements of the elderly. About 80 percent of the males and less than 40 percent of the females are living with their spouse (see Figure 16.2). Over one-third of the women and about one-

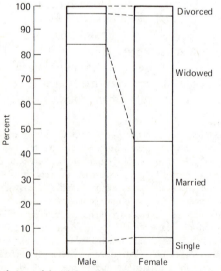

Figure 16.1. Percent Distribution of the Male and Female Population 65 Years Old and Over by Marital Status, 1975.
Source: U.S. Bureau of the Census (1976), P-23, No. 59:45.

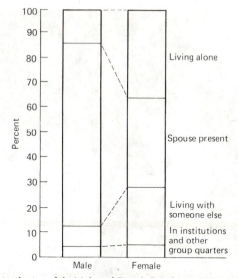

Figure 16.2. Percent Distribution of the Male and Female Population 65 Years Old and Over by Living Arrangements: 1975.
Source: U.S. Bureau of the Census (1976), P-23, No. 59:45.

seventh of the men are living alone. Another large group of women over sixty-five (22 percent) are living with "someone else" (relative or friend). Thus, the difference in survival makes a dramatic difference in kinship ties toward the end of one's life. Males are likely to die while married and thus have closer interaction patterns still prevailing with many of their kin. Females are more likely to die widowed, often living alone and often in serious financial difficulties (U.S. Bureau of the Census, 1976, Series P–23, No. 59, Lopata, 1979).

The reader should note that the differences between males and females at these older ages would be even more extreme if we looked only at people age seventy-five and above, instead of the total group aged sixty-five and above. The older the group, the more the female longevity makes itself apparent. For example, by age seventy-five almost 70 percent of women are widowed and only 23 percent are married (U.S. Bureau of the Census, 1976, Series P–23, No. 59:46). Clearly, the period of old age is likely to involve crises due to the death of a spouse as well as economic crises and health problems (Lopata, 1973; 1979; Hiltz, 1978). These crises of old age are in part related to the mid-life crises of people in their forties (Hallberg, 1978; Lowenthal, et al., 1976; Levinson, 1978). People in their forties are the children of elderly parents and when those parents have problems these children are often called upon to help. This sort of role reversal of the parent-child background is stressful and demanding. At this same time these same middle-aged parents have teenage children going through their own growing-up crises and in need of financial help to obtain an education and become economically self-sufficient.

It is no wonder that the focus in recent years has been on the mid-life crisis because it is so central to both the adolescent and aging crises. It would appear

Photo by Ira Reiss.

obvious that the ties among these three generations are closely interwoven and strains for any one generation places pressures on the other two generations. Reuben Hill's rare type of study of three generations documents many of the specifics of three generational interaction (Hill, 1970). To understand the kinship ties among people one must gain insight into the place in society that each generation occupies. My own opinion is that we have oversimplified the life crises picture by thinking of it as a series of fixed stages and as fixed types of crises. The range of variation is wide by economic levels, by age groups, and by life plans and values. I suspect that for most people there would be in any five-year period of their life a crisis at work, or at home with the children, or with one's mate or parents, or with friends, or with one's health. So life can be viewed as a series of crises. Adolescence, middle age, and old age are surely three common periods when perhaps there is a clustering of problems, but I would not let this fact force the conclusion that there are only fixed common crises or that these three periods (adolescence, middle age, and old age) would necessarily be the most difficult. Many Americans may well plan more carefully to avoid problems at these three known crisis periods. The crises that catch us off-guard may be the more disturbing. But the important point for this chapter on kinship is that those who are kin to us are the most likely to be involved as both the cause of many problems and as those who will provide the greatest assistance in overcoming many problems. In all societies, people are taught to rely most, in times of greatest need, upon those who are related to them through descent.

Summary and Conclusions

The examination of the old Parsonian arguments highlights what has changed in American society. The rigid separation of male and female roles has been altered. Thus, both males and females are now much more likely to be employed in the outside occupational structure. This change alters the traditional situation in two ways. First, it means that the prestige and status of the family is now determined by both the male and the female occupational participation. The last chapter noted that one-third of the employed wives earn as much or more than their husband and millions of women are the sole support for their children. Secondly, the greater female occupational participation means that the separation of the family and the occupational world is not possible because both husband and wife perform in both institutions. The occupational system is surely a most powerful feature of our society, yet despite this fact there are pressures to change the hours of work so as to be more responsive to the needs of getting children off to school. There are also pressures to encourage business firms to employ both husbands and wives in the same unit and to allow positions to be split between a married couple. Increasingly, pregnancy leaves are part of a normal employment contract. In short, there are indications that the family and industry are integrated and that the influence flows both ways, even if not equally so.

Kinship ties, in many ways, can assist young people who wish to advance in the occupational world. The need for committed kinship attachments is perhaps most apparent at the beginning of life and at the end of life. Infants are helpless creatures and kin ties are their guarantee of protection, support, and survival. In time, the elderly become increasingly helpless. The infants these elderly people once nurtured are the very people society calls upon to give nurturance and meaning to the final acts of their parents' lives.

References

Adams, Bert N. 1968. *Kinship in an Urban Setting*. Chicago: Markham.

———. 1970. "Isolation, Function and Beyond: American Kinship in the 1960's," *Journal of Marriage and the Family* 32 (November):575–597.

Arling, Greg. 1976. "The Elderly Widow and Her Family, Neighbors and Friends," *Journal of Marriage and the Family* 38 (November):757–768.

Bott, Elizabeth. 1957. *Family and Social Network*. London: Tavistock.

Broderick, Carlfred. 1953. "A Study of the Friend-Family Clusters in a Mobile Urban Population." Unpublished honors thesis, Harvard University.

Burch, Thomas K. 1967. "The Size and Structure of Families: A Comparative Analysis of Census Data," *American Sociological Review* 32 (June):347–364.

Coale, Ansley J., et al. 1965. *Aspects of the Analysis of Family Structure*. Princeton, NJ: Princeton University Press.

Dore, Ronald P. 1958. *City Life in Japan*. Berkeley: University of California Press.

Elliot, Thomas D. 1930. "The Adjustive Behavior of Bereaved Families: A New Field for Research," *Social Forces* 8:543–549.

Firth, Raymond (ed.). 1956. *Two Studies of Kinship in London*. London: Athlone Press.

Gibson, Geoffrey. 1972. "Kin Family Network: Overheralded Structure in Past Conceptualizations of Family Functioning," *Journal of Marriage and the Family* 34 (February):13–23.

Glenn, Norval D. 1975. "Psychological Well-Being in the Postparental Stage: Some Evidence from National Surveys," *Journal of Marriage and the Family* 37 (February):105–110.

Greenfield, Sidney M. 1961. "Industrialization and the Family in Sociological Theory," *American Journal of Sociology* 67 (September):312–322.

Hallberg, Edmond D. 1978. *The Gray Itch: The Male Metapause Syndrome*. New York: Stein & Day.

Hill, Reuben. 1970. *Family Development in Three Generations*. Cambridge, MA: Schenkman.

Hiltz, Starr R. 1978. "Widowhood: A Roleless Role," *Marriage and Family Review* 1 (November/December):1–10.

Homans, George. 1961. *Social Behavior: Its Elementary Forms*. New York: Harcourt, Brace and World.

Irwin, Theodore. 1975. "Male Menopause: Crises in the Middle Years." Public Affairs Pamphlets, No. 526. New York.

Klatzky, Sheila R. 1972. *Patterns of Contact with Relatives*. Washington, DC: American Sociological Association.

Kohn, Melvin L. 1977. *Class and Conformity: A Study in Values*, 2nd ed. Chicago: University of Chicago Press.

Laslett, Peter, et al. 1972. *Household and Family in Past Time*. New York: Cambridge University Press.

Levinson, Daniel J. 1978. *The Seasons of a Man's Life*. New York: Knopf,

Litwak, Eugene. 1960a. "Occupational Mobility and Extended Family Cohesion," *American Sociological Review* 25 (February):9–21.

———. 1960b. "Geographic Mobility and Extended Family Cohesion." *American Sociological Review* 25 (June):385–394.

Lopata, Helena Z. 1973. *Widowhood in an American City*. Cambridge, MA: Schenkman.

———. 1979. *Women as Widows: Support Systems*. New York: Elsevier Press.

Lowenthal, Majorie, Majde Thurnher, and David Chiriboga. 1976. *Four Stages of Life*. San Francisco: Jossey-Bass.

Parron, Eugenia M., and Lillian E. Troll. 1978.

"Gold Wedding Couples: Effects of Retirement on Intimacy in Long-Standing Marriages," *Alternative Lifestyles* 1 (November):447–464.

Parsons, Talcott, 1953. "A Revised Analytical Approach to the Theory of Social Stratification," in Reinhard Bendix and Seymour M. Lipset (eds.), *Class, Status and Power*. New York: Free Press.

Petrowsky, Marc. 1976. "Marital Status, Sex, and the Social Networks of the Elderly," *Journal of Marriage and the Family* 38 (November):749–756.

Pfeiffer, Eric, and Glenn C. Davis. 1972. "Determinants of Sexual Behavior in Middle and Old Age," *Journal of the American Geriatrics Society* 20:151–158.

Plath, David W. 1964. *The After Hours: Modern Japan and the Search for Enjoyment*. Berkeley: University of California Press.

Sauer, William. 1975. "Morale of the Urban Aged: A Regression Analysis by Race." Unpublished Ph.D. dissertation, University of Minnesota.

Schneider, David M. 1968. *American Kinship: A Cultural Account*. Englewood Cliffs, NJ: Prentice-Hall.

_____, and George C. Homans. 1955. "Kinship Terminology and the American Kinship System," *American Anthropologist* 57 (August):1194–1208.

Seward, Rudy R. 1978. *The American Family: A Demographic History*. Beverly Hills, CA: Sage Publications.

Shanas, Ethel, et al. 1968. *Old People in Three Industrial Societies*. New York: Atherton.

_____. 1973. "Family-Kin Networks and Aging in Cross-Cultural Perspective," *Journal of Marriage and the Family* 35 (August): 505–511.

Strodtbeck, Fred L. 1958. "Family Interaction, Values, and Achievement," in Marshall Sklare (ed.), *The Jews: Social Patterns of an American Group*. New York: Free Press.

Sussman, Marvin B., and Lee Burchinal. 1962. "Kin Family Network: Unheralded Structure in Current Conceptualizations of Family Functioning," *Journal of Marriage and the Family* 24 (August):231–240.

Sweetser, Dorrian Apple. 1966. "The Effect of Industrialization on Intergeneration Solidarity," *Rural Sociology* 31:156–170.

U.S. Bureau of the Census. 1976. "Demographic Aspects of Aging and the Older Population in the U.S.," *Current Population Reports*, Series P-23, No. 59. Washington, DC: Government Printing Office.

_____. 1979. "Special Studies on Family and Aging," *Current Population Reports*, Series P-23, No. 78. Washington, DC: Government Printing Office.

Vogel, Ezra F. 1963. *Japan's New Middle Class*. Berkeley: University of California Press.

Wilmott, Peter, and Michael Young. 1960. *Family and Class in a London Suburb*. London: Routledge and Kegan Paul.

Wood, Vivian, and Joan F. Robertson. 1978. "Friendship and Kinship Interaction: Differential Effect on the Morale of the Elderly," *Journal of Marriage and the Family* 40 (May):367–375.

Young, Michael, and Peter Wilmott. 1964. *Family and Kinship in East London*. Baltimore, MD: Pelican Books.

Part Five   MODELS OF THE FUTURE

Sweden: The Western Model

SEVENTEEN

In the opening section of this book, I made the point that the entire Western world was heading toward greater male-female equality in their Family Systems. In this final section I have chosen to examine one of the leaders in this movement toward equality. There are other countries with similar records of change; for example, Denmark. I chose Sweden because it is accepted as a leader, and after spending a year there (1975–76) and having maintained many professional contacts over the years, I feel best able to discuss the Family Systems in that country. I should say at the outset that I am not proposing that Sweden *ought* to be the model for the United States. It is a homogeneous country of some 8 million people and we are a heterogeneous country of 222 million people. What I am suggesting is that we are moving in the same direction and in many respects changes in the Family Systems have occurred a decade sooner in Sweden. As a country we can learn much about the way we may or may not want to go by examining the experience of Sweden as she copes with decisions that are confronting all Western countries.

Historical Background

Let us look first at gender roles in Sweden. The basic question that I am asking is *not* why gender roles have become more equalitarian in Sweden in this century; that general question would be relevant to any country in the Western world, for all countries have experienced an increase in gender-role equality, especially in the last twenty years. The question is why has Sweden been a *leader* in this movement and why has her rate of change seemingly been so much faster than that in the non-Scandinavian Western countries?

One could refer to historical developments during the last one thousand years in answering such a question (Kälvemark, 1978a, 1978b). After all, there is more evidence of equalitarianism in the distant history of Sweden than in many other Western countries (Andersson, 1970). Nevertheless, there is also evidence of a male-dominated society in the late nineteenth and early twentieth centuries. I will avoid the historical debates and focus predominantly on the twentieth century and comment only rarely upon earlier periods of time.

One of the most significant explanatory events is the late arrival of industrialization in Sweden. Industrialization did not take place until the late nineteenth and early twentieth centuries. This enabled Sweden to take advantage of the mistakes that other Western countries had made when they industrialized for she could better integrate her production with the market needs of the already industrialized nations. The timing of industrialization is important for another reason. It was precisely in the late nineteenth century that the great exodus from Sweden to America began. Over one million Swedes—25 percent of the citizens—left their homeland and most of them came to America. Economic hardships led to their departure but those reasons began to recede as Sweden became industrialized. In less than a century, Sweden had changed from the "poor house" of Europe to one of its wealthiest countries. Partially as a result of the emigration and partially due to rapid industrialization, there was a labor shortage in twentieth-century Sweden. Labor shortages are one factor that seem to promote greater economic opportunities for women. Most of the countries which have witnessed a rise in female equality in the last twenty years have also witnessed a labor shortage that encouraged women to enter the working world in larger numbers (Galenson, 1973).

Another factor that contributed to the labor shortages in Sweden was the traditionally low birthrate (*Statistiska Central Byrån 1969*). Sweden has had one of the lowest birthrates in Europe and as of 1978 had a crude birthrate of only about 12 per 1,000 compared to the U.S. birth rate of about 15 per 1,000, an all-time low for both countries (*Statistiska Central Byrån*, 1975b:73; *Social Change in Sweden*, Feb. 1978:1; U.S. Dept. of HEW, 1978 Vol. 26, No. 12:1). Furthermore, Sweden has had a high proportion of people who never marry—that percentage has ranged close to 20 percent for much of this century (Schoen and Urton, 1979). The percent who never marry in the United States has hovered about 5 percent for the past thirty years or so (see Chapter 9). The age at marriage in Sweden was also later than in the United States. In 1978 the average age at first marriage for men was twenty-seven and for women twenty-five (*Statistiska Central Byrån*, 1975b:116–117). Thus, with a high proportion of people who never marry, an older age at marriage, a very low birthrate, and a very high emigration rate, the labor shortage during the early decades of industrialization and beyond had been aggravated (*Social Change in Sweden*, February 1978).

During the second decade of this century—particularly from 1915–1920—Sweden passed a number of quite radical laws changing the marital institution (Linner, 1967). Historians do not all agree (Frykman, 1975; Andersson, 1970) on just why these laws were passed but one major motivation seems to have been to make marriage and the family more attractive and thereby to raise the birthrate. This concern with increasing births is evident even in the depression years of the 1930s in the writings of Gunnar and Alva Myrdal (1934).

The laws that were passed entailed many changes. First, the rights of the wife were increased so that at age twenty-one she could take independent legal action. The new laws revoked the husband's guardianship over the wife. The wife thus became less of a chattel of the male than was the case in the rest of the Western world. Divorce laws were changed to allow for the possibility of divorce by mutual consent. In addition, illegitimacy was taken off the birth certificate of infants whose parents were not legally married (Frykman, 1975; *Current Sweden*, April 1977, No. 157). All of these changes had the possibility of making marriage more attractive and encouraging childbearing. Because of this legislation in the early decades of this century, Sweden was labeled as being radical in terms of gender roles and this reputation has been extended over the years to all aspects of male-female relationships. As shall be pointed out later, much of the popular view of Swedish sexuality and other gender-role aspects is distorted by this misleading reputation of being radical on these matters.

Another important reason for the high degree of gender equality is the present weak position of the Lutheran church (*Profile of Sweden*, 1972). Only about 10 percent of Swedes are regular churchgoers. All Swedes are automatically members of the Lutheran church, unless they officially fill out a form and resign. One and one-half percent of their income goes to the church. All this may sound like the church is rather powerful but that is not really the case. The money that goes to the church is predominantly for keeping statistical records of the population. A visit to the places where these records are kept reveals little of a religious or church atmosphere. Such places are typical bureaucracies and the church is only nominally in control. The church has kept such records since 1749, and they are among the best historical data for any Western country.

Christianity came very late to Sweden and it did not gain the total dominance that it had in other parts of Europe. Historians point out that for many centuries the engagement agreement by the parents of a young couple was considered the most important sanction for the legitimation of the union (*Fataburen*, 1969:9–24). A church wedding was expected to eventually take place but it took a long time before the church wedding became a socially important legitimation device. The wedding became compulsory only in 1734. But by 1909 civil marriage became an alternative to religious marriage. In addition common-law marriage was recognized up until 1915 (Lewin, 1979:171). During the nineteenth century and in the early part of this century the church did seem to have considerable power but today it is clearly not a dominant force. The basic Christian ethics have, of course, permeated the population but the observances of religious holidays today are strongly secularized. In many neighborhoods Christmas and Easter are observed by a series of parties and social get-togethers of family and friends and by very little else that is of orthodox religious significance.

The importance of this disengagement from organized religion is that the Swedish culture is now freer to choose a definition of gender roles that is not in line with the segregated, nonequalitarian views of the church. Traditionally, organized religion in the West has promoted a view of male and female roles that places the man in the dominant role and the woman in the home. Thus, the more powerful traditional religion is, the more difficult it would be for a culture to move away from the traditional religious conception of gender roles.

There are other factors (see Reiss, 1980) that could be added but the above affords the reader a general background for the remarkable changes that have occurred in Sweden in the twentieth century.

Gender Roles: Attitudes versus Behaviors

There is an attitudinal and a behavioral aspect to gender roles and it would be well to examine how close the two are in Swedish society. At the attitudinal level there is a vast difference between Sweden and America regarding gender-role equality. The official position in Sweden is in favor of "human liberation," which is to say that both males and females are considered equal and both have to be treated in a way that promotes their "liberation" from restrictive gender-role conceptions (*Social Change in Sweden*, September 1977). There was an increasing debate on gender roles in Sweden starting in the late 1950s and the early 1960s. In the late 1950s there was a compromise attempted which asserted that women should accept two roles: one in the home and one at work (Myrdal and Klein, 1956). This compromise was questioned in the early 1960s by people like Eva Moberg (1962) who felt that it was unfair to burden women with two roles and that women could never be liberated unless men, too, were liberated from traditional roles. A new equalitarian role structure was proposed wherein both men and women would participate in both the home and in the outside work world (*Sweden Today*, 1968; Sandberg, 1975; Dahlström, 1971). The concept then became one of *human* liberation rather than simply *female* liberation.

Equalitarian gender roles are the official position of the political parties in power and the people in general; particularly those with higher education (*Sweden Today*, 1968; Allardt, 1975; *Social Change in Sweden*, March 1979; Swedish Information Service, July 1979). The furtherance of equalitarianism can be seen in customs like flexible time which many industries adopt to allow people to get children off to school and still put in an eight-hour day. It can be seen in the strong government support for the growth of day-care centers (*Current Sweden*, December 1975; May 1976, Nos. 115 & 116; October 1976; and March 1977). In the 1976 national election each party vied with the other promising more and more day-care centers if they were elected. As of 1979 there were over 134,000 children in day nurseries and this represented about half of the preschool children whose mothers worked twenty or more hours per week (Swedish Information Service, July 1979). In 1965 there were only 25,000 places and even in 1974 there were but 105,000 day-care places. The goal was to reach 200,000 places for children by 1980 (*Current Sweden*, October 1976). This goal had not been achieved as of late 1979.

As of 1974 there was in effect a law which allowed either parent to take six months off upon the birth of a child and still receive 90 percent of their base pay

(*Swedish Ministry of Health and Social Affairs*, 1977). Further, one can take an additional three months off before the child is eight years old and also receive 90 percent of base pay. Such laws are aimed at affording more time for the family and encouraging fathers to stay home and become more involved with their young children. Also, as of January 1979, parents could work a six-hour day instead of an eight hour day or take a leave of absence until their child was eighteen months old. Thus, there is ample evidence of a strong Swedish equalitarian ideology with legal enactments behind it. But what are the actual outcomes of these efforts?

The actual outcomes are a long way from achieving the goals of gender-role equality. For example, after five years of permitting either or both parents to take a leave with 90 percent pay at the birth of a child, the percentage of fathers who took advantage of this possibility was only 10 to 12 percent. Further, even that small percent took advantage of it only for about forty days of the total possible period of 180 days (*Swedish Ministry of Health and Social Affairs*, 1977). Also, those fathers who do take advantage are the higher-educated professional workers.

The gap between attitude and actual outcomes can perhaps be best seen in the educational and occupational world. There is very little difference by gender, in terms of the percentage of women and men who finish the required nine years of education, or who finish gymnasium (senior high school), or graduate from the University (*Statistiska Central Byrån*, 1975c). But when one looks at the fields in which men and women major, the difference is dramatic (*Current Sweden*, April 1975). By 1980 female university graduates will make up over 20 percent of the people receiving medical and law degrees (see Table 17.1). That is only somewhat higher than here in the United States (see Table 3.3). Thus, the traditional distinctions of more men entering the sciences and the higher-paid professions are still prevalent despite the strong equalitarian attitudes (*Statistiska Central Byrån*, 1975c:136–137; *Current Sweden*, November 1975; November 1976).

In terms of income, the same gap between equalitarian goals and achievement appears. In the United States the average salary of a full-time employed woman is about 60 percent of what a man earns (U.S. Department of Labor, 1977). In Sweden, the average full-time employed woman in 1975 earned about 70 percent of what a man earned (*Statistiska Central Byrån*, 1975c:61, 72). Thus, there is greater equality but still a far cry from complete male-female equality. There are higher proportions of women working in Sweden as compared to the U.S.A., over 60 percent as compared to about 50 percent. But in both countries only about half the women who were employed worked full time, year round. The Swedes do not show the sharp difference between the percentage of women with preschoolers who work and other women; it is over 60 percent for all groups of women (Trost, 1978). However, in the United States, 42 percent of the women with preschoolers work as compared to about 57 percent of women with school-age children (see Chapter 15, Figure 15.4). This is an important difference because the strongest norms against female work are those which apply to mothers of preschool children (Mason and Bumpass, 1975). Even in Sweden this pressure can be seen in that the preschool mothers work the fewest hours per year (*Statistiska Central Byrån*, 1975c; Trost, 1978).

TABLE 17.1

Estimated Percent of Swedish University Graduates in 1980, with a Degree in Various Fields, Who Are Female

(percent)

23	Doctors
4	Engineers
35	Dentists
98	Lower Pharmacy Degrees
39	of Pharmacists
21	Law Graduates
69	of Humanities Graduates

Source: Women in Sweden in Light of Statistics (August 1973):25.

Another indication that equalitarian ideology has not fully penetrated the day-to-day interactions of the Swedish family can be seen in recent data on the proportion of work done in the home by husbands when the wife is employed part-time as compared to when she is employed full-time (Nordlund and Trost, 1975; Haas, 1978). The question by Nordlund and Trost concerns who takes care of the children at night, when they are ill, when they need consolation, when they need to be played with, and so forth (see Table 17.2 for the full set of questions). In all areas the mother performed these tasks much more often than did the father. There was a small difference when the mother worked full-time as opposed to part-time but none of these tasks was "mostly done" by more than 16 percent of the fathers regardless of how much time the mother worked. Perhaps if we looked only at very

Even in Sweden it is the mother who is usually seen with the baby carriage. Photo by Bo Lewin.

TABLE 17.2

Mothers with at Least One Child Ten Years Old or Younger, Living with the Father of the Child, in Families Where Both Spouses Are Gainfully Employed, Differentiating between Part-time and Full-time Employment among the Mothers.

	(percent) THE MOTHER'S EMPLOY- MENT	MOSTLY THE FATHER	MOSTLY THE MOTHER	BOTH	N
Who takes care of the	Full-time	12.5	51.6	35.9	(64)
children at night?	Part-time	3.2	54.8	41.9	(62)
Who stays at home when	Full-time	5.1	61.0	33.9	(59)
the children are ill?	Part-time	3.4	86.4	10.2	(59)
Who consoles the	Full-time	0.0	28.1	71.9	(64)
children?	Part-time	4.8	41.9	53.2	(62)
Who plays with the	Full-time	15.6	14.1	70.1	(64)
children?	Part-time	11.3	29.9	59.7	(62)
Who has the responsibility	Full-time	0.0	65.8	34.4	(64)
for the children's food?	Part-time	1.6	93.5	4.8	(62)
Who has the responsibility	Full-time	0	93.8	6.3	(64)
for the children's clothes?	Part-time	0	100	0	(62)
Who goes to the physician/	Full-time	4.8	68.3	27.0	(63)
dentist with the children?	Part-time	4.9	78.7	16.4	(61)

Source: Nordlund and Trost (1975):173.

young parents the situation would be more equalitarian. But it is nevertheless clear that there is a wide gap between day-to-day family practices and equalitarian attitudes.

The composition of the Riksdag, the national parliament, is also indicative of male dominance despite a trend toward equality. In 1973 about 20 percent of the Riksdag seats were held by women (see Figure 17.1) The comparable figures for the United States indicate that a high was reached in the 1960s and 1970s of about 1 or 2 percent of the Senate and 3 or 4 percent of the House of Representatives (*Statistical Abstract of the U.S.*, 1976:463).

I believe that even in *performance* there is still more gender equality in Sweden than in the States. But the difference between Sweden and the United States is much greater in gender-role *expectations*. Such equalitarian expectations are not without consequences and perhaps in time the performances will reflect these expectations much more than they do today.

We need to examine in depth one aspect of gender roles in order to open to view the network that connects to the other aspects of gender roles. Since we have covered a good deal about sexuality I have chosen to use it as a focus for our analysis.

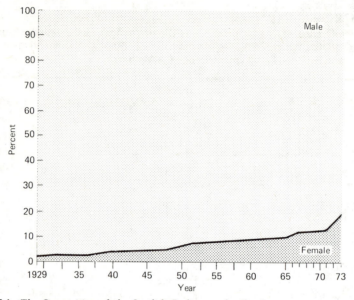

Figure 17.1. The Composition of the Swedish Parliament by Gender.
Source: Statistiska Central Byrån, 1975c:154

Sexuality in Sweden

PREMARITAL SEXUALITY

Premarital intercourse is virtually universal in Sweden. As far back as 1947 over sixty percent of adult Swedes considered premarital intercourse not to be wrong (Linner, 1967:19). In 1967 Zetterberg found that only 2 percent of the married males and females had not experienced premarital coitus. In this same national sample, Zetterberg reports 90 percent felt it was acceptable to have coitus if in love and 70 percent of the males and over 40 percent of the females felt it was acceptable even if not in love (Zetterberg, 1969). In a more recent study, only 6–7 percent felt that both genders should abstain from coitus before marriage (Eliasson, 1971). In the United States in 1975 roughly 70 percent of a national sample felt that premarital coitus was acceptable under some conditions (NORC, 1975). In 1963 the percentage approving premarital intercourse was only about 20 percent (Reiss, 1967: Chap. 2). The change to acceptance of premarital coitus had occurred a decade earlier in Sweden. Today the countrywide *occurrence* in Sweden of premarital coitus, plus the countrywide *expectation* of premarital coitus, colors the relationship between the genders differently than in the States. There is an impression of greater friendship between males and females in Sweden. The possibility of friendship between boys and girls seems greater than it is in America. Sexual orientations do differ between males and females in the same general direction as in this country (Zetterberg, 1969). However, there is seemingly less emphasis on the sexual aspects of relationships—perhaps because it is understood that if a couple does come to like each other, they will naturally have intercourse. Thus intercourse becomes less of a central issue.

One characteristic of sexuality in Sweden is that the sexual standards that apply to weekdays and to nonholidays are different than those that apply to weekends and to holidays. Now, to some extent this is surely true in America as well—we have our TGIF clubs and our Saturday night "fever." But the contrast seems greater in Sweden. Part of the reason for this contrast is acceptance of a "realistic" or "naturalistic" philosophy. The belief is frequently voiced that it is natural for people to seek some form of sexual excitement. Also, it is considered natural that people will enjoy drinking alcohol and it is expected that drinking alcohol will bring out more sexual desires. The same person who during the week will go to bed early and work diligently during the day, may go out drinking and looking for a sexual partner on Friday or Saturday night. The heterosexual interactions one may have during the week seem to proceed rather slowly, involving a long process of getting to know each other. However, that same person, at a dance or on a holiday, may be interested in finding a new partner for the night. We all have seen this type of contrast in America. Nevertheless, there are two characteristics that distinguish it in Sweden: (1) the difference is more dramatic and more widespread, and (2) there is more expectation and toleration of it. A visit to Sweden on a Tuesday night would yield a quite different picture of the country than a visit on a Saturday night.

Thus, although young people in Sweden do value long-term stable relationships and deep affection, they also accept the reality of "letting loose" on weekends and holidays. The research evidence of Zetterberg (1969) and my own impressions support the view that although sexuality with affection is preferred, sexuality for pleasure is accepted by many. As might be expected, this is more often the case for males but there are many females who share this perspective. I noted above that 70 percent of the men and 40 percent of the women accepted coitus without love in Zetterberg's 1967 national survey. Today the acceptance would likely be even higher. But more recent national data are not available. Zetterberg reported that as of 1967 only about one in ten women, but almost half the men, had had more than five premarital partners (Zetterberg, 1969:39). This frequency of partner change seems comparable to Americans (see Chapter 7). There is no lack of discrimination for most Swedes but there is an attitudinal acceptance of the fact that one may on occasion be less discriminating than usual. There is also an element of the double standard in that the emphasis on careful selection of partners seems more strongly aimed at females than males. The average age at first coitus was about seventeen in 1967 and it is estimated to be about sixteen today for both genders (*Current Sweden*, July 1976). The average age for females in America is about 18 (see Chapter 8). Nevertheless, there is more public concern with females starting "too early" than with males. It is interesting to note that births to young Swedish teenage females do not display the high risks to mother and child that young teenage females in America experience (*Current Sweden*, July 1976; Bremberg, 1977). Despite the fact that American doctors believe this higher risk is physiologically based, in reality the reason for the higher risk in America is apparently the poorer health care given such young mothers in America. Sweden's National Health Care Program ensures better health care for such youthful mothers.

One of the major reasons for the greater tolerance of premarital sexuality in Sweden is the view of sexuality as private behavior. Of course, the entire Western world in some sense views sexuality as private behavior. But in America we have laws that intrude on sexual behavior. Many of our state statutes outlaw premarital intercourse, oral and anal sexuality, and extramarital intercourse. In short, in America we view sexuality as private but still as an area that the state can freely enter into via laws. In Sweden the sense of privacy is stronger, and therefore the state is kept out of the area and laws regarding sexuality are rare. There are laws as to the legal age (fifteen) for premarital heterosexual coitus and laws against incest, but little else. Prostitution on a one-to-one basis is accepted—again because in that form it is a private arrangement. The pornography regulations also stress that pornographic material should be inside the store and not displayed outside where it could be imposed visually upon others. Thus, the *privacy* view of sexuality encourages the Swedish culture to accept much sexual behavior that our *regulatory* view would not tolerate. I would stress here that this does not mean that the average Swede believes that casual sexuality or pornography should be endorsed—no, rather they believe it is not their business and they will tolerate it, even if they dislike it, as long as it is not imposed on them.

Swedes give a very high degree of autonomy to young people in their sexual lives and, as we discussed in Chapter 7, autonomy is an excellent predictor of premarital sexual permissiveness (Reiss, 1967; 1979). The Swedes even have laws that assert that striking your own child is an illegal practice. The schools have a long-standing program of sex education which supports this private-autonomous view applied to sexuality. (For the old and the new views see: *Handbook on Sex Instruction in Swedish Schools*, 1956; *Sexual and Samlevnadsundervisnug*, 1974; and *Samlevnadsundervisning*, 1977. They teach the fundamentals of contraception to their teenagers. The availability of contraception in Swedish society is very high. For example, one can purchase condoms from machines on the street, in department stores, in magazine stores, and in many other public places. There is also the element of rational choice more clearly present in Swedish premarital sexuality. Since it is accepted that intercourse will occur, the focus of attention is upon the conditions under which it occurs. Males are encouraged to use condoms and take responsibility for protecting themselves and their partners from VD and from pregnancy. Zetterberg in 1967 found that 56 percent of the people said they used contraception the first time they had coitus. About 80 percent felt contraception should be used every time one had coitus. This is a much more procontraception approach than we have here in America. In point of fact, the VD rate has been falling in Sweden since 1970 and the sale of condoms has risen (RFSU, 1974 Samlevnads Undervisning 1977:195). The number of gonorrhea cases dropped from 38,885 in 1970 to 24,288 in 1975. Condoms alone do not account for the entire drop in VD—it is also likely that greater awareness of symptoms leads to earlier treatment and less spread of VD to others (Juhlin and Danielsson, 1975).

There is some indication of increased condom use in the United States but on a much smaller scale (Redford et al., 1974).

In cultures that are more conflicted about accepting premarital sexuality, responsibility for consequences of premarital sexuality often takes a back seat to the attempt to contain premarital sexual behavior. Individuals who themselves are not sure of the legitimacy of their sexual orientation are less likely to take a rational, planned approach to their sexual lives (see Chapter 8 for the discussion of contraceptive usage). We are surely changing in America, for the polls indicate that we increasingly believe that premarital intercourse is acceptable for unmarried people under some conditions. But we still are more ambivalent about premarital sexuality than the Swedes are and our weaker emphasis on contraception for young people is clear evidence of this.

MARITAL SEXUALITY

Cohabitation is an excellent transition between premarital and marital sexuality for it has elements of both institutions. Cohabitation in America is largely a premarital custom (see Chapter 4). Among American cohabitators, there is little acceptance of children being born into a cohabiting relationship. We defined marriage as an institution which universally sanctions childbirth. As we have previously discussed, most cohabitants in America will abort or get legally married or feel very bad if pregnancy occurs during cohabitation and therefore cohabitation in America is largely a new form of courtship.

The situation in Sweden is considerably different. It is estimated by Jan Trost (1978) that as of 1977 approximately 15 percent of the marriagelike unions in Sweden were cohabitation unions (85 percent were legal marriages). The comparable figure for the United States would be 2 percent (Glick and Norton, 1977). Many of the Swedish cohabitants eventually end up in legal marriage (Trost and Lewin, 1978). In a recent study by Trost of one hundred newly married couples it was found that ninety-nine of them had cohabitated prior to legal marriage. Although the marriage rate dropped sharply from 1966 to 1973, it has begun to rise again. However, it is difficult to predict the likelihood of legal marriage for cohabitants (Lewin, 1979). Trost reports that having children in a cohabitation relationship is acceptable to most people in Sweden. However, it still is but a minority who have babies this way and the general belief is that commitment to the relationship is less in cohabitation than it is in legal marriage (Trost, 1976; Lewin, 1979). Legal marriage is still the preferred way to cohabit but nonlegal cohabitation is acceptable (Lewin, 1979). In a study done in 1970 it was found that 75 percent of the cohabiting couples had been together less than five years whereas only 25 percent of the legally married couples had been together less than five years. This indicates the transitory nature of much of cohabitation even in Sweden (*Statistiska Central Byrån*, 1975c:53).

It was reported by Kajsa Sundström, of the National Swedish Board of Health and Welfare, that of all Swedish mothers giving birth in 1973, 72 percent were legally married, 19 percent were cohabiting, and 9 percent were neither legally married nor cohabiting (*Current Sweden*, July 1976). Thus, a sizable minority of births in Sweden are occurring in cohabiting relationships. Sweden has for most of this century had a high rate of births out of legal wedlock ranging from 11 percent in 1900 to over 30 percent in the 1970s (*Statistiska Central Byrån*, 1969; 1975b). However, in the earlier decades, legal marriage very often followed within a few years of the "illegitimate birth." Today there is a more acceptable attitude toward single mothers (*Current Sweden*, April 1977, Nos. 154 & 157). In America almost 16 percent of births were out of legal wedlock in 1978 compared to about 3 percent in 1920 (Cutright, 1972; U.S. Department of HEW, 1978). We have no way of knowing how many of those births occurred in cohabiting relationships. The current evidence would indicate that it is a minority of illegitimate births that occur in cohabiting relationships. Our acceptance of single parents has increased but not to the level that it has in Sweden (see Chapter 8).

The entire trend toward cohabitation is very new. Prior to 1966, even in Sweden, cohabitation was nowhere near as widespread. The same was true here. In the years since then cohabitation grew at a very rapid rate and seems to be continuing to increase. The years 1965–75 are the years during which a radical change in Western premarital sexual attitudes and behavior occurred and thus it is not surprising to find this custom growing close to the same time period.

Legal changes and interpretation are occurring in both Sweden and America in connection with cohabitation. There is concern for the welfare of the "weaker" parties, namely, women and children (see Chapter 4). Judicial decisions in the States indicate that under some conditions males *may* be held economically responsible for females with whom they cohabit and may be required to share the wealth accumulated during the years of cohabitation, just as they would be if they were legally married (Weitzman, 1974). There are already precedents for the requirement that a male who fathers a child should support that child until adulthood. These legal decisions are gradually moving cohabitation from the nonlegal to the legal sphere. We have pointed out (Chapter 4) that our current form of legal marriage arose in precisely the same fashion. As long as cohabitation involves only courtship behavior of a temporary sort, it is unlikely to be legally regulated, but as it extends into the area of prolonged relationship and serves as a context for childbirth, it is increasingly likely to be legally regulated and to thereby become a form of legal marriage. It will be particularily interesting to follow these developments in Sweden since cohabitation is more common there than anywhere else in the Western world and therefore the pressure for the government to act is great.

Hans Zetterberg's 1967 national study of some two thousand Swedes did ask direct questions about marital sexuality. There is very little of more recent date so we shall rely heavily on this study. Zetterberg divided his sample into those eighteen to twenty-nine years old and those thirty to sixty years of age. The younger married group averaged (mean) 7.6 times intercourse in the "last month"; the older married group averaged 4.9 times in the last month (Zetterberg, 1969:40). The best comparison for the United States would be Westoff's national samples of married women. Westoff's sample, though an excellent one for representing America, only includes women and only those under forty-five years of age. His sample reported a mean frequency of coitus "during the last four weeks" of 6.8 times in 1965 and in 1970 a mean frequency of 8.2 times (Westoff, 1974). This rate is very comparable to that of the younger group of married people in the Swedish sample. If one averages the 1965 and 1970 rates, one obtains a figure of 7.5 times in the last four weeks as compared to 7.6 times in the last month for the younger Swedish sample. The American sample is probably about an average of five years older than the young Swedish sample but even allowing for that the averages are very close.

Another area of similarity between American and Swedish married couples is that the wives in both cultures, more than their husbands, stress love as a prerequisite for sexual satisfaction (Clark and Wallin, 1965; Hunt, 1974). However, in Sweden the differences are not large, e.g., only 5 percent of the men and 14 percent of the women said their last coitus was "not at all satisfying" because love was not present. Also, 46 percent of the men and 24 percent of the women said their last coitus without love was "very satisfying" (Zetterberg, 1969:42). Thus, although love is more important to women than to men, there was much overlap in the responses of both genders.

The finding that only a small proportion of women report no satisfaction in intercourse if love is not present may be due to the fact that almost all Swedish women experience premarital intercourse, and thus they are more sexually awakened than is the case for American women. I would estimate that 25 percent of American women are virginal at marriage, compared to 1 percent of Swedish women (Reiss, 1980).

Marital sexuality in Sweden or in America is an area where very little research exists. It seems that researchers are not as interested in marital sexuality as they are in premarital or extramarital sexuality. Thus, there is very little that one can add to the above brief analysis of marital sexuality. Overall, the scanty information available supports the traditional gender-role differentiation in marital sexuality with perhaps less differentiation being present in Sweden.

EXTRAMARITAL SEXUALITY

Extramarital sexuality is a strategic area to examine because strong feelings about it exist in the Western world, and they generally fit with a traditional gender-role differentiation. Although premarital intercourse is all but universally accepted and practiced in Sweden, the situation is quite different regarding extramarital sexuality. Roughly 90 percent of the Swedes in the Zetterberg 1967 national study rejected extramarital intercourse (see Table 17.3). Whether this has changed at the present is hard to say but it is likely that there is less opposition today. It was the higher educated and economically better-off individuals who were most likely to accept extramarital coitus and those groups have grown since 1967; such individuals also influence public opinion. Nevertheless, the orientation to extramarital sexuality contrasts with the views toward premarital coitus. My own impression is that in extramarital sexuality there is considerable tolerance even though only about 5 percent of the married individuals have engaged in this behavior in the last year

TABLE 17.3

Acceptance of Extramarital Coitus by Generation

| | RESPONDENTS | | | |
| | Younger Generation 18–29 | | Older Generation 30–60 | |
Percent Accepting Extramarital Sexual Relations Between:	Man	Woman	Man	Woman
Married man–unmarried woman	13	6	9	3
Unmarried man–married woman	13	7	8	3
Both married to others	12	7	7	3

Source: Zetterberg, (1969):26.

(Zetterberg, 1969:82–85). I have noted that the general Swedish emphasis on privacy supports a tolerant view toward what others do. In addition, Zetterberg (1969:76) cites data indicating that over 25 percent of the sample felt that occasional, casual marital infidelity should be excused for both males and females. Thus, there is evidence of a *tolerance* level that prevails despite low overall *endorsement*. This tolerance is likely part of an overall "naturalistic" view of sexuality which asserts that sexuality is not something which people can perfectly control. Therefore, occasional missteps can be expected and should be excused even if not endorsed. In this sense the Swedes are more flexible but less idealistic and romantic than we are.

In terms of extramarital sexual intercourse Zetterberg (1969:85) found that 6 percent of the husbands and 4 percent of the wives had had extramarital intercourse in the last twelve months. This seems to be a lower rate than is the case in America. Kinsey (1953:437) found that an average of 28 percent of the husbands had extramarital intercourse in the five years between ages thirty-six and forty and 17 percent of the wives had extramarital coitus during the ages thirty-six to forty (Kinsey et al., 1953:439). Thus, the five-year American rate is four and one-half times the one-year Swedish rate. If one assumes that almost all of the men and women who had had extramarital intercourse in the last year in Sweden stopped that behavior within a year and therefore the people who engaged in that practice the next year were almost all new, then the Swedish rate would approach the Kinsey rate. But that is not a reasonable assumption and thus it appears that at the Swedish rate of extramarital coitus it would take more than five years to reach the five-year American rates. I would estimate the overall five-year Swedish rate to be about 15 percent compared to the American rate of about 23 percent.

The above does not mean that extramarital coitus is widely accepted in America or even that it is more accepted here than in Sweden. Recent national surveys by NORC (1976) indicate that 68 percent of the adult U.S. population say that extramarital coitus is "always wrong," and another 16 percent says it is "almost always" wrong (NORC, 1976). It is likely that we have in America a situation in which many of the people who engage in extramarital coitus do not believe it is right, but their extramarital behavior exceeds their levels of extramarital acceptance.

In Sweden the situation may well be reversed, wherein there is *more* tolerance for extramarital coitus but the behavior still occurs *less* often than would be tolerated.

Lack of opportunity may be one reason for low rates of extramarital relationships in Sweden. Swedes seem much less geographically mobile compared to Americans and such lack of mobility may lessen opportunities for extramarital coitus. Sweden has more of an equalitarian culture and that may make husbands more fearful that if they have extramarital coitus then their wives would have the right to do so. The privacy orientation to sexuality may also be involved and may inhibit people from making the moves necessary to start an affair.

Changes may be taking place in Sweden today because we know that divorced people are more acceptant of extramarital relationships and divorces are increasingly common in Sweden. Sweden has the highest divorce rate in Europe—about 14 per 1,000 married women in 1975 (Trost, 1977). But still not up to the U.S. rate! The Swedish divorce rate rose significantly during the 1970s but, like the American rate, it now seems to be stabilizing.

Urban dwellers are more sexually permissive and so are higher-educated people. These groups have increased significantly in the last decade and this too may well have promoted higher extramarital rates for the 1970s. The Zetterberg data showed greater similarity between males and females in extramarital coital rates for the eighteen- to twenty-nine-year-olds as compared to the thirty- to sixty-year-olds. United States data cited in Chapter 11 showed increases in female but not male rates in recent years and this too would lead to greater equality. In any case, it is clear that the acceptance of extramarital coitus is far below the level of the acceptance of premarital coitus. The typical Swede will say that one ought not to enter into a sexual relationship that threatens an existing and valued sexual relationship. This seems to be not only a Swedish but a general Western value. The question being debated today in both the United States and Sweden is, What are the conditions under which extramarital coitus does not threaten an existing marital relationship? We discussed this issue in some depth in Chapter 11.

Summary and Conclusions

Perhaps the first thing that should be noted is that many of the overall trends and characteristics that have been spoken of here are most applicable to the higher-educated groups in Sweden. In addition, what has been stressed are ideas and policies which are promulgated as the official policies of the Swedish government. While there is a great deal of respect for the government and for the higher-educated groups, there are, of course, also dissenters. I have pictured what I believe to be the dominant trends and ones that are likely to continue to grow but it should be clear that there are also opposition elements in Swedish society.

It is important to keep in mind that the forces that promoted gender-role equality in Sweden are the same forces that are assumed to have promoted it throughout the Western world during this century. Forces like labor shortages and weakening of traditional religions and equalitarian ethics are put forth as important. These forces were seemingly more powerful in Sweden and the homogeneous Swedish people had the ability to respond to them. Other Scandinavian countries seem to fit with these ideas. However, although Norway, Finland, and Denmark all accept premarital intercourse, they differ in many other ways. Denmark is most like Sweden in general permissiveness, whereas Norway and Finland are generally more conservative (Allardt, 1975).

The fact that Sweden is considerably more equalitarian than the United States in attitudinal beliefs but less different in actual relationships between men and women is worth remembering. Nevertheless, I would expect that this attitudinal acceptance will eventually lead to structural changes and equalitarian behavior. The reasons why a culture like Sweden, which genuinely wants gender equality, has fallen short of achieving that equality, are in dire need of research. It is possible that the answer is in part that it simply takes more time. Many of the changes in Sweden are but fifteen to twenty years old and it may take another twenty years to raise a generation more fully imbued with these newer ideas.

I also believe there are other factors that are impeding the rate of change toward gender role equality. Most basic is the fact that a nonequalitarian gender-role system weaves itself throughout the institutional framework of all Western societies and thus change toward an equalitarian gender-role system requires very fundamental changes in the *total* institutional system. For example, equal pay for equal work is relatively easy to gain approval for but to get equal proportions of women into the top-ranked professions is much more difficult. It is true that Sweden and the West are moving in that direction but those moves are partially muted by the fact that when women enter a profession they often are "assigned" to subspecialties that have low prestige. For example, in medicine they go into pediatrics and not into surgery; in politics they become local officials and not senators; and in universities they become instructors and not vice-presidents. We have discussed the case of medicine in the Soviet Union (Chapter 3). Women now comprise 80 percent of the medical doctors in the U.S.S.R. However, over the decades as that percentage has risen the prestige and pay of the medical profession has accordingly fallen. In Russia today a nonspecialized medical doctor earns less than a skilled industrial worker. In addition, the top medical specialties have remained in the control of men as have the administration of the hospitals and of the medical profession. Clearly, the male dominance was such that the medical profession, instead of yielding to equalitarian pressures, merely accommodated women into a new version of a still male-dominated profession. This occurrence supports the point that a new system of gender equality first necessitates equality of power and prestige in the overall culture. This is a "Catch–22" type of situation because, seemingly, before the overall culture will assign equal power to men and women, the individual institutions have to incorporate such equality. Furthermore, there is an enigma as to how such a shift can occur when those who must change are not just the women in the culture but the very men who are in power.

Another fundamental problem that Sweden has faced in its effort to achieve male-female equality is that equality demands changes that even many of those who are equalitarian in their thinking are not yet ready to make. One good example of this is the Western concept of a career. As it now stands, a career to most people means a profession to which one is so devoted that almost every spare moment of one's life will be spent in its pursuit. As we discussed in Chapter 15, the model of the career pictures a married man whose wife does virtually everything connected with the home and children and with entertaining his colleagues so that he may pursue his career. The idea of working part-time at a career such as surgery, law, the ministry, or college teaching strikes a discordant note with many people. The logic is that "real" career people would be unable to work part-time because they would be so driven by devotion to their career that they would feel compelled to work at it full-time. True, there have been some starts made in the direction of reducing the full-time career conception. But these attempts are few and far between (Levine, 1976). In Sweden, at the Huddinge Clinic in Stockholm in the mid-1970s, the kidney-transplant surgeons were put on a schedule of forty hours a week. If they worked more than forty hours they would lose 90 percent of the extra money which they earned. This situation was planned to encourage the doctors to spend more time with their families and to change their career conception to make it less demanding than it had been. There is some dissatisfaction with this schema and it is hard to say how far it will go but it is precisely the kind of redefinition that seems to be needed if one wishes to achieve gender equality in careers.

As careers are now structured, women who are married can only compete if they have a husband who would assume the traditional supportive female role and such husbands are not abundantly present. Thus, the current concept of a career helps maintain male dominance. The difficulties for women in careers is evidenced by their very high divorce rates and very low rates of marriage, compared to men in the same careers. This problem illustrates some of the reasons that Sweden may be having difficulty in altering the institutional system in a more equalitarian direction. Some who support gender equality, also support traditional career notions.

One major aspect of gender roles which we have examined is that of sexual relationships. In one sense the Swedish approach to sexuality allows for more individual freedom than our own. They have a naturalistic, less idealistic, less demanding, conception of sexuality. They also have much less in the way of puritanical sets of laws defining "normal sexuality." But there are areas where we in America have greater permissiveness and greater experimentation. Despite popular opinion to the contrary, it was not until 1975 that Sweden legally liberalized its abortion laws to accept "abortion on demand." The U.S. Supreme Court decision changed our laws in this direction two years earlier—in January 1973. However, abortion is free in Sweden and this is not the case here so there is still another difference. Our culture is much more pluralistic. More opposing groups exist, each with very different ideas and thus clean-cut decisions that are accepted by the overwhelming majority are less likely in America.

One other area where we are more experimental is sterilization for males. In

America, for couples married ten years or more, the most common method of contraception is for either the wife or husband to be sterilized (Westoff and Jones, 1977 and see Chapter 13). In half the cases it is the husband who is sterilized. In Sweden it is only in the past few years that sterilization of males has even been a minor contraceptive method. This is an anomalous situation since one would think that a more equalitarian culture would be more likely to have male sterilization. Perhaps other factors are involved in Sweden, such as willingness to use alternative contraceptive methods.

There are then no easy generalizations regarding consistencies among the various aspects of gender roles. Even just within the sexual area one cannot assume that because a culture is permissive premaritally it will also be permissive extramaritally. Nor can one assume that because a culture is permissive regarding sexuality it will be public about its sexuality. One thing that seems clear is that broad cultural changes in gender roles do affect sexual relationships. People whose integration into occupations, politics, religion, and education differ will not view sexuality alike. We can document this *within* each gender as well as between the genders. The Swedes are aware of this and their efforts are aimed at creating equality in all these domains by reducing gender-role differentiation. It remains to be seen how well they will succeed. We face the same issues and decisions regarding the many aspects of gender roles as do the Swedes. Clearly, we are a different society, but I believe we can learn much from the experience of Sweden.

A Swedish family celebrate their daughter's graduation from gymnasium. Photo by Ulla Fors.

References

Allardt, Erik. 1975. *Att Ha, Att Alska, Att Vara: Om Valfard i Norden* (To Have, To Love, To Be: About Welfare in Scandinavia). Lund, Sweden: Argos Forlag AB.

Andersson, Ingvar. 1970. *A History of Sweden*. Stockholm: Natur och Kultur.

Bremberg, Sven. 1977. "Pregnancy in Swedish Teenagers: Perinatal Problems and Social Situations," *Scandinavian Journal of Social Medicine* 5, No. 1:15–19.

Christensen, Harold T. 1962. "Value Behavior Discrepancies Regarding Premarital Coitus in Three Western Cultures," *American Sociological Review* 27 (February):66–74.

_____. 1973. "Attitudes Toward Marital Infidelity: A Nine Culture Sample," *Journal of Comparative Family Studies* 4 (Autumn):197– 214.

Clark, Alexander L., and Paul Wallin. 1965. "Women's Sexual Responsiveness and the Duration and Quality of Their Marriages," *American Journal of Sociology* 21 (September):187– 196.

Current Sweden. 1975. Göran Beckerus. "To Swedish Men on the Situation of Women University Graduates in Sweden" 67 (April):1– 7. Swedish Institute, Stockholm.

_____. 1975. Maria Salmson. "Free Choice: Theory and Reality: Summary of a Report from the Sex Roles Project, Swedish National Board of Education" 95 (November):1–6. Swedish Institute, Stockholm.

_____. 1975. Camilla Odhnoff. "Equality is for Children Too" 98 (December):1–6. Swedish Institute, Stockholm.

_____. 1976. Lars-Gören Engström. "New Penal Provisions on Sexual Offenses Proposed in Sweden" 118 (April):1–7. Swedish Institute, Stockholm.

_____. 1976. Birgitta Wittorp and Karin Lund. "Children's Policy in Sweden" 115 (May):1–6. Swedish Institute, Stockholm.

_____. 1976. Birgitta Wittorp and Karin Lund. "Some Facts About Swedish Children and Their Parents" 116 (May):1–6. Swedish Institute, Stockholm.

_____. 1976. Kajsa Sundström. "Young People's Sexual Habits in Today's Swedish Society" 115 (July):1–8. Swedish Institute, Stockholm.

_____. 1976. Bodil Rosengren. "More Time for the Children: A Survey of Recent Developments in the Care of Young Children" 131 (October):1–15. Swedish Institute, Stockholm.

_____. 1976. "From Words to Action: Practical Measures to Improve the Status of Women in the Swedish Civil Service" 135 (November): 1– 4. Swedish Institute, Stockholm.

_____. 1977. Sven Svensson. "A New Regime After 44 Years" 92 (January) 1–8. Swedish Institute, Stockholm.

_____. 1977. Siv Thorsell. "Pre-School Education and Child Care in Sweden" 155 (March):1– 9. Swedish Institute, Stockholm.

_____. 1977. Birgitta Ologsson. "Child and Juvenile Delinquency in Sweden" 154 (April):1– 6. Swedish Institute, Stockholm.

_____. 1977. Birgitta Linner. "No Illegitimate Children in Sweden" 157 (April):1–7. Swedish Institute, Stockholm.

Cutright, Phillips. 1972. "Illegitimacy in the U.S.: 1920–1968," in C. F. Westoff and R. Parke, Jr. (eds.), *Demographic and Social Aspects of Population Growth.* Vol. 1. Washington, DC: U.S. Government Printing Office.

Dahlström, Edmund (ed.). 1971. *The Changing Roles of Men and Women.* Boston: Beacon Press.

Derry, T. K. 1979. *A History of Scandinavia.* Minneapolis: University of Minnesota Press.

Eliasson, Rosmari. 1971. "Sex Differences in Sexual Behavior and Attitudes Toward Sexuality," Ph.D. dissertation, Lund University, Sweden.

Fataburen, Nordiska Museets Och Skansens Årsbok, 1969. 1969. (The Storeroom: Nordic Museum and Skansens Yearbook.) Stockholm.

Frykman, Jonas. 1975. "Sexual Intercourse and Social Norms: A Study of Illegitimate Births in Sweden, 1831–1933." *Ethnologia Scandinvica: A Journal for Nordic Ethnology.* 110–150.

Galenson, Marjorie. 1973. *Women and Work: An International Comparison.* Ithaca, NY: Cornell University.

Glick, Paul C. 1975. "A Demographer Looks at American Families," *Journal of Marriage and the Family* 37 (February):15–26.

_____, and Arthur J. Norton. 1977. "Marrying, Divorcing and Living Together in the U.S. Today," *Population Bulletin* 32.5 (October):3– 39.

Haas, Linda. 1978. "Sexual Equality in the Family: A Study of the Extent and Determinants of Role-Sharing Behavior in Sweden." Paper presented at the Ninth International Sociological Association Meetings in Uppsala, Sweden.

Handbook on Sex Instruction in Swedish Schools. 1956. Royal Board of Education in Sweden. Stockholm. (English translation, 1964, of this old guide to sex education).

Herman, Sondra R. 1972. "Sex Roles and Sexual Attitudes in Sweden: The New Phase." *Massachusetts Review* (Winter/Spring).

Hunt, Norton. 1974. *Sexual Behavior in the 1970's.* Chicago: Playboy Press.

Juhlin, Lennart, and G. Danielsson (eds.). 1975. *Genital Infections.* Stockholm: Almqvist and Wiksell.

Kälvemark, Ann Sofie. 1978a. "Aktenskap och familj i Sverige i historiskt perspektiv" (Marriage and Family in Sweden in Historical Perspective), in *History Teachers Association Annual* :23–31 Stockholm.

———. 1978b. "Den Ogifta modern i Sverige i Historiskt Perspektiv" (Present Day Singlehood in Sweden in Historical Perspective), in *Historical Journal.* :83–101 Stockholm.

Kalvesten, Anna Lisa. 1962. *Social Structure of Sweden* (mimeo). Stockholm: Swedish Institute.

Kinsey, Alfred C, Wardell Pomeroy, Clyde Martin, and Paul Gebhard. 1953. *Sexual Behavior in the Human Female.* Philadelphia: Saunders.

Levine, James A. 1976. *Who Will Raise the Children?* Philadelphia: Lippincott.

Levitt, Eugene E., and Albert D. Klassen, Jr. 1974. "Public Attitudes Toward Homosexuality," *Journal of Homosexuality* 1.1:29–43.

Lewin, Bo. 1979. *Om Ogift Samboende i Sverige.* (On Unmarried Cohabitation in Sweden.) Doctoral Dissertation, Uppsala University, Sweden.

Liljeström, Rita, et al. 1975. *Sex Roles in Transition.* Stockholm: Swedish Institute.

Linner, Birgitta. 1967. *Sex and Society in Sweden.* New York: Random House.

Macklin, Eleanor D. 1972. "Heterosexual Cohabitation Among Unmarried College Students," *Family Coordinator* (October):463–473.

Mann, William E. 1967. "Sexual Standards and Trends in Sweden," *Journal of Sex Research* 3.3 (August):191–200.

Mason, Karen, and Larry Bumpass. 1975. "U. S. Women's Sex Role Ideology, 1970," *American Journal of Sociology* 80 (March):1212–1219.

Moberg, Eva. 1962. *Women and Human Beings.* Stockholm: Bonniers.

Myrdal, Alva, and Viola Klein. 1956. *Women's Two Roles.* Stockholm.

Myrdal, Alva, and Gunnar Myrdal. 1934. *Crises in the Population Question.* Stockholm.

NORC (National Opinion Research Center). 1975. *Codebooks for General Social Surveys.* Chicago: University of Chicago Press.

———. 1976. *Codebooks for General Social Surveys.* Chicago: University of Chicago Press.

Nordlund, Agnethe, and Jan Trost. 1975. "Some Data on Sex Role Socialization in Sweden," *International Journal of Sociology of the Family* 5.2 (Autumn):168–177.

Pietropinto, Anthony, and Jacqueline Simenauer. 1977. *Beyond the Male Myth: A Nationwide Survey.* New York: Times Books.

Profile of Sweden. 1972. Stockholm: Swedish Institute.

Rainwater, Lee. 1966. "Some Aspects of Lower-Class Sexual Behavior," *Journal of Social Issues* 22 (April):96–108.

Redford, Myron H., Gordon W. Duncan, and Denis J. Prager. 1974. *The Condom: Increasing Utilization in the United States.* San Francisco: San Francisco Press.

Reiss, Ira L. 1960. *Premarital Sexual Standards in America.* New York: Free Press.

———. 1967. *The Social Context of Premarital Sexual Permissiveness.* New York: Holt, Rinehart and Winston.

———. 1980. "Sexual Customs and Gender Roles in Sweden and America: An Analysis and Interpretation," in H. Lopata (ed.), *Research on the Interweave of Social Roles: Women and Men.* Greenwich, CT: JAI Press.

———, W. Burr, I. Nye, and R. Hill. 1979. *Contemporary Theories About the Family.* Vols. 1 and 2. New York: Free Press.

RFSU (Riksförbundet for Sexuell Upplysning). The National Federation for Sexual Information. 1969. *Verksamhetsberättelse.* (Activity Report). Stockholm.

———. 1973. "Det Finns Inga Homosexuella!" ("There Are No Homosexuals!") *RFSU Bulletin* 3.4 (September):1–12. Stockholm.

———. 1974. *Verksamhetsberättelse* (Activity Report). Stockholm.

Samlevnads-Undervisning (Education for Living Together). 1977. Stockholm: LiberLaromedel. (The report by the Board of Education, and is the current Guide to Sex Education)

Sandberg, Elisabet. 1975. *Equality is the Goal.* Stockholm: Swedish Institute.

Schoen, Robert, and William Urton. 1977. "Marriage, Divorce and Mortality: The Swedish Experience." International Population Conference, Mexico.

―――. 1979. "A Theoretical Perspective on Cohort Marriage and Divorce in Twentieth-Century Sweden," *Journal of Marriage and the Family* 41 (May):409–415.

Sexuella Övergrepp. 1976. No. 9 (Sexual Intrusion.) (A Report of a State Commission on New Sex Laws.) Stockholm, SOU.

Sexual Och Samlevnadsundervisning. 1974. (Education for Sexuality and Living Together: A Report by the State Commission on Sex Education.) Stockholm, SOU.

Social Change in Sweden. 1977. Rita Liljeström. "Children, Parents, Jobs: Rearranging the Swedish Society" (May):1–4. New York: Swedish Information Service.

―――. 1977. Rose-Marie G. Oster. "Human Liberation: Swedish Society in Transition" 1 (September):1–8. New York: Swedish Information Service.

―――. 1978. Ingvar Holmberg. "Births Down, Aging Up: What's the Impact?" 4 (February):1–6. New York: Swedish Information Service.

―――. 1979. Kenneth Jaffe. "The Politics of Child Care" 11 (March): 1–6. New York: Swedish Information Service.

Statistical Abstract of the U.S., 1976. 1976. Washington, DC: Government Printing Office.

Statistiska Central Byrån. 1969. *Historisk Statistisk för Sverige, Del 1. Befolkning 1720–1967.* Stockholm, Sweden. (Historical Statistics for Sweden, Part I. Population.)

―――. 1975a. *Statistisk Årsbok 62.* Stockholm, (Statistical Abstract of Sweden.)

―――. 1975b. *Befolknings-Förändringar, 1974.* (Population Change.) Del. 3. Stockholm

―――. 1975c. *Levnadsforhållanden Årsbok, 1975.* (Living Conditions Yearbook 1975). Stockholm

Sweden Today. 1968. "The Status of Women in Sweden, Report to the United Nations, 1968." Stockholm: Swedish Institute.

Swedish Information Service. "Swedish Family Policy" by Lillemor Melsted. (July) 1979. New York: Swedish Consulate General.

Swedish Ministry of Health and Social Affairs. 1977. "Parental Insurance in Sweden: Some Data." 1–9. Stockholm.

Talmon, Yonina. 1972. *Family and Community in the Kibbutz.* Cambridge, MA: Harvard University Press.

Tavris, Carol, and Susan Sadd. 1977. *The Redbook Report on Female Sexuality.* New York: Delacorte.

Trost, Jan. 1975. "Married and Unmarried Cohabitation: The Case of Sweden with Some Comparisons," *Journal of Marriage and the Family* 37 (August):677–682.

―――. "Attitudes to and Occurrence of Cohabitation Without Marriage." Paper presented at VI World Congress of Social Psychiatry, October 4–10, 1976, Yugoslavia.

―――. 1977. "Divorce in Sweden," in Robert Chester (ed.). *Divorce in Europe.* Leiden, The Netherlands: Martinus Nyhoff Co.

―――. 1979. "The Changing Role of Women in Family and Society: Sweden," in Eugene Lupri (ed.), *The Changing Role of Women in Family and Society: A Cross Cultural Comparison* (in press).

―――, and Bo Lewin. 1978. *Att Sambo och Gifta Sig* (To Live Together and to Marry). Stockholm: Justice Department. SOU, No. 55 (Report Published by Family Law Experts)

U.S. Department of Health, Education, and Welfare. 1978. "Final Natality Statistics, 1976." *Monthly Vital Statistics Report* 26.12 Supplement (March 29, 1978). Washington, DC: Government Printing Office.

U.S. Department of Labor, Bureau of Statistics. 1977. *U.S. Working Women: A Databook.* Washington, DC: Government Printing Office.

Weitzman, Lenore J. 1974. "Legal Regulation of Marriage: Tradition and Change," *California Law Review* 62:1169–1288.

Westoff, Charles F. 1974. "Coital Frequency and Contraception," *Family Planning Perspectives* 6.3 (Summer):136–141.

―――, and Elise F. Jones. 1977. "Contraception and Sterilization in the U.S., 1965–1975," *Family Planning Perspectives* 9.4 (July/August):153–157.

Women in Sweden, In the Light of Statistics. 1973 (August):1–98. Stockholm: Joint Female Labour Council.

Zelnik, M., and J. F. Kantner. 1972. "Sexuality, Contraception and Pregnancy Among Young Unwed Females in the U.S.," in U.S. Commission on Population Growth and the American Future. *Demographic and Social Aspects of Population Growth.* Vol. 1. Washington, DC: Government Printing Office.

_____, and _____ 1977. "Sexual and Contraceptive Experience of Young Unmarried Women in the U.S., 1976 and 1971," *Family Planning Perspectives* 9 (March/April):55–71.

Zetterberg, Hans L. 1969. *Om Sexuallivet i Sverige* (On Sexual Life in Sweden). Stockholm: Statens Offentiliga Utredningar (SOU).

The Future of the Family Systems in America

EIGHTEEN

This chapter involves both a challenge and a pleasure. It is a challenge because predicting the future is always a most delicate and difficult operation and it is a pleasure because after being constrained by the structure of the previous seventeen chapters, I am now free to try to assess the meaning of this investigation of our Family Systems. Of course, the reader should be aware that I am allowed to be more speculative in this chapter than I have been before.

Gender Equality

One theme has predominated over all others in this book. I have stressed the centrality of gender roles for the understanding of the Family Systems. It should by now be obvious that the major role positions that males and females occupy in their lifetimes are interrelated in very powerful ways. It is no accident that the women's rights movement was revived in the last twenty years at the very same period of history when female participation in the labor force was growing at an unprecedented rate. The increase in this century from 5 million women employed in 1900 to more than 40 million employed by 1980 has had a significant impact on the shared conception of the female gender role. The direct impact is perhaps best seen in the data covered in Chapter 15 which points out that in the past thirty years the proportion of mothers of preschool-age children who are employed rose from 12 percent to 42 percent. A change in the obligatory tie of females to small children is a change of first importance for gender roles.

Another important aspect of gender-role change is the widespread cultural support for more alternatives in male and female lives. There is strong grass-roots support for women not being so fully tied down to their small children as they were in the past. This feeling exists, I believe, for both employed and nonemployed mothers. Suggestive evidence for this can be seen in Figure 18.1 Note that between 1967 and 1976 the percent of three and four-year-old children enrolled in nursery schools virtually doubled from about 15 percent to over 30 percent. The point of greatest interest here is that the upward curve is just as sharp for those mothers who were not employed! It is true that the employed mothers utilize such schools more than full-time housewives but this is to be expected and is easily understood. What is more impressive is the increase among mothers who are not employed. The acceptance of being free from small children even though not employed can be interpreted as a step toward less rigid ties of the female gender role to the care of small children. At the very least it shows greater flexibility, even if mothers claim that they send their child to nursery schools for the child's benefit. It is worth adding that the responsibilities of mothers to five- and six-year-olds has already been largely altered by increases in kindergarten enrollments. Almost 95 percent of all children aged five to six are now enrolled in school (U.S. Bureau of the Census, 1979, Series P–20, No. 335:8). I would speculate that the role of various types of schools as socializer of children will grow in the future as increasing numbers of women desire more time for themselves and enroll their children at younger and younger ages in day-care programs.

Another major force that aids in the development of less traditional female gender roles is the level of female education. In 1968 women made up less than 40 percent of all college students *under* age thirty-five. By 1978 women comprised

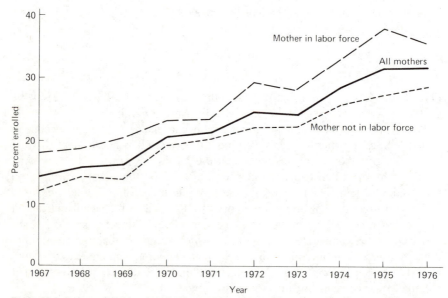

Figure 18.1. *Percent of Children 3 and 4 Years Old Enrolled in Preprimary School by Labor Force Status of Mother: October 1967 to 1976.*
Source: *U.S. Bureau of the Census (1978), Series P-20, No. 318:4.*

almost half of all such college students. Between 1972 and 1978 the number of women in college *over* age thirty-four doubled, while the number of comparable males increased by only one quarter. Accordingly, in 1978, there were 850,000 females but only 460,000 males over age thirty-four in college (U.S. Bureau of the Census, 1979, Series P–20, No. 335:2). This increase of females in college at all ages is impressive. Enrollment at age thirty-five and above is evidence of a resocialization process wherein women are learning new skills at the very time when their children are all in school. This appears to be preparation on the part of women for new activities like outside jobs that they will seek as their children get older. This trend evidences a further inroad upon the traditional mother role. I would suggest that the educational change for mothers is related to the greater school enrollment for young children. They are both processes that increase the flexibility of the female role.

It is the higher-educated females who have been the leaders in the new feminist movement of the last twenty years. The college education process can open up vistas of role alternatives as well as developing skills that are helpful in obtaining employment. The larger the proportion of educated women, the larger the support for gender-role alternatives. In 1977 over 40 percent of the women in their late twenties had completed at least one year of college (for men it was 51 percent) (U. S. Bureau of the Census, 1977, Series P–20, No. 314:1). The comparable percentage for that age group of females in 1970 was only 26 percent (and for males 35 percent). When one adds to this the rapid rise in women thirty-five and older who are returning to college, it is clear that female educational advances are impressive.

The nursery-school and college-education trends taken together are only two indices but two important ones of what I believe will be the continued growth of more flexible female gender-role models. In most cases, the change will modify the traditional bond of obligation between mothers and children, rather than breaking it. Much more problematic is the question of trends in the male gender role. Will males increase their felt responsibilities for child rearing and thereby compensate for the weakening of the female bond? Although such sharing is ideologically accepted in many cultures, it does not occur very often in practice (see Chapter 17 on Sweden). Part of this reluctance may be attributable to males feeling that child care would interfere with their career development. Relatedly, females will hesitate to drastically change their responsibility patterns as long as males hesitate to assume more of the parental responsibility. I expect child rearing will be an area wherein we will see greater equality but the changes will be gradual (Duncan and Duncan, 1978; Simmons, et al., 1977).

Courtship Changes

Cohabitation is a custom "whose time has come," as the historians say. In a little over a decade cohabitation has swept over the Western world and come to dominate the courtship scene. It appeared at the time when the immense cohort of war babies were entering their late teenage years—the late 1960s. I feel sure that the very size of this cohort gave it a share of power not previously possessed by youth. The affluence of the late 1960s no doubt aided this process of allocating greater power to young people. We have examined other reasons for the changes of the late 1960s in the area of love and sexuality. But no change better symbolizes the ethos of the youth culture than the cohabitation custom. It embodies fully the sense of autonomy that is so central to youth culture. Cohabitation also expresses the feeling that public control of private love and sexual relationships is inappropriate.

Cohabitation will continue to grow but I do not believe it will become a viable alternative to legal marriage. The recent Ph.D. dissertation in Sweden by Bo Lewin (1979) reported on a longitudinal study (begun in 1974) of 101 newly married couples and 111 cohabiting couples in Gävle, Sweden. One of Lewin's findings is that despite tolerance for cohabitation as a relationship in which to have children, there was agreement that involvement is greater in legal marriage and that legal marriage is "more proper," "more secure," and shows more "sincerity of the involvement" (Lewin, 1979:173–176). Most of the cohabitors intended to legally marry someday. Now these results are from Sweden, the country with the highest rate of cohabitation in the Western world and the most favorable attitudes toward cohabitation. From these results I conclude that cohabitation, even in Sweden, will largely stay a courtship custom and only a minority will substitute cohabitation for legal marriage. Surely, cohabitation will continue to grow in this country. It is virtually a universal practice before legal marriage in Sweden and I believe it will become much more common in this country—perhaps being premaritally practiced by over 50 percent of the young people by the late 1980s.

In the area of premarital sexuality we seem to be entering a plateau period in terms of the percentage of participants. I would judge that, in 1980, three-quarters of the females and nine-tenths of the males enter marriage nonvirginal. This will likely remain relatively stable but the attitudinal acceptance as well as the variety of partners and activities may well change. The examination of Sweden in the last chapter should have made it apparent that the acceptance of premarital intercourse in the Western world is not part of an orgiastic rite of Bacchus. Many people have qualifications for the acceptance of premarital intercourse. Some accept coitus only with the person they are engaged to—some only if they are in a stable, affectionate relationship. The major change of the last twenty years is really in the area of tolerance—in the area of *legitimation of choice*. Even those who choose not to have premarital intercourse are likely to accept the right of others to choose differently. Thus, what we have is more tolerance for a wider range of choices. We do not have an endorsement of promiscuous sexuality. Sexuality is still taken very seriously by most young people.

However, there are changes occurring in the direction of nonlove sexual relationships. In part I believe this is occurring because our notions of love have been modified and deromanticized. The importance to females of a career, for example, means that occupation as well as love increasingly guides female life plans. The recognition by both genders that many marriages end in divorce leads to the realization that love per se is far from a guarantee of favorable life outcomes. These sort of changes in the meaning of life and life plans, I believe, increase the likelihood of accepting pleasure-based sexuality. The pursuit of pleasure fits in with a life-style aimed at self-actualization much more than with a life-style aimed at obedience to traditional roles. Love-based sexuality will beyond a doubt remain the "higher quality" sexuality. But the pleasure-based sexuality is becoming a more legitimate second choice.

Both genders are ambivalent in this time of change. Females want to be admired physically but they fear that if the physical attraction is the focus of the relationship, then there is little "respect" for them as total persons. This feeling is based on the reality that to many people women are second-class citizens and are valued predominantly for their physical attributes. Males do not react to body-centered approaches with similar reluctance for they know they are valued for more than their physical appearance in our society. Thus, as females come to be valued more as a total participant in the society, they will be less sensitive to being "used." Conversely, as males come to value females in more diverse ways, they will be less likely to view themselves as "seducing" an ambivalent female. In the meantime, it is only by open communication that either gender can discern just where on this changing continuum the other exists.

From a societal view, one can see the supports for these courtship changes in the forms of love and sexuality. As we noted earlier, individuals, for at least large parts of their lives, live more separate from their families than they used to. We have the wealth to do this, and we have the divorce and widowhood rates to encourage it. Such an increase in private dwellings increases the opportunity and ability to be independent of others. In fact, it is precisely such independence that is one major purpose of living separately. Privacy and autonomy increase the individual's chances for starting a cohabiting relationship or for having a weekend affair with a friend, or for just being alone. It is this increased individualism which Scanzoni (1975:Chap. 6) has contrasted with the familism of earlier generations. Familism was closer binding and allowed for more controls over each family member's behavior. Thus, it is no accident that the change toward individualism is closely related to the demographic dispersion of our population.

The Marital Institution

Dyadic relationships are still the name of the game in American society. There is today an emphasis on the satisfactions available from dyadic relationships that rivals anything we've had in our history as a nation. I would submit that our expectations are quite high and our tolerance of dissatisfaction is low. We want to obtain a great deal of satisfaction from marriage and if that is not clearly forthcoming, we often do not stay around. In terms of our discussion of dyadic commitment in Chapter 10, "normative inputs" have declined in importance. In former generations there was more emphasis upon staying together because that was our duty or it was expected of us by our relatives and friends. That sort of normative input to dyadic commitment has been drastically reduced. At the same time, the pressures from structural constraints that decrease dyadic commitment have risen in the occupational sector. We now have a higher proportion of workers in demanding professional and managerial positions. Also half the marriages involve dual-earner situations of various types. Such developments add stresses and strains that may further reduce dyadic commitment. Finally, our desired *lifetime* output from the reward-tension balance of the marital relationship is significantly higher than it was in the past. This is so even though many Americans seem to accept the view that love cannot satisfy all our needs. They still wish for as much satisfaction as possible.

If the above analysis is correct, it is no wonder that our divorce rate has risen. Nevertheless, there is a stabilizing trend now. The divorce rate has not been rising to any significant degree since 1976. I believe that what has happened is that many Americans have tried the alternatives of divorce and the stresses and strains of the divorce process have made an impression on them and on others who were married. The emotional and economic costs of divorce are high and this fact may not have been realized by those whose ideology stressed "doing one's own thing." This may be part of the reason for the delay in entering a first marriage. Nevertheless, the married person seems better able to manage life strains and avoid depressions (Pearlin and Johnson, 1977; Campbell, et al., 1976). Finally, our ability to manage dual-earner marriages may well have increased in recent years. My position here simply asserts that a decade of experimenting and trying new alternatives and choices has led to some general reactions which have fed back on each of us and altered our outlooks. For better or worse, I feel we are entering a period of greater satisfaction with what is and less idealistic striving for the "total marriage." The experience with new choices and new ideals has probably made us more aware of what we are likely to obtain from a dyadic relationship and thus perhaps increased our self-knowledge.

One dimension of marriage which married couples in the 1960s and 1970s have explored with relish is the sexual aspect. I believe we will continue at this relatively high level of marital sexual experimentation. Our contraceptive practices have dramatically risen in effectiveness and this is a major contributor to feeling free to enjoy sexuality without fear of pregnancy. Also, the reduced birthrates of the past twenty years have afforded each couple more time with each other and thereby places less constraints on marital dyadic commitment. I expect our extramarital sexuality orientation will move toward the Swedish approach, which is high on toleration but low on endorsement of extramarital relationships. Fewer people in the 1980s will break a marriage over an extramarital affair of their partner. A small minority may even endorse some degree of permission for extramarital relations although the fear of such relationships will likely keep the conditions rather stringent.

The Family Institution

I believe the zero population birthrate of about two children per family will continue. A strong support of this low birthrate resides with the involvement of wives in the labor force. The more flexible female gender role places less emphasis on the mother-child relationship and therefore allows a woman more legitimate choice regarding the size of her family. We saw in our discussion of fertility that it is the woman rather than the man, both in the childless marriage and child-present marriage, who is more certain about the number of children desired. Thus, the wife is the key to future fertility and as her interests outside the home rise, her motivation for children will fall.

Just as Americans' expectations from marriage have risen in the recent past, so have our standards for a "good parent." For example, we are becoming much less tolerant of violence between parents and children. Further, we expect more than just financial support from fathers. We expect mothers to set flexible female role models for their daughters. In all these ways Americans seem to be asking more of themselves as parents than did previous generations. The ultimate outcome seems to be that we are taking parenthood more seriously. The parental role now is more of a choice than a foregone conclusion or an accident.

In Sweden it is taken for granted that the right to work belongs to both parents. Thus, if parental employment produces strains on the child, the Swedes do not conclude that the mother should stop working and take care of the child's needs. Rather, they conclude that both parents are involved in the problem and both must somehow strive to resolve it. The government programs in Sweden have aimed at allowing both parents to take time off to be with their children. But more important than that is the fact that the official view in Sweden is that the psychological health of the child is not the mother's responsibility alone, it is both parents' responsibility. Even in Sweden this normative position is violated in practice and the woman is the one to quit work and to feel guilty when a child is having a problem. But the ideology that contends that employment and parenthood are roles that both husbands and wives have a right and obligation to, is a major innovation in Western culture. The traditional view—still quite popular in the States—is that the mother may be employed but only if she first has worked out a method of taking care of "her" family. Americans are moving in the direction of the Swedish position. However, I believe that any approximation to equal rights of men and women to both parenthood and employment will prevail mainly in those families with dual professional careers. This is so because there is more of an equalitarian ideology in such groups.

We are one of the few Western societies without a coherent government policy on the family. Our "moralistic" approach to the family leads Congress to desire legislation that supports only the traditional, stable, two-parent family. Americans understood when President Nixon vetoed Walter Mondale's child-care act. Nixon stated that to develop child-care facilities might undermine the family as we know it by encouraging mothers to work outside the home. In Sweden political parties vie with each other to see who can promise to add the greatest number of child-care places. The Swedish policy is more pluralistic and does not try to promote any one type of family. First priority on day-care places is given to one-parent families. Our government has begun to move in the direction of forming a family policy. There is a national conference on the family called by President Carter for 1980. Family-planning facilities supported by the government became visible in the mid-1960s and have grown up to date. Thus, there are elements of a family policy here and there but they are far from integrated. I expect our political divisions in this country are such that we will continue, at least through the 1980s, to have a piecemeal set of legislative acts rather than any organized, coherent family policy. (See Appendix 1 for a discussion of value judgments.) We are 222 million people and we are quite diverse by almost any measure one applies. Ultimately, such diversity may force tolerance upon us in order for us to coexist in the family area and this may bring pressure toward the formulation of a set of policies that will promote the welfare of more than one type of family. But as of this moment we are far from agreeing on just what the family's welfare consists of. A glance at the dispute over abortion and the Equal Rights Amendment (ERA) exemplify our divisions today. I do believe that some of this divisiveness will subside because the strong drift of the entire Western world toward gender equality will very likely prevail and help organize our values concerning the family.

The New Dogma

One of the characteristics of any new social philosophy is that it tends to develop its own dogmas at the very same time as it decries the dogmas of the traditional philosophies against which it is fighting. This is surely the case for some people in the area of the new family forms that we have discussed in many different parts of this book. Many of those who are into the newer philosophy of love or into open marriage or childless marriage are prone to think of those who disagree with them as narrow-minded, conventional, thoughtless people. On the other side, those living the more traditional forms of the family view the innovators as reckless, lacking in good moral judgment, and prone to excess. From a sociological point of view, we must expect this conflict, but as sociologists we have an opportunity to gain an objective point of view and not be merely participants in the debate.

The difference between discrimination and inhibition is almost always lost sight of in such debates. Those who are into the new family forms are likely to call those who do not experiment with these forms "inhibited." Now there is a difference, from an objective point of view, that should not be lost sight of, between inhibition and discrimination. The difference centers about being *unable* to allow oneself to do something because of the inability to even entertain certain thoughts and, on the other hand, the *desire* not to do something because one *has examined* a behavior and decided that it is not appropriate for oneself. Discriminating people and in-hibited people can be found *on both sides* of this debate over new family forms. There are people who have carefully thought out and planned their life and decided on a new life-style as best for them as well as people in the traditional family forms who have also thoughtfully arrived at their position. In both traditional and new positions there are also people who are emotionally blocked from any new life-style and cannot even entertain the possibility of change. In the sexual area this becomes apparent with at least some of the new "therapists" who view anyone who has not experimented with a wide variety of sexual behaviors as inhibited. Such people do not entertain the possibility that such a choice may be a question of discrimination and not inhibition. The line between the two is, of course, vague, and one can rationalize oneself into one camp or the other, but the line is real and for an objective understanding of different life-styles this is an important point to understand.

Another set of concepts that needs to be considered if we are to understand how new dogmas develop is the difference between acceptance and endorsement. One may well find that he or she comes to the position that a wide variety of behavior in new family forms is *acceptable* for other people to choose. But that is a different position from *endorsing* all new family forms just by virtue of the fact that they are acceptable or new. There is an emotional aspect to a new idea that would tend to promote endorsement rather than acceptance; it would tend to make a member of the new movement feel that not only are the new family forms a possible choice but one *should endorse* all of them as good and right. On the opposite end would be those who feel that the traditional forms are acceptable and *should* also be endorsed as *the* good or right set of choices. The difference between acceptance and endorsement is an important one. It is endorsement as *the* right way for everyone that leads to dogma. Rather than any increase in real freedom, this position restricts freedom. Freedom involves choice, and choice is more in line with the concept of acceptance and (as discussed above) with the concept of discrimination rather than the concept of forced choice or endorsement of some life-style simply because it is old or new. The history of social movements would indicate that although new dogmas are often established in the interest of freedom, these dogmas may come to restrict freedom as much as the old dogmas. It will be interesting to see if the current social scene will repeat this pattern or if there will be more of a presence of freedom of choice.

We need some kind of objective definition of prejudice in order to be aware of the presence of prejudicial dogmas, new or old. I believe the definition of prejudice given by Allport a number of years ago is an excellent one. Allport (1954) defined a prejudice as an antipathy based upon a false and inflexible generalization or, in less formal language, a dislike based upon an emotional feeling which doesn't easily change and which becomes generalized to apply to all people of a certain type. The beauty of this definition is that it permits one to separate out someone who may have a view that is unfavorable to a group but who is open to change and to reason. Such people are not inflexible in their opinion and in this sense are not prejudiced. Thus, someone can say I don't like that particular black person, or that particular woman. That person may or may not be sexist and racist. The test would be whether or not that individual was applying that dislike to all people of a group and applying it in a way that was inflexible and unchangeable regardless of evidence. In a social movement people will reject as hostile to their movement anyone who does not say all blacks, all women, all Jews, all Catholics are "good." Anyone who would question this "positive" prejudice would be seen as hostile to the movement. As a sociologist I would say that we can expect this positive prejudice to be present in the new family forms movement and probably on both sides of any debate. It is a task for the sociologist to study the current changing new family forms scene to see to what extent this inflexibility in allowing for individual differences is present and to interpret its causes and consequences. Allport's clarification of prejudice helps ensure that we will avoid in our research becoming adherents of the positive prejudice that is present in all ideologies, both old and new. (See Appendix 1 for more on research dealing with value judgments.)

Range of Choices

If I had to pick one characteristic that was a trademark of the family in twentieth-century America, I would pick the *legitimation of choice*. There is no question in my mind that as I write these words, the range of truly legitimated choices is far greater than it was in 1950, 1960, or even in 1970. In that sense, the social movement involving changes in the Family Systems is seemingly one in which there is less dogma than is usual in such movements and in which there is a greater amount of legitimate freedom of choice. We have covered relevant evidence on this in sexuality, the areas of employed wives, attitudes toward divorce and abortion, and elsewhere. What this legitimation of choice means is that one psychological comfort once available to many Americans is fast disappearing. The comfort was the belief that one's way of life was *the* one right way of life. We are involved now in a society with a variety of life-styles that necessitates people being able to feel that their own life-style is proper for them, *even though* it may not be a proper life-style for other people. That position is psychologically much more difficult to live with, and it is the reason for some of the stresses and strains felt by many people today. One of the major causes of divorce is the lack of standardization concerning the role conceptions of what husbands and wives should be like. The potential for conflict and disillusionment is much greater when gender roles are in transition. We must learn to live with this, and we must learn to arrive at a judgment of our own preferences if we are to adjust to the type of society that has developed at this point in time. This does not necessarily call for a relativistic type of ethic in the sense of denying common values. What it does call for is the realization that although people feel that they can agree upon values such as integrity, honesty, concern for other human beings, happiness, and so forth, they may still disagree as to how best to achieve those values in their personal lives.

There is, as part and parcel of this greater legitimation of choice, a greater emphasis on experimentation. If there were only one right way to do things, there would be very little need to experiment. But when there are multiple ways of doing things, then one may often feel the need to try different life-styles before settling upon one that is felt to be best. It is just this experimentation that startles so many parents when it occurs with their teenage children in the area of sexuality. However, the evidence that exists and that we have covered in this book indicates that experimentation with a wide variety of sexual partners or practices is for a great majority of people a transition period, perhaps a learning period, but not a permanent style of life. To try to eradicate experimentation would be most difficult in the type of society that we have. Experimentation is likely to be a lasting hallmark of our type of Family Systems.

Some Americans interpret the battles over abortion and ERA as indicative of a backlash of conservatism and a restriction of choices. They believe that perhaps we are returning to a period similar to the way of life that existed in the early 1950s. I have a different interpretation of what these heated debates are about. I believe that the increased legitimation of new choices since 1965 has been of such magnitude that those who opposed this trend were literally backed into a corner. Given the enormity of the change, the traditionalists had no choice but to battle for their point of view or abandon their traditional position. Thus, the debates we are witnessing are simply a sign that our society in 1980 is vastly different than it was in 1960 and those who like the 1960 life-style are understandably upset. In a country as pluralistic as ours, we will never be without such encounters. Both sides have learned that they must organize and gain political strength in order to have their way of life prevail as a viable option. I suspect we will see a great deal of power politics in the 1980s as the traditionalists and the innovators continue to battle for their particular visions of the good life.

China: A Comparison and Contrast

I would like to end with a brief foray into the People's Republic of China. After the last chapter's comments on Sweden, this may not seem like quite so distant a voyage. China is a country that has been fighting the traditional versus the innovative type of battles for over thirty years. I believe that this excursion to China will highlight some of the important points about family change which we have been discussing. Often such changes can best be grasped after one has the added perspective of a more distinct culture.

First, we must realize the immensity of China—a country of over 900 million people who speak many distinct languages and who have been under communist rule only since 1949. The reports that are available on China today are few although their number is increasing (Freedman, 1962; Sidel, 1972; Kessen, 1975; Parish, 1975; Liu and Yu, 1977; Walstedt, 1978; Jaffe and Oakley, 1978; Parish and Whyte, 1978). China is an agricultural nation with 80 percent of its population living in rural areas. I will describe the way the government's family policy has worked out in rural areas. I rely heavily on the recent research on Kwangtung province by Parish and Whyte (1978). Kwangtung is one of the twenty-six Chinese provinces. It has a population of 50 million people. It is located adjacent to Hong Kong. The capital of Kwangtung is the city of Canton, a city of 2 million people. This is the area from which most of the Chinese came who immigrated to America. The Parish and Whyte study of China is based upon interviewing sixty-five Chinese who left Kwangtung province and came to Hong Kong. There was no social-science research permitted in China from 1957 to 1979. In 1979 it was announced that sociological research could now be undertaken. Sociology courses were stopped in 1952, but now they are being reinstated and a Chinese Society of Sociology was founded in 1979. It is still too early to know what types of research will be encouraged. Parish and Whyte had little choice but to use their Hong Kong informants. Such informants are not necessarily political refugees who oppose the communist regime. They are more likely to be people who have relatives in Hong Kong and who may be lured there by the greater economic opportunities.

The communist leadership in the People's Republic of China promulgated a policy in which women and men are supposed to be equal, marriage should not be before age twenty-three for females and twenty-five for males, births are to be limited to one or two, and all work is for the benefit of the Republic. The old patrilocal, patrilineal, and patriarchal customs are declared to be decadent and should be destroyed. Now let us see just how this policy has been implemented since the great land reforms of the early 1950s.

Old customs die slowly—this is amply illustrated by the case of China today. The economic structure of rural China in part works against the family policy of the government. To be specific, the government today encourages the peasants to marry late and have only one or two children. But the decentralized Chinese collective farms consisting typically of production teams of twenty to forty families working together, divide food by the amount of work done. The Marxian ideology of work according to one's ability and pay according to one's needs is *not* abided by in China, as it is in the Israeli kibbutzim. Now, what this method of food

Two brothers in Nanking, China, 1978. Photo by Jerry Fisher.

payment encourages is early marriage and many sons. This is so because the sooner one marries the sooner one will have help in the fields and receive better food rations. Further, if the child is a boy, he will do the heavier work and be given more food rations than would a girl (Parish and Whyte, 1978:Chap. 5). Also, the welfare system of the Republic is not extensively developed and thus one's family is still the guarantee of support in illness and old age. Parents want to be assured of being able to live with one of their sons in their old age. This, too, motivates toward having more children.

The collective production teams of twenty to forty families is made up largely of people related to each other through a common male ancestor. In short, they are a traditional patrilineal descent group. In the beginning the communists tried to break up these lineages and to utilize larger groups of cooperative workers. The agriculture experiment of the Great Leap Forward (1958–1961) proved that method to be a disaster. The smaller groups of closely related kin were much more productive and they have remained the key rural working teams ever since. This system of small production teams of kinsmen promotes patrilocal residence wherein a male brings his bride to live with him in his village. Therefore, sons are more valuable than daughters because sons do not leave home after marriage. Migration to the cities is restricted in order to maintain the necessary rural labor force and this, too, encourages children to stay with their families and to become economically important to those families. Public nurseries are rare, and therefore paternal grandmothers are in demand for child-care tasks. Once again the family structure fills the needs not satisfied by the government.

This very brief description of the Family System in present-day China points out how the old kinship ties helped structure the new collectives and how the distribution of food and lack of governmental welfare further encourage early marriage and desire for male children. From 1966 to 1969 there occurred the "Cultural Revolution" aimed at ridding China of "old customs." Since 1969 there has been an intense birth-control campaign in China (Parish and Whyte, 1978:141). China desires to reach a birthrate similar to ours (15 births per 1,000 people) and there is evidence (Parish and Whyte, 1978; Jaffe and Oakley, 1978) that they have been moving gradually toward that goal. Their current birthrate can only be estimated at about 20–25 per 1,000 (Jaffe and Oakley, 1978).

There have been significant changes in male-female relationships since 1949. The degree of male dominance is much less than it was in the pre-Republic days. There is an attitude-behavior conflict here similar to what we noticed in Sweden. The official communist party attitudes are much more equalitarian than the actual peasant behaviors. But there is no question that, despite compromises, the 1950 marriage law created major breaks with the past patriarchal traditions. Arranged marriage, filial obedience, and patrilineal servitude have all been radically reduced. The ideal family for the present-day Chinese is quite close to the ideal family in America. Marriage is to be freely chosen on the basis of mutual affection. When a husband brings his bride to live in his home, he is supposed to protect her from the demands of his mother. Both husband and wife are expected to work in the fields. Divorce is available if the marriage cannot be saved by counseling. Thus,

Waving at the Panda bears in the Peking Zoo, 1978. Photo by Jerry Fisher.

the model family of the Republic is similar in many ways to the Western family model!

But the reality of village life often fell short of the ideal. One of the young female informants in the Parish and Whyte study (1978:204–205) gave the following picture of the division of labor in 1974 in the rural areas:

> Women did all the housework such as cooking, washing, tending the children. In the morning before work, at noon, and in the evening from nine to eleven or twelve, the men would be gathered about in groups of three to five just chatting away. The women, meanwhile, were home working. . . . No, no one talked about men doing the work in the home. It was just about doing the heavy work in the fields that the women complained. We . . . women pointed out that in Canton husbands helped with dishwashing and even cleaning up the diapers of the children. The village men just laughed and said they wouldn't be men anymore if they did that. The village women couldn't even think of such a change, so they didn't express any opinion.

This was twenty-five years after the communist takeover of China. There is little question that the new social structure has not been able to eliminate many ancient ideas.

What I have described above regarding the Chinese Family System is based on a study of people from just one province in China. We know there is a great deal of variety even within the Kwangtung province. The twenty-five other provinces of China may differ considerably (Walstedt, 1978; Liu and Yu, 1977).

Summary and Conclusions

My purpose in the above comments on China was not to afford the reader a comprehensive view of China but to drive home some of the major propositions of this book. First, attitudes are powerful and important parts of a social group. The communist ideology was the key motivating force for the changes in land reform and family policies that occurred during the last thirty years in China. We have seen in the case of Sweden how the equalitarian ideology of the government has also effected many changes in that country. In addition, behavior in the Family System in any country results from more than just the government's ideology. Ancient beliefs have power. Economic and political pressures are particularly important. We saw that illustrated by the restrictions imposed in Sweden and America on females due to the Western concept of careers that dominate the top-ranked professions. That economic situation has kept women at a disadvantage in career professions. We have just seen it again in the payment for work rules in China. Those rules give males greater return for their work than females receive. Female power is again restricted by the patrilineal nature of the production teams. It is just such structural conditions of life that place severe limits on changing toward more equalitarian gender roles.

Knowledge of specific causal relationships are important but the sociological perspective also demands that emphasis be placed on the relevance of the broader social context in which such relationships operate. The other major parts of our social system—political, educational, economic, religious—place dramatic limits on the operation of the Family System in a particular culture. Nevertheless, it should be emphasized that the Family System does not simply react to the pressures of these other institutions. The Family System also initiates change in these other institutions. For example, the very presence of the nuclear family in nineteenth-century America made it easier for industrialization to occur. Therefore, the total causal nexus is complex and interrelated. The total institutional structure is the macro level of human society. We have also spoken of the related micro level consisting of the particular attitudes and behaviors of individuals. These two levels of analysis help clarify each other.

It may seem to the reader a bit unusual to end a book on American Family Systems with a section on the People's Republic of China. Nevertheless, I would suggest that you can better grasp the broad social forces that affect our attitudes and behaviors by becoming familiar with the social systems of other societies. The Swedish social system is perhaps easier to grasp, since it is part of the Western world. But the Chinese social system makes it even more apparent just how much there is in common in all human societies. All societies have to deal with the realities of the institutional network in which Family Systems are embedded. With the advantage of this broadened sociological perspective, we should all be better able to comprehend the reasons for the changes that are occurring in our own society and in many of the other societies on this planet. The comprehension of our Family Systems and their fit into our overall social system is a puzzle which I have found to be fascinating and intriguing. I hope by now that many of you who have read this book share my feelings.

References

Allport, Gordon. 1954. *The Nature of Prejudice.* Cambridge, MA: Addison-Wesley.

Araji, Sharon K. 1977. "Husbands' and Wives' Attitude Behavior Congruence on Family Roles," *Journal of Marriage and the Family* 39 (May):309–322.

Bernard, Jessie. 1975. "Notes on Changing Lifestyles 1970–74," *Journal of Marriage and the Family* 37 (August):582–594.

Bradford, David L., and Simon Klevansky. 1975. "Non-Utopian Communities: The Middle-Class Commune," in Kenneth C. W. Kammeyer (ed.), *Confronting the Issues: Sex Roles, Marriage and the Family.* Boston: Allyn & Bacon.

Campbell, Angus, Philip E. Converse, and Willard L. Rodgers. 1976. *The Quality of American Life.* New York: Sage Foundation.

Clarke-Stewart, Allison. 1977. *Child Care in the Family: A Review of Research and Some Propositions for Policys.* New York: Academic Press.

Duncan, Beverly, and Otis D. Duncan. 1978. *Sex Typing and Social Roles: A Research Report.* New York: Academic Press.

Freedman, Maurice. 1962. "The Family in China, Past and Present." *Public Affairs* 39 (Winter):323–336.

Glick, Paul C. 1975. "A Demographer Looks at American Families," *Journal of Marriage and the Family* 37 (February):15–26.

Jaffe, Frederick S., and Debrah Oakley. 1978. "Observations on Birth Planning in China, 1977," *Family Planning Perspectives* 10 (March/April):101–108.

Kessen, William (ed.). 1975. *Childhood in China.* New Haven, CT: Yale University Press.

Lewin, Bo. 1979. "Om Ogift Samboende i Sverige" (About Unmarried Cohabitation in Sweden). Unpublished Ph.D. dissertation, Uppsala University, Sweden.

Liu, William T., and Elena S. H. Yu. 1977. "Variations in Women's Roles and Family Life Under the Socialist Regime in China," *Journal of Comparative Family Studies* 8 (Summer):201–215.

Meeker, B. F., and P. A. Weitzel-O'Neill. 1977. "Sex Roles and Interpersonal Behavior in Task-Oriented Groups," *American Sociological Review* 42 (February):91–105.

Meisner, Maurice. 1977. *Mao's China: A History of the People's Republic.* New York: Free Press.

Olson, David H. 1972. "Marriage of the Future: Revolutionary or Evolutionary Change?" *Family Coordinator* 21 (October):389.

Parish, William L., Jr. 1975. "Socialism and the Chinese Peasant Family," *Journal of Asian Studies* 34 (May):613–630.

_____, and Martin K. Whyte. 1978. *Village and Family in Contemporary China.* Chicago: University of Chicago Press.

Pearlin, Leonard L., and J. S. Johnson. 1977. "Marital Status, Life Strains and Depression," *American Sociological Review* 42 (October):704–715.

Ramez, James. 1978. "Experimental Family Forms—The Family of the Future," *Marriage and Family Review* 1 (January/February):1–9.

Scanzoni, John H. 1975. *Sex Roles, Life Styles, and Childbearing: Changing Patterns in Marriage and the Family.* New York: Free Press.

Sidel, Ruth. 1972. *Women and Child Care in China.* New York: Hill & Wang.

Simmons, Roberta G., Susan D. Klein, and Richard L. Simmons. 1977. *Gift of Life: The Social and Psychological Impact of Organ Transplantation.* New York: Wiley.

Stein, Peter J. 1978. "The Lifestyle and Life Chances of the Never Married," *Marriage and Family Review* 1 (July/August):1–11.

Strong, Leslie D. 1978. "Alternative Marital and Family Forms: Their Relative Attractiveness to College Students and Correlates of Willingness to Participate in Nontraditional Forms," *Journal of Marriage and the Family* 40 (August):493–503.

U.S. Bureau of the Census. 1976. "Daytime Care of Children: October 1974 and February 1975," *Current Population Reports*, Series P–20, No. 298 (October). Washington, DC: Government Printing Office.

_____. 1977. "School Enrollment—Social and Behavior Characteristics of Students: October 1976," *Current Population Reports*, Series P–20, No. 309. Washington, DC: Government Printing Office.

_____. 1977. "Educational Attainment in the U.S.: March 1977 and 1976," *Current Population Reports*, Series P–20, No. 314 (December). Washington, DC: Government Printing Office.

_____. 1978. "Nursery School and Kindergarten Enrollment of Children and Labor Force Status of Their Mothers: October 1967 to October

1976," *Current Population Reports*, Series P–20, No. 318 (February). Washington, DC: Government Printing Office.

———. 1979. "School Enrollment—Social and Economic Characteristics of Students: October 1977," *Current Population Reports*, Series P–20, No. 333 (February). Washington, DC: Government Printing Office.

———. 1979. "School Enrollment—Social and Economic Characteristics of Students: October 1978," *Current Population Reports*, Series P-20, No. 335 (April). Washington, DC: Government Printing Office.

Walstedt, Joyce J. 1978. "Reform of Women's Roles and Family Structures in Recent History of China," *Journal of Marriage and the Family* 40 (May): 379–392.

Whyte, Martin King. 1978. *The Status of Women in Preindustrial Societies*. Princeton, N.J.: Princeton University Press.

Value Judgments and Science

APPENDIX ONE*

Those readers who have had an introductory course in sociology will have been exposed to some of the ideas in this appendix. However, research has shown that individuals often do not fully retain knowledge from a previous course. Thus, I feel it important at least to review this area.

When dealing with the values people hold and the behavior patterns present in various groups, one inevitably becomes involved in controversial material. One comes to see the range of viewpoints that various groups hold concerning "the good life." To some the good life includes the right to premarital coitus, free abortion, and marital equality; to others the good life includes premarital chastity, restricted abortion, and patriarchy. The sociologist is presented with two basic paths to follow: (1) choosing a particular conception of the good life and arguing, as eloquently and convincingly as possible, the merits of that choice or (2) trying to remain impartial while analyzing the reasons for the varying positions present and the trends that are developing.

At the time of the debates over divorce, in the first decade of this century, sociologists were much more likely to choose the first option. At the 1908 meetings of the American Sociological Association (ASA), the comments of sociologists were heavily value laden on the topic of divorce. Of course, sociologists also took the second option to some extent, for that option involves the basic research approach that all agree is a fundamental part of the role of sociologists. However, on the issue of divorce, sociologists did take a value position mainly in favor of freer divorce. The situation today has changed a good deal. One way to illustrate the difference is to note that in 1967, at the ASA meetings in San Francisco, a proposal was brought up asking the ASA to go on record against the war in Vietnam. The council of the ASA voted against making such a resolution; the vote was then put to the entire membership, and they, too, voted against making such a resolution. The major reason for this negative vote was not that sociologists approved of the war in Vietnam. Rather, it was predominantly because of the belief that sociologists must try to be objective and impartial and not take sides on such issues. There is nothing in the skills of sociologists *qua*

*The four appendixes are not essential to the understanding of the text but they are quite helpful in getting more out of it. They are available for use at the option of the instructor and student.

474

sociologists that would allow them to arrive at a conclusion concerning the *justness* of the Vietnam War. They could, of course, describe the ways in which the United States became involved, the various group pressures, the likely outcome of the conflict, the cost in monetary and attitudinal terms— but there was no sociological way to weigh all these factors on some universal scale of justice and conclude that the war was unjust.

I am quick to add that sociologists are human, and often they do not adhere so closely to their creed of objectivity as they might. There have been cases of sociological reports that have been far from objective. In Part II of this book I mentioned the bias in many older marriage and family textbooks on the subjects of sex and love. Nevertheless, the norm of objectivity is endorsed, and the effort is made and honored.

Definition of Value Judgments

To better understand the reasons for the objective stance of sociologists, let us start by defining what we mean by value judgments. First and foremost, a value judgment is a statement that suggests, directly or indirectly, how one ought to behave. For example, a direct form would be: "You ought to go to church every week"; the indirect form would be: "Those who don't go to church every week are damned." Both statements imply that one ought to behave a certain way. Thus, the "ought" quality is one essential element in a value-judgment type of statement.

A second quality of value judgments is that they are stated in such a way that they are not empirically testable. By "empirically testable" I am referring, of course, to scientific testing, that is, to tests done by means of the scientific examination of sensory responses. "Empirical" refers to knowledge gained by observation or experimentation—the two key approaches of modern-day science. Look at the above example concerning going to church: There is no empirical way to test the assertion that one ought to go to church. What observation or experiment would suffice to test such an assertion? Nothing in the statement points to what specific evidence is relevant for an empirical test.

Now if the reader applies these two criteria, he or she will have an objective way of identifying value judgments. This is rather important, for although it is quite easy to spot value judgments that we do not agree with, it is often difficult to notice value judgments that we do agree with. For example, if we do not go to church, we can clearly see how that is an "ought" statement and not empirically testable. But if we were opposed to the war in Vietnam and someone asserted we ought to get out of there, then we would likely think that this is a "rational," "intelligent," and "logical" thing to do. Because of the appeal the view has to us, we may fail to note that it is a value judgment and come to think of it as empirical fact. (We shall shortly talk of the differences and similarities of values and facts.)

If value judgments contain assertions that are not empirically testable, then what is the referent of the statement? And, what is the possible support for such statements? The *implied* referent of a value judgment is to an ultimate, objective realm of values. By this I mean that the person saying you ought to go to church is also saying, by implication, that going to church is in line with the correct values as they would appear if we were aware of what was ultimately and objectively morally correct. The assertion is that an objective realm of ultimately true values exists and that the person making the statement has awareness of that realm and thus knows what is objectively correct. This objective realm of values is the yardstick by which one measures what is called "right" or "wrong."

All cultures make an assumption that there is some objective basis for morality. They all assert that under certain circumstances a given action is correct, and that it is "correct" because it is in line with ultimate values. In short, they all assert a belief in an ultimate, objective yardstick by which to measure the worth of various actions. When people make a value judgment, they mean precisely this: They mean that what they believe to be moral is so because it is in line with some objective measure of morality.

There is one other major implication that could underlie a value judgment: One could simply mean that this way of behaving suits his or her taste. One could, in such an instance, simply be making a subjective statement of taste and not assert anything about any objective yardstick. However, if that is what is meant, then one would hardly ever try to convince someone else about the correctness of one's own value judgments. If you like chocolate ice cream more than vanilla and someone else has the reverse preference, you will probably not feel any compulsion to convince the other party of the error of his or her ways and the rightness of your preference. You will simply assert that your preference is a subjective judgment and realize that since the other person's preference is also a subjective judgment, there is no need for them to be alike. Although some people contend that when they make a value judgment they are asserting only a subjective preference, almost all people act as if they are asserting something objectively true. For example, those who opposed the war in Vietnam did not act as if their opposition was purely subjectively based. They acted as if their opposition was based on objective moral principles that apply to all regardless of their subjective feelings. In the late 1960s, the radical students on campus did not simply assert that they subjectively felt change was needed. Rather, they asserted that change *was* needed, and that was objectively true—true for those who realized it and also for those who subjectively did not realize it. Thus, the way almost all humans all over the world act about their value judgments implies that they believe in some sort of objective realm of values that can act as a yardstick for human value judgments.

This objective realm of values, which is universally assumed to exist, is then the area that needs to be examined in order to check the validity of one's value judgments. If one wants to find out if a value judgment is correct, the task consists of seeing if it fits with this objective realm of values. Since this objective realm of values does not exist in the empirical (observable) world, there is no scientific way to test value assertions. Value judgments, then, are analogous to statements about God's existence. They have referents to the nonempirical world, and all a scientist can say is that from a scientific point of view he has no way of accepting *or* refuting such statements.

Relativism

Some people, notably some anthropologists (Hartung, 1954), have responded to the impossibility of scientifically proving value judgments by stating that because of this situation we ought to treat every culture as being of equal moral worth. This, they believed, was the only fair, impartial way to proceed. Since we cannot scientifically assert that our culture is better than all others, then we should assert that all cultures are of equal moral worth. This position appeals to many Americans because it is in line with our moral norms. I mentioned earlier how easy it is to be blind to our own accepted value judgments and to see them as empirical facts. One of our values is tolerance of other people's viewpoints. America is a "melting pot" of scores of other cultures, and this has made a tolerant approach to others an essential feature of our culture. Protestants are not supposed to tell other people that Protestantism is the best religion, but rather they should assert that there are many different religious ladders leading to the good life. Democrats are not supposed to call Republicans idiots. Rather, they are supposed to assert their belief in a two-party system and say that it is perfectly proper to choose either political party as one's own. Accordingly, the relativistic approach of saying all cultures are of equal moral worth appeals to many Americans.

Does the relativistic approach really contain less dogma, less assertion of knowledge of what the objective realm of moral values is like? I think not. The assertion of equality requires just as much knowledge of what is morally correct as does the assertion of individual superiority. Analogously, if one asserts that he is the tallest person in the room, it is clear that he must have a yardstick and have applied it to everyone and found himself coming out on top. If a person asserts that everyone in the room is of the same height, what does he then need? Exactly the same thing. He must have a yardstick and measure everyone and find that they are identical in height. Thus, in either case one needs an accepted yardstick. The same holds true in the moral realm. One must have knowledge of a moral yardstick by which every culture can be measured, before one can assert that all cultures are of *equal* moral worth. Thus, the same problems arise concerning how one can scientifically validate the yardstick and demonstrate that it is the true one. This cannot be done scientifically, and thus the relativistic approach is not a scientific approach. Although one may want to take it as a personal philosophy, it cannot be scientifically supported. On the question of ultimate values, science must remain agnostic. Not only can science not assert which set of values is correct but it cannot even assert that there is *any* correct set of moral values.

Scientific Assumptions and Scientific Proof

America in the twentieth century has come to worship science in the same blind way that people often worshiped other gods. We therefore tend to not see some of the assumptions that we are making and fail to realize that other approaches to the world in which we live are possible. All systems of thought (science, religion, philosophy) are based upon certain assumptions about the nature of the world. These assumptions are in themselves unprovable, for they are the starting points of our reasoning. Science is based upon three such assumptions which almost all scientists accept implicitly or explicitly: (1) The world is knowable through the senses; (2) the world we study is external; and (3) the world is orderly. Since the prestige of science and the "believability" of science are so high today, these three assumptions are taken by most of us as incontestably "true." But let us briefly look at them in order to become better aware of their tenuousness.

The first assumption cited above is that the world is knowable through the senses. Plato was one of the first philosophers to question this assumption, and his position has continued down to the present day in one or another philosophical tradition. Plato illustrated his view best in his analogy of the cave. He pictured man as facing the wall of the cave with the opening and the sun behind him. Man walked by the fire in the cave and saw the shadows of things portrayed on the wall of the cave. But the reality was not contained in those shadows. Reality was *outside* the cave. However, here, too, the senses do not yield reality because the sun is too bright to be understood by staring up at it. The path to reality, said Plato, was therefore of necessity a path consisting of the life of contemplation. The senses deceived one by presenting shadows or illusions such as the stick that appears bent when under water. Reality comes from thought, from contemplation that informs one when to trust one's senses and when not to and what the sense images mean in terms of a comprehensive philosophy of life. Here then is a basis for questioning the assumption that by use of the senses one can know the world. Now, one can argue with Plato and accept the assumption of science, but one begins to realize how arbitrary that assumption is, how much it rules out, and how easily its validity can be questioned. Thus, one must take this assumption on faith and assert belief in it without any scientific way to demonstrate the truth of such a belief.

The second assumption stated that the world is external. This may seem the most obvious of the three assumptions. But this, too, philosophers in the past and present have questioned. Berkeley, the eighteenth-century English philosopher, when still a young man in his twenties questioned this assumption. He stated that there was no external world and that people's thoughts were put there by God. The external world consisted not of hard matter, but of ideas implanted in the minds of people by God. This sounds fantastic to present-day readers, for most of us have come to accept this second assumption on faith and have not thought much about it. But recall that there are people in mental hospitals who claim to see things that others do not; there are things we see in dreams, but not in waking states; and who is to say which state is reality? One can assert that he "sees" other people and buildings, and this therefore proves that there is an external reality. One can kick a stone, as did Samuel Johnson, and say that this proves external reality. But none of these approaches scientifically "proves" the point. It can always be said that these are merely illusions that one subjectively feels. There is a branch of philosophy called "solipsism" in which one asserts the most subjective position of all. In this view one is the only pebble on the beach and there really is not even any beach! The self in this view is the only existing thing. Now, I am not trying to argue this position any more than I was arguing Plato's position. Rather, I am trying to make the reader aware that it is quite possible to deny this assumption and to make a contradictory assumption about the nature of the world. Whether one accepts the assumption as stated by science or the assumption stated by Berkeley is purely a matter of where one wishes to place one's faith. There is no scientific way to prove that one is inherently "better" than another. They are merely different starting points and they create different worlds in which to believe.

The third, and final, assumption of science affirms that the world is orderly. The first assumption is necessary because science operates via the observable sensory world. The second assumption is necessary because science wants to affirm that its observations are not merely illusions. The third assumption is necessary because science must assert that the order it finds at Time One will not vanish at Time Two, one second later. The world must be orderly if one is to be able to generalize about its nature. Order must be present; and it cannot entirely vanish after it is discovered. Basically this assumption involves faith in cause-and-effect relationships, for such relationships are the essence of scientific order in the world. Cause-and-effect relationships are invariant relationships; that is, they assert that when the cause, or causes, are present, then the effect must show itself. David Hume, an eighteenth-century Scottish philosopher, when not much older than many of the students reading this book, pointed out the impossibility of fully demonstrating cause and effect. He noted that if one strikes a match on a surface and it lights 100 times, one would assume a cause-and effect relationship. But all one knows is that this happened 100 times. It is altogether possible that the one hundred and first time the match would not light. In short, science arrives at causal relationships by observing that two or more things were correlated closely in all the checks that were made. Then it is assumed that these things are causally related. But all one really has is a high probability of obtaining the effect when the cause is present. As noted above, the next time one checks out the relationship, it may work differently, or not at all. Inductive reasoning cannot give one certainty, only probability. Almost all modern science has partially incorporated this view of Hume by using probability-type statements rather than absolute cause-and-effect statements. However, science still assumes cause and effect, but merely acknowledges that it is not possible to demonstrate this with certainty. Here too, then, one makes an assumption that can be questioned and that cannot be proved. Here, too, we have an article of faith of the scientific approach.

Two very important conclusions follow from the above examination of the assumptions of science: (1) Science is based on faith in certain key assumptions about the nature of the world. One must accept these before science can be accepted. (2) Since the assumptions from all systems of thought are accepted on faith, there is ultimately no inherent priority to the scientific system of thought. The first conclusion ought to be obvious to the reader by now. It simply shows the tentativeness of science and, hopefully, removes some of the dogmatic aspects of the scientific faith. The second conclusion is of equal importance, for it points out that there are many other possible approaches to the world. This is an important aid to our understanding, because it makes us aware that scientific proof and scientific tests are but one kind of proof and one kind of test. Many people are so enamored of science that they fail to realize that there are other approaches to reality that are based on different assumptions. Once we realize that science itself is based on faith in certain assumptions, then we are less likely to think it is the only possible approach to the world.

When I speak of value judgments being *scientifically* untestable, I mean just that. They certainly *are* testable in terms of other approaches. For example, one can test value judgments concerning church attendance by reference to the orthodox religious approach to reality.

The orthodox religious approach accepts the Bible as divine, and one could refer to the Bible as the justification for going to church to worship God and in this sense "test" that value judgment. Now, surely this would not be a scientific, empirical test. But it is a test of a different sort. And let us remember that science and religion are alike in their both being based on faith in certain assumptions about the universe. Thus, the conclusion that one arrives at by following out one of these approaches is no more certain or "true" than the other. The truth or certainty of such conclusions depends on one's willingness to accept certain assumptions.

Differences between Science and Religion

One basic difference between the scientific and the religious approach to reality is the greater willingness of the scientific enterprise to incorporate change. While I fully agree that scientists do not change their views as quickly as the rules of science might dictate, the willingness to change one's generalizations about the world when observation and experimentation show one's views to be false is a normative aspect of science. It is not a normative aspect of the Christian church, or at least it is less so. The Church has surely changed over the past 2,000 years, but it has done so in response to societal pressures and not because of a normative acceptance of change. Another basic difference between science and religion is that there is much more agreement on the assumptions of science than there is on the assumptions of religion. The assumptions of science that we reviewed are accepted by almost all Americans. The assumptions of Western religion regarding the existence of God, the divinity of the Bible, the nature of creation, and so on, are much less widely accepted. This difference has consequences of importance. It means that science will be taken as the source of truth, whereas religion will have to work at convincing people of its worth and of its truth qualities.

Ultimately the answers to questions posed by either the scientific or the religious approach depend on accepting certain assumptions. What this means is that the answer to the value-judgment type of question that religion is often concerned with, and the answer to the factual questions that science is concerned with, are both only as acceptable as are the assumptions underlying these two approaches to reality. The lesser felt certainty of the answer to the value-judgment questions stems from the greater lack of unanimity on the fundamental assumptions concerning the nature of the ultimate set of objective values, as compared with the unanimity of belief concerning the assumptions underlying science.

Facts and Values

What is the relationship between facts and values? Can we support a value judgment by factual evidence? A relevant illustration would be cigarette smoking. The evidence from various sources on the causal connection between cigarette smoking and lung cancer is quite strong and convincing. Each year over 50,000 people die of lung cancer, and almost all of them are smokers. Roughly estimating that over 50 million people smoke enough to increase their risks of lung cancer, it seems that each year one in every thousand of these people will contract lung cancer. Of those people who get lung cancer, about 95 percent die.

Now, can we take the above findings as factual proof of the value judgment that it is wrong to smoke cigarettes? The answer is no. But the reason many of us (particularly those of us who are nonsmokers) find this evidence convincing is because of our hierarchy of values. We simply rank the pleasures of smoking as being unworthy of the risk of death from lung cancer. If one has a different hierarchy of values and enjoys smoking so much that she feels it is worth the risk to her life, then what can we say to her? Clearly, the decision as to whether the health hazard justifies a value judgment that one ought not to smoke depends on the value weights that one assigns to the variables involved. The only way we could resolve such a dispute over value weights would be to appeal to some objective and ultimate set of established value weights. Such a set does not exist in the empirical world. Thus, one must resort to his or her own conception of the ultimately true value weights, and one can always argue that one's grasp of those weights is more accurate than that of one's opponent. Although there is no objective way for facts to prove value judgments to be correct, the facts may be relevant to the value judgments and may help clarify the nature of the choice. However, the ultimate basis of choice is the weight given to each consequence of the situation.

There is an element of probability in choices. The person racing beyond the speed limit on the highway figures the advantages of the time saved is worth the risk of a speeding ticket. Clearly, though, such a person does not expect to get caught. If one knew that he or she would get caught speeding or get lung cancer, then one might well be less willing to participate in the related behavior. But—and this is the point—even then, even if death from lung cancer were certain, this fact would not prove that smoking was wrong; it would merely show that it was suicidal. Although this is an extreme example, one could still decide to smoke because the rewards were worth it or because one wanted to commit suicide. There are cases on record where people have been told by doctors that smoking would kill them in a matter of months and they have not stopped. Almost all of us, of course, have value systems that would make us stop under these circumstances, and we might question the sanity of people who killed themselves in this fashion. But it is true that the facts of the situation tell us only the likely consequences; such consequences do not prove value judgments, but are the material that must be weighed in order to arrive at a value judgment. Thus, while facts help to show us what is involved in a value choice, our conception of a proper value hierarchy is the basis for that choice.

Value Judgments in Science

Up to this point, I have stressed the ways in which science as such avoids making value judgments. In order to give an accurate view of science, it is now necessary to show where science does make value judgments. Science is a human institution. It is composed of people in patterned role relationships to one another. It is literally impossible to have scientists engaged in research, publication, and training and yet not have any norms—that is, any standards for behavior. Clearly there must be rules and regulations concerning what is the proper way to carry on research, to publish one's work, and to train others in one's discipline. Such rules and regulations must involve value judgments.

Some value judgments are at the heart of science. They consist of statements that say that a more valid or reliable measuring instrument is *better* than a less valid or less reliable measuring instrument. Another scientific type of value judgment is that one ought to publish research findings so as to aid other scientists. Also, what we have been talking about in this entire appendix is another value judgment, namely, that one ought not allow his or her personal value judgments to bias one's research. So the very statement "Be objective!" in itself contains a value judgment.

Thus, science certainly contains value judgments as part and parcel of its operations. What is being ruled out in the attempt to be impartial are those value judgments that are not part of the scientific enterprise and that may bias the research operation. Personal values like one's religious or political preference are the kind of values that science rules out. Now, when I say "rules out," I do not mean that no scientist can have a religious or political preference; not at all. I simply mean that *when in the role of scientist*, one is supposed to not allow such preferences to block obedience to scientific norms of research. The role of scientist is but one role a person plays. A scientist may also be a husband or wife, a father or mother, a member of a religious and a political group, and a citizen of a community. In these roles many other value systems come into play (Lundberg, 1952).

Science demands as much single-minded allegiance from the scientists as the monastery role demands from the anchorite. The difference is that the scientist has other roles to play outside of the pursuit of science. But while in the scientific role, the requirement is that the values from these other roles be temporarily set aside. In the monastery case, the demand is similarly that other values besides that role be set aside.

There is a possibility of role conflict for the scientist. For example, when Carleton Coon (1962) published his book on the history of the races, he reported evidence that the Caucasoid race (white) had evolved into Homo sapiens sooner than did the Negroid race (black). Some people criticized Coon for publishing these research findings. These critics believed that such findings could be used by prejudiced people to argue against integration because blacks had evolved so much more recently than whites. It is true that such an argument has no factual support. The years since one's race evolved into Homo sapiens need not be directly correlated with intelligence or such. But some people argued that it nevertheless gave ammunition to prejudiced people and should not have been published. Now, this is a clear case of the demands of two different role systems being in conflict. There is first the demand of the scientific role, which states that one should publish research findings. Then there is the demand of one's role as a private citizen, which states that one should avoid giving information that can be used for "harmful" purposes. The individual must make the choice and decide which role demands are more important and this must be in terms of the person's overall values. Coon chose to honor the values of science, and others have indicated they would have chosen to honor their conception of the role of private citizen. This type of dilemma should help show the reader the specific limits of the scientific role. Often, in the general mind, the scientific role is taken to be the only role. People ask how a scientist can believe in God, as if one can only accept in other roles those things that are supported in the scientific role. We have seen the limits of the kind of questions with which science can deal. No one can live by scientific norms alone, for one would then have no guidelines regarding how to behave toward friends and family and nation.

Summary and Conclusions

There are several sysems that claim to be ways of understanding reality. One of these is science. All such systems of thought have assumptions that are taken on faith and that lay the foundation for the type of approach that will be followed. In addition, all such systems of thought have norms or value judgments that one is supposed to follow while in that role. It is particularly important to show young people today that science is but one of the several approaches that claim to yield truth. This is important to learn because our culture has come to accept science in a blind, unquestioning fashion. Just a few centuries ago this blind, unquestioning acceptance was directed toward the religious approach to truth. The reader is probably familiar with the classic case of Galileo. He reported seeing four moons near Jupiter through his telescope. The religious officials said this was not possible. It was agreed by the Church that there were only seven heavenly bodies and if Jupiter had four moons, that would bring the total up to eleven. The fact that one could "see" those moons was unconvincing. The moons were taken to be illusions, or errors in judgment, because they could not be real since the standard of reality, religion, stated that they could not be.

Today we have shifted toward viewing science with almost the same awe as we once did religion. We interpret everything scientifically, and if a scientific interpretation does not fit, then we say, as was once said of the four visible moons around Jupiter, that the phenomenon does not exist. We wonder about positing an objective realm of values or a God. These things clearly cannot be scientifically tested or proved. If science is our only guide to truth, then we cannot accept such things—we must remain agnostic. I would not argue for or against taking such a position. I would merely note that we should be aware that the science that is used as *the* standard of truth must itself be accepted by our having faith in its assumptions. Thus, we must be in this sense nonscientific and accept something (the assumptions) on a nonscientific basis, in order to be able to accept anything on a scientific basis. Once this is realized one may be more willing to entertain other sets of assumptions regarding the world and add other approaches to the scientific approach.

In a very real sense we make the kind of world in which we live. We do this by our choice of what assumptions regarding the world we are willing to accept. We can create a very limited or broad, a consistent or contradictory, a meaningful or meaningless world in this fashion. Whatever choices we make here, our discussion can be helpful. By knowing each role we perform and the assumptions underlying each, we can avoid mixing our value judgments from other roles with our scientific value judgments. We can also gain a deeper understanding of ourselves and of the possible approaches to reality.

References

Bahm, Archie J. 1974. *Ethics as a Behavioral Science*. Springfield, IL: Charles C Thomas.

Burtt, Edwin A. 1954. *The Metaphysical Foundations of Modern Science*. New York: Anchor Books.

Coon, Carleton. 1962. *The Origin of Races*. New York: Knopf.

Durant, Will. 1951. *The Story of Philosophy*. New York: Simon & Schuster.

Edel, Abraham. 1955. *Ethical Judgment*. New York: Free Press.

Foss, Dennis C. 1977. *The Value Controversy in Sociology*. San Francisco: Jossey-Bass.

Furfey, Paul H. 1959. "Sociological Science and Problems of Values," in L. Gross (ed.), *Symposium on Sociological Theory*. New York: Harper & Row, pp. 509–530.

Goode, William J., and Paul K. Hatt. 1952. *Methods in Social Research*. New York: McGraw-Hill, Chaps. 3 and 4.

Gouldner, Alvin. 1968. "The Sociologist as Partisan: Sociology and the Welfare State," *The American Sociologist* 3 (May 1968):103–117.

Hartung, Frank. 1954. "Cultural Relativity and Moral Judgments," *Philosophy of Science* 11 (April):118–126.

Hyman, Herbert. 1955. *Survey Design and Analysis*. New York: Free Press, pp. 49–59.

Jowett, Benjamin (trans.). 1937. *The Dialogues of Plato*. New York: Random House.

Lundberg, George. 1952. "Science, Scientists, and Values," *Social Forces* 30 (May): 373–379.

McKeon, Richard (ed.). 1941. *The Basic Works of Aristotle*. New York: Random House.

Meehan, Eugene J. 1969. *Value Judgment and Social Science*. Homewood, IL: Dorsey Press.

Reiss, Ira L. 1960. *Premarital Sexual Standards in America*. New York: Free Press, Chap. 3.

———. 1963. "Personal Values and the Scientific Study of Sex," in H. Beigel (ed.), *Advances in Sex Research*. New York: Harper & Row, pp. 3–10.

Russell, Bertrand. 1945. *A History of Western Philosophy*. New York: Simon & Schuster.

Schwartz, George, and P. W. Bishop (eds.). 1958. *Moments of Discovery* (vols. 1 & 2). New York: Basic Books.

Werkmeister, W. H. 1959. "Theory Construction and the Problem of Objectivity," in Llewellyn Gross (ed.), *Symposium on Sociological Theory*. New York: Harper & Row, pp. 483–508.

An Elementary Approach to Probability

Statistics

Few subjects arouse fear in the hearts of students as much as mathematics. The fear of mathematics is really groundless in the sense that much of math does *not* present a way of thinking very different from that utilized in our everyday thinking. This connection to everyday life is especially true for statistical reasoning. What I propose to do here is to present a simple introduction to probability statistics so that students will be able to read the research tables that appear in this book, and in most research reports, with greater ease and understanding. In doing this I hope to help remove some of the trepidations the student may have concerning statistical reasoning. However, the student should be aware that I am presenting a simplified version and that further study will require consultation of the sources listed at the end of this appendix.

The one essential question that probability statistics attempts to answer is the likelihood that an event will occur, given a particular state of affairs. We all try to make such judgments in our everyday existence, and, thus, this is a very familiar way of thinking. For example, when a woman twice says no to a man's invitation to dinner, the man reasons how likely it is that a woman who wants to see him would turn him down twice. The woman, too, is aware of such probability type of reasoning and will often act to encourage the man to reach the "correct" conclusion. To illustrate: If the woman is not interested, she may well say: "I am busy this Saturday night and every Saturday for the rest of the quarter." If she is interested, her response may be: "I have a date this Saturday night but I'm free on Wednesday, Thursday, and Friday." She thereby informs him that her refusal is "circumstantial," and he should not reject "chance" as his explanation.

If an acquaintance asks us to lend him $10 and he has failed to pay back two previous loans, what is our reaction? Typically, we would hesitate and wonder if his failure to pay back the previous loans was evidence that he was a "deadbeat." In short, here as in the dating situation, we estimate the odds that despite his failure to pay back two previous loans he could still be reliable. Could the two failures simply be "accidental"? This type of reasoning is really all that is involved in probability statistics, except that in such statistics we try to be more precise in arriving at our conclusions.

If we note in a sample of delinquents and a sample of nondelinquents that the delinquents come from broken homes more often than the nondelinquents, is the difference great enough so that we can say it is not the result of "chance"? That is, can we say that these two samples come from overall populations that are significantly different in terms of broken homes?

Two samples can differ because of a sampling variability. We know that for every 1,000 samples drawn, there will be a certain number that will differ rather radically due to the sampling process. The principle can be seen in coin tossing where some samples of 10 coin tosses will turn up all heads or all tails, even though such samples, if drawn often enough would average out half heads and half tails. In other words, although the total groups (the populations) from which samples are randomly drawn are identical in terms of a certain variable, it is possible that the sample may differ due to "accidental" factors in the sampling process, or what is technically called "sampling variability."

How much sampling variability do we accept before rejecting chance? This is a key question. In extreme cases this is rather easy to answer. The same holds true in everyday life. If a woman turns down a man ten times for a date, if a person fails to pay back a loan a dozen times, then we are strongly convinced that this sort of result is *not* due to chance but is due to something else. The same holds true in the above research example. If delinquents came from broken homes in 95 percent of the cases and nondelinquents came from broken homes in only 15 percent of the cases, we would find such an extreme difference a basis upon which to conclude that "chance" or sampling variability was not the reason but that broken homes were really more prevalent among delinquents.

Levels of Significance

Obviously, one cannot operate in science and make these judgments about chance by "the seat of one's pants." A more precise method is needed for arriving at the conclusion to reject or to not reject sampling variability as the cause of one's results. The basic question to be answered concerns the probability that differences of a certain amount could be found between two samples that are drawn from populations that are the same on the variable being examined. Such a question can be answered with precise odds; that is, one can say that there are three chances out of one hundred that such and such a difference could occur between samples that are drawn from populations that are really the same on the variable being examined. What must be decided then is a cutoff point. The profession has generally agreed on the .05 level of significance. The phrase "level of significance" refers to a statistical level at which one is willing to reject sampling variability. The decimal .05 literally means 5 out of 100 or 5/100. Put these together and it means that when the odds are such that a difference of this size could occur due to sampling variability 5 (or fewer) times out of 100 between samples that are drawn from populations that are really the same, then we will reject sampling variability and say that something else is involved. The assertion that the samples come from the same type of population is called the "null hypothesis." To reject the null hypothesis is to reject sampling variability as the explanation for your findings. We call it the null hypothesis because it is the hypothesis we are trying to nullify.

Let us go back to our illustration concerning broken homes and delinquency. If the delinquent group had many more individuals from broken-home backgrounds than the nondelinquent group did, and there were 5 or fewer chances in 100 for a difference that large to occur due to sampling variability in samples drawn from overall populations that were the same on the proportion of broken homes, then we would reject sampling variability (the null hypothesis). In such a case we would assert that the delinquent group does have a greater likelihood to come from broken homes and that this difference in samples is not just the result of sampling variability. On an analogous basis, one can pose the question: How many times does a player have to exceed the other player in tossing a winning throw of the dice before one concludes that the difference is not due to sampling variability but is due to something else (like cheating)?

Now, the reader may wonder how does one figure out the odds that a certain difference can occur when samples are drawn from similar populations. I shall preface my remarks here by saying that it is not necessary for the student to be able to compute these measures.

It is necessary for the student to understand the logic underlying the measure. By now I hope the essentials of that logic are becoming clear. Chi square (X^2) is the most common measure utilized for purposes of estimating the likelihood that an observation occurred due to sampling variability. The reader will have noticed this figure below some of the tables in this book. Basically, the chi square measures the difference between what results one would have theoretically expected from samples drawn from populations that are the same on a variable and what results one actually obtained. Thus, the bigger the chi square, the bigger the difference between theoretical expectation and what one found. The bigger this difference between expectations and observations, the more likely are the results to reach the .05 level of significance. In short, the larger the chi square, then the more likely we are to have a result significant at the .05 level, and thus the more likely it is that we shall reject sampling variability as the explanation.

To illustrate, let us say we have samples of 100 delinquents and 100 nondelinquents, and we ask them about their home backgrounds. These samples should be chosen so as to represent the larger populations from which they were drawn. Random selection is one procedure used to accomplish this. Let us further say that of the total of 200 respondents, 100 individuals respond that they are from broken homes and 100 respond that they are not from broken homes. If our two samples come from populations that are really the same on the variable of broken homes, how many of those 100 who are delinquent would be from broken homes and how many who are nondelinquents would be from broken homes? In this simple example the answer is clearly that over a long series of such tests, the theoretical expectation would be an equal number from both samples would be from broken homes. Table A2.1 presents this result in the top table. If this were the actual result we found when we asked the question, then our expected results and our observed results would be the same, and the chi square would be 0. If, however, we found that 90 of the 100 individuals who reported that they were from broken homes were also delinquent, but only 10 of the individuals from unbroken homes were delinquent, then we would have a quite different situation. This case is shown in the lower table in Table A2.1. The difference between the theoretical results (50–50) and what we actually found (90–10) would be rather large, and the chi square would accordingly be large and would easily come out significant at the .05 level. We would then reject sampling variability and assert that delinquents are more likely

TABLE A2.1

Theoretical and Oberved Tables

	THEORETICAL TABLE		
	From Broken Homes	Not From Broken Homes	
Delinquent	50	50	100
Nondelinquent	50	50	100
	100	100	200 Total cases

	OBSERVED TABLE		
	From Broken Homes	Not From Broken Homes	
Delinquent	90	10	100
Nondelinquent	10	90	100
	100	100	200 Total cases

to come from broken homes and that this is not just due to sampling variability. In such a case we would conclude that in terms of the percent of broken homes, the population of *delinquents* from which one sample was drawn was not similar to the population of *non-delinquents* from which the other sample was drawn. In short, we would accept the conclusion that delinquent groups are more likely to come from broken homes and therefore reject the null hypothesis.

One can simply look up the chi square in the back of almost any statistics book and find a table that will specify whether this size chi square is significant at the .05 level. In most published research tables, one need not even do that. Below the chi square is usually given another notation such as P<.05. The letter "P" stands for the following phrase: "The probability that this finding could occur due to sampling variability in samples drawn from populations that are alike on this variable is . . . " The sign following P is a "less than" sign, and then comes the .05 value. Thus, the entire notation means that the probability that this finding could occur because of sampling variability in groups that are drawn from the same type of population is less than 5 in 100. In short, it meets the .05 level of significance, and one would, therefore, reject sampling variability.

If the relationship does not meet the .05 level of significance, then one can note this fact by "P > .05," which simply substitutes a "greater than" sign for the "less than" sign. Another way of denoting that the relationship does not reach the .05 level of significance is to use the initials "N.S." which stands for "nonsignificant." In the case where the relationship did not meet the .05 level of significance, one would be unable to reject sampling variability and would assert that whatever difference was found was simply due to sampling variability and not to any real difference that exists in the population from which the sample was drawn. In other words, such a result occurs when there are 6 or more chances in 100 that a result like the one found could occur in sample groups that really are from similar populations. Thus, the social scientist in using the .05 level of significance is saying that she will be correct at least 95 times out of 100 when she rejects sampling variability, but that 5 times out of 100 she may be in error; for a result this extreme *could* occur 5 times out of 100 even when the groups sampled were from the same type of population. Even a very unusual event does not necessitate our rejection of sampling variability. Sampling variability, in rare instances, can lead to two samples being radically different on the proportion from broken homes, even though they are drawn from two total populations that are actually identical on the proportion of broken homes. So even at the .05 level we are risking 5 out of 100 erroneous conclusions.

Now, some social scientists want to minimize the chances of affirming a relationship that should be rejected, and thus they adopt what is called the .01 level of significance. The meaning is the same as the .05 level of significance except that at the .01 level one will not reject sampling variability until there are only one or fewer chances in 100 of getting such a result from sampling variability. Out of 100 such judgments, one would be wrong in rejecting sampling variability only once out of 100 times. However, this "higher" level of significance is not an unmixed blessing, for one *increases* the possibility of rejecting a real relationship by refusing to reject sampling variability. By reducing the possibility of error in not rejecting false relationships, one increases the possible error in rejecting a real relationship. These two kinds of errors are respectively called Type One and Type Two errors (Loether and McTavish, 1976:478).

The key point to bear in mind is that the .05 level is generally the most widely used, but that one can utilize other levels such as the .01 or even the .001. These are all just arbitrarily agreed upon levels to adopt as a basis for the possible rejection of the null hypothesis (which asserts sampling variability as the reason for your results). One can choose between them on the basis of the particular nature of the research project. Whichever way one chooses, there is always the possibility of error, but the level of significance one adopts is important as I shall illustrate below.

A recent news event illustrates the importance of choosing carefully the level of significance for your research problem. In 1978 a congressional commission was set up to investigate the 1963 assassination of President Kennedy. One of the issues that confronted this committee was the question of whether there had been a conspiracy to kill President Kennedy. The decision on this question depended heavily on whether there were four or only three shots fired at the President. If there were four shots, then it could be concluded that a second gunman was involved and there was a conspiracy. The major evidence on the possibility of a fourth shot was an audio tape from a police motorcycle present at the assassination. Audio experts were brought in to analyze that tape and decide if it indicated that three or four shots had been fired. Clearly, this was a crucial decision. The experts stated that there were only 5 chances out of 100 of having the particular sounds present on that audio tape if there were only three shots fired. Therefore, using the .05 level of significance would lead one to reject sampling variability (the null hypothesis) as the reason for that audio tape sounding as it did and to conclude that there was a fourth shot fired. That conclusion would lead the congressional committee to decide that there was a conspiracy. However, had the committee decided that they wanted to minimize the chance of rejecting a true null hypothesis (Type One error), they might then decide to utilize the .01 level of significance. Using the .01 level of significance, the conclusion would be just the opposite of that using the .05 level of significance. Since there are 5 chances out of 100 that such an audio tape was due to sampling variability, then one would conclude that it is too common an event to meet the .01 level of significance and we would not reject the null hypothesis. Then the decision would be that there was no conspiracy. Of course, by adopting the .01 level of significance, you increase the chances of rejecting a true relationship (Type Two error). Thus, there is no errorless level of significance but if the consequences of a decision are drastic (e.g. death), one would likely use a higher level of significance before risking those consequences. This illustration shows how the decision on an important event can be completely altered depending on which level of significance one chooses. It is important to realize the need for multiple checks and careful choosing of the level of significance in accord with the consequences of the decision.

Some means whereby one distinguishes results due to sampling variability from results due to real differences in the populations sampled are essential. Without this we could never make any statement about causal relationships because we would never know whether, for example, broken homes went with being delinquent as a result of sampling variability or because of some real relationship between broken homes and delinquency. At this point the reader should be aware that what we are dealing with here are probabilities and not certainties. We know the probability that a result could occur. We can never be certain that the result was, or was not, due to sampling variability. All we can say is that the odds are this small, or this large, that such an event could occur in samples that come from the same type of population. Then we choose our level of significance and make our decisions by it. We play the odds, as the bookmakers call it, but this can never be done with full certainty that we are correct. That is why we call this "probability" statistics. Such statistics add an element of agreed-upon standards and more objective calculations to the everyday quessing on probabilities. All of us are involved in calculating the odds of one thing or another. The social scientist has merely developed a more precise way of doing what everyone does. Since such probabilistic thinking is essential in our reasoning about human affairs, it is a vital part of sociological research.

Strength and Nature of Relationships

One final point concerns the strength of statistical relationships. The chi square does not tell one how strong a relationship is; rather, it informs one how rare or unusual a relationship is. But in order to causally understand the phenomenon we are investigating, we must know more than just how unusual an event is. We must also know how strongly related the two variables are. For example, it is valuable to know that there are fewer than 5 chances out of 100 that delinquents in this sample could come from broken homes to the extent they do, if delinquents and nondelinquents really come from similar home backgrounds. However, that does not tell us how strong the relationship is between broken homes and delinquency; that is, it does not inform us regarding precisely how much of an increase in one variable (delinquency) will result from an increase in the other variable (broken homes). To measure this aspect we need a measure of the strength of association.

Instead of covering a variety of measures, I will simply comment on gamma (G), which is used in some of the tables in this book. Gamma varies from -1.0 to $+1.0$. The minus result would, of course, indicate a negative relationship; that is, as one factor went up, the other would go down. A plus result would indicate a positive relationship wherein as one variable went up, so would the other, and as one went down, so would the other. To illustrate: "As the proportion of broken homes increased, the proportion of delinquency in the group increased" is an example of a positive relationship. "As the proportion of broken homes increased, the proportion of delinquency *decreased*" is an example of a negative relationship.

The closer to 1.0 that the gamma is, the stronger the relationship (positive or negative). A gamma of ± 0.7 is stronger than one of 0.6. The choice of gamma as a measure of strength is determined by the type of data one is examining. It is appropriate for data wherein we know how to rank people, but we are not sure of the exact distance between each rank. For more precise data one can use "r" (product-moment correlation). Any standard statistics textbook will have full explanations of these choices. Gamma is not usuable for curvilinear relationships. A curvilinear relationship is one in which, instead of a straight positive or negative relationship, one may find that the middle category of one variable is the most likely to go with either the highest or lowest category of the other variable. For example, it would be a curvilinear relationship if having a moderate amount of broken homes in an area went with the very highest delinquency rates, while having a low amount of broken homes went with very low delinquency rates and a high amount of broken homes also went with low delinquency rates. A gamma is not a good measure of strength for such a relationship, and one would thus have to choose another statistic. Curvilinear relationships are discussed and illustrated in Appendix 4. There are also other ways of choosing which measure of strength best fits one's data, but I will not go into them here. The interested reader can follow through on the list of references for this purpose.

Summary and Conclusions

One final suggestion: Read over this appendix again if you have any remaining confusions; disregard the elaborations and try to follow the key points. It is essential to know these in order to be able to read intelligently the research literature or even the daily newspapers today. If one is actually going to conduct research, then a much greater depth of inquiry is essential. But for the average student, all that is needed is a basic understanding of the logic of probability statistics. However, the reader should realize that for purposes of clarity I have simplified the picture. I suggest following this appendix review with a reading of Appendix 3, which is logically related.

References

Anderson, Theodore R., and Morris Zelditch, Jr. 1975. A *Basic Course in Statistics with Sociological Application*. (2nd ed.). New York: Holt, Rinehart and Winston.

Blalock, Hubert M. 1979. *Social Statistics* (3rd ed.). New York: McGraw-Hill.

Cohen, Jacob, and Patricia Cohen. 1975. *Applied Multiple Regression, Correlation Analysis for the Behavioral Sciences*. New York: Wiley.

Dornbusch, Sanford M., and Calvin F. Schmid. 1955. A *Primer of Social Statistics*. New York: McGraw-Hill.

Duggan, Thomas J., and Charles W. Dean. 1968. "Common Misinterpretations of Significance Levels in Sociological Journals," *The American Sociologist* 3 (February):45–46.

Huff, Darrell. 1954. *How to Lie with Statistics*. New York: Norton.

———. 1959. *How to Take a Chance*. New York: Norton.

Kerlinger, Fred N., and Elazar J. Pedhazur. 1973. *Multiple Regression in Behavioral Research*. New York: Holt, Rinehart and Winston.

Loether, Herman J., and Donald G. McTavish. 1976. *Descriptive and Inferential Statistics: An Introduction*. Boston: Allyn & Bacon.

Reynolds, H. T. 1977. *The Analysis of Cross-Classification*. New York: Free Press.

Siegel, Sidney. 1956. *Nonparametric Statistics for the Behavioral Sciences*. New York: McGraw-Hill.

Skipper, James K., et al. 1967. "The Sacredness of .05: A Note Concerning the Uses of Statistical Levels of Significance in Social Science," *American Sociologist* 2 (February):16–19.

Sterne, Richard S., 1964. *Delinquent Conduct and Broken Homes*. New Haven, Conn: College & University Press.

Wilkinson, Karen. 1974. "The Broken Family and Juvenile Delinquency: Scientific Explanation or Ideology," *Social Problems* 21 (June): 726–739.

Causal Analysis: The Fascinating Search for Answers

APPENDIX THREE

The fundamental question raised in social research is a causal question: "What produced this effect?" The effect may be delinquency, a high marriage rate, or a free courtship system, but the question always involves the same causal quest. Thus, to understand research reports, such as those included in this or any other sociology book, it is essential that one understand the logic of causal inquiry. This appendix is devoted to a simple exposition of that point. The reader should realize the need to consult other sources, such as those listed at the end of this appendix, for a deeper understanding.

Spuriousness: Correlation and Causation

The first key problem that confronts one in causal analysis is the necessity of distinguishing correlation from causation. One classic illustration of this problem can be seen in the oft-found correlation of high birthrates and the presence of storks. Such a correlation has been reported in several parts of the world. Now, we do not accept storks as causally related to birthrates, and so, although there is a statistically significant correlation between these two variables, we feel the need for some kind of causal explanation. The explanation turns out to be rather simple: Rural areas have many more storks than urban areas and rural areas also have higher birthrates than urban areas. The causal connections, then, are that living in a rural area involves style-of-life factors that produce higher birthrates than are found in urban areas. At the same time, living in a rural area means that there will be more storks present. There is no causal relationship between storks and the birthrate, but rather a third factor (rural-urban residence) determines both the birthrate and the presence of storks. The correlation between birthrates and storks, then, is not an indication of a causal relationship, but rather a result of the common rural-urban residence factor.

One other example may help illustrate the difference between correlation and causation. There is a reasonably high correlation between the murder rate and the size of the separations between the blocks in sidewalks. It is a negative relationship: the smaller the cracks between the sidewalk blocks, the higher the murder rate. Once again, we cannot intellectually accept such a relation as causal, and so we are forced to search for some third factor that may be producing both of the variables that are correlated. The third factor in this example turns

490

out to be the weather. As the weather gets warmer, people get out more and interact more with one another. As a result of such increased interaction, the murder rate goes up. At the same time, the warmer weather causes the concrete to expand, and this narrows the cracks between the blocks. Once again we see that the original correlation was a result of some third factor that was causally related to each of the correlated variables.

Any two variables that are causally related must be correlated with each other; that is, one must vary when the other one does. However, not all variables that are correlated to each other are causally related. We have seen this in the above two examples. Thus there are two types of correlations that we are talking about: (1) correlations that involve causally related variables and (2) correlations that involve variables that are correlated because of some third factor. The second type of correlation, which we have illustrated above, is commonly referred to as a "spurious" correlation. The first type involves causal relationships and is what we are searching for. A causal relation is defined as an invariant relation; that is, when one variable varies, the other *must* also vary, for they are causally connected. In order to find causal variables, one thing we must do is check to be sure that we are not dealing with a spurious type of correlation. Much of sociological analysis is concerned with just such a search.

I will use the relation of broken homes and delinquency to illustrate further the nature of the causal search. I will use hypothetical findings. (The real findings can be found in Chapter 14). Table A3.1 presents the basic "zero-order" correlation between broken homes and delinquency in our hypothetical example. Note in the total table (called "zero order") that there clearly is a positive relationship between broken homes and delinquency rates. For simplicity, I have not calculated any measures of significance or any measures of strength of association. However, it is quite clear that the total table presents a strong relationship and a statistically significant one: 77 percent of those who are "Yes" on broken homes are "Yes" on delinquency (1,020 of 1,320), and 77 percent of those "No" on broken homes are "No" on delinquency (1,020 of 1,320). For simplicity's sake we can assume that "Yes" on delinquency will be defined as having any convictions for juvenile offenses and "No" is having none. Also, "Yes" on broken homes can be defined as being in a home with only one parent, and "No" is being in a home with two parents. Clearly, one can improve upon these crude measures, but that is not our concern here. For the samples, we will assume we sampled randomly chosen households of 1,320 young people with delinquency records and a second sample of 1,320 randomly chosen households of young people without de-

TABLE A3.1

A Case of an Antecedent or Intervening Variable in the Correlation of Broken Homes and Delinquency

				Broken Home	
				No	Yes
(Zero-order table)	Delinquency		No	1,020	300
			Yes	300	1,020

		LOWER CLASS Broken Home			UPPER CLASS Broken Home	
		No	Yes		No	Yes
(First-order partial tables)	Delinquency			Delinquency		
	No	20	200	No	1,000	100
	Yes	100	1,000	Yes	200	20

linquency records. Our chief hypothesis would be: Broken homes influence delinquency rates in a positive direction. Thus, we would expect more people in the delinquent group to be from broken homes.

Now we raise here the same question raised in the sidewalk and stork examples: "Is there a third factor that is causally related to both these variables in a way that indicates that this correlation is spurious?" Here is where one's knowledge of an area is all-important. From such knowledge come the insights as to what third factors might be involved. One such factor is social class. It is possible that social class sets up a style of life that causes a certain tendency toward broken homes and social class may also cause tendencies toward a certain rate of delinquency. More specifically, being from the lower class may expose one to economic and physical hazards that make divorce, death and desertion more likely. These same hazards may create tensions that also lead to delinquency. The upper-class setting may have opposite effects. I have set up this example to indicate that class causes both broken homes and delinquency, and there is no direct causal relationship between delinquency and broken homes. The correlation between these two factors is merely an accidental result of their being related to the same third factor (social class). In short, this explanation argues that social class is the true cause of both the delinquency and the broken homes and that the correlation between those two factors is therefore spurious.

Now, if this interpretation is correct—that social class is the third factor that causally explains the zero-order correlation—then when we divide the sample into groups that contain only one class, the original correlation should disappear. In short, if social class is causing the relationship between broken homes and delinquency, then if it is controlled (that is, if one looks at only one social-class category at a time), the cause will be absent and so the relationship will disappear. I have set up the hypothetical example in Table A3.1 to show exactly this in the two partial tables in the bottom half of Table A3.1. In actual situations, a relationship will probably not completely vanish as it does in this example. There usually is more than one cause of a correlation, and control categories are really only crude controls. But for simplicity, I have made the example extreme.

The reader should look at the two "partial tables at the lower part of Table A3.1. The one on the left is the original relationship as it appears for the 1,320 lower-class respondents, and the right-hand table is the original relationship as it appears for the 1,320 upper-class respondents. Neither table shows any relationship whatsoever. This lack of relationship can be seen by reading down any column or across any row on either table. For example, examine the lower-class table. Of those not in broken homes, 20 of 120 are not delinquent (one out of every six cases); of those in broken homes, 200 of 1,200 are not delinquent (also one out of every six cases). Thus, one out of every six people is not delinquent in both the "Yes" or the "No" categories of broken homes. Clearly, whether an individual is "Yes" or "No" on broken homes is having absolutely no effect on being delinquent. The same can be seen by reading across the rows of this table. Note that 20 out of the 220 respondents who are not delinquent are also not in broken homes (one out of every eleven respondents) and that 100 out of the 1,100 delinquent respondents are not in broken homes (also one of every eleven respondents in this row). Thus, one of every eleven respondents is not in a broken home no matter what the response is to delinquency. Once again the lack of any relationship should be obvious.

How can it be that two tables that show no relationship can produce a relationship when put together? The answer can be easily seen in the two partial tables. Note that in the lower-class table 1,000 of the total of 1,320 cases in this table (76 percent of all cases in this table) are in the cell that indicates being "Yes" on both broken homes and delinquency. This fits with our theoretical explanation above as to how social class could cause both broken homes and delinquency. It is shown that 76 percent of these lower-class respondents are in broken homes and are delinquent, *but* there is no correlation between the two conditions in the table. Thus, it seems that both factors are merely characteristics that go with being a member of the lower class.

Note an analogous situation in the upper-class partial table. (These two tables produced by the control variable of social class are called "partial tables" because they are the two partials that, if put together, produce the zero-order table.) The upper-class table shows that 1,000 or 1,320 respondents appear in the cell that indicates not being in a broken home and not being delinquent. This is just the opposite of the lower-class table. Once again, one can interpret this to mean that being upper class causes one to be unlikely either to be delinquent or to come from a broken home. There is no correlation between these two variables. Instead, the "No" response on both these variables appears as simply a distinctive characteristic of upper-class people.

When one places these two radically different tables together, the correlation is produced by the fact that the lower-class cases cluster in the cell opposite from the upper-class cases. If the total table represented a causal relationship, it would look exactly as it does now. But in this illustration we know it not to be causal, for we know that the "No–No" cell cluster of cases is produced by upper-class people, and the "Yes–Yes" cell cluster of cases is produced by lower-class people. If social class were not causally involved, there would be a more random distribution of lower-class and upper-class cases in each of these two key cells of the table. As it is, the cells are each largely the product of one particular social class, and thus social class reveals itself to be the causal factor.

The full nature of this causal relationship can be seen in Table A3.2, which shows the relation of social class to the two other variables. If our theoretical explanation is correct and social class is causally related to each of these two variables, then a correlation should show up in the subtables in Table A3.2. Both tables indicate a strong relationship in a negative direction. Being high on social class goes with both not being delinquent and not being in a broken home. This is precisely what our theoretical explanation asserted. The figures for the two subtables in Table A3.2 come from the row and column totals (the "marginals") of the two partial tables in Table A3.1. The interested reader can try to work this out. I shall elaborate on the procedure shortly.

One way to further grasp the logic of the above analysis is to take the simple case of the correlation between the storks and the birthrate. You can translate the three tables in Table A3.1 so as to illustrate that situation by simply changing the labels. Change "delinquency" to "birthrates" and change "broken homes" to "storks." Assume the numbers in each cell of the table remain the same. The zero-order table now shows that storks and birthrates are correlated. Then do the same relabeling for the two partial tables also and change the control variable of "social class" to "rural-urban residence." The left-hand table would be rural residence (because it is high on both storks and birth rates) and the right-hand table would be urban residence (because it is low on both storks and birthrates). Do the same for Table A3.2, making the same label substitutes so that the top table is relating birthrates to rural-urban residence and the bottom table is relating storks to rural-urban residence. The rea-

TABLE A3.2

The Relation of Social Class to Both Delinquency and Broken Homes

		SOCIAL CLASS	
		Low	High
Delinquency	No	220	1,100
	Yes	1,100	220

		SOCIAL CLASS	
		Low	High
Broken home	No	120	1,200
	Yes	1,200	120

soning implied by Tables A3.1 and A3.2 should be even clearer using the stork and birthrate example. Since you know this relation cannot be causal, you can more quickly grasp the notion of how a third factor is operating. Go over the table a few times if necessary, looking at it when it represents the storks and birthrate example and then when it represents the broken homes and delinquency example. This should clarify the specifics of the type of causal relationships we are analyzing here.

Intervening Variables

Were spuriousness the only aspect to be checked in causal analysis, life would be much simpler for the social scientist. However, the very check for spuriousness that we illustrated in Tables A3.1 and A3.2 raises another important causal question. This question springs from the fact that in many instances the results shown in these tables can be interpreted differently. For example, we found that social class is correlated with both delinquency and broken homes and that the correlation between delinquency and broken homes disappears when social class is controlled. Our interpretation was that social class is an *antecedent variable* to both delinquency and broken homes. In other words, we assumed that social class comes earlier in time and, through time, produced the two other variables (delinquency and broken homes). However, one could argue that social class is an *intervening variable*. In this case, social class would intervene between broken homes and delinquency. The explanation would be that when a home is broken by death, divorce, or desertion, one's social class tends to be lowered because of the strains involved. This lowered social class then, in turn, produces a higher tendency toward delinquency.

Note that in this new explanation social class temporally comes between the two other variables. The relation between the two other variables in this explanation is *not* spurious; rather, it is simply that social class is a necessary link between them. Broken homes still do not *directly* causally relate to delinquency in this new explanation. Broken homes relate only *indirectly* to delinquency through the action of the intervening variable of social class. This is a quite different explanation than previously given. Nevertheless, the statistical tables that would result if this "intervening" explanation is true are identical to those that result when the "antecedent" view is correct. This is so because in each explanation social class is correlated to both broken homes and delinquency (as shown in Table A3.2), and in both explanations the original correlation will therefore disappear when one controls on social class. If social class is the cause, then when it is controlled there will be no effect. In both cases the relation between broken homes and delinquency depends upon social class for its existence, but the nature of that dependency is quite different in the two explanations. How then does one choose between them?

One key basis for deciding between the two explanations consists of previous knowledge. For example, if one knows from research studies that the experience of death, divorce, and desertion of a mate does not affect one's social-class position, then one can conclude that the view of social class as an intervening variable must be rejected. We do know that divorce, desertion, and death of a husband often lowers the economic resources of the woman. So this is a possible explanation. I would still favor the former explanation wherein the social-class level produced the strain that led to divorce, for we do know that divorce rates are higher for the lower classes. Also, the drop in income that follows the loss of a husband may be temporary and, in part, alleviated by help from relatives. But the reader can see that these two competing explanations need to be carefully examined, and empirical findings can help one choose between them.

In other instances the choice between an antecedent or intervening explanation can be easier. For example, if the control factor is race or genetic sex, it is clear that race and genetic sex cannot be produced by another factor that comes earlier in time. Genetic sex and race, being assigned at birth, are obviously antecedent variables (unless one thinks of them in terms of attitudes associated with being male or female, black or white, and so on). Other variables create much more difficulty than did our social-class example. To illustrate: think of a variable called "number of times in love." This can be viewed as coming earlier in time (antecedent variable) than, say, one's sexual attitudes; or it can be viewed as being a product of such sexual attitudes and itself causing some outcome (being an intervening variable). Only careful research and reasoning can guide one in causal analysis and aid in making one's explanation. [Lazarsfeld (1955) refers to the antecedent case as "explanation" and the intervening case as "interpretation." I do *not* follow his usage in this appendix.]

Interaction

There is one additional way that a third factor (the control variable) can be causally involved in the explanation of a particular correlation. This way differs from the case of an antecedent variable or an intervening variable. A third factor can specify the conditions under which the relationship holds. This type of third factor is called an *interaction variable,* and it literally specifies when the relationship will, and will not, occur. To illustrate this I present Table A3.3. In the lower-class partial table the relationship holds up and is even stronger than it is in the zero-order table. In the upper-class partial table the relationship has vanished and is totally nonexistent. This hypothetical result illustrates interaction. The social-class control specifies the relationship by showing that it holds only for lower-class people.

One could make sense out of this result by contending that only among poorer people does the advent of a broken home have enough of an impact to lead to increased delinquency. In such a case the "third factor" does does not cause broken homes or delinquency but rather interacts with this relationship in such a way as to *specify the conditions* under which the relationship will hold. Since the third factor does not cause either broken homes or delinquencies, if we correlate the control variable (social class) with each of the other two variables, we should find no relationship. In the case of an intervening or antecedent variable, we would expect a relationship, and Table A3.2 showed this to be true. Table A3.4 shows the relationship that derives from the case of interaction, and it is zero. Table A3.4 is derivable from the partial tables in Table A3.3 in ways that I shall comment upon shortly.

TABLE A3.3

A Case of Interaction

		Broken Home						
		No	*Yes*					
	No	1,020	300					
Delinquency								
	Yes	300	1,020					

		LOWER CLASS				UPPER CLASS		
		Broken Home				Broken Home		
		No	Yes			No	Yes	
	No	750	30		No	270	270	
Delinquency				Delinquency				
	Yes	30	750		Yes	270	270	

TABLE A3.4

The Relation of Social Class to Delinquency and Broken Homes

		SOCIAL CLASS	
		Low	High
Broken home	No	780	540
	Yes	780	540

		SOCIAL CLASS	
		Low	High
Delinquency	No	780	540
	Yes	780	540

Such an interaction could work in other ways than that presented. For example, compared to the zero-order table, one of the partial tables could display a weakened, instead of an absent, relationship, and the other one a slightly stronger relationship. In a crude sense, the two partial tables in an interaction situation balance out to make up the total table. If the total table shows a moderate relationship and one partial shows no relation, then the other partial must show a strong relationship (this is the illustration I presented). Or if the total shows a moderate relationship, then one partial could show a moderately weak relationship and the other a moderately strong relationship. One could even have the case wherein the total table shows no relationship, but one partial table shows a positive relationship and the other partial table shows a negative relationship. When the positive and negative relationships are joined in the total table, they cancel each other out. (See Reiss, 1967:58–66 for an example of this. See also Rosenberg, 1968, Chap. 4 for another rare type of interaction.)

The case of interaction is quite different from the case of an antecedent and intervening third factor. In the "intervening" and "antecedent" case the partial tables do not average out to the total table. This is so because in such cases the relationship is not present in the partial tables, but is present in the "marginals" of these tables. By "marginals" is meant the row and column totals. Table A3.2, discussed earlier in this appendix, indicates this fact by showing the relation of the third factor (social class) to both broken home and delinquency. The relationships shown in Table A3.2 are formed from the row and column totals of the two partial tables in Table A3.1. For example, the number of cases in Table A3.2 in the low-class and no-delinquency cell is 220. This number comes from the row total of the no-delinquency cases in the low-class table in Table A3.1. Thus, the tables in A3.2 can be composed from the marginals in Table A3.1. In this sense, the relationships in Table A3.2 are present in the marginals of Table A3.1. Correspondingly, one can look at the relations of social class to broken homes in Table A3.4 and see that a cell like "No" on broken homes and "Low" on social class obtains its 780 cases from Table A3.3. This is done by adding the 750 and the 30 cases in the "No" column of broken homes in the lower-class partial table of Table A3.3. In this case one sees in Table A3.4 that no relationship exists in the tables composed from these marginals. It is in this sense that Lazarsfeld has said that the relationship between two variables exists either in the partials or the marginals. In interaction situations the relation is in the partials tables, and in antecedent or intervening cases it is in the marginals of these tables. Of course, in actual cases it can exist in part in both the marginals and the partials. I am using polar types for simplicity. The reader need not be able perfectly to follow this particular point on partials and marginals in order to understand causal analysis. I present it here for those who are interested, and I suggest the references listed at the end of this appendix for further elaboration.

Summary and Conclusions

First, a brief review: When one finds two variables correlated to each other, one has necessary, but not sufficient, evidence of causality. In order to be causally related to each other, two variables must be correlated, but being correlated does not guarantee causal connection. Third factors may be producing a spurious correlation. An antecedent variable is such a third factor. It comes earlier in time than either of the two variables that are correlated and produces both of these variables. This common relation of the antecedent variable to the two originally correlated variables is what produces the spurious correlation. In such a case there is no causal connection between the two originally correlated variables. In terms of our example, this would be causally diagrammed as follows:

$$\text{Social class} \nearrow^{\displaystyle \text{Broken homes}}_{\displaystyle \searrow \text{Delinquency}}$$

A second type of third factor is an intervening variable. This is a variable that comes later in time than the independent variable in the original correlation, but earlier in time than the dependent variable in the original correlation. This intervening variable is influenced by the independent variable, and the intervening variable, in turn, influences the dependent variable. Here, then, there is an indirect causal connection between the two originally correlated variables, but the connection necessitates an intervening variable. In terms of our example this would be causally diagrammed as follows:

Broken homes ⟶ Social class ⟶ Delinquency

A third type of factor that can occur in causal analysis is an interaction factor (Lazarsfeld calls this "specification"). In this case the new variable acts as a condition of the relationship, and only a certain value or category of that new variable permits the original relationship to occur. In terms of our example this would be causally diagrammed as follows:

Social class (low)   (Specified Conditions)   *Social class (high)*
Broken homes ⟶ Delinquency   Broken homes ⟶̸ Delinquency

If one controls on a third factor and any of these three types of results occurs, one will know how to make causal sense out of such findings. There is, of course, a fourth possibility when one controls, and that is that the original relationship remains unchanged in the partial tables. In such an instance, if one had exhaustively tested for third factors, one would conclude that the original relationship is probably causal and that no other causal connections are apparent. In an actual research situation it would be necessary to try controlling more than just one variable. One would control all the variables that one felt might be causally involved with the original relationship. One would also control more than one variable at a time. I have avoided these complexities for pedagogical reasons.

The basic logic of causal analysis presented here is modeled after that utilized in the physical sciences in their experimental methods. In the social sciences we are more often limited to survey data gathered in a particular locale, and experimentation is more difficult. However, we still strive to fit the experimental model. To illustrate: The independent or causal variable in my illustration (broken homes) was divided into two subcategories of "Yes" and "No." The "Yes" category can be thought of as that containing the stimuli (the experimental group), and the "No" category as the control group. If the variable is causally related, then the "Yes" category will affect the dependent variable (delinquency) differently than will the "No" category. Now, in an experimental setting the experimental group and the control group would have been carefully matched on other variables that might be causally relevant. In survey research this cannot be fully done, and so the use of statistical controls is an attempt to make up for that. By controlling these potentially causally relevant variables, we are eliminating their effect. This is exactly what one does when matching the control and experimental groups on such key variables. If the relationship still holds unaltered even when a variable is controlled, then we know that this control variable is not important. If the relationship is altered, then we decide whether it is an antecedent, intervening, or interacting variable.

Causal analysis is always incomplete. One can always go back further in time to factors that are more distantly causally involved. Also, one can usually find intervening variables if one wants to get specific enough about the full nature of the causal relationship. Where we stop in a causal analysis is largely a matter of what our research problem requires. Beyond this, how far one goes becomes a matter of personal interest and taste. It is customary in sociology to start with an independent variable that represents some type of social fact and end with an effect that also is a social fact (Durkheim 1938; Merton, 1957). One may insert between these two social facts intervening variables of a social-psychological nature. I have generally followed this type of pattern in this book.

There are other approaches to causal analysis utilizing regression analysis, path analysis, and most recently Goodman (1972, 1973), and Bishop et al. (1974), and others have put forth a new contingency table analysis called log-linear analysis (for an illustration see Reiss et al., 1975). However, the basic logic of causality is always the same. Also, in all approaches the causal quest is endless. It is not possible to be certain that one has the full causal picture of any relationship.

I hope that when the reader looks over some of the tables in this book, or elsewhere, he or she will apply this logic of causal analysis. One can do this by asking oneself if the author has analyzed the correlations by utilizing controls and if the findings are carefully explained. When we discussed in Part II that the way love affects sex attitudes differs for males and females, we were reporting an interaction situation. When we discuss in Chapter 12 that interfaith marriages between college students, as compared with interfaith marriages between those having less education, have a smaller increased risk of divorce, we are also specifying the relationship of divorce and interfaith marriage. When we go further and say that much of the higher divorce rate of interfaith marriages results from the young age of the people involved and their social-class background, then we are saying that the relation between divorce and interfaith marriage is to this extent spurious, that it tends to disappear when the social class of the couple and the age of the bride are controlled. As the above examples indicate, we have discussed causal relationships throughout this book. *The key aspect of causal analysis is the attempt to discern if a basic relationship holds up when examined in various subgroups.* The way the relationship alters and whether it alters give us the beginning answers to the causal quest. I hope that by reading this appendix the reader will become more conscious of the process and more capable of critically evaluating and understanding research reports.

Like probability statistics, we utilize causal analysis in our everyday thinking. The mass media constantly present causal statements that bear examination. For example, one frequently hears that since those with a college education earn much more money during their lifetimes than those with less education, it is economically advisable to go to college. One is here assuming that the correlation between college education and financial income is causal. After reading this appendix the reader should immediately think that this relationship would surely have to be controlled by social class. We know that being in an upper social class increases the likelihood that one will go to college and may also increase the likelihood of earning a higher income because of direct and indirect help from one's family. In short, it may be that social class is an antecedent variable to both college attendance and earned income, and that these two variables are only spuriously related to each other. I am not offering this as the answer to the correlation examined, but rather as an illustration of causal thinking in everyday life. To the extent that we understand causal analysis we can more deeply grasp the realities of the social world in which we live. My presentation here is simplified and incomplete. It is intended only as an introduction. The reader should consult the sources listed at the end of this appendix in order to gain a deeper understanding.

References

Asher, Herbert B. 1976. *Causal Modeling*. Beverly Hills, CA: Sage Publications.

Bishop, Y. M., S. E. Fienberg, and P. W. Holland. 1974. *Discreet Multivariate Analysis: Theory and Practice*. Cambridge, MA: Massachusetts Institute of Technology Press.

Blalock, Hubert M., Jr. 1964. *Causal Inferences in Nonexperimental Research*. Chapel Hill, NC: University of North Carolina Press.

_____ (ed.). 1971. *Causal Models in the Social Sciences*. Chicago: Aldine.

_____, and Ann B. Blalock (eds.). 1968. *Methodology in Social Research*. New York: McGraw-Hill.

Duncan, Otis D. 1975. *Introduction to Structural Equation Models*. New York: Academic Press.

Durkeim, Emile. 1938. *The Rules of Sociological Method*. New York: Free Press. (Originally published in 1895.)

Goode, William J., and Paul K. Hatt. 1952. *Methods in Social Research*. New York: McGraw-Hill. (See especially Chaps. 7 and 8.)

Goodman, Leo A. 1972. "A General Model for the Analysis of Surveys," *American Journal of Sociology* 77 (May):1035–1086.

_____. 1973. "Causal Analysis of Data from Panel Studies and Other Kinds of Surveys," *American Journal of Sociology* 78 (March):1135–1191.

Heise, David R. (ed.). 1974. *Sociological Methodology 1975*. San Francisco: Jossey-Bass.

_____. 1975. *Causal Analysis*. New York: Wiley.

Hirschi, Travis, and Hanan C. Selvin. 1967. *Delinquency Research: An Appraisal of Analytic Methods*. New York: Free Press.

Hyman, Herbert. 1955. *Survey Design and Analysis*. New York: Free Press. (See especially Chaps. 5, 6, and 7.)

Kendall, Patricia L., and Paul F. Lazarsfeld. 1950. "Problems of Survey Analysis," in Robert K. Merton and Paul F. Lazarsfeld (eds.), *Continuities in Social Research*. New York: Free Press, pp. 133–196.

Kerlinger, Fred N. 1973. *Foundations of Behavioral Research* (2nd ed.). New York: Holt, Rinehart and Winston.

Lazarsfeld, Paul F. 1955. "Interpretation of Statistical Relations as a Research Operation," in Paul F. Lazarsfeld and Morris Rosenberg (eds.), *The Language of Social Research*. New York: Free Press, pp. 115–125.

Merton, Robert K. 1957. *Social Theory and Social Structure*. New York: Free Press.

Reiss, Ira L. 1967. *The Social Context of Premarital Sexual Permissiveness*. New York: Holt, Rinehart and Winston.

_____, Albert Banwart, and Harry Foreman. 1975. "Premarital Contraceptive Usage: A Study and Some Theoretical Explorations," *Journal of Marriage and the Family* 37 (August):619–630.

Rosenberg, Morris. 1968. *The Logic of Survey Analysis*. New York: Basic Books.

Sonquist, John A. 1970. *Multivariate Model Building*. Ann Arbor, MI: Survey Research Center.

Sterne, Richard S. 1964. *Delinquent Conduct and Broken Homes*. New Haven: Conn: College and University Press.

Wilkinson, Karen. 1974. "The Broken Family and Juvenile Delinquency: Scientific Exploration or Ideology," *Social Problems* 21 (June):726–739.

Zeisel, Hans. 1957. *Say It with Figures*. New York: Harper & Row, Chaps. 8 and 9.

Theory Construction: The Building

of Explanations

APPENDIX FOUR

Appendix 3 introduced the reader to the area of causal analysis. One important way to understand causal analysis is to have an overall grasp of the meaning of theory construction. Theory construction is basically the attempt in science to build explanations. These explanations are most often posed in causal terms. This is so whether what we are explaining is an event in the physical, the biological, or the social universe. A great deal of what has been said in this textbook is theory in the sense of being explanations. When we explain why the higher-educated groups have become more acceptant of premarital sexuality, we are theorizing. We are using concepts, variables, and propositions, and we are interrelating them in various ways to explain the subject we are talking about. We have done the same throughout the book for the various new forms of the family as well as for traditional forms of the family. In Appendix 3 we explained some of the fundamental ways that variables can relate to each other, namely, by one variable being antecedent to two other variables or by one variable intervening between the other two or interacting and specifying the conditions under which the relationship between the two other variables holds. Of course there is also the simple case of two variables that relate to each other without involving other variables. With this as background the work of this chapter is greatly simplified. This section is designed to clarify some fundamental terms that are used in most all scientific writings and to show how they fit into the theory construction that we have informally done throughout this book. I recommend that the reader who wishes to gain elementary insight and who has no background in this area look at the book in the references by Hardy and Jensen (1974). It is by far the most elementary, simple, and straightforward explanation that is available in the literature. I have also included other references for those students who wish to further increase their own awareness.

Parts of Theory and Diagramming

Now let's start with defining some basic parts of theory. The most fundamental part of a theory is what is called a "concept." A sociological concept is a relatively abstract idea that represents a social phenomenon of some kind. Examples of this are present throughout the book: the concept of premarital sexual permissiveness, the concept of group marriage, and the concept of the nuclear family. In fact, at the very opening of the book we take the concepts of the courtship, marital, and family institutions and define them. One particular

500

kind of concept that we are concerned with is what is called a *variable*. The most common kind of variable we deal with is one that ranges from low to high—for example, low to high dyadic commitment or low to high premarital sexual permissiveness. There is another kind of variable that we also deal with where the presence or absence of the variable is really what is being discussed. This could be called a *nominal variable*. The variation in this case is not in degree but in kind, so that one can be male or female, white or black, Republican or Democrat. Thus, nominal variables are also variables but not variables that range from low to high degree but variables that distinguish types or kinds of things or people.

In theory construction these very elementary things called variables are related to each other. It is this interrelationship of two or more variables that is generally called a proposition (or by some people a hypothesis or generalization). This book is of course replete with propositions asserting that Variable A is causing Variable B, such as in our discussion in Chapter 7 about autonomy influencing premarital sexual permissiveness. In Chapter 10, on dyadic commitment, we diagrammed variables such as reward-tension balance and showed its influence in a positive direction on the degree of dyadic commitment. A proposition, then, simply relates two or more variables. You will recall that in Appendix 3, for illustrative purposes, we related the presence of broken homes to the presence of delinquency. Propositions are the raw material of scientific theory, that is, of scientific explanation. It is formulating these propositions, interrelating them, testing them, refining them, testing the refined version, and so on, that forms the essence of the scientific enterprise.

Other very elementary definitions of terms that the reader should be aware of are "dependent variable" and "independent variable." These two terms are very simple to grasp. A dependent variable is a variable that is being influenced by some other variable. The independent variable is the variable that is doing the influencing. In the hypothetical example in Appendix 3 of broken homes and deliquency, the proposition that was being examined was that the presence of broken homes influences the presence of delinquency in a positive direction. In that proposition then, broken homes was the independent variable and delinquency the dependent variable.

There is also the question of the direction of the relation between variables. We have touched upon this in the appendixes and the text, and this should be clear to the reader. If the influence of one variable on another is such that as the independent variable increases so does the dependent variable and as the independent variable decreases so does the dependent variable, then that is called a positive or direct relationship. On the other hand, if an increase in the independent variable influences a dependent variable to decrease and, further, if a decrease in the independent variable causes the dependent variable to increase, then we have what is called a negative or inverse relationship. A positive relationship is represented with a plus sign, the negative relationship with a minus sign.

We can have variables that are nominal variables and are either present or absent, like male–female or black–white, or like our discussion of broken homes and delinquency where we simply spoke of the presence or absence of a broken home or of delinquency. The same positive and negative relationships can be conceived to exist between such variables. For example, we could define one category of a variable as high (like presence of a broken home) and another category as low (like absence of a broken home). This same logic can be arbitrarily applied to any nominal variable.

There are other types of relationships that we should at least briefly comment upon. For example, to illustrate a curvilinear relationship involving our two familiar variables of broken homes and delinquency, we would have to divide broken homes and delinquency each into three categories. In this sense we could divide broken homes into low, medium, or high categories and divide delinquency into low, medium, or high categories. This could easily be done by utilizing the length of time one had been exposed to a broken home as the basis for dividing it into low, medium, and high and by defining delinquency in terms of the low, medium, or high seriousness of the offense. Now in relating these variables, if the low category of broken homes was associated with a low degree of delinquency, and if the high category of broken homes was also associated with a low degree of delinquency, but the middle category of broken homes was associated with a high degree of delinquency, then we would have one common type of curvilinear relationship.

The first part of Figure A4.1 illustrates what a positive relationship between broken homes and delinquency would look like. The second part of this figure indicates what a negative relationship would look like. The third part of the diagram illustrates one type of curvilinear relationship, and you will note in this case the line, instead of being straight, does have an inverted V-shape curve to it. This is but one type of curvilinear relationship. Many others are possible, and the reader is directed to the references at the end of this appendix for further elaboration (Reiss and Miller, 1974; Burr et al., 1979; Burr, 1973).

Figure A4.2 shows how to diagram a positive relationship between broken homes and delinquency. The arrow is the symbol that indicates causality. The plus sign on the line indicates a positive relationship. In the same diagram, farther down, one can see a negative relationship distinguished by the minus sign on the line. A possible notational system for a curvilinear relationship is represented in the third part of Figure A4.2 by a plus sign, a dash, and a minus sign on the line. This symbol indicates that the first part of the curve goes in the form of a positive relationship, pointing diagonally up. The second part of the symbol is a negative sign, indicating a diagonal line pointing down. The two lines together form an inverted V, indicating one particular type of curvilinear relationship. (See Figure A4.1.) The reader can reason out other alternative symbols for curvilinear relationships using the logic of the same notation (see also Burr, et al., 1979: Chapter 2).

As we noted in the last Appendix, one type of relationship that at times needs to be represented is that of an interaction variable. This adds more complexity and requires some new symbolism in a diagram. Figure A4.3 presents this interactive situation using one of the hypothetical examples from Table A3.3 in Appendix 3. In this example broken homes are related to delinquency but predominantly under the condition of low social class. This is presented by the usual line with a plus sign between broken homes and delinquency, indicating that there is a positive influence of broken homes on delinquency. In addition, there is a perpendicular arrow from social class which intersects the basic relation and indicates that social class interacts with this particular relationship of broken homes and delinquency. The symbol parallel to the interacting line is an arrow pointing down and a letter S following it, with both enclosed in a circle. This symbol ⊕S represents the idea that as the interacting variable decreases (which is what the downward pointing arrow indicates), the relationship between broken homes and delinquency is strengthened (which is what the S indicates). The general symbolism used then is as follows: A downward-pointing arrow indicates that the interacting variable decreases; an arrow pointing up means that the interacting variable increases; and an S indicates a strengthening of the relationship being intersected. Thus, a downward-pointing arrow with an S means that as the interacting variable decreases, the relationship it interacts with is strengthened. An arrow pointing up with an S means that as the interacting variable increases, the relationship between the two variables is strengthened. In the example given above, the interacting variable is social class. The symbol ⊕S means that a decrease in social class (going toward the lower social

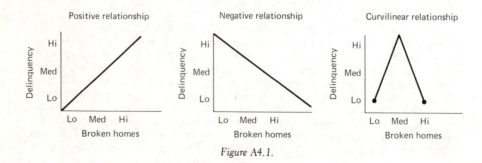

Figure A4.1.

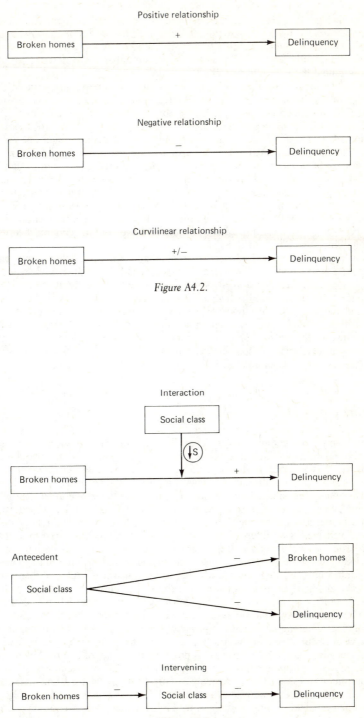

Figure A4.2.

Figure A4.3.

classes) strengthens the relationship between broken homes and delinquency. Conversely, as you go toward the upper classes, the relationship of broken homes and delinquency is weakened. Therefore, the relationship between broken homes and delinquency is specified to hold predominantly for the lower classes. These are rather straightforward concepts and should cause no difficulty to the reader after a little practice.

The reader should know that some authors do illustrate interaction by use of a plus or minus sign on the interacting line instead of our symbol of an arrow with an S. However, there are difficulties with that practice, for the plus or minus sign is used with all diagrams to indicate a positive or negative relationship between *two* variables. In a situation of interaction, that same sign would refer to an effect on a *relationship* and not on a *single variable*. The effect in interaction is to strengthen or weaken a *relationship* and not to just show a positive or negative relationship to a *variable*. Thus the plus or minus sign, if used in interacting situations, would be used differently than it normally is. Giving more than one meaning to the exact same symbol can add confusion. That is why I have introduced our method of representing interaction. This method was developed together with Brent Miller in the course of writing our 1974 article on heterosexual permissiveness (Reiss and Miller, 1974) and is utilized throughout in the recent two volume work on theories about the family (Burr, Nye, Hill and Reiss, 1979).

Also in Figure A4.3 we see a presentation of an antecedent variable that was presented in Table A3.2 in Appendix 3. This is graphically represented in Figure A4.3 by social class displaying a negative relationship to broken homes and also a negative relationship to delinquency. This means that the higher the social class the lower the likelihood of broken homes and the lower the likelihood of delinquency. Intervening relationships were also discussed in Appendix 3 and are diagrammed in Figure A4.3 by placing the social class variable between the broken homes and delinquency variables. We find here a negative relationship of social class to both broken homes and delinquency as was the case when social class was treated as an antecedent variable.

The Theorizing Process

There are many other complexities in causal diagramming that could be gone into here, but the above should be sufficient so that most readers can more fully understand the causal diagrams that they will find in this book and elsewhere. The question may come up as to the value of such technical diagrams. I believe, throughout the course of the book, we have illustrated some of the value. Basically, such diagramming forces one to be clear about the ideas being put into words. For example, one can say that social class has some relationship to broken homes and delinquency. But in what way? In an interaction situation, as an antecedent variable, as an intervening variable, or what? If you are forced to diagram this situation, you are forced to make this answer more explicit. Anyone who has presented a talk has found that some ideas that seemed lucid in one's mind were not so lucid when they were put into words. Further, anyone who has written an article has found that some ideas that were lucid when put into words were not so lucid when written down. Finally, some ideas that seem crystal clear when written down seem not so clear when one attempts to present them in the form of a causal diagram. Causal diagrams force one to gain precision and clarity regarding one's theoretical explanations and that is one of their important values.

Now what about theorizing itself? Is it a simple statement of propositions which we diagrammatically represent? Not exactly. A proposition is a part of theory. The theory itself is an interrelated set of propositions. In short, the relationship of several causal variables is what constitutes an explanation or a theory. Figure 10.6 in Chapter 10 interrelates several variables as part of a theory of dyadic commitment. On a very primitive level, Figure A4.3 presents three variables in three possible ways of interrelating. In that sense, it presents three alternative theories. There are multiple propositions in each of these possibilities—propositions regarding the relationship of broken homes to delinquency as well as propositions regarding the relationships of social class to broken homes and social class to delinquency. In a more developed theory we would point out the necessity of involving a wider variety of other variables that are causally involved with the three variables in these propositions. The interested reader may want to refer to Burr, et al., 1979: Chap. 4, where the propositions on premarital sexual premissiveness presented in Reiss (1967) were clarified and interrelated into a much more advanced theory of premarital sexual premissiveness. The original propositions did have one common dependent variable, namely, premarital sexual premissiveness, but they were not carefully interrelated to one another. Also, some of the terms of the original propositions needed further clarification regarding how they might be measured. This process of clarifying and interrelating propositions is at the heart of theory construction.

Clarity in concepts is another very important feature of theory construction. One must define precisely how one goes about measuring a particular term. For example, the reader may have wondered what is meant by broken homes, how would we measure it? Do we mean people who are in a home where there has been a divorce, a death, a desertion, a remarriage, or exactly how would we measure this particular variable? Thus, another benefit of causal diagramming is that one is forced to clarify terms, for once one writes them down in causal form, people will look at them and think through exactly what a particular concept means and how they will measure that concept. The pressure toward precision of thought is thereby increased greatly by the diagrammatic process.

Finally, we should note that one arrives at particular propositions in two related fashions. One method is called deduction and simply means that you have the idea first and then you deduce propositions from it. For instance, you may have the general idea that attitudes will influence behavior, and then you *deduce* from that that premarital sexual attitudes will influence premarital sexual behavior. Another way of arriving at propositions is by induction. You might find that in the course of research that political attitudes seem to have an influence on political behavior, religious attitudes influence religious behavior, sexual attitudes influence sexual behavior, and from those several empirical findings you *induce* the more general proposition that attitudes influence behavior. Both methods are part of science. Both methods are used in almost all research. One is constantly inducing new propositions from one's examination of previous propositions. One almost always ends a research work with new propositions or new theories that one has induced from the findings. Another scientific researcher would then test those propositions and other propositions that one can deduce from them. That researcher would ultimately also induce some new propositions for further researchers to further test and elaborate upon. This process comprises the never-ending chain of arriving at explanation in science.

Summary and Conclusions

Just as an exercise one might go through several of the chapters of this book and try more formally to pull out the propositions that are put forth there in verbal form. I have deliberately tried to make verbally explicit the propositions that I have discussed throughout the book and to diagram several of them. I tried to clarify terms and to raise issues of theorizing like those we have discussed in this appendix. But there is still more that can be done in this direction in each chapter. In addition, one can pick several of the verbally stated propositions and further interrelate them into theories that can be tested in one's own research.

It would also be an interesting exercise to see if a group of people examining the same research findings would produce the same set of propositions and would integrate them the same way. I feel sure there would be some variation. That variation is the creative element in science. Some people are much more perceptive at both induction and deduction and at generalization. Some people are more knowledgeable of existing theories with which they can interrelate a theory they are working upon. In all of these ways there is a creative and an artistic element in science that we should not lose sight of, for it is a particularly important element in the area of theory construction. Careful scientific checks on computers will test the logic of these creative theories, but it takes professionally trained, imaginative, and knowledgeable human beings to formulate viable theories and to program the computers.

References

Berger, Joseph, Morris Zelditch, Jr., and Bo Anderson. 1966. *Sociological Theories in Progress.* Boston: Houghton Mifflin.

Blalock, H. M., Jr. (ed.). 1971. *Causal Models in the Social Sciences.* Chicago: Aldine.

Burr, Wesley R. 1973. *Theory Construction and the Sociology of the Family.* New York: Wiley.

———, R. Hill, I. Nye, and I. L. Reiss (eds.). 1979. *Contemporary Theories About the Family.* New York: Free Press. (Two Volumes)

Chafetz, Janet S. 1978. *A Primer on the Construction and Testing of Theories in Sociology.* Itasca, IL: F. E. Peacock.

Gibbs, Jack. 1972. *Sociological Theory Construction.* Hinsdale, IL: Dryden.

Hage, Jerold. 1972. *Techniques and Problems of Theory Construction in Sociology.* New York: Wiley.

Hardy, Hazel, and Margaret Jensen. 1974. *Theory Without Pain: A Programmed Instruction Guide to Using Theory.* Provo, UT: Brigham Young University Press.

Mullins, Nicholas C. 1971. *The Art of Theory: Construction and Use.* New York: Harper & Row.

Reiss, Ira L. 1967. *The Social Context of Premarital Sexual Premissiveness.* New York: Holt, Rinehart and Winston.

———, and Brent Miller. 1974. "A Theoretical Analysis of Heterosexual Permissiveness." University of Minnesota, Family Study Center (Technical Bulletin No. 2), Minneapolis.

Reynolds, Paul Davidson. 1971. *A Primer in Theory Construction.* Indianapolis: Bobbs-Merrill.

Zetterberg, Hans. 1962. *Social Theory and Social Practice.* New York: Bedminster.

Bibliography

Aberle, David F., A. K. Cohen, A. K. Davis, M. J. Levy, and F. X. Sutton. 1950. "The Functional Prerequisites of a Society," *Ethics* 60 (January): 100–111.

Ackerman, Charles. 1963. "Affiliations: Structural Determinants of Differential Divorce Rates," *American Journal of Sociology* 69 (July):13–21.

Acosta, Frank X. 1975. "Etiology and Treatment of Homosexuals: A Review," *Archives of Sexual Behavior* 4 (January):9–29.

Acton, William. 1857. *The Functions and Disorders of the Reproductive Organs.* London: J & A Churchill.

Adams, Bert N. 1968. *Kinship in an Urban Setting.* Chicago: Markham.

———. 1970. "Isolation, Function and Beyond: American Kinship in the 1960's," *Journal of Marriage and the Family* 32 (November):575–597.

Albrecht, Stan L. 1980. "Reactions and Adjustments to Divorce: Differences in the Experiences of Males and Females," *Family Coordinator*, Vol. 29 (in press).

Aldous, Joan. 1978. *Family Careers: Developmental Changes in Families.* New York: Wiley.

———, Thomas Condon, Reuben Hill, Murray Straus, and Irving Tallman (eds.). 1971. *Family Problem Solving.* Hinsdale, IL: Dryden Press.

Allardt, Erik. 1975. Att Ha, Att Alska, Att Vara. Om Valfard i Norden (To Have, To Love, To Be: About Welfare in Scandinavia). Lund, Sweden: Argos Forlag AB.

Allport, Gordon. 1954. *The Nature of Prejudice.* Cambridge, MA: Addison-Wesley.

Anderson, Theodore R., and Morris Zelditch, Jr. 1975. A *Basic Course in Statistics with Sociological Application.* New York: Holt, Rinehart and Winston.

Andersson, Ingvar. 1970. A *History of Sweden.* Stockholm: Natur och Kultur.

Araji, Sharon K. 1977. "Husbands' and Wives' Attitude Behavior Congruence on Family Roles," *Journal of Marriage and the Family* 39 (May):309–322.

Archives of Sexual Behavior 7.4 (July 1978). This entire issue is on "Transsexualism." Based on the Fourth International Conference on Gender Identity.

Arling, Greg. 1976. "The Elderly Widow and Her Family, Neighbors and Friends," *Journal of Marriage and the Family* 38 (November): 757–768.

Aronoff, Joel, and William D. Crano. 1975. "A Re-examination of the Cross-Cultural Principles of Task Segregation and Sex Role Differentiation in the Family," *American Sociological Review* 40 (February):12–20.

Asayama Shin'ichi. 1975. "Adolescent Sex Development and Adult Sex Behavior in Japan," *Journal of Sex Research* 11 (May):91–112.

Asher, Herbert B. 1976. *Causal Modeling.* Beverly Hills, CA: Sage Foundation.

Atwater, Lynn. 1979. "Getting Involved: Women's Transition to First Extramarital Sex," *Alternative Lifestyles* 2 (February):33–68.

Bachofen, J.J. 1948. *Das Mutterrecht.* Basel: Benno Schwabe. (Originally published in 1861.)

Back, Kurt. 1972. *Beyond Words.* New York: Russell Sage.

Bahm, Archie J. 1974. *Ethics as a Behavioral Science.* Springfield, IL: Charles C Thomas.

Bailyn, Lotte. 1970. "Career and Family Orientations of Husbands and Wives in Relation to Marital Happiness," *Human Relations* 23 (April):97–114.

Bales, Robert F., and Philip E. Slater. 1955. "Role Differentiation in Small Decision-Making Groups," in Talcott Parsons (ed.), *The Family: Socialization and Interaction Process.* New York: Free Press.

Bane, Mary Jo. 1976. *Here to Stay: American Families in the Twentieth Century.* New York: Basic Books.

Barry, H., and L. M. Paxson. 1971. "Infancy and Early Childhood: Cross Cultural Codes," *Ethnology* 10:466–508.

Barry, Herbert, M. K. Bacon, and I. L. Child. 1957. "A Cross-Cultural Survey of Some Sex Differences in Socialization," *Journal of Abnormal and Social Psychology* 55 (November):327–332.

Bartell, Gilbert. 1970. "Group Sex Among the Mid-Americans," *Journal of Sex Research* 6 (May):113–130.

———. 1971. *Group Sex.* New York: Wyden Books.

Bartz, Karen W., and Elaine S. Levine. 1978. "Childrearing by Black Parents: A Description and Comparison to Anglo and Chicano Parents," *Journal of Marriage and the Family* 40 (November): 709–721.

Bates, Alan. 1942. "Parental Roles in Courtship," *Social Forces* 20 (May):483–486.

Beach, Frank A. (ed.). 1965. *Sex and Behavior*. New York: Wiley.

———— (ed.). 1977. *Human Sexuality in Four Perspectives*. Baltimore: Johns Hopkins University Press.

Becker, Howard, and H. E. Barnes. 1938. *Social Thought From Lore to Science* (two vols.). Washington, DC: Harren Press.

Beckman, Linda J. 1978. "The Relative Rewards and Costs of Parenthood and Employment for Employed Women," *Psychology of Women Quarterly*, Vol. 2, No. 3 (Spring):215–234.

————. 1979. "Fertility Preferences and Social Exchange Theory," *Journal of Applied Social Psychology* (in press).

Bell, Alan P., and Martin S. Weinberg. 1978. *Homosexualities*. New York: Simon & Schuster.

Bell, Daniel. 1960. "Crime as an American Way of Life: A Queer Ladder of Social Mobility," in Daniel Bell (ed.), *The End of Ideology*. New York: Free Press.

————. 1973. *The Coming of Post-Industrial Society: A Venture in Social Forecasting*. New York: Basic Books.

Bell, Howard W. 1938. *Youth Tell Their Story*. Washington, DC: American Council on Education.

Bell, Robert, and Jay B. Chaskes. 1970. "Premarital Sexual Experience Among Coeds, 1958 and 1968," *Journal of Marriage and the Family* 32 (February):81–84.

————, and Dorothyann Peltz. 1974. "Extramarital Sex Among Women," *Medical Aspects of Human Sexuality* 5 (March):10–31.

————, Stanley Turner, and Lawrence Rosen. 1975. "A Multivariate Analysis of Female Extramarital Coitus," *Journal of Marriage and the Family* 36 (May):375–384.

Bem, Sandra L. 1974. "The Measurement of Psychological Androgyny," *Journal of Consulting and Clinical Psychology* 42 (April):155–162.

Benjamin, Harry. 1966. *The Transsexual Phenomenon*. New York: Julian.

Berger, Bennett, et al. 1972. "Child Rearing Practices of the Communal Family," in I. L. Reiss (ed.), *Readings on the Family System*. New York: Holt, Rinehart and Winston.

Berger, Joseph, Morris Zelditch, Jr., and Bo Anderson. 1966. *Sociological Theories in Progress*. Boston: Houghton Mifflin.

Bermann, E., and D. R. Miller. 1967. "The Matching of Mates," in R. Jesser and S. Feschback (eds.), *Cognition, Personality and Clinical Psychology*. San Francisco: Jossey-Bass.

Bernard, Jessie. 1956. *Remarriage: A Study of Marriage*. New York: Holt, Rinehart and Winston.

————. 1974. "Infidelity: Some Moral and Social Issues," in James and Lynn Smith (eds.), *Beyond Monogamy*. Baltimore: Johns Hopkins Press.

————. 1975. "Notes on Changing Lifestyles 1970–74," *Journal of Marriage and the Family* 37 (August):582–594.

Berscheid, Ellen, and Elaine Walster. 1969. *Interpersonal Attraction*. Reading, MA: Addison-Wesley.

————, and George Bohrnstedt. 1972. "Your Body Image: A Questionnaire," *Psychology Today* 6 (July):57–64.

Bieber, Irving, et al. 1962. *Homosexuality: A Psychoanalytic Study*. New York: Basic Books.

Bierstedt, Robert. 1959. "Nominal and Real Definitions and Sociological Theory," Chap. 4 in Llewellyn Gross (ed.), *Symposium on Sociological Theory*. Evanston, IL: Row, Peterson.

Billingsley, Andrew. 1968. *Black Families in White America*. Englewood Cliffs, NJ: Prentice-Hall.

Birchler, Gary R., Robert L. Weiss, and John P. Vincent. 1975. "Multidimensional Analyses of Social Reinforcement Exchange Between Maritally Distressed and Nondistressed Spouse and Stranger Dyads," *Journal of Personality and Social Psychology* 31 (February): 348–360.

Bishop, Y.M., S. E. Fienberg, and P. W. Holland. 1974. *Discreet Multivariate Analysis: Theory and Practice*. Cambridge, MA: Massachusetts Institute of Technology Press.

Blackwell, James E. 1975. *The Black Community*. New York: Dodd, Mead.

Blake, Judith. 1961. *Family Structure in Jamaica: The Social Context of Reproduction*. New York: Free Press.

————. 1971. "Abortion and Public Opinion: The 1960–1970 Decade," *Science* 171 (February):540–549.

————. 1979. "Is Zero Preferred? American Attitudes Toward Childlessness in the 1970's." *Journal of Marriage and the Family* 41 (May):245–257.

Blalock, Hubert M., Jr. 1964. *Causal Inferences in Nonexperimental Research*. Chapel Hill: University of North Carolina Press.

———— (ed.). 1971. *Causal Models in the Social Sciences*. Chicago: Aldine.

_____. 1979. *Social Statistics* (3rd ed.). New York: McGraw-Hill.

_____, and Ann B. Blalock (eds.). 1968. *Methodology in Social Research*. New York: McGraw-Hill.

Blitsten, Dorothy R. 1963. *The World of the Family*. New York: Random House.

Blood, Robert O., Jr. 1955. "A Retest of Waller's Rating Complex,"*Marriage and Family Living* 17 (February):41–47.

_____, and Donald M. Wolfe. 1960. *Husbands and Wives: The Dynamics of Married Living*. New York: Free Press.

Booth, Alan. 1977. "Wife's Employment and Husband's Stress: A Replication and Refutation," *Journal of Marriage and the Family* 39 (November):645–650.

Borland, Dolores M. 1975. "An Alternative Model of the Wheel Theory," *The Family Coordinator* 24 (July):289–292.

Bott, Elizabeth. 1957. *Family and Social Network*. London: Tavistock.

Bower, Donald W., and Victor A. Christopherson. 1977. "University Student Cohabitation: A Regional Comparison of Selected Attitudes and Behavior," *Journal of Marriage and the Family* 39 (August):447–453.

Bowerman, Charles E., and Barbara R. Day. 1956. "A Test of the Theory of Complementary Needs as Applied to Couples During Courtship," *American Sociological Review* 21 (October):602–605.

Bowlby, John. 1951. *Maternal Care and Mental Health*. Geneva: World Health Organization.

_____. 1969. *Attachment*. New York: Basic Books.

_____. 1973. *Separation*. New York: Basic Books.

Bowman, Henry A., and Graham B. Spanier. 1978. *Modern Marriage*, 8th ed. New York: McGraw-Hill.

Bracken, Michael, et al. 1972. "Correlates of Repeat Induced Abortions," *Journal of Obstetrics and Gynecology* 40 (December):816–825.

Bradburn, Norman M. 1969. *The Structure of Psychological Well-Being*. Chicago: Aldine.

Bradford, David L., and Simon Klevansky. 1975. "Non-Utopian Communities: The Middle Class Commune," in Kenneth C. W. Kammeyer (ed.) *Confronting the Issues: Sex Roles, Marriage and the Family*. Boston: Allyn and Bacon.

Brain, Robert. 1976. *Friends and Lovers*. New York: Basic Books.

Bram, Susan. 1978. "Through the Looking Glass: Voluntary Childlessness as a Mirror of Contemporary Changes in the Meaning of Parenthood,"

Chap. 24 in Warren B. Miller and Lucile F. Newman (eds.), *The First Child and Family Formation*. Chapel Hill, NC: Carolina Population Center.

Bremberg, Sven. 1977. "Pregnancy in Swedish Teenagers: Perinatal Problems and Social Situations, *Scandinavian Journal of Social Medicine* 5 (1):15–19.

Brim, Orville G., Jr. 1968. "Family Structure and Sex Role Learning by Children," in Normal W. Bell and Ezra F. Vogel (eds.), *A Modern Introduction to the Family* (2nd ed.). New York: Free Press.

Broderick, Carlfred. 1953. "A Study of the Friend-Family Clusters in a Mobile Urban Population." Honors thesis, unpublished, Harvard University, Cambridge, MA.

_____. 1966. "Socio-sexual Development in a Suburban Community," *The Journal of Sex Research* 2 (April):1–24.

Bronfenbrenner, Urie. 1958. "Socialization and Social Class Through Time and Space," in Eleanor Maccoby, et al. (eds.), *Readings in Social Psychology*. New York: Holt, Rinehart and Winston.

_____. 1977. "Toward an Experimental Ecology of Human Development," *American Psychologist* (July):513–531.

Broude, Gwen J., and Sarah J. Green. 1976. "Cross-Cultural Codes on Twenty Sexual Attitudes and Practices," *Ethnology* 15.4 (October): 409–429.

Broverman, Inge K., S. R. Vogel, D. M. Broverman, F. E. Clarkson, and P. S. Rosenkrantz. 1972. "Sex Role Stereotypes: A Current Appraisal," *Journal of Social Issues* 28.2:59–78.

Brown, Prudence, Lorraine Perry, and Ernest Harburg. 1977. "Sex Role Attitudes and Psychological Outcomes for Black and White Women Experiencing Marital Dissolution," *Journal of Marriage and the Family* 39 (August):549–561.

Brownmiller, Susan. 1975. *Against Our Will: Men, Women and Rape*. New York: Simon & Schuster.

Budd, L. S. 1976. "Problems, Disclosure, and Commitment of Cohabiting and Married Couples." Doctoral dissertation, unpublished, University of Minnesota.

Bukstel, Lee H., Gregory D. Rolder, Peter R. Kilmann, James Laughlin, and Wayne M. Scotell. 1978. "Projected Extramarital Sexual Involvement in Unmarried College Students," *Journal of Marriage and the Family* 40 (May):337–340.

Bumpass, Larry L., and James A. Sweet. 1972. "Differentials in Marital Instability: 1970,"

American Sociological Review 37 (December): 754–767.

_____, and R. Rindfuss. 1979. "Children's Experience of Marital Disruption," *American Journal of Sociology* 85 (July) 49–65.

Burch, Thomas K. 1967. "The Size and Structure of Families: A Comparative Analysis of Census Data," *American Sociological Review* 32 (June):347–364.

Burchinal, Lee G. 1964. "Characteristics of Adolescents from Unbroken, Broken, and Reconstituted Families," *Journal of Marriage and the Family* 26 (February):44–51.

_____, and Loren E. Chancellor. 1962. "Survival Rates Among Religiously Homogamous and Interreligious Marriages," *Iowa Agricultural and Home Economics Experiment Station Research Bulletin* 512 (December):743–770.

Burgess, Ernest W., and Leonard S. Cottrell, Jr. 1939. *Predicting Success or Failure in Marriage.* New York: Prentice-Hall.

_____, and Paul Wallin. 1953. *Engagement and Marriage.* Philadelphia: Lippincott.

Buric, Olivera, and Andjelka Zecevic. 1967. "Family Authority, Material Satisfaction and the Social Network in Yugoslavia," *Journal of Marriage and the Family* 29 (May):325–337.

Burke, Ronald J. 1976. "Some Personality Differences Between Members of One-Career and Two-Career Families," *Journal of Marriage and the Family* 38 (August):453–459.

_____, and Tamara Weir. 1976. "Relationship of Wives' Employment Status to Husband, Wife and Pair Satisfaction and Performance," *Journal of Marriage and the Family* 38 (May):279–287.

Burr, Wesley R. 1970. "Satisfaction With Various Aspects of Marriage Over the Life Cycle," *Journal of Marriage and the Family* 32 (February):29–37.

_____. 1973. *Theory Construction and the Sociology of the Family.* New York: Wiley.

_____, Reuben Hill, Ivan Nye, and Ira L. Reiss (eds.). 1979. *Contemporary Theories About the Family.* Vols. I and II. New York: Free Press.

Burtt, Edwin A. 1954. *The Metaphysical Foundations of Modern Science.* New York: Anchor Books. (Published by Doubleday and Company.)

Calderone, Mary. 1958. *Abortion in the U.S.* New York: Harper & Row.

Calhoun, Arthur W. 1945. *A Social History of the American Family.* New York: Barnes & Noble. (Three volumes; originally published in 1917.)

Campbell, Angus. 1975. "The American Way of Mating: Marriage Si, Children Only Maybe," *Psychology Today* 8 (May):37–43.

_____, Philip E. Converse, and Willard L. Rodgers. 1976. *The Quality of American Life.* New York: Sage Foundation.

Capellanus, Andreas. 1959. *The Art of Courtly Love.* Trans. by John Jay Parry. New York: Ungar.

Carden, Maren L. 1974. *The New Feminist Movement.* New York: Sage Foundation.

_____. 1977. *Feminism in the Mid-1970's.* New York: Ford Foundation.

_____. 1978. "The Proliferation of a Social Movement," pp. 179–196 in *Research in Social Movements, Conflicts and Change* (vol. 1). Greenwich, CT: JAI Press.

Carpenter, Clarence R. 1953. "Life in the Trees: The Behavior and Social Relations of Man's Closest Kin," in Carleton S. Coon (ed.), *A Reader in General Anthropology.* New York: Holt, Rinehart and Winston.

Carter, Hugh, and Paul C. Glick. 1976. *Marriage and Divorce: A Social and Economic Study* (rev. ed.). Cambridge, MA: Harvard University Press.

Castiglione, Baldesar. 1959. *The Book of the Courtier.* Trans. by Charles S. Singleton. New York: Doubleday.

Center for the American Woman in Politics. 1979. 1521 New Hampshire Avenue N.W., Washington, D.C. 20036.

Centers, Richard. 1975. *Sexual Attraction and Love.* Springfield, IL: Charles C Thomas.

_____, Bertram H. Raven, and Aroldo Rodrigues. 1971. "Conjugal Power Structure: A Re-Examination," *American Sociological Review* 36 (April):264–278.

Chafetz, Janet S. 1978. *A Primer on the Construction and Testing of Theories in Sociology.* Itasca, IL: F. E. Peacock.

Chase, Ivan D. 1975. "A Comparison of Men's and Women's Intergenerational Mobility in the U.S.," *American Sociological Review* 40 (August): 483–505.

Cherlin, Andrew. 1978. "Remarriage as an Incomplete Institution," *American Journal of Sociology* 84 (November):634–650.

_____. 1979. "Work Life and Marital Dissolution," Chap. 9 in George Levinger and Oliver C. Moles (eds.), *Divorce and Separation: Context, Causes and Consequences.* New York: Basic Books.

Chesser, Eustace. 1957. *The Sexual, Marital, and Family Relationship of the English Woman.* New York: Roy.

Chester, Robert (ed.). 1977. *Divorce in Europe.* Leiden, Netherlands: Martinus Nyhoff Co.

Child, Irvin L. 1973. *Humanistic Psychology and the Research Tradition: Their General Virtues.* New York: Wiley.

Christensen, Harold T. 1962. "A Cross-Cultural Comparison of Attitudes Toward Marital Infidelity," *International Journal of Comparative Sociology* 3 (September):124–137.

Christenson, Cornelia V. 1971. *Kinsey: A Biography.* Bloomington: Indiana University Press.

———. 1962. "Value Behavior Discrepancies Regarding Premarital Coitus in Three Western Cultures," *American Sociological Review* 27 (February):66–74.

———. 1966. "Scandinavian and American Sex Norms: Some Comparisons with Sociological Implications," *Journal of Social Issues* 22 (April):60–75.

———. 1973. "Attitudes Toward Marital Infidelity: A Nine Culture Sample," *Journal of Comparative Family Studies* 4 (Autumn):197–214.

———. 1978. "Recent Data Reflecting Upon the Sexual Revolution in America," paper presented at the International Sociological Association in Uppsala, Sweden, August 1978.

———, and Kenneth E. Barber. 1967. "Interfaith versus Intrafaith Marriage in Indiana," *Journal of Marriage and the Family* 29 (August):461–469.

———, and Christina F. Gregg. 1970. "Changing Sex Norms in America and Scandinavia," *Journal of Marriage and the Family* 32 (November): 616–627.

———, and Kathryn Johnson. 1971. *Marriage and the Family.* New York: Ronald.

Churchill, Wainwright. 1967. *Homosexual Behavior Among Males: A Cross-Cultural and Cross-Species Investigation.* New York: Hawthorn.

Clanton, G., and L. Smith (eds.). 1977. *Jealousy.* Englewood Cliffs, NJ: Prentice-Hall.

Clark, Alexander L., and Paul Wallin. 1965. "Women's Sexual Responsiveness and the Duration and Quality of Their Marriages," *American Journal of Sociology* 21 (September):187–196.

———. 1964. "The Accuracy of Husbands' and Wives' Reports of Frequency of Marital Coitus," *Population Studies* 18 (November):165–173.

Clark, John P., and Eugene Wenninger. 1962. "Socio-economic Class and Area as Correlates of Illegal Behavior Among Juveniles," *American Sociological Review* 27 (December):826–834.

Clark, Robert A., F. Ivan Nye, and Viktor Gecas. 1978. "Husbands' Work Involvement and Marital Role Performance," *Journal of Marriage and the Family* 40 (February):9–21.

Clarke-Stewart, Allison. 1977. *Child Care in the Family: A Review of Research and Some Propositions for Policy.* New York: Academic Press.

Clayton, Richard R., and Harwin L. Voss. 1977. "Shacking Up: Cohabitation in the 1970's," *Journal of Marriage and the Family* 39 (May):273–283.

Clemmer, Donald. 1958. "Some Aspects of Sexual Behavior in the Prison Community," *Proceedings of the Eighty-Eighth Annual Congress of Correction of the American Correctional Association.* Detroit, MI.

Clinard, Marshall. 1978. *The Sociology of Deviant Behavior.* New York: Holt, Rinehart and Winston.

Cloward, Richard A., and Lloyd E. Ohlin. 1960. *Delinquency and Opportunity.* New York: Free Press.

Coale, Ansley J., et al. 1965. *Aspects of the Analysis of Family Structure.* Princeton, NJ: Princeton University Press.

Cochran, William G., Frederick Mosteller, and John Tukey. 1954. *Statistical Problems of the Kinsey Report on Sexual Behavior in the Human Male.* Washington, DC: The American Statistical Association.

Cogswell, Betty E., and Marvin B. Sussman. 1979. "Family and Fertility: The Effects of Heterogeneous Experience," in Wes Burr, R. Hill, I. Nye, and I. R. Reiss (eds.), *Contemporary Theories About the Family.* Vol I. New York: Free Press.

Cohen, Albert K. 1955. *Delinquent Boys.* New York: Free Press.

Cohen, Jacob, and Patricia Cohen. 1975. *Applied Multiple Regression, Correlation Analysis for the Behavioral Sciences.* New York: Wiley.

Collins, John K., Judith R. Kennedy, and Ronald D. Francis. 1976. "Insights into a Dating Partner's Expectations of How Behavior Should Ensue During the Courtship Process," *Journal of Marriage and the Family* 38 (May):373–378.

Comfort, Alex. 1967. *The Anxiety Makers: Some Curious Preoccupations of the Medical Profession.* London: Thomas Nelson.

Constantine, Larry L, and Joan M. Constantine. 1973. *Group Marriage: A Study of Contemporary Multilateral Marriage:* New York: Macmillan.

Cooley, Charles Horton. 1909. *Social Organization.* New York: Schocken Books.

Coombs, Robert H. 1962. "Reinforcement of Values in the Parental Home as a Factor in Mate

Selection," *Marriage and Family Living* 24 (May):155–157.

Coon, Carleton. 1962. *The Origin of Races.* New York: Knopf.

Crano, William D., and Joel Aronoff. 1978. "A Cross-Cultural Study of Expressive and Instrumental Role Complementarity in the Family," *American Sociological Review* 43 (August):463–471.

Cromwell, Ronald E., and David H. Olson (eds.). 1975. *Power in Families.* New York: Halsted Press.

Cuber, John, and Peggy Harroff. 1965. *The Significant Americans.* New York: Penguin.

Current Sweden. 1975. Göran Beckerus. "To Swedish Men on the Situation of Women University Graduates in Sweden," 67 (April):1–7. Swedish Institute, Stockholm.

———. 1975. Camilla Odhnoff. "Equality is for Children Too," 98 (December):1–6. Swedish Institute, Stockholm.

———. 1975. Maria Salmson. "Free Choice: Theory and Reality: Summary of a Report from the Sex Roles Project, Swedish National Board of Education," 95 (November):1–6. Swedish Institute, Stockholm.

———. 1976. Lars-Gören Engström. "New Penal Provisions on Sexual Offenses Proposed in Sweden," 118 (April):1–7. Swedish Institute, Stockholm.

———. 1976. Bodil Rosengren. "More Time for the Children: A Survey of Recent Developments in the Care of Young Children," 131 (October):1–15. Swedish Institute, Stockholm.

———. 1976. Kajsa Sundström. "Young People's Sexual Habits in Today's Swedish Society," 115 (July):1–8. Swedish Institute, Stockholm.

———. 1976. Birgitta Wittorp and Karin Lund. "Children's Policy in Sweden," 115 (May):1–6. Swedish Institute, Stockholm.

———. 1976. Birgitta Wittorp and Karin Lund. "Some Facts About Swedish Children and Their Parents," 116 (May):1–6. Swedish Institute, Stockholm.

———. 1976. "From Words to Action: Practical Measures to Improve the Status of Women in the Swedish Civil Service," 135 (November): 1–4. Swedish Institute, Stockholm.

———. 1977. Birgitta Linner. "No Illegitimate Children in Sweden," 157 (April):1–7. Swedish Institute, Stockholm.

———. 1977. Birgitta Ologsson. "Child and Juvenile Delinquency in Sweden," 154 (April):1–6. Swedish Institute, Stockholm.

———. 1977. Sven Svensson. "A New Regime After 44 Years," 92 (January):1–8. Swedish Institute, Stockholm.

———. 1977. Siv Thorsell. "Pre-School Education and Child Care in Sweden," 155 (March):1–9. Swedish Institute, Stockholm.

Cutright, Phillips. 1971. "Income and Family Events: Marital Stability," *Journal of Marriage and the Family* 33 (May):291–306.

———. 1972. "The Teenage Sexual Revolution and the Myth of an Abstinent Past," *Family Planning Perspectives* 4 (January):24–31.

———. 1972. "Illegitimacy in the U. S.: 1920–1968," in Charles Westoff and Robert Parke (eds.), *Demographic and Social Aspects of Population Growth.* Washington, DC: Government Printing Office.

Dahlström, Edmund (ed.). 1971. *The Changing Roles of Men and Women.* Boston: Beacon Press.

Danielsson, Bengt. 1956. *Love in the South Seas.* New York: Reynal.

Davidson, Laurie, and Laura Kramer Gordon. 1979. *The Sociology of Gender.* Chicago: Rand McNally.

Davis, Kingsley. 1939. "Illegitimacy and the Social Structure," *American Journal of Sociology* 45 (September):215–233.

———. 1940. "Extreme Social Isolation of a Child," *American Journal of Sociology* 45 (January):544–564.

———. 1947. "Final Note on a Case of Extreme Isolation," *American Journal of Sociology* 50 (March):432–437.

———. 1950. *Human Society.* New York: Macmillan.

———, and Judith Blake. 1956. "Social Structure and Fertility: An Analytic Framework," *Economic Development and Cultural Change* 4 (April):211–235.

Day, Donald. 1954. *The Evolution of Love.* New York: Dial.

De Rougemont, Denis. 1940. *Love in the Western World.* Trans. by Montgomery Belgion. New York: Harcourt, Brace & World.

De Tocqueville, Alexis. 1954. *Democracy in America.* New York: Vintage Books. (Originally published as four volumes between 1835 and 1840.)

Dean, Gillian, and Douglas T. Gurak. 1978. "Marital Homogamy the Second Time Around," *Journal of Marriage and the Family* 40 (August):559–570.

Degler, Carl N. 1974. "What Ought to Be and What Was: Woman's Sexuality in the Nineteenth Century," *American Historical Review* 79 (December):1467–1490.

Delamater, John, and Patricia MacCorquodale. 1978. "Premarital Contraceptive Use: A Test of Two Models," *Journal of Marriage and the Family* 40 (May):235–247.

———. 1977. *Premarital Sexuality*. Madison, Wisc.: University of Wisconsin Press.

Demos, John. 1977. "The American Family in Past Time," Chap. 2 in A. S. Skolnick and J. H. Skolnick (eds.), *Family in Transition*. Boston: Little, Brown.

Denfield, Duane. 1974. "Dropouts from Swinging," *The Family Corodinator* 23 (January):45–49.

Derry, T. K. 1979. *A History of Scandinavia*. Minneapolis: University of Minnesota Press.

Devereux, George. 1955. *A Study of Abortion in Primitive Societies*. New York: Julian.

Diamond, Milton, et al. 1973. "Sexuality, Birth Control and Abortion: A Decision-Making Sequence," *Journal of Biosocial Science* 15 (July):347–361.

Dinitz, Simon, et al. 1960. "Mate Selection and Social Class: Changes During the Past Quarter Century," *Marriage and Family Living* 22 (November):348–351.

Ditzion, Sidney. 1953. *Marriage, Morals and Sex in America*. New York: Bookman Associates.

Dore, Ronald P. 1958. *City Life in Japan*. Berkeley: University of California Press.

Dornbusch, Sanford M., and Calvin F. Schmid. 1955. *A Primer of Social Statistics*. New York: McGraw-Hill.

Doten, Dana. 1938. *The Art of Bundling*. New York: Holt, Rinehart and Winston.

Driver, Harold H. 1961. *The Indians of North America*. Chicago: University of Chicago Press.

Druckman, Joan. 1979. "Premarital Relationships: Interaction Types and Processes," Ph.D. dissertation, unpublished, University of Minnesota.

Duberman, Lucile. 1975. *The Reconstituted Family: A Study of Remarried Couples and Their Children*. Chicago: Nelson-Hall.

Duggan, Thomas J., and Charles W. Dean. 1968. "Common Misinterpretations of Significance Levels in Sociological Journals," *American Sociologist* 3 (February):45–46.

Dumon, Wilfried A. 1978. "When Two Become Three," Paper presented to the International Union of Family Organizations, Vienna (June).

Duncan, Beverly, and Otis Dudley Duncan. 1969. "Family Stability and Occupational Success," *Social Problems* 16 (Winter):273–285.

———, and ———. 1978. *Sex Typing and Social Roles: A Research Project*. New York: Academic.

Duncan, Greg J., and James N. Morgan. 1978. *Five Thousand American Families: Patterns of Economic Progress*. Ann Arbor, Mich.: University of Michigan Press.

Duncan, Otis D. 1975. *Introduction to Structural Equation Models*. New York: Academic.

Durant, Will. 1951. *The Story of Philosophy*. New York: Simon & Schuster.

Durkheim, Emile. 1897. *Suicide*. Paris: Felix Alcan.

———. 1938. *The Rules of Sociological Method*. New York: Free Press. (Originally published in 1895.)

Duvall, Evelyn. 1967. *Family Development* (4th ed.). Philadelphia: Lippincott.

Dyer, Everett D. 1963. "Parenthood as Crises: A Re-study," *Marriage and Family Living* 25 (May):196–201.

Edel, Abraham. 1955. *Ethical Judgment*. New York: Free Press.

Edwards, John. 1973. "Extramarital Involvement: Fact and Theory," *Journal of Sex Research* 9 (August):210–226.

Ehrmann, Winston W. 1959. *Premarital Dating Behavior*. New York: Holt, Rinehart and Winston.

Eliasson, Rosmari. 1971. "Sex Differences in Sexual Behavior and Attitudes Toward Sexuality," Ph.D. dissertation, unpublished, Lund University, Sweden.

Elliot, Thomas D. 1930. "The Adjustive Behavior of Bereaved Families: A New Field for Research," *Social Forces* 8:543–549.

Ellis, Albert. 1949. "A Study of Human Love Relationships," *Journal of Genetic Psychology* 75 (September):61–71.

———. 1972. *The Civilized Couple's Guide to Extramarital Adventure*. New York: Pinnacle Books.

Ellis, Havelock. 1954. *Psychology of Sex: A Manual for Students*. New York: New American Library of World Literature. (Originally published in 1891.)

Emerson, R. M. 1976. "Social Exchange Theory," in A. Inkeles, J. Coleman, and N. Smelser (eds.), *Annual Review of Sociology*. Palo Alto, CA: Annual Reviews.

Engels, Friedrich. 1902. *The Origin of the Family, Private Property, and the State*. Chicago: Charles H. Kerr. (Originally published in 1884.)

Epstein, Cynthia F. 1970. "Encountering the Male Establishment: Sex Status Limits on Women's Careers in the Professions," *American Journal of Sociology* 75 (May):965–982.

Ericksen, Julia A., William L. Yancey, and Eugene P. Ericksen. 1979. "The Division of Family Roles," *Journal of Marriage and the Family.* 41 (May):301–313.

Evans-Pritchard, E. E. 1951. *Kinship and Marriage Among the Nuer.* London: Oxford University Press.

———. 1965. *The Position of Women in Primitive Societies and Other Essays in Social Anthropology.* New York: Free Press.

Farber, Bernard. 1964. *Family: Organization and Interaction.* San Francisco: Chandler.

Farley, Reynolds. 1971. "Family Types and Family Headship: A Comparison of Trends Among Blacks and Whites," *Journal of H man Resources* 6.3:275–296.

Fataburen, Nordiska Museets Och Skansens Årsbok, 1969. 1969. (The Storeroom: Nordic Museum and Skansens Yearbook.)

Featherman, David L., and R. M. Hauser. 1976. "Sexual Inequalities and Socio-Economic Achievement in the U.S., 1962–1973," *American Sociological Review* 41 (June):462–483.

Feldman, Harold. 1966. "Development of the Husband-Wife Relationship," research report, unpublished, Cornell University, Ithaca, NY.

———, and M. Feldman. 1973. *The Relationship Between the Family and Occupational Functioning in a Sample of Rural Women.* Ithaca, NY: Department of Human Development and Family Studies, Cornell University.

———. 1978. "The Effect of Father Absence on Adolescents," unpublished manuscript.

Ferber, Marianne, and Joan Huber. 1979. "Husbands, Wives and Careers," *Journal of Marriage and the Family* 41 (May):315–325.

Ferriss, Abbott L. 1971. *Indicators of Trends in the Status of American Women.* New York: Sage Foundation.

Firth, Raymond (ed.). 1956. *Two Studies of Kinship in London.* London: Athlone Press.

Flavell, John H., et al. 1975. *The Development of Role-Taking and Communication Skills in Children* (2nd ed.). New York: Wiley.

Ford, Clellan S., and Frank A. Beach. 1953. *Patterns of Sexual Behavior.* New York: Harper & Row.

Ford, Kathleen. 1978. "Contraceptive Use in the U.S., 1973–1976," *Family Planning Perspectives* 10 (September/October):264–269.

Forrest, Jacqueline D., Christopher Tietze, and Ellen Sullivan. 1978. "Abortion in the U.S., 1976–1977," *Family Planning Perspectives* 10 (September/October):271–279.

Foss, Dennis C. 1977. *The Value Controversy in Sociology.* San Francisco: Jossey-Bass.

Freedman, Deborah S., and Arland Thornton. 1979. "The Long Term Impact of Pregnancy at Marriage on the Family's Economic Circumstances," *Family Planning Perspectives* 11 (January/February):6–21.

Freedman, Maurice. 1962. "The Family in China, Past and Present," *Public Affairs* 39 (Winter):323–336.

Freedman, Mervin B. 1965. "The Sexual Behavior of American College Women: An Empirical Study and an Historical Survey," *Merrill-Palmer Quarterly of Behavior and Development* 11 (January): 33–39.

Freedman, Ronald, and L. Coombs. 1970. "Social and Economic Correlates of Family Building Patterns in Detroit," Final Report Project No. 312-6-207, unpublished, U.S. Department of Health, Education, and Welfare (plus Appendixes A through F).

French Institute of Public Opinion. 1961. *Patterns of Sex and Love.* New York: Crown.

French, J. R. P., and B. H. Raven. 1959. "The Bases of Social Power," in D. Cartwright (ed.), *Studies in Social Power.* Ann Arbor: University of Michigan Press.

Freud, Sigmund. 1962. *Three Contributions to the Theory of Sex.* New York: Dutton. (Originally published in 1905).

Friedan, Betty. 1963. *The Feminine Mystique.* New York: Dell.

Frykman, Joan. 1975. "Sexual Intercourse and Social Norms: A Study of Illegitimate Births in Sweden, 1831–1933," *Ethnologia Scandinavica: A Journal of Nordic Ethnology* 110–150.

Fuchs-Epstein, Cynthia. 1971. "Law Partners and Marital Partners: Strains and Solutions in the Dual Career Family Enterprise," *Human Relations* 24:549–563.

Fuller, C. J. 1976. *The Nayars Today.* Cambridge, England: Cambridge University Press.

Furtey, Paul H. 1959. "Sociological Science and Problems of Values," in L. Gross (ed.), *Symposium on Sociological Theory.* New York: Harper & Row.

Furstenberg, Frank F. 1966. "Industrialization and the American Family: A Look Backward," *American Sociological Review* 31 (June):326–337.

Furstenberg, Frank F., Jr. 1976. *Unplanned Parenthood.* New York: Free Press.

———. 1978. "Recycling the Family: Perspectives for Researching a Neglected Family Form " paper presented at the American Sociological Association meeting in San Francisco.

Gadpaille, Warren J. 1972. "Research into the Physiology of Maleness and Femaleness," *Archives of General Psychiatry* 26 (March): 193–206.

Galenson, Marjorie. 1973. *Women and Work: An International Comparison*. Ithaca, NY: Cornell University Press.

Gebhard, Paul H., W. Pomeroy, C. Martin, and C. Christenson. 1958. *Pregnancy, Birth, and Abortion*. New York: Harper & Row.

———, J. H. Gagnon, W. B. Pomeroy, and C. V. Christenson. 1965. *Sex Offenders: An Analysis of Types*. New York: Harper & Row.

Gebhard, Paul. 1966. "Factors in Marital Orgasm," *Journal of Social Issues* 22 (April):88–95.

Gecas, Viktor, and F. Ivan Nye. 1974. "Sex and Class Differences in Parent-Child Interaction: A Test of Kohn's Hypothesis," *Journal of Marriage and the Family* 36 (November):742–749.

Geiger, Kent. 1968. *The Family in Soviet Russia*. Cambridge, MA: Harvard University Press.

Gelles, Richard J., and Murray A. Straus. 1979. "Determinants of Violence in the Family: Towards a Theoretical Integration," in W. Burr, R. Hill, I. Nye, and I. Reiss (eds.), *Contemporary Theories About the Family*. New York: Free Press.

Gersick, Kelin E. 1979. "Divorced Men Who Receive Custody of Their Children," Chap. 18 in George Levinger and Oliver C. Moles (eds.), *Divorce and Separation: Context, Causes and Consequences*. New York: Basic Books.

Giallombardo, Rose. 1966. *Society of Women: A Study of a Women's Prison*. New York: Wiley.

Gibbs, Jack. 1972. *Sociological Theory Construction*. Hinsdale, IL: Dryden.

Gibson, Geoffrey. 1972. "Kin Family Network: Overheralded Structure in Past Conceptualizations of Family Functioning," *Journal of Marriage and the Family* 34 (February):13–23.

Gilford, Rosalie, and Vern Bengston. 1979. "Measuring Marital Satisfaction in Three Generations: Positive and Negative Dimensions," *Journal of Marriage and the Family* 41 (May):387–398.

Gilmartin, Brian. 1974. "Sexual Deviance and Social Networks," in James Smith and Lynn Smith (eds.), *Beyond Monogamy*. Baltimore: Johns Hopkins Press.

———. 1975. "That Swinging Couple Down the Block," *Psychology Today* 8 (February):55–58.

———. 1978. *The Gilmartin Report*. Seacaucus, N.J.: Citadel Press.

———, and D. V. Kusisto. 1973. "Some Personal and Social Characteristics of Mate-Sharing Swingers," in R. Libby and R. Whitehurst (eds.), *Renovating Marriage*. San Francisco: Consensus Publishers.

Glass, Shirley P., and Thomas L. Wright. 1977. "The Relationship of Extramarital Sex, Length of Marriage, and Sex Differences on Marital Satisfaction and Romanticism: Athanasiou's Data Reanalyzed," *Journal of Marriage and the Family* 39 (November): 691–703.

Glenn, Norval D. 1975. "Psychological Well-Being in the Postparental Stage: Some Evidence from National Surveys," *Journal of Marriage and the Family* 37 (February):105–110.

———. 1975. "The Contribution of Marriage to the Psychological Well-Being of Males and Females," *Journal of Marriage and the Family* 37 (August):594–601.

———, and Charles N. Weaver. 1979. "Attitudes Towards Premarital, Extramarital and Homosexual Relations in the U.S. in the 1970's," *Journal of Sex Research* 15 (May):108–118.

Glick, Paul C. 1973. "Perspectives on the Recent Upturn in Divorce and Remarriage," *Demography* 10 (August):301–314.

———. 1975. "A Demographer Looks at American Families," *Journal of Marriage and the Family* 37 (February):15–26.

———. 1977. "Updating the Life Cycle of the Family," *Journal of Marriage and the Family* 39 (February):5–13.

———. 1979. "Children of Divorced Parents in Demographic Perspective," *Journal of Social Issues* (in press).

———. 1980. "Who Are the Children in One Parent Households?" Unpublished manuscript.

———, and Arthur J. Norton. 1977. "Marrying, Divorcing and Living Together in the U.S. Today," *Population Bulletin* 32 (October): 1–39.

Glock, Charles Y., and Rodney Stark. 1966. *Christian Beliefs and Anti-Semitism*. New York: Harper & Row.

Glueck, Sheldon, and Eleanor Glueck. 1968. *Delinquents and Nondelinquents in Perspective*. Cambridge, MA: Harvard University Press.

Goldberg, Steven. 1973. *The Inevitability of Patriarchy*. New York: Morrow.

Goldscheider, Calvin. 1971. "Religion, Minority Group Status and Fertility," in *Population, Modernization and Social Structure*. Boston: Little, Brown.

Goldstein, Sidney, and Calvin Goldscheider. 1968. *Jewish Americans: Three Generations in a Jewish*

Community. Englewood Cliffs, NJ: Prentice-Hall.

Golod, S. I. 1969. "Sociological Problems of Sexual Morality," *Soviet Sociology* 8 (Summer):3.

Goode, William J. 1951. "Economic Factors and Marital Stability," *American Sociological Review* 16 (December):802–812.

———. 1956. *After Divorce*. New York: Free Press.

———. 1959. "The Theoretical Importance of Love," *American Sociological Review* 24 (February):37–48.

———. 1960. "Illegitimacy in the Caribbean," *American Sociological Review* 25 (January):21–30.

———. 1961. "Illegitimacy, Anomie, and Cultural Penetration," *American Sociological Review* 26 (December):910–925.

———. 1963. *World Revolution and Family Patterns*. New York: Free Press.

———, and Paul K. Hatt. 1952. *Methods in Social Research*. New York: McGraw-Hill.

Goodman, Leo A. 1972. "A General Model for the Analysis of Surveys," *American Journal of Sociology* 77 (May):1035–1086.

———. 1973. "Causal Analysis of Data from Panel Studies and Other Kinds of Surveys," *American Journal of Sociology* 78 (March): 1135–1191.

Gordon, Michael. 1978. *The American Family: Past, Present and Future*. New York: Random House.

———, and Tamara Haraven. 1973. "New Social History of the Family," *Journal of Marriage and the Family* 35 (special section) (August): 393–495.

Gordon, Thomas. 1970. *Parent Effectiveness Training*. New York: Wyden.

Gottlieb, David, et al. 1966. *The Emergence of Youth Societies: A Cross-Cultural Approach*. New York: Free Press.

Gough, Kathleen E. 1960. "Is the Family Universal: The Nayar Case," in Norman Bell and Ezra Vogel (eds.), *A Modern Introduction to the Family*. New York: Free Press.

———. 1971. "The Origins of the Family," *Journal of Marriage and the Family* 33 (November):760–770.

Gouldner, Alvin. 1968. "The Sociologist as Partisan: Sociology and the Welfare State," *American Sociologist* 3 (May):103–117.

Greeley, Andrew M., W. C. McCready, and K. McCourt. 1976. *Catholic Schools in a Declining Church*. Kansas City, MO: Sheed & Ward.

Green, Richard. 1974. *Sexual Identity Conflict in Children and Adults*. New York: Basic Books.

Greenfield, Sidney M. 1961. "Industrialization and the Family in Sociological Theory," *American Journal of Sociology* 67 (November): 312–327.

Gross, Edward. 1968. "Plus ca change. . . ? The Sexual Structure of Occupations Over Time," *Social Problems* 16 (Fall):198–208.

Guttman, Louis. 1950. "The Bases for Scalogram Analysis," in Samuel A. Stouffer, et al., *Measurement and Prediction*. Princeton, NJ: Princeton University Press.

Haas, Linda. 1978. "Sexual Equality in the Family: A Study of the Extent and Determinants of Role-Sharing Behavior in Sweden." Paper presented at the Ninth International Sociological Association meetings in Uppsala, Sweden.

Hage, Jerold. 1972. *Techniques and Problems of Theory Construction in Sociology*. New York: Wiley.

Hallberg, Edmund D. 1978. *The Gray Itch: The Male Menapause Syndrome*. New York: Stein & Day.

Hammond, Boone. 1965. "The Contest System: A Survival Technique," Master's thesis, unpublished, Washington University, St. Louis, MO.

Hammond, Dorothy, and Alta Jablow. 1975. "Women: Their Familial Roles in Traditional Societies." A Module of Cummings Publishing Co. Menlo Park, CA.

Hampe, Gary, and Howard Ruppel. 1974. "The Measurement of Premarital Sexual Permissiveness; A Comparison of Two Guttman Scales," *Journal of Marriage and the Family* 36 (August):451–464.

Handbook on Sex Instruction in Swedish Schools. 1956. Royal Board of Education in Sweden. Stockholm, Sweden. (English translation, 1964.)

Hardy, Hazel, and Margaret Jensen. 1974. *Theory Without Pain: A Programmed Instruction Guide to Using Theory*. Provo, UT: Brigham Young University Press.

Hardy, Kenneth R. 1964. "An Appetitional Theory of Sexual Motivation," *Psychological Review* 71 (January):1–18.

Harlow, Harry F. 1958. "The Nature of Love," *American Psychologist* 13 (December):673–685.

———. 1962. "The Heterosexual Affection System in Monkeys," *American Psychologist* 17 (January):1–9.

———, and Margaret K. Harlow. 1962. "Social Deprivation in Monkeys," *Scientific American* 206 (November):1–10.

Harry, Joseph. 1976. "Evolving Sources of Happiness for Men Over the Life Cycle: A Structural

Analysis," *Journal of Marriage and the Family* 38 (May):289–296.

Hartley, Ruth E. 1960. "Children's Concepts of Male and Female Roles," *Merrill-Palmer Quarterly* 6 (January):83–91.

Hartley, Shirley F. 1975. *Illegitimacy*. Berkeley: University of California Press.

Hartung, Frank. 1954. "Cultural Relativity and Moral Judgments," *Philosophy of Science* 11 (April):118–126.

Havens, Elizabeth M. 1973. "Women, Work, and Wedlock: A Note on Female Marital Patterns in the U.S.," *American Journal of Sociology* 78 (January):975–981.

Heckman, Norma A., Rebecca Bryson, and Jeff B. Bryson. 1977. "Problems of Professional Couples: A Content Analysis," *Journal of Marriage and the Family* 39 (May):323–330.

Heer, David M. 1958. "Dominance and the Working Wife," *Social Forces* 36 (May):341–347.

———. 1962. "The Trend of Interfaith Marriages in Canada, 1922–1957," *American Sociological Review* 27 (April):245–250.

———. 1963. "Dominance and the Working Wife," in F. Ivan Nye and Lois W. Hoffman (eds.), *The Employed Mother in America*. Skokie, IL: Rand McNally.

———. 1963. "The Measurement and Basis of Family Power: An Overview," *Journal of Marriage and the Family* 25 (May):133–139.

———. 1966. "Negro-White Marriage in the United States," *Journal of Marriage and the Family* 28 (August):262–273.

———. 1974. "The Prevalence of Black-White Marriage in the U.S., 1960 and 1970," *Journal of Marriage and the Family* 36 (May):246–258.

Heilbrun, Alfred B. 1965. "An Empirical Test of the Modeling Theory of Sex Role Learning," *Child Development* 36 (September):789–799.

Heise, David R. 1967. "Cultural Patterning of Sexual Socialization," *American Sociological Review* 32 (October):726–739.

——— (ed.). 1974. *Sociological Methodology 1975*. San Francisco: Jossey-Bass.

———. 1975. *Causal Analysis*. New York: Wiley.

Heiss, Jerold S. 1960. "Premarital Characteristics of the Intermarried," *American Sociological Review* 25 (February):47–55.

———. 1962. "Degree of Intimacy and Male-Female Interaction," *Sociometry* 25 (June):197–208.

Henze, Laura F., and John W. Hudson. 1974. "Personal and Family Characteristics of Cohabiting and Noncohabiting College Students,"

Journal of Marriage and the Family 36 (November):722–737.

Herberg, Will. 1956. *Protestant-Catholic-Jew*. New York: Doubleday.

Herbert, P. G. 1952. "The Measurement of Family Relationships," *Human Relations* 5:3–35.

Herman, Sondra R. 1972. "Sex Roles and Sexual Attitudes in Sweden: The New Phase," *Massachusetts Review* (Winter/Spring):45–64.

Hicks, Mary, and Marilyn Platt. 1970. "Marital Happiness and Stability: A Review of Research in the Sixties," *Journal of Marriage and the Family* 32 (November):553–575.

Hill, Charles T., Zick Ruben, and Letitia Anne Peplou. 1976. "Breakups Before Marriage: The End of 103 Affairs," *Journal of Social Issues* 32 (January):147–168.

Hill, Reuben. 1949. *Families Under Stress*. New York: Harper & Row.

———. 1966. "The Significance of the Family in Population Research," in William T. Liu (ed.), *Family and Fertility*. Notre Dame, IN: University of Notre Dame Press.

———. 1970. *Family Development in Three Generations*. Cambridge, MA: Schenkman.

———, and Roy H. Rodgers. 1964. "The Developmental Approach," in Harold T. Christensen (ed.), *Handbook of Marriage and the Family*. Skokie, IL: Rand McNally.

———, and Joan Aldous. 1969. "Socialization for Marriage and Parenthood," in David A. Goslin (ed.), *Handbook of Socialization Theory and Research*. Skokie, IL: Rand McNally.

Hill, W. W. 1935. "The Status of the Hermaphrodite and Transvestite in Navaho Culture," *American Anthropologist* 37:273–279.

Hiltz, Starr R. 1978. "Widowhood: A Roleless Role," *Marriage and Family Review* 1 (November/December):1–10.

Himes, Norman E. 1963. *Medical History of Contraception*. New York: Gamut Press.

Hinkle, Dennis E., and Michael J. Sporakowski. 1975. "Attitudes Toward Love: A Reexamination," *Journal of Marriage and the Family* 37 (November):764–768.

Hirschi, Travis, and Hanan C. Selvin. 1967. *Delinquency Research: An Appraisal of Analytic Methods*. New York: Free Press.

Hobbs, Daniel F. 1965. "Parenthood as Crisis: A Third Study," *Journal of Marriage and the Family* 27 (August):367–372.

———. 1968. "Transition to Parenthood: A Replication and an Extension," *Journal of Marriage and the Family* 30 (August):413–418.

———, and Sue Peck Cole. 1976. "Transition to

Parenthood: A Decade Replication," *Journal of Marriage and the Family* 38 (November):723–731.

Hoffman, Lois W., and Martin L. Hoffman. 1973. "The Value of Children to Parents," Chap. 2 in James T. Fawcett (ed.), *Psychological Perspectives on Population*. New York: Basic Books.

———, and F. Ivan Nye. 1974. *Working Mothers*. San Francisco: Jossey-Bass.

Hollingshead, August B. 1949. *Elmtown's Youth*. New York: Wiley.

Holmstrom, Lynda L. 1972. *The Two-Career Family*. Cambridge, MA: Schenkman.

Holter, Harriet. 1970. *Sex Roles and Social Structure*. Oslo, Norway: University Publishers.

Homans, George. 1961. *Social Behavior: Its Elementary Forms*. New York: Harcourt, Brace & World.

Hooker, Evelyn. 1965. "Male Homosexuals and Their 'Worlds'," in Judd Marmor (ed.), *Sexual Inversion: The Multiple Roots of Homosexuality*. New York: Basic Books.

Hornick, Joseph D. 1978. "Premarital Sexual Attitudes and Behavior," *Sociological Quarterly* 19 (Autumn):534–544.

———, Louise Doran, and Susan H. Crawford. 1979. "Premarital Contraceptive Usage Among Male and Female Adolescents," *Family Coordinator* 28 (April):181–190.

Houseknecht, Sharon K. 1977. "Reference Group Support for Voluntary Childlessness: Evidence for Conformity," *Journal of Marriage and the Family* 38 (May):285–292.

———. 1978. "Voluntary Childlessness," *Alternative Lifestyles* 1 (August):379–402.

———. 1979. "Childlessness and Marital Adjustment," *Journal of Marriage and the Family* 41 (May):259–265.

Hudson, John W., and Laura F. Henze. 1969. "Campus Values and Mate Selection: A Replication," *Journal of Marriage and the Family* 31 (November):772–775.

Huff, Darrell. 1954. *How to Lie with Statistics*. New York: Norton.

———. 1959. *How to Take a Chance*. New York: Norton.

Humphreys, Laud. 1970. *Tearoom Trade*. Chicago: Aldine.

Hunt, Morton M. 1959. *The Natural History of Love*. New York: Knopf.

———. 1969. *The Affair*. New York: World Publishers.

———.1974. *Sexual Behavior in the 1970's*. Chicago: Playboy Press.

Huston, Ted L. (ed.). 1974. *Foundations of Interpersonal Attraction*. New York: Academic.

Hyman, Herbert. 1955. *Survey Design and Analysis*. New York: Free Press.

Ihinger, Marilyn. 1975. "The Referee Role and Norms of Equity: A Contribution Toward a Theory of Sibling Conflict," *Journal of Marriage and the Family* 37 (August):515–525.

Inkeles, Alex. 1960. "Industrial Man: The Relation of Status to Experience, Perception, and Value," *American Journal of Sociology* 66 (July):1–31.

Irwin, Theodore. 1975. "Male Menopause: Crises in the Middle Years," Public Affairs Pamphlets, No. 526. New York.

Jacobson, Paul H. 1959. *American Marriage and Divorce*. New York: Holt, Rinehart and Winston.

Jaffe, Frederick S., and Debrah Oakley. 1978. "Observations on Birth Planning in China, 1977," *Family Planning Perspectives* 10 (March/April):101–108.

Johnson, Michael P. 1969. "Courtship and Commitment: A Study of Cohabitation on a University Campus," Master's thesis, unpublished, University of Iowa, Iowa City.

Johnson, Miriam. 1963. "Sex Role Learning in the Nuclear Family," *Child Development* 34 (June):319–333.

Johnson, Nan E., and C. Shannon Stokes. 1976. "Family Size in Successive Generations: The Effects of Birth Order, Intergenerational Change in Lifestyle and Familial Satisfaction," *Demography* 13 (May):175–187.

Johnson, P. B. 1974. "Social Power and Sex-Role Stereotyping," Ph.D. dissertation. University of California, Los Angeles.

Johnson, Ralph E. 1970. "Extramarital Sexual Intercourse: A Methodological Note," *Journal of Marriage and the Family* 32 (May):279–283.

———. 1970. "Some Correlates of Extramarital Coitus," *Journal of Marriage and the Family* 32 (August):449–457.

Jourard, Sidney M. 1968. *Self Disclosure: An Experimental Analysis of the Transparent Self*. New York: Wiley.

———. 1971. *The Transparent Self* (2nd ed.). New York: Van Nostrand.

Journal of Marriage and the Family. November 1978. This entire issue is devoted to studies of the black family.

Jowett, Benjamin (trans.). 1937. *The Dialogues of Plato*. New York: Random House.

Juhlin, Lennart, and G. Danielsson (eds.). 1975.

Genital Infections. Stockholm: Almqvist and Wiksell.

Jurich, Anthony P., and Julie A. Jurich. 1974. "The Effect of Cognitive Moral Development Upon the Selection of Premarital Sexual Standards," *Journal of Marriage and the Family* 36 (November): 736–741.

Kagan, Jerome. 1964. "Acquisition and Significance of Sex Typing and Sex Role Identity," in Martin L. Hoffman and Lois W. Hoffman (eds.), *Review of Child Development Research.* New York: Sage Foundation.

———. 1978. *The Growth of the Child: Reflections on Human Development.* New York: Norton

———, and Howard A. Moss. 1962. *Birth to Maturity.* New York: Wiley

Kälvemark, Ann Sofie. 1978. "Aktenskap och familj i Sverige i historiskt perspektiv" (Marriage and Family in Sweden in Historical Perspective), in *History Teachers Association Annual:*23–31. Stockholm.

———. 1978. "Den Ogifta modern i Sverige i Historiskt Perspektiv" (Present Day Singlehood in Sweden in Historical Perspective), In *Historical Journal:*83–101. Stockholm.

Kalvesten, Anna Lisa. 1962. *Social Structure of Sweden* (mimeo). Stockholm: Swedish Institute.

Kandel, Denise, and Gerald S. Lesser. 1969. "Parent-Adolescent Relationships and Adolescent Independence in the United States and Denmark," *Journal of Marriage and the Family* 31 (May): 348–358.

Kanter, Rosabeth. 1972. *Commitment and Community.* Cambridge, MA: Harvard University Press.

———. 1977. *Men and Women of the Corporation.* New York: Basic Books.

Kantner, John F., and Melvin Zelnik. 1972. "Sexual Experience of Young Unmarried Women in the United States," *Family Planning Perspectives* 4 (October):9–18.

Kaplan, Helen Singer. 1974. *The New Sex Therapy.* New York: Brunner/Mazel.

Katz, Joseph, et al. 1968. *No Time for Youth.* San Francisco: Jossey-Bass.

Kelley, Jonathan. 1978. "Sexual Permissiveness: Evidence for a Theory," *Journal of Marriage and the Family* 40 (August):455–468.

Kelley, Robert K. 1979. *Courtship, Marriage and the Family* (3rd ed.). New York: Harcourt.

Kendall, Patricia L., and Paul F. Lazarsfeld. 1950. "Problems of Survey Analysis," in Robert K. Merton and Paul F. Lazarsfeld (eds.), *Continuities in Social Research.* New York: Free Press.

Kennedy, Robert. 1973. *The Irish.* Berkeley: University of California Press.

Kerckoff, Alan C. 1972. *Socialization and Social Class.* Englewood Cliffs, NJ: Prentice-Hall.

———, and Keith E. Davis. 1962. "Value Consensus and Need Complementarity in Mate Selection," *American Sociological Review* 27 (June):295–303.

Kerlinger, Fred N. 1973. *Foundations of Behavioral Research* (2nd ed.). New York: Holt, Rinehart and Winston.

———, and Elazar J. Pedhazur. 1973. *Multiple Regression in Behavioral Research.* New York: Holt, Rinehart and Winston.

Kessen, William (ed.). 1975. *Childhood in China.* New Haven, CT: Yale University Press.

Kiefer, Otto. 1934. *Sexual Life in Ancient Rome.* London: Routledge.

King, Karl, Jack O. Balswick, and Ira E. Robinson. 1977. "The Continuing Premarital Sexual Revolution Among College Females," *Journal of Marriage and the Family* 39 (August):455–459.

Kinsey, Alfred C., Wardell Pomeroy, and Clyde Martin. 1948. *Sexual Behavior in the Human Male.* Philadelphia: Saunders.

———, and Paul Gebhard. 1953. *Sexual Behavior in the Human Female.* Philadelphia: Saunders.

Kirkpatrick, Clifford, and Theodore Caplow. 1945. "Courtship in a Group of Minnesota Students," *American Journal of Sociology* 51 (September):114–125.

———, and Charles Hobart. 1954. "Disagreement, Disagreement Estimate, and Nonempathic Imputations for Intimacy Groups Varying from Favorite Date to Married," *American Sociological Review* 19(February):10–19.

Klatzky, Sheila R. 1972. *Patterns of Contact with Relatives.* Washington, D.C.: American Sociological Association.

Kobrin, Frances E. 1976. "The Fall of Household Size and the Rise of the Primary Individual in the U.S.," *Demography* 13 (February): 127–138.

———. 1976. "The Primary Individual and the Family: Changes in Living Arrangements in the U.S. Since 1940," *Journal of Marriage and the Family* 39 (May):233–239.

———, and Gerry E. Hendershot. 1977. "Do Family Ties Reduce Mortality? Evidence from the United States, 1966–68," *Journal of Marriage and the Family* 39 (November):737–745.

Kohn, Melvin L. 1959. "Social Class and Parental Values," *American Journal of Sociology* 64 (January):337–351.

———. 1963. "Social Class and Parent-Child Relationships: An Interpretation," *American Journal of Sociology* 68 (January): 471–480.

———. 1969. *Class and Conformity*. Homewood, IL: Dorsey Press.

———. 1971. "Bureaucratic Man: A Portrait and an Interpretation," *American Sociological Review* 36 (June):461–474.

———. 1977. *Class and Conformity: A Study in Values* (2nd ed.). Chicago: University of Chicago Press.

———, and Carmi Schooler. 1973. "Occupational Experience and Psychological Functioning: An Assessment of Reciprocal Effects," *American Sociological Review* 38 (February):97–118.

———, and ———. 1978. "The Reciprocal Effects of the Substantive Complexity of Work and Intellectual Flexibility: A Longitudinal Assessment," *American Journal of Sociology* 84 (July):24–52.

Kolb, Trudy M., and Murray A. Straus. 1974. "Marital Power and Marital Happiness in Relation to Problem-Solving Ability," *Journal of Marriage and the Family* 36 (November):756–766.

Komarovsky, Mirra. 1964. *Blue-Collar Marriage*. New York: Random House.

———. 1974. "Patterns of Self-Disclosure of Male Undergraduates," *Journal of Marriage and the Family* 36 (November):677–686.

———. 1976. *Dilemmas of Masculinity*. New York: Norton.

Kraemer, Helena C., et al. 1976. "Orgasmic Frequency and Plasma Testosterone Levels in Normal Human Males," *Archives of Sexual Behavior* 5 (March):125–132.

Krafft-Ebing, Richard von. 1965. *Psychopathia Sexualis: A Medico-Forensic Study* (trans. Harry E. Wedeck). New York: Putnam. (Originally published in 1886.)

Krain, Mark, Jeffery Bagford, and Drew Cannon. 1975. "Communication Among Premarital Couples at Three Stages of Dating," *Journal of Marriage and the Family* 37 (August):609–618.

———, et al. 1977. "Rating-Dating or Simply Prestige Homogamy?", *Journal of Marriage and the Family* 39 (November):663–677.

Kramer, Judith R., and Seymour Leventman. 1961. *Children of the Gilded Ghetto*. New Haven, CT: Yale University Press.

Kuhn, Manford H. 1955. "Kinsey's View of Human Behavior," in Jerome Himelhoch and Sylvia F. Fava (eds.), *Sexual Behavior in American Society*. New York: Norton.

Labovitz, Sanford. 1968. "Criteria for Selecting a Significance Level: A Note on the Sacredness

of .05," *American Sociologist* 3 (August):220–222.

Landis, Judson T. 1949. "Marriages of Mixed and Non-Mixed Religious Faith," *American Sociological Review* 14 (August):401–407.

———. 1962. "A Comparison of Children from Divorced and Nondivorced Unhappy Marriages," *Family Life Coordinator* 21 (July):61–65.

Landy, David. 1959. *Tropical Childhood*. Chapel Hill, NC: University of North Carolina Press.

Larson, Richard F., and Gerald R. Leslie. 1968. "Prestige Influences in Serious Dating Relationships of University Students," *Social Forces* 47 (December):195–202.

Laslett, Peter. 1972. *Household and Family in Past Time*. New York: Cambridge University Press.

———. 1977. *Family Life and Illicit Love in Earlier Generations*. Cambridge, England: Cambridge University Press.

Lavori, N. 1976. *Living Together, Married or Single: Your Legal Rights*. New York: Harper & Row.

Laws, Judith Long, and Pepper Schwartz. 1977. *Sexual Scripts: The Social Construction of Female Sexuality*. New York: Holt, Rinehart and Winston.

Lazarsfeld, Paul F. 1955. "Interpretation of Statistical Relations as a Research Operation," in Paul F. Lazarsfeld and Morris Rosenberg (eds.), *The Language of Social Research*. New York: Free Press.

Lee, David. 1968. "Marital Disruption Among Medical Faculty and Liberal Arts Faculty," Ph.D. dissertation, unpublished, University of Iowa, Iowa City.

Lee, Gary. 1975. "The Problem of Universals in Comparative Research: An Attempt at Clarification," *Journal of Comparative Family Studies* 6 (Spring):89–100.

———. 1977. *Family Structure and Interaction: A Comparative Analysis*. Philadelphia: Lippincott.

Lee, John. 1974. *Colours of Love*. Toronto: New Press.

Lecky, William E. H. 1955. *History of European Morals from Augustus to Charlemagne*. New York: Braziller.

Leik, Robert K. 1963. "Instrumentality and Emotionality in Family Interaction," *Sociometry* 26 (June):131–145.

LeMasters, Ersel E. 1957. "Parenthood as Crises," *Marriage and Family Living* 19 (November):352–355.

Lemert, Edwin M. 1967. *Human Deviance, Social Problems and Social Control.* Englewood Cliffs, NJ: Prentice-Hall.

Lenski, Gerhard. 1961. *The Religious Factor: A Sociological Study of Religion's Impact on Politics, Economics, and the Family Life.* New York: Doubleday.

Levine, Gene N., and Leila A. Sussmann. 1960. "Social Change and Sociability in Fraternity Pledging," *American Journal of Sociology* 65 (January):391–399.

Levine, James A. 1976. *Who Will Raise the Children?* Philadelphia: Lippincott.

Levinger, George. 1964. "Task and Social Behavior in Marriage," *Sociometry* 27 (December):433–446.

———. 1966. "Systematic Distortion in Spouses' Reports of Preferred and Actual Sexual Behavior," *Sociometry* 29 (September):291–299.

———. 1975. "Marital Cohesiveness and Dissolution: An Integrative Review," *Journal of Marriage and the Family* 27 (February):19–28.

———, D. J. Senn, and B. W. Jorgensen. 1970. "Progress Toward Permanence in Courtship: A Test of the Kerckhoff-Davis Hypothesis," *Sociometry* 33 (December):427–433.

———, and Oliver C. Moles (eds.). 1979. *Divorce and Separation: Context, Causes and Consequences.* New York: Basic Books.

Levinson, Daniel J. 1978. *The Seasons of a Man's Life.* New York: Knopf.

Lévi-Strauss, Claude. 1969. *The Elementary Structures of Kinship.* Boston: Beacon.

Levitt, Eugene E., and Albert D. Klassen, Jr. 1974. "Public Attitudes Toward Homosexuality: Part of the 1970 National Survey by the Institute for Sex Research," *Journal of Homosexuality* 1.1:29–43.

Levy, Marion J., Jr., and Lloyd A. Fallers. 1959. "The Family: Some Comparative Considerations," *American Anthropologist* 61 (August):647–651.

Lewin, Bo. 1979. *Om Ogift Samboende i Sverige* (On Unmarried Cohabitation in Sweden). Ph.D. Dissertation. Uppsala University, Sweden.

Lewis, Robert A. 1973. "A Longitudinal Test of a Developmental Framework for Premarital Dyadic Formation," *Journal of Marriage and the Family* 35 (February):16–27.

———. 1973. "Social Reaction and the Formation of Dyads: An Interactional Approach to Mate Selection," *Sociometry* 36 (September): 409–419.

Libby, Roger. 1973. "Extramarital and Comarital Sex," in R. Libby and R. Whitehurst (eds.),

Renovating Marriage. San Francisco: Consensus Publishers.

———, and Robert Whitehurst (eds.). 1973. *Renovating Marriage.* San Francisco: Consensus Publishers.

———, and ——— (eds.). 1977. *Marriage and Alternatives.* Glenview, IL: Scott, Foresman.

———, Louis Gray, and Mervin White. 1978. "A Test and Reformulation of Reference Groups and Role Correlates of Premarital Sexual Permissiveness Theory," *Journal of Marriage and the Family* 40 (February):79–92.

Licht, Hans. 1953. *Sexual Life in Ancient Greece.* New York: Barnes & Noble.

Liljeström, Rita, G. F. Mellström, and G. L. Svensson. 1975. *Sex Roles in Transition.* Stockholm: Swedish Institute.

Linner, Birgitta. 1967. *Sex and Society in Sweden.* New York: Random House.

Linton, Ralph. 1936. *The Study of Man.* New York: Appleton.

———. 1955. *The Tree of Culture.* New York: Knopf.

Lipset, Seymour M. 1960. *Political Man: The Social Bases of Politics.* New York: Doubleday.

Litwak, Eugene. 1960. "Occupational Mobility and Extended Family Cohesion," *American Sociological Review* 25 (February):9–21.

———. 1960. "Geographic Mobility and Extended Family Cohesion," *American Sociological Review* 25 (June):385–394.

Liu, William T., and Elena S. H. Yu. 1977. "Variations in Women's Roles and Family Life Under the Socialist Regime in China," *Journal of Comparative Family Studies* 8 (Summer):201–215.

Livsey, Clara G. 1979. "Coping with Adultery that Threatens Marriage," *Medical Aspects of Human Sexuality* (April):8–23.

Loether, Herman J., and Donald G. McTavish. 1976. *Descriptive and Inferential Statistics: An Introduction.* Boston: Allyn and Bacon.

Longfellow, Cynthia. 1979. "Divorce in Context: Its Impact on Children," Chap. 17 in George Levinger and Oliver C. Moles (eds.), *Divorce and Separation: Context, Causes and Consequences.* New York: Basic Books.

Lopata, Helenaz. 1971. *Occupation: Housewife.* New York: Oxford University Press.

———. 1973. *Widowhood in an American City.* Cambridge, MA: Schenkman.

———. 1979. *Women as Widows: Support Systems.* New York: Elsevier.

Lowenthal, Marjorie, Majde Thurnher, and David

Chiriboga. 1976. *Four Stages of Life*. San Francisco: Jossey-Bass.

Lowrie, Samuel H. 1951. "Dating Theories and Student Responses," *American Sociological Review* 16 (June):334–340.

Luckey, Eleanor B., and Gilbert D. Nass. 1969. "The Comparison of Sexual Attitudes and Behavior in an International Sample," *Journal of Marriage and the Family* 31 (May):348–359.

Lundberg, George A. 1939. *Foundations of Sociology*. New York: Macmillan.

———. 1952. "Science, Scientists, and Values," *Social Forces* 30 (May):373–379.

Lynn, David B., and William I. Sawrey. 1958. "The Effects of Father-Absence on Norwegian Boys and Girls," *Journal of Abnormal Social Psychology* 59 (September):258–262.

Maccoby, Eleanor E. 1960. "Effects Upon Children of Their Mothers' Outside Employment," in Norman W. Bell and Ezra F. Vogel (eds.), *A Modern Introduction to the Family*. New York: Free Press.

——— (ed.). 1966. *The Development of Sex Differences*. Stanford, CA: Stanford University Press.

———, and Carol Jacklin. 1974. *The Psychology of Sex Differences*. Stanford, CA: Stanford University Press.

MacCorquodale, Patricia, and John DeLamater. 1979. "Self-Image and Premarital Sexuality," *Journal of Marriage and the Family* 41 (May):327–339.

MacIver, Robert M. 1942. *Social Causation*. Boston: Ginn.

Macke, Ann S., George W. Bohrnstedt, and Ilene N. Bernstein. 1979. "Housewives' Self-Esteem and Their Husbands' Success: The Myth of Vicarious Involvement," *Journal of Marriage and the Family* 41 (February):51–57.

Macklin, Eleanor D. 1972. "Heterosexual Cohabitation Among Unmarried College Students." *Family Coordinator* 21 (October):463–473.

———. 1976. "Unmarried Heterosexual Cohabitation on the University Campus," in J. Wiseman, *The Social Psychology of Sex*. New York: Harper & Row.

———. 1978. "Nonmarital Heterosexual Cohabitation," *Marriage and Family Review* 1 (March/April):1–12.

MacNamara, Donald E. J., and Edward Sagarin. 1977. *Sex, Crime and the Law*. New York: Free Press.

Maison, Sally. 1976. "Jealousy: A Theoretical and Cross-Cultural Review," research paper, unpublished, University of Minnesota, Minneapolis.

Malinowski, Bronislaw. 1929. *The Sexual Life of Savages in North-Western Melanesia*. New York: Harvest Books. (Published by Harcourt Brace Jovanovich.)

———. 1930. "Parenthood, the Basis of Social Structure," in V. F. Calverton and Samuel Schmalhausen (eds.), *The New Generation*. New York: Citadel.

Mancini, Joy A., and Dennis K. Orthner. 1978. "Recreational Sexuality Preferences Among Middle Class Husbands and Wives," *Journal of Sex Research* 14 (May):96–106.

Mandel, William M. 1975. *Soviet Women*. New York: Anchor Books.

Mann, William E. 1967. "Sexual Standards and Trends in Sweden," *Journal of Sex Research* 3 (August):191–200.

Manosevitz, Martin. 1974. "Early Sexual Behavior in Adult Homosexual and Heterosexual Males," in Nathaniel M. Wagner (ed.), *Perspectives on Human Sexuality*. New York: Behavioral Publications.

Marini, Margaret M. 1978. "The Transition to Adulthood: Sex Differences in Educational Attainment and Age at Marriage," *American Sociological Review* 43 (August):483–507.

Marshall, Donald S. 1971. "Sexual Behavior on Mangaia," in Donald S. Marshall and Robert C. Suggs (eds.), *Human Sexual Behavior: Variations in the Ethnographic Spectrum*. New York: Basic Books.

———, and Robert C. Suggs (eds.). 1971. *Human Sexual Behavior: Variations in the Ethnographic Spectrum*. New York: Basic Books.

Martin, M. Kay, and Barbara Voorhies. 1975. *Female of the Species*. New York: Columbia University Press.

Martin, Thomas W., Kenneth J. Berry, and R. Brooke Jacobsen. 1975. "The Impact of Dual-Career Marriages on Female Professional Careers: An Empirical Test of a Parsonian Hypothesis," *Journal of Marriage and the Family* 37 (November):734–742.

Martinson, Floyd M. 1976. "Eroticism in Infancy and Childhood," *Journal of Sex Research* 12 (November):251–262.

Marwell, Gerald. 1975. "Why Ascription? Parts of a More or Less Formal Theory of the Functions and Dysfunctions of Sex Roles," *American Sociological Review* 40 (August):445–455.

Maslow, Abraham. 1962. *Toward a Psychology of Being*. New York: Van Nostrand.

Mason, Karen O., and Larry Bumpass. 1975.

"U.S. Women's Sex Role Ideology, 1970," *American Journal of Sociology* 80 (March):1212–1220.

_____, J. L. Czajka, and Sara Arber. 1976. "Change and U.S. Women's Sex-Role Attitudes, 1964–1974," *American Sociological Review* 41 (August):573–596.

Massarik, Fred. 1974. "National Jewish Population Study: A New U.S. Estimate," in *American Jewish Yearbook 1974–75*. Philadelphia: Jewish Publication Society of America.

_____, and Alvin Chenkin. 1973. "United States' National Jewish Population Study: A First Report," in *American Jewish Yearbook 1973*. Philadelphia: Jewish Publication Society of America.

Masters, William H., and Virginia F. Johnson. 1966. *Human Sexual Response*. Boston: Little, Brown.

_____, and _____. 1970. *Human Sexual Inadequacy*. Boston: Little, Brown.

_____, _____, and Robert Kolodny (eds.). 1977. *Ethical Issues in Sex Therapy and Research*. Boston: Little, Brown.

_____. 1979. *Homosexuality in Perspective*. Boston: Little, Brown.

_____, _____, and _____. 1980. *Ethical Guidelines for Sex Therapy and Research*. Boston: Little, Brown.

Mathes, Eugene W. 1975. "The Effects of Physical Attractiveness and Anxiety on Heterosexual Attraction Over a Series of Five Encounters," *Journal of Marriage and the Family* 37 (November): 769–773.

Matza, David. 1964. *Delinquency and Drift*. New York: Wiley.

Mayer, John E. 1961. *Jewish-Gentile Courtships*. New York; Free Press.

Mazur, Ronald. 1973. *The New Intimacy*. Boston: Beacon Press.

McCord, Joan, and William McCord. 1958. "The Effects of Parental Role Models on Criminality," *Journal of Social Issues* 14 (July):66–75.

McDowell, Sophia F. 1971. "Black-White Intermarriage in the U.S.," *International Journal of Sociology of the Family* (May):49–58 (special issue).

McKeon, Richard (ed.). 1941. *The Basic Works of Aristotle*. New York: Random House.

McLaughlin, Steven D. 1978. "Occupational Sex Identification and the Assessment of Male and Female Earning Inequality," *American Sociological Review* 43 (December):909–921.

Mead, George Herbert. 1934. *Mind, Self and Society*. Chicago: University of Chicago Press.

Mead, Margaret. 1928. *Coming of Age in Samoa*. New York: Morrow.

_____, and Frances B. Kaplan (eds.). 1965. *American Women: The Report of the President's Commission on the Status of Women*. New York: Scribner.

Meehan, Eugene J. 1969. *Value Judgment and Social Science*. Homewood, IL: Dorsey Press.

Meeker, B. F., and P. A. Weitzel-O'Neill. 1977. "Sex Roles and Interpersonal Behavior in Task Oriented Groups," *American Sociological Review* 42 (February):91–105.

Meisner, Maurice. 1977. *Mao's China: A History of the People's Republic*. New York: Free Press.

Mencher, Joan P. 1965. "The Nayars of South Malabar," in Meyer F. Nimkoff (ed.), *Comparative Family Systems*. Boston: Houghton Mifflin.

Merton, Robert K. 1938. "Social Structure and Anomie," *American Sociological Review* 3 (October):672–682.

_____. 1957. *Social Theory and Social Structure*. New York: Free Press.

Meyenburg, Bernd and Volkmar Sigusch. 1977. "Sexology in Germany," *Journal of Sex Research* 13 (August):197–209.

Meyer-Bahlburg Heino, F. L. 1977. "Sex Hormones and Male Homosexuality in Comparative Perspective," *Archives of Sexual Behavior* 6 (July):297–323.

Michel, Andree. 1967. "Comparative Data Concerning the Interaction in French and American Families," *Journal of Marriage and the Family* 29 (May):337–345.

Middleton, Russell. 1962. "Brother-Sister and Father-Daughter Marriage in Ancient Egypt," *American Sociological Review* 27 (October):603–611.

Miller, Brent C. 1975. "Types of Marriage Interaction and Their Relation to Contextual Characteristics in a Sample of Young Married Couples," Ph.D. dissertation, unpublished, University of Minnesota, Minneapolis.

Miller, Daniel R., and Guy E. Swanson. 1958. *The Changing American Parent*. New York: Wiley.

Miller, Joanne, Carmi Schooler, Melvin Kohn, and Karen Miller. 1979. "Women and Work: The Psychological Effects of Occupational Conditions," *American Journal of Sociology* 85 (July):66–94.

Miller, Kent S., and Ralph M. Dreger (eds.). 1973. *Comparative Studies of Blacks and Whites in the U.S.* New York: Seminar Press.

Moberg, Eva. 1962. *Women and Human Beings.* Stockholm: Bonniers.

Modell, John, Frank Furstenberg, and Theodore Hershberg. 1976. "Social Change and Transitions to Adulthood in Historical Perspective," *Journal of Family History* 1 (Autumn):7–33.

Monahan, Thomas P., and William M. Kephart. 1954. "Divorce and Desertion by Religious and Mixed Religious Groups," *American Journal of Sociology* 59 (March):454–465.

_____. 1957. "Family Status and the Delinquent Child: A Reappraisal and Some New Findings," *Social Forces* 35 (March):250–258.

Money, John, and Anke Ehrhardt. 1972. *Man and Woman: Boy and Girl.* Baltimore: Johns Hopkins Press.

Money, John, and Herman Musaph (eds.), 1977. *Handbook of Sexology.* New York: Elsevier-North Holland Co.

Moore, Barrington, Jr. 1958. *Political Power and Social Theory.* Cambridge, MA: Harvard University Press.

Moore, Kristin A. 1977. "The Effect of Government Policies on Out of Wedlock Sex and Pregnancy," *Family Planning Perspectives* 9 (July/August):164–169.

_____, and Steven B. Caldwell. 1976. "Out of Wedlock Pregnancy and Childbearing," Working Paper 992–02. Washington, DC: Urban Institute.

_____, Sandra L. Hofferth, Steven B. Caldwell, and Linda J. Waite. 1979. *Teenage Motherhood: Social and Economic Consequences.* Washington, DC: Urban Institute.

Morgan, Lewis Henry. 1877. *Ancient Society.* Chicago: Charles H. Kerr.

Mortimer, Jeylan. 1976. "Social Class, Work and the Family: Some Implications of the Father's Occupation for Familial Relationships and Sons' Career Decisions," *Journal of Marriage and the Family* 38 (May):241–256.

_____. 1978. "Dual Career Families—A Sociological Perspective," in S. S. Peterson, J. M. Richardson, and G. V. Kreuter (eds.), *The Two Career Family: Issues and Alternatives.* Washington, DC: University Press of America.

Moynihan, Daniel P. 1965. *The Negro Family: The Case for National Action.* Washington, DC: Government Printing Office.

Mueller, Charles W., and Blair G. Campbell. 1977. "Female Occupational Achievement and Marital Status: A Research Note," *Journal of Marriage and the Family* 39 (August):587–593.

_____, and Hallowell Pope. 1977. "Marital Instability: The Study of Its Transmission Between Generations," *Journal of Marriage and the Family* 39 (February):83–92.

Mullins, Nicholas C. 1971. *The Art of Theory: Construction and Use.* New York: Harper & Row.

Murdock, George P. 1949. *Social Structure.* New York: Macmillan.

_____. 1957. "World Ethnographic Sample," *American Anthropologist* 59 (August):664–687.

_____. 1967. "Ethnographic Atlas: A Summary," *Ethnology* 6 (April): 109–236.

_____. 1975. *Outline of World Cultures.* New Haven, CT: Human Relation Area Files.

Murray, Henry A., et al. 1938. *Explorations in Personality.* New York: Oxford University Press.

Murstein, Bernard (ed.). 1967. "Empirical Tests of Role Complementary Needs and Homogamy Theories of Marital Choice," *Journal of Marriage and the Family* 29 (November):689–696.

_____. 1971. *Theories of Attraction and Love.* New York: Springer Publishing.

_____. 1976. *Who Will Marry Whom?* New York: Springer Publishing.

Mussen, Paul H. 1961. "Some Antecedents and Consequents of Masculine Sex Typing in Adolescent Boys," *Psychological Monographs* 75.2 (entire no. 506).

_____. 1962. "Long-Term Consequents of Masculinity of Interests in Adolescence," *Journal of Consulting Psychology* 26 (October):435–440.

_____ (ed.). 1970. *Carmichael's Manual of Child Psychology* (3rd ed.; vols. 1 and 2). New York: Wiley.

_____, and L. Distler. 1959. "Masculinity, Identification and Father-Son Relationships," *Journal of Abnormal Social Psychology* 59 (November):350–356.

Myrdal, Alva, and Gunnar Myrdal. 1934. *Crises in the Population Question.* Stockholm, Sweden.

_____, and Viola Klein. 1956. *Women's Two Roles.* Stockholm, Sweden.

Nablandov, A. V. 1964. *Reproductive Physiology.* San Francisco: W. H. Freeman.

Nason, Ellen M., and Margaret M. Poloma. 1976. *Voluntarily Childless Couples: The Emergence of a Variant Lifestyle.* Beverly Hills, CA: Sage Publications.

National Opinion Research Center. 1975. *Codebooks for General Social Surveys.* Chicago: University of Chicago Press.

_____. 1976. *Codebooks for General Social Surveys.* Chicago: University of Chicago Press.

_____. 1977. "Cumulative Codebook for the

1972–77 General Social Surveys," Chicago: University of Chicago Press.

Neubeck, Gerhard (ed.). 1969. *Extramarital Relations*. Englewood Cliffs, NJ: Prentice-Hall.

Newton, N. 1967. "Psychological Aspects of Lactation," *New England Journal of Medicine* 277:4–12.

Nimkoff, Meyer F. (ed.). 1965. *Comparative Family Systems*. Boston: Houghton Mifflin.

———, and Russell Middleton. 1960. "Types of Family and Types of Economy," *American Journal of Sociology* 6 (November):215–255.

Noonan, John T., Jr. 1966. *Contraception*. Cambridge, MA: Harvard University Press.

Nordlund, Agnethe, and Jan Trost. 1975. "Some Data on Sex Role Socialization in Sweden," *International Journal of Sociology of the Family* 5 (Autumn):168–177.

Norem, Rosalie. 1979. "A Longitudinal Study of Premarital Couple Interaction," University of Minnesota Ph.D. dissertation, unpublished.

Nye, F. Ivan. 1957. "Child Adjustment in Broken and in Unhappy Unbroken Homes," *Marriage and Family Living* 19 (August):356–361.

———. 1958. *Family Relationships and Delinquent Behavior*. New York: Wiley.

———. 1974. "Emerging and Declining Family Roles," *Journal of Marriage and the Family* 36 (May):238–245.

———, and Lois W. Hoffman (eds.). 1963. *The Employed Mother in America*. Skokie, IL: Rand McNally.

Olson, David H. 1972. "Marriage of the Future: Revolutionary or Evolutionary Change?", *Family Coordinator* 21 (October):383–393.

———. 1981. *Typologies of Marriage and Family Systems* (forthcoming).

———, and R. G. Ryder. 1970. "Inventory of Marital Conflicts (IMC): An Experimental Interaction Procedure," *Journal of Marriage and the Family* 32 (August):443–448.

O'Neill, William L. 1967. *Divorce in the Progressive Era*. New Haven, CT: Yale University Press.

———. 1969. *Everyone Was Brave: The Rise and Fall of Feminism in America*. Chicago: Quadrangle.

Oppenheimer, Valerie K. 1977. "The Sociology of Women's Economic Role in the Family," *American Sociological Review* 42 (June):387–406.

Orden, S. R., and N. M. Bradburn. 1969. "Working Wives and Marital Happiness," *American Journal of Sociology* 74 (January):392–408.

Osborn, Candice A., and Robert H. Pollack. 1977.

"The Effects of Two Types of Erotic Literature on Physiological and Verbal Measures of Female Sexual Arousal," *Journal of Sex Research* 13 (November):250–256.

Osmond, Marie, and Pat Martin. 1975. "Sex and Sexism: A Comparison of Male and Female Sex-Role Attitudes," *Journal of Marriage and the Family* 37 (April):744–758.

Otterbein, Keith F. 1965. "Caribbean Family Organization: A Comparative Analysis," *American Anthropologist* 67 (February):66–79.

Otto, Luther, and David L. Featherman. 1972. "On the Measurement of Marital Adjustment Among Spouses," working paper, unpublished, Center for Demography and Ecology, University of Wisconsin, Madison.

Ovid. 1957. *The Art of Love* (trans. Rolfe Humphries). Bloomington: Indiana University Press.

Papanek, Hanna. 1973. "Men, Women and Work: Reflections on the Two-Person Career," *American Journal of Sociology* 78 (January):852–872.

Parish, William L., Jr. 1975. "Socialism and the Chinese Peasant Family," *Journal of Asian Studies* 34 (May):613–630.

———, and Martin K. Whyte. 1978. *Village and Family in Contemporary China*. Chicago: University of Chicago Press.

Parron, Eugenia M., and Lillian E. Troll. 1978. "Gold Wedding Couples: Effects of Retirement on Intimacy in Long-Standing Marriages," *Alternative Lifestyles* 1 (November):447–464.

Parsons, Talcott. 1953. "A Revised Analytical Approach to the Theory of Social Stratification," in Reinhard Bendix and Seymour M. Lipset (eds.), *Class, Status and Power*. New York: Free Press.

———. 1959. "The Social Structure of the Family," in Ruth N. Anshen (ed.), *The Family: Its Function and Destiny*. New York: Harper & Row.

———, and Robert F. Bales (eds.). 1955. *Family Socialization and Interaction Process*. New York: Free Press.

Parven, Theophilus. 1883–1884. "Hygiene of the Sexual Functions," *New Orleans Medical and Surgical Journal* 11:92–95.

Paxton, Anne Lee, and Edward J. Turner. 1978. "Self Actualization and Sexual Permissiveness: Satisfaction, Prudishness and Drive Among Female Undergraduates," *Journal of Sex Research* 14 (May):65–80.

Payne, Donald E., and Paul H. Mussen. 1956. "Parent-Child Relations and Father Identification Among Adolescent Boys," *Journal of Ab-*

normal and Social Psychology 52 (May):358–362.

Pearlin, Leonard L., and Melvin L. Kohn. 1966. "Social Class, Occupation and Parental Values: A Cross National Study," American Sociological Review 31 (August):466–479.

———, and J. S. Johnson. 1977. "Marital Status, Life Strains and Depression," American Sociological Review 42 (October):704–715.

Perlman, Daniel. 1974. "Self-Esteem and Sexual Permissiveness," Journal of Marriage and the Family 36 (August):470–474.

———, 1978. "Cross Cultural Analyses of Students' Sexual Standards," Archives of Sexual Behavior 7 (November):545–558.

Perry, Joseph B., and Erdwin H. Pfuhl. 1963. "Adjustment of Children in Solo and Remarriage Homes," Marriage and Family Living 25 (May):221–224.

Peterman, Don J., Carl A. Ridley, and Scott M. Anderson. 1974. "A Comparison of Cohabiting/Non-Cohabiting College Students," Journal of Marriage and the Family 36 (May):344–354.

Petros, John W. 1975. Sex Male, Gender Masculine. Port Washington, NY: Alfred.

Petrowsky, Marc. 1976. "Marital Status, Sex, and the Social Networks of the Elderly," Journal of Marriage and the Family 38 (November):749–756.

Pfeiffer, Eric, and Glenn C. Davis. 1972. "Determinants of Sexual Behavior in Middle and Old Age," Journal of the American Geriatrics Society 20:151–158.

Pietropinto, Anthony, and Jacqueline Simenauer. 1977. Beyond the Male Myth: A Nationwide Survey. New York: Times Books.

Pineo, Peter C. 1961. "Disenchantment in the Later Years of Marriage," Marriage and Family Living 23 (February):3–11.

Pinkney, Alphonso. 1975. Black Americans. Englewood Cliffs, NJ: Prentice-Hall.

Plath, David W. 1964. The After Hours: Modern Japan and the Search for Enjoyment. Berkeley: University of California Press.

Plato. 1956. Symposium (trans. Benjamin Jowett). Indianapolis: Bobbs-Merrill.

Playboy Report on American Men. 1979. Chicago: Playboy Enterprises. (Analysis and interpretation by William Simon and Patricia Y. Miller.)

Poloma, Margaret. 1971. "The Married Professional Woman: A Study on the Tolerance of Domestication," Journal of Marriage and the Family 33 (August):531–540.

———, and Neal Garland. 1971. "The Myth of the Egalitarian Family: Familial Roles and the Professionally Employed Wife," in A. Theodore (ed.), The Professional Woman. Cambridge, MA: Schenkman.

Pope, Hallowell. 1967. "Unwed Mothers and Their Sex Partners," Journal of Marriage and the Family 30 (August):555–567.

Preston, Samuel H., and John McDonald. 1979. "The Incidence of Divorce Within Cohorts of American Marriages Contracted Since the Civil War," Demography 16 (February):1–25.

Profile of Sweden. 1972. Stockholm: Swedish Institute.

Psychology of Women Quarterly 3 (Fall 1978). This entire issue is on dual-career couples.

Quadagno, David M., Robert Briscoe, and Jill S. Quadagno. 1977. "Effect of Perinatal Gonadal Hormones on Selected Nonsexual Behavior Patterns: A Critical Assessment of the Nonhuman Literature," Psychological Bulletin 84, No. 1:62–80.

Queen, Stuart A., and Robert Habenstein. 1974. The Family in Various Cultures (4th ed.). Philadelphia: Lippincott.

Quinley, Harold E., and Charles Y. Glock. 1979. Anti-Semitism in America. New York: Free Press.

Rabb, Theodore K., and Robert I. Rotberg (eds.). 1971. The Family in History: Interdisciplinary Essays. New York: Harper Torchbooks.

Radcliffe-Brown, A. R. 1959. African Systems of Kinship and Marriage. New York: Oxford University Press.

———, and Daryll Forde (eds.). 1950. African Systems of Kinship and Marriage. New York: Oxford University Press.

Rains, Prudence M. 1971. Becoming an Unwed Mother. Chicago: Aldine.

Rainwater, Lee. 1966. "Some Aspects of Lower Class Sexual Behavior," Journal of Social Issues 22 (April):96–108.

———, and William L. Yancey. 1967. The Moynihan Report and the Politics of Controversy. Cambridge: Massachusetts Institute of Technology Press.

Ramey, James W. 1972. "Communes, Group Marriage and the Upper Middle Class," Journal of Marriage and the Family 34 (November):647–655.

———. 1976. Intimate Friendship. Englewood Cliffs, NJ: Prentice-Hall.

———. 1978. "Experimental Family Forms—The Family of the Future," Marriage and Family Review 1 (January/February):1–9.

Rapoport, Robert, and R. Rapoport. 1965. "Work and Family in Contemporary Society,"

American Sociological Review 30 (June):381–394.

——. 1978. "Dual Career Families: Progress and Prospects," *Marriage and Family Review* 1 (September/October):1–12.

Raschke, Helen, and Vern Raschke. 1979. "Family Conflict and Children's Self-Concept: A Comparison of Intact and Single-Parent Families," *Journal of Marriage and the Family* 41 (May):367–375.

Raschke, Vern. 1972. "Religiosity and Sexual Permissiveness," Ph.D. dissertation, unpublished, University of Minnesota, Minneapolis.

——, and Angelina Li. 1976. "Premarital Sexual Permissiveness of College Students in Hong Kong," *Journal of Comparative Family Studies* 7 (Spring):65–74.

Rausch, Harold L., William A. Barry, Richard K. Hertel, and Mary Ann Swain. 1974. *Communication, Conflict and Marriage*. San Francisco: Jossey-Bass.

Rausch, Harold L., Ann C. Grief, and Jane Nugent. 1979. "Communication in Couples and Families," in W. Burr, R. Hill, I. Nye, and I. Reiss (eds.), *Contemporary Theories About the Family*. Vol. I. New York: Free Press.

Raven, Bertram H., Richard Centers, and Aroldo Rodrigues. 1975. "The Bases of Conjugal Power," in Ronald E. Cromwell and David Olson (eds.), *Power in Families*. New York: Halsted Press.

Redford, Myron H., Gordon W. Duncan, and Denis J. Prager. 1974. *The Condom: Increasing Utilization in the United States*. San Francisco: San Francisco Press,

Reichelt, Paul A. 1978. "Changes in Sexual Behavior Among Unmarried Teenage Women Utilizing Oral Contraception," *Journal of Population* 1:57–68.

Reiss, Albert J. Jr. 1961. "The Social Integration of Queers and Peers," *Social Problems* 9 (Fall):102–120.

Reiss, Harriet M. 1973. "Contraception and Parental Communication," unpublished research paper.

Reiss, Ira L. 1956. "The Double Standard in Premarital Sexual Intercourse: A Neglected Concept," *Social Forces* 34 (March):224–230.

——. 1957. "The Treatment of Premarital Coitus in 'Marriage and Family' Texts," *Social Problems* 4 (April):334–338.

——. 1960. *Premarital Sexual Standards in America*. New York: Free Press.

——. 1960. "Toward a Sociology of the Het-erosexual Love Relationship," *Marriage and Family Living* 22 (May):139–145.

——. 1963. "Personal Values and the Scientific Study of Sex," in H. Beigel (ed.), *Advances in Sex Research*. New York: Harper & Row.

——. 1964. "Premarital Sexual Permissiveness Among Negroes and Whites," *American Sociological Review* 29 (October):688–698.

——. 1964. "The Scaling of Premarital Sexual Permissiveness," *Journal of Marriage and the Family* 26 (May):188–198.

——. 1965. "Social Class and Campus Dating," *Social Problems* 13 (Fall):193–205.

——. 1965. "Social Class and Premarital Sexual Permissiveness: A Re-examination," *American Sociological Review* 30 (October):747–756.

——. 1965. "The Universality of the Family: A Conceptual Analysis," *Journal of Marriage and the Family* 27 (November):443–453.

——. 1967. *The Social Context of Premarital Sexual Permissiveness*. New York: Holt, Rinehart and Winston.

——. 1970. "Premarital Sex as Deviant Behavior: An Application of Current Approaches to Deviance," *American Sociological Review* 35 (February):78–87.

——. 1973. *Heterosexual Permissiveness Inside and Outside of Marriage*. Morristown, NJ: General Learning Press, pp. 1–29.

——. 1976. "Premarital Sexual Standards," *Sex Information and Education Council of the U.S.* Study Guide No. 5, pp. 1–24. (Revised edition.)

——. 1980. "Sexual Customs and Gender Roles in Sweden and America: An Analysis and Interpretation," in H. Lopata (ed.), *Research on the Interweave of Social Roles: Women and Men*. Greenwich, CT: JAI Press.

——, and Brend Miller. 1974. "A Theoretical Analysis of Heterosexual Permissiveness," Technical Report No. 2. Minneapolis: University of Minnesota, Family Study Center.

——. Albert Banwart, and Hartty Foreman. 1975. "Premarital Contraceptive Usage: A Study and Some Theoretical Explorations," *Journal of Marriage and the Family* 37 (August):619–630.

——, and Brent C. Miller. 1979. "Heterosexual Permissiveness: A Theoretical Analysis," in W. Burr, R. Hill, I. Nye, and I. Reiss (ed.), Vol. I. New York: Free Press.

——, W. Burr, R. Hill, and I. Nye. 1979. *Contempory Theories About the Family*. Vols. I and II. New York: Free Press.

——, Ronald Anderson, and G. C. Sponaugle.

1980. "A Multivariate Model of the Determinants of Extramarital Sexual Permissiveness, *Journal of Marriage and the Family* (May) (in press).

———, R. Walsh, M. Zey-Ferrell, W. Tolone, and O. Pocs. 1980. "A Guide to Research on Heterosexual Relationships," Chap. 4 in R. Green and J. Wiener (eds.), *The Methodology of Sexual Research* (in press).

———, and Frank F. Furstenberg. 1980. "The Sociology of Human Sexuality for Medical Doctors," in H. Lief (ed.), *Human Sexuality and the Physician*. Chicago, IL: American Medical Association Press (in press).

Renne, Karen. 1970. "Correlates of Dissatisfaction in Marriage," *Journal of Marriage and the Family* 32 (February):54–67.

Reynolds, H. T. 1977. *The Analysis of Cross-Classifications*. New York: Free Press.

Reynolds, Paul Davidson. 1971. *A Primer in Theory Construction*. Indianapolis, IN: Bobbs-Merrill.

Ridley, J. C. 1969. "The Changing Position of American Women: Education, Labor Force Participation and Fertility," in *The Family in Transition*. Fogarty International Proceedings No. 3. Washington, DC: Government Printing Office.

Ridley, Carl A., Dan J. Peterman, and Arthur W. Avery. 1978. "Cohabitation: Does It Make for a Better Marriage?", *Family Coordinator* 27 (April):129–136.

Riksförbundet för Sexuell Upplysning (RFSU). National Federation for Sexual Information. 1969. *Verksamhetsberättelse* (Activity Report). Stockholm.

———. 1973. "Det Finns Inga Homosexuella!" ("There Are No Homosexuals!"). *RFSU Bulletin* 3 (September):1–12. Stockholm.

———. 1974. *Verksamhetsberättelse* (Activity Report). Stockholm.

Rindfuss, Ronald R., and Charles F. Westoff. 1974. "The Initiation of Contraception," *Demography* 11 (February):75–87.

———, and Larry L. Bumpass. 1977. "Fertility During Marital Disruption," *Journal of Marriage and the Family* 39 (August): 517–528.

———, and James A. Sweet. 1977. *Postwar Fertility Trends and Differentials in the U.S.* New York: Academic Press.

Robbins, Mina B., and Gordon D. Jensen. 1978. "Multiple Orgasm in Males," *Journal of Sex Research* 14 (February):21–26.

Rodman, Hyman. 1963. "The Lower-Class Value Stretch," *Social Forces* 42 (December):205–215.

———. 1966. "Illegitimacy in the Caribbean Social Structure: A Reconsideration," *American Sociological Review* 30 (October): 673–683.

———. 1967. "Marital Power in France, Greece, Yugoslavia, and the United States: A Cross-National Discussion," *Journal of Marriage and the Family* 29 (May):320–325.

———. 1969. "Fidelity and Forms of Marriage: The Consensual Union in the Caribbean," in Gerhard Neubeck (ed.), *Extramarital Relations*. Englewood Cliffs, NJ: Prentice-Hall, pp. 108–127.

———. 1972. "Marital Power and the Theory of Resources in Cultural Context," *Journal of Comparative Family Studies* 3 (Spring):50–69.

———. 1978. "Social Class and Parents' Range of Aspirations for Their Children," *Social Problems* 25 (February):333–344.

———, and Paul Grams. 1967. "Juvenile Delinquency and the Family: A Review and Discussion," in *Task Force Report: Juvenile Delinquency and Youth Crime*. The President's Commission on Law Enforcement and Administration of Justice. Washington, DC: Government Printing Office.

Roebuck, J., and S. L. Spray. 1967. "The Cocktail Lounge: A Study of Heterosexual Relations in a Public Organization," *American Journal of Sociology* 72 (January):388–395.

Rogers, Carl. 1972. *Becoming Partners*. New York: Delacorte.

Rogers, Everett M., and A. Eugene Havens. 1960. "Prestige Rating and Mate Selection on a College Campus," *Marriage and Family Living* 22 (February):55–59.

Rollins, Boyd C., and Stephen Bahr. 1976. "A Theory of Power Relationships in Marriage," *Journal of Marriage and the Family* 38 (November):619–627.

———, and Kenneth L. Cannon. 1974. "Marital Satisfaction Over the Family Life Cycle: A Reevaluation," *Journal of Marriage and the Family* 35 (May):271–284.

———, and Darwin L. Thomas. 1975. "A Theory of Parental Power and Child Compliance," in Ronald E. Cromwell and David H. Olson (eds.), *Power in Families*. New York: Halsted Press.

———, and Darwin L. Thomas. 1979. "Parental Support, Power and Control. Techniques in the Socialization of Children," in Wes Burr, R. Hill, I. Nye, and I. L. Reiss (eds.), *Contemporary Theories About the Family*. Vol. I. New York: Free Press.

———, and Harold Feldman. 1970. "Marital Satisfaction Over the Family Life Cycle," *Journal of Marriage and the Family* 32 (February):20–28.

Rosen, David H. 1974. *Lesbianism: A Study of Female Homosexuality*. Springfield, IL: Charles C Thomas.

Rosenberg, Morris. 1965. *Society and the Adolescent Self-Image*. Princeton: Princeton University Press.

———. 1968. *The Logic of Survey Analysis*. New York: Basic Books.

Rosenfeld, Rachel A. 1978. "Women's Intergenerational Occupational Mobility," *American Sociological Review* 43 (February):36–47.

Rosow, Irving. 1957. "Issues in the Concept of Need-Complementarity," *Sociometry* 20 (September):216–233.

———, and K. Daniel Rose. 1972. "Divorce Among Doctors," *Journal of Marriage and the Family* 34 (November):587–598.

Rossi, Alice S. 1977. "A Biosocial Perspective on Parenting," *Daedalus* (Spring):1–31.

Rubin, Lillian. 1976. *Worlds of Pain: Life in the Working Class Family*. New York: Basic Books.

Rubin, Zick. 1973. *Liking and Loving*. New York: Holt, Rinehart and Winston.

Russell, Bertrand. 1945. *A History of Western Philosophy*. New York: Simon & Schuster.

Russell, Candyce S. 1974. "Transition to Parenthood: Problems and Gratifications, *Journal of Marriage and the Family* 36 (May):294–302.

Safilios-Rothschild, Constantina. 1967. "A Comparison of Power Structure and Marital Satisfaction in Urban Greek and French Families," *Journal of Marriage and the Family* 29 (May):345–353.

———. 1970. "The Study of Family Power Structure: A Review 1960–1969," *Journal of Marriage and the Family* 32 (November):539–552.

———. 1977. *Love, Sex and Sex Roles*. Englewood Cliffs NJ: Prentice-Hall.

Saghir, Marcel T., and E. Robbins. 1973. *Male and Female Homosexuality*. Baltimore: Williams & Wilkins.

Samlevnads—Undervisining. 1977. (Education for Living Together). Stockholm: Liber Laromedel. (This report was prepared by the Board of Education; it is the current guide to Sex Education in Sweden.)

Sampson, William A., and Peter H. Rossi. 1975. "Race and Family Social Standing," *American Sociological Review* 40 (April):201–214.

Sandberg, Elisabeth. 1975. *Equality is the Goal*. Stockholm: Swedish Institute.

Sarvis, Betty, and Hyman Rodman. 1974. *The Abortion Controversy*. New York: Columbia University Press.

Sauer, William. 1975. "Morale of the Urban Aged: A Regression Analysis by Race," Ph.D. dissertation, unpublished, University of Minnesota, Minneapolis.

Savage, James E., Jr., Alvis V. Adair, and Philip Friedman. 1978. "Community-Social Variables Related to Black Parent-Absent Families," *Journal of Marriage and the Family* 40 (November):779–785.

Scanzoni, John. 1970. *Opportunity and the Family*. New York: Free Press.

———. 1971. *The Black Family in Modern Society*. Boston: Allyn and Bacon.

———. 1972. *Sexual Bargaining*. Englewood Cliffs, NJ: Prentice-Hall.

———. 1975. "Sex Roles, Economic Factors and Marital Solidarity in Black and White Marriages," *Journal of Marriage and the Family* 37 (February):130–144.

———. 1975. *Sex Roles, Life Styles, and Childbearing*. New York: Free Press.

———. 1976. "Sex Role Change and Influences on Birth Intentions," *Journal of Marriage and the Family* 38 (February):43–60.

———. 1976. "Gender Roles and the Process of Fertility Control," *Journal of Marriage and the Family* 38 (November):677–692.

———. 1979. "A Historical Perspective on Husband-Wife Bargaining Power and Marital Dissolution," Chap. 2 in George Levinger and Oliver C. Moles (eds.), *Divorce and Separation: Context Causes and Consequences*. New York: Basic Books.

———. 1979. "Social Processes and Power in Families," Chap. 13 in W. Burr, R. Hill, I. Nye, and I. L. Reiss (eds.), *Contemporary Theories About the Family*. Vol. I. New York: Free Press.

Schafer, Siegred. 1977. "Sociosexual Behavior in Male and Female Homosexuals: A Study in Sex Differences," *Archives of Sexual Behavior* 6 (September):355–364.

Schlegel, Alice (ed.). 1977. *Sexual Stratification: A Cross-Cultural View*. New York: Columbia University Press.

Schlesinger, Yaffa. 1977. "Sex Roles and Social Change in the Kibbutz," *Journal of Marriage and the Family* 38 (November):771–780.

Schmidt, Gunter. 1975. "Male-Female Differences in Sexual Arousal and Behavior During and After Exposure to Sexually Explicit Stimuli," *Archives of Sexual Behavior* 4 (July):353–365.

————, and Volkmar Sigusch. 1970. "Sex Differences in Response to Psycho-sexual Stimulation by Films and Slides," *Journal of Sex Research* 6 (November): 268–283.

Schneider, David M. 1968. *American Kinship: A Cultural Account*. Englewood Cliffs, NJ: Prentice-Hall.

————, and Kathleen E. Gough (eds.). 1961. *Matrilineal Kinship*. Berkeley: University of California Press.

————, and George C. Homans. 1955. "Kinship Terminology and the American Kinship System," *American Anthropologist* 57 (August): 1194–1208.

Schneider, Harold K. 1971. "Romantic Love Among the Turu," in Donald Marshall and Robert Suggs (eds.), *Human Sexual Behavior*. New York: Basic Books.

Schoen, Robert. 1975. "California Divorce Rates by Age at First Marriage and Duration of First Marriage," *Journal of Marriage and the Family* 37 (August):548–555.

————. 1979. "A Theoretical Perspective on Cohort Marriage and Divorce in Twentieth Century Sweden," *Journal of Marriage and the Family* 41 (May):409–415.

————, and William Urton. 1977. "Marriage, Divorce and Mortality: The Swedish Experience," paper presented at International Population Conference, Mexico.

Schofield, Michael. 1965. *The Sexual Behavior of Young People*. Boston: Little, Brown.

————. 1965. *Sociological Aspects of Homosexuality: A Comparative Study of Three Types of Homosexuals*. Boston: Little, Brown.

Schram, Rosalyn W. 1979. "Marital Satisfaction Over the Family Life Cycle: A Critique and Proposal," *Journal of Marriage and the Family* 41 (February):7–12.

Schulz, Barbara, George W. Bohrnstedt, Edgar F. Borgatta, and Robert E. Evans. 1977. "Explaining Premarital Sexual Intercourse Among College Students: A Causal Model," *Social Forces* 56 (September):148–165.

Schusky, Ernest L. 1965. *Manual for Kinship Analysis*. New York: Holt, Rinehart and Winston.

Schutz, William C. 1958. *A Three-Dimensional Theory of Interpersonal Behavior*. New York: Holt, Rinehart and Winston.

Schvaneveldt, Jay D., and Marilyn Ihinger. 1979. "Sibling Relationships in the Family," In W. Burr, R. Hill, I. Nye, and I. L. Reiss (eds.),. *Contemporary Theories About the Family*. Vol. I. New York: Free Press.

Schwartz, George, and P. W. Bishop (eds.). 1958. *Moments of Discovery*, 2 vols. New York: Basic Books.

Schwartz, Pepper. 1973. "Female Sexuality and Monogamy," in R. W. Libby and R. N. Whitehurst (eds.), *Renovating Marriage: Toward New Sexual Life Styles*. Danville, CA: Consensus Publishers.

Sears, Robert T., Eleanor E. Maccoby, and Harry Levin. 1957. *Patterns of Child Rearing*. White Plains, NY: Row, Peterson.

Seward, Rudy R. 1978. *The American Family: A Demographic History*. Beverly Hills, CA: Sage.

Sewell, William H. 1961. "Social Class and Childhood Personality," *Sociometry* 24 (December):340–356.

Sexuella Övergrepp (Sexual Intrusion). 1976. No. 9. Stockholm, Sweden, SOU. (A Report of a State Commission on New Sex Laws.)

Sexual Och Samlevnadsundervisning (Education for Sexuality and Living Together: A Report by the State Commission on Sex Education). 1974. Stockholm, Sweden, SOU.

Shanas, Ethel. 1973. "Family-Kin Networks and Aging in Cross-Cultural Perspective," *Journal of Marriage and the Family* 35 (August):505–511.

————, et al. 1968. *Old People in Three Industrial Societies*. New York: Atherton.

Shaplen, Robert. 1954. *Free Love and Heavenly Sinners*. New York: Knopf.

Shepher, Joseph. 1971. "Mate Selection Among Second Generation Kibbutz Adolescents and Adults: Incest Avoidance and Negative Imprinting," *Archives of Sexual Behavior* 1 (January):298–307.

Short, James F., Jr., and Fred L. Strodtbeck. 1965. *Group Process and Gang Delinquency*. Chicago: University of Chicago Press.

Shorter, Edward. 1975. *The Making of the Modern Family*. New York: Basic Books.

Sidel, Ruth. 1972. *Women and Child Care in China*. New York: Hill & Wang.

Siegel, Sidney. 1956. *Nonparametric Statistics for the Behavioral Sciences*. New York: McGraw-Hill.

Sigusch, Volkmar, et al. 1970. "Psychological Stimulation: Sex Differences," *Journal of Sex Research* 6 (February):10–24.

Silka, Linda, and Sara Kiesler. 1977. "Couples Who Choose to Remain Childless," *Family Planning Perspectives* 9 (January/February):16–25.

Simmons, Roberta G., Susan D. Klein, and Richard L. Simmons. 1977. *Gift of Life: The Social*

and Psychological Impact of Organ Transplantation. New York: Wiley.

Simon, William, and John H. Gagnon. 1967. "Homosexuality: The Formulation of a Sociological Perspective," *Journal of Health and Social Behavior* 8 (September):177–185.

———, Alan Berger, and John Gagnon. 1972. "Beyond Anxiety and Fantasy: The Coital Experiences of College Youth," *Journal of Youth and Adolescence* 1, No. 3:203–222.

Singh, B. Krishna, Bonnie L. Walton, and J. Sherwood Williams. 1976. "Extramarital Sexual Permissiveness: Conditions and Contingencies," *Journal of Marriage and the Family* 38 (November):701–712.

Skinner, B. F. 1959. *Science and Human Behavior.* New York: Macmillan.

Skipper, James K., A. L. Guenther, and G. Nass. 1967. "The Sacredness of .05: A Note Concerning the Uses of Statistical Levels of Significance in Social Science," *The American Sociologist* 2 (February):16–19.

Sklar, June, and Beth Berkov. 1974. "Abortion, Illegitimacy, and the American Birth Rate," *Science* 185 (September 13):909–915.

Slater, Philip. 1961. "Parental Role Differentiation," *American Journal of Sociology* 67 (November):296–311.

Smith, Daniel Scott. 1978. "The Dating of the American Sexual Revolution: Evidence and Interpretation," in Michael Gordon (ed.), *The American Family in Social-Historical Perspective* (2nd ed.). New York: St. Martins.

———, and Michael S. Hindus. 1975. "Premarital Pregnancy in America, 1640–1971: An Overview and Interpretation," *Journal of Interdisciplinary History* 4 (Spring):537–570.

Smith, James R., and Lynn G. Smith (eds.). 1974. *Beyond Monogamy.* Baltimore: Johns Hopkins Press.

Smith, William M., Jr. 1952. "Rating and Dating: A Restudy," *Marriage and Family Living* 14 (November):312–317.

Smith-Lovin, Lynn, and Ann R. Tickamyer. 1978. "Nonrecursive Models of Labor Force Participation, Fertility Behavior and Sex Role Attitudes," *American Sociological Review* 43 (August):541–557.

Sobol, Marion G. 1963. "Commitment to Work," in F. Ivan Nye and Lois W. Hoffman (eds.), *The Employed Mother in America.* Skokie, IL: Rand McNally.

Social Change in Sweden. 1977. Rita Liljeström. "Children, Parents, Jobs: Rearranging the Swedish Society," (May):1–4. New York: Swedish Information Service.

———. 1977. Rose-Marie G. Oster. "Human Liberation: Swedish Society in Transition," 1 (September):1–8. New York: Swedish Information Service.

———. 1978. Ingvar Homberg. "Births Down, Aging Up: What's the Impact?", 4 (February):1–6. New York: Swedish Information Service.

———. 1979. Kenneth Jaffe. "The Politics of Child Care," 11 (March):1–6. New York: Swedish Information Service.

Sonquist, John A. 1970. *Multivariate Model Building.* Ann Arbor: Survey Research Center.

Sorensen, Robert. 1973. *Adolescent Sexuality in Contemporary America.* New York: World Publishing.

Spanier, G. B. 1976. "Measuring Dyadic Adjustment," *Journal of Marriage and the Family* 38 (February):15–28.

———, Robert A. Lewis, and Charles L. Cole. 1975. "Marital Adjustment over the Family Life Cycle; The Issue of Curvilinearity," *Journal of Marriage and the Family* 37 (May):263–277.

———, William Sauer, and Robert Larzelere. 1979. "An Empirical Evaluation of the Family Life Cycle," *Journal of Marriage and the Family* 41 (February):27–38.

Spence, Janet T., Robert Helmreich, and Joy Stapp. 1975. "Ratings of Self and Peers on Sex Role Attributes and Their Relation to Self-Esteem and Conceptions of Masculinity and Femininity," *Journal of Personality and Social Psychology* 32, No. 1:29–39.

Spiro, Melford E. 1956. *Kibbutz: Venture in Utopia.* Cambridge, MA: Harvard University Press.

———. 1958. *Children of the Kibbutz.* Cambridge, MA: Harvard University Press.

Spock, Benjamin. 1947. *Child and Baby Care.* New York: Pocket Books.

Sponaugle, G. C. 1976. "Extramarital Sexual Relations," unpublished paper, University of Minnesota, Minneapolis.

Sprenkle, Douglas H., and David H. Olson. 1978. "Circumplex Model of Marital Systems: An Empirical Study of Clinic and Non-Clinic Couples," *Journal of Marriage and Family Counseling* (April):59–74

Stafford, Rebecca, Elaine Backman, and Pame[l]a V. Debona. 1977. "The Division of Lab[or] Among Cohabiting and Married Couple[s]," *Journal of Marriage and the Family* 39 (F[eb]ruary):43–57

Staples, Robert. 1978. "Race, Liberalism-C[o]

vatism and Premarital Sexual Permissiveness: A Bi-Racial Comparison," *Journal of Marriage and the Family* 40 (November):733–742.

Statistical Abstract of the U.S., 1976. 1976. Washington, DC: Government Printing Office.

Statistical Bulletin. 1978. Metropolitan Life Insurance Co. 59 (October-December):12–15.

Statistiska Central Byrån. 1969. *Historisk Statistisk för Sverige, Del. 1. Befolkning 1720–1967* (Historical Statistics for Sweden, Part I, Population). Stockholm, Sweden.

———. 1975. *Statistick Årsbok 62* (Statistical Abstract of Sweden). Stockholm, Sweden.

———. 1975. *Befolknings Förändringer, 1974* (Population Change). Del. 3. Stockholm.

———. 1975. *Levnadsförhallånden Årsbok, 1975* (Living Conditions Yearbook 1975). Stockholm.

Steffensmeir, Darrell. 1970. "Male and Female Attitudes Toward Homosexuality," Master's thesis, unpublished, University of Iowa, Iowa City.

Stein, Peter J. 1978. "The Lifestyle and Life Changes of the Never Married," *Marriage and Family Review* 1 (July/August):1–11.

Steinmetz, Suzanne K. 1978. "Violence Between Family Members," *Marriage and Family Review* 1 (May):1–16.

Stephens, William N. 1963. *The Family in Cross-Cultural Perspective.* New York: Holt, Rinehart and Winston.

Sterne, Richard S. 1964. *Delinquent Conduct and Broken Homes.* New Haven, Conn: College and University Press.

Stetson, Dorothy M., and Gerald C. Wright, Jr. 1975. "The Effects of Laws on Divorce in American States," *Journal of Marriage and the Family* 37 (August):537–547.

Stillerman, Eric D., and Colin M. Shapiro. 1979. "Scaling Sex Attitudes and Behavior in South Africa," *Archives of Sexual Behavior* 8 (January):1–13.

Stouffer, Samuel A., et al. 1949. *The American Soldier* (4 vols.). Princeton: Princeton University Press.

Straus, Murray A. 1979. "Measuring Intrafamily Conflict and Violence: The Conflict Tactics (CT) Scales," *Journal of Marriage and the Family* 41 (February):75–88.

Strauss, Anselm. 1947. "Personality Needs and Marital Choice," *Social Forces* 25 (March):332–335.

Strodtbeck, Fred L. 1951. "Husband-Wife Interaction Over Revealed Differences," *American Sociological Review* 16 (December):468–473.

———. 1958. "Family Interaction, Values, and Achievement," in Marshall Sklare (ed.), *The Jews: Social Patterns of an American Group.* New York: Free Press.

Strong, Leslie D. 1978. "Alternative Marital and Family Forms: Their Relative Attractiveness to College Students and Correlates of Willingness to Participate in Nontraditional Forms," *Journal of Marriage and the Family* 40 (August):493–503.

Stryker, Sheldon. 1964. "The Interactional and Situational Approaches," in Harold T. Christensen (ed.), *Handbook on Marriage and the Family.* Skokie, IL: Rand McNally.

———. 1968. "Identity Salience and Role Performance: The Relevance of Symbolic Interaction Theory for Family Research," *Journal of Marriage and the Family* 30 (November):558–564.

Suggs, Robert C. 1966. *Marquesan Sexual Behavior: An Anthropological Study of Polynesian Practices.* New York: Harcourt, Brace & World.

Sussman, Marvin. 1953. "Parental Participation in Mate Selection and Its Effect Upon Family Continuity," *Social Forces* 32 (October): 77–81.

———, and Lee Burchinal. 1962. "Kin Family Network: Unheralded Structure in Current Conceptualizations of Family Functioning," *Journal of Marriage and the Family* 24 (August):231–240.

Sutherland, Edwin H., and Donald R. Cressey. 1960. *Principles of Criminology.* Philadelphia: Lippincott.

Swafford, Michael. 1978. "Sex Differences in Soviet Earnings," *American Sociological Review* 43 (October):657–673.

Sweden Today. 1968. "The Status of Women in Sweden, Report to the United Nations, 1968." Stockholm: Swedish Institute.

Swedish Information Service. July 1979. "Swedish Family Policy" by Lillemor Melsted. New York: Swedish Consolate General.

Swedish Ministry of Health and Social Affairs. 1977. "Parental Insurance in Sweden: Some Data" 1–9. Stockholm.

Sweet, James A. 1973. *Women in the Labor Force.* New York: Seminar Press.

Sweetser, Dorrian Apple. 1966. "The Effect of Industrialization on Intergenerational Solidarity," *Rural Sociology* 31 (June):156–170.

Symonds, Carolyn. 1968. "Pilot Study of the Peripheral Behavior of Sexual Mate Swappers," Master's thesis, unpublished, Riverside College, University of California.

Talmon, Yonina. 1964. "Mate Selection in Col-

lective Settlements," *American Sociological Review* 29 (August):491–508.

———. 1972. *Family and Community in the Kibbutz*. Cambridge, MA: Harvard University Press.

Tavris, Carol, and Susan Sadd. 1977. *The Redbook Report on Female Sexuality*. New York: Delacorte.

Taylor, Patricia A., and N. D. Glenn. 1976. "The Utility of Education and Attraction for Females' Status Attainment Through Marriage," *American Sociological Review* 41 (June):484–498.

Terman, Lewis M. 1938. *Psychological Factors in Marital Happiness*. New York: McGraw-Hill.

Tharp, B. F. 1963. "Dimensions of Marriage Roles," *Journal of Marriage and the Family* 25 (November):389–404.

Theodorson, George A. 1965. "Romanticism and Motivation to Marry in the United States, Singapore, Burma and India," *Social Forces* 44 (September):17–28.

Thomas, Darwin, Viktor Gecas, Andrew Weigert, and Elizabeth Rooney. 1974. *Family Socialization and the Adolescent*. Lexington, MA: Heath.

Thomas, John L. 1956. *The American Catholic Family*. Englewood Cliffs, NJ: Prentice-Hall.

Thompson, Linda, and Graham B. Spanier. 1978. "Influence of Parents, Peers and Partners on the Contraceptive Use of College Men and Women," *Journal of Marriage and the Family* 40 (August):481–492.

Thornton, Arland, and Deborah S. Freedman. 1979. "Changes in the Sex Role Attitudes of Women 1962–1977," *American Sociological Review* 44 (October):831–842.

Thwing, C. F., and C. F. B. Thwing. 1887. *The Family: An Historical and Social Study*. Boston: Lee & Shepard.

Tibbits, Clark. 1965. "The Older Family Member in American Society," in H. Lee Jacobs (ed.), *The Older Person in the Family: Challenges and Conflicts*. Iowa City: Institute of Gerontology.

Tietze, Christopher. 1978. "Teenage Pregnancies: Looking Ahead to 1984," *Family Planning Perspectives* 10 (July/August):205–207.

Trost, Jan. 1967. "Some Data on Mate-Selection: Complementarity," *Journal of Marriage and the Family* 29 (November):730–738.

———. 1975. "Married and Unmarried Cohabitation: The Case of Sweden with Some Comparisons," *Journal of Marriage and the Family* 37 (August):677–682.

———. 1976. "Attitudes to and Occurrence of Cohabitation Without Marriage," paper presented at VI World Congress of Social Psychiatry, Yugoslavia, October 4–10.

———. 1977. "Divorce in Sweden," in Robert Chester (ed.), *Divorce in Europe*. Leiden, Netherlands: Martinus Nyhoff Co.

———. 1978. "Attitudes Toward and Occurrence of Cohabitation Without Marriage," *Journal of Marriage and the Family* 40 (May):393–400.

———. 1979. "The Changing Role of Women in Family and Society: Sweden," in Eugene Lupri (ed.), *The Changing Role of Women in Family and Society: A Cross Cultural Comparison* (in press).

———, and Bo Lewin. 1978. *Att Sambo och Gifta Sig* (To Live Together and to Marry). Stockholm: Justice Department. SOU No. 55. (Report published by Family Law Experts.)

Turk, James L., and Norman W. Bell, 1972. "Measuring Power in Families," *Journal of Marriage and the Family* 34 (May): 215–222.

Turnbull, Colin. 1972. *The Mountain People*. New York: Simon & Schuster.

Udry, J. Richard, Karl E. Bauman, and Naomi M. Morris. 1975. "Changes in Premarital Coital Experiences of Recent Decade of Birth Cohorts of Urban American Women," *Journal of Marriage and Family* (November):783–787.

Ullerstam, Lars. 1966. *The Erotic Minorities*. New York: Grove.

United Nations. 1979. *Demographic Yearbook 1978*. New York: United Nations Publisher.

U.S. Bureau of the Census. 1949. *Historical Statistics of the U.S. 1789–1945*. Washington, DC: Government Printing Office.

———. 1958. *Current Population Reports*, Series P-20, No. 79 (February 2). Washington, DC.: Government Printing Office.

———. 1964. *U.S. Census of Population 1960, Vol. 1: Characteristics of the Population, Part 1*. Washington, DC: Government Printing Office.

———. 1966. *1960 Census of Population*, Vol. 2, 4D, "Marital Status." Washington, DC: Government Printing Office.

———. 1969. "Marriage, Fertility and Childspacing: June 1965," *Current Population Reports*, Series P-20, No. 186. Washington, DC: Government Printing Office.

———. 1972. *1970 Census of Population* PC(2)-4C, "Marital Status." Washington, DC: Government Printing Office.

———. 1973. *1970 Census of Population* PC(2)-7a, "Occupational Characteristics." Washington, DC: Government Printing Office.

———. 1974. *Current Population Reports*, Series

P-60 (for the years 1939–1972). Washington, DC: Government Printing Office.

———. 1974. *1970 Census of Population* PC(2)-7c. "Occupation by Industry." Washington, DC: Government Printing Office.

———. 1975. *Historical Statistics of the United States: Colonial Times to 1970, Part 1 and Part 2.* Washington, DC: Government Printing Office.

———. 1975. "The Social and Economic Status of the Black Population in the U.S., 1974," *Current Population Reports*, Series P-23, No. 54. (July) Washington, DC: Government Printing Office.

———. 1976. "Daytime Care of Children: October 1974 and February 1975," *Current Population Reports*, Series P-20, No. 298 (October). Washington, DC: Government Printing Office.

———. 1976. "Demographic Aspects of Aging and the Older Population in the U.S.," *Current Population Reports*, Series P-23, No. 59 (May) Washington, DC: Government Printing Office.

———. 1976. "Fertility History and Prospects of American Women: June 1975," *Current Population Reports*, Series P-20, No. 288 (January). Washington, DC: Government Printing Office.

———. 1976. "Number, Timing and Duration of Marriages and Divorces in the U.S.: June 1975," *Current Population Reports*, Series P-20, No. 297 (October). Washington, DC: Government Printing Office.

———. 1977. "Educational Attainment in the U.S.: March 1977 and 1976," *Current Population Reports*, Series P-20, No. 314 (December). Washington, DC: Government Printing Office.

———. 1977. "Fertility of American Women: June 1976," *Current Population Reports*, Series P-20, No. 308 (June). Washington, DC: Government Print ng Office.

———. 1977. "Marital Status and Living Arrangements: March 1976," *Current Population Reports*, Series P-20, No. 306 (January). Washington, DC: Government Printing Office.

———. 1977. "Marriage, Divorce, Widowhood and Remarriage by Family Characteristics: June 1975," *Current Population Reports*, Series P-20, No. 312 (August). Washington, DC: Government Printing Office.

———. 1977. "Population, Profile of the U.S.: 1976," *Current Population Reports*, Series P-20, No. 307 (April). Washington, DC: Government Printing Office.

———. 1977. "School Enrollment—Social and Behavior Characteristics of Students: October 1976," *Current Population Reports*, Series P-20, No. 309. Washington, DC: Government Printing Office.

———. 1978. "Characteristics of American Children and Youth: 1976," *Current Population Reports*, Series P-23, No. 66. (January) Washington, DC: Government Printing Office.

———. 1978. "Fertility of American Women: June 1977." *Current Population Reports*, Series P-20, No. 325 (September). Washington, DC: Government Printing Office.

———. 1978. "Fertility of American Women: June 1978 (Advance Report)," *Current Population Reports*, Series P-20, No. 330. (November) Washington, DC: Government Printing Office.

———. 1978. "Household and Family Characteristics: March 1977," *Current Population Reports*, Series P-20, No. 326 (August). Washington, DC: Government Printing Office.

———. 1978. "Households and Families by Type: March 1978 (Advance Report)," *Current Population Reports*, Series P-20, No. 327 (August). Washington, DC: Government Printing Office.

———. 1978. "Marital Status and Living Arrangements, March 1977," *Current Population Reports*, Series P-20, No. 323 (April). Washington, DC: Government Printing Office.

———. 1978. "Nursery School and Kindergarten Enrollment of Children and Labor Force Status of Their Mothers: October 1967 to October 1976," *Current Population Reports*, Seriers P-20, No. 318 (February). Washington, DC: Government Printing Office.

———. 1978. "Perspectives on American Fertility," *Current Population Reports*, Series P-23, No. 70 (July). Washington, DC: Government Printing Office.

———. 1978. "Perspectives on American Husbands and Wives," *Current Population Reports*, Series P-23, No. 77 (December). Washington, DC: Government Printing Office.

———. 1978. "Population Profile of the U.S.: 1977," *Current Population Reports*, Series P-20, No. 324 (April). Washington, DC: Government Printing Office.

———. 1978. *Statistical Abstracts of the United States: 1978.* Washington, DC: Government Printing Office.

———. 1979. "Marital Status and Living Arrangements: March 1978," *Current Population Reports*, Series P-20, No. 338 (May). Washington, DC: Government Printing Office.

———. 1979. "Money Income in 1977 of Families

and Persons in the United States," *Current Population Reports*, Series P-60, No. 118. Washington, DC: Government Printing Office. (See also earlier annual issues of this report.)

———. 1979. "Population Profile of the U.S.: 1978," *Current Population Reports*, Series P-20, No. 336 (April). Washington, DC: Government Printing Office.

———. 1979. "School Enrollment—Social and Economic Characteristics of Students: October 1977," *Current Population Reports*, Series P-20, No. 333 (February). Washington, DC: Government Printing Office.

———. 1979. "School Enrollment—Social and Economic Characteristics of Students: October 1978," *Current Population Reports*, Series P-20, No. 335 (April). Washington, D.C.: Government Printing Office.

———. 1979. "Special Studies on Family and Aging," *Current Population Reports*, Series P-23, No. 78. Washington, DC: Government Printing Office.

———. 1979. "Fertility of American Women: June 1978," *Current Population Reports*, Series P-20, No. 341, (October). Washington, D.C.: Government Printing Office.

U.S. Department of Health, Education, and Welfare, Center for Disease Control. 1974. "Venereal Disease Statistical Letter: August 1974," No. 120 (October). Atlanta, GA Bureau of State Services.

———. 1975. "Abortion Surveillance 1973" (May). Atlanta, GA.

———. 1978. "Abortion Surveillance, 1976. (August). Atlanta, GA.

———. 1978. "Reported Mortality and Mortality in the U.S." Center for Disease Control 26 (September). Atlanta, GA.

U.S. Department of Health, Education, and Welfare, National Center for Health Statistics. 1964. *Natality Statistics Analysis: United States 1962*, Series 21, No. 1 (October). Washington, DC: Government Printing Office.

———. 1967. *Divorce Statistics Analysis: United States 1963*, Series 21, No. 13. Washington, DC: Government Printing Office.

———. 1968. *Trends in Illegitimacy: United States 1940–1965*, Series 21, No. 15 (February). Washington, DC: Government Printing Office.

———. 1970. "Interval Between First Marriage and Legitimate First Birth, U.S., 1964–66," *Monthly Vital Statistics Report*, Vol. 18, No. 12 (March 27). Washington, DC: Government Printing Office.

———. 1971. "Marriage: Trends and Characteristics," *National Center for Vital Statistics*, Series 21, No. 21 (September). Washington, DC: Government Printing Office.

———. 1973. "Divorces: Analysis of Changes in U.S.: 1969," *Vital and Health Statistics*, Series 21, No. 22 (April). Washington, DC: Government Printing Office.

———. 1973. "Remarriages: United States," *Vital and Health Statistics*, Series 21, No. 25 (December). Washington, DC: Government Printing Office.

———. 1973. "Teenagers: Marriage, Divorce, Parenthood and Mortality," *Vital and Health Statistics*, Series 21, No. 23 (August). Washington, DC: Government Printing Office.

———. 1974. "Summary Report: Final Natality Statistics, 1970." *Monthly Vital Statistics Report*, Vol. 22, No. 12, Supplement. (March 20). Washington DC: Government Printing Office.

———. 1975. "Summary Report: Final Natality Statistics, 1973." *Monthly Vital Statistics Report*, Vol. 23, No. 11 (January 30). Washington, DC: Government Printing Office.

———. 1975. "Summary Report: Final Marriage Statistics, 1973." *Monthly Vital Statistics Report*, Vol. 24, No. 5 (July 30). Washington, DC: Government Printing Office.

———. 1978. "Final Divorce Statistics, 1976," *Monthly Vital Statistics Report*, Vol. 27, No. 5 (August 16). Washington, DC: Government Printing Office.

———. 1978. "Advanced Report: Final Natality Statistics, 1976," *Monthly Vital Statistics Report*, Vol. 26, No. 12. Supplement. (March 29). Washington, D.C.: Government Printing Office.

———. 1979. *Monthly Vital Statistics Report*. "Final Natality Statistics 1977," Vol. 27, No. 11 (February 5). Washington, DC: Government Printing Office.

———. 1979. "Births, Marriages, Divorces and Deaths for 1978," *Monthly Vital Statistics Report*, Vol. 27, No. 12 (March 15). Washington, DC: Government Printing Office.

———. 1979. "Final Divorce Statistics, 1977," *Monthly Vital Statistics Report*, Vol. 28, No. 2 (May 16). Washington, DC: Government Printing Office.

U.S. Department of Labor. 1963. *American Women*. Washington, DC: Government Printing Office.

———. 1967. *Handbook of Labor Statistics*. Washington, DC: Government Printing Office.

————. Bureau of Labor Statistics. 1974. *Special Labor Force Report 164*. Washington, DC: Government Printing Office.

————. 1977. *U.S. Working Women: A Databook*. Washington, DC:Government Printing Office.

————. 1979. "Employment and Unemployment During 1978: An Analysis," Special Labor Force Report 218. Washington, DC: Government Printing Office.

————. 1979. *News* (May 4). Washington, DC: Government Printing Office.

————. 1979. Report 565, No. 1, First Quarter 1979. Washington, DC: Government Printing Office.

————. 1979. "Women in the Labor Force: Some New Data Series." Report 575 (October). Washington, D.C.: Government Printing Office.

————, Employment and Training Administration, and Department of Health, Education, and Welfare. 1978. *Employment and Training Report of the President*. Washington, DC: Government Printing Office.

————. 1978. "Women in Traditionally Male Jobs: The Experience of Ten Public Utilities," R & D Monograph No. 65. Washington, D.C.: Government Printing Office.

————, Manpower Administration, and Department of Health, Education, and Welfare. 1975. *Manpower Report of the President*. Transmitted to the Congress (April). Washington, DC: Government Printing Office.

Van Der Velde, T. H. 1929. *Ideal Marriage: Its Physiology and Techniques*. New York: Random House.

Vance, Ellen B., and Nathaniel N. Wagner. 1976. "Written Descriptions of Orgasm: A Study of Sex Differences," *Archives of Sexual Behavior* 5 (January):89–98.

Vaughan, Barbara, James Trusell, Jane Menken, and Elise F. Jones. 1977. "Contraceptive Failure Among Married Women in the U.S., 1970–73," *Family Planning Perspectives* 9 (November/December):251–258.

Veevers, Jean E. 1973. "Voluntary Childless Wives: An Exploratory Study," *Sociology and Social Research* 57 (April):356–366.

————. 1974. "The Life Style of Voluntary Childless Couples," in L. Larson (ed.), *The Canadian Family in Comparative Perspective*. Toronto: Prentice-Hall.

Veroff, Joseph, and Sheila Feld. 1970. *Marriage and Work in America: A Study of Motives and Roles*. New York: Van Nostrand.

Vincent, Clark E. 1961. *Unmarried Mothers*. New York: Free Press.

Vogel, Ezra F. 1963. *Japan's New Middle Class*. Berkeley: University of California Press.

Voydanoff, Patricia, and Hyman Rodman. 1978. "Marital Careers in Trinidad," *Journal of Marriage and the Family* 40 (February):157–163.

Waite, Linda J., and R. M. Stolzenberg. 1976. "Intended Childbearing and Labor Force Participation of Young Women: Insights from Non-Recursive Models," *American Sociological Review* 41 (April): 235–252.

Walker, Kenneth N., Joy Rogers, and William Messinger. 1977. "Remarriage After Divorce: A Review," *Social Casework* (May):276–285.

Waller, Willard. 1937. "The Rating and Dating Complex," *American Sociological Review* 2 (October):727–734.

Wallin, Paul, and Alexander L. Clark. 1958. "Cultural Norms and Husbands' and Wives' Reports of Their Marital Partner's Preferred Frequency of Coitus Relative to Their Own," *Sociometry* 21 (September):247–254.

————, and ————. 1958b. "Marital Satisfaction and Husbands' and Wives' Perception of Similarity in Their Preferred Frequency of Coitus," *Journal of Abnormal and Social Psychology* 47 (November): 370–372.

Walsh, Robert H. 1970. "A Survey of Parents and Their Own Children's Sexual Attitudes," Ph.D. dissertation, unpublished, University of Iowa, Iowa City.

————, Mary Zey-Ferrell, and William L. Tolone. 1976. "Selection of Reference Group, Perceived Reference Group Permissiveness, and Personal Permissiveness Attitudes and Behavior: A Study of Two Consecutive Panels (1967–71; 1970–74)," *Journal of Marriage and the Family* 38 (August):495–507.

Walshok, Mary L. 1971. "The Emergence of Middle Class Deviant Subcultures: The Case of Swingers," *Social Problems* 18 (Spring): 488–496.

Walstedt, Joyce J. 1978. "Reform of Women's Roles and Family Structures in Recent History of China," *Journal of Marriage and the Family* 40(May):379–392.

Walster, Elaine, and G. William Walster. 1978. *A New Look at Love*. Reading, MA: Addison-Wesley.

Walster, Elaine, V. Arenson, D. Abrahams, and L. Rottman. 1966. "Importance of Physical Attractiveness in Dating Behavior," *Journal of Personality and Social Psychology* 4 (November):508–516. Ward, David A., and Gene G. Kassenbaum. 1965. *Women's Prison: Sex and Social Structure*. Chicago: Aldine.

Weber, Max. 1930. *The Protestant Ethic and the Spirit of Capitalism*. London: G. Allen. (Originally published in 1904.)

Weeks, H. Ashley. 1943. "Differential Divorce Rates by Occupation," *Social Forces* 21 (July):334–337.

Weinberg, Martin S., and Collin J. Williams. 1974. *Male Homosexuals*. New York: Oxford University Press.

Weiner, Annette. 1976. *Women of Value: Men of Renown*. Austin: University of Texas Press.

Weinstock, Edward, Christopher Tietze, Frederick S. Jaffe, and Joy S. Dryfoos. 1975. "Legal Abortions in the United States Since the 1973 Supreme Court Decisions," *Family Planning Perspectives* 7 (January/February):23–31.

Weiss, Robert S. 1975. *Marital Separation*. New York: Basic Books.

Weitz, Shirley. 1977. *Sex Roles*. New York: Oxford University Press.

Weitzman, Lenore J. 1974. "Legal Regulation of Marriage: Tradition and Change," *California Law Review* 62:1169–1288.

_____. 1978. *The Marriage Contract*. Englewood Cliffs, NJ:Prentice-Hall.

_____, et al. 1978. "Contracts for Intimate Relationships," *Alternative Lifestyles* 1 (August):303–378.

Weller, Robert H., and Frank B. Hobbs. 1978. "Unwanted and Mistimed Births in the U.S.: 1968–1973," *Family Planning Perspectives* 10 (May/June):168–172.

Werkmeister, W. H. 1959. "Theory Construction and the Problem of Objectivity," in Llewellyn Z. Gross (ed.), *Symposium on Sociological Theory*. New York: Harper & Row.

West, Donald J. 1968. *Homosexuality*. Chicago: Aldine.

Westermarck, Edward. 1922. *The History of Human Marriage* (5th ed.; 3 vols.). New York: Allerton Book Co. (Originally published in 1891.)

Westoff, Charles F. 1974. "Coital Frequency and Contraception," *Family Planning Perspectives* 6 (Summer):136–141.

_____. 1977. "The Secularization of U.S. Catholics Birth Control Practices," *Family Planning Perspectives* 9 (September/October): 203–207.

_____, and Elise F. Jones. 1977. "Contraception and Sterilization in the U.S., 1965–1975," *Family Planning Perspectives* 9 (July/August):153–157.

Westoff, Leslie Aldridge. 1977. *The Second Time Around*. New York: Viking.

_____, and Charles F. Westoff. 1971. *From Now to Zero*. Boston: Little, Brown.

Whalen, Richard E. 1966. "Sexual Motivation," *Psychological Review* 73, No. 2:151–163.

Whitehurst, Robert. 1969. "Extramarital Sex: Alienation or Extension of Normal Behavior," in Gerhard Neubeck (ed.), *Extramarital Relations*. Englewood Cliffs, NJ: Prentice-Hall.

Whiting, Beatrice B. (ed.). 1963. *Six Cultures: Studies in Child Rearing*. New York: Wiley.

Whitley, Marily P., and Susan B. Poulsen. 1975. "Assertiveness and Sexual Satisfaction in Employed Professional Women," *Journal of Marriage and the Family* 37 (August):573–582.

Whyte, Martin K. 1978. *The Status of Women in Preindustrial Societies*. Princeton, NJ: Princeton University Press.

Wiley, Philip. 1935. *As They Reveled*. New York: Avon.

Wilkinson, Karen. 1974. "The Broken Family and Juvenile Delinquency: Scientific Explanation or Ideology," *Social Problems* 21 (June): 726–739.

Willie, Charles V., and Susan L. Greenblatt. 1978. "Four 'Classic' Studies of Power Relationships in Black Families: A Review and Look to the Future," *Journal of Marriage and the Family* 40 (November): 691–694.

Wills, Thomas A., Robert L. Weiss, and Gerald R. Patterson. 1974. "A Behavioral Analysis of the Determinants of Marital Satisfaction," *Journal of Consulting and Clinical Psychology* 42 (December): 802–811.

Wilmott, Peter, and Michael Young. 1960. *Family and Class in a London Suburb*. London: Routledge.

Winch, Robert F. 1958. *Mate Selection: A Study of Complementary Needs*. New York: Harper & Row.

_____. 1967. "Another Look at the Theory of Complementary Needs in Mate Selection," *Journal of Marriage and the Family* 29 (November):756–762.

_____. 1977. *Familial Organization*. New York: Free Press.

_____, and Rae Blumberg. 1972. "Societal Complexity and Familial Complexity: Evidence for the Curvilinear Hypotheses," *American Journal of Sociology* 77 (March):898–920.

Wise, Jeff. 1975. "The Relationship Between Extramarital Coitus and Marital Happiness," graduate paper, unpublished, University of Minnesota, Minneapolis.

Wolf, Wendy C., and Neil D. Fligstein. 1979. "Sex and Authority in the Workplace: The

Causes of Sexual Inequality," *American Sociological Review* 44 (April):235–252.

Wolfe, D. M. 1959. "Power and Authority in the Family," in D. Cartwright (ed.), *Studies in Social Power*. Ann Arbor: University of Michigan, Institute for Social Research.

Women in Sweden, In the Light of Statistics. 1973 (August):1–98. Stockholm: Joint Female Labour Council.

Wood, Vivian, and Joan F. Robertson. 1978. "Friendship and Kinship Interaction: Differential Effect on the Morale of the Elderly," *Journal of Marriage and the Family* 40 (May):367–375.

Wright, Gerald C., Jr., and Dorothy M. Stetson. 1978. "The Impact of No-Fault Divorce Law Reform on Divorce in American States," *Journal of Marriage and the Family* 40 (August):575–580.

Wright, James D. 1978. "Are Working Women Really More Satisfied? Evidence from Several National Surveys," *Journal of Marriage and the Family* 40 (May):301–313.

Yankelovich, Daniel. 1974. *The New Morality.* New York: McGraw-Hill.

Yarrow, Leon J. 1964. "Separation from Parents During Early Childhood," in Martin L. Hoffman and Lois W. Hoffman (eds.), *Review of Child Development Research* (Vol. 1). New York: Russell Sage.

Yarrow, Marion, et al. 1962. "Childrearing in Families of Working and Nonworking Mothers," *Sociometry* 25 (June):122–140.

Yllo, Kersti A. 1978. "Nonmarital Cohabitation," *Alternative Lifestyles* 1 (February):37–54.

Yorburg, Betty. 1974. *Sexual Identity.* New York: Wiley.

Young, Michael, and Peter Wilmott. 1964. *Family and Kinship in East London.* Baltimore: Pelican Books.

Zeisel, Hans. 1957. *Say It with Figures.* New York: Harper & Row.

Zelditch, Morris, Jr. 1955. "Role Differentiation in the Nuclear Family: A Comparative Study," in Talcott Parsons and Robert F. Bates (eds.),

The Family: Socialization and Interaction Process. New York: Free Press.

Zelnik, Melvin and John F. Kantner. 1972. "Sexuality, Contraception and Pregnancy Among Young Unwed Females in the United States," in U.S. Commission on Population Growth and the American Future, *Demographic and Social Aspects of Population Growth* (Vol. 1). Washington, DC: Government Printing Office.

———. 1974. "The Resolution of Teenage First Pregnancies," *Family Planning Perspective* 6 (Spring):74–80.

———. 1977. "Sexual and Contraceptive Experience of Young Unmarried Women in the U.S., 1976 and 1971," *Family Planning Perspectives* 9 (March/April):55–71.

———. 1978. "First Pregnancies to Women Aged 15–19: 1976 and 1971," *Family Planning Perspectives* 10 (January/February):11–20.

———. 1978. "Contraceptive Patterns and Premarital Pregnancy Among Women Aged 15–19 in 1976," *Family Planning Perspective* 10 (May/June):135–142.

Melvin Zelnik, Y. J. Kim, and J. F. Kantner, 1979. "Probabilities of Intercourse and Conception among U.S. Teenage Women 1971–1976," *Family Planning Perspectives*" (May/June):177–183.

Zetterberg, Hans L. 1962. *Social Theory and Social Practice.* New York: Bedminster.

———. 1969. *Om Sexuallivet i Sverige* (On Sexual Life in Sweden.). Stockholm: Statens Offentiliga Utredningar. (State Public Report).

Zey-Ferrell, Mary O., William L. Tolone, and Robert H. Walsh. 1977. "Maturational and Societal Changes in the Sexual Double-Standard: A Panel Analysis (1967–71; 1970–74)," *Journal of Marriage and the Family* 39 (May):255–271.

Zimmerman, Carle C., and Lucius F. Cervantes. 1956. *Marriage and the Family: A Text for Moderns.* Chicago: Regnery.

Ziskin, J., and M. Ziskin. 1973. *The Extramarital Sex Contract.* Los Angeles: Nash Publications.

NAME INDEX

SUBJECT INDEX